The Peace of God

The Peace of God

*Social Violence and Religious Response
in France around the Year 1000*

EDITED BY

Thomas Head *and*
Richard Landes

Cornell University Press

ITHACA AND LONDON

This volume is dedicated to our teachers

Contents

Maps   ix

Acknowledgments   xi

A Note on Citations and Sources   xiii

Introduction   1
Thomas Head and Richard Landes

1. History, Historians, and the Peace of God   21
   Frederick S. Paxton

2. The Cult of Relics and Pilgrimage in Burgundy and
   Aquitaine at the Time of the Monastic Reform   41
   Bernhard Töpfer

3. The Enemies of the Peace: Reflections on a Vocabulary,
   500–1100   58
   Elisabeth Magnou-Nortier

4. The Chiaroscuro of Heresy: Early Eleventh-Century
   Aquitaine as Seen from Auxerre   80
   Guy Lobrichon

5. Peace from the Mountains: The Auvergnat Origins of
   the Peace of God   104
   Christian Lauranson-Rosaz

6. The Castellan Revolution and the Peace of God
   in Aquitaine   135
   André Debord

7. The Peace of God and the Cult of the Saints in Aquitaine
   in the Tenth and Eleventh Centuries   165
   Daniel F. Callahan

8. Between Aristocracy and Heresy: Popular Participation
   in the Limousin Peace of God, 994–1033   184
   Richard Landes

9. The Judgment of God: Andrew of Fleury's Account of
   the Peace League of Bourges   219
   Thomas Head

10. Monks, Feuds, and the Making of Peace in Eleventh-
    Century Flanders   239
    Geoffrey Koziol

11. Protection of the Church, Defense of the Law, and
    Reform: On the Purposes and Character of the Peace
    of God, 989–1038   259
    Hans-Werner Goetz

12. Pollution, Purity, and Peace: An Aspect of Social Reform
    between the Late Tenth Century and 1076   280
    Amy G. Remensnyder

    Postscript: The Peace of God and the Social Revolution   308
    R. I. Moore

    Appendix A: Selected Documents on the Peace of God
    in Translation   327

    Appendix B: "To Control Military Requisitions": A Letter
    from Hincmar of Reims to Charles the Bald (859)   343

    Appendix C: The Latin Texts of the "Letter"
    of Heribert   347

    Contributors   351

    Index   355

Maps

1. Places associated with the early Peace of God   5

2. Western Aquitaine   137

3. Flanders and the *delatio* performed by the monks of Lobbes, 1060   241

Acknowledgments

The editors wish to express their thanks to the many people and institutions whose help and support have been essential in the preparation of this volume. The Medieval Institute of Western Michigan University provided us, as it has many medievalists, with our first forum for this collective endeavor. S. K. Johannesen, Evilou Hill, and the rest of the editors and staff at *Historical Reflections / Réflexions historiques* worked hard to bring an earlier version of this volume to fruition. Their enthusiasm and efforts are fondly remembered. Janos Bak, Phillippe Buc, Hans-Werner Goetz, and Amy G. Remensnyder have donated generously of their abilities and time in preparing translations for this volume. Bernard Bachrach graciously allowed the editors to substitute Christian Lauranson-Rosaz's essay for Professor Bachrach's own work on the Peace of God in the Auvergne (included in the earlier *Historical Reflections / Réflexions historiques* volume), even though, in the final analysis, they took very different approaches. Eliza McClennen's mapmaking skills have been greatly appreciated. Picard Editeur has graciously consented to the use of the graph reproduced on page 143. The anonymous readers for Cornell University Press provided thoughtful and useful critiques. John Ackerman, Kay Scheuer, Joanne Hindman, and their colleagues at the Press have displayed almost infinite patience at seeing this book through to its conclusion. John Thomas showed equal patience and expertise in copyediting the manuscript.

The academic institutions at which the editors held positions during earlier stages in the editorial process, the University of Pittsburgh (Landes) and Pomona College (Head), provided generous support that Boston University and Yale University continued. Richard Landes thanks his colleagues at Pittsburgh for their ready ears and penetrating questions, as well as Faye Schneider, whose lightning fingers and cheerful disposition are now sorely missed. Columbia University and the MacArthur Foundation awarded him two Faculty Grants in "Peace and Conflict Studies," which provided a medievalist a chance to say something on the matter. The American Council of Learned Societies provided funds for travel to a conference in France where many of the European contributions were first secured. Thomas Head thanks Harry Liebersohn for his sympathetic and sage advice. He also thanks Heather Barkley and Mark Rabuck, who provided yeoman service in the correction of proof.

Our most heartfelt gratitude goes to Paula Fredriksen and Virginia Reinburg, who have received little peace from this project in which they were perhaps unwilling participants and who, in both work and friendship, have turned the bad to the good, and the good to the better. And finally we thank each other for the patience, perseverance, and (mostly) good humor which have been in evidence during the gestation of this volume.

T. H. and R. L.

A Note on Citations and Sources

As in any work of medieval history, many of the sources cited in the footnotes of the essays in this book have been consulted in the editions found in such standard collections as the *Monumenta Germaniae historica* and the *Patrologia latina*. In such cases, the citation is provided in two parts, separated by a semicolon. The first part gives the author and title of the work, followed by the relevant book, chapter, or other section number. The second part provides the volume and page (or column) numbers in the source collection. The references within the text itself and within the printed edition are separated. Thus "Abbo of Fleury, *Collectio canonum*, chap. 40; *PL* 139:496" is a reference to the fortieth chapter of Abbo's collection, which may be found at the cited volume and column of the *Patrologia latina*. The canons of Peace councils and other synods or assemblies are similarly cited in two parts: first, the place and date of the council, followed by the numbers of the relevant canons; second, a citation where the canons might be found in *Sacrorum conciliorum nova, et amplissima collectio*, ed. Giovanni Mansi, revised by J. Martin and L. Petit, or in the relevant volumes of the *Monumenta Germaniae historica*. Thus "Bourges (1031), can. 5; Mansi 19:501–2" is a reference to the fifth canon of the council held at Bourges in 1031 and may be found at the cited volume and column in the Mansi collection. When the precise date is unknown, a range within which the assembly likely took place is provided, as in "Poitiers (1000/14)." It should be noted that in many cases alternative editions (or alternative publications of the same edition) are available. When a modern critical edition has been used, the citations follow more standard form, with both types of citation combined. Thus "*The Epistolae Vagantes of Pope Gregory VII*, ed. H. E. J. Cowdrey (Oxford, 1972), no. 9,

p. 20" is a reference to the ninth letter of this collection, to be found on page 20 of the Cowdrey edition. Our intention has been to aid the reader in tracing cited passages; we hope that these conventions produce the desired result, and not complete confusion.

The primary sources listed here are cited throughout this volume in the shortened form shown on the left. Bibliographic information on secondary sources and on less frequently cited primary sources appears in the footnotes.

AASS   *Acta sanctorum quotquot toto orbe coluntur.* Ed. Jean Bolland et al. Antwerp and Brussels, 1643–present.

Ademar of Chabannes, *Chronicon   Chronique d'Ademar de Chabannes.* Ed. Jules Chavanon. Collection des textes pour servir à l'étude et à l'enseignement de l'histoire, 20; Paris, 1897.

AH   Analecta hymnica medii aevi. 55 vols. Ed. G. M. Dreves and C. Blume. Leipzig, 1886–1922.

Cartulaire de Sauxillanges   Cartulaire de Sauxillanges. Ed. Henri Doniol. Clermont-Ferrand, 1864.

Chartes et docs. de Saint-Maixent   Chartes et documents pour servir à l'histoire de l'abbaye de Saint-Maixent. 2 vols. Ed. Alfred Richard. Archives historiques du Poitou, 1; Poitiers, 1886.

Rodulphus Glaber, *Historiarum   Raoul Glaber: Les cinq livres de ses histoires (900–1044).* Ed. Maurice Prou. Paris, 1886. See also *Historiarum libri quinque.* Ed. and trans. John France. Oxford Medieval Texts; Oxford, 1989, and *Rodolfo il Glabro: Cronache dell'anno mille.* Ed. and trans. G. Cavallo and G. Orlandi. Milan, 1989.

Liber mirac. s. Fidis   Liber miraculorum sanctae Fidis. Ed. Auguste Bouillet. Collection des textes pour servir à l'étude et à l'enseignement de l'histoire, 21; Paris, 1897.

Mansi   *Sacrorum conciliorum nova, et amplissima collectio.* 31 vols. Ed. Giovanni Mansi. Florence and Venice, 1759–1798. Rev. ed. and cont. J. Martin and L. Petit. 60 vols. Paris, 1899–1927. Rpt., Graz, 1961–present.

MGH   Monumenta Germaniae historica.

MGH SRM   MGH Scriptores rerum merovingicarum.

MGH SS   MGH Scriptores, in folio.

Mirac. s. Benedicti   Les miracles de saint Benoît écrits par Adrevald, Aimon, André, Raoul Tortaire et Hugues de Sainte Marie, moines de Fleury. Ed. Eugène de Certain. Paris, 1858.

Paris, BN lat.   Paris, Bibliothèque nationale, codex latinus.

PL   Patrologia latina. 221 vols. Ed. J.-P. Migne. Paris, 1844–1864.

RHF   Recueil des historiens des Gaules et de la France. 2d ed., 24 vols. Ed. Léopold Delisle. Paris, 1864–1904.

Trans. et mirac. s. Viviani   Translatio sancti Viviani episcopi in coenobium Figiacense et eiusdem miracula. Analecta Bollandiana 8 (1889), 256–84.

Vatican, Reg. lat.   Vatican, Bibliotheca Apostolica, codex Reginensis latinus.

The Peace of God

Introduction

THOMAS HEAD AND
RICHARD LANDES

In the summer of 987, the West Frankish nobility passed over the claims of the last Carolingian and elected a new king. Although few at the time may have realized it, they had inaugurated a new royal dynasty, the Capetians. Whether this dynastic change triggered the changes that followed or merely provided added vigor to them, the next two generations mark a fundamental turning point in French, and beyond that in European, history. This transformation of all levels and all aspects of society—the "mutation of the year 1000" as one historian described it—occurred during a period that seemed to marry disorder and creativity.[1] During the slow and awkward consolidation of Capetian power, the lesser nobility (castellans) and their mounted warriors (milites) asserted their independence and power. In the long run, the resultant feuding and pillage proved a symptom of fundamental change in the basic structures of Frankish society. To many contemporaries, particularly the clerics who left written testimony, however, it seemed to mark a headlong slide into anarchy: "With the world coming to an end, since men are driven by a briefer life, so does a more atrocious cupidity burn in them. Whence it occurs that they take away the possessions of the holy church, now by force, now by extortion, now by the claims of unjust ministers, so that only the name of the holy church remains."[2]

Among the many responses to the perceived disorder at the turn of the millennium, one of the earliest, and perhaps the most intriguing, was the Peace of God. Rather than rely solely on the protection

---

[1] Guy Bois, *La mutation de l'an mil* (Paris, 1989).

[2] *Documents pour l'histoire de l'église de Saint-Hilaire de Poitiers (768–1300)*, ed. L. Rédet (Mémoires de le Société des Antiquaires de l'Ouest; Poitiers, 1847), no. 65, p. 74.

the spiritual sanctions that later characterized the Peace of God. Nevertheless, the oath sworn at Le Puy serves as an important precursor of the Peace movement. Subsequent events in the Auvergne indicate that Guy and other bishops continued to call such mass gatherings and eventually began to use relics as a means of drawing larger crowds. In discussing these events in Chapter 5, Christian Lauranson-Rosaz draws a detailed picture of the initiatives undertaken by the high clergy of the Auvergne to cope with disorder in a region where no king, indeed no count, could guarantee stability.

The earliest council from which Peace canons survive was that held at Charroux in 989. According to its decree, three crimes were to be punished by excommunication: robbery of church property, assaults on clerics, and theft of cattle from peasants.[6] The decrees of later councils, which generally followed the model laid down at Charroux, bear witness to an increasingly coherent concept of God's peace. At Le Puy in 994, the bishops opened their legislation with the statement, "Since we know that without peace no man may see God, we adjure you, in the name of the Lord, to be men of peace."[7] They then proceeded to outlaw, in far greater detail, the same actions earlier proscribed at Charroux. As Hans-Werner Goetz suggests in his discussion of the legacy of Charroux found in the acts of Peace councils through the 1030s (Chapter 11), on one level the bishops simply intended their decrees to be one means of reasserting the rule of law in their society. They thus hoped to protect themselves, their clerics, the property of their churches, and the productive output of their peasants from the consequences of social violence. Beyond this, Amy G. Remensynder reminds up in Chapter 12 how much the acts of these Peace councils shared with the concerns of the more widely disseminated monastic and papal reform movements associated with the names of the abbey of Cluny and Pope Gregory VII.

The canons of the councils themselves provide only one lens through which to observe the Peace of God; at Charroux, in addition to the promulgated edicts, we also find the assembly of a large number of saints' relics and the enthusiastic participation of the *populus*.[8] These characteristics also marked most subsequent councils. Narrative descriptions, such as the following from the council of Héry, allow us to observe the circumstances in which the unarmed clergy and the *populus* could extract oaths to observe God's peace from the *milites*:

[6] For a translation of this document and other relevant sources, see Appendix A.

[7] *Cartulaire de Sauxillanges*, p. 52.

[8] The charged atmosphere found at this assembly can be sensed in Letaldus of Micy's *Delatio corporis s. Juniani ad synodem Karoffensem*, a translation of which may be found in Appendix A.

Introduction

THOMAS HEAD AND
RICHARD LANDES

In the summer of 987, the West Frankish nobility passed over the claims of the last Carolingian and elected a new king. Although few at the time may have realized it, they had inaugurated a new royal dynasty, the Capetians. Whether this dynastic change triggered the changes that followed or merely provided added vigor to them, the next two generations mark a fundamental turning point in French, and beyond that in European, history. This transformation of all levels and all aspects of society—the "mutation of the year 1000" as one historian described it—occurred during a period that seemed to marry disorder and creativity.[1] During the slow and awkward consolidation of Capetian power, the lesser nobility (castellans) and their mounted warriors (*milites*) asserted their independence and power. In the long run, the resultant feuding and pillage proved a symptom of fundamental change in the basic structures of Frankish society. To many contemporaries, particularly the clerics who left written testimony, however, it seemed to mark a headlong slide into anarchy: "With the world coming to an end, since men are driven by a briefer life, so does a more atrocious cupidity burn in them. Whence it occurs that they take away the possessions of the holy church, now by force, now by extortion, now by the claims of unjust ministers, so that only the name of the holy church remains."[2]

Among the many responses to the perceived disorder at the turn of the millennium, one of the earliest, and perhaps the most intriguing, was the Peace of God. Rather than rely solely on the protection

---

[1] Guy Bois, *La mutation de l'an mil* (Paris, 1989).
[2] *Documents pour l'histoire de l'église de Saint-Hilaire de Poitiers (768–1300)*, ed. L. Rédet (Mémoires de le Société des Antiquaires de l'Ouest; Poitiers, 1847), no. 65, p. 74.

afforded by secular princes, ecclesiastical lords turned to their neighboring patron saints and the populace of their territories for assistance in keeping the peace. Leading regional bishops convoked councils of their fellow bishops, meetings that were also attended by the abbots of important monastic communities and by various secular leaders. Monks from the region raised up the relics enshrined in their churches and took them to the sites of the councils, where the saints could serve as witnesses and representatives of divine authority. The presence of such treasures drew large numbers of men and women from an enthusiastic *populus*.[3] All converged on the large open fields that were the favored sites of Peace councils. There—surrounded by clerical and lay magnates, by saints, and by their social inferiors—members of the warrior elite took oaths of peace, framed in a context that mobilized what a modern observer might call popular opinion.[4]

Concerning as it did many aspects of contemporary culture—the feud, the developing power of the warrior elite, conciliar legislation, relic cults, the ascendency of the crowd, and religious revival—the Peace of God has been studied by scholars from a variety of differing and even contradictory critical perspectives. Frederick Paxton (Chapter 1) describes the major trends within this literature and analyzes them within a wider intellectual context. He details the many ways in which political and historiographic concerns have shaped the interpretation of the Peace offered by historians. Over the course of more than a century, this movement has served as a sort of lightning rod, attracting representatives of virtually every major school in the interpretation of medieval French history. At a moment when the question of social change in France around the turn of the millennium is being debated with renewed fervor, it seems appropriate to offer the collective reexamination of the Peace represented by the articles in this volume.

Much of the variety in scholarly presentation of the Peace of God results from differing interpretations of an all-too-scarce documentation. For the early period of the Peace movement, on which this volume focuses, there are two main types of source material: legal (oaths, conciliar canons, and charters) and narrative (hagiography, histories, and sermons). Each has its own limitations. Texts composed in an administrative setting tended to use conservative and laconic language as their authors consciously strived to suggest continuity with the past.

[3] This rather anonymous Latin term refers to all those free laypeople of relatively low social status whom we might call commoners, that is, to wealthy merchants and impoverished peasants alike; see Anne-Marie Bautier, " 'Popularis' et la notion de 'populaire'," *Acta Antiqua Academiae Scientiarum Hungaricae* 23 (1975), 285–303.

[4] Loren MacKinney, "The People and Public Opinion in the Eleventh Century Peace Movement," *Speculum* 5 (1930), 181–206.

Such texts rarely, for example, mentioned the presence of the *populus* at councils. On the other hand, narrative sources, especially miracle stories, dwelt on the size and excitement of the crowds. Their authors used an exaggerated, even polemical, rhetoric that may reflect only a narrow clerical perspective. Those historians who downplay the originality and significance of the Peace of God characteristically favor the legal documents, while those who prefer a more dramatic picture favor the narrative sources.[5] It seems only fair to alert the reader that the editors favor the latter approach, although we have included the foremost representatives of the former school in this volume.

The best way to introduce the essays that follow is to present a general picture, not only of the Peace movement, but also of the society into which it was born. It is in the nature of such summaries to gloss over many disputed points. The works Paxton discusses here could be cited to corroborate, or to qualify, or even to dispute virtually every assertion we make below with seeming confidence. But to let the reader judge, we have tried to bring together a representative spectrum of studies in this volume; each of them further refines, refocuses, and reframes our rough introductory portrait of the Peace in varied, and often surprising, ways.

The Development of the Peace of God

Peace councils were first held in Aquitaine and Burgundy during the last quarter of the tenth century. In 975, Bishop Guy of Le Puy convoked a large meeting in an open field outside his episcopal city to deal with those who had pillaged the churches of his diocese. Backing his threat of excommunication with the troops of his nephews, the counts of nearby Gévaudan and Brioude, Guy forced those gathered, both knights and armed peasants (*milites ac rustici*), to take an oath to maintain the peace. Since he acted with secular support rather than that of his fellow bishops, he was unable to enact the formal canons or threaten

---

[5] For an example of a historian who favors legal documentation, see Karl-Ferdinand Werner, "Observations sur le rôle des évêques dans le mouvement de la paix au Xe et XIe siècles," in *Mediaevalia Christiana XIe–XIIe siècles: Hommages à Raymonde Foreville*, ed. Coloman Viola (Paris, 1989), pp. 155–95. His assertion that the early Peace movement has little popular participation rests, however, on incomplete documentation; he inexplicably claims (p. 159), for example, that there were no relics brought to the council of Charroux (989) and makes no mention of the council of Limoges (994). The presence of relics and the *populus* at both councils is amply attested in the narrative sources; see, for example, the works by Letaldus of Micy and Ademar of Chabannes included in Appendix A.

the spiritual sanctions that later characterized the Peace of God. Nevertheless, the oath sworn at Le Puy serves as an important precursor of the Peace movement. Subsequent events in the Auvergne indicate that Guy and other bishops continued to call such mass gatherings and eventually began to use relics as a means of drawing larger crowds. In discussing these events in Chapter 5, Christian Lauranson-Rosaz draws a detailed picture of the initiatives undertaken by the high clergy of the Auvergne to cope with disorder in a region where no king, indeed no count, could guarantee stability.

The earliest council from which Peace canons survive was that held at Charroux in 989. According to its decree, three crimes were to be punished by excommunication: robbery of church property, assaults on clerics, and theft of cattle from peasants.[6] The decrees of later councils, which generally followed the model laid down at Charroux, bear witness to an increasingly coherent concept of God's peace. At Le Puy in 994, the bishops opened their legislation with the statement, "Since we know that without peace no man may see God, we adjure you, in the name of the Lord, to be men of peace."[7] They then proceeded to outlaw, in far greater detail, the same actions earlier proscribed at Charroux. As Hans-Werner Goetz suggests in his discussion of the legacy of Charroux found in the acts of Peace councils through the 1030s (Chapter 11), on one level the bishops simply intended their decrees to be one means of reasserting the rule of law in their society. They thus hoped to protect themselves, their clerics, the property of their churches, and the productive output of their peasants from the consequences of social violence. Beyond this, Amy G. Remensynder reminds up in Chapter 12 how much the acts of these Peace councils shared with the concerns of the more widely disseminated monastic and papal reform movements associated with the names of the abbey of Cluny and Pope Gregory VII.

The canons of the councils themselves provide only one lens through which to observe the Peace of God; at Charroux, in addition to the promulgated edicts, we also find the assembly of a large number of saints' relics and the enthusiastic participation of the *populus*.[8] These characteristics also marked most subsequent councils. Narrative descriptions, such as the following from the council of Héry, allow us to observe the circumstances in which the unarmed clergy and the *populus* could extract oaths to observe God's peace from the *milites:*

[6] For a translation of this document and other relevant sources, see Appendix A.

[7] *Cartulaire de Sauxillanges*, p. 52.

[8] The charged atmosphere found at this assembly can be sensed in Letaldus of Micy's *Delatio corporis s. Juniani ad synodem Karoffensem*, a translation of which may be found in Appendix A.

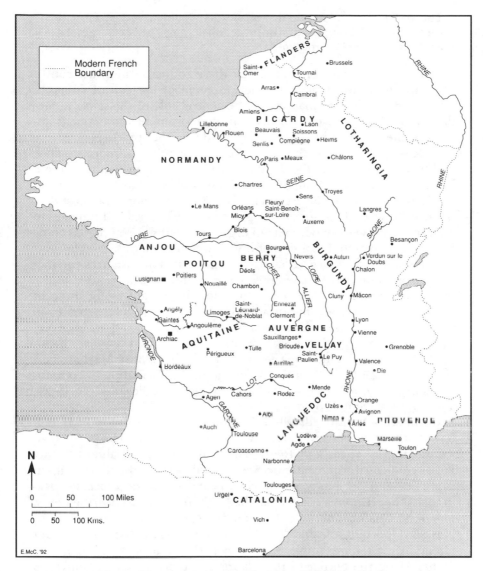

Map 1. Places associated with the early Peace of God

Crowds of common people without number, of every age and both gen-
ders, hurried there. In order that the devotion of these laypeople might be
increased on their journey, men of faith began to bring the bodies of many
saints as well. Along with such venerable relics, [the monks of Montier-en-
Der] did not neglect to bring along the relics of the holy body of our patron Bercharius, which were fittingly placed for their journey on a litter.

This was done, moreover, so that our leaders could make a proclamation about a certain count, Landric by name, concerning the booty he had stolen from our blessed protector.[9]

Given the prominent role of relics at these councils, the Peace constitutes an important stage in the development of the cult of saints. In Chapter 7, Daniel Callahan traces the central role of the saints in mediating the Peace in Aquitaine as well the movement's consequent impact on the shape of both liturgical and devotional practice.

At least a half dozen similar gatherings of bishops, monks, saints, and people occurred in the decade following the council at Charroux. They were scattered throughout the French Midi, from Narbonne and the Rouergue to the Auvergne and Burgundy. Perhaps the most dramatic of these early councils took place outside the walls of Limoges in 994. In response to an outbreak of ergotism—a disease known as "holy fire" and interpreted as a sign of divine wrath—the duke and bishops of Aquitaine summoned relics from monasteries at distances ranging to over one hundred kilometers. A mass healing was attributed to the miraculous powers of the relics, the most important being those of Saint Martial, an early bishop of the city. Richard Landes argues in Chapter 8 that these events galvanized Limousin society in unprecedented ways. He traces how, in one region, an aroused populace influenced, on the one hand, the rise of an "apostolic" cult of Martial, their city's patron saint, and, on the other hand, the formation of communities dedicated to the *vita apostolica* who rejected relic cults, crucifixes, and the sacramental structure of the church itself.

In the decades immediately following the turn of the millennium, few Peace councils were held, but the movement underwent a revival during the 1020s and 1030s. There are records of almost twenty Peace councils during these decades. Councils were held not only in Aquitaine and Burgundy, the original heartland of the Peace, but also in such other regions as Catalonia, the Narbonnais, Provence, the Berry, Flanders, Champagne, and Normandy. Territorial princes came to play an important role and "peace" ideology became the transcendant idiom; in 1024, for example, King Robert the Pious met with Emperor Henry II on the border of their lands to proclaim such a "universal peace." Writing a few years after the fact, Rodulphus Glaber noted that it was in Aquitaine in 1033 that

bishops, abbots, and other men devoted to holy religion first began to gather councils of the whole people [*populus*]. At these gatherings the bod-

---

[9] *De diversis casibus coenobii Dervensis et miracula s. Bercharii*, c. 27; *Acta sanctorum ordinis sancti Benedicti*, 9 vols., ed. Luc d'Archéry and Jean Mabillon (Paris, 1668–1701), 2:859.

ies of many saints and shrines containing holy relics were assembled. From there through the provinces of Arles and Lyon, then through all of Burgundy, and finally in the farthest corners of Frankland, it was proclaimed in every diocese that councils would be summoned in fixed places by bishops and by the magnates of the whole land for the purpose of reforming both the peace and the institutions of the holy faith.[10]

But the Peace movement was changing. In 1038, for the first and perhaps only time, its adherents took arms to enforce the Peace, in the so-called Peace militia organized by Archbishop Aimon of Bourges. As Thomas Head points out in his study of this incident (Chapter 9), the creation of the Peace militia marked a major turning point in the course of the Peace movement. Moreover, the only detailed source for this episode comes from the pen of Andrew of Fleury, the first spokesman for the monastic reform movement to oppose a Peace measure. In Chapter 4, Guy Lobrichon analyzes another piece of propaganda produced, or at least used, by monastic reformers of this time. A vitriolic attack on heretics, it reveals under probing analysis that many of the concerns that preoccupied Andrew, such as the protection of monastic property and a distrust of lay religious enthusiasm, played a vital role in the battles fought by monks within the orbit of Cluny.

In the 1040s, the Peace movement underwent profound changes. The Peace of God had been an attempt to protect the unarmed, particularly the clergy, at all times. What followed was the proclamation of the Truce of God, an attempt to outlaw all fighting, but only during certain periods of religious significance. The Truce first appeared in 1027 at the council of Elne (or Toulouges).[11] It later became a dominant feature of the Peace movement at the synod of Arles (ca. 1041), where the bishops prohibited all Christians from engaging in combat from Thursday to Monday morning (in commemoration of Christ's passion), on important feast days, and in the seasons of Advent and Lent. Once again excommunication was threatened, but the importance of relics and the *populus* was considerably diminished. Unlike earlier councils, whose canons were limited to the jurisdictions of the bishops there summoned, the bishops who gathered at Arles suggested that their actions be applied throughout the kingdom of France. The idea soon spread to neighboring kingdoms, particularly by means of the efforts of Cluniac monks.

The Truce of God was both more and less ambitious in its aims than the Peace promulgated at earlier councils. The bishops of the early

[10] Rodulphus Glaber, *Historiarum*, 4.5.14. See Appendix A for a longer excerpt from Glaber's work.
[11] See the translation of the canons of this council in Appendix A.

Peace movement had been first and foremost concerned with the unarmed. They had not punished violence perpetrated against armed
men, and thus they had in essence failed to question the right of the
milites to take up arms at will. The Truce of God, however, suggested
that the very shedding of Christian blood was sinful. As a canon of the
council of Narbonne (1054) phrased it, "No Christian should kill another Christian, since whoever kills a Christian doubtless sheds the
blood of Christ."[12] With such restraints on his actions within Christendom, the knight found the prospect of battle against Christ's enemies
increasingly attractive, for the Truce encouraged the idea that combat
pleased God only in defense of Christendom. When, at the council of
Clermont in 1095, Urban II called on the knights of western Europe to
aid their Christian brethren in the east through the First Crusade, his
first canon proclaimed the renewal of the Truce of God.

In addition to this change from a focus on protected groups to one
on protected times, the Truce also shifted the means by which it enforced its measures from hierarchic command to communal consent:
often the police forces of the prince were specifically exempted from
the proscription on combat. The Truce thus appealed to lay lords, who
embraced it as an ecclesiastical support for enforcing law and order
through centralized government. In the empire, for example, both emperors and dukes disseminated and enforced the Truce, known in German as the *Landfrieden,* as part of their efforts to redirect the military
power of their knights against foreign enemies. Thus, over the course
of the twelfth century, the Truce of God was inexorably co-opted by
secular authorities and became part of the emerging constitutional order of governance and peacekeeping. By the mid-twelfth century in
France, the Peace of God had become the king's Peace.[13] In fact, truce
days constituted the first moments at which, at least in theory and by
legal definition, public authority held a monopoly on the legitimate
use of violence, an idea that was to become one of the cornerstones of
the modern concept of the state.

The spread of the Truce and the slow cessation of formal Peace
councils did not, however, mark an abrupt end, to the general concerns
of the Peace movement. Geoffrey Koziol in Chapter 10 examines an
event that most treatments of the Peace movement would not include,
the journey (*delatio*) of the relics of Saint Ursmer in 1060. Placing the
episode in the context of contemporary civil disorder within the Ottonian empire, Koziol shows how monks used relics, and the large

---

[12] Mansi 19:827.
[13] Aryeh Graboïs, "De la trève de Dieu à la paix du roi: Etude sur les transformations
du mouvement de la paix au XIIe siècle," in *Mélanges offerts à René Crozet* (Poitiers, 1966),
1:585–96.

crowds those relics drew, as a means to pressure recalcitrant warriors into reconciliation—a technique pioneered in the Peace movement.

The Truce of God has to some extent overshadowed the earlier Peace of God in historical memory. In its most domesticated forms it was part of the governmental order of late medieval society. Many modern scholars have investigated it as one of the building blocks of the Christian ideology of holy war which led to the undertaking of the Crusades. In 1915, one historically minded member of the British army recalled it in a letter home that described the remarkable events surrounding the celebration of Christmas on the western front: "All at once Germans came scurrying from their trenches and British from theirs, and a marvellous thing happened. . . . a sudden friendship had been struck up, the truce of God had been called, and for the rest of Christmas day not a shot was fired along our section."[14]

France and Western Europe at the Turn of the Millennium

Since the 1950s, we have witnessed a quiet revolution in the historiography of the Middle Ages. Robert Fossier summarized the fruits of this research when he sought

> to underline . . . the leading place the late tenth and eleventh centuries ought to occupy in our vision of the Middle Ages. Personally, I am convinced that, in those hundred years, there took place an overturning both of ideologies and of economic and social infrastructures to a degree even greater than that which occurred during the late Roman Empire or the sixteenth century. And I would not hesitate to compare it to that which, beginning at the end of the last century, so harshly jolted our own world.[15]

Historians once favored the twelfth century as a time of renaissance and renewal. They have come more recently to recognize, with Fossier, that momentous, if less immediately striking, social and cultural change began in the latter half of the tenth century, change that gained its full momentum only over the course of the following century. The titles of surveys of this period illustrate the point: Jean-Pierre Poly and Eric Bournazel's *Mutation féodale* and Robert Fossier's *Enfance de l'Europe*

[14] A letter from a member of the Sixth Gordon Highlanders quoted in Modris Ecksteins, *Rites of Spring: The Great War and the Birth of the Modern Age* (New York: 1989), p. 123.

[15] Robert Fossier, "Les mouvements populaires en Occident au XIe siècle," *Académie des Inscriptions et Belles-Lettres: Comptes rendus des séances de l'année 1971*, 1971, pp. 257–69. For the expression of similar sentiments, see J. Dhondt and Michel Rouche, *Le haut moyen âge: VIIe–XIIe siècles* (Paris, 1968), pp. 245–56.

supposedly treat the entire period from the early tenth to the close of the twelfth century, but both focus closely on the decades around the turn of the millennium.[16]

The picture of western Europe from the late tenth through the eleventh century emerging from this research has four main components. First, Europe ceased to be the victim of periodic foreign invasion and, in a dramatic reversal, became the aggressively imperial and colonial power it has continued to be to the present day.[17] Second, the region's economy experienced unprecedented growth in both agriculture and mercantile commerce, an expansion that included a steady increase of population, the rise of autonomous cities, and the widespread use of old and new technologies.[18] Third, a profound shift in mental structures engendered the growth of literacy and texts, the beginnings of a new awareness of the self, and the reestablishment of public modes of governance.[19] Most important, the practice of Christianity itself pro-

[16] Jean-Pierre Poly and Eric Bournazel, *La mutation féodale: Xe–XIIe siècles* (Nouvelle Clio, 16; Paris, 1980) (in English, *The Feudal Transformation, 900–1200* [New York, 1991]); Robert Fossier, *L'enfance de l'Europe (Xe–XIIe siècles): Aspects économiques et sociaux,* 2 vols. (Nouvelle Clio, 17; Paris, 1982). Both works contain excellent bibliographies that can orient the reader to the broad scope of recent research. Insight into current research can be found in two volumes published for the millennial anniversary of the Capetian accession: *La France de l'an mil,* ed. Robert Delort (Paris, 1990), and *Religion et culture autour de l'an mil: Royaume capétien et Lotharingie,* ed. Dominique Iogna-Prat and Jean-Charles Picard (Paris, 1990).

[17] Scholars have paid surprisingly little attention to the cessation of the so-called second age of invasion, but the volume of works on the First Crusade, the most obvious symptom of European expansion, is staggering. Useful summary treatments may be found in Jonathan Riley-Smith, *The Crusades: A Short History* (New Haven, Conn. 1987), and Hans-Eberhard Mayer, *The Crusades,* 2d ed., trans. J. Gillingham (Oxford, 1988), which is particularly good on the relationship of the First Crusade to the Peace of God.

[18] See, for example, such works as Georges Duby, *Guerriers et paysans, VIIIe–XIIe siècle: Premier essor de l'économie européene* (Paris, 1973) (in English, *The Early Growth of the European Economy: Warriors and Peasants from the Seventh to the Twelfth Century,* trans. Howard Clarke [London, 1974]), Lynn White, *Medieval Technology and Social Change* (Oxford, 1962), and André Chédeville, "Le rôle de la monnaie et l'apparition du crédit dans les pays de l'Ouest de la France, XIe–XIIIe siècle," *Cahiers de civilization médiévale* 17 (1974), 305–25.

[19] On these related problems, see such different works as M. T. Clanchy, *From Memory to Written Record: England, 1066–1307* (Cambridge, 1979); Brian Stock, *The Implications of Literacy: Written Language and Models of Interpretation in the Eleventh and Twelfth Centuries* (Princeton, N.J., 1983); Colin Morris, *The Discovery of the Individual, 1050–1200* (London, 1972); Caroline Bynum, "Did the Twelfth Century Discover the Individual?" *Journal of Ecclesiastical History* 31 (1980), 1–17; Alexander Murray, *Reason and Society in the Middle Ages,* 2d ed. (Oxford, 1985); Susan Reynolds, *Kingdoms and Communities in Western Europe, 900–1300* (Oxford, 1984); Peter Brown, "Society and the Supernatural: A Medieval Change," *Daedalus* 104 (1975), 133–51; and Charles Radding, *A World Made by Men: Cognition and Society, 400–1200* (Chapel Hill, N.C. 1985). These authors adopt a wide variety of theoretical stances, from functional anthropology (Brown) to psychohistory (Radding). Many of them have located the decisive changes they study in the twelfth century, although a recent trend is to see the more culturally visible changes of the twelfth in relation to those of the previous century.

foundly changed. The impulse for reform, associated with such centers as Cluny and Gorze, spread among traditional monasteries. Similar movements reshaped canonical life, and eremitic monasticism experienced a strong revival. By the end of the eleventh century, these developments had led to the birth of the Premonstratensian and Cistercian orders, novelties in terms of ecclesiastical organization. This transformation of religious life aided and abetted the parallel efforts of the Gregorian reformers in the papal curia, efforts that in turn helped to shape the growth of papal monarchy. At the same time, laypeople expressed growing religious enthusiasm in ways both traditional and novel, ranging from pilgrimage and relic cults to the pursuit of the apostolic life.[20] And tragically, as R. I. Moore has eloquently shown, in responding to these changes, members of the ecclesiastical and secular hierarchies formulated means for repressing dissent.[21]

This focus on the turn of the millennium is not a creation of modern historiography. One eleventh-century historian associated with Cluny, Rodulphus Glaber, seemed acutely aware that society was undergoing epochal changes. He noted that western Europe was a specially blessed region for the growth of Christianity because Christ had faced west and had held his right hand to the north while on the cross at Calvary.[22] He depicted the decades that followed the millennial anniversary of Christ's birth as a time of religious revival, reporting how in the "third year after the aforementioned millennium . . . there occurred throughout the whole world, and most particularly in Italy and Gaul," a profusion of church building.[23] It was as if "the world itself, shaking off the old, had covered itself with a shining white mantle [*candida uestis*] of churches."[24] If Glaber had been simply commenting on the color of those churches, he could have used the more usual adjective *albus*,

[20] A general orientation to these religious changes may be found in Etienne Delaruelle, *La piété populaire au moyen âge* (Turin, 1975); André Vauchez, *La spiritualité du moyen âge occidental (VIIIe–XIIe siècles)* (Paris, 1975); Jacques Paul, *L'Eglise et la culture en occident*, 2 vols. (Nouvelle Clio, 15; Paris, 1986); and Colin Morris, *The Papal Monarchy: The Western Church from 1050 to 1250* (Oxford, 1989). On some of the specific points mentioned here, see Henrietta Leyser, *Hermits and the New Monasticism: A Study of Religious Communities in Western Europe, 1000–1150* (London, 1984); John Van Engen, "The 'Crisis of Cenobitism' Reconsidered: Benedictine Monasticism in the Years 1050–1150," *Speculum* 61 (1986), 269–304; Thomas Head, *Hagiography and the Cult of Saints: The Diocese of Orléans, 800–1200* (Cambridge Studies in Medieval Life and Thought, 4th ser., 14; Cambridge, 1990); and Lester Little, *Religious Poverty and the Profit Economy in Medieval Europe* (Ithaca, N.Y., 1978).

[21] R. I. Moore, *The Origins of European Dissent* (London, 1977), as modified by his more recent *The Formation of a Persecuting Society: Power and Deviance in Western Europe, 950–1250* (London, 1987).

[22] Glaber, *Historiarum*, 1.5.24.

[23] Glaber, *Historiarum*, 3.6.19.

[24] Glaber, *Historiarum*, 3.4.13.

whereas the term *candidus* recalled biblical passages describing the coming of the kingdom of heaven.[25] He thus implicitly shared with the monks of Cluny the association of the renewal of the cults of saints, the rebuilding of churches, and the reform of the monastic life which occurred during his own lifetime as a kind of realized eschatology.[26] In his prologue, dedicated to Abbot Odilo of Cluny, Glaber assured his readers that the Savior would bring about such "new things" (*nova*) until the last hour of the last day.[27] These comments contradicted an almost universally accepted historiographic tradition, hallowed by Augustine, which taught that the world was growing old (*mundus senescit*). On the verge of the final judgment, according to the old wisdom, new things could only be bad. For Glaber and his contemporaries, even the concept of renewal had to be reinvented.

The kingdom of France, under the uncertain rule of its new Capetian dynasty, was at the very center of these transformations. Since George's Duby's study of the Mâconnais was published in the 1950s, a generation of historians—schooled in the methodology of Marc Bloch, Lucien Febvre, and their journal *Annales: Economies, sociétés, civilisations*—has produced dense studies of other regions of Capetian France and its neighbors.[28] Collectively these works provide a comprehensive history of the transformation of west Frankish society.[29] These historians usually tell the story in terms of a "castellan revolution." Somewhere between 970 and 1030, local lords in many regions of west Frankland began to build motte and bailey castles, often forgoing or extorting the traditional permission of their overlords. From these fortifications they established their personal authority over the surrounding countryside. They constrained free and servile peasantry alike and, at the same time, ceased to participate regularly in the courts of their counts, gatherings that had previously constituted the political and judicial center of the rural countryside. This devolution of public power (*bannum*) to the smallest unit of political organization (the castellan's *districtio*) marks the collapse of the *pagus* (the area governed by a

---

[25] Mark 9:3; 16:5. James 2:2. Rev. 1:14; 2:17; 10:30; 14:14; 15:6; 19:8; 20:11. In Mark, for example, the word is used to describe Christ's garments during the transfiguration and the garments of the angel who guarded Christ's tomb; in Revelation, it describes the clothing of the saints and angels, the throne of God, and the cloud on which the Son of Man sits.

[26] Edmond Ortigues and Dominique Iogna-Prat, "Raoul Glaber et l'historiographie clunisienne," *Studi medievali*, 3d ser., 26 (1985), 537–72.

[27] Glaber, *Historiarum*, preface.

[28] Georges Duby, *La société aux XIe et XIIe siècles dans la région mâconnaise* (Paris, 1953; 2d ed., 1971).

[29] A useful guide to these regional studies may be found in Jean Dunbabin, *France in the Making, 843–1180* (Oxford, 1985), pp. 421–26.

count), which had served as the last remnant of the Carolingian empire and its elaborate system of governance.[30] It also marked the beginning of the manorial regime that characterizes what Marc Bloch has called "the second feudal age."[31]

Although in some areas of west Frankland this development predated the election of Hugh Capet to the throne in 987, the accession of the Capetians, occurring as it did under circumstances of dubious legitimacy, provided added impetus to the collapse of central authority, which in turn gave rise to intensified warfare among castellans and knights fighting for land, peasants, and power. Both Christian Lauranson-Rosaz and André Debord draw in Chapters 5 and 6 on regional studies to show how, in the Auvergne and the Aquitaine, processes of social change helped to give birth to the Peace of God.[32]

The consequences of this change in the locus and exercise of power reached all levels of Frankish society. The high nobility (king, dukes, counts, and even viscounts) saw their traditional authority, especially their claim to exercise justice according to the rights of the *bannum*, eroding. In particular, they found themselves forced to come to new accommodations with those who were in theory their subordinates.[33] But even the supposed winners in this affair, the castellans, paid a heavy price: to maintain their new power they had to reorganize inheritance patterns. They thus shifted from loosely defined aristocratic clans to rigid agnatic lineages in which one son inherited the whole patrimony. The full and painful consequences of primogeniture and

---

[30] Jean-François Lemarignier, "La dislocation du 'pagus' et le problème des 'consuetudines' (X–XI siècles)," in *Mélanges d'histoire du moyen âge dédiés à la mémoire de Louis Halphen*, ed. Charles-Edmond Perrin (Paris, 1951), pp. 401–10.

[31] Bloch dated the beginning of this age to ca. 1050; see *La société féodale*, 2 vols. (Paris, 1939–40) (in English, *Feudal Society*, trans. L. A. Manyon [London, 1961]). Historians use Bloch's terminology and chronology widely, but, as Thomas Bisson has pointed out, recent research has shifted the beginning of this manorial regime to ca. 1000; see Bisson's introduction to Georges Duby, *The Three Orders: Feudal Society Imagined,* trans. Arthur Goldhammer (Chicago, 1985), p. ii. For an excellent discussion of the issues involved, see R. I. Moore, "Duby's Eleventh Century," *History* 69 (1984), 36–49.

[32] And see Christian Lauranson-Rosaz, *L'Auvergne et ses marges (Velay, Gévaudan) du VIIIe au XIe siècle. La fin du monde antique?* (Le Puy-en-Velay, 1987), and André Debord, *La société laïque dans les pays de Charente: Xe–XIIe siècles* (Paris, 1984).

[33] This process has been traced, with local variations, in many of the various lands that once constituted the Carolingian empire. See particularly Jean-François Lemarignier, *Le gouvernement royal aux premiers temps capétiens (987–1108)* (Paris, 1965); Eric Bournazel, *Le gouvernement capétien au XIIe siècle: Structures sociales et mutations institutionnelles* (Paris, 1975); Karl Leyser, *Rule and Conflict in an Early Medieval Society: Ottonian Saxony* (Bloomington, Ind. 1979); and Giovanni Tabacco, *Egemonie sociali e strutture del potere nel Medioevo italiano* (Rome, 1973) (in English, *The Struggle for Power in Medieval Italy: Structures of Political Rule,* trans. Rosalind Jensen [Cambridge, 1989]).

the resulting disinheritance of younger sons were to be played out over subsequent centuries.[34]

The concomitant reorganization of the countryside had equally powerful effects on the peasantry. For them, the lord's new exercise of the *bannum* meant the imposition of so-called evil customs (*malae consuetudines*), a wide array of demands, exactions, and extortions.[35] In the most general terms, these "customs" involved a homogenization of status among the tillers of the soil. At the time the last remnants of slavery were disappearing, so too were those free, and armed, peasants who had once attended the courts of the counts. By absenting both themselves and their peasants from these comital courts and thus causing their demise, the castellans struck another blow at the power of both the high nobility and the free peasantry. In a sense, all the *rustici* or *agricolae* thus became servile. They were subject to the local lord's power to impose his justice and to demand labor, payments, or lodging for his troops. They had descended from a position of relative, albeit inferior, autonomy to one of closely regulated control.[36]

The ecclesiastical hierarchy also suffered at the hands of the castellans and their expanding military power. Although the appropriation of church property by lay lords was by no means new, the scale of such pillage seems to have become larger during this period, the perpetrators came ever more from the lesser nobility, and, most important, church leaders could hope for little help from their so-called protectors. On the contrary, castellans often enough interpreted their temporal rights (*advocatia et vicaria*) over ecclesiastical lands as a virtual licence to plunder. As Abbo of Fleury complained, "Those who are these days called defenders of churches [*advocati*] defend that which by law belongs to the church only for their own use against the authority of laws and canons. They thus inflict violence on clerics and monks,

---

[34] For the consequences in French society, see, in particular, Léopold Genicot, "The Nobility in Medieval Francia: Continuity, Break, or Evolution?" in *Lordship and Community in Medieval Europe*, ed. Fredric Cheyette (New York, 1975), pp. 128–36; Janet Martindale, "The French Aristocracy in the Early Middle Ages: A Reappraisal," *Past and Present* 75 (1977), 5–45; and Constance Bouchard, "The Origins of the French Nobility: A Reassessment," *American Historical Review* 86 (1981), 501–32.

[35] For divergent views on this subject, see Elisabeth Magnou-Nortier, "Les mauvaises coutumes en Auvergne, Bourgogne méridionale, Languedoc et Provence au XIe siècle: Un moyen d'analyse sociale," in *Structures féodales et féodalisme dans l'Occident méditerranéen (Xe–XIIIe siècles)* (Collection de l'Ecole française de Rome, 44; Paris, 1980), pp. 135–72, and Christian Lauranson-Rosaz, "Les mauvaises coutumes d'Auvergne (fin Xe–XIe siècles)," *Annales du Midi* 102 (1990), 557–86.

[36] See particularly Pierre Dockès, *Medieval Slavery and Liberation*, trans. Arthur Goldhammer (Chicago, 1982), and Pierre Bonassie, *From Slavery to Feudalism in South Western Europe*, trans. Jean Birrell (Cambridge, 1991).

and they rob the property of churches and monasteries for their own use and profit."[37]

The Peace movement was not, of course, the only available means of resolving property disputes and feuds. In many cases, charges of violence were merely topoi invoked by ecclesiastical writers against lay donors who attempted to regain some lost, disputed, or misunderstood rights over property. More important, as the Carolingian legal system was disintegrating over the course of the tenth and early eleventh centuries, a new set of legal customs and traditions began to take their place. Disputes between aristocratic lineages and monastic communities over property could extend for generations; Barbara Rosenwein concludes that such records require a redefinition of the very concept of ownership. Fredric Cheyette has shown how litigants in such cases sought to reach compromises acceptable to both sides, and Stephen White and Patrick Geary have demonstrated that individual laymen, and sometimes women, acted as representatives of lineages, constrained by the ties of kinship. In such circumstances it is often more accurate to speak of families than of individuals, of custom than of law.[38] One striking example of how this new scholarship in legal history can enrich our understanding of the Peace of God and its relationship to various means of peacekeeping may be found in Geoffrey Koziol's analysis (Chapter 10) of feuds in mid-eleventh-century Flanders.

Although many of the new legal customs were not to develop fully until well after the flowering of the Peace movement, it is necessary for us to place the Peace within a wide range of attempts to resolve conflict in Frankish society. Central to this problem was the feud (*faida*). From the premigration period until the turn of the millennium and well beyond, the feud served as one of the central forces in Frankish society. As one historian has remarked, "It is not difficult to arrive at . . . a working definition of feud. We may call it, first, the threat of hostility between kins; then, the state of hostility between them; and finally the

---

[37] Abbo of Fleury, *Collectio canonum*, chap. 2; *PL* 139:476–77.

[38] Barbara Rosenwein, *To Be the Neighbor of Saint Peter: The Social Meaning of Cluny's Property, 909–1049* (Ithaca, N.Y., 1989); Fredric Cheyette, "Suum cuique tribuere," *French Historical Studies* 6 (1970), 287–99; Patrick Geary, "Vivre en conflit dans une France sans état: Typologie des mécanisms de règlement des conflicts (1050–1200)," *Annales: E.S.C.* 41 (1986), 1107–33; Stephen White, " 'Pactum . . . Legem Vincit et Amor Judicium': The Settlement of Disputes by Compromise in Eleventh-Century Western France, " *American Journal of Legal History* 22 (1978), 281–308; and idem, *Custom, Kinship, and Gifts to Saints: The "Laudatio parentum" in Western France, 1050–1150* (Chapel Hill, N.C., 1988). For similar conclusions on the resolution of conflicts in another medieval society, see William Ian Miller, "Avoiding Legal Judgment: The Submission of Disputes to Arbitration in Medieval Iceland," *American Journal of Legal History* 28 (1984), 95–134. On the problem of conflict resolution in the early Middle Ages, see the model of collaborative argument provided in the essays collected in Wendy Davies and Paul Fouracre, eds., *The Settlement of Disputes in Early Medieval Europe* (Cambridge, 1986).

satisfaction of their differences and a settlement on terms acceptable to both."[39] It was at base the state of dispute between kindred; thus it imposed numerous and onerous obligations on a society, particularly a nobility, which understood itself in kinship terms. It carried within it the threat of bloodshed but did not necessarily lead to violence. Despite its deceptively simple and relatively consistent form, the feud emerged in myriad ways according to its social and political context. Historians have thus treated it in similarly varied ways; it has become a crucial and controversial issue in the interpretation of Frankish, and more generally Germanic, society.[40]

Since similar combinations of dispute, vengeance, and resolution are to found in varied forms throughout tribal societies, the feud has also proved to be of great interest to anthropologists. A generation of functionalists portrayed it as a potential stabilizing force in society, since people caught in a web of conflicting obligations strive to resolve the conflict. In a famous phrase, Max Gluckman talked of the resulting "peace in the feud."[41] No such easy peace, however, was to be found in the Capetian kingdom. Indeed, recent anthropologists have criticized the "extraordinary optimism" of the functionalist approach.[42] Such anthropologists might welcome the possible insights provided by the historical study of social change over time which the Peace movement provides.

These issues of conflict resolution and the feud underline one major problem in assessing the importance of the Peace of God: much depends on how serious one judges the threat posed by violence to have been. Some historians, pointing to the long-term stability of new forms of lordship and the consistency of other forms of conflict resolution, deny the existence of any "castellan revolution" or "feudal anarchy." They portray the shift in power around the turn of the millennium—whether it be the dynastic one from Carolingian to Ottonian or Capetian, or the more regional change from count to castellan—as relatively

[39] J. M. Wallace-Hadrill, "The Bloodfeud of the Franks," in *The Long-Haired Kings* (London, 1962), pp. 121–47 (quotation on p. 122).

[40] The classic, and still useful, statement of the problem was provided by Marc Bloch, *Feudal Society*, pp. 125–30. The bibliography on the subject since the work of Bloch is extensive; for useful orientation, see Stephen White, "Feuding and Peace-Making in the Touraine around the Year 1100," *Traditio* 42 (1986), 195–263, particularly p. 195, note 1. Some of the most interesting recent analyses of feuding concern Iceland, making use of the rich material provided by the sagas; see, for example, Jesse Byock, *Feud in the Icelandic Saga* (Berkeley, 1982), and William Ian Miller, *Bloodtaking and Peacemaking: Feud, Law, and Society in Saga Iceland* (Chicago, 1990).

[41] Max Gluckman, *Custom and Conflict in Africa* (Oxford, 1956), pp. 1–26.

[42] The phrase is that of Renato Rosaldo, *Ilongot Headhunting, 1883–1974: A Study in Society and History* (Stanford, Calif., 1980), p. 273. Rosaldo's own work provides a model of diachronic analysis in ethnography. Orientation to recent anthropological literature may be found in Laura Nader and Harry Todd, *The Disputing Process in Ten Societies* (New York, 1978), particularly in the introduction by the editors on pp. 1–40.

smooth and orderly. Such interpretations, represented here by the essays of Elisabeth Magnou-Nortier and Hans-Werner Goetz, may offer
an important antidote to the more dramatic readings. They point to
strong continuities between the Peace of God and earlier judicial institutions, as well as to contemporary peacekeeping efforts by secular
lords. In the calm and measured cadences of their analyses, the Peace
of God, while still important, emerges as less innovative than it does
elsewhere in this collection. These authors show that the Peace was one
of several institutional means used by the secular and ecclesiastical hierarchies to contain and channel social change.

At the same time, it is important to remember that historical hind-
sight may mask the depth of social convulsion, thus making moments
of genuine crisis seem inevitable and their solutions obvious. After all,
the following century produced a vast array of cultural and political innovations for which the depiction of continuity offers little explanation.
Rather, disorder somehow gave rise to a more creative and dynamic society. Some scholars, seeking to explain this change, have turned to the
religious fervor among the *populus:* at the turn of the millennium one
finds commoners—singly, in small communities, in large crowds—tak
ing the initiative in organizing relic cults, vowing themselves to pilgrimage to both local shrines and Jerusalem, and searching for the apostolic
life. Bernhard Töpfer presents one, but only one, side of this activity in
Chapter 2 when he charts the growth of new and renewed relic cults at
the turn of the millennium. The extraordinary interest in relics that
period witnessed was to play an enormous role in the Peace of God, as
the essays of Christian Lauranson-Rosaz, Daniel Callahan, Richard
Landes, Thomas Head, and Geoffrey Koziol all document.

Yet, there was another side to lay, and indeed to clerical, religious
enthusiasm. In addition to pious pilgrims, the documents also speak
for the first—but not the last—time of executions of heretics in the
early years of the eleventh century Guy Lobrichon's redating of the
"Letter" of Heribert—long thought to be simply a symptom of twelfth-
century concerns—to the early eleventh century provides added evidence, not only of the strength of religious change among the laity, but
of the harsh reaction such creativity met among the ecclesiastical hierarchy. Landes and Head explore yet other ways in which religious enthusiasms, judged both orthodox and heretical by the clergy, took hold
of the *populus* in close conjunction with the Peace of God.

All these issues might seem arcane and quite irrelevant to the social
and economic historian. But the strong links between religion and its
social context are undeniable. It was in the presence of both the relics
of saints and the *populus* that the lay and clerical aristocracy prevailed
on the warriors of a region to abjure violence and maintain God's

peace. The leaders combined religious with social pressure to enforce
compliance: curses threatened the *milites* with chastisement from the
saints whose relics had been present, excommunications entailed exclusion from the sacramental means to salvation, and both meant social
ostracism through the hostility of the paraded masses and even of one's
fellow fighting men.

In describing the climactic wave of Peace activity that marked the
millennium of Christ's Passion in 1033, Glaber told of the jubilant
throngs who gathered on these occasions and, believing that they were
joining in a covenant with God, raised the palms of their hands sky-
ward and shouted "Peace! Peace! Peace!"[43] This startling picture has
led historians to call the Peace of God "the first mass religious movement of the Middle Ages."[44] They thus emphasize how, in dramatic
and perhaps unprecedented ways, the Peace of God introduced the
populus as an actor on the stage of European history and helped to
teach that group how to organize itself. If, as Loren MacKinney first
pointed out a half century ago and as R. I. Moore has forcefully emphasized more recently, the great revolutionary movements of the late
eleventh century—the Gregorian reform, the communes, and the crusades—all shared elements in common, foremost among them was the
active role of the *populus,* a role first played in the Peace movement.[45]
It would be a curious kind of ethnocentrism not to understand that the
behavior of the lower classes in western European culture—their vigor,
initiative, and even aggression—constitutes one of that civilization's
most unique features.

The Plan of This Book

The great strides made in interpreting the social change that
marked the world of the year 1000 have impelled us and our collaborators to reexamine the place of the Peace of God in the development
of Frankish, and more generally of western European, society. It has
been over twenty-five years since Hartmut Hoffmann published his
Gottesfriede und Treuga Dei, the last full-scale treatment of the Peace
movement and the Truce to have appeared, which, to its credit, raised

---

[43] Glaber, *Historiarum,* 4.5.16.

[44] Carl Erdmann, *Die Entstehung des Kreuzzungsgedankens* (Forschungen zur Kirchen-
und Geistesgeschichte, 6; Stuttgart, 1935), p. 66. See also the similar remark of Bernhard
Töpfer, *Volk und Kirche zur Zeit der beginnenden Gottesfriedensbewegung im Frankreich* (Neue
Beiträge zur Geschichtswissenschaft, 1; Berlin, 1957), p. 105.

[45] See MacKinney, "People and Public Opinion," as well as the more recent comments
of R. I. Moore, "Family, Community and Cult on the Eve of the Gregorian Reform,"
Transactions of the Royal Historical Society, 5th ser. 30 (1980), 49–69.

more questions than it resolved. As editors we have chosen to limit this volume to the Peace of God itself and not take up the very different problems posed by its institutionalization under the Truce of God in the mid-eleventh and twelfth centuries.[46] The essays collected here focus on, although they are not limited to, events between the 980s and 1040s.

Earlier versions of the essays by Frederick Paxton, Guy Lobrichon, Daniel Callahan, Richard Landes, Thomas Head, and Geoffrey Koziol appeared in an issue of the journal *Historical Reflections / Réflexions Historiques.*[47] Reaction to that collection provided impetus to the solicitation of further contributions, particularly from French and German scholars. The result is a mix of methods which spans the range of research on western Europe in the tenth and early eleventh centuries. With certain exceptions—Berhard Töpfer's seminal article published in German in 1956, Amy G. Remensynder's essay, written expressly for this volume in response to the *Historical Reflections* collection, and R. I. Moore's Postscript—the articles contained here present significantly revised versions of work published in the past decade. All the essays by French and German scholars appear here in English translation for the first time.

The collection begins with a historiographic essay by Frederick Paxton which sets the work of our collaborators against the backdrop of a century of historical research and debate. The remaining contributions fall roughly into three groupings: first, three introductory discussions that set the Peace of God in the specific contexts of the histories of relic cults and pilgrimage, of legal vocabulary, and of heresy; second, six regional studies of the Peace—some focused on specific incidents, others on more general themes—presented in loosely chronological sequence; finally, two general assessments of the Peace councils, one as a coherent movement in itself and the other as part of wider currents of ecclesias-

[46] On the later developments, see Thomas Bisson, "The Organized Peace in Southern France and Catalonia, ca. 1140–ca. 1233," *American Historical Review* 82 (1977), 290–311; Roger Bonnaud-Delamare, "La légende des associations de la paix en Rouergue et en Languedoc au début du XIIIe siècle (1170–1229)," *Bulletin philologique et historique, Comité des travaux historiques et scientifiques* (1938), 47–78; Michel de Boüard, "Sur les origines de la Trève de Dieu en Normandie," *Annales de Normandie* 9 (1959), 169–89; André Joris, "Observations sur la proclamation de la Trève de Dieu à Liège à la fin du XIe siècle," in *La Paix* (Recueils de la Société Jean Bodin, 14; Brussels, 1962), pp. 503–45; Roger E. Reynolds, "Odilo and the *Treuga Dei* in Southern Italy: A Beneventan Manuscript Fragment," *Mediaeval Studies* 46 (1984), 450–62; and Bernhard Töpfer, "Die Anfange der Treuge Dei in Nordfrankreich," *Zeitschrift für Geschichtswissenschaft* 9 (1961), 876–93.

[47] *Essays on the Peace of God: The Church and the People in Eleventh-Century France,* ed. Thomas Head and Richard Landes (Historical Reflections / Réflexions historiques, 14.3; Waterloo, Ontario, 1987). One essay in the first volume, Bernard Bachrach's "The Northern Origins of the Peace Movement at Le Puy in 975," has not been included here from lack of space and overlap with Lauranson-Rosaz's essay.

tical reform. The volume concludes with one forceful reading of these essays in the form of a postscript by R. I. Moore—one of the leaders in the revolution in historical research outlined above—which places the dozen individual works into the context of recent historiography.

We do not pretend that any single or simple view of the Peace movement will emerge here. One of the most interesting aspects of interpreting this movement is that such interpretation requires the historian to take a stand, either implicit or explicit, on a host of related issues, from the class structure of Frankish society to the reality of the problems posed by violence and social disorder. The essays challenge many long-accepted opinions; in doing so they often disagree with one another. Different ways of reading the proffered evidence and interpretations will surely suggest themselves to each reader.

1

History, Historians, and
the Peace of God

FREDERICK S. PAXTON

The beginning of modern historiography on the early medieval Peace of God can be precisely dated to 1857.[1] In that year two monographs devoted to the subject appeared: in Paris, Ernest Semichon's *La paix et la trêve de Dieu;* in Leipzig, August Kluckhohn's *Geschichte des Gottesfriedens.* The impetus for Kluckhohn's work, shared by most German investigators, was the possibility that the ecclesiastical peace legislation of the late tenth and early eleventh centuries had given rise to the institution of the territorial peace (known in German as *Landfrieden*), which had long been regarded as one of the foundations of German constitutional development. Convinced that the nature of "so strange an institution" as the Peace of God could not be understood apart from the historical realities of the time and place of its origin, Kluckhohn began his work with a survey of the sociopolitical conditions prevailing in France around the turn of the millennium.[2] What he saw was unparalleled disorder in governmental, legal, and social institutions. In the face of incessant private warfare, against which the king was unable and the nobility unwilling to act, the French people, imbued with a "national spirit" peculiarly creative in the fight against political and social ills, turned to spiritual sanctions as the only available means to limit violence.[3] Since he defined the Peace as the containment

---

[1] Some earlier works are cited in Dolorosa Kennelly, "The Peace of God: Fact or Fiction?" (Ph.D. diss., University of California, Berkeley, 1962), p. 242, note 7. I owe my basic orientation in this subject to the historiographic essay that forms the first chapter of Kennelly's thesis.

[2] August Kluckhohn, *Geschichte des Gottesfriedens* (Leipzig, 1857; rpt., Aalen, 1966), pp. 1–12.

[3] Kluckhohn, *Geschichte*, pp. 18, 22; on the "franzözischer Geist," see p. 56.

of the feud, Kluckhohn did not place its inception before the first manifestations of the Truce of God, which put limitations on actual fighting rather than just sanctioning violence to ecclesiastical lands and dependents.[4] In the end, his research led him to reject the notion that the Peace of God was either the spiritual or formal basis of the *Landfrieden*, which, he argued, both preceded and coexisted with the Peace.[5]

Semichon's book was, by his own admission, something less than a work of pure scholarship[6] and has been described as "polemical and romantic."[7] Semichon was disturbed by the processes of industrialization and secularization in nineteenth-century French society. To the positivist vision of progress as achievement in science and technology, he opposed the notion that progress should be measured by the extent to which the principles of Christianity were applied to civil and political institutions.[8] His reading of medieval conciliar and narrative sources had convinced him that the "nouvelle barbarie" that he saw forming around him could be halted only by a return to the spirit of Christian association that had, in the form the Peace and Truce of God, saved medieval Europe from "la barbarie féodale."[9] Like Kluckhohn, Semichon argued that the origins of the Peace lay in the failure of public authority in the face of rampant private warfare during the later tenth and early eleventh centuries. Into the fray stepped the church, which created a civil code, a judiciary, and armed associations to keep the peace in each diocese. From these diocesan associations evolved diocesan communes, and from the latter evolved the municipal communes of the twelfth century.[10] By the thirteenth century, the French monarchy had grown strong enough to assume responsibility for public order, and the institutions of the Peace of God declined. The peacemaking activity of the medieval Church was so important, however, that Semichon was willing to credit it, not only with the origins of bourgeois

---

[4] Kluckhohn, *Geschichte*, pp. 37–42, especially p. 42, note 2.

[5] Kluckhohn, *Geschichte*, pp. 74–86.

[6] Ernest Semichon, *La paix et la trêve de Dieu: Histoire des premiers développements du tiers-état par l'église et les associations* (Paris, 1857), p. ix. In a second edition (Paris, 1869), Semichon reorganized his discussion and added chapters on Germany, scholastic philosophy, and the church as a source of social reform—a theme pursued even more vigorously than in the first edition.

[7] Kennelly, "Peace of God," p. 1.

[8] Semichon, *La paix et la trêve*, pp. 352–53.

[9] Semichon, *La paix et la trêve*, pp. 356–57.

[10] Semichon, *La paix et la trêve*, pp. 256–86; Kennelly points out the reasonableness of Semichon's belief in the existence of peace associations given his uncritical reading of the scholarship available to him, for his "scholarly contemporaries without exception derived the communes from associations of some kind, whether from free peasant communities or from Teutonic guilds"; "Peace of God," pp. 3–4.

liberties, but with all the cultural accomplishments of the West—in particular, of modern France.[11]

Such extravagant claims could not go unanswered, for they cut directly against the grain of French liberal traditions. The rise of the medieval communes was a particularly sensitive issue. French historiography on the communes, which had begun in earnest after the July Revolution of 1830, saw the self-governing communes as the vanguard of opposition to seigneurial oppression, identified as much with the power of the church as with that of the feudal aristocracy.[12] Semichon's rehabilitation of the role of the Catholic church in the history of liberty may have had a ready audience in the early years of the Second Empire, but the end of the marriage between throne and altar also saw the rejection of his thesis by eminent scholars of medieval urban life and institutions such as Achille Luchaire and Henri Pirenne.[13] Luchaire maintained that, although the Peace may have acclimatized common people to work together against the weight of lordship, it had little or no practical effect. The church and the communes were diametrically opposed in nature and purpose, and in point of fact churchmen had opposed communes at every turn. Pirenne fully agreed, and proposed a different explanation. The communes owed their origins to the intrinsic need of the merchants for peace; they had no connections with the Peace of God.[14]

While Semichon's work fell under the attack of liberal historians of urban institutions, Kluckhohn was criticized in 1892 by Ludwig Huberti in the first (and only) volume of a work on the legal history of the Peace of God and the *Landfrieden*.[15] Huberti traced the development of Peace legislation in France from the tenth to the thirteenth centuries, and his inclusion of extended citations from a vast array of medieval documents has, in the absence of a systematic collection of original sources on the Peace, kept his book a useful tool up to the present time.

[11] Semichon, *La paix et la trêve*, p. 318: "Le monde, et surtout la France moderne, sont sortis de l'église et du clergé catholique comme un fleuve sort de sa source."

[12] Albert Vermeesch, *Essai sur les origines et la signification de la commune dans le nord de la France (XIe et XIIe siècles)* (Studies Presented to the International Commission for the History of Representative and Parliamentary Institutions, 30; Heule, 1966), p. 17.

[13] Although not as radical a Catholic as Louis Veuillot, the editor of the journal *L'Univers*, Semichon certainly expressed a point of view that coincided with the high hopes of French Catholic supporters of the Second Republic and Napoleon III. On the alliance of throne and altar after 1848, see Ross Collins, *Catholicism and the Second French Republic* (New York, 1933), pp. 266–344; George P. Gooch, *The Second Empire* (London, 1960), pp. 230–51; and Alain Plessis, *The Rise and Fall of the Second Empire, 1852–1871*, trans. Jonathan Mandelbaum (Cambridge, 1985), pp. 135–37.

[14] On the views of Luchaire and Pirenne, see Vermeesch, *Essai sur les origines*, pp. 15–21.

[15] Ludwig Huberti, *Studien zur Rechtsgeschichte der Gottesfrieden und Landfrieden*, Vol. 1: *Die Friedensordnungen in Frankreich* (Ansbach, 1892).

Huberti saw the Peace of God as a *Kampf um Recht*—a struggle to transform the state of feud into one of peace and from there to one of law.[16] In opposition to Kluckhohn, Huberti argued that the Peace had no connection with social disorder but developed as a phase in a natural evolution of legal forms that had prepared the way for a territorial, rather than a personal (tribal), law to emerge in late tenth-century Aquitaine.[17] The church acted as the agent in this transformation by exercising judicial powers granted to it by Merovingian and Carolingian kings.[18] Once established through the regulations of the ecclesiastical Peace of God, the principle of territorial law was absorbed by secular rulers and made the basis of the *Landfrieden*. Thus, the Peace of God was a stage in an evolutionary process by which the barbarian law of the feud, under which individuals could prosecute their own disputes, was displaced by the "law of the land."[19]

Huberti disagreed fundamentally with Kluckhohn and conceived his work as a corrective to that of his German predecessor. He was less critical of Semichon, confining himself to (numerous) corrections on matters of dating and some remarks on Semichon's tendency to exaggerate the role of the clergy in medieval Europe and the connection between the Peace and the rise of the communes.[20] Whatever their differences of opinion or approach, though, all these scholars worked within the prevailing intellectual and political climate of the late nineteenth century. In such a climate, it was difficult for French historians to approach the question of the relation of the Peace to the communes dispassionately. The liberal interpretation of the origins of the communes that had emerged after the July Revolution was not likely to be recast after the events of 1870. Scholars on all sides of the issues believed, moreover, that only institutions of the most precise sort—that is, those definable in strictly legal terms—could be regarded as essential to the definition and development of a phenomenon like the Peace. Most operated on the added assumption that the presence of an institution at one time demanded a previous institution out of which it had developed. That is why Semichon sought to uncover the links in a causal chain that led from Peace councils to diocesan peace associations to communes. Huberti worried less about such concrete connections. In his view, the law had its own history, evolving of itself in a Hegelian

---

[16] Huberti, *Studien*, pp. 32–33.
[17] Huberti, *Studien*, pp. 70–79.
[18] Huberti, *Studien*, pp. 45–53.
[19] Huberti, *Studien*, p. 33: "Von hier aus scheint als Zweck der Bewegung die 'rechtliche Umbildung der Selbsthilfe' und zwar handelt es sich zunächst um Umbildung des Fehdezustandes in einen Friedenszustand, dann um Umbildung des Friedenszustandes in einen Rechtszustand."
[20] Huberti, *Studien*, pp. 327, 358–61.

pursuit of higher forms. In contrast, Kluckhohn's desire to root the history of the Peace within the context of *die menschlichen Kulterwelt* sounds rather modern.[21] Nevertheless, Kluckhohn's strictly legal definition of the Peace and his recourse to the vague, and romantic, notion of a French national spirit to explain its origins place him squarely among his contemporaries.

The nineteenth-century scholars who worked on the Peace of God left a mixed legacy. On the one hand, they laid the groundwork for all further study. They identified the Peace as a distinct object of historical interest, gathered the medieval records that referred to it, and raised several central issues: the precise legal nature of the Peace, the role of the church and feudal violence in its inception, and the relationship between the movement and such subsequent events as the rise of the communes and the creation of territorial rule. On the other hand, the rejection of Semichon and Kluckhohn by Luchaire, Pirenne, and Huberti left the Peace without much of a role in the history of France in the eleventh century. In their rush to discredit Semichon, Luchaire and Pirenne presented the Peace as ephemeral and inconsequential, a matter of churchmen only. By presenting the Peace as a transitional episode in the history of more enduring legal structures, Huberti's historical idealism had a similar effect. Kluckhohn's "strange institution" remained so.

This legacy from the past is apparent in the small quantity of works on the Peace produced in the early decades of this century, the best of which explored the patristic origins of its conceptions and rooted the desire for peace within an intellectual tradition stretching back to Augustine.[22] Gerhard Görris, for example, argued that a common adherence to this tradition was the glue that bound the coalition of churchmen and their allies among the nobility who first instituted the Peace of God.[23] Others saw the Peace as a primitive law of nations. Frédéric Duval contrasted the humanity of the Christian law of peace with the armed truce that preceded World War I.[24] Duval was romanticizing in the manner of Semichon, but Görris noted well the contours of religious thought that underlay the organization of the Peace. Nonetheless, Görris and his contemporaries still approached the Peace solely from within the history of law and legal institutions.[25]

[21] Kluckhohn, *Geschichte*, p. 1.
[22] Kennelly, "Peace of God," pp. 6–9.
[23] Gerhard Görris, *De denkbeelden over oorlog en de bemoeiingen voor vrede in de elfde eeuw* (Nijmegen, 1912).
[24] Frédéric Duval, *De la paix de Dieu à la paix du fer* (Paris, 1923); Kennelly, "Peace of God," p. 8.
[25] Kennelly, "Peace of God," p. 9; Görris, *Denkbeelden*, pp. 178–81.

In 1930, *Speculum* (then only in its fifth year) published an article by an American scholar from Louisiana State University, Loren MacKinney.[26] MacKinney noted that there was barely anything in English on "the popular aspects of the movement and its connection with public opinion."[27] He could have said the same for historiography in European languages.[28] His study implicitly criticized both the narrowness of strictly legal interpretations like Huberti's and the idealism of those who ascribed purely religious or ethical motivations to leaders of the Peace movement. Although MacKinney recognized an element of idealism in the movement, he did not extricate medieval churchmen from the social and economic structures of their day. After all, he reminded his readers, the Peace councils set out first and foremost to protect the lands and dependents of the church, "the greatest property-holder in Christendom."[29]

MacKinney's main purpose was to investigate the social context of the Peace movement from the viewpoint of popular participation. He noted, almost for the first time,[30] that there were large numbers of commoners at the Peace councils, and that relics of saints brought there by monks were the source of numerous miracles and outbursts of religious enthusiasm. He noted also that, when seen from this point of view, there were important similarities between the gatherings of the late tenth and early eleventh centuries and those that attended the calling of the First Crusade. He argued that the medieval churchmen who orchestrated the early Peace councils first awakened and then harnessed public opinion. Through the Peace movement, as he put it, "an apparently inactive populace was transformed into a positive ally of the Church and of social reform."[31] The movement reached its culmination in 1095 when Urban II "gave universal application, leadership, and publicity to the peace movement by combining it with another popular cause."[32] By bringing into focus the participation of the populace and the importance of popular religion in the Peace, MacKinney broke away from strictly legal interpretations and gave the Peace a place on the agenda for research in the social history of medieval Europe.

And MacKinney was not alone. At the same time, the German scholar Carl Erdmann was investigating the Peace movement from the point of view of the social history of the Crusades. In his famous work

---

[26] Loren C. MacKinney, "The People and Public Opinion in the Eleventh-Century Peace Movement," *Speculum* 5 (1930), 181–206.

[27] MacKinney, "People and Public Opinion," p. 181.

[28] Semichon had mentioned it; see *La paix et la trêve*, p. 323.

[29] MacKinney, "People and Public Opinion," p. 182.

[30] Cf. Huberti, *Studien*, pp. 230–31.

[31] MacKinney, "People and Public Opinion," p. 204.

[32] MacKinney, "People and Public Opinion," p. 201.

on the origins of the crusading idea, he characterized the Peace of God as a necessary precondition for the holy wars.[33] The Peace movement enrolled the warrior class of Europe in Christian society; it set limits to their fighting but sanctified its use against the enemies of Christendom. Like MacKinney, Erdmann recognized the depth of popular participation at both the Peace councils and at Clermont in 1095. Like him, Erdmann felt that neither the Peace movement nor the Crusades would have existed without popular support.

While Erdmann and MacKinney were opening up the social history of the Peace of God, a French scholar, Roger Bonnaud-Delamare, was picking up the thread of the intellectual-historical approach inaugurated by Görris. Bonnaud-Delamare began his work on the Peace of God by demolishing the documentary case for the peace associations in which Semichon had seen the origins of diocesan and urban communes.[34] The evidence for the existence of such associations was based on misreadings of primary sources and dissolved into mist when Bonnaud-Delamare checked into them. This led him to reject the basic premise of the legal historians—the essentially juridical nature of the Peace—and to look to the history of ideas for its meaning. The result was two theses, one for the University of Montpellier and the other for the Ecole des Chartes, which traced the nature and evolution of the idea of peace from the Carolingian age to the twelfth century.[35] Bonnaud-Delamare never published the second of the two studies, but in a short statement of his conclusions he expressed the view that a juridical understanding of the Peace of God misrepresented the depth of religious consciousness in the Middle Ages.[36] He concluded that the desire for peace was not motivated by opposition to private warfare, but by the conviction that "peace had to reign . . . because it represented a form of the glory of God on earth."[37] Any actual alleviation of the lawlessness of the time was an unexpected by-product of the

[33] Carl Erdmann, *Die Entstehung des Kreuzzugsgedankens* (Stuttgart, 1933; rpt., 1955), pp. 51–85 (in English, *The Origins of the Idea of Crusade*, trans. Marshall Baldwin and Walter Goffart [Princeton, 1977], pp. 57–94); Erdmann's conclusions had been foreshadowed by both Semichon, *La paix et la trêve*, pp. 298–305, and Duval, *La paix de Dieu*, pp. 33–43.

[34] Roger Bonnaud-Delamare, "La légende des associations de la paix en Rouergue et en Languedoc au début du XIIIe siècle (1170–1229), *Bulletin philologique et historique: Comité des travaux historiques et scientifiques, année 1936/37*, 1938, pp. 47–78. The nature of Semichon's "peace association" had been further elaborated by Georges Molinié in *L'organisation judiciaire, militaire et financière des associations de la paix* (Toulouse, 1912); for discussion, see Kennelly, "Peace of God," pp. 6–10.

[35] Roger Bonnaud-Delamare, *L'idée de paix à l'époque carolingienne* (Paris, 1939), and "L'idée de paix au XIe et XIIe siècles" (Ph.D. diss., Paris, 1945).

[36] Roger Bonnaud-Delamare, "Fondement des institutions de paix au XIe siècle," in *Mélanges d'histoire du moyen âge dédiés à la mémoire de Louis Halphen* (Paris, 1951), pp. 19–26.

[37] Bonnaud-Delamare, "Fondement," p. 20.

movement for peace, one that arose from neither the breakdown of civil order nor the evolution of legal forms but from the religious expectations connected with the millennial anniversary of Christ's life on earth. Thus the movement was directed not only against war but against "all forms of disorder: famine, epidemics, the death of the body and the death of the soul."[38]

Although his focus was on the religious character of the Peace, Bonnaud-Delamare did not completely ignore its social dimension. While maintaining his opposition to narrowly legal interpretations, he nonetheless noted that the Peace of God drove a wedge between the upper class (both lay and clerical) and the lower, between those who exercised power and the powerless who were in need of protection.[39] But such a cursory acknowledgment of the social dimensions of the movement was unacceptable to Bernhard Töpfer, an East German scholar who introduced the perspective of Marxist historiography into the discussion. Töpfer praised MacKinney for his attention to the popular aspects of the Peace but criticized him for assuming that public opinion had been created by churchmen.[40] He scorned Bonnaud-Delamare's conclusions on the religious orientation of the Peace as typical of bourgeois historical scholarship. To give priority to such evidence was to miss the real thing for the cloak of ideological expression in which it was garbed.[41] Where did the particular emphasis on the return of Christ and the heightened desire for peace come from, he asked. Eschatological longings were as common to the Middle Ages as lice; the people did not read Augustine. The only reasonable explanation lay in the social and economic realities of the time. The loosening of the social order, the sharpening of class differences, and conditions of famine and disease which uprooted people and sent them searching for food and succor around the countryside led not only to the Peace movement but also to the rise of pilgrimages, the appearance of heresy, and monastic reform. The ecclesiastical authorities were able, in every case except radical heresy, to direct all these folk movements into channels that would not harm the feudal social order, but the movements arose from the populace itself.[42] The church did not create public opinion, although it did set out to mold it to its own purposes and to gain its support. Indeed, without the support of the people, the churchmen would have been utterly unable to put any force at all behind their religious sanctions of excommunication and interdict. In the Peace movement itself, monks played an essential role in gathering

[38] Bonnaud-Delamare, "Fondement," p. 36; cf. Kennelly, "Peace of God," pp. 10–14.
[39] Bonnaud-Delamare, "Fondement," p. 23.
[40] Bernhard Töpfer, *Volk und Kirche zur Zeit der beginnenden Gottesfriedensbewegung in Frankreich* (Neue Beiträge zur Geschichtswissenschaft, 1; Berlin, 1957), pp. 81–82.
[41] Töpfer, *Volk und Kirche*, p. 83.
[42] Töpfer, *Volk und Kirche*, p. 40.

popular support. By displaying the relics of the saints at peace assemblies, they provided huge crowds to witness and put force behind the decrees of the prelates and nobles.

Töpfer need not have worried about the religious interpretation of the Peace presented by Bonnaud-Delamare in his 1951 article cited above, because the author himself came, at least implicitly, to repudiate the views expressed therein. In a series of articles published between 1956 and 1961,[43] Bonnaud-Delamare set out to place the Peace within a totally different context—that of the emergence of new structures of authority and power within and between secular and ecclesiastical hierarchies. In the latest of these, he carried out a detailed analysis of the political and ecclesiastical alliances that lay behind the Aquitanian peace councils of the period 989–1034 and the great denouement at Bourges in 1038 when the forces of the count of Déols defeated a "peace" army organized by the archbishop of Bourges. There is little talk of the Christian desire for peace in this analysis. Instead, these central events in the history of the Peace are presented as moves in a struggle for authority among the bishops and archbishops of Bordeaux and Bourges, their allies among the local counts and viscounts, and the dukes of Aquitaine. In this struggle, the right to proclaim the peace was both prize and sign of the success of one party over another.

When Dolorosa Kennelly surveyed the state of the question in 1962, she found herself in agreement with Töpfer and Bonnaud-Delamare that the older juristic interpretations of the Peace were inadequate but decided that what most needed clarification was the practical effect of the Peace. This could be ascertained, she reasoned, through a comparative study of other means of controlling violence in the eleventh and twelfth centuries. She concluded that, compared with feudal oaths, arbitration, and urban institutions, the movement, although "an eminently practical approach to problems of disorder in its day, was unequal to the task of enforcing peace in feudal Europe."[44] In an article published a year later, Kennelly took up the vexed question of the Peace and the origins of the communes.[45] Continuing her comparative approach and drawing on her earlier work, she presented evidence

---

[43] Roger Bonnaud-Delamare, "La paix d'Amiens et de Corbie au XIe siècle," *Revue du Nord* 38 (1956), 167–78, "La paix en Flandre pendant la première croisade," *Revue du Nord* 39 (1957), 147–52, "Les institutions de paix dans la province ecclésiastique de Reims au XIe siècle," *Bulletin philologique et historique: Comité des travaux historiques et scientifiques*, année 1955/56, 1957, pp. 143–200, and "Les institutions de paix en Aquitaine au XIe siècle," *Recueils de la Société Jean Bodin pour l'histoire comparative des institutions* 14 (1961), 415–87.

[44] Kennelly, "Peace of God," p. 238.

[45] Dolorosa Kennelly, "Medieval Towns and the Peace of God," *Medievalia et Humanistica* 15 (1963), 35–53.

from charters, oaths, and communal seals. The language of communal charters as it turned out, makes constant use of the themes of the Peace. Although communal oaths differ from those of the Peace, they share a common abhorrence of the depredations of goods and persons by feudal lords. Finally, communal seals illustrate the self-conception of the towns as places of peace. Kennelly's conclusion was cautious, but significant: the Peace of God was "of considerable, although not decisive importance for the development of an urban law of peace in the twelfth century."[46]

The results of Kennelly's work were telling. Although the Peace movement may not have succeeded in attaining its stated goals, and whereas there was no foundation for the view that communes were the direct outgrowth of institutions set up under its aegis, Kennelly nevertheless showed that it established a language of sign, gesture, and action that lived on among those who established the first communes. This kind of indirect contribution of the Peace to the history of the eleventh century, however difficult to document and fraught with methodological and conceptual pitfalls, has since come increasingly to interest historians.

A welcome boost to new investigations came in 1964 when Hartmut Hoffmann laid a new foundation for all further work in his thorough and comprehensive study of the Peace and Truce which appeared in the Schriften series of the *Monumenta Germaniae historica.*[47] Hoffmann steered clear of large generalizations on the nature and meaning of the Peace in favor of detailed presentations of sources and problems. In his view, the Peace comprised a spectrum that covered much, grew unevenly, and was differently received in different areas.[48] Bishops, who had assumed secular power over maintenance of the peace, were its leaders, and in its later form—the Truce of God—it ultimately worked to the benefit of the new configurations of power that arose at the end of the eleventh and throughout the twelfth centuries—that is, the principalities and kingdoms of high medieval Europe. Hoffmann rejected Töpfer's notion that popular activity had given rise to the Peace, but he agreed with Erdmann that it had played a role in the process by which the church gave up its opposition to war and conceived the holy wars of the twelfth century. As to its practical efficacy, Hoffmann (like Kennelly) concluded that, although the Peace failed to achieve its stated goals, it made substantial indirect contributions to the crusading

---

[46] Kennelly, "Medieval Towns," p. 53.

[47] Hartmut Hoffmann, *Gottesfriede und Treuga Dei* (Schriften der Monumenta Germaniae historica, 20; Stuttgart, 1964).

[48] A position first articulated by Huberti, *Studien*, pp. 219–33.

movement, the rise of the communes, the development of church law, and the organization of feudal principalities.[49]

Georges Duby significantly advanced the level of discussion on the social history of the Peace in a 1965 study on the laity and the Peace of God.[50] Duby's analysis is set against the background of weakening royal power in the south of France at the end of the tenth century, but his sense of what that meant is far richer than that of his predecessors. The Peace movement coincided, not just with a period of weakened royal power, but with what amounts to a major turning point in European history—that point at which the older Carolingian structures of governance broke down and feudalism emerged as both a social and political order. It was not just a matter of private warfare; it was also a matter of the end of a worldview that saw the king as the embodiment of both spiritual and social order. The loss of royal power meant the end of royal immunities set up to protect church lands and dependents and the assumption of regalian rights by feudal nobles who could not embody both sacred and secular authority as had the Carolingian kings. Thus, the ecclesiastical leaders of the Peace acted to take over the spiritual function of peacekeeping which Carolingian rulers had seen to in the past. In so doing, they began to draw lines between clergy and laity, between sacred and secular, and effectively "announced" the attitudes of the Gregorian reform.[51]

To understand the effect of the Peace on the laity, Duby argued, one must take into account both the spiritual and the temporal aspects of the movement.[52] The social effect of the Peace was to aid in the emergence of the knights as a distinct group within the society of the time. The Peace was directed both from above and from below at the free class of mounted warriors, the *milites*. In its earliest stage, the Peace movement acted to separate the armed and mounted horsemen from the unarmed—that is, the increasingly servile peasant class and the clergy (to whom it prohibited the use of arms)—and added to the sharpening of distinctions between laity and clergy in general. In a second phase, as the millennium of Christ's death approached, and within a mounting atmosphere of purification and penance, the knights were formed into an *ordo* of Christian society. In its final phase, these new *milites Christi* were given a holy purpose—the defense of Christendom and the liberation of the Holy Land. By separating churchmen and la-

---

[49] Hoffmann, *Gottesfriede*, p. 250.

[50] Georges Duby, "Les laïcs et la paix de Dieu," *I laici nella 'societas christiana' dei secoli XI e XII* (Miscellanea del Centro di Studi Medioevali, 5; Milan, 1968), pp. 448–61; rpt. in *Hommes et structures du moyen âge* (Paris, 1973), pp. 227–40, and in *The Chivalrous Society* trans. Cynthia Postan (Berkeley, 1977), pp. 123–33.

[51] Duby, *Hommes et structures*, pp. 229–31 (*Chivalrous Society*, pp. 125–26).

[52] Duby, *Hommes et structures*, p. 228 (*Chivalrous Society*, p. 124).

ity and by legitimizing the activity of the knights, the Peace helped to
form and cement the conception of the division of society into three
orders—*oratores, bellatores, laboratores*—and to lay the foundation for the
feudal order of the following centuries.[53]

The appearance in 1966 of Albert Vermeesch's essay on the origins
of the northern French communes finally cleared the decks of the de-
bris of nineteenth-century debates.[54] Vermeesch did not resurrect
Semichon's theory of diocesan peace associations, but he argued that in
criticizing Semichon's views French historians had fallen into the trap
of defining communes as bourgeois creations and as such antipathetic
to the church.[55] Rejecting such a definition as anachronistic, Vermeesch presented the case that in the eleventh and twelfth centuries
no distinction was drawn between the diocesan and urban communes.
These and other means of keeping the peace stemmed from a common
source, the early eleventh-century Peace movement.[56] To Vermeesch,
the point of contact was not the territory—diocese or town—but the
"peace pact" guaranteed by the oaths of lords and knights and protected by the people.[57]

Nineteenth-century French historians had falsely identified the parties of 1789, 1830, and 1870 with their medieval predecessors. In Vermeesch's analysis, eleventh-century churchmen were neither as liberal
as Semichon had painted them nor as reactionary as his opponents
maintained. The churchmen did not oppose the cause of liberty, yet
neither were they (or the burghers) the vanguard of revolution. The
communes did not seek to overthrow the feudal order, only to regulate
it.[58] The lines of contact between the communes and the Peace are
more direct in Vermeesch's analysis than in Kennelly's—perhaps too
much so—but the combined effect of their work clearly rid the interpretive field of anachronism and restored to the evidence something
more like its own voice. As had Duby, Vermeesch realized that medieval

[53] Duby, *Hommes et structures*, p. 233 (*Chivalrous Society*, p. 128). Duby later elaborated
on this point in his *Les trois ordres ou l'imaginaire du féodalisme* (Paris, 1978), pp. 168–74 (in
English, *The Three Orders: Feudal Society Imagined*, trans. Arthur Goldhammer [Chicago,
1980], pp. 134–39), where he linked the Peace with monastic reform and heresy as "com-
peting systems" that led to the formulation of the tripartite image of society. This position is further elaborated by Jean-Pierre Poly and Eric Bournazel, *La mutation féodale:
Xe–XIIe siècles* (Nouvelle Clio, 16; Paris, 1980), pp. 220–50.
[54] Vermeesch, *Essai sur les origines*; cf. Bryce Lyon, "Commune," *Dictionary of the Middle
Ages*, 13 vols. (New York, 1982–89), 3:493–503, where Vermeesch's view is presented as
one of several theories on the origins of the communes.
[55] Vermeesch, *Essai sur les origines*, pp. 15–21.
[56] Vermeesch, *Essai sur les origines*, p. 175: "Il semble normal sinon évident qu'elle n'a
pu chercher son inspiration que dans les initiatives de l'époque et qu'elle s'insère dans le
contexte général du mouvement de paix."
[57] Vermeesch, *Essai sur les origines*, p. 176.
[58] Vermeesch, *Essai sur les origines*, pp. 178–79.

Europeans did not draw lines between the sacred and the secular in the way we do.

The 1970s produced several studies elaborating the various aspects of the peace that had emerged from previous analysis and adding significant new dimensions. In an article published in *Past and Present* in 1970, H. E. J. Cowdrey returned to Bonnaud-Delamare's insight that the Peace was a response not only to social and political violence but also to the violence of nature, above all famine and disease.[59] Like Vermeesch, Cowdrey sought to differentiate between modern interpretations of the Peace and those of its participants. Although the Peace might appear to us primarily a matter of bishops extending their traditional rights of jurisdiction in the absence of royal power by means of such new sanctions as interdict, that is not at all the way an eleventh-century observer would have seen it.[60] The works of such monastic writers as Rodulphus Glaber and Ademar of Chabannes demonstrated that "at least in the minds of churchmen, the search for peace . . . came to embody something approaching their total view of Christianity."[61] Once established, however, the Peace became an integral part of the renewal of structures of secular and religious authority in the eleventh and twelfth centuries. The spiritual ideology propagated under the banner of the Peace helped prepare the ground for the reform papacy to claim the French church. This was especially true at Limoges, where the monks' fight for the apostolicity of their patron Saint Martial both supported and drew support from devotion to Saint Peter and conceptions of the supremacy of the Roman church, and where, on becoming a dependency of the abbey of Cluny, the monastery of Saint Martial came under the ultimate protection of the apostolic see.[62]

A similar process led to the coupling of the Peace with emerging structures of secular authority. Drawing on a growing body of regional studies of the Peace,[63] Cowdrey argued that the attempts by the dukes of Aquitaine to use the Peace at an early date in support of their

[59] H. E. J. Cowdrey, "The Peace and the Truce of God in the Eleventh Century," *Past and Present* 46 (1970), 42–67.

[60] Cowdrey, "Peace and the Truce," p. 44. The article by A. C. Howland, "The Origin of the Local Interdict," *Annual Report of the American Historical Association* 1 (1899), 431–48, is still valuable; see especially pp. 445–48.

[61] Cowdrey, "Peace and the Truce," p. 50.

[62] Daniel Callahan, "Adémar de Chabannes et la paix de Dieu," *Annales du Midi* 89 (1977), 21–43, has pointed out the connection between the cult of Saint Martial at Limoges and the protection afforded to pilgrims by the Peace, thus illuminating one of the bases of support for the movement among the *populus*.

[63] Eugen Wohlhaupter, *Studien zur Rechtsgeschichte der Gottes- und Landfrieden in Spanien* (Heidelberg, 1933); Michel de Boüard, "Sur les origines de la trêve de Dieu en Normandie," *Annales de Normandie* 9 (1959), 169–89; Bonnaud-Delamare, "La paix en Aquitaine," and "La paix en Flandre"; Aryeh Graboïs, "De la trêve de Dieu à la paix du roi: Étude sur la transformation du mouvement de la paix au XIIe siècle," in *Mélanges offert à René Crozet*, ed. P. Gallais and Y. -J. Riou (Poitiers, 1966), 1:585–96.

authority were followed later by more successful but essentially similar policies in the Norman duchy and Sicily, the counties of Flanders and Barcelona, Capetian France, and the German empire.[64] The Peace of God of the first half of the eleventh century increasingly became the Peace of dukes, counts, kings, and emperors thereafter.

Cowdrey's analysis revealed a deep division in the history of the Peace movement which was both conceptual and, at least in part, chronological. Thomas N. Bisson characterized the nature of that divide when he defined and described two basic structural forms of the Peace.[65] From its inception, the Peace had an institutional character, since it emerged in and around councils that had themselves legislative functions; but at times the institutional aspects of the Peace were accompanied by a "characteristic associative structure" that Bisson called the "sanctified peace." Inspired by monks, marked by participation of people at all levels of society, and expressed in waves of religious enthusiasm that built steadily in the first third of the eleventh century, the sanctified peace appeared only fitfully after ca. 1050, most notably at Clermont in 1095.[66] The "instituted peace," however, because of its written statutory character and its utility to those magnates seeking to establish some form of territorial authority, soon overtook the sanctified peace.[67] Its most innovative features—the peace oaths and the prohibitions of the Truce of God—were directed not to the people as a whole but to the armed horsemen who were the source of social disorder. Thus, where the Peace succeeded, it did so by virtue of its assumption into evolving institutions of justice and order. In southern France and Catalonia in the later twelfth century, for example, the maintenance of public security had come "to rest on the instituted obligations in service and money of the regional community," obligations that had their origins in the Peace movement.[68]

In a study of the place of oaths in the Peace movement published in 1977, Theodore Körner revived the German tradition of legal-historical studies on the Peace.[69] Over the years, German histories of

---

[64] Cowdrey, "Peace and the Truce," pp. 58–67.

[65] Thomas Bisson, "The Organized Peace in Southern France and Catalonia, ca. 1140–ca. 1233," *American Historical Review* 82 (1977), 290–311.

[66] Bisson, "Organized Peace," p. 293.

[67] Cf. Thomas N. Bisson, "Peace of God, Truce of God," *Dictionary of the Middle Ages*, 9:473–75; here he speaks only of the instituted peace.

[68] Bisson, "Organized Peace," p. 292; see also note 4, in which he credits Georges Molinié (above, note 34) with a similar thesis, which had been missed in the general critique of his work.

[69] Theodor Körner, *Iuramentum und frühe Friedensbewegung (10.–12. Jahrhundert)* (Münchener Universitätsschriften: Juristische Fakultät, Abhandlungen zur rechtswissenschaftlichen Grundlagenforschung, 26; Berlin, 1977). Körner's book had been preceded by significant works by, among others, Joachim Gernhuber, *Die Landfriedensbewegung in*

law had come to present the manifestations of the Peace in Germany after 1081 as linked to the earlier movement in the West via a common tradition of swearing the peace.[70] Körner, through an analysis of who was involved in making the peace and how they did so, set out to test those assumptions. On the basis of his results, he argued that oaths could not have been the link between West Frankish and East Frankish Peace movements. Oaths played a very small role in the German Peace and none at all in its first appearance in Liège (1082), Cologne (1083), and Mainz/Bamberg (1085). Even more valuable than these negative results, however, was Körner's success in detailing the variety of means by which the leaders of the Peace sought to proscribe certain actions. By rejecting the distinction between the Peace of God and the *Landfrieden* as artificial, and by organizing his data under the general heading of peacemaking, Körner uncovered a whole conglomerate of *Verpflichtungsformen* which included, besides oaths, episcopal decrees, cooperation between secular and ecclesiastical powers, and various types of popular, imperial, or papal support.[71]

This emphasis on the variety of local manifestations of peacemaking in the eleventh century is also evident in several important works with a regional focus that appeared in the 1970s. Elisabeth Magnou-Nortier's study of the Narbonnais, for example, revealed the ingenuity with which churchmen in the south set out to make peace: through extending the right of asylum connected with churches, drawing up contracts of peace (*convenientiae*) with laypeople whom they both feared and needed to administer and protect their estates, and holding Peace councils.[72] Pierre Bonnassie regarded the innovations of peacemakers

---

Deutschland bis zum Mainzer Reichslandfrieden von 1235 (Bonn, 1952), and Victor Achter, *Über den Ursprung der Gottesfrieden* (Krefeld, 1955). Körner (*Iuramentum*, pp. 3–4) criticized Gernhuber for treating the evidence in accordance with a modern model of law. Achter's interpretation of the origins of the Peace illustrates the longevity of interpretive models like that of Huberti. Achter argued that the Peace emerged from the breakdown of an old pagan-religious legal structure rooted in antiquity, that it signaled a new sacralization of law along Christian lines, and that it was a transitional stage to a new concept of law that developed in the twelfth century wherein people were seen as capable of creating law and securing its demands with real penalties.

[70] Körner, *Iuramentum*, pp. 2–3, 129–30.

[71] Körner, *Iuramentum*, pp. 123–28.

[72] Elisabeth Magnou-Nortier, *La société laïque et l'église dans la province ecclésiastique de Narbonne (zone cispyrénéenne) de la fin du VIIIe à la fin du XIe siècle* (Publications de l'Université de Toulouse-Le Mirail, ser. A, 20; Toulouse, 1974), pp. 292–312. See also Magnou-Nortier, "La place du Concile du Puy (v. 994), dans l'évolution de l'idée de paix," in *Mélanges offerts à Jean Dauvillier* (Toulouse, 1979), pp. 489–506, in which she argues that, at least at Le Puy, the decrees of the council were meant to extend the Carolingian restriction on the abuse of the right of "seizure" by which the army was able to provision itself in the field to an abolition of the right itself, insofar as church lands and dependents were concerned; and idem, "Les mauvaises coutumes en Auvergne,

in Catalonia, which eventually helped to establish the authority of the counts of Barcelona, as responses to the revolutionary potential of the changes that convulsed Catalan society before and after the year 1000.[73] At least in one case, however, an incident long regarded as an important, even fateful, innovation in peacemaking was called into question. Guy Devailly's work on the Berry convinced him that the famous militia of Archbishop Aimon of Bourges had nothing to do with the Peace but was instead an ad hoc reinforcement to his forces in a "feudal quarrel of the classic type" that pitted the archbishop and the viscount of Bourges against the count of Déols.[74]

New avenues of exploration into the connections among the Peace, the populace, and the general movement for reform in the eleventh century were opened up by R. I. Moore in an extraordinary essay published in 1980.[75] Moore's earlier work on medieval heresy and his use of the provincial studies of Devailly, Magnou-Nortier, Bonnassie, and others along with works in social and cultural anthropology give an unusual twist to his interpretation, both precise in detail and broad in implication. In Moore's view, mass participation at Peace councils and demands for the purification of the clergy (even its outright rejection by some) flowed from the same source. The processes of social change that had placed the power of the ban in the hands of the *milites* had broken up communities and kin groups and brought about a crisis of community. People at the parish level came to equate peace with purity and to demand an end to simony and clerical marriage for the same reasons that they sought to limit the destructiveness of private warfare. At the core of all these actions was a new ideal of sanctity—a mirror image of social reality—in which the powerful voluntarily renounced their power, all shared in the common life, and priests, shorn of their ties to wives, children, and feudal lords, represented their communities both socially and symbolically.[76] Herein lay the connection between the

---

Bourgogne méridionale, Languedoc et Provence au XIe siècle: Un moyen d'analyse sociale," *Structures féodales et féodalisme dans l'occident méditerranéen (XIe–XIIIe siècles)* (Collection de l'École Française de Rome, 44; Rome, 1980), pp. 135–72, in which she interprets the *malae consuetudines* so often mentioned in eleventh-century sources in the same manner.

[73] Pierre Bonnassie, *La Catalogne du milieu de Xe à la fin du XIe siècle: Croissance et mutations d'une société,* 2 vols. (Publications de l'Université de Toulouse-Le Mirail, ser. A, 24; Toulouse, 1975–76), pp. 653–62.

[74] Guy Devailly, *Le Berry du Xe siècle au milieu du XIIIe siècle: Étude politique, religieuse, sociale et economique* (Civilisations et Sociétés, 19; Paris, 1973), pp. 142–48.

[75] R. I. Moore, "Family, Community and Cult on the Eve of the Gregorian Reform," *Transactions of the Royal Historical Society,* 5th ser. 30 (1980), 49–69.

[76] Moore, "Family, Community and Cult," p. 65.

Peace and the reform of the church: for priests to be peacemakers, they must stand outside the social network of family, sexuality, and power.

The apparent welter of interpretations of the Peace has led one scholar recently to ask whether "historians may have conferred on the peace movement greater significance that it had," tending "to incorporate it into whatever scheme they have been weaving."[77] There are two questions here, one directed at the overall significance of the Peace in the process of adjustment to changes in society, economy, spirituality, and political life before and after the year 1000, and the other directed at specific interpretations of the Peace as essentially a matter of law, politics, religion, or social change. The first question is more easily settled than the second.

Although it took generations before anyone could see beyond the limits set by Kluckhohn, Semichon, and their critics, their conclusions have slowly been superseded, as have the nineteenth-century commitments and intellectual structures to which they conformed. The tendency to romanticize the Peace that persisted until World War I clouded the issues,[78] as did the understandable predominance of strictly legal interpretations up to that time. But since then, chronological difficulties have been clarified,[79] a much wider range of sources has been combed, and scholars have analyzed the data from a variety of perspectives. Have they made too much of what they have found? The insights of MacKinney and Erdmann into the part played by the Peace in the formation of the crusading ideal and the mass participation in the First Crusade have been corroborated and fleshed out by Duby. Kennelly and Vermeesch have established a route from the Peace councils to the communes. MacKinney, Töpfer, Duby, and Moore have brought to light the extent and significance of popular participation in the Peace and the deep connections that led from there to the general reform movement that transformed church and society in the eleventh and twelfth centuries. Area and provincial studies have shown the use made of the Peace by territorial princes in building effective means of secular control. In the face of these results, there can be little doubt about the overall historical significance of the Peace. The later tenth and early eleventh centuries brought changes all through the social

[77] Jean Dunbabin, *France in the Making, 843–1180* (Oxford, 1980), p. 152.
[78] Duval lost his life in the war that was spawned by the "paix de fer." See the Preface to *La paix de Dieu*, by Emile Chenon, who saw to its posthumous publication in 1923.
[79] But not completely; there is still disagreement over the dating of important councils, such as those held at Verdun-sur-le-Doubs (1016, Duby, Magnou-Nortier; 1019/23, Hoffmann; 1021/23, Töpfer) and Poitiers (1011/14, Bonnaud-Delamare, Duby; 1000/14, Hoffmann; 1000, Jean Becquet, "Les évêques de Limoges aux Xe, XIe, XIIe siècles," *Bulletin de la Société archéologique et historique du Limousin* 105 [1978], 85–86).

system of the West Frankish lands. The old structures of Carolingian order, both material and ideological, were rapidly disintegrating, and the result was disruption but also opportunity. Each individual and group looked to the tools at hand—the horse and sword, the relics of the saints, the traditions of ecclesiastical jurisdiction, the courts of the dukes, counts, viscounts, and castellans—to secure a place in the evolving order. The Peace developed within and around these changes, both shaping and being shaped by them. Whatever mistakes have been made in the study of the Peace of God, the cumulative evidence points to it as one of the seminal institutions of the age, one that roots many of the great events of the later eleventh and twelfth centuries—the reform of the church, the Crusades, the rise of the communes, and the formation of stable feudal principalities (all of which have been portrayed as emerging almost out of nowhere after the year 1050 or so)—in the process of adjustment to the changes that marked the turn of the millennium.

But what about the Peace movement itself? Do its various interpretations conflict to such a degree that a synthesis is impossible? Is it possible to characterize the Peace, to reduce its manifold expressions to one or more essential qualities? The most recent major work on the subject, by Hans-Werner Goetz, attempts to do just that, characterizing the Peace in terms of its primary goals (the protection of churches, churchmen, and church lands), the means of their achievement (support for existing structures of law), and the general climate in which it occurred (the eleventh-century reform movement).[80] Goetz's arguments are specifically aimed at correcting certain tendencies in earlier scholarship, especially the tendency to see the Peace as a response to the absence of law primarily aimed at controlling feuds. In line with recent research, Goetz argues that, although royal authority was in abeyance in southern France in the late tenth century, chaos did not follow. Although there was disorder and violence, it did not attend the total breakdown of public law, over which the church was then forced to take control, but rather the emergence of a new feudal order in which everyone in positions of lordship sought to protect and consolidate their lands and dependents.[81] Töpfer's claim that the early Peace was a movement of churchmen and populace against the nobility and Bonnaud-Delamare's that it was a struggle between ecclesiastical and secular aristocrats were equally wrong.[82] Churchmen worked together

---

[80] Hans-Werner Goetz, "Kirchenschutz, Rechtswahrung und Reform: Zu den Zielen und zum Wesen der frühen Gottesfriedensbewegung in Frankreich," *Francia* 11 (1983), 193–239. An English version of this article appears as chapter 11 in this volume.

[81] Goetz, "Kirchenschutz," pp. 203–8.

[82] Goetz, "Kirchenschutz," p. 238.

with local authorities to add religious sanctions to public legal measures against peacebreakers. Thus, although the ecclesiastical leaders of the Peace were innovative, they worked entirely within existing structures of law to adopt them to changing circumstances.

Goetz, like Cowdrey, maintains that those who participated in the Peace movement expressed their goals in purely religious terms—the establishment of some measure of eternal peace and heavenly order in this world—and that this attitude connects the Peace to the larger movement for church reform getting under way in the same period.[83] His analysis of the conciliar decrees leads him, however, to suggest that, whatever its participants may have said, the goals of the movement were really quite modest and practical, that they were not unlike those of other lords and sought only to maintain the safety and provisioning of church lands.[84] What is the source of the contradiction here? In part, it lies in the fact that Goetz never fully escapes from the legal-historical tradition he sets out to correct. By fully exploiting conciliar degrees in the light of recent revisions of the institutional history of the early eleventh century, Goetz is able to present a more subtle and finely tuned interpretation of them, but the fact remains that behind the conciliar decrees lay a social reality that encompassed more than they could encode. Goetz is aware of this, and he grapples with the problem of popular participation in the movement; but if the goals of the movement went no farther than his analysis suggests, it is hard to understand why so many people of every social background were drawn to the Peace councils or what they expected to find there.

The questions raised by Goetz's study go right to the heart of the issue. Almost from the outset, scholarship on the Peace has oscillated between the poles of legal, social, and religious history. If the Peace had been solely a social-religious movement, or if it had been solely a matter of laws and institutions, there would be less of a problem giving a coherent account of it. The evidence, however, suggests that it was both. The sanctified peace and the instituted peace were one and the same for much of the eleventh century, and perhaps for longer that that. What is needed is a mode of historical discourse that can encompass the Peace in all its aspects—legal, social, and religious—without reducing its essential character to any one of them. One element of that discourse must certainly be a commitment to seeing the Peace in its own terms. Early medieval men and women did not draw sharp lines

---

[83] Goetz, "Kirchenschutz," pp. 232–39.
[84] Goetz, "Kirchenschutz," pp. 209–20.

between the sacred and secular,[85] and they did not behave with the exigencies of modern disciplinary boundaries in mind. Another element of that discourse might be the acceptance of some overarching concept, such as "peacemaking" or "the search for order in Christian society," which would facilitate the integration of the various aspects of the Peace brought to light by its many investigators. In any case, until the Peace is understood and anchored within the network of political, economic, social, religious, and perhaps even psychological realities of the period—as much as that is possible—its nature will remain, at least in part, unclear.

The Peace of God did not create the circumstances that led to the monumental changes of the eleventh century, but it acted as a focus for all the forces—social, economic, political, religious, popular, ideological—that did. The religious enthusiasm generated by the one thousandth anniversary of Christ's life on earth, the profound social adjustments brought on by the devolution of power and the emergence of the *milites* as a distinct group, the traditions of episcopal jurisdiction over church lands, the shared administrative and family histories of the prelates and nobles, the desires of monks to promote their cult centers and protect the pilgrims who flocked to them—all these had a share in shaping the Peace movement. That is why no one interpretation has been completely satisfactory. That is also why a complete analysis of the Peace is a necessary precondition for an understanding of this pivotal period in European history.

[85] See, for example, Goetz, "Kirchenschutz," p. 238: "Die weltlich-geistliche Charakter der Gottesfrieden ist typisch für die mittelalterliche Verknüpfung von 'Staat' und 'Kirche' (weltlicher und geistlicher Gewalt) und zugleich Ausfluss der familiären und verfassungsrechtlichen Abhängigkeit der Bischöfe von den hohen adligen Machthabern."

2

The Cult of Relics and Pilgrimage
in Burgundy and Aquitaine
at the Time of the Monastic Reform

BERNHARD TÖPFER

Although one of the most interesting questions of medieval church history is that of the relationship between the church and the lower strata of society, it has not been studied sufficiently. Clearly the main task of the church was to implant its ideology among the masses and secure control over them. It is therefore a most worthwhile object of study to establish how this task was performed by the clergy in different times and places, as well as to determine the means by which they spread the ecclesiastical word among the laity. This has, of course, to be augmented by an inquiry into the reception of these ideas by the people and their reactions to them. Such an investigation is particularly promising for periods in which ecclesiastical life underwent significant changes and new forces made themselves felt. Eventually this may help to clarify the structure of these renovations: to what extent were they symptoms or consequences of certain social conditions and their transformation rather than results of the action of a few devoted and pious men and women.

In this essay I discuss some aspects of ecclesiastical life in France, particularly in Burgundy and Aquitaine during the late tenth and

The original version of this essay was published as "Reliquienkult und Pilgerbewegung zur Zeit der Klosterreform im burgundisch-aquitanischen Gebiet," in *Vom Mittelalter zur Neuzeit: Zum 65. Geburtstag von Heinrich Sprömberg*, ed. Hellmut Kretzschmar (Berlin, 1956), pp. 420–39. That article was taken from Professor Töpfer's dissertation, which was itself later published as *Volk und Kirche zur Zeit der beginnenden Gottesfriedensbewegung in Frankreich* (Neue Beiträge zur Geschichtswissenschaft, 1; Berlin, 1957). The present translation is by Janos Bak of the University of British Columbia, with the editorial assistance of Thomas Head. The text has been slightly abbreviated. In some cases, additions have been made to the notes to take into account more recent publications; all such additions have been placed in brackets.

early eleventh centuries, with these questions in mind. There is no
need to justify at length the choice of area and date. In that place and
time the Cluniac reform flourished and the Peace of God movement
had its beginning. The significance of these events is well established,
and so is the central role the church played in the society of the time.
Our question can, then, be formulated as, how far did the church in
these conditions reach the lower strata of society, and what were its
methods? Georg Schreiber has demonstrated that the Cluniacs were
successful in bridging the gap "between *monasterium* and laity" and that
their reform movement achieved "a wide expansion and a deep rooting
even among the common men."[1] This is a rather general statement,
however, one that offers no suggestion as to the actual methods used by
the ecclesiastics to grow these deep roots.

Surely the parishes played a role in this matter. Although the institution of proprietary churches (*Eigenkirche*) had strongly diminished
the effectiveness and influence of the parish clergy, steps were taken to
restore them. The reformed monasteries were particularly active in acquiring proprietary churches from the secular nobility and in founding new parishes themselves.[2] But this tendency, although vigorously
pursued by Cluniac priories, did not culminate until the mid-eleventh
century, when it brought about an extensive "emancipation of the local church [*Niederkirche*] from lay domination."[3] In the first half of the
century, the conditions in the parishes left much to be desired, as is
shown by a decree of the synod of Limoges (1031) insisting that the
parish priest preach regularly on Sundays and holidays and not leave
this task to the clerics attached to cathedrals alone.[4] Considering such
shortcomings, even if they were gradually eliminated, the lines of communication between church and people have to be found elsewhere.
One is naturally tempted to suspect that the monasteries, which were
in the forefront of the ecclesiastical movements of their times, used
their own enhanced position and strength to influence the minds of
the lower classes.

In this respect, the veneration of the saints and the cult of their relics
offer a good point of departure.[5] The history of each is as old as the

---

[1] Georg Schreiber, "Cluny, Cîteaux, Prémontré zu Eigenkirche, Parochie und Seel-
sorge," *Zeitschrift für Rechtsgeschichte* 65 (1947), 118.

[2] Georg Schreiber, "Gregor VII, Cluny und die Eigenkirche: Zur Würdigung der Tra-
ditionsnotizen des hochmittelalterlichen Frankreich," *Archiv für Urkundenforschung* 17
(1941–42), 359–418; Guillaume Mollat, "La restitution des églises privées au patrimonie
ecclésiastique en France du IXe au XIe siècle," *Revue historique de droit français et étranger*,
4th ser., 27 (1949), 399–423.

[3] Schreiber, "Gregor VII," p. 369.

[4] Mansi 19:544.

[5] Heinrich Fichtenau, "Zum Reliquienwesen im früheren Mittelalter," *Mitteilungen des
Instituts für österreichische Geschichtsforschung* 60 (1952), 60–89.

Christian church.[6] In the tenth century, however, there was a conspicuous rise in this most popular side of piety.[7] There was no distinction between classes and estates when the assistance of a saint was called for. Where could one make such a call better than at the place where the appropriate relics were kept? No wonder leading churchmen often looked down with reservation, if not disapproval, on these examples of popular piety. Yet, the cult of saints could serve as a promising means to tie the masses closer to the church, just because of its resonance in the mentality of the lower classes. In a period marked by the church's increasing worry over its material basis and the growth of disquieting popular movements, nothing was more logical for the clergy than to make use of these popular forms of devotion to reach the widest audience effectively. This logical step was indeed taken. The lead was assumed, as one would expect in this age, not by the episcopate but by monks. In the tenth and eleventh centuries the monasteries became the centers of a highly elaborate cult of relics and of pilgrimages connected to it, embracing the whole society.

Monasteries usually kept relics of at least one saint, their patron. The people of the neighborhood naturally wished to visit these, and by the time of the synod of Frankfurt of 794 regulations required that oratories (chapels) be built in the monasteries where relics were kept and special services held there.[8] This rule is clarified by the words of a capitulary of 789, which prescribes that the chapel of the relics be a distinct place where the brethren (the clerics or the monks) could pray in peace.[9] The formulation suggests that some monasteries with venerable relics were already so frequented by the laity that special care had to be taken to secure undisturbed devotion of the monks or clerks. Special holidays were observed on the feast day of the patron saint and also on the feast of that saint's translation (*translatio*)—the anniversary of the ritual transfer of the relics to the monastery. These holidays brought great crowds to the monastic church. A miracle story composed at Fleury around 880 by the monk Adelerius records that on the feast of Saint Benedict's translation (July 11) "many groups of various

---

[6] On the early history of the cult of relics, see André Grabar, *Martyrium: Recherches sur le culte des reliques et l'art chrétien antique*, 2 vols. (Paris, 1946, and London, 1972), 1:34, and Hippolyte Delehaye, *Sanctus* (Subsidia Hagiographica, 17; Brussels, 1927), pp. 196–207. [Also Victor Saxer, *Morts, martyrs, reliques en Afrique chrétienne aux premiers siècles: Les témoignages de Tertullien, Cyprien, et Augustin à la lumière de l'archéologie africaine* (Théologie historique, 55: Paris, 1980), and Peter Brown, *The Cult of the Saints: Its Rise and Function in Latin Christianity* (Chicago, 1981).]

[7] Albert Hauck, *Kirchengeschichte Deutschlands*, 7th ed., 5 vols. (Berlin, 1952), 2:771.

[8] "De monasterio, ubi corpora sanctorum sunt: ut habeat oratorium intra claustra ubi peculiare officium et diuturnum fiat"; *MGH Capitularia* 1:76.

[9] "Ut ubi corpora sanctorum requiescunt aliud oratorium beatorum, ubi fratres secrete possint orare"; *MGH Capitularia* 1:63.

sizes came together, not only from the adjacent areas but also from various distant places."[10]

Famous monasteries such as Fleury or Saint-Martin in Tours were visited by numerous pilgrims from all walks of life. The cult of relics therefore served as a significant link between monastery and laity and offered the monks ready opportunities to spread ecclesiastical influence. And so one must ask, what was the attitude of the reform monasteries of the late tenth century to these matters? Were they anxious to utilize the vehicle of relic cults to influence the lower strata or even to disseminate and propagate that very cult? If this was so, then during this period of considerable growth monasteries may very well have had a significant impact on the masses. This influence would be the more important for coming not from an inefficient and dependent parish priest of some *Eigenkirche* but from a community of monks devoted to the ideas of profound ecclesiastical reform.

Let us survey the evidence offered by the history of the abbey of Saint-Philibert in Tournus. In the 940s the monks left their monastery after quarrels with Gilbert, count of Autun and later duke of Burgundy, and they took their relics with them. Catastrophes in the following years—bad harvests, epidemics, high prices—were seen as consequences of the departure of the holy remnants, and a synod decided, in the presence of a great multitude, to call back the monks. They returned and were received by a "copious multitude of people," as the chronicler records.[11] The day the relics returned was declared a holiday for the dioceses of Chalon-sur-Sâone and Mâcon. The population from the vicinity had to come to Tournus; those from more distant places were not bound by the date, but they had to visit the abbey at least once a year with donations according to their wealth.[12]

A few decades later, in 979, Abbot Stephen undertook to augment the treasury of relics at Saint-Philibert. He exhumed the remnants of the martyr Valerian from a forgotten grave near the monastery and had them appropriately buried; that is, he instituted a ritual translation. We are told that a great crowd of people from different

---

[10] *Mirac. s. Benedicti*, 1.40, p. 83.

[11] Falco of Tournus, *Chronicon Trenorchiense*, chaps. 34–35, in *Monuments de l'histoire des abbayes de Saint-Philibert (Noirmoutier, Grandlieu, Tournus)*, ed. René Poupardin (Collection de textes pour servir à l'étude et à l'enseignement de l'histoire, 38; Paris, 1905), pp. 93–96, quotation from p. 95.

[12] Falco of Tournus, *Chronicon Trenorchiense*, chap. 36, p. 96. On these useful donations, see Fichtenau, "Reliquienwesen," p. 75. For example, in the second half of the eleventh century the greatest source of income for the abbey of Saint-Trond were such donations; see Edouard de Moreau, *Histoire de l'église en Belgique*, 5 vols. (Brussels, 1945), 2:402, and *MGH SS* 10:234.

towns assisted the monks on the festive day.[13] However primitive such events may sound to us, they were obviously very effective in mobilizing large numbers of people. The earthly remains of the saint were placed in a precious shrine and set on the main altar, enabling the faithful to offer their prayers. Later, however, the head of Saint Valerian was enshrined in a bust and probably placed on a special altar in the main monastic church, making it accessible at all times to the people. The remaining bones were deposited in a separate reliquary on another altar in the crypt, which was enlarged and renovated by Abbot Stephen. Our sources report that subsequently the crypt was "ceaselessly frequented by the people" (*indesinenter a populo frequentabatur*).[14] Some time later, the abbot found another grave worthy of his attention and translated the relics of Saint Porcian.[15]

These events suggest a quite conscious pattern: the relics of famous saints, or of saints who had been made famous, proved to be the best tools for reaching out to the broadest circles of the population. The translation of the treasures was used to institute an annual pilgrimage, the hitherto inaccessible remains of Valerian and Porcian were displayed for worship: all this had the obvious purpose of making the abbey a repository of famous relics and drawing the laity to its church.

Saint-Philibert was no exception; similar procedures were reported at other French monasteries. The author of *Translatio sancti Viviani episcopi* (ca. 1000) describes the cult of the saint of the abbey of Figeac in the southern French diocese of Cahors.[16] We read there that to the annual feast of Saint Vivian "crowds of innumerable people used to come from all directions."[17] On one of these occasions the abbey church became so overcrowded that the "*maiestas* [a reliquary made in the form of a bust] of the venerable confessor" had to be carried outside into a tent built in an open place so that the pilgrims could gain access to the relics.[18]

There is a remarkable story about Anzy-le-Duc, a priory of the abbey of Saint-Martin of Autun. By the end of the tenth century, the monk Hugh, who had probably served as the first prior of the house, had come to be regarded as a saint and was buried in the church of Anzy.

[13] "Affuit nichilominus copiosa plebis diversarum urbium multitudo"; Falco of Tournus, *Chronicon Trenorchiense*, chap. 38, p. 98.

[14] Falco of Tournus, *Chronicon Trenorchiense*, chap. 40, p. 99. There is also a report (chap. 41, p. 99) of miracles occurring when "the people attended, as usual, the service in the upper church," that is, in the monastic church itself, not in the crypt. This was also on a feast day, so laypeople found themselves in the monastery's church.

[15] Falco of Tournus, *Chronicon Trenorchiense*, chap. 44, p. 100.

[16] *Trans. et mirac. s. Viviani, passim.*

[17] *Trans. et mirac. s. Viviani*, chap. 21, p. 267.

[18] *Trans. et mirac. s. Viviani*, chap. 30, pp. 271–72. [On the technical meaning of the term *maiestas*, see below, note 47.]

When the monks entered the church one Christmas night, we are told, they found all the candles lit, although no one had been in the hall earlier, and the lid of Hugh's grave seemed to have been moved. There was no little wonder over all this and the news reached, surely not by mere chance, the ears of the bishop of Autun. He decided, together with the prior of Anzy-le-Duc, that the remains of the saint should be transferred from the grave and given more appropriate repose in the church. The planned event became widely known and a year later the *elevatio* of the relics took place "with greatest splendor and in the presence of all the people." This event proved more successful than the monks could have hoped, and "from then on invalids and sick came from great distances as well as from the neighborhood, spent two or three nights and left with restored health, praising the saint that their hopes had been fulfilled."[19] This example is instructive; it shows the conscious efforts of the monks to increase the popularity of their priory, through miracle stories, magnificent feasts, and easily accessible reliquaries with healing power. And indeed Anzy-le-Duc soon became a rather important center of pilgrimage.

It would, however, be wrong to assume that such efforts were limited to the generally acclaimed and famous pilgrimage centers. The same kind of activity can be observed in more minor monasteries, in accordingly smaller scope. The abbey of Saint-Genou-de-Lestrée (near Bourges) had owned relics of Saint Genulph since the ninth century. In the tenth century, reports of miracles performed there spread, and on the saint's day the population of the adjacent districts visited the abbey in great numbers bringing many offerings.[20] The translation in 985 of the relics of a holy woman, named Valeria, into a more conspicuous and precious reliquary brought many people to Chambon, a priory of Saint-Martial of Limoges.[21] Another case was that of Paray-le-Monial: when the new church was to be consecrated in 977, the "place was badly in need of relics of saints."[22] The founder of the abbey, Count Lambert of Chalon-sur-Sâone, anxious to mend this shortcoming, obtained permission from the bishop to transfer relics of Saint Gratus, a

[19] *Translatio s. Hugonis prioris Enziacensis; AASS*, April II, pp. 761–69, quotations from p. 769. Also see Emile Mâle, *L'art religieux de XIIe siècle en France: Etudes sur les origines de l'iconographie du Moyen Age* (Paris, 1922), pp. 220–21.

[20] "Instante solemnitate sancti confessoris, ac plurimis ad eius sacrosanctum properantibus sepulchrum et devotionis suae munera . . . deferentibus"; *Miracula s. Genulphi*, chap. 46; *AASS*, January II, p. 470.

[21] *Miracula s. Valeriae*, chap. 2; *Analecta Bollandiana* 8 (1889), 279–80. On the dating of this event, see Louis Duchesne, "Saint-Martial de Limoges," *Annales du Midi* 4 (1892), 316.

[22] Ernst Sackur, *Die Cluniacenser in ihrer kirchlichen und allgemeingeschichtlichen Wirksamkeit bis zur Mitte des 11. Jhs.*, 2 vols. (Halle, 1892), 1:241. *Vita s. Grati*, chap. 7; *AASS*, October IV, p. 287.

former bishop of Chalon, to the monastery. The valuable remains were enshrined in a silver reliquary and placed in the new abbey church. The monks took care that the news of the event reached the dioceses of Lyon, Autun, Vienne, and Mâcon, whence great numbers of laypeople "of both sexes came along."[23] This initial success of mobilization promised to secure a flow of visitors from all over Burgundy and beyond.

The priory of Souvigny, which became a favored goal of many pilgrimages, belonged to the immediate circle of Cluny. This rather small community was the burial place of Abbot Maiolus (†944).[24] An altar built above his grave was consecrated by Bishop Bego of Clermont, and soon reports about miracles spread. "People from the surroundings gathered" as early as the ritual of consecration, but by the saint's feast day an "uncountable multitude" was present.[25] This monastic church was open to the laity for Sunday mass and services as well.[26] It was reported that once a paralyzed man arrived on Saturday evening and spent the night in front of the church doors; when the door was opened for matins, he walked in with the rest of the people.[27] After another miracle at the grave, the healing of a mentally deranged man, "prayers to God were offered by the monks . . . and the people around," which again suggests the regular presence of laity.[28]

A few more examples may be added from the *Liber miraculorum sanctae Fidis* of Conques, one of the greatest centers of pilgrimage on the road to Compostela. Naturally, there were great gatherings on the saint's feast day, and we are told that "there was a crowd of many people from various regions" in attendance.[29] For example, a peasant from the Auvergne made a pilgrimage to Conques.[30] From a miracle story about a widow who came to spend the night with her blind daughter in the church of Saint Faith, we know that monks had to keep all-night watches because of the presence of the pilgrims. They sang psalms with other literate clergy, while the pilgrims, mostly unlettered peasants, could not be kept from spending the long night singing

[23] "Hac . . . translatione manifesta Lugdunensium, Viennensium, Matisconensium, Aeduorum, Biennensiumque populis, ingenti volitante fama omnes utriusque sexus obviam venientes"; *Vita s. Grati*, chap. 7; AASS, October IV, p. 288.

[24] See the *Miracula s. Maioli;* AASS, May II, pp. 689–700. Also see Sackur, *Cluniacenser,* 1:251. [On the cult of Saint Maiolus, see also Dominique Iogna-Prat, *Agni Immaculati: Recherches sur les sources hagiographiques relatives à saint Maieul de Cluny (954–994)* (Paris, 1988).]

[25] *Miracula s. Maioli,* 1.9, p. 690, and 2.18, p. 697.

[26] *Miracula s. Maioli,* 2.20, p. 698.

[27] *Miracula s. Maioli,* 1.19, p. 691.

[28] *Miracula s. Maioli,* 1.1, p. 689.

[29] *Liber mirac. s. Fidis,* 4.16, p. 202.

[30] *Liber mirac. s. Fidis,* 4.2, p. 177.

rather unholy songs and telling jokes.[31] When the author of the first part of the *Liber miraculorum,* Bernard of Angers, complained to the monks about such inappropriate and blasphemous behavior, the abbot retorted with a story. The monastic community had been trying to stop the "abominable shouting and unruly singing of peasants," but when their efforts failed they decided to lock up the church after vespers and force the *rusticana multitudo* to spend the night outdoors. This worked for a time, but once, when the crowd of pilgrims was particularly great, the doors unlocked by themselves during the night, while the monks were sleeping. Even the special entrance to the altar of the church at Conques, which was not to be visited without a guide, fell open. When the monks entered the church for matins they found, to their great surprise, the nave so full of people that they had great difficulty getting through to the choir. This miracle, in which the pilgrims could have hardly been completely passive, convinced the monks that they should not attempt to hinder the entrance of the faithful to the church.[32]

This story points to the considerable rift between popular culture and ecclesiastic civilization but also proves that the church was, in spite of this difference, able to keep the masses under its influence.[33] How successful they were can be seen from such events as that in Lent in 1018, when the crowd, waiting for the early morning mass, poured into the abbey church of Saint-Martial in Limoges with such vehemence that fifty-two people were overrun and killed.[34]

Great excitement caused by natural catastrophes, such as famines and epidemics, was often reflected in events of this sort. When a particularly severe epidemic of ergotism was taking a heavy toll in the area of Orléans, the people came in masses to the abbey of Micy. There were so many of them that the monks could not perform the regular service; the "pilgrims" were camping everywhere, including the crypt. Finally temporary roofs were erected in a courtyard to house the

[31] *Liber mirac. s. Fidis,* 2.12, p. 120.

[32] *Liber mirac. s. Fidis,* 2.12, pp. 120–22.

[33] On the independent character of the culture of the lower classes, see N. A. Sidorova, "Narodnie ereticheskie dvizheniia vo Frantsii v XI i XII vekakh," *Srednie veka* 4 (1953), 74–103.

[34] Ademar of Chabannes, *Chronicon,* 3.49, p. 173, also p. 210. See also *Chroniques de Saint-Martial de Limoges,* ed. Henri Duplès-Agier (Paris, 1874), p. 46, and *Commemoratio abbatum Lemovicensium; PL* 141:83. It is worth noting that in all likelihood this accident occurred in the old basilica, not yet designed for such an influx of people. A newer and larger building was just begun in 1017–18. [On this event, see Richard Landes, "The Dynamics of Heresy and Reform in Limoges: A Study of Popular Participation in the 'Peace of God' (994–1033)," *Historical Reflections / Réflexions historiques* 14 (1987), 497–503, and Chapter 8 in this volume.]

crowd overnight.[35] Similar scenes are reported from such monasteries as Saint-Genou and Saint-Martial, where hope for assistance from the saint against disease brought a great many people to the church portals.[36]

These examples may suffice to prove that in the tenth century the relics of saints kept and displayed in the abbey churches drew visitors to the monasteries from all levels of society; the reports are unanimous in telling about the lay crowds attending the abbey churches, which grew in number and importance during this period. We have also seen that many abbots consciously augmented an abbey's treasury of relics and increased their attraction by appropriate elevation feasts, displays, and miracle stories. The monastic movement thus became, by spreading the cult of relics, a driving force in the development of pilgrimages. Some of the abbeys became famous centers of pilgrimage—Conques, Saint-Sernin of Toulouse, Vézelay, Figeac, Aurillac, Saint-Martial of Limoges, and Saint-Jean-d'Angely, to name only the best known. In the late tenth and early eleventh centuries, the ancient tradition of visiting holy places grew into a veritable mass movement. According to Bernard of Angers, in the years preceding ca. 980 "the place was rather lonely and remote from the visit of pilgrims"[37]; the enthusiastic mass pilgrimages to Conques apparently did not begin until the end of the century. Similarly the cult of Saint Valeria began around 985 at the earliest. Etienne Delaruelle suggests that perhaps in the tenth century the cult of relics achieved the apex of its development.[38]

The movement grew rapidly in the first half of the eleventh century. Two events of that time reflect the methods that enhanced the growth of pilgrimage centers. In 1010, the abbot of Saint-Jean-d'Angély made known that the head of John the Baptist had been found and that "all Aquitaine, Gaul, Italy, and Spain should hasten there moved by the news."[39] The spread of the news and the good advertising of the monks of Angély is remarkable; they managed to mobilize an incredible number of lay and clerical pilgrims, among them the monks of Saint-Martial from Limoges, some sixty miles away, who carried the relics of their patron accompanied by nobles and *innumerabilis populus* in procession to Angély. Still, they were overshadowed by the monastery of Vézelay, which was claimed in 1037 to possess the relics of Mary

[35] Letaldus of Micy, *Miracula s. Maximini*, chap. 49; *PL* 137:820.

[36] *RHF* 10:361. *AASS*, January II, p. 470. Sackur, *Cluniacenser*, 1:392.

[37] *Liber mirac. s. Fidis*, 1.26, p. 69.

[38] Etienne Delaruelle, "La pietà popolare nel secolo XI," in *Relazioni del X° Congresso internazionale di scienza storiche 1955* (Florence, 1955), 3:326.

[39] Ademar of Chabannes, *Chronicon*, 3.56, pp. 179–82.

Magdelene; multitudes of pilgrims came from near and far.[40] Related to this event, and one of the most interesting cases of medieval credulity, is another rather naive one—the attempt of the monks of the abbey of Saint-Martial to improve their patron from the status of a *confessor* to that of an apostle, hence a contemporary and disciple of Christ.[41] That such an absurd dispute could keep minds excited for decades shows the extent to which the cult of relics and the prestige associated with their possession permeated ecclesiastical life in the 1020s.

Parallel to these local developments, pilgrimages over great distances increased, for example to Santiago de Compostela,[42] and above all to Jerusalem. Pilgrimages to the Holy Land were not novel, of course, but they grew into a movement of considerable size only from the late tenth century.[43] Characteristically, the people from France supplied the greatest numbers, as they did later to the first crusades. The presence of the lower classes among the travelers to the Holy Land is recorded by many, for example by Rodulphus Glaber, who puts the *ordo inferioris plebis* on top of his list, followed by the *mediocres*, then the kings and lords, and finally women, both rich and poor.[44] Pilgrimages to Compostela and Jerusalem, which have received the attention of many historians, were, however, the pinnacles of a movement based on innumerable local pilgrimages to major and minor French monastic

[40] Louis Duchesne, *Fastes épiscopaux de l'ancienne Gaule*, 3 vols. (Paris, 1900–15), 1:328; *Monuments inédits sur l'apostolat de sainte Marie-Madelaine en Provence*, 2 vols., ed. Etienne Faillon (Paris, 1859), 2:737. Also see J. Lestocquoy, "Vézelay," *Annales: E.S.C.* 7 (1952), 67–70.

[41] Karl Josef von Hefele, *Histoire des conciles d'après les documents originaux*, 2d ed., 11 vols., trans. Henri Leclercq (Paris, 1907–52), 4.2:936–39, 950–59; Louis Duchesne, *Fastes épiscopaux de l'ancienne Gaule*, 3 vols. (Paris, 1900–15), 2:104-17. [See also Landes, "Dynamics of Heresy and Reform," pp. 467–87, and Chapter 8 in this volume.]

[42] Mâle, *L'art religieux*, p. 291; Yves Renouard, "Le pèlerinage à Saint-Jacques-de-Compostelle et son importance dans le monde médiéval," *Revue historique* 206 (1951), 257. [A comprehensive study, the lack of which was regretted by Professor Töpfer, has yet to be written, but see Elie Lambert, *Le pèlerinage de Compostelle: Etudes d'histoire médiévale* (Toulouse, 1959), and T. D., Kendrick, *St. James in Spain* (London, 1960). Also see the articles collected in *Santiago de Compostela: 1000 ans de pèlerinage européen* (Ghent, 1985), which contains a full bibliography on the pilgrimage on pp. 488–95.]

[43] On pilgrimage to the Holy Land before the year 1000, see Anton Baumstark, *Abendländische Palästinapilger des 1. Jahrtausends und ihre Berichte* (Cologne, 1906). On later increases in the number of pilgrims, see Carl Erdmann, *Die Entstehung des Kreuzzugsgedankens* (Stuttgart, 1935), p. 280, and Christian Pfister, *Etudes sur le règne de Robert le Pieux* (Paris, 1885), pp. 345–50. [For an overview of the history of pilgrimage to Jerusalem, see E. D. Hunt, *Holy Land Pilgrimage in the Later Roman Empire AD 312–460* (Oxford, 1982), and F. E. Peters, *Jerusalem* (Princeton, 1985).]

[44] "Primitus enim ordo inferioris plebis, deinde vero mediocres, post hec permaximi quique reges et comites, marchiones ac presules, ad ultimum vero, quod numquam contigerat, mulieres multe nobiles cum pauperioribus illuc perrexere"; Rodulphus Glaber, *Historiarum*, 4.6.18.

churches. These abbeys played for the people of their surroundings the same role that Compostela and Jerusalem did for the whole of western and central Europe. Without these continuous processions and pilgrimages, however inconspicuous they may seem in the fragmentary records that come down to us, the great movements of the pilgrims would hardly have been possible.

The history of art and architecture offers additional evidence about the development of the relic cult and its impact. It is a long-established fact that church construction experienced a unique upsurge around the year 1000. Contemporaries such as Rodulphus Glaber noted it too.[45] Most of this building activity was sponsored by monastic communities, a fact that may be explained by the riches acquired through lavish donations and efficient economic activity. But also, as we have seen, many abbeys became centers of growing pilgrimages and therefore had to increase the capacity of their churches. The lack of space for the pilgrims at the shrine of Saint Vivian recurred elsewhere. A historian of architecture went so far as to suggest that "romanesque architecture was the consequence of the cult of relics. . . . The narrow, early medieval church halls where the masses of pilgrims got crowded in had to be widened: the result was the type of gigantic abbey church that we find at Vézelay, Autun, Saint-Gilles, or Arles, all of which clearly transcend the actual needs of the monastic community."[46]

The reports cited above frequently refer to new, precious shrines for the relics. In southern France it was usual to have whole statues made for the saints, as had been done for Saint Faith at Conques (where this statue still exists). When the author of the *Liber miraculorum sanctae Fidis*, Bernard, traveled from Angers—north of the Loire—to Conques, he recorded his bewilderment about and distaste for the statues made of gold, silver, and other metals which he saw in the Auvergne, in the Rouergue, and around Toulouse. These contained relics, mostly the skull, of the saint. He met the first one, which he regarded as an idol, in Aurillac, where the bust of Saint Gerald, made of gold and adorned with precious stones, stood on the altar. Having become accustomed to the southern practice, Bernard mentioned a gold "majesty" (*majestas*) of Saint Faith, another of Saint Amantius, also in Conques, and he called the statue of Saint Marius in the abbey of Babres (Rouergue) a *majestas* as well. The word seems to have been the technical term for

---

[45] Rodulphus Glaber, *Historiarum*, 3.4.13. See also Robert de Lasteyrie du Saillant, *L'architecture religieuse en France à l'époque romane*, 2d ed. (Paris, 1929), p. 228.

[46] L. Hourticq as cited in Philibert Schmitz, *Histoire de l'Ordre de saint Benoît*, 2d ed., 7 vols. (Zurich, 1948–56), 2:238.

busts with relics in them.[47] If this is correct, then Figeac also had a bust of Saint Vivian by the end of the tenth century, and the *imago* of Saint Valerian in Tournus (sponsored by the busy Abbot Stephen) may have been similar.[48] From Limoges we even have a description of "a golden image of Saint Martial, sitting above the altar, his right hand blessing the people, and holding the Gospel in his left."[49]

For our inquiry, it is most significant that such reliquaries were not made to be kept in the crypts—which remained, in spite of some additions in these times, fairly small spaces—but rather in the upper church.[50] (Some reliquaries were still placed in the crypt, even, as mentioned above, in Tournus.) The emergence of new elaborate forms was clearly necessitated by the wish to display the relics of the abbey in an accessible place and in splendid works of art, which would appropriately impress the thousands of pilgrims visiting the shrine. These changes in art and architecture fully support the suggestion that around the turn of the millennium it became the main function of abbey churches to accommodate masses of lay pilgrims.

The study of literary genres points to the same conclusion. Max Manitius wrote in his standard *Geschichte der lateinishchen Literatur des Mittelalters,* "In Carolingian times it was still possible to write a saint's life without adding miracles to it. In this period [the tenth and eleventh centuries] this was still done in a few isolated cases, but the addition of miracles had grown enormously."[51] Indeed, books of miracles now became the favorite type of hagiography: the *Liber miraculorum sanctae Fidis,* the continuation of the *Miracula sancti Benedicti* (written at Fleury), the *Miracula sancti Viviani* (Figeac), and the *Miracula sancti Valeriae*

[47] Simpler reliquaries, probably just cases, were referred to as *capsa,* as in the case of that of Saint Saturninus. [On such images, see in particular Ilene Forsyth, *The Throne of Wisdom: Wood Sculptures of the Madonna in Romanesque France* (Princeton, 1972) on the art historical questions, and Amy G. Remensnyder, "Un problème de cultures ou de culture? La statue-reliquaire et les *joca* de sainte Foy de Conques dans le *Liber miraculorum* de Bernard d'Angers," *Cahiers de civilisation médiévale (Xe–XIIe siècles)* 33 (1990), 351–79, on the social historical questions.]

[48] Falco of Tournus, *Chronicon Trenorchiense,* chap. 41, pp. 99–100. See also Jean Hubert, " 'Cryptae inferiores' et 'cryptae superiores' dans l'architecture religieuse de l'époque carolingienne," in *Mélanges d'histoire du Moyen Age dédiés à la mémoire de Louis Halphen,* ed. Charles-Edmond Perrin (Paris, 1951), pp. 355–57.

[49] "Iconem auream sancti Martialis fecit, sedentem super altare, et manu dextra populum benedicentem, sinistra librum tenentem Evangelii"; *Commemoratio abbatum Lemovicensium; PL* 141:82.

[50] Rolf Wallrath, "Zur Entwicklungsgeschichte der Krypta," *Jahrbuch des Kölnischen Geschichtsvereins* 22 (1940), 278; Léon Maître, "Le culte des saints sous terre et au grand jour," *Revue de l'art chrétien,* 5th ser., 45 (1902), 15; Hubert, " 'Cryptae inferiores'," p. 355; François Deshoulières, "Les cryptes en France et l'influence du culte des reliques sur l'architecture religieuse," *Mélanges en hommage à la mémoire de F. Matroye* (Paris, 1940), p. 235.

[51] Max Manitius, *Geschichte der lateinishchen Literatur des Mittelalters,* 3 vols. (Berlin, 1911–33), 2:414.

(Chambon) were all written around this time, as were the *Miracula sancti Maximini* by Letaldus of Micy. The function of these collections was basically to augment and propagate the fame of the saints and thus enhance the draw of their relics. Consequently, there was a great need for this type of literature in late tenth-century France, where monasteries were actively engaged in advertising their relics, as our examples have shown. Naturally, these Latin works were not read by the laity, but they supplied the clergy with an extensive treasury of miracle stories needed for the formulation and enrichment of their preaching. There is ample evidence that popular sermons at the great festivities of the saint's days, often preached by the abbots themselves in the vernacular, were built around the praise of the miraculous events at the grave or shrine of the saints.[52] Baudouin de Gaiffier points out that the hagiography of the eleventh century "played a very definite part in social life."[53] The popularity of these stories is vouched for by a reference in the *Liber miraculorum sanctae Fidis* in which we read that the several miracles of the saint were current among the peasants of the area as *joca sanctae Fidis* (jokes of the saint).[54]

The French clergy were, then, unlike their more aristocratic German counterparts, analyzing means that promised to find resonance among the laity in order to bind the lower classes to the church.[55] Miracle stories were exactly the type of literature that offered effective communication to all elements of society. Secular lords, always eager to grab ecclesiastical property, could be scared off by the terrible accidents that befell likeminded lords through the intervention of patron saints.[56] At the same time, the exploited peasants gained confidence in

[52] Preaching to the laity was typically done in the vernacular; see A. Lecoy de la Marche, *La chaire française au XIIIe siècle*, 2d ed. (Paris, 1886), pp. 235–46; L. Bourgain, *La chaire française au XIIe siècle* (Paris, 1879), p. 176; Baudouin de Gaiffier, "L'hagiographie et son public au XIe siècle," in *Miscellanea historica in honorem Leonis van der Essen* (Brussels, 1947), p. 154. [On this problem, see Thomas Head, *Hagiography and the Cult of Saints in the Diocese of Orléans, 800–1200* (Cambridge Studies in Medieval Life and Thought, 4th ser., 14; Cambridge, 1990), pp. 129–32, 173–74. More generally, on the relationship of vernacular and Latin cultures in this period, see Brian Stock, *The Implications of Literacy: Written Language and Models of Interpretation in the Eleventh and Twelfth Centuries* (Princeton, N.J., 1983).]

[53] Gaiffier, "L'hagiographie et son public," p. 152, where the author correctly notes that hagiographic writing "plays a sort of public function in social life."

[54] *Liber mirac. s. Fidis*, 1.23, p. 60, and 1.26, p. 66.

[55] Ludwig Zoepf, *Das Heiligen-Leben im 10. Jahrhundert* (Leipzig, 1908), p. 144.

[56] For examples, see *Liber mirac. s. Fidis*, 1.6, pp. 26–29, 1.11 and 1.12, pp. 38–46. *Mirac. s. Benedicti*, 3.13, pp. 158–59, 3.16, pp. 163–64, 4.4, p. 179. [On this problem, see Pierre André Sigal, "Un aspect du culte des saints: Le châtiment divin aux XIe et XIIe siècles d'après la littérature hagiographique du Midi du France," in *La religion populaire en Languedoc du XIIIe à la moitié du XIVe siècle*, ed. M. -H. Vicaire (Cahiers de Fanjeaux, 11; Toulouse, 1976), pp. 49–59, and Head, *Hagiography and the Cult of Saints*, pp. 172–81. These authors consider respectively the stories cited by Töpfer.]

the saint and hence in the clergy by the promise of comfort and help from the patron against the violence of their insatiable lords. Such examples were told as that of a knight who was flung from his horse for having robbed a poor widow of a sack of oats; the intervention of the holy Benedict was self-evident to the author.[57] "The lord hears the call of the poor," wrote another hagiographer.[58] There were also stories intended to warn the lower classes not to neglect their Christian duties; the peasant who worked on Sunday (instead of attending mass) or was otherwise disrespectful to a saint was smitten by that saint's vengeance, just as was the serf who attempted to escape feudal dependence by flight.[59] In all these respects, the miracle story proved to be a most suitable medium for conveying the ecclesiastical message to the laity.

These different kinds of evidence substantiate the proposal that the regular clergy were positioned to exert a strong influence on the lay population and to form their religious attitudes effectively. Adolf Harnack was right when he said, "The history of medieval piety was the history of monasticism."[60] We have seen that this role did not fall into the lap of ecclesiastical institutions by chance but resulted from conscious efforts to develop and utilize the means of mass communication which can reasonably be compared with modern propaganda. The relics, hagiography, miracle stories, ritual festivities, and ecclesiastical architecture all served this end.

In the early eleventh century an additional practice became widespread: on various occasions the shrines or statues of the saints were carried around in festive processions. The first instances of such relic processions may have been caused by the Viking raids of the ninth and tenth centuries, when many relics had to be moved from their graves to security elsewhere. There is also evidence that relics were carried to besieged walls—in Tours and Paris, for example—to protect the cities and scare the enemy. But in the eleventh century these processions became regular festivals and were intended, with the methods discussed above, to draw the laity nearer the church.[61]

[57] *Mirac. s. Benedicti*, 2.14, pp. 116–17.

[58] *Miracula s. Genulphi*, chap. 37, p. 469.

[59] *Liber mirac. s. Fidis*, 4.21, pp. 212–13. *Trans. et mirac. s. Viviani*, chap. 9, p. 261. *Mirac. s. Benedicti*, 5.8, pp. 205–7, and 6.2, pp. 218–21. See also Baudouin de Gaiffier, "Les revindications de biens dans quelques documents hagiographiques du XIe siècle," *Analecta Bollandiana* 50 (1932), 131–38 [and the added bibliography in note 56 above].

[60] Adolf von Harnack, *Lehrbuch der Dogmengeschichte*, 2d ed., 3 vols. (Tübingen, 1909–20), 3:9.

[61] [On this topic, see Pierre Héliot and M. -L. Chastang, "Quêtes et voyages de reliques au profit des églises françaises du moyen âge," *Revue d'histoire écclésiastique* 59 (1964), 789–822, and 60 (1965), 5–32; and Pierre-André Sigal, "Les voyages des reliques aux XIe–XIIe siècles," in *Voyage, quête, pèlerinage dans la littérature et la civilisation médiévale* (Senefiance, 2; Paris, 1976), pp. 75–104.]

The *Liber miraculorum sanctae Fidis* again supplies us with good examples. When the monastery obtained some possessions as a grant from Count Robert of the Rouergue, the often-mentioned statue of Saint Faith was taken there, because—so the report adds—it was the practice of the community to carry the relics of the saint to all newly acquired churches and other properties, in order to place them under the saint's protection through her taking actual and eternal possession of them. Naturally we hear of a great multitude gathering and accompanying the monks' procession; the sick and infirm were brought along, and many healings and other miracles happened.[62] Similarly, in the early eleventh century, when the estate of Pallas was given to the monastery by Count Raymond (before he left for a pilgrimage to Jerusalem), Saint Faith again performed several miracles in the course of the procession from Conques to her new acquisition. This time the monks and their saint had to spend the night en route; the peasants of the nearby village flocked to the camp to venerate the relics.[63]

The reasons for such procedures in the case of newly acquired properties are quite obvious: the presence of a great crowd served more than one end. It was, like the methods just discussed, one more occasion to establish contact with the peasants. But, in those insecure times, it was also safer to have the transaction witnessed by as many people as possible, and nothing drew a greater crowd than the famous statue of the saint. Finally, the corporal presence of the saint, in the form of her venerated relics, promised a guarantee against usurpation, making any trespass on her property a sacrilege. By this method, the monks secured in advance the condemnation of future usurpers by the widest possible range of public opinion.

Such measures were especially necessary when a manor of the abbey had already been occupied by an aggressive neighbor. This was the reason for carrying the relics of Saint Faith to the village of Molompise in the Auvergne. As Bernard of Angers wrote, "It was an accepted and time-hallowed practice to carry the shrine to a place that had been alienated from Saint Faith by a lawless intruder." Accordingly, a festive procession of clergy and people which was to proceed to the usurped estate with the shrine, tapers, torches, cymbals, and trumpets was therefore announced. The news traveled fast, and a "whole army of sick arrived from all parts of the country." At their destination, miracles happened in such numbers that the monks could not get away to take a meal, since it was usual to intone psalms and sound the horns and cymbals whenever a wondrous healing occurred. The description

[62] *Liber mirac. s. Fidis*, "Récits speciaux au Codex Londinensis," chap. 3, pp. 252–56.
[63] *Liber mirac. s. Fidis*, 2.4, p. 104.

of this folk festival suggests that such events had little in common with
traditional Christian piety, but they proved the facility of the monks in
fascinating the crowds with nothing less than a circus.[64]

Space forbids detailed discussion of the role of relic processions and
the display of holy statues in the Peace movement of the tenth century.
The synods and councils called for the constitution of a *treuga* or *pax
Dei*. This first veritable mass movement sponsored by the church and,
above all, by monasteries has been dealt with elsewhere. The assembly
of relics at these gatherings served the same dual purpose as recorded
above: to draw the greatest possible public and secure the widest publicity and supernatural sanction to the Peace regulations issued by the
hierarchy.[65]

In summary, one can say that in the tenth century the relics played
an eminent role in the minds of the people, and that the regular clergy
was particularly active in utilizing this fact for building close contacts
between the population and the monastery, or, more generally, between church and laity. The examples cited above certainly—at any
rate, for the southern and southwestern areas of France—dispel the
idea, still not entirely abandoned by historians, that central medieval
monasticism was a retiring proposition isolated from the lay world.
This does not mean that Cluniac monasticism did not offer the monks
a silent and secluded life in the community of the cloister, opposed to
all activities that would lead the religious into the secular world; it certainly did, but the more pious and otherworldly the monks appeared,
the greater was their appeal to the laity.

The possibilities inherent in the cult of relics were utilized by many
monasteries, not only by the Cluniacs. The great pilgrimage centers of
Saint Faith at Conques, Saint Philibert at Tournus, and Saint Vivian at
Figeac were not reformed by Cluny. Conversely, the reports from Souvigny prove that the immediate vicinity of Cluny was as active in this
respect as that of any other French abbey. The religious movement of
the late tenth century in western Europe was evidently not created by
Cluny; rather, Cluny was carried by this mighty wave and—this should
not be denied—in turn added much to its force and impact.

Still, it is remarkable how strongly the masses reacted to the different
manifestations of the cult of relics. The reports of the immeasurable
multitudes present at translations, processions, Peace councils, and
other festivals certainly exaggerated in the same manner the authors of
the miracle books did, but there is ample evidence that pilgrimages did
indeed embrace the widest circles of the population and that consid-

---

[64] *Liber mirac. s. Fidis*, 2.4, pp. 100–101.

[65] This topic is further discussed in the author's dissertation [published in *Volk und
Kirche*, pp. 54–58]. See also Fichtenau, "Reliquienwesen," p. 69.

erable crowds gathered at monasteries with famous relics. Such a movement would not have been possible, even with the most cunning influence of ecclesiastical propaganda, had the social conditions not been ripe for an increased participation of the lower classes in public life. It would lead us too far here to discuss the social and economic situation of the working population in Burgundy and Aquitaine, or to analyze the elements of social tensions in the late tenth century. It may suffice to mention the emergence of heretics in exactly the same period, which points to the increased unrest among the people and to the sharpening of contradictions.[66] This may very well have been the main reason for the increased efforts of the church to utilize the cult of the relics in reaching out to the laity. These efforts were, as we have seen, extremely successful. The appearance of the first Cathars in the same period is only an apparent contradiction. The pilgrimage movement, monastic reform, and heresy were only different manifestations of essentially identical trends. Their common root was in the displacements in the social structure and in the sharpening of class conflicts that mobilized the lower classes and also moved the church to develop new means of exerting its influence.

For the time being, the French church succeeded—mainly through the efforts of the monasteries—to channel the movement of the masses into forms approved from above, and at the same time to achieve much greater prestige and influence for itself. Heretics, particularly the Cathars of southern France, were only the left wing of the same movement from below—that is, the part of the movement the church failed to co-opt. In the eleventh century, this left wing was still considerably weaker than the mainstream of the movement, which remained under ecclesiastical control in the form of pilgrimages, the Peace movement, and the like.

[66] Ernst Werner, *Die gesellschaftlichen Grundlagen der Klosterreform im 11. Jahrhundert* (Berlin, 1953), pp. 71 ff.; Arno Borst, *Die Katharer* (Schriften der Monumenta Germaniae historica, 12; Stuttgart, 1953), pp. 71–80. [The literature on the topic of heresy in the eleventh century has grown massively in recent years. On the class aspects of this problem, see Jean Musy, "Mouvements populaires et hérésies au XIe siècle en France," *Revue historique* 513 (1975), 33–76, and R. I. Moore, *The Formation of a Persecuting Society: Power and Deviance in Western Europe, 950–1250* (London, 1977).]

3

The Enemies of the Peace:
Reflections on a Vocabulary, 500–1100

Elisabeth Magnou-Nortier

Historians appear to believe that they can fully and satisfactorily explain the Peace of God by presenting it as an initiative on the part of several bishops in southern France intended to exorcise feudal anarchy, reestablish order in lands devastated by private wars, and force nobles to give back their ill-gotten plunder. Were not laypeople incessantly accused of being *invasores, depraedatores, raptores,* and *oppressores?* In choosing to express myself this way, I paraphrase the pages that Hartmut Hoffmann dedicated some twenty-five years ago to the "Peace and Truce of God."[1] Despite the necessity of some retouching and the addition of a few complementary details, Hoffmann's remains a work to which historians are indebted.

Some doubt about this picture of the Peace, however, creeps into one's mind as soon as one examines the condition of the great southern principalities that are supposed to have given birth to the Peace of God at the end of the tenth and during the eleventh centuries. Whether one considers the duchy of Aquitaine, the county of Toulouse, or the counties of the Pyrenees, no evidence exists that would permit one to speak of endemic disorders. On the contrary, the great aristocratic families were firmly implanted in the "states" that were their power bases. It is impossible to label as anarchy the simple quarrels of succession or the tensions between lineages which are the common lot of all societies, even those highly organized. It becomes difficult to maintain the view

This essay has been translated by Amy G. Remensnyder. The author gratefully acknowledges her work.

[1] Hartmut Hoffmann, *Gottesfriede und Treuga Dei* (Schriften der Monumenta Germaniae historica, 20; Stuttgart, 1964).

that the Peace of God originated in a desire to fight against feudal disorders, given that these latter are impossible to find.

Let us make a second observation. The vocabulary used in the sources pertaining to the Peace of God to brand the fomenters of discord—*raptores, pervasores, usupatores, violatores ecclesiarum,* and so on— was an archaic and ecclesiastical one. By the sixth century, Frankish bishops employed it to designate those people who, despite ecclesiastical legislation, thought that they could dispose as they wished of offerings made to churches. These same bishops also spoke of peace, not the Peace of God, but the peace of the Church: *pax ecclesiae,* or *pax ecclesiastica.* The curious constants of vocabulary and context have provoked me to reexamine the history of the Peace, which began much earlier than the eleventh century.[2]

Furthermore, eleventh-century sources relating to the Peace are problematic in their usage of terms such as *praeda, rapina,* and *violentia,* which seem to indicate plundering, that is, the violent and illicit seizure of property. My first inquiry into so-called *malae consuetudines* engendered thorny questions.[3] I found that plundering (*praedare* or *praedas facere*) was licit from the feast of All Saints to Easter, but not from Easter to All Saints. In addition, the *institutores pacis* did not establish peace on their own lands, where they were actually in control. It became evident to me that the scope of my research would have to be broadened.

I was all the more encouraged in this project because a hardly insignificant commentator on the Peace of God, Ademar of Chabannes, spoke of peace in terms that do not seem at all consonant with historians' traditional analyses.[4] In his ponderings, Ademar was led to reflect on the ideal relationships between clergy and laity. "The laymen," he wrote, "are subordinated to the clergy in religious matters; they should obey their bishops who are the Lord's representatives." Not a word about the so-called anarchy, the mother of all the abuses; not a word against the "right of might" and the unbounded power of the nobles over the defenseless poor. When he thought of peace, Ademar employed the old Gelasian doctrine of the distinction of powers. The

[2] Elisabeth Magnou-Nortier, "La place du concile du Puy (v. 994) dans l'évolution de l'idée du paix," in *Mélanges offerts à Jean Dauvillier* (Toulouse, 1979), pp. 489–506; "Les évêques et la paix dans l'espace franc (VIe–XIe siècles)," in *L'évêque dans l'histoire de l'Eglise* (Angers, 1984), pp. 33–50; and "Les princes, les évêques et la paix dans le royaume de France (IXe–début XIIe siècles)," unpublished paper delivered at the Colloque de Mayence organized by the Mission française en Allemagne, March 1985.

[3] Elisabeth Magnou-Nortier, "Les mauvaises coutumes en Auvergne, Bourgogne méridionale, Languedoc et Provence au XIe siècle: Un moyen d'analyse sociale," in *Structures féodales et féodalisme dans l'occident méditerranéen (Xe–XIIIe siècles)* (Rome, 1980), pp. 135–72, particularly 143–44.

[4] Daniel Callahan, "Adémar de Chabannes et la paix de Dieu," *Annales du Midi* 89 (1977), 21–43.

disjunction between the discourse of this contemporary observer and the commentaries of modern historians is obvious.

All these considerations have led me to analyze the semantic contexts of the vocabulary of the Peace more carefully. Through such an examination, one can identify the sources that inspired the Peace movement during the eleventh century. Here, however, my focus is the vocabulary used relative to the enemies of the peace.

Terms Used for the Offenders: *Raptores, Pervasores, Usurpatores, Oppressores Ecclesiarum et Pauperum*

We can easily reconstruct the vocabulary that served to brand the enemies of the peace in the canons of the Frankish councils of the sixth century. *Pervasores, raptores,* and similar terms were applied to Christians who took away or took back offerings made to churches. The bishops declared that such people were excluded from the "peace of the church."

The "peace of the church" was a perfectly unambiguous expression used since the sixth century (and perhaps even earlier) to designate the status enjoyed by the Christians who were faithful to God's law and that of the church. Whoever transgressed these laws was cast outside the peace of the church and could reenter only by means of penitence and the amendment of his or her ways. Canon law gradually defined the misdeeds for which Christians could be deprived of the peace of the church, that is, those for which they could be excommunicated from the society of the faithful. In the sixth century, conciliar provisions imposed this penalty on the laity for four major offenses: idolatry or heresy,[5] incest,[6] infraction of the right of asylum,[7] and the seizure of offerings made by Christians to churches.[8]

We need to examine the latter two cases in more detail. It can only be considered just that those who violated the peace of the church while actually within consecrated buildings should have been punished. It is,

---

[5] Orléans (533), can. 20; *MGH Concilia* 1:64. Orléans (538), can. 34; *MGH Concilia* 1:83. Orléans (541), cans. 15, 16; *MGH Concilia* 1:90. Orléans (549), can. 1; *MGH Concilia* 1:101.

[6] Clermont (535), can. 12; *MGH Concilia* 1:68. Orléans (538), can. 11; *MGH Concilia* 1:76–77.

[7] Orléans (511), cans. 1–3; *MGH Concilia* 1:2–4. Orléans (541), can. 21; *MGH Concilia* 1:92. Orléans (549), can. 22; *MGH Concilia* 1:107–8.

[8] Clermont (535), can. 4; *MGH Concilia* 1:67. Orléans (538), cans. 13, 25; *MGH Concilia* 1:77, 80–81. Orléans (541), cans. 19, 25, 32; *MGH Concilia* 1:91–94. Orléans (549), cans. 13, 15, 16; *MGH Concilia* 1:104–6. Tours (567), cans. 25–27; *MGH Concilia* 1:134–35. Lyon (567–700), can. 2; *MGH Concilia* 1:140. Paris (556–73), cans. 1, 2, 7; *MGH Concilia* 1:142–44.

however, rather surprising that the same penalty was imposed on those who merely stole offerings. This is scarcely a petty matter that we can safely ignore; instead, it presents us with the enormous and difficult question of the uses for which ecclesiastical patrimonies were intended and the respective authority of church and state over these properties. Any historian studying questions relative to the Peace cannot lose sight of this issue; it constitutes the central matter of debate, the battlefield on which those who wielded ecclesiastical authority (*auctoritas*) and secular authority (*potestas*) confronted one another through the centuries. Here, due not only to the struggles but also to the compromises, the so-called Peace legislation was gradually forged.

In contrast to the clarity of the nature of the ecclesiastical peace, the status and intended uses of ecclesiastical properties were matters of insoluble debate, for roughly the following reasons. In 506, the council of Agde proclaimed an important, though certainly not novel, principle of canon law—"Let it be known that consecrated things belong to God"—thereby rendering ecclesiastical goods inalienable.[9] Canon law thus declared that, whether it was a humble offering made by a dying person for the remission of sins or a royal grant to a church, this property had been definitively acquired by God. The Theodosian Code, however, and judicial practices inherited from Rome allowed simple citizens as well as the powerful to oppose this canonical precept by legal means if they thought it would be to their advantage. Indeed, some well-known provisions of the code forbade clerics from trying to inveigle inheritances from widows or orphans and prohibited women *deo sacratae* from disinheriting their legal heirs.[10] Otherwise, Roman law always designated the public power as the sole trustee of the right to determine the reasons of state which could occasion the withdrawal of

[9] "Diacones vel presbiteri in parochia constituti de rebus ecclesiae sibi crediti nihil audeant commutare, vendere vel donare, quia res sacratae Deo esse noscuntur. Similiter et sacerdotes nihil de rebus ecclesiae sibi commissae . . . alienare praesumant"; Agde (506), can. 49; Mansi 8:333. If clerics were not able to touch the patrimony, still less would laypeople have had the right. On women *deo sacratae*, see Elisabeth Magnou-Nortier, "Formes féminines de vie consacrée dans les pays du midi jusqu'au début du XIIe siècle," in *La femme dans la vie religieuse du Languedoc (XIIe–XIVe s.)* (Cahiers de Fanjeaux, 23; Toulouse, 1988), pp. 193–216.

[10] *Theodosiani libri cum constitutionibus Sirmondis et leges novellae*, 2 vols., ed. Theodor Mommsen and Paul Meyer (Berlin, 1905), 16.2.20, 16.2.27, pp. 841, 843–44. Disinheritance justly figured among the abuses for which Charlemagne reproached his clergy with great severity in 811: see *Capitula de causis*, chap. 5; *MGH Capitularia* 1:163. The Theodosian Code also inspired the following capitulary: "Statutum est ut nullus quilibet ecclesiasticus ab his personis res deinceps accipere praesumat, quarum liberi aut propinqui hac inconculta oblatione possint rerum propriarum exheredari. Quod si aliquis deinceps hoc facere temptaverit, a sinodali vel imperiali sententia modis omnibus feriatur"; Ansegisus, *Capitularium* 1.83; *MGH Capitularia* 1:406. This might be attributed to Charlemagne or to Louis the Pious.

fiscal privileges granted by the government to ecclesiastical or lay beneficiaries. Churches obviously had all the more reason to fear the possible exercise of this right, since their patrimonies were generally public in origin and administered in the same manner as the fisc.[11]

Two laws, two sets of rights, thus constantly risked being at loggerheads. There could be minor conflicts between a church and the heirs of one of its benefactors. In much more serious clashes, the natural defenders of churches—the bishops—could find themselves forced to confront kings and obliged to oppose to reasons of state (*necessitas* or *utilitas*) the real purposes for which princes and men of power gave properties to the church: prayer, charitable works, and the maintenance of the clergy and churches. Certain of the provisions of the great Frankish councils of the sixth century best illustrate such conflicts. The councils held at Orléans in 538 and 541 stipulated that a Christian, even if the legitimate heir, was forbidden to take back any offering made to a church or to retain for any other purpose posthumous offerings.[12]

Two canons of the council of Tours of 567 demonstrate the kind of difficulties which could cause bishops and princes to clash. One specified that kings were responsible for the "civil wars" that tore kingdoms apart: "Since our lords rage at one another like wild animals and are incited by evil men and attack each other's possessions with devouring greed, in order that they do not presume to attack or contaminate ecclesiastical domains with their violence, we make the following provision which is to be observed inviolably . . ."[13] The remainder of this canon and the whole of the next analyzed the actions of those who stole ecclesiastical property (*pervasores rerum ecclesiasticarum*), in whom we must see kings, royal agents, and clients who seized, claimed, and confiscated offerings made to churches. After a third warning directed to the guilty parties, the bishops decreed that "because we have no other weapons, with Christ aiding us, let the choir of the church be closed off and Psalm 108 recited so that the curse which fell upon Judas who

[11] It is necessary to give renewed attention to the fundamental clause which Charles the Bald stated in 873 with clarity and equal rigor, and which always guided the princes in administering those fiscal dealings with churches bordering on their patrimonies: "Quia sicut et per scripturas et per auctoritatem et per rationem manifestum est, duo sunt, quibus principaliter mundus hic regitur, regia potestas et pontificalis auctoritas, et in libro capitulorum avi et patri nostri coniuncte ponitur, ut res et mancipia ecclesiarum eo modo contineantur sicut res ad fiscum dominicum pertinentes contineri solent, iuste et rationabiliter de rebus et mancipiis quae in regia et in ecclesiastica vestitura fuerunt, uniformiter et uno modo tenendum est"; Quierzy (873), chap. 8; *MGH Capitularia* 2:345.

[12] Orléans (538), can. 25; *MGH Concilia* 1:80–81. Orléans (541), cans. 14, 18, 19; *MGH Concilia* 1:90–91.

[13] "Dum inter se saeviunt domini nostri ac malorum hominum stimulo concitantur et alter alterius res rapida cupiditate pervadit, non ista caduca actionem, qua inter sese agunt, ecclesiastica rura contingere aut contaminare praesumant, inviolabiliter observandum censemus, ut . . ."; Tours (567), can. 25; *MGH Concilia* 1:134.

filled his purse by depriving the poor of their means of sustenance will descend upon whoever murders poor people and seizes ecclesiastical property."[14]

We should carefully note the set of terms and expressions with which the bishops branded those bad Christians who considered it their right to take back or retain for themselves offerings made to churches: *rapere, auferre, tollere, prendere, pervadere; substantia aegentium, orrenda cupiditas, res pervasa, pauperum alimenta; pervasores, invasores, necatores pauperum.* Indeed, in the eyes of the bishops, whoever impoverished the clergy was at the same time robbing the poor, who were in the care of the church. Property of the poor and property of the church represented equally the livelihood of the clergy and the price paid for sins. Therefore, the misuse of ecclesiastical property was a grave misdeed, threatening the church's very mission. In addition, the bishops used their most formidable spiritual weapons when faced with the danger of princes absconding with ecclesiastical revenues to pay their military expenses. The bishops menaced these princes with exclusion forever from the peace of the church.

But did this severest of sanctions have any effect? That notorious *pervasor* Chilperic died within the peace of the church.[15] In fact, episcopal justice was hedged in by a barrier that could not, as of yet, be crossed: the free will of the prince. The prince remained within the peace of the church even if he committed deeds contrary to the canonical prescriptions—but justified by reasons of state (*necessitas*).

During the Carolingian period these givens did not alter appreciably, but tensions between the prince and the church increased. With an iron fist Charlemagne managed to keep both the lay and ecclesiastical subjects of his vast empire under control. But his son, Louis the Pious, had to confront a current of virulent opposition which the imperial guardianship of the Frankish church had inevitably aroused. It is significant that the subject of the first polemics against the emperor, which began ca. 820, was the proper use of ecclesiastical patrimonies: Agobard of Lyon wrote his *Liber de dispensatione ecclesiarum rerum*, condemning to spiritual death those who misused ecclesiastical properties.[16] Jonas of Orléans composed his *De rebus ecclesiasticis non invadendis.*[17] Paschasius Radbertus informs us that Wala, for his part, wrote a small tract (*parva schedula*) that dealt with the same issue.[18] The

---

[14] "[E]t quia arma nobis non sunt altera, auxiliante Christo, circumsepto clericali choro, necaturi pauperum, qui res pervadit ecclesiae, psalmos CVIII dicatur, ut veniat super eum illa maledictio quae super Iudam venit, qui, dum loculos faceret, subtrahebat pauperum alimenta"; Tours (567), can. 26; *MGH Concilia* 1:134–35.

[15] Gregory of Tours, *Historia francorum*, 6.46; *MGH SRM* 1:286–87.

[16] *PL* 104:227–50.

[17] *MGH Concilia* 2.2:724–67. The attribution of the work remains probable.

[18] *PL* 120:1608.

collection *Formulae imperiales* contains numerous models for acts of restitution of ecclesiastical property.[19] If we add to this list the formal letter of doctrine the influential members of the Frankish episcopate addressed to Louis the Pious in 829, in which they modified in their own favor the role of the spiritual authority in relation to the imperial power, we can see that all these works highlight just how important the stakes were for each party.[20] Either the Frankish state would remain master of its own decisions and means and thus force the church to comply, or the church would impose its will on the state.

The resulting duel involved the judgment and condemnation of Louis the Pious and the consequent fabrication of the pseudo-Isidorian decretals and forged capitularies. And it was always with the same words that the clerics reproved laypeople who retained ecclesiastical properties. Louis the Pious was treated as a disturber of peace (*perturbator pacis*).[21] In 845, the synod of Beauvais entreated Charles the Bald to act severely "against the attackers and oppressors of churches and their property."[22] The pseudo-Isidorian decretals were drawn on for the first time at the council of Quierzy to produce what was aptly called the *Collectio de raptoribus*.[23] As for the pseudo-Isidorian decretals themselves, their author(s) constantly repeated the condemnation of the evil people (*pravi homines*) who seized the goods of churches and those of the poor. They were guilty of murder and sacrilege and incurred the same damnation as Ananias and Saphira or Judas:

> Therefore whoever steals or seizes the revenues of Christ and the church or defrauds the church of them is a murderer in the eyes of the Just Judge.[24]

[19] *MGH Formulae imperiales*, nos. 6, 18, 21, 25, 26, 27, 36, 46. To these should be added the formulas of immunity from litigation and hospitality.

[20] *MGH Concilia* 2.2:606–80. See also the *Relatio* of the bishops in *MGH Capitularia* 2:26–51.

[21] Sources cited in Elisabeth Magnou-Nortier, *Foi et fidélité* (Toulouse, 1976), p. 78.

[22] Beauvais (845), chaps. 17–19; *MGH Capitularia* 2:403–4. The last canon reads as follows: "Ut contra depraedatores et obpressores ecclesiarum et rerum ad easdem pertinentium defensores secundum ministerium vestrum . . . existatis."

[23] *MGH Capitularia* 2:285: "Collectio de raptoribus, quae dicitur, re vera exemplar admonitionis est, quam episcopi populo adnuntiarent et proclamarent." The same arguments were brandished by the bishops in a letter addressed to Louis the German in November 858: "eos, qui facultates ecclesiasticas diripiunt et res ecclesiasticas indebite sibi usurpant Iudae traditori Christi similes computant . . . divino iudicio tanquam necatores pauperum ab ecclesiae liminibus et a coelesti regno secludunt"; *MGH Capitularia* 2:433. In light of this, one must reread canon 25 of the council of Tours (567) in *MGH Concilia* 1:134.

[24] "Ergo qui Christi pecunias et ecclesie rapit, aufert vel fraudat, homicidia est ante conspectu Iusti Iudicis"; Paul Hinschius, *Decretales pseudo-isidorianae et capitula Angilramni* (Leipzig, 1863), p. 78.

All who persecute the saintly fathers . . . God hates . . . as *invasores* and *destructores* of the fathers.[25]

Anyone who injures the church, who plunders its *praedia* and the offerings made to it, is considered sacrilegious.[26]

These possessions of the faithful are called offerings because they are offered to God. Therefore, they should not be turned to any other uses than those benefiting the aforementioned Christian brethren and the indigent. This is because they represent the votive offerings of the faithful and the payments of sinners given to churches for the abovementioned purposes. Moreover, if anyone (God forbid!) should act otherwise, let him take care lest he receive the same damnation as Ananias and Saphira.[27]

Such is the core of the pseudo-Isidorian doctrine—which I call the "Isidorian spirit"—relative to the intended usages of ecclesiastical patrimonies. No agreement was possible between such a conception and the public power. The authors of this collection of forgeries claimed full authority over ecclesiastical patrimonies and condemned all withholding or withdrawal of ecclesiastical properties as so much sacrilege, even if justified by "necessity" or reasons of state.

Nonetheless, then as now, there was a great distance between dogmatic, intransigent conceptions and the exigencies of reality. In the middle of the ninth century, one "necessity" above all weighed heavily on Francia; the realm had become the victim of repeated Norman attacks. Thus, churches had to contribute to their own defense —one of fate's ironies, in the era in which the pseudo-Isidorians reminded clerics of the old prohibition of clerics bearing arms—and to that of the kingdom, just as all other domains, fiscal or not, were compelled to do.

The key document for this sombre epoch is certainly the "peace" of Pîtres in 862. Confronted with the tragedy of the invasions, Charles the Bald proposed at first an anagogical reading of events. He could not disregard the fact that he and his people had disobeyed God's law by having diverted ecclesiastical possessions from their proper uses. Nor

[25] "Omnes qui sanctos patres persecuntur . . . sic odit eos Deus . . . ut patrum invasores vel destructores"; Hinschius, *Decretales pseudo-isidorianae*, p. 97.

[26] "Qui ecclesiam vastat, eius praedia et donaria expoliat et invadit, fit sacrilegus"; Hinschius, *Decretales pseudo-isidorianae*, p. 118.

[27] "Ipse enim res fidelium oblationes appellantur, quia Domino offeruntur. Non ergo debent in aliis usibus quam ecclesiasticis et predictorum christianorum fratrum vel indigentium converti, quia vota sunt fidelium et pretia peccatorum adque ad praedictum opus explendum Domino traditae. Si quis autem, quod absit, secus egerit, videat ne dampnationem Ananiae et Saffirae percipiat"; Hinschius, *Decretales pseudo-isidorianae*, p. 144. These examples could be multiplied. On the pseudo-Isidorian decretals, one must also consult the fundamental work of Horst Fuhrmann, *Einfluss und Verbreitung der pseudo-isidorischen Fälschungen* (Stuttgart, 1972).

could he deny his responsibility and that of his magnates for having used such property for military purposes. In a moving passage, he promised that he and all the other men of the kingdom would set out on the road of penitence in order to appease God's just wrath, which had manifested itself in the terrible trials inflicted on the realm:

> In the midst of all these misfortunes, our Father has shown us that through these external ravages we ought to discern those of the soul and, having thus understood them, return to him. . . . He, being truth, has said "Return to me and I, I shall return to you." When we have acquired the habit of returning from these many military expeditions to our houses, soaked, with our heads shaven like monks and our clothes and shoes in tatters, then we will regain our strength. . . . Each of us will refresh himself with contrition and heartfelt repentance and confession, by doing good works and by adhering to the will of God.[28]

Here we see the origin of all penitential developments later linked with the Peace of God.

Nevertheless, the king presented at the same time an objective reading that impelled him to assume his function as the defender of the realm and of the churches. How could he possibly renounce military and financial contributions from churches and still fill this role effectively? Everyone, of whatever status and function, had the duty of supporting the defense and war efforts. Thus, the king sought a compromise, a peace between the contradictory exigencies of the rights of the church and the duty of the state. He seemed to have found it in a condemnation of the recent abuses perpetrated by his followers and a firm insistence on the prerogatives of the state.[29] Nine years previously he had formulated this regulation: "If, due to various reasons of state, properties which are proven with reliable evidence to belong to churches cannot be restored fully, then at least their tithes [*nonae et decimae*] should be granted [to the churches]."[30] Charles the Bald ensured that the most flagrant abuses would be remedied, but he intended to remain the only one to determine the necessities of state and their importance. For their part, the bishops warned, "Whoever then seizes any ecclesiastical possessions shall be judged the more

---

[28] Pitres (862); *MGH Capitularia* 2:302–10. A brief analysis of this text is provided in Magnou-Nortier, "Les évêques et la paix," pp. 44–45. The *placitum* of Pîtres of 862 is called the "peace" in 864, by Charles the Bald himself: "et quia pacem quam iam praeterito anno hic communiter confirmavimus"; Pitres (862); *MGH Capitularia* 2:312.

[29] Charles the Bald recalled the military regulations issued by Charlemagne and Louis the Pious relating to the movement of troops; see *MGH Capitularia* 2:289–91. Here it was principally a matter of controlling *praedae* or *rapinae* and of imposing a reprieve in the compensation of victims. The penalties for transgressors were heavy.

[30] Soissons (853), chap. 8; *MGH Capitularia* 2:266 (text B).

harshly for this reason, . . . [that] thieves . . . shall not possess the kingdom of God."[31]

Ultimately, a new method of legislating developed; the king and the
bishops and abbots jointly issued practical measures which they described as "medicine" to reestablish "peace with God." Henceforth the
ecclesiastical peace and the royal peace tended to blend together.
These emergency measures were aimed at the *raptores, rapaces,* and *depraedatores,* in other words, at those who did not respect the immunities
of churches and their goods. These provisions required such people to
make reparations according to public law and to receive the appropriate penance from their bishops. They were granted a grace period
from June to the Kalends of October to "reestablish peace with God."

When King Odo swore his oath to the bishops at his consecration in
888, he too made a promise: "I will carry out the defense of your
churches against *depraedatores et oppressores.*"[32] The king thus continued
to embody the best possible defense for the churches in his kingdom.
But did the vocabulary change in the tenth and eleventh centuries?

At Trosly in 909, Hervaeus, archbishop of Reims, and the attending
bishops of his province pronounced a long exhortation on behalf of
churches and their rights, one directly inspired by the pseudo-
Isidorian decretals. Accordingly, it is hardly surprising that the "oppression" and the "pillaging" of ecclesiastical properties by the laity
were denounced in the by now familiar terms and that the sanction
against the sacrilegious *raptor* was reiterated. At Coblenz in 922,
Sainte-Macre in 935, and Senlis in 989/90, those who stole church
property were declared to be excommunicated and constrained to do
penance.[33] With scarcely different words, Flodoard described the sad
fate of the diocese of Reims during the confrontation of the archbishop
Artaud with Hugh, the son of Herbert of Vermandois: "He plundered
[*depraedabatur*] the villas of the bishopric of Reims . . . and was excommunicated by this bishop on account of the properties he had stolen
[*invaserat*] from the church." Two chapters later he repeated himself,
using expressions such as *res [clericorum] aufere atque diripere, rapinae per
totam urbem perpetrari.* Those who attacked the monastery of Montfaucon were *praedones* who came to *praedare.*[34]

When the earliest of the so-called Peace councils regulated in their
turn the usage of ecclesiastical patrimonies, they merely retrieved

[31] The words of Paul had already been cited in the dispositions of Charlemagne and of
Louis the Pious; see above, note 29.
[32] *MGH Capitularia* 2:376.
[33] Mansi 18:263–307 (Trosly); 18:343–46 (Coblenz); 18:373–74 (Sainte-Macre);
19:95–100 (Senlis).
[34] Flodoard, *Historia Remensis ecclesiae,* 4.33, 35, 40; *MGH SS* 13:584, 585–86, 591–92.

expressions that had already been repeated hundreds of times and reiterated old and familiar desires. A brief list is enough to demonstrate this:

Charroux, ca. 990	*infractores ecclesiarum; per vim abstrahere, praedare*[35]
Le Puy, ca. 994	*ecclesiam infringere; predam facere; malas consuetudines [exigere]; raptor*[36]
Anse, ca. 994	*qui sanctuaria Dei diripiunt; maligni homines; ecclesias desolatas; auferre*[37]
Poitiers, ca. 1000	*res sanctae Dei ecclesiae fraudulenter aut violenter possederat aut iniuste rapuerat*[38]
Poitiers, ca. 1030	*res . . . ecclesiae fraudulenter aut violenter possidere; iniuste rapere; [novas] consuetudines [exigere]: pauperes condemnare*[39]
Narbonne, 1054	*invasores bonorum monasterii* (Saint Michel de Cuxa); *assiduae depraedationes, invasiones, hospitationes atque rapinae a perversis et pravis hominibus [factae]*[40]
Province of Narbonne, 1043	*pravi homines; violenter auferre, rapere, depraedare; res et terras [ecclesiasticas] invadere, rapere aut tollere; rapinas et praedas [facere]*[41]

In approximately 1038, Aimon, archbishop of Bourges, proposed a "pact of peace" to his clergy and swore that he himself would endeavor to accomplish its aim: "I will fight with all my will against *pervasores aecclesiasticarum rerum, incentores rapinarum, oppressores* of monks, nuns, and clerics until they repent."[42]

To describe what were always the same evils, it appears that the clerics used an unchanging language. We can extrapolate from this one certainty: it was not one of the major axes of the politics of the Peace of God to fight against private wars and the brigandage and pillaging of feudal lords; it was, rather, as in the sixth, ninth, and tenth centuries, to force the laity—described as *raptores, rapaces,* and *praedatores*—to renounce the rights they claimed over the ecclesiastical lands of which they were the legal defenders, or over those lands which, as was more often the case, they had seized to ensure the defense of their re-

---

[35] Mansi 19:90.
[36] *Cartulaire de Sauxillanges,* p. 53.
[37] Mansi 19:177–78.
[38] Mansi 19:265–66.
[39] *Chartes et docs. de Saint-Maixent,* 1:109–11.
[40] Mansi 19:827–32.
[41] Mansi 19:599–600.
[42] *Mirac. s. Benedicti,* 5.2, p. 193.

gion when it was threatened. In the latter instance, it is by no means improbable that they were guilty of various abuses. The Peace was intended to return control of ecclesiastical patrimonies to the clergy. Thus, at the heart of these struggles we find the Gelasian doctrine of the respective competence of *auctoritas* and *potestas* and the long history of compromises and peaces these two had established between themselves in the course of five centuries.

Terms Used for the Offenses: *Praeda, Rapina;*
Rapere, Praedare, Tollere

In proposing such continuity of vocabulary and meaning, can we be sure that we have not gone astray by seemingly ignoring the pillaging and excesses of violence denounced in all the sources relating to the Peace? These texts use the words *praeda, rapina,* and *violentia* so frequently that one would have to be blindfolded not to notice them. The problem, however, is to grasp exactly what such terms mean. We can try to find out in two complementary ways. One is to take up the line of argument of one of the most recent historians to write about the Peace; another is to reread some of the sources.

Hans-Werner Goetz has recently published a fundamental article on the Peace of God movement.[43] He argues, first of all—as his predecessors have done since Huberti and as the majority of his contemporaries do—that the Peace movement was born at the end of the tenth century in southern France. Thus, it represents to him a new phenomenon with no relation to any preexisting tradition. Hence, he finds it necessary to answer a basic question: why did it emerge? Goetz believes the answer to be inscribed in a causal chain: famine (or other disaster), pious supplications, peace that translates into a desire expressed mainly by clerics to establish an "inner peace." The goal of the clerics' legislative efforts, "as banal as it may seem," he writes, "was none other [than] the maintenance and reestablishment of peace itself . . . which served as self-protection for the church and for society, but was at the same time a deeply religious matter."[44]

Goetz's proposed causal chain, however, hardly works for all the councils and peace oaths. The events in the Limousin, for which Richard Landes has written a commentary of all the necessary rigor and

[43] Hans-Werner Goetz, "Kirchenschutz, Rechtswahrung und Reform: Zu den Zielen und zum Wesen der frühen Gottesfriedensbewegung in Frankreich," *Francia* 11 (1983):193–239.
[44] Goetz, "Kirchenschutz," p. 227.

depth, constitute almost the only case that fits such a chain.[45] There is
even a contemporaneous instance of famine which appears to be completely different: the diocese of Lodève suffered from a severe famine
near the end of the episcopacy of its holy bishop, Fulcran (ca. 971–
1006); the bishop merely bought wheat in the neighboring province of
the Rouergue and distributed it to his grateful flock.[46]

Nonetheless, Goetz is right to insist that councils and oaths proposed
all sorts of measures intended to protect farm animals, harvested
crops, vineyards, mills, and people transporting foodstuffs (especially
wine and wheat).[47] It is exactly at this point, however, that the attempt
to answer the second basic question about the Peace of God—how
these provisions and those relative to the protection of the poor were
actually implemented—runs into an obstacle, namely, the clauses of
reservation. Indeed, these clauses so restricted the scope of these measures that Goetz is forced to infer that they encouraged the lords to
protect not so much the poor as themselves. Thus, he concludes that
the Peace of God was of much more limited consequence than historians usually believe. It maintained rather than transformed the extant
social order. The current of reform, stimulated in particular by the
great monastery of Cluny, was in the end more dynamic.

Goetz comes to such conclusions because he wisely takes into account
the restrictive clauses that figure in both the conciliar records and the
oaths but which so far have not been explained. It seems to me that
such clauses, if understood fully, can shed as much light on the nature
and goals of the Peace as do the statutes themselves.

Ten years ago I showed to one of my mentors canon 27 of the 1054
council of Narbonne: "We repeat that this regulation as it is written
above should be obeyed without fail by everyone, except by those who
are the administrators of their own allod, fief, or baille."[48] In my study
of *malae consuetudines,* I presented an interpretation of this canon
which did not meet with unanimous agreement. My mentor suggested
to me the possibility that there had been an error in the transcription
of the text of the council: the scribe had written *praeter* ("except") in
place of *propter* ("because of, by means of"). In response, I pointed out
that the provision of 1054 merely reiterated and synthesized the

[45] Richard Landes, "The Dynamics of Heresy and Reform in Limoges: A Study of Popular Participation in the 'Peace of God' (994–1033)," *Historical Reflections/Réflexions historiques* 14 (1987), 467–511.
[46] Elisabeth Magnou-Nortier, *La société laïque et l'Eglise dans la province ecclésiastique de
Narbonne (VIIIème–XIème siècles)* (Toulouse, 1974), p. 325.
[47] Goetz, "Kirchenschutz," pp. 215–20.
[48] "Dicimus iterum ut haec institutio ab omnibus firmiter teneatur, sicut superius
scriptum est, praeter eos qui de suo alode, vel fevo, sive baiulia institutores extiterint";
Mansi 19:832.

clauses of reservation of the canons of the council of Le Puy in 994. At the time, however, I had no other comparable evidence at my disposal.

In short, if one accepts this evidence and the conclusions of Goetz's excellent study, one realizes that historians both have not yet succeeded in identifying the causes of the Peace movement and are uneasy about their estimates of its potential impact. On the one hand, the conciliar assemblies, the penitential atmosphere, the practices focusing on saints' relics, and the spread of the movement to embrace the north as well as the south show its exceptional importance. On the other, its actual effects seem to have been so derisory that the wave of Cluniac foundations appears to have been of more consequence.

What do these clauses of reservation actually say? If we transpose them into a positive form, we can summarize those stipulated by the council of Le Puy as follows: (1) Bishops had the right of plunder (*predam facere*) to obtain their rents, and those who led a military escort (*conductum*) had the right to slaughter animals and requisition food supplies along the way. (2) One could seize whatever one wished to, build or lay siege to a fortified place, as long as one was on one's own land, allod, benefice, or domain for which one had the *comanda*. (3) One could exercise the right of seizure over male and female serfs (*villanus; villana*) or demand from them a ransom (*redemptio*) if they were dependents of one's own domain or benefice or of a territory that was the object of dispute. (4) One could establish a *mala consuetudo*, which thus became legal, over ecclesiastical lands retroceded to laypeople.[49]

The stipulations of the aristocratic peace oaths and their clauses of reservation set before their readers the same exercise. Thus Warin, bishop of Beauvais, could seize male and female serfs (*prendere villanos et villanas*) and their money if their lord was not engaged by the same oath as Warin was. He could confiscate (*tollere*) horses and mules from the feast of All Saints to the Kalends of March. He could kill animals for his *conductum* and seize (*rapere*) wheat mills during certain periods. He could at any time seize (*rapere*) his own mills.[50] In other words, he formally declared that he could pillage himself. He excluded quite precisely in his oath his own properties (*alloda, beneficia, franquisia,*

---

[49] The text of the canons of the council of Le Puy (994) can be found in Magnou-Nortier, "La place du councile du Puy," pp. 499–500.

[50] This text has been edited by Christian Pfister, *Etudes sur le règne de Robert le Pieux (996–1031)* (Paris, 1895), pp. lx–lxi. It has been reedited, along with a similar text from Verdun-sur-le-Doubs, by Roger Bonnaud-Delamare, "Les institutions de paix dans la province ecclésiastique de Reims au XIe siècle," *Bulletin philologique et historique: Comité des travaux historiques et scientifiques, années 1955–1956* (1957), pp. 148–53. Bonnaud-Delamare has neglected to include the contemporary oath of Count Humbert aux Blanches Mains.

commenda et vicaria), where none of the peace measures would apply. Count Humbert aux Blanches Mains swore such an oath with similar conditions.[51]

This was certainly an odd sort of peace. Violence, rapine, and pillage were legal in precisely the territories over which a bishop or count exercised full authority—their allods, benefices, or the regions they administered and for which they had assumed the guard. Peace thus existed (but how exactly?) wherever the magnates did not have direct power. What did it mean to legislate so determinedly to ensure peace, to promise with such solemnity to uphold peace, to bring to the councils so many saints' relics—and then to refuse to create peace in the domains where one was actually master? The paragraph Goetz devotes to feud demonstrates clearly the absurdity of such a form of legislation: the poor were the most mistreated and injustices were the least often redressed on the lands of the *institutores pacis* themselves (to borrow the words of the council of Narbonne of 1054). Even worse, such actions were corroborated, legitimated, and supported by conciliar provisions and the oaths. All this combined is certainly enough to make us insist on the very limited scope of the peace measures.

Goetz has, however, raised a very important issue. As always, the contradiction does not arise from the sources themselves; rather, it originates in the accepted translations of certain words. Goetz himself realizes that a *villanus* or *villana* could certainly no longer be translated as *Bauer*, but he still has in mind the traditional concept of the seigneury and the celebrated "great domain." He is not aware of the history of such key terms as *praeda* and *rapina*, translated in French as *pillage* or *vol*, in German as *Raub* or *Einbrauch*, and in English as "plunder"; *redemptio*, translated as *rançon* or *Freikauf*; *mala consuetudo*, rendered as "exaction" or "violence" in French and English and as *Erpressung* in German. We can add the following observation. If it was merely a matter of curbing theft and brigandage, why was it necessary to invent a new form of legislation called "of the Peace," given that all the extant older laws had ample sanctions for such offenses?

The existence of reservation clauses in the peace legislation thus places before the modern historian an exceptionally clear-cut dilemma: either this legislation was absurd and indeed completely useless—an interpretation difficult to accept in light of the broad diffusion of such legislation in the course of the eleventh century—or it has not yet been fully understood.

[51] This text has been edited by Georges de Manteyer, "Les origines de la Maison de Savoie en Bourgogne (910–1060): La Paix en Viennois (Anse [17 Juin?] 1025) et les additions à la bible de Vienne (ms. Bern A 9)," *Bulletin de la Société de Statistique des Sciences naturelles et des Arts industriels du Département de l'Isère*, 4th ser., 7 (1904), 87–192 (here 91–98). A new edition is needed.

I do not present here in its full detail an analysis I intend to develop elsewhere, nor do I reiterate previous relevant conclusions, in particular those concerning extraordinary taxes.[52] But I can use this opportunity to draw historians' attention to the meaning of the expressions *praedas* (or *rapinas*) *facere* and also, of course, *praedare, rapere,* and *tollere.* I analyze these terms in two different contexts.

One context is that of the Carolingian capitularies. About 823 or 825, Louis the Pious addressed to all the subjects of his realm an *admonitio,* reminding them that according to their rank and competence (bishops and clergy, counts and laity, abbots) they all participated in the imperial ministry and thus assumed responsibility for it. Consequently, they should obey the principal regulations in force in the empire, especially those concerning the peace of the roads used by the armies, hospitality due to foreign envoys, currency, tolls, bridges, tithes (*decimae et nonae*), and the maintenance of churches.[53] The first of these regulations is relevant here.[54] The emperor announced that all those who in the preceding year had suffered damages from the passage of the army and who could supply the name of the guilty party would be recompensed. In the following article, he specified the penalties to be inflicted on the *pacis violator,* that is, on the person who had not respected the military peace. The penalties applied to two social levels, the offender and his superior (*senior*), and were graded accordingly. We can imagine that the latter may have had some difficulty enforcing the obedience of the former, for example, in ensuring compliance with the emperor's directives, especially that no seizure of goods (*praeda*) be committed in the realm. To understand this, it is necessary to return to the capitularies of Charlemagne and Louis the Pious, later recovered integrally by Charles the Bald, which dealt with military discipline along the roads used by the army.[55] One of these capitularies stipulated, "If within the kingdom anyone in the army without an order from us has the intention of using armed force to seize [*praedare*] anything or to take [*tollere*] hay or grain or any type of farm animals, large or small . . . we completely prohibit this."[56] Here it is clear that, although an imperial or royal command could legitimate seizures (*praedae*), they were illegal without such authority (*sine iussione dominica*). Thus one could, if so authorized by the king or emperor, make requisitions for the royal host (*tollere foenum, granum, et pecora*).

---

[52] See Elisabeth Magnou-Nortier, "Le grand domaine: Des maîtres, des doctrines, des questions," *Francia* 15 (1987), 659–700 (esp. 688–694).

[53] *Admonitio ad omnes regni ordines* (823/25); *MGH Capitularia* 1:303–7.

[54] *Admonitio ad omnes regni ordines* (823/25), chaps. 16, 17; *MGH Capitularia* 1:305.

[55] Quierzy (857); *MGH Capitularia* 2:289–91.

[56] "Si quis in exercitu, infra regnum, sine iussione dominica, per vim hostilem aliquid praedare voluerit, aut foenum tollere, aut granum sive pecora maiora vel minora . . . omnino prohibemus"; Quierzy (857), chap. 10; *MGH Capitularia* 2:290.

Moreover, another capitulary specified that "if any member of the host has exceeded the rights of a lord [*super bannum dominicum*] in what grain or standing crops he has seized or stolen or trampled down [*rapuerit, vel paverit, aut furaverit*] or ruined with his horses, according to law he should pay three times the estimated damage."[57]

It is important to note the similarities between these military laws and those of emperor Maurice's *Strategicon;* they hardly seem to be pure coincidence.[58] In each case, it was a matter of reminding soldiers and their leaders of the disciplinary regulations they were supposed to obey. Equally, these provisions attempted to curb the abuses armies were the most likely to commit, among which were those hardly surprising ones related to requisitions. The men in charge of requisitions and provisions could have more goods and supplies delivered than necessary and then sell the excess at a profit; they could lie about quantities received or prices, steal livestock, and seize agricultural produce. Moreover, they could exploit the fear armed men have always aroused in civilians. Using their armed force (*vis hostilis*) in service of their greed, they could act *per vim* or *per violentiam*. Hence the ambivalence of the term *praeda:* it meant not only legal requisitioning but also goods extorted by means of threats. The case is the same for *rapina,* a term used in similar contexts.

The letter written by Archbishop Hincmar of Reims to Charles the Bald in 859 highlights this ambiguity.[59] This powerful prelate had evidently just learned that the king was preparing either to pass through the diocese of Reims or to stay there for several days. This royal plan emerges clearly in *Les annales de Saint-Bertin.*[60] Hincmar communicated to Charles the disquieting rumors aroused by these proposed

[57] "Si quis messes aut annonas in hoste, super bannum dominicum, rapuerit vel paverit, aut furaverit, aut cum caballis vastaverit, aestimato damno secundum legem in triplum componat"; Quierzy (857), chap. 9; *MGH Capitularia* 2:290.

[58] François Aussaresses, *L'armée byzantine à fin du VIème siècle d'après le Strategicon de l'empereur Maurice* (Bordeaux, 1909), p. 46: "Discipline first, then organization and tactics: this is the principle of the military code. . . . This abbreviated code comprises twenty articles, which we can easily divide into four categories: obedience, military honor, internal service, relations with the civilian population. . . . As to relations with the civilian population, whoever does not give back the stolen animal or object or who inflicts damage on a civilian, is punished and pays a compensation estimated at twice the value of the stolen object [the Frankish capitularies prescribed triple the value]. The *strategus* is to avoid centers of habitation, to spare cultivated fields, and when he must cross them is to remedy the damages inflicted. . . . To save the peasants' fields and to protect civilians against harassment by military personnel—this is the general's duty." These regulations were not new. This subject should be studied in greater depth.

[59] *De coercendis militum rapinis, ad Carolum regem; PL* 125:953–56. We have rendered the title "To Control Military Requisitions." The author's summary and partial rendering of the entire letter may be found in Appendix B.

[60] *Les annales de Saint-Bertin,* ed. Felix Grat, Jeanne Veilliard, and Suzanne Clémenet (Paris, 1964), p. 80 (for the year 859).

movements. He informed the king of the abuses he knew had occurred and of the measures he had taken to protect his diocese. In view of the bad reputation royal journeys had, he addressed to Charles a confidential letter in which he described his written instructions to the priests in the villages. The priests were to read these aloud to the men in charge of provisioning the royal army (*homines caballarii*). The archbishop described these latter as *cocciones*—highway robbers and plunderers of the villages from which they were to make requisitions for the royal household. Here Hincmar qualified these *homines caballarii* as *raptores*.[61]

The area subject to requisitioning was specified: the *villae*, at least those Hincmar had chosen from among those dependent on the archbishopric to support the requisitions for the royal army. He made sure to send to the priests of the *villae* (most probably because they could read) written instructions dealing with royal agents in charge of provisions (*propter fodrarios*) in reaction to the royal injunction concerning the required *hospitium*. Unfortunately, the royal order and, even more important, the written directions of the archbishop have not survived. They would have shown us how in practice the amount of goods and supplies required from each *villa* was deducted from the total sum of general taxes they owed. The extant letter of Hincmar, however, proves at least two things:

1. *Rapinae* were strictly controlled by provisions emanating from the sovereign (the *iussio dominica* of the capitularies) and from the local functionaries of the *res publica* (the state) who had the duty of actually enforcing these regulations (hence Hincmar's *admonitio* to the priests of the *villae* and the copy he sent to the king). The archbishop's evident concern that no one know in advance of these provisions—he told the king that they should be read aloud to the public in the king's presence—demonstrates that he took all possible measures to ensure that, while in the lands of the church of Reims, the royal purveyors would not undergo their usual transformation into robbers or *cocciones*. Was it for the kingdom's benefit, he wondered aloud in his letter to Charles, that the imminent arrival of the king should be felt to be a curse? Was it desirable that the king exhaust with unbridled and crushing demands the resources of the tiny part of the kingdom still subject to him? The king should thus have an army in proportion to the capacities of his subjects to support and supply it. And he should dismiss as quickly as possible his followers who lived like parasites from the fruits of the labor of others and send them back to their own lands.

---

[61] "Id est Dei misericordiam inde peto, et vox exinde commoneo, et per villas, in quibus non solum homines caballarii, sed etiam ipsi cocciones rapinas faciunt, admonitiones presbyteris ut eas raptoribus relegant dirigo"; *PL* 125:954A.

2. Hincmar indeed had reason to be worried about *rapinae,* and he felt it his duty to communicate his anxiety to the king. The archbishop had heard that the king had said that he was not obliged to intervene in disputes engendered by *rapinae* and that, furthermore, the palace tribunal turned a deaf ear to such complaints. But did not one article of the capitulary (cited above) make provisions precisely for the indemnification of all those who had suffered damages during the preceding year due to the passage of the royal host? Certainly Hincmar rejected these two accusations as false. Nonetheless, he took advantage of this opportunity to remind his sovereign of several fundamental precepts of Christian wisdom and politics. At the same time, however, he declared that he had no choice but to admit the truth of a third accusation, perhaps because he himself had had the opportunity to verify it. After having collected from the *villae* the amount of goods and supplies stipulated in their instructions, the royal purveyors demanded from the churches who had already made their contributions a supplementary *redemptio* (which we interpret to mean a payment in money). Otherwise, they threatened, they would forcibly break into the church, no doubt to carry out the most arbitrary of requisitions. Now Hincmar emphasized that his instructions "are the words of God" and that transgressors commit sacrilege (*sacrilegium accumulant*). Indeed, in the eyes of the archbishop, deeds such as demanding twice the fixed amount from ecclesiastical lands, violating the rights of ecclesiastical immunity and asylum, and extorting from churches more than they owed constituted more than mere injustice—they were sacrilege. The *raptor* guilty of such offenses was identical to the *raptor* who kept for his or her own benefit property that had been conceded to churches, whether this property was fiscal in origin or represented offerings made by Christians and contested by their heirs. Both committed the same sin: they held the church of God and the poor in contempt. Both were thus subject to the same spiritual sanctions.

We can see from Hincmar's letter that he did not contest the king's right as a prelate to levy on those ecclesiastical lands he administered the lawful exactions and contributions owed him. But the archbishop argued vehemently that these levies should not turn into occasions for extortions that had absolutely nothing to do with this royal right or with law. This latter sort of exaction demeaned the royal office and in the end could only call down God's wrath on the kingdom.

Respect for the rights of ecclesiastical immunity and asylum, respect for ecclesiastical patrimonies, strict control of (or, even better, the reduction of) public exactions related to the royal host, spiritual punishment of those who transgressed these regulations, a call for general penitence if the kingdom was afflicted with misfortunes on account of too many such offenses—such is the causal chain I propose for the peace movement in the ninth century and then again two centuries later. The advantage clerics had over the other subjects in the kingdom who suffered the same abuses was that they could lean on the solid tradition of canon law. Those people on fiscal lands, or indeed all those subject to public exactions, had no lawyers capable of defending them as the ecclesiastics could do for themselves in relation to the lands they administered. There existed only the most indirect and general defense of the poor against the powerful—assured by the clergy who traditionally took the part of the poor. And some of these may have been led to reason and moderation when reminded of the moral duty of every human being and of divine judgment and punishment.

Here we perceive the spirit and intention of the dispositions relating to *praedae, rapinae,* and *violentiae* in the peace legislation of the eleventh century. These provisions have lost their seeming incoherence. We can now understand how it could have been legal to *praedare* or *praedas seu rapinas facere*—to exact requisitions—from the feast of All Saints to March, but illegal from March to All Saints.[62] The reinforcement of military discipline by the regulations of the Peace of God allowed *praedas* to be made after the harvest and during the winter from the stored harvests but prohibited them during the period of planting and the harvest, which was itself the season for military expeditions. The requisitions thus had more chance of being conducted "in accordance with justice" and with market prices. Unfortunately, we can catch only a few glimpses of the prices actually paid for requisitioned foodstuffs and livestock, through such indirect means as the regulations relative to the *conductum* applicable to the markets,[63] or the estimate made for a

---

[62] The oath of Bishop Warin of Beauvais to Robert the Pious reads: "Mulum aut mulam et caballum et equam et pullum qui in pascuis fuerunt, per exfortium non tollam ulli homini a kalendis martii usque festivitatem omnium sanctorum"; Bonnaud-Delamare, ed., "Institutions de paix," p. 150. The same language appears in the oath of Count Humbert aux Blanches Mains; de Manteyer, ed., "Origines de Maison de Savoie," p. 93. A canon of the council of Toulouse (1041, a date that should be corrected to 1068) reads: "Similiter confirmaverunt, ut nullus homo in isto episcopatu illo praedam non faciat de equabus vel pullis earum usque ad medium annum"; Claude Devic and J.-J. Vaissète, *Histoire générale de Languedoc avec des notes et les pièces justificatives,* augmented edition, 16 vols. (Toulouse, 1872–1904), 5:220. A full translation of this text appears in Appendix A.

[63] The oath of Bishop Warin of Beauvais: "et salvamenta ecclesiarum in supradictis hostibus non infringam, nisi mercatum mihi aut conductum victus vetaverint"; Bonnaud-Delamare, ed., "Institutions de paix," p. 152. The oath of Count Humbert: "et si mutare non potuero, et ibi albergariam per necessitatem fecero, et ad rationem missus fuero, infra XV dies ad possibilem emendationem veniam"; Manteyer, ed., "Origines de Maison de Savoie," p. 95.

redemptio,[64] or the description of the poultry taken for feeding falcons and hawks.[65] The measures proclaimed to protect merchants and those who transported foodstuffs originated in the same concern as those that sought to control and reduce, or even eliminate, military requisitions on ecclesiastical lands.[66]

We can also now understand how the leaders of the army, the bishops, the counts, the viscounts, and the *vicarii* desired to retain the right to make such lawful exactions on the lands subject to their authority (*dominatio*). Accordingly, Bishop Warin's oath to Robert the Pious, which includes an important reciprocity clause, should be considered a contract dealing with the voluntary reduction of the military resources of each party, with the royal interest and host excepted. In the presence of the king, the bishop and the other party who took this oath promised each other that they would not provision their host on the lands of the other. Nonetheless, each was allowed to seize grain (*rapere annonam*) from his own mills, to take by force (*tollere per exfortium*) horses and mules, to seize (*prendere*) merchants and female and male serfs or make them pay a ransom (*redimere facere*), and to build fortresses.[67] Those responsible for the maintenance of peace and order, above all the king in the north of the realm, were not allowed to diminish in any other way the military capabilities of the parties who swore such an oath. Consequently, if they engaged themselves in a peace pact, they retained rights on their own lands which they renounced elsewhere. One tangible result of the policies of the Peace of God was thus to diminish the taxes due for the support of the host and to limit warfare in space as well as time.

Finally, in this "war on wars," the monks were in the front line because they did not bear as heavy a burden of public and above all military exaction as did the bishops (at least those in the north). In addition, the theme of ecclesiastical liberties so dear to the author(s) of the pseudo-Isidorian decretals was recuperated and revivified by the

[64] Le Puy (994), can. 6: "Villanum et villanam propter redemptionem non [prendat homo] nisi per suum forspactum"; *Cartulaire de Sauxillanges*, p. 53. The *conventia pacis* of Verdun-sur-le-Doubs: "Villanum et villanam, vel servientes, aut mercatores non prendam, nec denarios eorum tollam, nec redimere eos faciam"; Bonnaud-Delamare, ed., "Institutions de paix," p. 150.

[65] The *conventia pacis* of Verdun-sur-le Doubs: "De auca, de gallo et de gallina nisi pro accipitribus; et si propter eos accepero, emam illam duos denarios"; Bonnaud-Delamare, ed., "Institutions de paix," p. 150.

[66] The oath of Bishop Warin: "Illis autem qui vinum cum carro duxerunt non tollam illud, neque boves qui duxerint. Venditores non prendam nec caballos eorum neque canes tollam"; Bonnaud-Delamare, ed., "Institutions de paix," p. 151. The oath of Count Humbert includes "venatores, piscatores, aucellatores, navigatores in ascendendo et descendendo"; see the text in Manteyer, ed., "Origines de Maison de Savoie," p. 94.

[67] Bonnaud-Delamare, ed., "Institutions de paix," p. 150.

monks. They exploited the vast possibilities offered by the canons and especially those pseudo-Isidorian decretals—including the potential of Christian belief in the justice, both salvific and punitive, of God—to expand their immunities and regain portions of their patrimony confiscated for military purposes.[68] The recent work by scholars in North America on Ademar of Chabannes best illustrates this aspect of the politics of the Peace.

This brief examination of the vocabulary used to designate the enemies of the peace reveals two major axes of the movement historians label "the Peace of God": (1) Increasingly elaborate and specific military regulations demanded that ecclesiastical immunities be respected and accordingly caused definitive restrictions of the right to requisition men, animals, and supplies. (2) The clerics, and above all the monks, repeated incessantly that offerings made to God and to the saints were inalienable and that people who kept them or used them for other purposes were excluded from the communion of the faithful. In the eleventh century, in a kingdom delivered from the threat of invasion, ecclesiastical law intervened at exactly the right moment to reinforce the tendency toward restricting military requisitions.

[68] The influence of the pseudo-Isidorian decretals among the Cluniac monks has been particularly well analyzed by Fuhrmann, *Einfluss und Verbreitung*, pp. 758–68.

4

The Chiaroscuro of Heresy:
Early Eleventh-Century Aquitaine
as Seen from Auxerre

GUY LOBRICHON

History abounds with heresies. Sudden utterances of men still in the flesh, expressions of their dream to be released or of their melancholic awareness of the impossible—they are ever the bitter fruit of the establishment of a new order. Yet at times they are induced by imagination: censorship and its ideologues are all too swift in creating the source of their own fears. And since the most verbose documents (not necessarily the most reliable) emanate from would-be judges of every ilk—lay or ecclesiastical law courts, public assemblies, or writers of polemical fiction—the historian who too readily trusts these (themselves naive) sources is likely to be deceived. Such has been the fate of the interpreters of a famous account of heresy in twelfth-century Périgord. The story is historiographically instructive, for a modicum of attention and inquiry would have prevented many blunders in interpreting the "Letter" of the monk Heribert. As soon as one follows the trail of this reputedly reliable source back through its early manuscripts, the "Letter" is revealed to be the untrustworthy vehicle of a slander campaign. A literal interpretation becomes unsatisfactory; the text demands to be read with an eye to the rhetoric of polemics and of literary fiction.[1]

The author expresses his full appreciation to Phillippe Buc, who translated this article, and to Amy G. Remensnyder and Thomas Head, who reviewed the English version.
[1] To give a full bibliography on heresy is beyond the abilities of an individual and beyond the scope of an article. See Carl Berkhout and Jeffrey Burton Russell, *Medieval Heresies: A Bibliography, 1960–1979* (Toronto, 1981), which brings the work of Herbert Grundmann up to date. Every year the volumes published in the Cahiers de Fanjeaux series contain articles on heresy in southern France. More recently, see M. Zerner, "Du court moment où on appela les hérétiques des *bougres*: Et quelques déductions," *Cahiers de civilisation médiévale* 32 (1989), 305–24.

The "Facts" and Their Dissolution

First the facts, as recounted (after much preliminary prose) in a recently published study. The presentation is instructive. Between 1145 and 1163, a certain monk Heribert denounced in an inflammatory letter the nefarious deeds of a sect infesting the province of Périgord in southwestern France. The sect, according to this modern account, "pretended that it was returning to the apostolic life, condemned the eating of meat and the drinking of wine, rejected the Eucharist and the worship of the cross; noblemen, clerics, monks and nuns had joined its ranks; its leader was called Poncius."[2] Not much more is known about the event. Yet, starting with Mabillon, historians' imaginations have latched onto this report. This precise and concise document seemed to throw a new light on Saint Bernard's preaching in the Bordelais, the Périgord, and the Toulousain (1145). The abbot of Clairvaux was known to have violently clashed in those areas with followers of Henry the Monk (Henry of Lausanne). Mabillon intuited—and his conclusion was received as Gospel by subsequent historians—that the enemy unmasked by Heribert had to correspond to diehards that the saint had been unable to bring back into the fold. Given this "fact," one could endow the letter with a likely date and deduce its actual referent.[3] Later historians found yet better: in Heribert's "Letter" one had the rock-hard proof that there had been, from as early as the middle of the twelfth century, contacts between the Cathars and the Eastern Bogomils. Did Heribert not cite the odd doxology of the Périgord heretics? Did this creed not contain a typical prayer formula that was recognizably eastern? Away with Henry the monk; there stood the birth certificate of Catharism in the Latin west—this thanks to the birthdate obligingly supplied by the Henrician hypothesis![4] One cannot help but find the logic leading to this discovery somewhat disconcerting.

The historian who prefers commentaries and glosses to the simple bareness of primary sources runs a heavy risk: the very ground can

[2] Bernard Guillemain, "Le duché d'Aquitaine hors du catharisme," in *Effacement du Catharisme? (XIIIe–XIVe s.)* (Cahiers de Fanjeaux, 20; Toulouse, 1985), pp. 58–59.

[3] Jean Mabillon, *Vetera analecta* (Paris, 1682), 3:467 (1723 ed., p. 483). Cf. R. I. Moore, *The Birth of Popular Heresy* (London, 1975), p. 79.

[4] Malcolm Lambert, *Medieval Heresy: Popular Movements from Bogomil to Hus* (London, 1977), pp. 62–63. The new edition has moved discussion of this letter back to the early eleventh century; *Medieval Heresy: Popular Movements from the Gregorian Reform to the Reformation* (2d ed., Oxford, 1992), p. 30. Reading what Gregory of Tours (ca. 585) reports about Visigothic beliefs, one will understand that Lambert's original speculations are unfounded: "You do not answer the Gloria correctly," a Spaniard tells him, "for we, following the Apostle Paul, say 'Glory to God the Father through the Son.' But you say 'Glory to the Father, to the Son, and to the Holy Spirit' "; *Historia Francorum*, 6.40, translation adapted from the French translation of Robert Latouche (Paris, 1965), 2:62.

disappear underfoot. We can simulate this sad happening by following the document's trail backward. Heribert's "Letter" was first published by Mabillon in 1682, then again by Martène and Durand in 1717. The two editions were based on two different (albeit related) manuscripts.[5] Our knowledge of the case rests on these editions. The *Annales de Margan* provide an additional, later testimony: the annalist dates the discovery of the Périgord heretics to precisely 1163.[6] This yields a useful *terminus ad quem,* which becomes rock solid when one unearths two further facts: that the 1163 council of Tours was stirred by the news of heretical activities, and that William of Newburgh reported (ca. 1198) the arrival of the *publicani* in England ca. 1163. According to William, they came from Gascony and then were quickly discovered and condemned at an Oxford synod.[7] This is all so well known and so often repeated by historians that it must be authentic. But is it really? The council of Tours spoke of a cancer gnawing at the Toulousain, not the Périgord, and its prime worry was the backers of the German antipope. As for the Oxford heretics, one should remark that they came from Gascony, of which the Périgord is no part. Furthermore, theirs was an opportune emergence that coincided with the interests of Henry II, providing the king with a timely certificate of orthodoxy. Where, then, are Heribert's men from the Périgord?

At least two twelfth-century manuscripts contain Heribert's text. They might have caused accepted wisdom to be questioned. Toward the end of the century, a cleric (probably in Paris) recopied the letter in a set of contemporary *prognostica* and prophecies. Kindly enough, he corroborated the date of 1163. He may have been the Margam annalist's source, but his text differed markedly from that of the Maurists—Mabillon, Martène, and Durand.[8] Somewhat earlier, in the third quarter of the twelfth century, another scribe, a monk of Luxeuil, had transcribed Heribert's "Letter" into the abbey's lectionary. It happens that his version is quite close to that of the Maurists. In all like-

---

[5] Dom Mabillon did not indicate the manuscript he had used. Edmund Martène and Ursinus Durand, *Thesaurus novus anecdotorum,* 5 vols. (Paris, 1717–26), 1:453, say that they are transcribing a manuscript from the monastery of Saint-Amand. Mabillon's text seems the better of the two editions. *PL* 181:1721–22, however, reprints the Martène-Durand version.

[6] *Annales de Margan* (year 1163), in *Annales monastici,* ed. H. R. Luard, 5 vols., Rolls series, 36 (London, 1864–69), 1:15.

[7] William of Newburgh, *Historia rerum Anglicarum; MGH SS* 27:231–32. Also see *The Letters and Charters of Gilbert Foliot,* ed. Adrian Morey and Christopher Brooke (Cambridge, 1967), pp. 208–9. The chronicles of the late twelfth century do not say a word about the heretics of the Périgord. For the year 1163 they speak of *schismatici,* that is, partisans of the antipope Victor and of Frederick I.

[8] Paris, BN lat. 16208 (late twelfth century; Sorbonne), fol. 135v. See Appendix C for an edition of this text.

lihood, it represents the form in which the text circulated toward the middle of the century. Yet there is no mention of 1163 (or, for that matter, of any date whatsoever) in either the text of the Luxeuil monk or the Mabillon and Martène-Durand editions. Furthermore, the Luxeuil manuscript bears the marks of the message's adaptation to a public in the German empire.[9] Printed editions and manuscripts do agree on the name of the heretics' *princeps* (Poncius). But can one blindly trust the letter as a whole, given the fluctuations in the data provided by the manuscript tradition?

It is hardly credible that Heribert's "Letter," being such a brief pamphlet, could vary so much from one version to another. This first astonishing fact is already ground for strong doubt, but there is worse: Heribert's words do not allude to any of the character traits specific to twelfth-century heresies. They can, however, apply to a timeless and numerous crowd that had existed since the origins of Christianity—the opponents of the institutional face of the church. There is nothing specific about the material wealth of the churches or of the faithful, nothing about the ecclesiastical hierarchy, nothing about marriage. The sole trait that might be dated would be the Périgord heretics' strong disgust for the Eucharist, were it not for the fact that reflections on the body and blood of Christ have ever been fertile fields for dispute. Thus, even if it has to be granted that right around the birthdate commonly ascribed to the pamphlet contemporary observers did witness such critiques and rejections, one should be wary of seeing in the target of Heribert's fulminations actual heretical antieucharistic pronouncements and attitudes. Indeed, the embers of the ninth-century controversies on the Eucharist between Ratramnus of Corbie and Paschasius Radbertus had burst into flame again before 1100; the condemnation of Berengar of Tours († 1088) is proof of the endemic nature of the eucharistic issue.[10] And there were always orthodox thinkers ready to remind Christians that sacramental realism might indeed be the logical consequence of the Christian tenet of the Incarnation but was also (and much more) a divine concession to the all too human thirst for material signs. Furthermore, debates on the sacraments, in which clerics of unimpeachable loyalty to the church took part, permeated the whole breadth of the twelfth century. Heretical fringe groups had no monopoly on criticism of the Eucharist. To fall back on the aforementioned identifications of our heretics as either

[9] Vesoul, Bibliothèque municipale, 1 (third quarter of the twelfth century; scriptorium of the abbey of Luxeuil), fol. 165r. See Appendix C for an edition of this text.
[10] See Jaroslav Pelikan, *The Christian Tradition: A History of the Development of Doctrine*, Vol. 3: *The Growth of Medieval Theology (600–1300)* (New Haven, Conn., 1978), pp. 74–80, and 186–202; on Ratramnus, see J. P. Bouhot, *Ratramne de Corbie* (Paris, 1976).

the Henricians or the Oxford *publicani* (also known as *popelicani*) is tempting but unsound.[11] The Henricians have only one point in common with the Périgord sect—their spite for the crucifix. But there have always been iconoclastic movements within Christianity. The coincidence is just that; it cannot lead to the identification of the Périgord heretics with a historically attested sect. Between the Oxford heretics and ours, there is one essential difference: the *popelicani* based their antisacramentalism on intellectual and dogmatic grounds that the Périgourdins seemed to lack. They indulged rather in sarcastic irony (see their mocking of the crucifix). Read it and reread it as one may, it seems strangely insubstantial; one hesitates to recognize historical reality behind Heribert's diatribe. It rings hollow. It is not aimed at an identifiable group that is clearly defined by a coherent body of doctrines, a label, individual qualities, or a set of practices that set it apart from other sects.

An Earlier Heribert

The sands shift, treacherous for the historian treading without caution, without a scaffolding of facts and dates. One cannot plead dearth of sources and (convenient) disappearances of documents; for, long forgotten, behold a sixth witness of Heribert's "Letter"! This sixth version forces one back almost a century and a half earlier; it is transcribed in a beautiful hand, even and clean, which modern paleographic science readily attributes to the beginning of the eleventh century. The manuscript itself is a repository of documents ranging from the mid-ninth to the mid-eleventh century; it belonged to the abbey of Saint-Germain in Auxerre around 1050. It is there that a scribe, locally trained and fully immersed in the calligraphic conventions that had ruled the scriptorium since the mid-ninth century, copied Heribert's "Letter."[12] Here is the text in full:

---

[11] Some twelfth-century sources called them *popelicani*, as in the case of the heretics at Vézelay (1167); see *Monumenta Vizelaciensia*, ed. R. B. C. Huygens (Corpus Christianorum, Continuatio Mediaeualis, 42; Turnhout, 1976), pp. 228, 606.

[12] Paris, BN lat. 1745 (ninth to eleventh century; Saint-Germain of Auxerre), fol. 31r. See Guy Lobrichon, "Culture et société à Saint-Germain d'Auxerre, du IXe au XIe siècle: Enquête sur un manuscrit parisien," *Bulletin de la Société des fouilles archéologiques et des monuments historiques de l'Yonne* 2 (1985), 9–16, which includes a facsimile of Heribert's "Letter" and a detailed description of the codex. Both Bernhard Bischoff and Jean Vezin have corroborated the date—arrived at on paleographic grounds—of this manuscript. On the manuscripts from Auxerre, see also Guy Lobrichon, "L'atelier auxerrois," in *L'école carolingienne d'Auxerre de Murethach à Remi, 830–908* (Paris, 1991), pp. 59–69.

To all Christians in the Orient and in the Occident, North and South, who believe in Christ, Peace and Mercy in God the Father, in His only Son our Lord, and in the Holy Ghost.

A new heresy is born in this world and in our days; its source is pseudo-apostles; through their origin, these mens are the ministers of all iniquity. Considering this, we have sought to write you, intending to make you cautious and on all points wary, lest you fall into their heresy.

In our own time indeed, in the area of Périgueux, numerous heretics have arisen. Truly, it is so. To subvert the Christian religion at its very roots, they pretend that they are leading the apostolic life. They do not eat meat, do not drink wine (except on the third day); a hundred times a day do they genuflect; not only do they refuse money, but the funds they (seemingly honestly) possess they put in common.

Yet their sect is most perverse; it is hidden and deceptive. For they do not enter churches, unless they want to corrupt. They never say "Glory to the Father and to the Son and to the Holy Ghost," but instead they say, "For yours is the Kingdom, and you rule all creatures for ever and ever, Amen." They say alms are worthless, for since there should be no property, whence can they [legitimately] come? They hold the mass to be nothing and say that one should perceive the Eucharist as fragments of blessed bread. They assert that liturgical chant is a vanity, invented to please men. If one of them (in order to corrupt) sings the mass, he does not say the canon, and turns his back, behind or on the side of the altar. As for the host, he throws it in the missal or behind the altar. They do not worship the cross or the effigy of the Lord [the crucifix], and they even forbid (as much as they can) others to worship them, to the extent that, standing in front of the effigy, they lament aloud: "How unfortunate those who worship you," according to the word of the Psalmist, "the idols of the nations [are man-made, of gold and of silver]."[13]

Thus have they corrupted and brought to them numerous people, not only laypeople, who have given up all their belongings, but also clerics, priests, monks, and nuns. They have been swallowed up [by heresy] to the extent that they seek to find men who might torture and deliver them unto death. For they perform many wonderous feats. Indeed, no one (no matter how rustic) adheres to their sect who does not become, within eight days, wise in letters, writing, and action, [so wise] that no one can overcome him in any way. They cannot be harmed, because if they are caught no bounds can hold them.

Indeed, I, Heribert, the least of all monks, and author of this letter, was there when they were loaded with chains, and put in a great wine barrel. It had an open bottom,[14] its top was shut, and guards had been set over it. In the morning, they were gone, and, furthermore, they left no tracks until their next appearance. A vase, emptied of its wine, in which a little bit

[13] Ps. 113:4, 134:15.
[14] Philippe Buc pointedly suggests that either this wine vat was turned over to make a prison or Heribert invented a parodic miracle (cf. the escape of Christ's body from the tomb) to mock his rivals at the same time he emphasized the threat they posed.

of wine was put, was found full the next morning. And they perform other
deeds marvelous indeed, which I cannot relate here. For right now, secretly, they are invading these parts and others.

Thus Heribert was already sounding the alarm around the year
1000. This fact invalidates all the interpretations heretofore put forward concerning the "realities" described by the document. Let there
be no ambiguity; this manuscript does not lead one onto firmer
ground. It ruins all hope of locating the heretics in the clear-cut timeframe of the twelfth century; yet, can one now, without preliminary reflection, seize on one of the early eleventh-century heretical groups?
Can one seek to match at all costs one of the groups of dissenters attested in that era with Heribert's targets? This would be to cloak oneself in the same uncritical certitudes as one's predecessors, and, having
transposed farther back in time their erroneous mode of reasoning, ex-
pose oneself to the same dangers. These pitfalls cannot be avoided unless one transforms the inquiry and asks different questions, which
may lead, possibly, but not necessarily, to other heretics.

A Methodological Aside

Essentially, it is necessary to read Heribert's "Letter" as a product of
early medieval writing and literary composition. This oral society confined the technicians of writing in scriptoria. Such tradition-bound
centers perpetuated constraining formalistic rules. Armed with the
pen and its literary techniques, the intellectual made manifest his ability to reveal all knowledge: his function among men was to open channels of communication between the hierarchized levels of reality, from
the most material to the most spiritual. Mere scribe or compiler and
author, the medieval intellectual always went beyond the depiction of a
reality a modern person would consider univocal. Analogy and metaphor were still in the twelfth century the means of the highest and
most scientific rationality. Thus, one should not evaluate the worth of
Heribert's "Letter" by testing whether it stands up to a literal reading—
the criteria and results of which would be the yielding of positivistic
contents anchored in some objective reality and ascribed to a precise
timeframe. Rather, the letter should be considered as a coded document; its keys are to be sought through a metaphorical reading, its interpretation to be found within the field of ideology. Such an approach
is legitimate, given both the eternal methods of propaganda and the
exegetical rules that governed thought in the eleventh century and
would still govern it in the twelfth. To be blunt, the historian should

not take Heribert's "Letter" at its (deceptively obvious) surface meaning before he or she has exhausted other hermeneutic possibilities. It needs a careful decoding, for it is a carefully composed structure; its form was such that it could serve the ends of all its recipients, who could adulterate it according to their own needs. And the manuscript tradition teaches that they did.[15] Be it fiction or veridical report, this written document is cast according to the rules of the time-tested rhetoric taught in the schools. One gets a sense of the letter's specific cast by merely glancing at it: it is a pamphlet.[16] It is closer to those early medieval "letters from Heaven" that fell on altars than it is to police reports, themselves far from reliable; lawyers and judges have long known how to see through their pretenses and lay bare their would-be objectivity. The letter's polemical intent is undeniable. Yet one must still follow the pamphleteer's tortuous maneuvers. His are indirect tactics: the enemy is too powerful to be named and attacked frontally.

For a thorough understanding of such a missive, the historian needs to take a roundabout approach. Then and only then will he or she be able to judge. A three-step tactic is required: one must first define the potential targets, then see where they actually belong within the set of categories provided by the literary tradition, and finally, looking at it from a progressively wider perspective, translate Heribert's indictment into the clearer terms of a social analysis.

Every written document earmarked for diffusion bears discrete, but perceptible, signs. They indicate the level of intelligibility and veracity the informer claims. Our letter must therefore contain a few hints supplied to avert its readers from misunderstandings. The initial step is to locate these signs; they define the rules according to which the readers (or listeners) are going to interpret the document. First, there is the way the author uses traditional formularies. A heavy yoke in all societies, formularies were especially restrictive in early medieval letter writing, a genre shaped by the conventions of the classical world. The authors of the successive versions of the "Letter" have cleverly sought to give it a plausible tone, as can be seen in the salutation. The early eleventh-century monk called out "to all Christians who dwell in the Orient and in the Occident, in the South and in the North." In the mid-twelfth century, it became: "I, Heribert the monk, want to let it be known to all Christians, that . . . " The Parisian scribe, around 1200, shortened the formula to a pithy "Heribert, to all Christians,

[15] Natalie Zemon Davis, *Fiction in the Archives: Pardon Tales and Their Tellers in Sixteenth-Century France* (Stanford, Calif., 1987), stimulates one to reflect on the narrative practices of the past. See also Jeanette Beer, *Narrative Conventions of Truth in the Middle Ages* (Geneva, 1981).

[16] The Latin text may be found as document 1 in Appendix C.

greetings!"[17] The reworking of the salutation was not simply motivated
by a desire to adapt it to the canons of the day. The twelfth-century
scribes followed contemporary usage, but the early eleventh-century
salutation was a total oddity. Its tone was foreign to both contemporary
and later diplomatic or letter-writing formulas. Hence, perceiving this
peculiarity, the twelfth-century scribes decided to modify it (we return
to this point). There is yet another clue that revisers were ill at ease: the
passage in which Heribert identified himself as the document's author
was advanced to become the letter's first line. But in the eleventh-
century letter, the description of the Périgord doctrines was located
where one would have normally expected to find a preamble; then followed Heribert's "subscription," itself prefacing a report on the *mira signa,* on the heretics' quasi-miraculous feats. Thus, their "law and
creed" (*lex et doctrina*) was alluded to without much detail, as a mere
reminder: the heresy's specificity was located in its paranatural *mira signa.* The informant, judge and witness, came forth ("I, Heribert the
monk") to testify to the actuality of those "miracles" and wonders.
Clearly, he had endowed these with a key role in his demonstration; he
was willing to risk blurring the lines between truth and falsehood. The
placing of the authority "Heribert" before the *mira signa* was a formal
sign to the audience that it had to focus on the wonders. A century
later, the adapters of the "Letter" were bothered by its structure. They
chose to revolutionize it.

The formulaic rules, the external trimming, are not the only agents
shaping interpretative rules. Heribert, it seems, sparsed his letter with
additional clues. These referred to a system of beliefs; contemporaries,
who shared in this system, would have immediately identified the al-
lusions. The eleventh-century Heribert was cautious. He did not
present himself in the guise of the ecclesiastical judge. He weighed his
words carefully; he did not want his readers to identify these "enemies
of the church" in a clear-cut manner. Taken individually, each of his
catchall sentences had been a commonplace in treatises against heresies since the beginnings of Christianity. Any police informant or dissident hunter could use them. Two singular details of the "Letter" urge
one to diverge from a literal reading; one perceives echoes to which
contemporary readers would have been sensitive. They show that
Heribert did not want his readers to identify the menace with any of
the groups of dissidents they might have found in traditional cata-

[17] "Omnibus christianis qui sunt in oriente et occidente, meridie et aquilone . . . " in
Paris, BN lat. 1745, f. 31r; see Appendix C, document 1, lines 1–2. "Omnibus Christianis notum esse cupio ego Heribertus monachus, ut se caute agant . . . " in Mabillon,
ed., 3:467; in Martène and Durand, eds., 1:453; in Vesoul, BM 1, f. 165r; see Appendix
C, document 2. "Omnibus christianis heribertus salus. Exierunt . . . " in Paris, BN lat.
16208, fol. 135v; see Appendix C, document 3.

logues of heresies. First, Heribert's Périgord heretics could not tolerate the inflation of "ecclesiastical chant." An eleventh-century Cluniac would have felt a personal attack in this rejection; the great Burgundian abbey had claimed changed liturgy as its specialty. Shortly after "Heribert," Rodulphus Glaber, an excellent publicist of Cluny, related a similar series of criticism against monastic chant. Yet his opponent was not a heretical conventicle but a group of clerics and bishops belonging to the established church.[18] Rodulphus and Heribert converge in an unexpected way. And what was the meaning of the puzzling salutation, "To all the Christians who dwell in the Orient and in the Occident, in the South and in the North, and who believe in Christ, Peace and Mercy in God the Father, in his only Son our Lord, and in the Holy Ghost"? This emphatic greeting endowed the "Letter" with the wonderous aura of a very specific set of texts: a genre colored with apocalyptic hues, examples of which date from the letters of Bourges and Palestine (419) to the missive of Prester John.[19] Its surviving representatives were extremely rare until the second half of the eleventh century; after this date, the quantity of such texts sharply increased. The genre would be extremely popular with Joachim of Fiore's followers in the thirteenth century. But let us return to the point: Heribert's preamble participated in the same ideology as did Rodulphus Glaber's later meditations on the "divine quaternity" and the golden globe of Henry II of Germany. The significance of this latter marvelous sphere is well known; it symbolized the Empire of Justice at work in this earthly world, a kingdom whose propagation Cluniac ideology sought to hasten.[20]

In the context of these fragmentary traces of its exterior setting, the nature of Heribert's "Letter" may change. Was it really a warning against a fully reported heresy, a description that would clearly point to a specific fringe group? When one edits a text, it is always dangerous to choose, a priori, the *lectio facilior*. The same lesson holds for polemical documents, and early medieval texts are no exception to this rule.

[18] Rodulphus Glaber, *Historiarum*, 3.3.12; also see 2.9.19.

[19] Although the letters themselves do not survive, two fifth-century historians refer to "letters sent everywhere" in 419 by the bishops of Bourges and Jerusalem to alert their fellow Christians of the "terrible signs and wonders" that occurred that year (on Bourges, Hydatius, *Chronicon*, 73; *MGH Auctores Antiquissimi* 11:20; on Jerusalem, *Consularia Constantinopolitana*, *MGH Auctores Antiquissimi* 9:246). One imagines that they contained an invocation similar to that of Heribert.

[20] Edmond Ortigues and Dominique Iogna-Prat, "Raoul Glaber et l'historiographie clunisienne," *Studi Medievali* 26 (1985), 537–72, particularly p. 558ff. Glaber's meditation on the divine quarternity is curiously echoed in a prologue that was added to the *Gesta episcoporum Leodiensium* a little after 1056 (*PL* 139:1668). Both refer to the declaratio of Rabanus Maurus in his *De laude sanctae crucis*, 1.7, which eleventh-century scribes recopied often (e.g., Paris, BN lat. 11685, fol. 15r; Saint-Germain des Près).

When it uses the appropriate commonplaces, a pamphlet is liable to foster the illusion of the historicity of the object to which it refers. And if one seeks polemicists who have diverted to their ends thematic labels normally attached to specific heresies, there is no dearth of examples: Jerome, around 400, against Rufinus; Agobard, in the ninth century, against Amalarius; closer to Heribert's time and place, Odorannus of Sens (ca. 1030–40).[21] Was Heribert, under the guise of the public prosecutor, spreading the early eleventh-century slogans of the Cluniac party with the help of his strange pamphlet? The monks, champions of ecclesiastical reform in France, backed by kings Hugh and Robert, were ready to come to blows with their opponents. These were not necessarily the institutional church's marginals. Could Heribert the monk's true target be lurking someplace other than where the historian would expect?

What can one do to move farther in the minefield of this definitely complex literary genre? It is necessary to find a second angle of approach; one must relocate Heribert's "Letter" in a wider setting. One will recall that the eleventh-century letter was copied in a manuscript corpus. The manuscript's raison d'être was to offer its reader a solid yet clear antiheretical set of texts.[22] Paris, Bibliothèque Nationale, codex latin 1745 starts with texts copied in the ninth century: Ambrose of Milan's *De fide ad Gratianum;* not unexpectedly, Augustine's *De haeresibus;* Agobard of Lyon's small treatise against his rival Amalarius's antiphonary. The drawing of two labyrinths has been pruned onto a blank folio, and early in the eleventh century a scribe has transcribed Heribert's document. The following quire contains an unpublished treatise on tithes and church offerings, composed and copied in the middle of the ninth century. A narrative charter of the mid-eleventh century—it clearly deals with similar issues—closes this series of texts. It was probably in the eleventh century that the monks of Saint-Germain of Auxerre bound together this very apposite codicological whole. The coherence of the final product is beyond doubt.[23]

Indeed, its intent was clearly polemical. Ambrose and Augustine supplied the necessary intellectual and patristic guarantees. Agobard of Lyon's worries demonstrated the permanent immanence of heresy. The anonymous author defended the rights of churches, and especially monasteries, to receive offerings and levy tithes. Finally, the two laby-

---

[21] See the instructive discussion by P. Lardet of Saint Jerome's polemical technique in the introduction to his edition of *Saint Jérôme: Apologie contre Rufin* (Sources chrétiennes, 303; Paris, 1983).

[22] See Lobrichon, "Culture et Société."

[23] In the Paris, BN lat. 1745, the only addition made after the mid-eleventh century is the table of contents, which was written in a hand from the beginning of the thirteenth century.

rinths were the iconographic symbols of the ways of falsity and error. The two eleventh-century documents concluded the textual case. They aimed at unmasking two types of evil doers. On the one hand were the heretics. Fortunately, their appearance had taken place in a faraway province; in every civilization, the immigrant and the *paganus* are the eternal source of all evils. On the other hand were the secular lords of the Auxerrois. At the end of the tenth century, the monks of Saint-Germain of Auxerre had been conquered by imperialistic Cluny. It seems that the king and the bishop had forced this hostile takeover. Intoxicated by the winds of reform that had forcibly swept the old halls of Saint-Germain, the new followers of Cluny indulged in finger pointing: the true enemies were the pseudoreformers and those who nibbled at monastic exemption and church liberties. Collusion between the monks' opponents would have been disastrous: political ambitions, but also an unrestrained rivalry between monks and secular clergy, tore Burgundy apart.[24]

Clerics are wont to accuse their opponents of being heretics for a mere trifle. Modern historians may have been impressed by Agobard sternly calling Amalarius a heretic, but his ninth century contemporaries were not; they had no qualms about copying Amalarius's treatise, even in Auxerre.[25] A heretic: the bishop of Orléans, fulminated Abbo of Fleury.[26] Heretics: kings Hugh and Robert, according to the papal legate Leo on the day following the council of Saint-Basle-de-Verzy (991).[27] Yet in these cases the issue was not doctrine but discipline. Furthermore, one will recall how loosely the protagonists of the so-called Gregorian reform used the concept of heresy. Thus one is correct to hesitate when faced with Heribert's heretics. They denied the church's right to receive alms, using as a pretext the claim that "since there should be no property, whence can they [legitimately] come?" "Not only do they refuse money, but the funds they (seemingly honestly) possess, they put in common." They were shaking the grounds of contemporary monastic power.[28] This was their real crime; how would monasteries survive if the flow of aristocratic bounty were to dry up, dammed up by criticism as old as religion itself? Through the pen of his eleventh-century scribe, Heribert countered those age-old attacks,

---

[24] Yves Sassier, *Recherches sur le pouvoir comtal en Auxerrois du Xe au début du XIIIe siècle* (Auxerre, 1980).

[25] Vatican, Reg. lat. 146 (end of the ninth or beginning of the tenth century, Saint-Julien of Auxerre).

[26] Abbo of Fleury, *Apologeticus; PL* 139:461–63, 468–69.

[27] *MGH SS* 3:686.

[28] "[E]lemosinam dicunt nihil esse, quia nec unde fieri possit debere possideri"; see Appendix C, document 1, line 12. "[P]ecuniam non solum non recipiunt, sed et habitam prout uidetur decenter dispertiunt"; see Appendix C, document 1, lines 8–9.

which one can also find reproduced in our manuscript's ninth-century layer. As for debates on tithes and offerings, they were also endemic. In the thirteenth century, the friars would be the villains; in the twelfth century, monks and clerics would fight over the control of the parish; in the eleventh century, the opponents were monks and lords: all of monasticism's rejuvenated forces versus all the "secular princes" who established *malae consuetudines,* new and evil taxes. Immunity and exemption were always present in the background. This constant wrestling was fundamentally the offspring of a dangerous doubt, to which many laypeople and secular clergy fell prey: were earthly riches useful to men and women on the steep and narrow road leading to the Lord? The question was yet another version of the delicate debate on the means and rules of Christian perfection. In this struggle, as one might expect, some took a high moral standpoint, and, brandishing the letter of the Gospel, unsettled the courteous game in which the old powers-that-be collude. For the monks, the danger loomed large. Their reaction was correspondingly violent. In those years of swift social mutation, any opponent could be branded a heretic.

We can now move on to the third approach. Heribert's clarity is a deceptive mask. For the historian, early eleventh-century monastic polemics are still almost virgin land. His "Letter" may well be rooted in this soil. What does Heribert tell us about the monks' reaction to contemporary movements?

The document clearly derived from a monastic milieu. In all the versions, Heribert is a monk. The message was diffused by a network of older monasteries (Saint-Germain of Auxerre, Luxeuil, Saint-Amand) and later by the important Cistercian house of Margam. All had considerable patrimonies to defend. Furthermore, our earliest copy of the text first appeared in Cluniac Auxerre, that is, in a place involved with reform politics. The voluntaristic leaders of the reform were the abbots of Cluny and their protectors. The bishop of Auxerre, Hugh of Chalon, organizer of the Peace assemblies of Verdun-sur-le-Doubs (1018) and Héry (1025), took care not to be left out of this group.[29] Thus Cluny and its propaganda arm may well have stood behind Heribert's pen—brilliant Cluny, which aroused a good number of northern French bishops to suspicion vis-à-vis the monks—ambitious Cluny, led by the great abbot Odilo, "King Odilo" to a disgusted Adalbero of Laon. Yet bishops and princes unanimously agreed with the monks on the need for religious reform to restore public peace, although episcopal power took little pleasure in the flight of prestigious monasteries into the bosom of a confederacy that guaranteed all its members liberty

---

[29] Sassier, *Recherches sur le pouvoir comtal,* p. 37.

and exemption—hence Bishop Hugh of Chalon's desire to be at the vanguard of the Peace movement in the lands he controlled, and in Auxerre his care to prevent too narrow a subjection of Saint-Germain to Cluny. He did not hesitate to breach one of the strictest Cluniac customs and bring the full weight of his considerable influence to bear on the choice of the abbot.[30] The fact shows the limits of the Cluniac spirit in Burgundy itself: tenacious resistance checked its influence in the very city where Cluny's newest recruits were adding Heribert's "Letter" to the aforementioned texts. Understandably, opposition was far from being less in Aquitaine, in this Périgord mentioned by all versions of the "Letter."

In Aquitaine, Cluny did not have much influence; the abbey of Sarlat in the Périgord seems to have been the one center that had fallen into its hands. Thus Cluny was not the local leader of reform. It spread from the older monastic centers of Poitiers, Limoges, and Charroux. And, until 1030, the dukes of Aquitaine jealously kept reform under their constant care. But the traditional structures had just started to show cracks. The duke was progressively losing control of the Peace movement; the competition between the bishops and the greater abbeys was becoming shriller, a rivalry in which the monks did not have the upper hand. A well-known example is Limoges and the abbey of Saint-Martial: by about 1030, the monks would have definitely lost the struggle for local hegemony. In the Périgord, at the beginning of the eleventh century, comital and episcopal office were in the hands of one man; this situation lasted until 1014, after which date counts and bishops became bitter rivals; their struggles would delay the establishment of the Truce of God and its actual acceptance in society. Thanks to the large-scale demise of public authority, bishops took control of the Peace movement and organized the "sanctified peace" and its many sanctions, including the interdict.[31]

About all this the eleventh-century Heribert was silent. His was not the voice of a faithful Christian deferring to traditional order. He did not call on the duke, the Aquitanian bishops, or the secular prelates of the neighboring dioceses to intervene. Rather, his "Letter" is representative of a well-known inflection of the Peace movement.

In this phase, the call to reform bypassed the customary leaders and aimed at all Christians. Events would soon follow that reflected this ideology. On the one hand, there were great uprisings against the

[30] Sassier, *Recherches sur le pouvoir comtal*, p. 39, note 158.
[31] Ademar of Chabannes, *Chronicon*, 3.68, p. 194; *The Letters and Poems of Fulbert of Chartres*, ed. and trans. Frederick Behrends (Oxford, 1976), no. 96 (1023/25), p. 174; Landes, "Making of a Medieval Historian," pp. 53–54, 103; and R. Kaiser, *Bischofsherrschaft zwischen Königtum und Fürstenmacht* (Bonn, 1981), pp. 227–28.

mounting pressure of banal lordship: in the Berry, in 1038, the archbishop of Bourges cunningly deflected the crowd's anger and directed
it against the other possessors of the *bannum,* the lay lords. On the
other hand, there was the much more revolutionary emergence of a
new higher authority—that of the pope represented in the kingdom by
his legates. Heribert was easily one of the leading voices of this phase
of the movement; born out of the failings of public power, it had been
carried away through an excess of momentum and was now outflank-
ing traditional religious institutions. His "Letter" expressed a monastic
ideal close to that developed by Cluniac propaganda: like the great
prose of Odilo's days, it called for reform of the *seculum.* This task
should have devolved on the leaders of the people; considering their
manifest powerlessness, one had to resort to other means. The actual
facts, local and regional circumstances were of no import. One had ur-
gently to wake up the world, "all Christians," and sternly warn against
the troublemakers.

Who were they? An indictment, to be efficient, ought to be precise.
This one was not. The heretics were anonymous. Heribert seems to
have covered them with an opaque mask. One may have to seek the key
in the neighboring elements of the codex. Could the real criminals be
those bishops and lay lords who used their power against immunities
and monasteries seeking exemption? Did those masters, freshly endowed with the *bannum,* not despise the elementary rules of society as
defined by Christian doctrine? This was probably how, in the first decades of the century, the monks perceived the kingdom's latest trends.
In the eleventh-century version, Heribert presented the main themes
of Cluniac ideology, but as if in a photographic negative. There is nothing surprising in this indirect tactic; it was common practice around
the turn of the millennium, as Gerbert of Reims's *Epistolae* and Odorannus of Sens's *Opusculae* attest.

Three Warnings

Drawing together the strands of interpretation, one sees that Heribert sounded three warnings. First, he solemnly warned against the in-
dolence of both public power and the bishops. Such was the meaning of
the address "to all Christians." Heribert did not call out, as one might
have expected, "to all prelates and princes," to those to whom Christendom had been entrusted. The pamphlet was a relative of the calls
for the establishment of the Peace of God, but Heribert apparently
thought that the *rectores* were no longer able to fulfill their duties. He
was not unlike Abbo of Fleury, who could say in the southwestern most

corner of France that he was "more powerful in that land than the king of France, whose domination no one here fears."[32] Heribert preserved no more than Abbo the fiction of public authority's survival at the local level. The situation is well known: the prince had not intervened yet, the archbishops and bishops were silent, the task devolved onto the monks. They were to reorganize the bases of the deficient powers and convoke the Peace assembly. But they needed extraordinary guarantors to make up for the absence of lay or ecclesiastical authority. Hence the monks' call on the saints to intervene; they brought them out of their fortresses, exhibiting their reliquaries. The saints were to provoke the crowds to enthusiasm.

The ostentation of these marvelously ornamented coffers containing holy bodies occurred precisely in Aquitaine—which was, according to non-Aquitanian chroniclers, a constantly insecure, unsalubrious region devoid of public peace. These saints specialized in miraculously liberating prisoners where lordly oppression was heavy. Thus, at Conques or at Saint-Léonard of Noblat, miraculous liberations opportunely accompanied the meteoric success of the new social contract. It is known that the heretics condemned at Orléans (1022) and Arras (1024–25) and mentioned in Ademar's *Chronicon* opposed relic veneration, something Heribert's "Letter" does not address. But Heribert's account of the heretics' miraculous liberation appears strangely akin to the wonders publicized by the pilgrimage centers' propagandists.[33] Heretics and monks in Aquitaine used the same means to proclaim the deficiencies of public institutions; they entrusted to the saints the establishment of a true peace. There was, however, one essential difference: the monks lauded traditional models, saints of the past. Heretics wanted to fill the earth with a new species of saints. The "Letter" shows Heribert's deep perplexity, for these disgusting new "saints-in-the-flesh" operated the same wonders as the real items. On the road of penitential practices and divine signs of approval, monks and holy relics were

[32] Aimo of Fleury, *Vita Abbonis*, chap. 20; *PL* 139:410.

[33] For Conques, see *PL* 141:143B; for Saint-Léonard of Noblat, see the stories of the miraculous liberations of prisoners in chains contained in the *Miracula sancti Leonardi*, which I have read in Paris, BN lat. 17007 (third quarter of the twelfth century; Burgundy), fols. 7v–8v, and which are described in Steven Sargent, "Religious Responses to Social Violence in Eleventh-Century Aquitaine," *Historical Reflections / Réflexions historiques* 12 (1985), 219–40. Also see the primitive backbone of the *Miracula beate Marie Magdalene*, composed for the Burgundian abbey of Vézelay in the second quarter of the twelfth century, which consists of a single liberation miracle; see Victor Saxer, "*Miracula beate Marie Magdalene Vizeliaci facta:* Etude de la tradition manuscrite des recueils de miracles de la Madeleine à Vézelay," *Bulletin philologique et historique (avant 1610)*, 1959, 69–82, and Guy Lobrichon, "La Madeleine des Bourguignons aux XIe et XIIe siècles," in *Marie Madeleine dans la mystique, les arts et les lettres*, ed. Eve Duperray (Paris, 1989), pp. 71–88.

about to be overtaken by another procession. Two ideals were compet-
ing: traditional sanctity, promoted and conveyed by clerical intermedi-
aries, and spontaneous sanctity, earned through asceticism and
martyrdom and legitimized by the crowds.[34] There were two ideological models. First was that of the monk; it praised the angelic *conversatio*
lived in monasteries and in so doing contributed to the defining of a
hierarchical order of society, the sole right order.[35] Second was that of
the heretics and their admirers; they refused any materialization of the
sacred and were about to overthrow an age-old order—a move made,
under the aegis of the Peace, in the Berry. In the Peace assemblies of
the 1020s and 1030s held in the center and the southwest of the kingdom, both models were certainly major bones of contention.

Heribert's second warning dealt with a deviationist trait of some ex-
tremists within the Peace movement. There was, he declared, a serious
attack against the divine service, the *opus christianum* and its mass liturgy. These Périgourdins "assert that liturgical chant is a vanity," yet it
was the essential part of liturgical practice and of liturgical innovation
in the tenth and eleventh centuries. Heribert's heretics shared the deviationist opinions of the intellectuals of Orléans: these clerics thought
that Christian homage to God inspired by piety or by duty was
useless.[36] For Heribert, for Rodulphus Glaber, for all the Cluniac party,
the denigration of ecclesiastical chant was blasphemy against the holi-
est rule of life—that of the monks, who lived divine service as a road to
perfection and as the sole work which might repel the forces of evil. A
Burgundian Cluniac might have smiled at the endless tropes sung in
Aquitanian monasteries, yet Cluny was that monastery which "in all
truly Christian lands is the most efficient in the freeing of souls from
demonic domination."[37] Indeed, Cluny celebrated mass permanently
and celebrated (better than any other place) the Eucharist, the prime
means of repelling demons and heretics.

Yet Heribert and his friends knew that their enemies' sole offense
was not their contempt for monastic service. These "heretics" had
practices of their own, in themselves quite benign, but which had to be
presented as senseless, as the fragments of an incoherent pseudolit-

---

[34] We might have written "popular" sanctity, meaning what is recognized by the
greater majority of the people (that is, a *fama sanctitatis*), were it not for historiographic
misunderstandings. On this problem, see André Vauchez, *La sainteté en Occident aux derni-
ers siècles du Moyen Age* (Rome, 1981), pp. 178–79.

[35] The monks exemplify how the wider society should be organized in order to be en-
gulfed into the heavenly Jerusalem.

[36] Glaber, *Historiarum*, 3.8.27: "Omne Christianorum opus, pietatis dumtaxat et iusti-
cie, quod estimatur precium remunerationis eterne, laborem superfluum indicabant
esse." The issue of the *canticum ecclesiasticum* is missing in the twelfth-century versions of
Heribert's letter.

[37] Glaber, *Historiarum*, 5.1.13; see also 2.9.19 and 3.3.12.

urgy. The letter's fasts and abstinences, odd ways of praying, endless genuflexions, were, for a Cluniac reader, clear pointers. They denoted two powerful contemporary currents: the penitential movement and the movement of the *vita apostolica*—that is, threats to, and direct rival of, the most modern elements of monasticism. The praise of penitential practices was a topos of hagiography, yet to whom was this *locus communis* applied at the beginning of the century? To important men: King Robert himself; two archbishops of Sens, Anstase († 977) and Seguinus († 999); the treasurer of the church of Tours, Hervaeus of Buzançais, and many others who passionately sought to transit from the earthly to the spiritual world through hair shirt, fasting, and prayer. They were the "friends of the monks" (*amatores monachorum*) and lived like monks.[38] The activists of the Peace of God shared in this desire.

Alas, so did Heribert's enemies. Holy excesses were unqualifiedly praiseworthy when they were collective behavior initiated by great abbots who kept them strictly within the orbit of their authority. Practiced by great secular prelates who dreamed of joining the Cluniacs' ranks, they were quite respectable. It became quite unbearable when the practitioners were laypeople, clerics, priests, and even wandering monks and nuns, who led this virtuous life outside the control of the traditional order. It was worse when such people claimed to belong to the other movement inspired by penitential ideals, the *vita apostolica*. Laying a claim to "live like the apostles," those Heribert called heretics presented themselves as the agents of a return to the primitive church's purity. The posture was not novel; it would reap rich harvests in later centuries; it always scared ecclesiastical leaders.

Yet, possibly to a greater extent than later centuries, the early Middle Ages had endowed it with the rich overtones of apocalypticism. Since at least the time of Amalarius of Metz—Agobard's rival—until the second half of the eleventh century and the *Liber quare*, the peace of the last days (which would follow the Antichrist and his persecutions) had been associated with the peace of the origins, that of the apostolic

---

[38] Odorannus of Sens, *Opera omnia*, ed. Robert-Henri Bautier and Monique Gilles (Paris, 1972), pp. 96–97 (Seguinus); *Chronique de Saint-Pierre-le-Vif de Sens*, ed. Robert-Henri Bautier and Monique Gilles (Paris, 1979), pp. 86 (Anstase) and 92 (Seguinus); Glaber, *Historiarum*, 3.4.15 (Hervé). Glaber praises the penitential dimension of the Peace movement (*Historiarum*, 4.5.14–16). See also L. Bornscheuer, *Miseriae Regum: Untersuchungen zum Krisen- und Todesgedanken in der herrschaftstheologischen Vorstellung der ottonisch-salischen Zeit* (Berlin, 1968), and Patrick Corbet, *Les saints ottoniens: Sainteté dynastique, sainteté royale et sainteté féminine autour de l'an mil* (Beihefte der Francia, 15; Sigmaringen, 1986).

community.[39] To live like the apostles of the post-pentecostal Jerusalem was to do violence to the timely course of history by locating oneself in those latter days. It could even imply a forcing open of the doors of the Kingdom. One may remember how ritual prostrations were to multiply at the approach of the Joachimite year, 1260. An avalanche of marvelous cures, wondrous portents, and prodigious signs would announce the Antichrist's coming (Matt. 24:24). These beliefs and practices make up a "consequent eschatology"—the end is near and this old world should be transformed. Whomsoever shared it was the rival of the other, "realized," eschatology, whose living (and innocuous) embodiment was monasticism, especially the Cluniac branch.[40]

Rivalry in aims entailed rivalry as to ranking: according to monastic terminology, the monks qua monks were the true disciples who "follow the Lamb wherever it goes" (Rev. 14:4). This meant that those who claimed to lead the apostolic life on the eve of the Last Judgment had to be necessarily pseudoapostles, the "ministers of all iniquity," the forerunners of the Antichrist. For both camps, the Last Days were near. But, unlike the monks who had abolished time and still granted the world the respite it needed to convert, the heretics wanted to accelerate the coming of the end. Two militias faced one another; hence the absolute need to present one's rival as dangerous.

And hence the third warning: the Périgord heretics were engaged in the subversion of the whole social order, in three ways according to Heribert. First, they imitated the monastic status; even laypeople insisting on giving up their belongings (*propria omnia relinquentes*); all fanatically sought martyrdom. Second, they abolished the ideal social disposition, the very one the Cluniacs were trying to realize: the hierarchy ascending from laypeople to clerics and priests, capped by monks and nuns. This was a solid model, which put the virgins per se—that is, the monks—on top. But the heretics blurred all categories, and their obscene social disorder was unbearable to the Cluniacs, heirs to the hi-

---

[39] Amalarius of Metz, *De ecclesiasticis officiis*, 3.2, which was available at Auxerre in Vatican, Reg. lat. 146 (end of ninth to beginning of tenth century; Saint-Julien of Auxerre), fol. 72. *Liber Quare*, ed. G. P. Goetz (Turnhout, 1983). On the subject of the church under the sixth seal of the Apocalypse, see Ambrose Autpert, *Expositio in apocalypsim*, ed. R. Weber (Corpus Christianorum, Continuatio Mediaeualis, 27; Turnhout, 1975), p. 292, and the pseudo-Alcuin in *PL* 100:1127C. For a fundamental revision of views on apocalyptic expectations around the year 1000, see J. Fried, "Endzeiterwartung um die Jahrtausendwende," *Deutsches Archiv für Erforschung des Mittelalters* 45 (1989), 385–473; and R. Landes, "*Millenarismus absconditus:* L'historiographie augustinienne et le millénarisme du Haut Moyen Age jusqu'en l'an mil," *Le Moyen Age* (to appear).

[40] For it was successful in finding an ideological formula for "realized eschatology"; see Ortigues and Iogna-Prat, "Raoul Glaber," and Dominique Iogna-Prat, "Le *Baptême* du schéma des trois ordres fonctionnels: L'apport de l'école d'Auxerre dans la seconde moitié du IXe siècle," *Annales:E.S.C.* 41 (1986), 101–26.

erarchical thought of John the Scot and Pseudo-Dionysius.[41] Finally, these people subverted the trinitarian order, as could be perceived in their doxology. The unity of He who reigns replaced the most holy Trinity that governed and guaranteed the world's disposition, the Trinity one invoked in the opening sentences of privileges and whose wonders in this world one recounted when promulgating a religious reform. A good formulary called for no less; so did a good reform, which from the standpoint of a good monk could only be monastic.

Les Mots ou les Choses?

There is no dearth of arguments in favor of the reality of the Périgord heresy. If one must bypass one's own methodological warnings, if one wants to brush aside all doubts on Heribert's "Letter," nothing is easier.[42] One can rehearse yet another time the eleventh-century chroniclers' testimonies of heretical outbursts. Our most reliable informants unhesitatingly dwelt on the theme of this dangerous plague. Ademar of Chabannes and Rodulphus Glaber (both ca. 1025–30) echoed Heribert's words. "Shortly thereafter [1018]," recalled Ademar,

> Manichees arose throughout Aquitaine, seducing the *promiscuous* populace, negating holy baptism and the power of the cross, *the Church and the Redeemer of the world, the honor of the saints of God, marriage and the eating of meat*, and whatever was sound doctrine. Abstaining from food, they seemed like monks, and faked chastity. But, in fact, among themselves they practiced every depravity and were the messengers of Antichrist; and they turned many simple people from the faith.[43]

[41] P. E. Dutton, "Raoul Glaber's De divina quaternitate: An Unnoticed Reading of Eriugena's Translation of the Ambigua of Maximus the Confessor," *Mediaeval Studies* 42 (1980), 431–52; Ortigues and Iogna-Prat, "Raoul Glaber"; Iogna-Prat, "Baptême"; idem, "Continence et virginité dans la conception clunisienne de l'ordre du monde autour de l'an mil," *Comptes-rendus de l'Académie des Inscriptions et Belles-Lettres*, 1985, pp. 127–46; idem, *Agni Immaculati: Recherches sur les sources hagiographiques relatives à saint Maieul de Cluny (954–994)* (Paris, 1988).

[42] This is how Richard Landes uses this document; "La vie apostolique en Aquitaine au tournant du millennium: Paix de Dieu, culte de reliques et communautés 'hérétiques'," *Annales: E.S.C.* 46 (1991), 579–87.

[43] "Paulo post exorti sunt per Aquitaniam Manichei, seducentes plebem. Negabant baptismum et crucem et quidquid sanae doctrinae est. Abstinentes a cibis, quasi monachi apparebant et castitatem simulabant, sed inter se ipsos omnem luxuriam exercebant, et nuncii Antichristi erant, multosque a fide exorbitare fecerunt"; Ademar of Chabannes, *Chronicon*, 3.49, p. 173. The italicized words in the translation appear only in the H manuscript (Paris, BN lat. 6190) of the *Chronicon*, which was not used in the Chavanon edition, whose Latin is cited here. On these differences, see Landes, "Making of a Medieval Historian," pp. 16, 88, 275, note 32.

Ademar sedulously accumulated a set of commonplaces deriving from Augustine's *De haeresibus,* polished and refined at length by tradition.[44] Did he really believe what one finds in a twelfth-century copy of his work—that a peasant from the Périgord was the spiritual leader of the Orléans heretics?[45] It may not matter, but one should remark that another version of Ademar (a mid-eleventh-century manuscript from Angoulême) did not contain this detail.[46] Rodulphus Glaber also cried out against the heresies of the day. They had caught hold of a vocal enemy of tithes and alms, Leutard of Vertus. And this disgusting heresy conjoined the peasant Leutard with the Orléans intellectuals in a similar blasphemy against the crucifix.[47]

The author of the Auxerre "Letter" kept his discourse within more moderate bounds. Craftily, he avoided giving a name to the deviationists, preferring to speak of a "new heresy," and bypassed the commonplaces of ecclesiastical catalogues of heresies.[48] Unlike his contemporaries, he refrained from spreading nonsense about the opponents' alleged sexual perversions. But he underlined how his rivals fascinated all sorts of people and especially the peasants—fair game in medieval pamphlets. The place of miracles in the letter (at the end) endowed the other facts with verisimilitude. Parenthetically, this role of the *mira signa* allows one to perceive that, in the eleventh century, educated churchmen and marginals shared a vision of the supernatural;

[44] Augustine, *De haeresibus, ad Quodvultdeum,* ed. R. Vander Plaetse and C. Beukers (Corpus Christianorum, Series Latina, 46; Turnhout, 1969). The edition refers to good manuscripts of the *De haeresibus* which were available in the early Middle Ages, but it finds little of interest in Paris, BN lat. 1745. Ademar made a copy of an abbreviated version of Augustine's list of heresies in his collection of ecclesiastical texts, Paris BN. lat. 2400, fols. 130–31.

[45] Richard Landes believes that this manuscript offers a later twelfth-century copy of a third version (Gamma) of Ademar's *Chronicon* which was originally executed in 1028–29; see Landes, "L'acession des Capétiens: Une reconsidération selon les sources," *Religion et culture autour de l'an mil: Royaume capéteian et Lotharingie,* ed. Dominique Iogna-Prat and J.-C. Picard (Paris, 1990), pp. 153–54. A new edition of Ademar's work, taking Gamma as a base, is in preparation under the direction of Pascale Bourgain, Georges Pon, and Richard Landes and will be forthcoming from Corpus Christianorum, Continuatio Mediaeualis.

[46] Landes, "Making of a Medieval Historian," pp. 94–95, 280, note 68. An interpolation in the third version of Ademar's *Chronicon* (Gamma) makes the leader of the Orléans heretics a Périgourdin. Since such additions probably come from Ademar himself (Landes, "Making of a Medieval Historian," p. 18), one must allow the possibility that Heribert's pamphlet and Ademar's historical work are either related textually or, more likely, independently describe the same phenomenon in the Périgord.

[47] Glaber, *Historiarum,* 2.11.22, 3.8.29–31. Jean-Pierre Poly and Eric Bournazel rightly insist on the important role literary motifs held in the narrations of the chroniclers; see *La mutation féodale: Xe–XIIe siècles* (Paris, 1980), pp. 421–25. Rodulphus Glaber is no exception.

[48] Paris, BN lat. 1745, fol. 31r: "Noua heresis horta est in mundo." The scribes of the following century struck out this comment. On this type of remark, see the remark of the annalist of Xanten *ad an.* 838: "haeretica pravitas orta est"; *MGH SS* 2:226.

it suggests the former group's anxieties, its inability to domesticate the extraordinary and to smother popular hopes.

In summary, the Auxerre letter has the reassuring look of yet another good piece of testimony; the solid reports on the famous heresies of the eleventh century—Orléans, Arras, Monteforte—support the trustworthiness of Heribert. It is in great part thanks to these texts' (postulated) authenticity that Heribert's "Letter" appears reliable.[49] That heterodox activity occurred in Aquitaine, indeed in the Périgord, during the 1010s and 1020s seems clear, since, in addition to the testimony of Heribert and Ademar, we have those of the *Liber miraculorum sanctae Fidis* and of a charter of the duke of Aquitaine for Saint-Hilaire of Poitiers in 1016.[50]

Yet are we certain that the convergences between the eleventh-century reports and the "Letter" outnumber the oddities of the latter document? Even granting this, one would have to admit that none of our sources—neither Ademar, nor Rodulphus, nor the notaries of the duke, nor Heribert—were "positivist" historians. The best one can say is that Heribert's "Letter," whether a literary fiction or an actual report, sounds as much like an ideological debate between known rivals as it does like a denunciation of a new heretical sect. In fact, in its codicological context, the ideological struggle seems to dominate the denunciation of the specific heresy. But to pursue such an analysis one needs to show what role such a redeployment of a circular letter denouncing the deviance of a group so far away might play in Auxerre. Were one to postulate when precisely this diatribe was felt to be of contemporary relevance, the most reasonable hypothesis (considering the echoes that associate Ademar of Chabannes, Rodulphus Glaber, and "Heribert") would point to the late 1020s or to the second quarter of the eleventh century: the Peace movement was broadening its scope and was then aiming at a generalized purification of society from its evils; yet soon enough public authorities would regain the initiative and divert the movement to their own ends—permanently so.

In the monks' hands, this pamphlet, apparently aimed at a heretical sect of the Périgord, could be used as the vehicle of an attack against a

[49] Definitive accounts of these heresies are contained in Robert-Henri Bautier, "L'hérésie d'Orléans et le mouvement intellectuel au début du XIe siècle: Documents et hypothèses," *Actes du 95e Congrès national des sociétés savantes, Reims, 1970: Section de philologie et d'histoire jusqu'à 1610* (Paris, 1975), pp. 63–88, and Huguette Taviani, "Le mariage dans l'hérésie de l'an mil," *Annales: E.S.C.* 32 (1977), 1074–89. See also the insightful remarks of Brian Stock, *The Implications of Literacy: Written Language and Models of Interpretations in the Eleventh and Twelfth Centuries* (Princeton, N.J., 1983), pp. 106–20.

[50] For a discussion and translation of both this charter and the material from Conques, see Pierre Bonnassie and Richard Landes, "Une nouvelle hérésie est née dans le monde," in *Les sociétés méridionales autour de l'an mil: Répertoire de sources et documents commentés*, ed. Michel Zimmermann (Toulouse, 1992).

much more dangerous enemy: the bishops or the monks' many rivals within the reform movement, including denizens of older monastic centers. The Cluniacs were also outflanked by charismatic groups: the new apostles embezzled, in the name of a sham *vita apostolica,* the precepts and the perfection that had, up until then, been the monk's lot. Mary's part, the worthiest lot, belonged to the monks. Until that point, this claim had been undisputed. Threatened, the monks counterattacked; all their rivals and opponents, indiscriminately, were branded as heretics. And it is possible that in the eleventh-century "Letter" the Cluniacs drew the confusing composite portrait of a heresy which borrowed its traits from the various groups of opponents in Aquitaine and from older catalogues. A maneuver known to all religions in history, calling one's competitors heretics was a time-tested tactic; it had been used from the very first days of Christendom. The motivations to use the "Letter" were lacking in the earliest phase of the Peace of God (990–1005); the monks and public institutions were the main promoters of the movement and had it under control. The second wave, however, adopted (ca. 1020) the values of the evangelical renewal; it advocated a real pact between society as a whole and God. Such may have been the context in which one composed or transcribed Heribert's "Letter." The place was Saint-Germain of Auxerre, a sanctuary Cluny had revived. Monasticism was ready there to use all means to suppress its enemies. It was ready to forge testimonies using large chunks of patristic commonplaces. This "noble lie" would have satisfied everybody. Since it provided its recipients with double readings, the "Letter" could be all things to all people. Who then was this Périgord heretic, this scapegoat, this reprobate? A real master of error, a live heretic doomed to death, or a strawman, the figure of high-placed enemies? No one can say for sure.

The document's historical interest lies equally in how a fact was perceived and reported and in how contemporary polemics could use the fact and its report. Its exceptional ideological density comes from its having been transcribed into the codex Bibliothèque Nationale, latin 1745. And, without any doubts, this version must be considered as one of the purest products of monastic ideology in the first third of the eleventh century. This interpretation seems to me to offer two insights not available from a reading that sees the text as a confirmation of an actual incidence of heresy. First, it addresses the issue of the copying and redeployment of texts for ideological purposes, which, as we know, is the polemicist's daily bread. Second, it forces us to deal with the complex forms of social response which confront heterodoxy without providing it too much publicity. This effort can take paradoxical forms: the grandiose liturgies of the cross and the development of the liturgical dramas and mystery plays for Christmas and Easter do not necessarily offend those apostolic cults that are purged of all materiality and virtually all images.[51] All these strange secretions doubtless contributed to the enrichment of possible alternatives to the cultic materialism that encumbered the history of the Eucharist and of holiness more generally, both then and for a long time afterward.

Whatever the case, and whatever solution one adopts for decoding Heribert's "Letter," this document reaffirms the imperious necessity of a persistently prudent and circumstantial exegesis of the heresies of the Middle Ages. One of positivist history's great lessons was to teach us to isolate concrete facts; it is a corollary of that lesson that we must beware mistaking for such facts the red herrings and masquerades invented by the learned of all ages to suppress the objects of their worst resentment. There are Heriberts in every age, in every culture; indignant prophets or liars and forgers, they deserve more than just a note at the end of repertories of sources, for their recorded jeremiads, as well as their lies, are history and the subject matter of history.

---

[51] That of Mary Magdalene offers one of the most curious examples in this regard.

5

Peace from the Mountains: The Auvergnat Origins of the Peace of God

CHRISTIAN LAURANSON-ROSAZ

How beautiful upon the mountains
are the feet of him who brings good tidings,
who publishes peace, who says to Zion:
"Your God reigns."
Isaiah 52:7

After the scholarly researches of the past century and the beginning of this one, one might have thought that the study of the Peace movement was essentially complete, particularly from an institutional point of view. In the past thirty years, however, research has not only continued to delve into the issue[1] but, in the wake of the *nouvelle histoire,* begun to use new approaches. Starting from a traditional analysis, and insisting above all on focusing on its origins, historians have been able to bring out the dual tonality that marks the first chords of the Peace, a clerical tonality to be sure, but also a popular one.[2]

In particular, Georges Duby, placing himself at the juncture of *Realpolitik* and the history of mentalities, has insisted on the social aspect of the Peace, showing the ideological opposition between the reforming bishops of the south, with their popular support, and their

The author expresses his full appreciation to Richard Landes, who edited and translated this article.

[1] Roger Bonnaud-Delamare, "Les institutions de paix en Aquitaine au XIe siècle," in *La paix* (Recueil de la Société Jean Bodin, 14; Bruxelles, 1962); Hartmut Hoffmann, *Gottesfriede und Treuga Dei* (Schriften der Monumenta Germaniae historica, 20; Stuttgart, 1964); more recently, Hans-Werner Goetz, "Kirchenschutz, Rechtswahrung und Reform: Zu den Zielen und zum Wesen der frühen Gottesfriedensbewegung in Frankreich," *Francia* 11 (1983), 193–239, an English adaptation of which appears in this volume as Chapter 11.

[2] The most important proponent of this analysis was Bernhard Töpfer, *Volk und Kirche zur Zeit der beginnenden Gottesfriedensbewegung in Frankreich* (Berlin, 1957). See Frederick S. Paxton's Chapter 1 of this volume, which highlights the gradual increase in attention among historians to the social element in Peace studies.

northern colleagues, who distrusted a popular movement they viewed as subversive of social order precisely when they were trying to prop up this order with the famous theory of trifunctionality.[3]

This dual focus, which is both social and political and emphasizes the role of ideology, is indispensable to an understanding of the Peace, and particularly of the stakes involved in the Peace movement against the backdrop of a troubled society at the turn of the millennium. The institutional once again rejoins the social and the mental: the nature of the first Peace assemblies is as interesting for the history of institutions as it is for the study of medieval communes or the peasant revolts of the eighteenth century.

Pierre Bonnassie has further emphasized the concretely popular tenor of the movement, the least documented in one sense but also the outstanding feature of the "primitive" Peace between the years 980, the time of the first councils, and 1040, the date of the institutionalization and transformation of the Peace into the Truce of God by Cluny. He has underlined "the importance of this phenomenon in terms of a history of the peasant masses still to be written," and his appeal for a more substantial investigation of this aspect of the Peace seems to have been heard.[4]

Whether it is the bishops of the Midi, the monks of Cluny, or the duke of Aquitaine who led the movement, in the period around the year 1000 the action of both lay and ecclesiastical rulers intervened in a context of popular agitation, even effervescence. The "odor of the church" which emanates from the councils of this first age of the Peace movement, drawing immense crowds in the wake of the relics offered for the people's devotion, should not make us lose sight of their necessarily confrontational aspect, the one so violently denounced by the bishops of the north.[5] For some, this meant a rejection of the new feudal society the lords were building, perhaps a desire to return to an older order; in any case, "this challenge to aristocratic violence essentially based itself on at least a momentary alliance between the clergy and the peasantry."[6]

---

[3] Georges Duby, "Les laïcs et la paix de Dieu," in *Hommes et structures du Moyen Age* (Paris, 1973), pp. 227–40, and idem, *Les trois ordres, ou l'imaginaire du féodalisme* (Paris, 1978).

[4] Pierre Bonnassie, *La Catalogne du milieu du Xe à la fin du XIe siècle: Croissance et mutations d'une société* (Toulouse, 1975), 1:357. Also see Robert Fossier, *Histoire sociale de l'Occident médiéval* (Paris, 1970), p. 137.

[5] In this volume, Richard Landes (Chapter 8) and Guy Lobrichon (Chapter 4) discuss the relations between the Peace and heresy; see also Richard Landes, "La vie apostolique en Aquitaine au tournant du millennium: Paix de Dieu, culte de reliques, et communautés 'hérétiques'," *Annales: E.S.C.* 46 (1991), 573–93.

[6] Bonnassie, *Catalogne*, 1:357, and idem, *Les cinquante mots clefs de l'histoire médiévale* (Toulouse, 1981), pp. 158–61.

I have earlier analyzed the political chronology of the Peace to demonstrate the logic of the movement's extension ca. 976–80, put in motion by Guy of Anjou, the bishop of Le Puy.[7] Leaving aside for the moment the *Realpolitik* aspect and also the polemic concerning the order of assemblies the question, for example, of whether Charroux was the first council), I here look again at the early Peace to begin to uncover its popular identity. To do this, I begin with a study of the genesis of the idea of the Peace itself, focusing on those regions of the center of Gaul which, for rather precise reasons, saw the first stirrings of the movement.

The Premises

The Declension of Power, 900–960

The goal of the Peace movement was to protect the "civilian" victims of warrior violence. The question of the Peace is therefore directly linked to problems of aristocratic violence, which in turn concerns issues of law and justice. The effort to repress aristocratic violence confronts the problem of justice, or rather, the lack of justice in a world where the traditional judiciary power, and traditional power in general, had failed. For if there is a "century of violence," the tenth century was it. As most of the recent monographs have shown, in the years 900–950 one can perceive throughout the Midi the first manifestations of the famous "feudal mutation," a transformation that would shake traditional society to its foundations and, in less than one astonishing century, transform both the structures of the countryside and the mentalities of its inhabitants.[8] In the Auvergne, violence committed by lords appears in isolated references in early tenth-century documents but becomes more frequent by mid-century. The gradual collapse of traditional authority freed the powerful from restraints, allowing them to institute new "customs" (usurpations, exactions, deputations, pillages) that challenged the economic and social equilibrium of the countryside and eventually led to the seigneury. From the peasant point of view, then, the need for peace was clearly urgent.[9]

[7] Christian Lauranson-Rosaz, *L'Auvergne et ses marges* (Velay, Gévaudan) *du VIIIe au XIe siècle: La fin du monde antique?* (Le Puy-en-Velay, 1987), pp. 409–56.

[8] From Georges Duby, *La société aux XIe et XIIe siècles dans la région mâconnaise* (Paris, 1956; rpt. 1972), to André Debord, *La société laïque dans la Charente, Xe–XIIe siècles* (Paris, 1984) and Lauranson-Rosaz, *L'Auvergne*.

[9] For the violence in the Auvergne, see Lauranson-Rosaz, *L'Auvergne*, p. 351. The first to speak of a feudal revolution was Marcellin Boudet, in his introduction to the *Cartulaire du prieuré de Saint-Flour* (Monaco, 1910), p. cxx. More recently, on the general crisis, see Jean-Pierre Poly and Eric Bournazel, *La mutation féodale (Xe–XIIe s.)* (Paris, 1980), pp. 220–74.

From the Royal Peace to the Episcopal Peace

In the Carolingian period, peace was still a rough and ready formula—peace in the interior of the empire, war against the pagans. Moreover, peace was above all the responsibility of the sovereign; it served as a monarchic justification for Pepin when he seized the throne and an imperial one for Charlemagne at his coronation.[10] With the end of expansion and the weakening of imperial authority, provisions for the internal peace fell to episcopal initiatives.[11] But even if the late Carolingian episcopal measures seemed for a while to maintain the fragile edifice put up by Charlemagne, they no longer worked by the beginning of the tenth century. The structures needed to implement them no longer responded: emperors, kings, and counts were becoming less credible, their agents less zealous. For the countries south of the Loire, more refractory than the others (in fact, never really assimilated into the Carolingian empire), the failure of the peace was directly linked to the collapse of political relations with the central power and the simultaneous distortion of the structure of local power. The "descent of power" brought with it an inexorable rise of lawlessness and violence.

When on 3 February 950, at Pouilly-sur-Loire near Nevers, Louis IV d'Outremer came to receive the homage of William III (Towhead), count of Poitiers and duke of Aquitaine, one might still think the ancient traditions lived. Louis presented himself as a real monarch taking control of a delicate situation. But, in fact, the countries of the Midi were already escaping any control of the kings in the north. The time of the territorial principalities had no sooner begun with the apparent acquisition of royal power by the regional ruling families than it devolved into dynastic struggles (houses of Poitou and Toulouse for the ducal title) and increasing disorder. It is significant that the magnates of Aquitaine did not come to Pouilly.[12] The only serious presence, that of Bishop Stephen II of Clermont, who gave homage to the king, his lord (*senior*), underlines this point. He represents one of the last royal vassals (*vassi regales*) mentioned in the south.

This analysis of the situation is confirmed four years later in an event, this time regional: the *placitum* (tribunal) of Ennezat. This was the last comital *placitum* in the Auvergne: the count and duke William

---

[10] Roger Bonnaud-Delamare, *L'idée de paix à l'époque carolingienne* (Paris, 1939).

[11] Elisabeth Magnou-Nortier, "La place du concile du Puy (v. 994) dans l'évolution de l'idée de paix," in *Mélanges offerts au Professeur Jean Dauvillier* (Toulouse, 1979), p. 489; idem, "Les évêques et la paix dans l'espace franc (VIe-XIe siècles)," in *L'évêque dans l'histoire de l'Eglise* (Publications du Centre de Recherches d'Histoire Religieuse et d'Histoire des Idées, 7; Angers, 1984), pp. 33–50; and Chapter 3 in this volume.

[12] Participants are mentioned in *Recueil des chartes de l'abbaye de Cluny*, 6 vols., ed. Auguste Bernard and Alexandre Bruel (Paris, 1876–1903), vol. 1, no. 763, and Richer *Historia francorum*, 2 vols., 2d ed. and trans. Robert Latouche (Paris, 1964–67), 2:98, 1:288.

took advantage of the death of King Louis (10 September 954) to attempt to impose his power. He took counsel with the leading men of the Auvergne (*seniores arvernici*), who gathered (*convenerunt*) and commended themselves to him (*commendaverunt*).[13] The context is still, one might say "Carolingian," given the presence of the territorial prince, the reference to the king, and the nature of the reunion: it was an affair of the magnates. It took place in an official site, the fiscal court of Ennezat, a comital residence. Around the count the great men (*optimates*) of the Auvergne gathered, bishop at the lead. One might even have thought oneself in the presence of the court of William the Pious at the beginning of the same century. But the illusion cannot be sustained. First there were debates and negotiations; only then came the traditional homage. Just as Pouilly was the symbol of the last royal illusions, so Ennezat shows the last attempts of a comital power, henceforth impotent. It is the transition between two political worlds: one, already passed, of Carolingian princes, and the other, already begun, of the lords—lords who were not susceptible to discipline and control, who could be reached only by appeals to morals or to their self-interest, or to both. Accordingly, Stephen appeared at Ennezat as a great authority in the diocese and as a mediator between duke and local lords rather than as a royal vassal.

Pax Quae Omnia Superat

Another four years later, in 958, a charter was issued at a *placitum* which throws important light on the developing situation. The *placitum* was held at Clermont, the episcopal city, and was no longer presided over by the count-duke assisted by the bishop; instead, the bishop presided alone.

The Auvergnat *seniores* apparently did not keep the agreement reached at Ennezat. "They rebelled" and command "passed" to Stephen, who managed, with God's help (*Domino adjuvante*), to reestablish order and revive "the peace which surpasses all."[14] The insurgents were again the lords and their *milites*, the heads of the most illustrious lineages of the countryside: the viscount Dalmas, the lay abbot of Bri-

---

[13] *Recueil de Cluny*, no. 825 (no date, but contemporary with the donations to Cluny of the domain of Reilhac by various people); no. 871 (relinquishing of Souvigny by Aimar of Bourbon, January 954); and nos. 872–76. For these five, Ferdinand Lot proposes a date of 955 (*Etudes sur le règne de Hugues Capet et la fin du Xe siècle* [Paris, 1903], p. 201 and note 4), while Hoffmann prefers 952 (*Gottesfriede*, p. 14), following Alfred Richard (*Histoire des comtes de Poitou (778–1204)* [Paris, 1903], 1:86), and Boudet (*Cartulaire de Saint-Flour*, p. cxxi).

[14] Archives départementales du Puy-de-Dôme, ser. 3G, arm. 18, sac. A, c. 4.

oude, the viscount Robert of Clermont, Aimar of Bourbon, Stephen of Thiers-Huillaux. Under cover of rebellion we find open violence, usurpation. The magnates behaved like genuine brigands, attacking the goods of the church in Basse-Auvergne and the lands of Sauxillanges. In 951, the lands of Saint-Julien of Brioude were ravaged by the lay abbot himself.[15] In 958 the lands of a canon of the cathedral chapter at Clermont were usurped by Calixte, the ancestor of the lineage of the Montmorin.

This *placitum* of Clermont demonstrates how the church found itself progressively forced to carry on the torch of collapsing authority. With princes and kings impotent, clerics turned to Rome and to pontifical powers;[16] or they clustered around Cluny, its agent, whose success was thereby assured; or the bishop even revived his role as *defensor civitatis* of the late empire—and, in the process, expanded his judicial authority.

The reestablishment of order and the search for peace demanded sanctions—and therefore an effective justice as well. But such a situation did not exist. The direct agent of power, the count, to whom theoretically the judicial function had devolved, could not or did not want to assume it. The immunity of ecclesiastical lands prohibited him from getting involved in church matters, and his actions as an advocate of certain abbeys (that is, judicial defender of their interests) became more and more random. He no longer concerned himself with anything but the justice of the magnates. Popular justice had passed into the hands of his *vicarii;* he no longer knew (or else he pretended to ignore) the vicissitudes of the peasants' world, and these latter saw less protection from his subordinate agents, who now became, as often as not, their oppressors.

Continuing a very old canonical tradition, some of the dioceses in the west had held "assemblies of peace." According to the Roman church, when there were "rebels to control," the bishop could convoke a public assembly convening all the classes of people in his diocese "in order to realize that which pleases God and serves the salvation of

---

[15] *Cartulaire de Sauxillanges,* no. 14; *Recueil de Cluny,* no. 792. *Cartulaire de Brioude,* ed. Henry Doniol (Clermont-Ferrand, Paris, 1863), nos. cccxlix (936–56) and ccxxix (945–70). This last work is complemented by the *Essai de restitution du Liber de Honoribus Sancto Juliano collatis,* ed. Anne-Marie Baudot and Marcellin Baudot (Mémoires de l'Académie de Clermont, 35; Clermont-Ferrand, 1935). On the political developments of the 950s in general, see Lauranson-Rosaz, *L'Auvergne,* p. 85.

[16] For the bull of protection of Agapetus II, see *Cartulaire de Sauxillanges,* no. 14, and *Monumenta Pontifica Arverniae decurrentibus IXe, Xe, XIe, XIIe saeculis,* ed. Chaix de Lavarène (Clermont-Ferrand, 1886), no. vii. Stephen II made a will in 959 and left for Rome; see Archives Départementales du Puy-de-Dôme, ser. 3G, arm. 11, sac. Q, c. 1. This was a period of many pilgrimages to Rome; see Lauranson-Rosaz, *L'Auvergne,* chap. 3.

souls."[17] We know that the clerics of the Auvergne knew the conciliar canons.[18] They were acting by virtue of church law. One can therefore already see a significant passage from political to judicial concerns behind the actions of Stephen II, who could act at the same time either as *defensor civitatis* or as *vassus regalis*, each role recuperating judicial prerogatives previously lost.

The Time of the Assemblies

Aurillac, 972

The Aquitanian origins of the Peace of God are widely accepted:[19] Charroux (989), followed closely by Narbonne, Limoges, and Anse (994).[20] If we are precise in defining "councils," Charroux is indeed the first example of an assembly of legislating bishops. But we see that these canons were not the birthplace of the movement—which they officially recorded—if we realize that the distinctive element of the Peace was an alliance of clergy and populace to resist aristocratic violence, or at least an acknowledgment by the clergy of the value of this popular element.[21]

For us, therefore, the discovery and first deployment of this popular element of the Peace appeared in the Auvergne. Many of the premises of the movement emerged in the ever more original line of action taken by the bishop of Clermont. Immediately before the first real councils of Peace in the last decade of the millennium we find more modest assemblies, diocesan or "peridiocesan" synods. By the 970s in the Auvergne, ecclesiastical authorities, assisted by lay groups, gathered around themselves considerable crowds of men and women. Held in open fields, at sites selected for their capacity to draw and accommodate such crowds, these assemblies were profoundly marked by the popular tone that serves as the focus of our inquiry.

The first Auvergnat gathering on the scale of a provincial council took place about fifteen years after Clermont. It has received little at-

---

[17] A Roman council of 904 used the terms here employed according to C. Du Cange, *Glossarium mediae et infinimae latinitatis* (Paris, 1845), 5:279. Cited by Auguste Fayard, "De Ruessium à St. Paulien," *Cahiers de la Haute-Loire*, 1976, pp. 43–127; 1978, pp. 27–28.

[18] The inventory of the library of the cathedral chapter of Clermont mentions the late tenth-century pontifical decrees (*Breve de libros sanctae Mariae*) in Archives départementales du Puy-de-Dôme, ser. 3G, arm. 18, sac. A, c. 6 (984–1010). On this document, see Marcel Brehier, *Deux inventaires du trésor de la cathédrale de Clermont au Xe siècle*, a supplement to *La revue d'Auvergne*, 1901, p. 34; and Lauranson-Rosaz, *L'Auvergne*, p. 254.

[19] Jean-Pierre Poly, "L'Europe de l'an mille," in *Le Moyen Age*, 3 vols., ed. Robert Fossier (Paris, 1982), 2:41.

[20] Hoffmann, *Gottesfriede*, pp. 24–31; and Bonnaud-Delamare, "Institutions de la paix," pp. 415–47.

[21] See, especially, Töpfer, *Volk und Kirche*.

tention from historians of the Peace, yet it differed significantly from the *placita* of the middle of the century. It was in fact a regional assembly (*conventus totius patriae*), held at Aurillac in 972 and presided over by the same Bishop Stephen II of Clermont, with the advice of local magnates (*cum consilio optimatum regionis*). The so-called Landeyrat charter that narrates the tale of this gathering must be treated critically.[22] It seems to be a contemporary piece. Nothing is fundamentally shocking in the text. Only the form—a bizarre preamble that curiously makes reference to miracles of Gerald and to the dedication of the church of Aurillac, followed by a donation—arouses suspicion. It is in fact a mixture of several texts, including a subsequent forgery intended to justify the dominion of the monks of Aurillac.

The charter's allusion to miracles is most significant; it evokes precisely the late tenth century, when the instigators of the Peace of God played the "miracle card" to draw crowds and impose respect. The site of the church founded by Gerald of Aurillac in 894, where he was subsequently buried, underlined the potential aristocratic contribution to peace. Gerald (ca. 855–904) was the first nonroyal layman ever to become a saint, a noble of surpassing Christian piety and generosity who went into battle with his spear reversed so as not to shed the blood even of a foe. In the early tenth century, no less a figure than Odo of Cluny had written the *Vita sancti Geraldi Auriliacensis* to propagate Gerald's life as a model of seigneurial virtue, a veritable mirror for knights.[23] How appropriate to launch a peace movement by exalting the abbey of that saint of peace par excellence. The choice of Aurillac was therefore not accidental. Nor were those figures assembled there at Stephen's side: Frotarius of Périgueux and Gauzbert of Cahors were surely required for the consecration of the church of Saint-Gerald. But they also give this manifestation a more than regional character; one might even speak of a synod. Finally, the assembly had a strong popular character, one of religious fervor rising up from this gathering of "an innumerable amount of clergymen and people." The charter actually cites the *nobiles* last, and even then it refers only to certain ones, for example, the brothers of the bishop.[24]

---

[22] *Cartulaire de Saint-Flour*, no. 1. This is a copy from the eighteenth century which cites a notation from 1347 (date of the creation of the bishopric of Saint-Flour); see the commentary of Boudet, *Cartulaire de Saint-Flour*, p. clvii.

[23] Odo of Cluny, *Vita sancti Geraldi Auriliacensis*, prologue; *PL* 133:639. On the impact of the *Vita sancti Geraldi*, see Georges Duby, "Les origines de la chevalerie," in *Hommes et structures*, p. 335.

[24] "Cum consilio clericorum Arvernensis sedis, aliorumque nobilium virorum," says the text rather ambiguously (*Cartulaire de Saint-Flour*, no. 1); did the nobles alone come? The expression *aliorumque nobiliumque virorum* seems to place them on the sidelines.

Peace and Popular Justice

Let us focus on the judicial dispositions the Landeyrat charter treats: it specifies the legal jurisdiction of the abbey of Aurillac, and it is decreed that synods and assemblies of the clergy and the magnates of Haute-Auvergne will be held three times a year at Aurillac. Both stipulations are noteworthy because they refer us to the great question of the end of the "old," Carolingian justice.

In terms of jurisdiction, one cannot doubt the base text: the abbey's judicial authority was not created all at once, although by the eleventh century these jurisdictions were already well established and could not be arbitrarily modified. At this point, however, the existence of this jurisdiction can be explained only as a transformation of the vicarial one, once held formally by Gerald, into the district of the abbey. And this passage from vicarial to abbatial power demonstrates clearly that the church was becoming in the process seigneurial, participating just as the castellans in the construction of the feudal order.[25]

To understand these regularly held assizes, however, we must go back approximately a century and recount the overturning of judicial habits brought about by the importation of Frankish structures of administrations. Since the end of the ninth century, official justice had changed considerably.[26] The count, no longer an itinerant *missus* (legate) subject to replacement by order of the king, but now an autonomous and hereditary local authority, began to delegate his judicial functions to one of his own men, a *vicarius*, whose tribunal became fixed by formal order of the Carolingian capitularies.[27] This displacement—at first consented to, then forced—of customary centers of sociability toward the official vicarial tribunal (*mallus*) (even if they may be related) contributed significantly to the distortion of primitive judicial structures.[28] In particular, this displacement entailed the progressive (eventually brutal) elimination of the popular elements of the older justice, the famous *boni homines* or *prud'hommes* responsible, since time immemorial, for representing the interest of free peasant

[25] *Cartulaire de Brioude*, no. cxiv (*placitum* of Langeac held by the count-missus Bernard concerning serfs of the fisc).

[26] On Carolingian justice, see François-Louis Ganshof, "Charlemagne et l'administration de la justice dans la monarchie franque," in *Karl der Grosse: Lebenswerk und Nachleben*, ed. W. Braunfels (Dusseldorf, 1966), 1:394–419. For its deformation in the Auvergne in particular, see Lauranson-Rosaz, *L'Auvergne*, pp. 343–51.

[27] Anne Lombard-Jourdan, "Du problème de la continuité: Y a-t-il une proto-histoire urbaine en France?" *Annales: E.S.C.* 25 (1970), 1121, and "Oppidum et banlieue: Sur l'origine et les dimensions du territoire urbain," *Annales: E.S.C.* 27 (1972), 373.

[28] See Ganshof, "Charlemagne," and Lauranson-Rosaz, *L'Auvergne*.

communities.[29] From the judicial level to the popular, we can understand the importance of this forced transformation of legal customs,
and once again we return to the more general question of the over-
throwing of social structures that characterized the feudal mutation.

From the time of Gerald of Aurillac, when the fixed vicarial tribunal
had become the rule, we can see the appearance of a social cleavage of
major proportions; if the assemblies, presided over by the vicarial judge
in the name of the count, still assembled such "vestiges" of the tribal
period as these *boni homines*, they dealt only with litigation between
people of humble origin. The popular assemblies, which originally
concerned themselves with all the free men of the *pagus*, now addressed
only commoners. The practice of the tenth century reveals a significant
division between pleas for the people and pleas for the greats. The nobles no longer came to the vicarial tribunal but to the comital one in
which power politics played an increasingly central role.[30] Since the
"popular" tribunal had also treated major causes as well as minor, one
thus passed from a competence *ratione materiae* to a competence *ratione
personae*. Gerald could condemn to death, although according to classic
Carolingian justice he should not have that right: capital punishment
was reserved, theoretically, for communal tribunals.[31]

A fixed site with an ever more sharply delimited jurisdiction, as well
as a judge soon to become a lord, thereby consolidating his authority
over the collectivity of (ever less) free men—it is not difficult to see
where this was going. From the *vicaria* to the castelleny and the seigneurial judge, the path was as clearly traced as the one from the *mallus*
of free men to the comital *mallus*.

The Scandalous Desire to Return to the Old Order

The destabilization of society this dislocation of traditional judicial
organization reveals, already launched in the eighth century, was well
under way in the middle of the tenth. With the *mallus* confiscated,
peasants had lost the most important part of their communal sociability, the last rampart against servility. The legitimate power to command, the *bannum*, until now justified by collective necessities, had, by

[29] For the *boni homines* and their role in rendering justice, see Poly and Bournazel, *La
mutation*, pp. 71–81, and Karin Nehlsen-Von Stryk, *Die boni homines des frühen Mittelalters,
unter besonderer Berucksichtigung der frankische Quellen* (Freiburger rechtsgeschichtliche
Abhandlungen, Neue Folge, 2; Berlin, 1981).

[30] "Ille necesse habebat ad quoddam placitum ex condictu venire, quo scilicet nobiles
quidam viri conventuri erant"; *Vita sancti Geraldi Auriliacensis*, 1.20; *PL* 133:649D.

[31] Gerald never exacted capital punishment because of his abhorrence for bloodlet-
ting; see *Vita sancti Geraldi Auriliacensis*, 1.20; *PL* 133:655.

slipping into the hands of the lords, become constraint. We move from a time of public peace to one of the castral system, from the time of the walled town (*oppidum*) as refuge to that of the castle as threat. Add to this the fact that social norms were ever more challenged and threatened within the very class of the *rustici*, where the free peasant could become a *miles* in the hire of some great man, while his neighbor, by choice or by necessity, could not. The unarmed peasant found himself more and more like an early medieval settler (*colonus*), that is, one who, increasingly subjugated over the past three centuries, had now become indistinguishable from a slave.[32]

This analysis also highlights what was so revolutionary in the action of the clergy: behind the bishops' desire to reestablish peace in their dioceses, we can also sense that of the rustics to once again gather in assemblies for all free men, a scandalous desire to return to an older way just as the cleavage between fighters (*bellatores*) and manual laborers (*laboratores*) was taking hold.[33] From that time on, there would always be latent ambiguity in the actions of clergy for the peace, in the popular support they provoked and which they could not do without. These clerics had a dual interest since, as unarmed lords, they were victims of this violence. Still, as lords of justice, clerics had much to gain from the new developments.

When he meted out justice, Gerald acted as a public functionary, resorting to force "in order to protect the unarmed people . . . to constrain by the right of war and by the force of justice those whom an ecclesiastical censure could not contain."[34] When a hundred years later Gerald's heir, the abbey of Aurillac, tried to take over justice from the seigneurial agents, it was motivated by more than charitable concerns; it could also make that justice an element of its own seigneurial power. Surrounding their maneuvers with all the necessary solemnity, the monks interpolated (or forged) an act that implicitly recognized that the possession of this public assembly lay with the abbey, as granted by the bishop of Clermont, he who had inherited comital power. And when their charter recalled the vast area subject to its jurisdiction, that of Gerald, it did so in order to better fix it. In a still greater centralization of the system, they had regrouped sites of justice, already fixed, and brought them to a single place, Aurillac, with the aim of controlling them. The abbey was already behaving as a seigneurial judge, un-

---

[32] On social structures and their transformations, see Poly and Bournazel, *La mutation*, pp. 194–219.

[33] Duby, *Les trois ordres*, pp. 168–74; more recently, Pierre Bonnassie, "D'une servitude à l'autre (Les paysans du royaume, 987–1031)," in *La France de l'an mil*, ed. Robert Delort (Paris, 1990), pp. 125–41.

[34] *Vita s. Geraldi Auriliacensis*, 1.8; *PL* 133:675.

der the guise of protecting the humble. At this same time, the abbey of Tulle handed over the right of collecting public fines (*freda regalia*) that they held by delegation of the king in the castle of Tulle.[35]

In the tenth century, these communities were still lively and resistant to the assaults of the aristocracy. When these latter were unable to suppress the vicarial assemblies of free people or to create them at will, as at Aurillac, they tried to denature them, an attempt to reorient the rustics' sociability which already heralded their submission to the banal seigneurie. This procedure reveals the judicial institution's last transformation before its complete privatization in the framework of the feudal system. Much more than an end to Carolingian structures, the subordination of the *boni homines* announced the end of the allodial landholders and of the primitive community-based system, at least what remained of it.

These were no longer the days of Gerald of Aurillac. The number of powerful great men who no longer respected the terms of the capitularies and rendered their own justice had become too numerous. Like Mafiosi, or some medieval version of the cattle barons in the American West, they behaved as lords of justice, diverting the *vicaria* from its original context, appropriating it, soon to make it a major source of pressure whereby they could impose their exactions. The customs they imposed were new, but bad because unjust; and yet, under cover of so great a level of open violence, they were no longer really illegal. A local lord, a *princeps*, could simply seize land, perhaps land given to the abbey by his family in the past. To his mind, it was a question of a trust, recuperable now that the abbey wanted to free itself of his patronage, his influence.[36]

No one challenged the lord's right to tithe, literally to decimate the people who lived on his lands, especially his slaves. But he went too far when he pillaged the goods of others, even if these others were lowly (*humiles*) or unarmed (*inermes*). Acts of violence, which an ecclesiastical, hence subjective, documentation reveals to us, seem above all to concern clerical property. But they also targeted the humble—peasants who owned even a little independent (allodial) property. As early as

---

[35] This creation of a judicial district for the abbey may have related to the oath the monks of Brioude would later demand of their lay dependants in order to delimit a free zone into which they could not penetrate. Thus immunity was recreated, which was already a form of exemption. See *Cartulaire de Brioude*, no. 74, Elisabeth Magnou-Nortier, *La société laïque et l'église dans la province ecclésiastique de Narbonne (zone cispyrénéenne) de la fin du VIIIe à la fin du XIe siècle* (Toulouse, 1974), p. 298, and Lauranson-Rosaz, *L'Auvergne*, p. 358. For the *freda regalia*, see Etienne Baluze, *Historiae Tutelensis libri tres* (Paris, 1717), col. 379 (pièces justificatives).

[36] Most recently on this topic, see Barbara Rosenwein, *To Be the Neighbor of Saint Peter: The Social Meaning of Cluny's Property, 909–1049* (Ithaca, N.Y., 1989).

958, the *placitum* held at Clermont had to deal with a usurped allod. The fact that it belonged to a canon suggests that this category of cleric arising from the free peasantry represents precisely that group most violently touched by this crisis.[37] The church had to react, to match the violence that plagued it and its poor with an equally powerful response.

Forcing the Issue: Laprade, 978/980

In his edition of the cartulaire of Saint-Flour, Marcellin Boudet emphasized the role played by the kinds of synods, that is, the *convenciones* we have just described, as precursors to the Peace.[38] Following his lead, the German historian Hartmut Hoffmann considered the two Auvergnat assemblies of Clermont in 958 and Aurillac in 972 as the juridical beginnings of the movement.[39] One can therefore consider these general peace *placita*, in which the bishop substituted himself for a failing comital power, the advance wave of the future provincial councils of the Peace. Hoffmann went still farther in affirming, as had Marc Bloch, that the true origins of the Peace movement are found in the Velay.[40] He did so by distinguishing between the traditionally recognized major council of nine bishops and two archbishops gathered by Bishop Guy of Le Puy around 993,[41] and a more precocious diocesan assembly gathered by the same bishop at the beginning of his episcopacy, ca. 975.[42]

The account of this earlier gathering at Laprade suggests some quite revolutionary ingredients:

> Scarcely having risen to the pontifical see and thinking about assuring the peace of the goods of the church, which the brigands of the area were tak-

[37] C. Lauranson-Rosaz, "Réseaux aristocratiques et pouvoir monastique dans le Midi Aquitain du IXe au XIe siècle," in *Naissance et fonctionnement des réseaux monastiques et canoniaux* (Actes du Premier Colloque International du C.E.R.C.O.M., Saint-Etienne, 1991), pp. 353–72. On the end of allodial holdings, see the synthesis of J.-P. Poly, "L'Europe de l'an mille," p. 47.

[38] Boudet, *Cartulaire de Saint-Flour,* p. cvii.

[39] Hoffmann, *Gottesfriede,* p. 16; see also Töpfer, *Volk und Kirche,* p. 18.

[40] Marc Bloch, *Feudal Society,* 2 vols., trans. L. A. Manyon (Chicago, 1961), 2:571.

[41] *Cartulaire de Sauxillanges,* no. 15. The conventional date of 990 assigned to the "council of Le Puy" derives from the logic of precedent, that is, that it occurred just after Charroux. See below for the application of similar logic to the council of 994.

[42] Saint-Germain-Laprade, ten kilometers to the east of Le Puy. See *Cartulaire de l'abbaye de Saint-Chaffre du Monastier, suivi de la Chronique de Saint-Pierre du Puy,* ed. Ulysse Chevalier (Paris, 1884), nos. ccclxxxv, ccccxiii. If there had been other bishops at Laprade along with Guy of Anjou, the chronicler, normally so concerned to aggrandize his hero, would certainly have mentioned it. For a more recent, local approach to these questions, one that makes a clear distinction between the two assemblies, see Fayard, "De Ruessium," 1976, p. 93.

ing by force, Guy ordered that all knights and rustics from his diocese should gather together, so that they might give him their advice
on the correct way to assure the peace. Asking his nephews to gather
their troops nearby in the *vicus* of Brioude, he called on all those from
his bishopric who were present in the field of Saint-Germain near Le
Puy to swear to a peace—to not oppress the goods of the church, to return those that had been taken, as it is appropriate for Christian faithful. But since those present resisted, he ordered his army to come during
the night from Brioude, wishing to force them to submit, and they were
therefore compelled to swear the Peace and leave pledges, and in this
way these people gave back the lands and the castle of Saint-Mari and
the goods of the church that they had taken. This was done with the help
of God.[43]

The meeting seems to have taken place between 978 and 980,[44] sometime before Guy's dedication of the chapel of Saint-Michel d'Aiguilhe
in 984.[45]

Guy, it seems, dove right into the atmosphere of the Peace from the
moment of his arrival in Le Puy. His own past as a reformer of the abbey of Cormery, not far from Tours, had probably put him in touch
with certain partisans of a reaction against the disorders of the day.[46]
Once enthroned, he strengthened his connections to the reforming circles in the region of Lyon and Vienne, which sought to sanction the
usurpations of a warrior aristocracy. Between 976 and 978 he attended
an assembly held in Provence with three other bishops and two archbishops who had come to support Aimo of Valence and to condemn a
certain Achardus, a powerful man with connections at the royal court
and a usurper of the land of Saint-Apollinaire in Vivarais whom the

---

[43] *Cartulaire de Saint-Chaffre*, no. ccccxiii, p. 152.

[44] Most likely, the chronicler of Saint-Pierre, Guy's biographer writing in the twelfth
century, worked from authentic documents. He seems to have had before him the formula for electing a prelate, the notice of the *placitum* at Laprade, the act of consecration of the sanctuary of Saint-Michel-d'Aiguilhe, and that of the foundation of the
abbey of Saint-Pierre-du-Puy (he gives a precise date—13 April 993—to this last and
crowning achievement of Guy's career and his chronicle). His narrative deserves our
confidence, if not for the form and manner of recounting events, at least for the basic
information. The order of events is probably chronological, since he was writing a chronicle. What I say below, about the assembly of Arles and what we know of the historical
context (divorce of Azalais from Louis V, see below note 57) argues for this narrow range
of 978/80.

[45] See Auguste Fayard, "La charte de Saint-Michel d'Aiguilhe," in *Saint-Michel d'Aiguilhe: Commémorations du millénaire de l'érection de la chapelle de Saint-Michel d'Aiguilhe* (Le
Puy, 1962), pp. 96–131. The chapel was founded by Guy's predecessor, Godechaud, in
961; the consecration took place in 984; see Odo de Gissey, *Discours historiques de la très
ancienne dévotion à Notre-Dame-du-Puy* (Lyon, 1620), p. 270.

[46] See Olivier Guillot, *Le comte d'Anjou et son entourage au XIe siècle*, 2 vols. (Paris, 1972),
2:138–46.

relevant bishops of Provence and the king refused to discipline.[47] This synod might have been of little relevance had it called only on the judgment of God. But it dared to draw up and solemnly place an edict of excommunication on the main altar of the cathedral of Arles, intended for that city's archbishop Ithier, who, like the other provincial bishops, had absented himself from such dangerous proceedings. In an effort to circumvent an impotent but prominent political system, one part of the episcopacy of the Midi had come to help the bishop of Valence, isolated in his own province as a partisan of locally assured peace. In this manner they put the other prelates of that province on notice. At the same time, their's was a desperate effort to work along traditional lines of hierarchy: they still appealed to the great archbishop; they even went all the way to Arles, *caput Gallie.*[48] We do not know what happened.

At Laprade (if in fact the assembly came later), Guy of Anjou drew certain lessons from the setback at Arles. Well before the first major Peace councils, which seem (like Charroux) to have limited themselves to legislating with the sole sanction of religious penalties, Guy forced the issue by imposing with the pressure of arms an oath guaranteed by hostages. By these truly effective means, with a more modest staging than at Arles (for Laprade was a purely diocesan reunion), he would structure the action of the peace in order to make a juridical reality. As Marc Bloch commented on the larger sweep of the Peace movement,

> Soon there was scarcely an assembly concerned with limiting violence, that was not concluded in this way by a great collective oath of reconciliation and good conduct. At the same time, the pledge inspired by the conciliar decisions, became more and more precise in its terms. Sometimes it was accompanied by the handing over of hostages. It was in these sworn associations, which endeavored to associate in the work of peace the entire population (represented, naturally, by its chiefs great and small), that the real originality of the Peace Movement resided.[49]

This all demanded daring. Such a coup could not have been carried out by just anyone. It could not have been affected just anywhere; one

---

[47] *Cartulaire de l'abbaye de Savigny,* ed. A. Bernard (Collection des documents inédits sur l'histoire de la France; Paris, 1853), no. 127. For an analysis and a transcription of the text, see Jean-Pierre Poly, *La Provence et la société féodale, 879–1166: Contribution à l'étude des structures dites féodales dans le Midi* (Paris, 1976), pp. 37–38, note 41. This marks Guy's first official appearance in the documentation of the region. The others included the archbishops Amblard of Lyon and Thibaud of Vienne and the bishops Isarn of Grenoble and Gerald of Geneva.

[48] Guy was not there to exert pressure by means of political leverage that would soon be his. His sister Azalais was not yet remarried to William of Arles; see Lauranson-Rosaz, *L'Auvergne,* pp. 87–96.

[49] Bloch, *Feudal Society,* 2:415.

needed a diocese outside the mainstream, a kind of experimental location. In the Velay, everything was ready, all the conditions necessary for an effective reaction finally coming from the clerics. What Stephen II had first set in motion at Clermont and Aurillac, and the bishops of Provence had dared not do at Arles, Guy brought to fruition.

This action of Guy of Anjou makes sense only if we consider his personality, his origins and alliances, and the political context of his own diocese. Guy was from one of the most illustrious lineages of the kingdom, that of the counts of Anjou. His action took place in a large network of alliances and enemies; and even his nomination to the episcopal seat of Le Puy in 975 was due to royal favor.[50] His sister Azalais, widow of a marriage with Stephen of Brioude, soon the wife of Count Raymond of Toulouse, ruled over a condominium that stretched from the southern Auvergne to the Pyrenees. It was her sons, Stephen's nephews, the counts Pons and Bertrand, *Aquitaniae clarissimi consules*, who commended themselves to him as soon as he came to Le Puy, who supported his action at Laprade; it was they who traveled through the night to be on hand and force the reluctant rustics and knights into accepting the Peace.[51]

Guy's Peace consisted of three programmatic points: (1) to swear peace (*ut pacem firmament, ut pacem jurarent*), (2) to demand the concrete assurances of hostages in order to ensure respect, and (3) to give back what had been unjustly seized. Only on fulfilling such conditions could one truly be a Christian.[52] One might object that juridically Laprade was not a council, and that is true. It was more a diocesan *placitum* irregularly assembled by a bishop in order to reestablish order, as Stephen II of Clermont had done in 958 and 972. But from another perspective, Laprade seems all the more important juridically, since for the first time the populace participated. All categories of the

[50] *Cartulaire de Saint-Chaffre*, no. ccccxii. In any case, it was during a period of plenty that Guy was able to act. The years following the 982 divorce of Azalais from her third husband, the young Louis (V) of France, son of king Lothaire, were rather somber for the Auvergne; see Lauranson-Rosaz, *L'Auvergne*, pp. 87–96, and Bernard Bachrach, "The Northern Origins of the Peace Movement at Le Puy in 975," *Historical Reflections / Réflexions historiques* 14 (1987), 405–22.

[51] On the political strategy of the Angevin clan, see Lauranson-Rosaz, *L'Auvergne*, pp. 409–42, and "Les manoeuvres angevines au service des premiers Capétiens dans le Midi (956–1020)," paper delivered at the Colloquium Hugues Capet, Barcelona, July 1987. Also see Bachrach, "Northern Origins," p. 405, and idem, "Some Observations on the Origins of Countess Gerberga of the Angevins: An Essay of the Tellenbach-Werner Prosopographical Method," *Medieval Prosopography* 7 (1986), 1.

[52] Oathtaking probably took place on local relics, perhaps those of Saint George. Gatherings for the restitution of ecclesiastical or peasant property (*convenientiae*), soon so widespread, must have followed, with exchange of hostages guaranteeing for at least some time fidelity to the oaths. The mentions of *fidejussores* multiply in the charters at this time.

population were convoked (*omnes, milites ac rustici*). The goods of the
lower classes (*res pauperum*) were protected there, in particular the
humble, the peasants who were the principle victims of the current
state of depredation. Those guilty of depradations, whether peasant
or castellan, had to give back what they had unjustly seized, that is,
the castles in Notre Dame of Le Puy and the goods of the churches
of the diocese. Who could these guilty ones be who lay a heavy hand on
the goods of the poor and the church if not powerful men helped by
their *milites*?[53]

But even if these rural goods were apparently the lands of Saint-
Mari (in contrast to the buildings of fortifications, *castella*), the con-
vocation of a *placitum* of all the *rustici* shows that the goods of the
church were not the only ones in question. Did not the bishop count at
least as much on the presence of these rustics as on the force of his
nephews' armies to impress the nobles and to inspire in them the councils of wisdom?

Ultimately, whether the poor were actually there may be less significant than the emphasis placed on their presence in the document.
When even a chronicler writing in the twelfth century, at a time when
the populace had rights of the city, would deceive us on their role,[54]
the important thing is the memory that remained of the event and of
its essentially popular impact. Moreover, the site chosen corroborates
this popular aspect. It is not far from Le Puy that the event took place,
in the fields of Saint-Germain, which one can easily identify with the
actual Saint-Germain-Laprade, a dozen kilometers to the east of the
city, in the suburbs in its medieval sense. It was a place perfectly suited
for deploying a vast assembly, especially given how narrow and con-
stricted the old city was at the time.

Nor was it entirely just a question of geography. A century later, in
1095, did not those calling for the First Crusade prefer Clermont to Le
Puy, to Laprade, or to Saint-Paulien, even though the official chief of
this crusade was in fact the bishop of Le Puy, Ademar of Monteil, pilgrim to Jerusalem? We believe in the profoundly symbolic meaning of
the choices people in the Middle Ages made. The site chosen is of the
highest interest because it concerns issues of local customs and popular
sociability. In fact, at the beginning of the twelfth century Saint-
Germain-Laprade was the destination of one of the earliest recorded
cases of a popular procession, annually performed with much noise

---

[53] Because the goods of the poor are the goods of the Lord, it was a sacrilege to pillage
peasants, whether or not they lived on ecclesiastical property. There may have been some
guilty among the *rustici*, a normal development in the context of the kinds of resistance
that characterize the countryside in times of raids.

[54] One thinks of the famous *Cappuciati* of Le Puy; see Duby, *Les trois ordres*, pp.
394–402.

and "charivari" by the confraternity of the Cornards. Each May they would travel from Le Puy to Saint-Germain to dance at a site called "Dear Saint John" under a sacred poplar.[55] This folklore, in which the tree was kissed and offered cakes, can only indicate old pagan practices, even if their original meaning had been forgotten. One can even imagine that under this tree, as in so many other such sites, the judicial assemblies of the people had taken place in "heroic" times.

Laprade would have been chosen, then, for its capacity to attract the *pagani*. The hypothesis is deduced. Even if the presence of relics was not recorded at Laprade, we can nevertheless consider a religious phenomenon, an effort to channel the sociability of the rural classes by the clerics. All the popular accents of the Peace were at play. It is after all, perfectly natural that one would take into consideration these poor, as at Aurillac, now that the disfunction of justice had deprived them of protection. Not forgotten, they were now deployed on the side of the church. The broad outlines—principles and applications—of the Peace of God were therefore already evident in this line of action of Guy of Anjou.

The Time of the Councils: Coler, ca. 980

As I have shown elsewhere, the councils of Charroux in 989, Narbonne around 990, and Anse in 994 all drew their political inspiration from Guy of Anjou's experiment at Laprade.[56] But even where Guy played a major role, he did not act alone. We see the importance of his connections, whether in the episcopate or in his family—connections well implanted in the south.[57] Among these, we find Guy's cousin and Stephan's successor, Bego of Calmont.[58] We might even expect that these two students of Stephen II might have cooperated in further reunions in the Auvergne sometime after Laprade (978) and before

[55] On the Cornards, see Albert Boudon-Lashermes, *Le vieux Puy: Les origines de la cité d'Anis, des origines à la conquête romaine* (Le Puy-en-Velay, 1923), p. 184. Saint-Germain was a parish church from the eleventh century. It was standard practice to blow trumpets at councils in the Rouergue; see Bernard of Angers, *Liber mirac. s. Fidis*, 2.11, p. 119–20.

[56] Lauranson-Rosaz, *L'Auvergne*, pp. 420–24.

[57] Azalais, Guy's sister, twice widowed (from Stephen of Brioude and Raymond of Toulouse), divorced from Louis V, married William of Arles, count of Provence, between 982 and 986. Through her husband, son, and son-in-law, she "ruled" over a condominium that extended from the Velay to the Pyrenees and from Toulouse to the Alps.

[58] Bego replaced Stephen as abbot of Conques and was probably his *chorepiscopus*, since Stephen was still cited in 972 (assembly of Aurillac) even though Bego, abbot of Conques, was called bishop in 959–60. On the issue of *chorepiscopi*, see Lauranson-Rosaz, *L'Auvergne*, p. 238; on the abbatial office in the south, see p. 242 and "Réseaux aristocratiques."

Saint-Paulien (ca. 993), where they would appear together (see below). And, in fact, after Laprade there is a trace of another assembly, indeed a "true" Auvergnat council, at Coler.

Although Hoffmann cited it, this council received little attention until Pierre Bonnassie and Anne-Marie Lemasson proposed for it both a precise site and date, in the upper Auvergne, right near Aurillac.[59] The only witness to this council comes from a hagiographic source, the miracles of Saint Vivian of Figeac:

> Sometime after, a great number of bishops came from various cities to hold a council in the Auvergne, to deliberate about the common good and the ways to reestablish a lasting peace. To add greater weight to their deliberations, they brought their holy relics, so that by the intercession of these God would confirm in the heavens what the authority of the church decreed, in their presence, on earth. The site chosen for this great solemnity was called Coler.[60]

The text is explicit. It was in fact a council that consisted of all the characteristic elements of the Peace of God: bishops from various dioceses, a program of durable peace, relics of the saints, crowds, and presumably miracles. As Bonnassie and Lemasson point out, the text clearly suggests Coler's anteriority to the council of Limoges (994),[61] and nothing contradicts the possibility that it could have come before Charroux (989).[62]

As far as the location, two possibilities stand out: Salers and Colin, respectively ten and twenty-three kilometers northwest of Aurillac.[63]

[59] Hoffmann, *Gottesfriede*, p. 19; Pierre Bonnassie and Anne-Marie Lemasson, "Répertoire des sources hagiographiques du Midi de la France antérieures à 1200: Fascicule I, Quercy" (typescript, 1987), p. 84.

[60] *Trans. et mirac s. Viviani*, chap. 13, p. 257. The original is to be found in Paris, BN lat. 2627, fols. 175v–85v.

[61] Later in the narrative Saint Vivian performs a miracle at that council; *Trans. et mirac. s. Viviani*, chaps. 32–36, pp. 272–75.

[62] A further textual argument favors the anteriority of Coler to Charroux. The *Trans. et mirac. s. Viviani* (chap. 21, p. 267) mentions abbot Adacius after recounting the story of the council. According to the *Gallia christiana*, 2d ed., 16 vols. (Paris, 1715–1865), 1:72, this Adacius was abbot at Figeac after 974 (date of the death of his predecessor, Calsto), and until 988 (date of his own death). If the hagiographer had written his work in chronological fashion, the council would have taken place during Adacius's abbacy or before, in any case before 988. Of course, it is difficult to have much confidence in the chronological accuracy of an early eleventh-century hagiographer. Whereas I earlier hypothesized a precocious reunion that would have included the famous *conventus* of Stephen II at Landeyrat in 972 (*L'Auvergne*, p. 413, note 12), I now incline toward a distinct gathering.

[63] Bonnassie and Lemasson, "Répertoire," p. 92, note 2, identify Coler with Colin (commune of Ayrens, canton of Laroquebrou), about ten kilometers northwest of Aurillac, close to Nieudan. According to them, Nantunemdinem is the place where the cortege stops (*Trans. et mirac. s. Viviani*, chap. 14, p. 264).

And I suggest a third choice: Aurillac, or its immediate surroundings. In fact, the council itself was marked by a quarrel between the monks of Figeac, who had brought their saint there, and those of Aurillac jealous of the miracles carried out by this new presence.

The rumor of these miracles spread in all directions; the monks of Saint-Gerald, aroused by jealousy, began to denounce them and pursue them with a Jewish hatred. But among them there was one, Benedict of good memory, who did not share their venomous condemnations, and who conceived a passion for the glory of the blessed pontiff [Vivian]. The monk took a small child deprived of the use of all his members, put in his atrophied hands some candles, and carried him wrapped in a cape to the remains of the holy confessor, giving back to this child little by little his natural state. His members came back to life and, blood having run from his mouth and his ears, he again was able to use his voice and his hearing. Bounding triumphantly, Benedict brought back the child to the incredulous monks and showed him completely healed without the slightest damage. At the sight of this, the stupefied monks repented. Barefoot and with the remains of their own glorious confessor of Christ, Gerald, they arrived at the feet of the holy confessor Vivian and, begging forgiveness for their faults, gave him worthy praise.

The monks of Figeac may have been camping close to Aurillac, exciting the jealousy of the locals, poaching as it were on the home territory of Saint Gerald. Benedict, the monk who reacted more generously, probably took a local child, and he could not have gone too far to take him to Saint Vivian, since he brought him back leaping.

Obviously one would not have chosen Aurillac itself, because it was the city of Saint Gerald. Would it have been conceivable for the bishops to hold a council in the holy precinct, that of the monks? These last, as much as those of Figeac, would undoubtedly have resisted it, given the jealousy that opposed those two communities, canonical and monastic. It was both natural and polite to set up near, but outside, the city. Moreover, such a site made the assembly of large numbers of people all the easier.

In this context, Coler may perhaps correspond to Cueilhes, situated on a hill to the west of Aurillac, an ideal site for the assembly, just as the field of Saint-Germain had served Guy outside Le Puy.[64] One might object that an out-of-the-way, hillside no matter how propitious it

[64] An act of 1230 mentions a *via de Coler* close to Aurillac; see *Documents relatifs à la vicomté de Carlat*, ed. Gustave Saige and Le comte de Dienne (Monaco, 1900), no. ix, p. 20. The other places mentioned in the act are found to the south of the city—most important, a neighborhood to the southwest known as les Malaudes, near which is the route du Collet.

might be for a popular gatherings, or perhaps even a correct site for a diocesan assembly like Laprade, is not a worthy site for a council. But this seems all the more an argument for dating Coler as one from the earliest conciliar age. To this day, Charroux remains this kind of rustic site.[65] Eventually it would be possible to pick more central political or religious sites, such as Narbonne or Limoges. But for the moment one could not necessarily hold a council anywhere, and certainly not in a capital, under the noses of the powerful. In fact, one still had to do without them, whether one was an archbishop, prince, or count. We have already seen in Arles that certain bishops did not want to compromise themselves; even at Charroux there was no real archbishop, Gunbaldus being only a pseudometropolitan ruling over a see devastated by Normans.[66]

The council of Coler was not a provincial council. With Aurillac and Figeac (and Conques, of which Bego was abbot?), the area involved was quite distinct: southern Auvergne, the Quercy, the Rouergue.[67] We are still dealing with a "marginal" council.

In the last analysis, the Coler event seems an affair of monks. Our witness does not even bother to name the bishops, who had come from all over in such great number, just as another scribe would not, later, in describing Saint-Paulien. If this is a lapse of memory, it also reveals a point of view: hagiography was entirely preoccupied with miracles.[68] This account was obviously subjective, but it was also significant, moving the regular clergy, as it were, up to the front line. In the overall question of the Peace, it is important to distinguish between clerical and popular elements, but also to keep in mind that only one faction of the clergy was engaged, as we saw in the case of the reluctant bishops at Arles. It is not by chance that these promoters of peace were so close to the monastic world not only by their first weapons (Guy at Cormery, Stephen and Bego at Conques) but also by their friendships and even their conception of the ecclesiastical world. The monastic circles where they found their support were therefore placed at the avant-garde of the reforming battle, whether it was a question of exemptions or of returning to the ascetic values of primitive Christianity, whether it was incarnated by an Odo, a Maiolus of Cluny, an Abbo of Fleury, or an

[65] Charroux was chosen by the organizing bishops as part of a political strategy, because of its proximity to the estates of the counts of Poitiers and to those of the lords of Charroux, future counts of La Marche, who at this time were the former's enemies; see Lauranson-Rosaz, *L'Auvergne*, p. 424.

[66] Lauranson-Rosaz, *L'Auvergne*, p. 424.

[67] One sick man came from Saint-Amans, which is unidentified, but probably Saint-Amant-des-Cots, in the Aveyron, to the east of Conques, southeast of Aurillac.

[68] If the monks of Figeac were there, their bishop was also; we have not yet reached the period of autonomous monasticism in the style of the Cluniacs.

Odalricus of Saint-Martial. Such monasticism would naturally find itself at the front lines of the Peace movement just as, under Cluny's leadership, it would eventually recuperate, reabsorb, and institutionalize it.

Coler seems like the next step on the path from Laprade to the Peace of God. Not a diocesan assembly, but not yet a provincial council, its size no longer came from the boundaries defined by an old order but from a catchment area created by the parading of relics; and it was brought to a site where the name itself evoked the peasantry ("It is called Coler by those who live there [*incolunt*]"). As at Laprade, they all came to work for the Peace, but here the crowd was larger and the lines of a division drawn differently. There, where no mention is made of relics, the *rustici* and *milites* both swore oaths (on portable relics?) and gave hostages; both categories were capable of troubling the peace. Here, the *rustici* were joined by still more anonymous people of both sexes, the poor, the defenseless. There, the decisive moment came with the appearance of a secretly prepared army, and hence the oaths were compelled; here, we hear only of miracles performed by the gathered saints' relics.[69]

The appearance of these first-class relics is the key element of the Peace of God as a popular movement. With the crowd they attracted, we touch on the global inclusivity of the Peace movement which made it so powerful a social force. As the hagiographer explained, these relics added the force of heaven's approval to the decrees of the church, pronounced in their presence, on earth. Guy's troops have been replaced by the troops of saints who will play so prominent a role in the southern Peace movement. For the first time, the historian can glimpse the emergence of that notion of a voluntary commitment to peace, decreed and enforced by ecclesiastical sanctions alone, which constitutes the most messianic of the Peace of God's aspirations. And the relics are at the heart of the matter. Everything revolved around the saints: the jealousy of the monks of Aurillac, the arrival of the ill and their healing, the legitimacy of the council's decrees—even our documentation. The reign of the saints was at hand.

The Reign of the Saints

The exacerbated religiosity of the southern regions around the year 1000—thinly veiled transformations of pagan idolatry—is well known.

---

[69] The sick man who came from Saint-Amans was also described as a *quidam*. See notes 53 and 92 on the anticastellan aspect of the Peace of Coler.

Richly enameled reliquaries, even statues of the Virgin and saints "in majesty," were so many testaments to this "hagiophilia."[70] Claudius, the bishop of Turin, had already denounced icons in more general fashion in the early ninth century, and 200 years later in the regions of the Auvergne the northern scholar Bernard of Angers discovered these reliquary statues with astonishment and disdain: "There is a venerable and antique custom, as much in the regions of the Auvergne, of Rodez and Toulouse, as in the neighboring regions: each raises up to his saints according to his means, a statue in gold, in silver, and in other metal, in which one encloses either the head of the saint or some other venerable part of his body."[71]

In the tenth century, Bishop Stephen II placed on the altar of his newly rebuilt and consecrated church a "majesty" (*maiestas*) of the Virgin; the monks of Aurillac, Conques, and Limoges made similar busts of Saint Gerald, Saint Faith, and Saint Martial. All these pious images would be carried in procession, exalted, even—in bad times— coerced.[72] It is therefore to be expected that in this land of Auvergne, where the Peace would be born, where the saints would reign, the Peace and the saints came together; with all this fetishism, one could use this popular imagery, even exploit it. As later in Latin American or in animist Africa, Christianity was able to recuperate the idolatry of the Auvergnat countryside only by means of an invading cult of saints, a deviation that would become, ironically, the principal characteristic of classic medieval catholicism.

In this perspective, the recuperation of public devotions, the phenomenon of the showing of relics that developed during the councils of Peace, takes on its true meaning. The assemblies in which one wanted people to gather became solemn occasions for the clergy to offer the precious remains of the martyrs for veneration by the *populus*, thereby channeling their excessive attraction for this kind of demonstration. The abbey holding these relics then took on a much greater authority in the entire diocese, and in similar fashion the episcopal see used the apostolicity of evangelizing saints of the region to better

---

[70] On this subject, see Bernard Töpfer (Chapter 2) this volume; Ilene H. Forsyth, *The Throne of Wisdom: Wood Sculptures of the Madonna in Romanesque France* (Princeton, N.J., 1972); and Clare W. Solt, "Romanesque French Reliquaries," *Studies in Medieval and Renaissance History*, n.s., 9 (1987), 167–95.

[71] Bernard of Angers, *Liber mirac. s. Fidis*, 1.13, pp. 46–47.

[72] See Daniel Callahan (Chapter 7) in this volume; and Patrick Geary, "La coercition des saints dans la pratique religieuse médiévale," in *La culture populaire au Moyen Age: Etudes présentées au 4e Colloque de l'Institut d'Etudes Médiévales de l'Université de Montréal* (Montreal, 1979), p. 146.

rule.[73] The *Liber miraculorum sanctae Fidis* from Conques shows us the relics of the woman who had become the patroness of the Rouergue, surrounded by throngs at diocesan synods, carried about to the sound of trumpets like the Ark of the Covenant, in ever more spectacular processions. The sponsors prepared the venues carefully and worked the crowds. The council near Rodez, reported in the same text, although later and more local gives a good sense of the ambiance of heightened spiritual expectations engendered by the presence of relics:

> Arnold, the bishop of Rodez, of good memory, having called a synod, so as to raise the solemnity of the event, ordered that the reliquaries of the saints be brought from all the parts of the diocese . . . by the various congregations of monks or canons. These reliquaries were marshaled in array under tents and pavilions, in the pastures of Saint-Felix situated about a mile from the city. This site was illuminated by the "majesties" in gold of Saint Marius, episcopal confessor, and of Saint Amantius, also episcopal confessor, by the golden statue of Saint Mary, mother of God, and finally by the golden "majesty" of Saint Faith. There were in addition a great number of other reliquaries of the saints which it is not worth detailing here.[74]

One rapidly moves beyond the abbatial or episcopal district to gather these charismatic totems. The translation of the bodies of the saints ignored diocesan frontiers: the Auvergne, avid for relics, received in great ceremony Saint Vivian of Figeac, Saint Barnard of Romans, or Saint Faith of Conques, whom one finds "crossing the Planèze from one side to the other even to Talizat and Moloplize."[75] Thus local assemblies could give way to true councils.

The Councils of Saint-Paulien

The council of Saint-Paulien, the second accomplishment of Guy of Anjou, takes its place in a general amplification of the Peace movement

---

[73] See the analysis of a most egregious case of this by Richard Landes (Chapter 8) in this volume.

[74] *Liber mirac. s. Fidis*, 1.28, pp. 71–73 (Bernard of Angers), and 4.11, pp. 195–97 (anonymous continuator). Bishop Arnaud, the organizer of this synod, was mentioned in 1025–31, but he probably succeeded Deusdet (latest mention 1004) considerably earlier. The countess Bertha of Rouergue, present at the council (*Liber mirac. s. Fidis*, 1.28 p. 73), was daughter of the marquis Boso of Tuscany and niece of Hugh of Arles.

[75] *Cartulaire de Sauxillanges*, in p. cci (based on the *Liber mirac. s. Fidis*).

which had begun shortly after the trial run at Laprade, gathered force at Coler, and spread to all of Aquitaine after the accession of the Capetians.[76] The second reunion directly orchestrated by Guy is this time a full-fledged conciliar assembly. It is the council incorrectly located at Le Puy, traditionally dated around 990, and often confused with that at Laprade.[77] It is known only by a single document, a Cluniac charter from Sauxillanges which gives an indication of neither place nor date. But another source, the *Miracula sancti Barnardi* of Romans, tells of a delation of the relics of that saint in the Velay at the end of the tenth century to Saint-Paulien, "where the Aquitanians and their bishops were there assembled in council."[78] Harmut Hoffmann suggested identifying this assembly with the council of Guy of Anjou at which the bishop of Valence was present, in whose diocese lay the abbey of Saint-Barnard. Other than Laprade and the council identified with Le Puy of 1036, we have no trace of other councils held in the Velay at the end of the millennium.[79]

Guy invited many people, no less than eight bishops and numerous laymen, and he chose each great man carefully. They were friends convoked for their numbers in the face of certain hostilities (which we discuss later). Guy was audacious to assemble under his leadership bishops from various provinces (Bourges, Vienne, Narbonne, and Embrun) without their metropolitan bishops (Thibaud of Vienne and Dagbert of Bourges, Guy's own metropolitan), who would later ratify the conclusions of the assembly.[80] He acted like an archbishop gathering a provincial synod, and it was a good section of the episcopacy of the Midi that he gathered around him. We find the famous combination of Angevin transplants who united various areas of the Midi. Peter of Viviers, Guigo of Valence, and Guigo of Glandèves were prelates devoted to the bishop of Le Puy and to his sister Azalais, to whom they

[76] Lauranson-Rosaz, *L'Auvergne*, pp. 420–31.

[77] E. Baluze, *Marca hispanica* (Paris, 1688), col. 418 (1002). J. Mabillon, *De re diplomatica* (Naples, 1789), 2:597 (976). The *Gallia christiana* provides four different dates: 2:1237 (976); 1:203 (990); 4:533 (ca. 1004); 6:1039 (1004). Also, Karl Josef Von Hefele *Histoire des conciles d'après les documents originaux*, 2d. ed., 11 vols., trans. Henri Leclercq (Paris, 1907–52), 4.2:870 n. (990); and Hoffmann, *Gottesfriede*, p. 17 (994), followed by Magnou-Nortier, "La place du concile du Puy," and Poly and Bournazel, *La mutation*, p. 234.

[78] *Miracula s. Barnardi; AASS*, January III, pp. 160–61. See also Charles Rocher, "Un concile vellave (1004)," in *Tablettes historiques du Velay* 3 (1872), 1–37.

[79] Hoffmann, *Gottesfriede*, p. 19. A council of the Peace–Truce of God was held at Le Puy in 1036; Fayard, "De Ruessium," 1976, p. 107, n. 20, and the *Miracula s. Privati*, chap. 7, ed. Clovis Brunel (Paris, 1912), pp. 14–16, from Paris, BN lat. 11748, fol. 13v.

[80] On Dagbert, see Guy Devailly, *Le Berry du Xe siècle au milieu du XIIIe* (Paris, 1973), p. 467, and Lauranson-Rosaz, *L'Auvergne*, p. 418.

owed their sees.[81] Fulcran of Lodève, Bego of Clermont, Deusdet of Rodez, Raymond of Toulouse, and Fredol of Elne were great reforming bishops or friends of Guy, and were linked, as he was, to the principality of the county of Toulouse.[82] It is in fact these presences that permit us to assign to the council of Saint-Paulien a fairly precise date: mid-October 993 or 994.[83]

The close relations between Guy of Anjou and the diocese of Viviers and Valence explain why the monks from Romans would be involved in the Velay: the abbot of Saint-Barnard was none other than Isarn, bishop of Grenoble and Guy's long-standing friend. The advocates and protectors of the monastery were the Clerieu, a powerful lineage with links to the Velay. The great Archbishop Leger of Clerieu, who had been abbot of Romans before his accession to the episcopacy and had passed his youth among the canons at Le Puy, would later include the Velay in his reforming campaigns.[84]

Why choose Saint-Paulien over Le Puy? Among the various reasons one might propose, the most likely is that it suited sociopolitical needs, here joining ecclesiastical and popular politics: one assembled crowds in open fields and bishops in prestigious places. Saint-Paulien was rural, but it had a prominent role in the political and the religious history of the Velay, the antique Ruessium of Gallo-Roman times, the *cité vieille* of apostolic times.[85] The selection was apt—a knowing dosage of the useful and the necessary, a skillful manipulation.

[81] Lauranson-Rosaz, *L'Auvergne*, p. 418.

[82] For the episcopates, see the relevant entries in the *Gallia christiana*, and in Bonifacius Gams, *Series episcoporum ecclesiae catholicae* (Ratisbonne, 1873; rpt. Leipzig, 1931; rpt. Graz, 1957). In particular, for Fulcran of Lodève, see *Gallia christiana* 6:272, Gams, *Series episcoporum*, p. 579; and Magnou-Nortier, *Société laïque*, pp. 323–29. For Thibaud of Vienne, see *Gallia christiana* 16:61, and Georges de Manteyer, *Les origines de la maison de Savoie en Bourgogne (910–1060): Notes additionelles* (Paris, 1901), pp. 8–12.

[83] The date of 993 would be interesting: on Good Friday, April 13 of that year, Guy, in the company of Guigo of Valence and Peter of Viviers, founded the monastery of Saint-Pierre-du-Puy. It was a good year for Guy. From 992 on, the Angevins enjoyed royal favor in the aftermath of the feud between the king and Odo of Blois, ally of the count of Poitiers. This could also explain how Bishop Dagbert, a *fidelis* of the king, would confirm, even though absent, the measures taken when he seems to have been hostile to the earlier council of Charroux. This does not eliminate the possibility of two simultaneous assemblies, a hypothesis that would explain the absence of Guy at Anse as well as that of Archbishop Thibaud at Saint-Paulien, who would also ratify the measures later. At the council of Anse, a charter was given to Saint-Barnard of Romans. The abbot, absent (might he have been at Saint-Paulien?), was represented by the protector of the abbey, Silvion of Clerieu; see Mansi 19:178; M. Giraud, *Essai historique sur l'abbaye de Saint-Barnard et sur la ville de Romans* (Lyons, 1856), p. 28; and Hoffmann, *Gottesfriede*, p. 46.

[84] Giraud, *Essai historique*, p. 24.

[85] Fayard, "De Ruessium," 1978, p. 39, and Ulysse Rouchon, *Le Velay gallo-romain et sa capitale Rouessio* (Le Puy-en-Velay, 1922), pp. 3–8.

Forgeries and Manipulations

The end of the tenth century inaugurated the great epoch of forgeries.[86] And one forges to manipulate—documents and facts, traditions and pious legends, beliefs and cults. One had to at once consolidate one's position when faced with lay lords and draw the people by exciting their devotion. Material motivations would drive the chapter of Brioude, the abbeys of Manglieu, of Mozac, of Saint-Chaffre, and of Aurillac to forge false diplomas of immunity based on ninth-century originals, to arm themselves against the intrusions of the lords, and to consolidate their own lordship (let us not forget the battle for monastic exemption).[87] More spiritual motivations, but with material implications, would drive the same establishments to review and correct, when they did not invent, the lives of their founding saints. The forgers wrote ceaselessly to historicize the mythical saints, to make credible the semilegendary facts, to apostolize the evangelizers of the diocese and give them more spectacular *vitae;* secular and regular clergy labored together to connect the merits of the apostolic evangelizers and the works of the founders of abbeys and hermits.

It was around the year 1000, at the same time as the Peace of God, that the *vitae* of the patron saints of the dioceses of central Gaul were rewritten: the life and translation of George in the Velay; of Marius and Austremoine in the Auvergne; of Front of Périgueux; of Martial, Justinian, Valeria, and Leonard in the Limousin. Also at this time Bernard of Angers composed the *Liber Miraculorum sanctae Fidis*, while another Bernard "found" a *Miracula* of Privat in the Gevaudan, and the miracles of Vivian at Figeac were composed along with those of Saint Barnard at Romans. It is also likely that at this time the cult of Saint Calmin was launched, in an area somewhere between Saint-Chaffre in the Velay, Mozac in the Auvergne, and Tulle in the Limousin, three abbeys whose foundations were attributed to him.[88]

---

[86] "The golden age of medieval forgery, however, was by common consent the eleventh and twelfth centuries"; Giles Constable, "Forgery and Plagiarism in the Middle Ages," *Archiv für Diplomatik* 29 (1983), 12.

[87] For diplomas of Pepin I of Aquitaine for Manglieu, Conques, and Brioude, and of Pepin II for Saint-Chaffre, Manglieu, and Mozac, see *Recueil des actes de Pepin Ier et de Pepin II, rois d'Aquitaine (814–848)*, ed. Leon Levillain (Paris, 1926), nos. xviii, xxv, xxxii, xlvi, li, liii, lviii. For diplomas of Charles the Bald for Brioude, Manglieu, and Saint-Chaffre, see *Recueil des actes de Charles II le Chauve, roi de France (840–877)*, 3 vols., ed. Georges Tessier, (Paris, 1943), nos. 373, 376, 392, 440, 405, 442. More generally on this subject, see Magnou-Nortier (Chapter 3) in this volume. On the absence of a clear-cut distinction between regular and secular clergy, just as between laity and clergy, see note 37. One understands thereby Abbo of Fleury's difficulties in obtaining exemptions.

[88] *Vita ss. Frontonis et Georgii; AASS*, October XI, p. 407. *Vita s. Theofredi; AASS*, October VIII, p. 256. *Vita s. Calminii; AASS*, August III, p. 758. *Vita s. Marii; AASS*, June I, p. 23.

All these literary works show us, as do the relic gatherings, the concerted action of ecclesiastical circles, the sustained relationships that linked the diocese whose bishops were friends. One late tenth-century text illustrates this cooperation nicely: written by a cleric of Limoges, it linked a Saint Front of Périgueux, whom it claimed had met Jesus with Saint George the evangelizer of the Velay.[89] Riding the crest of popular enthusiasm for the relic cults, clerics tried to offer their rural populations "correct saints," proper objects of veneration. The fashionability that saints whose cults were imported from Spain and Italy—such as Peter, Michael, and James—would soon enjoy in the Auvergne illustrates this point. They would be introduced into the patheon of Auvergnat sanctity to serve the good cause.[90] One can sense all the novelty that animated "traditional" Auvergnat religiosity.

But the autonomy of popular response, initially so welcome, rapidly became troublesome. In manipulating the religiosity of the countryfolk (*pagani*), one ran the risk that they would in turn refashion the saints they were encouraged to worship. Indeed, the local rustics soon imposed their own distortions on the new cults: Michael the archangel and dragonslayer became confused with George, the missionary to the Velay, through the latter's conflation with the mythical Saint George, dragon slayer.[91] And if in purely religious matters we can see unpredictable relationships arising between clergy and idolatrous peasantry, how much more trouble, then, arose when political issues were at stake? Without actually speaking of an ideology, we can certainly speak of an anticastellan protest for these early manifestations of the Peace: when, for example, we see the procession of pacifists at Coler attacked by bands of *milites*; or when, at Brioude, the rogues who dared attack the property of Saint Julian were denounced; or when, at Conques, a rebel villager actually killed a local *vicarius*.[92] Here we find once again

---

Liber mirac. s. Fidis, 1.28, pp. 71–73, and 4.11, pp. 195–97. Mirac. s. Privati, chap. 7, pp. 14–16. *Mirac. s. Barnardi; AASS*, January III, pp. 160–61. On Saint Martial, see Landes (Chapter 8) in this volume.

[89] Auguste Fayard, "Saint Georges: Les légendes et l'histoire," in *Cahiers de la Haute-Loire* (Le Puy, 1971), p. 7; given the late date for the Aurelian legend (early eleventh century; see Landes, Chapter 8), Saint Front's legend seems to have developed first.

[90] On the diffusion of the cult of Saint Michael, see Armando Petrucci, "Aspetti del culto e del pellegrinaggio di San Michele arcangelo sul monte Gargano," in *Pellegrinaggi e culto dei santi in Europa fino alla prima crociata* (IVe convengo del Centro di studi sulla spiritualita medievale; Todi, 1963), p. 147.

[91] Jean-Pierre Poly, "Le diable, Jacques Le Coupé et Jean des Portes, ou les avatars de Santiago," *Sénéfiance* 6 (1979), 445. On the confusion between the two Saint Georges, see Fayard, "Saint Georges."

[92] *Trans. et mirac. s. Viviani*, chap. 14, p. 264; *Cartulaire de Brioude*, no. 20; *Liber mirac. s. Fidis*, 4.3, pp. 178–79.

the popular side in all its complexity, the side that in the end still eludes our scrutiny.

As is not surprising, we do see the institutional church reacting, seeking to circumscribe more narrowly the manifestations of lay religiosity, and in the process structuring itself along lines that prefigure the Gregorian reform.[93] Its support for the people simultaneously conjured up and tried to contain their activity. Popular resistance existed independently; the clerics, like the nobles but in a different way, tried to absorb the sociability of a rural population penned in by the crisis, to control it within reasonably firm structures like the rural parishes and the liturgy. But it was no longer the old church of the Auvergne that acted in this fashion; it was a new church, a derivative of Cluny. By the mid-eleventh century, when the Peace was taken up again by Cluny under the more institutional form of the Truce, where relics and crowds played secondary roles at best, the popular movement would detach itself from politics without, however, losing its élan, remaining in the popular imagination only to burst forth once again in the Crusades.[94]

The Geography of the Peace Movement: The Mountains of the Auvergne

In this vast and fascinating question of the origins of the Peace of God movement, it is of central importance to consider regional specificity. The particular characteristics of the Auvergnat terrain go beyond the simple fact that it saw the Peace first spring up. After all, it had to arise somewhere. But why in the Auvergne? The documents force us to admit—the dates insist—not only to the precocity of the development in Auvergne but also to its originality. The matter is above all to be linked to the problem of rising violence, as we have seen. But others, the Normans, for example, had no need for councils: popular pressure, which sufficed on occasion, does not always express itself the same way. In the north, one did not even get indignant about the violence; it was a daily reality. Only the rich allodial landholder could be at ease, sheltered from it. In the south, however, if seigneurial justice struck people as unacceptably violent and abnormal, it was because it had fewer roots than in the north.[95]

[93] See Amy G. Remensnyder (Chapter 12) in this volume.

[94] This analysis rejoins that of Alphonse Dupront on the popular elements of the First Crusade in *La chrétienté et l'idée de Croisade* (Paris, 1954–59), 1.43–80.

[95] On a differentiated vision of the implantation of French feudalities, see *Structures féodales et féodalisme dans l'Occident méditerranéen (Xe-XIIIe siècles)* (Paris, 1980), especially the report of Pierre Bonnassie, "Du Rhone à la Galice: Genèse et modalités du régime féodal," p. 17.

The powerful men who wished to carve out a seigneury in the northern fashion lacked "banal" roots and had to act with all the more violence. They met dual resistance: on the one hand, from mountain folk, half Roman, half pagan; on the other, from members of their own class, stuck in a kind of sympathetic conservatism. And these opponents of the banal seigneurie, whether allodial landholders or nobles, joined quickly at the side of the reforming church, behind it, or even within it. In this sense, the Auvergne seems more meridional than the traditional Midi. The center of Gaul is a receptacle, a refuge for traditions, of a "vulgar" *Romanitas* in the sense of *vulgar Recht,* a receptacle of a certain kind of autonomous peasantry.

We are confronted at this point within the delicate question—which makes itself felt despite so miserly a documentation—of the persistence of the allodial class. The Auvergne is neither Champagne nor Provence, where great fiscs and rich aristocratic domains abound. It is rather a poor region, where uncultivated expanses covered the countryside—the *saltus*—with arable lands restricted to the fertile basins of an occasional valley. This geography gave small, often miserably unproductive, allodial holdings a firmer footing than elsewhere. And both wasteland and allods gained in prominence with altitude, in the upper Auvergne. It is not surprising that in these southern parts of the province, in the high often barren terrain of the Cantal and the Velay, the church launched the Peace by reviving a curious tradition (a scandalous innovation according to Adalbero), that of open-field assemblies and collective oaths.[96] The messengers of Peace had come down from the mountains.

This element is most interesting for our inquiry since it is eminently popular. The city at this time was the domain of ruling families, not of peasantry; it was also the site of official sanctuaries, not of vulgar cults. Closing oneself up in the cities, one lost the people at a time when the network of rural parishes was still tenuous. One therefore had to leave the cities and find the centers of popular sociability, to "get down" with this long-standing tradition of gatherings that marked the rural population from the earliest times. Popular religiosity demanded it: one no longer even conceived of an oath without relics, and for the same reason relics were venerated. At the same time, these aspects of a vibrant Christianity permitted the church to reorient the masses away from the still more egregiously pagan elements in their culture: dolmens, sacred groves, altars, witchcraft.

[96] The question of peasant communities is still to be explored; see Susan Reynalds, *Kingdoms and Communities in Western Europe,* 900–1300 (Oxford, 1984), pp. 101–54, and *Les communautés rurales* (Recueils de la Société Jean Bodin, 44; Brussels, 1987). There are for the Auvergne of the late Middle Ages, and even for more recent times, tangible signs of a solid tradition; see Henriette Dussourd, *Au même pot et an même feu: Etude sur les communautés familiales agricoles de Centre de la France* (Moulins, 1978).

A more favorable, popular ecclesiastical tradition? A free and fortified peasantry? Perhaps we find there a general situation that escapes
our documentation. It would, in any case, be interesting to link this
question to the specific structure of a mountainous region in the central zone, conditions that do not only apply to the Auvergne.

We conclude on what Adalbero would call the subversive aspect of
the first, popular Peace—its confrontational side. As Pierre Bonnassie
pointed out, one can see in these Peace assemblies "the emergence at
an institutional level of an enormous movement of resistance on the
part of the free peasants—still free in the face of attempts to subject
them."[97] But, *à la longue,* the egalitarian chant of the allodialists from
La Planèze of Saint-Flour carried too little weight in the face of Lord
Amblard of Nonette torching their huts. The genuine concern of certain prelates like Guy of Anjou to protect the unarmed was too com-
promised by their desire to legalize a new feudal order in which they
stood to profit handsomely.[98] The time of the *convenientiae* had come at
the same moment as the demise of the allodial tenures. Time for a kind
of peace—alas too banal.

[97] Bonnassie, "D'une servitude à l'autre," p. 138.
[98] Poly, "L'Europe en l'an mille," p. 42, sees the assemblies of 994 as the beginning of
the radical phase of seigneurialization. That seems an appropriate moment to end this
study of the first, primitive phase of the Peace movement.

6

The Castellan Revolution and
the Peace of God in Aquitaine

ANDRÉ DEBORD

When historians examine the documentation concerning the Peace of God, Aquitaine presents something of a paradox. The Peace, which scholars have traditionally understood as a response to a failure of authority at the top (king, duke, count), clearly began early and remained important in that region for at least a half-century. Yet the duke of Aquitaine and the count of Angoulême seem to have been among the most powerful and well-established rulers in early eleventh-century Frankland. My purpose in this essay is to examine this contradiction by investigating the impact of the newly emergent class of castellans on both the rulers and peasant population of Aquitaine. Understood in this context, the Peace appears as a response to the social and political transformations brought about by the proliferation of castle building that marked the early eleventh century.

Ducal and Comital Power, 980–1030

The impressive stature of Duke William V, "the Great" (993–1030), as well as his distinguished lineage, are well documented by both contemporaries and modern historians.[1] Count of Poitiers, he also ruled

This essay is based on the findings of my earlier published work, most notably *La société laïque dans les pays de la Charente, Xe–XIIe siècles* (Paris, 1984). Subsequent footnotes refer to material treated in more detail there. The author expresses his full appreciation to Richard Landes, who edited and translated this article.

[1] His father, William Ironarm died only in 995. He had already retired to the monastery of Saint-Maixent in December 992; see Alfred Richard, *Histoire des comtes de Poitou (778–1204)* (Paris, 1903), pp. 136–39. William V was first cousin to King Robert the Pious. By his third wife Agnes he was related to Otto-William, himself related to Adalbert the dethroned king of Italy. In addition, he was related to Richard II of Normandy and Odo of Blois.

the duchy of Aquitaine, which included the Poitou, western Berry, the Auvergne and its annexes, the Limousin, the Périgord, the Charente, and theoretically Gascony.[2] "All of Aquitaine he subjected to his rule," said Ademar of Chabannes at the end of his famous portrait of the duke of Aquitaine.[3] Walther Kienast has depicted him as a "personality of European stature" who underlined his authority, his prestige, and his pretentions by regularly taking the title of duke, already occasionally assumed by his father.[4]

Particularly in his relations with the church, the duke of Aquitaine played a role similar to that of the strongest Carolingian kings: he controlled some of the most prestigious monasteries in the region as lay abbot of Saint-Hilaire, Saint-Maixent, Nouaillé, and Saint-Jean-d'Angély, and he played a dominant role in the appointment of bishops.[5] In fact, as Ademar's account indicates, the duke attempted to detach Limoges from its archepiscopal superior at Bourges and bring it into the orbit of the group of bishops dependent on Bordeaux whom he convened as part of his suite.[6]

But, as other historians have already demonstrated, behind this masterful portrait lay a secular reality far less compelling.[7] In most cases the duke's authority derived largely from a personal bond that linked him to old and often independent families in the Angoumois and the Périgord, and he had no personal landholdings outside of the Poitou and the Aunis. The substantial benefices he handed out to friend (William of Angoulême) and rival (Fulk Nerra of Anjou)[8]

---

[2] In 1032, the second son of William the Great attempted to assert his claims on Gascony; see Charles Higounet, Bordeaux pendant le Haut Moyen Age (Toulouse, 1980), pp. 53–56, and Renée Mussot-Goulard, Les princes de Gascogne, 768–1070 (Marsolan, 1982), pp. 187–91.

[3] Ademar of Chabannes, Chronicon, 3.41, p. 163.

[4] Walther Kienast, Der Herzogtitel in Frankreich und Deutschland (9. bis 12. Jahrhundert) (Munich-Vienna, 1968), p. 203; Daniel Callahan, "William the Great and the Monasteries of Aquitaine," Studia Monastica 19 (1977), 321–42; Ademar, Chronicon, 3.41, 45; pp. 163, 176.

[5] At Limoges, Poitiers, Saintes, even Angoulême and Bordeaux. Bishop Rohon of Angoulême (consecrated 1018) came from Montaigu in the Poitou and did homage to the count of Poitiers.

[6] For examples of episcopal reunions in 1003, 1025, and 1029/31, see Debord, Société laïque, p. 107 and note 25. That the effort to detach Limoges eventually failed does not detract from the main point here: to even try, the duke had to have remarkable de facto control of the see of Limoges.

[7] Bernard Bachrach, "Toward a Reappraisal of William the Great, Duke of Aquitaine, 995–1030," Journal of Medieval History 4 (1979), 11–21, and " 'Potius Rex quam esse Dux putabatur': Some Observations Concerning Adémar of Chabannes' Panegyric on Duke William the Great," Haskins Society Journal 1 (1989), 11–21.

[8] For more details, see Bachrach, "Toward a Reappraisal," and Debord, Société laïque, pp. 107–8.

Map 2. Western Aquitaine

indicate how tenuous was his control of even limited institutional resources. And though counts and vicounts regularly frequented his court,[9] this authority did not come easily: William had to fight— not always successfully—against Audebert the First, count of the Marche, and Gui, the vicount of Limoges. Indeed, in his own backyard, so to speak, he experienced ongoing difficulties with

[9] Especially the counts of the Marche, the counts of Angoulême, and the viscounts of Limoges; see Debord, *Société laïque,* p. 105, notes 8–10.

belligerent vassals, the most famous of them Hugh the Chiliarc of Lusignan.[10]

One should not, then, conceive of the duchy of Aquitaine as a territorial principality, that is, "a veritable state in which the prince exercises the authority previously devolved from the king."[11] Although he might do without the king in his general policies, the duke of Aquitaine had no institutional authority outside the Poitou, no chancellery of his own.[12] Outside the Poitou, few private charters used his rule as a chronological referent.[13] The men he assembled at his court were vassals and clients, and when he intervened outside his own lands it was most often at the invitation of clients who had trouble with their own insubordinate vassals. He may have exercised the role of supreme arbiter, but he did so in a purely feudal sense.

The duke of Aquitaine's power was actually fairly great in the Angoumois region. The count there, William IV, Taillefer, was his best friend and faithful counselor, according to Ademar.[14] The count appeared often at the ducal court, and the two friends went together to investigate the Lombards' offer of the Italian throne to the duke. This close association with the duke gave Taillefer the role of brilliant second, for the time being an advantageous position for the counts of Angoulême.

Curiously, this relationship has not received much attention from those historians interested in vassalage and fiefs at the beginning of the eleventh century, particularly those commenting on the famous letter of Fulbert of Chartres to the duke of Aquitaine.[15] In fact, beyond personal links of friendship whose authenticity we have no reason to suspect, we can also discern the political reasons behind the duke's attitude. This was a period in which vassalic bonds did not involve positive obligations except where the vassal held a benefice from his lord,

[10] Debord, *Société laïque*, p. 105; Jane Martindale, "Notes and Documents: *Conventum inter Guillelmum Aquitanorum comes et Hugonem Chiliarchum*," *English Historical Review* 84 (1969), 528–49 (trans. George Beech in *Readings in Medieval History,* ed. Patrick Geary [New York, 1989], pp. 405–11).

[11] Jan Dhondt, *Etudes sur la naissance des principautés territoriales en France* (Ghent, 1948), p. 254.

[12] Note that outside the Poitou and the Aunis he never accorded a diploma to any monastery.

[13] For example, the charters of the cathedral of Angoulême and of Saint-Eparchius do not date by his rule even when they abandon dating by royal rule; see Richard Landes, "L'accession des Capétiens: Une reconsidération selon les sources," *Religion et culture autour de l'an mil: Royaume capétien et Lotharingie* (Paris, 1990), pp. 158–62.

[14] Debord, *Société laïque*, p. 108.

[15] Marcel Garaud, "Un problème d' histoire: A propos d'une lettre de Fulbert de Chartres à Guillaume le Grand comte de Poitou et duc d'Aquitaine," in *Etudes d'histoire de droit canonique dediées à Gabriel Le Bras*, 2 vols. (Paris, 1965), 1:559–62.

and often the extent of his obligations depended largely on the importance of that benefice.[16] William the Great accordingly made a concerted effort to bind his most powerful vassal, the only one (ducal title excepted) who could be compared to him inside Aquitaine, with clear reciprocal obligations. In other words, he concluded with William IV of Angoulême a *convenientia*. Unlike his other powerful vassal, Fulk Nerra, with whom the duke encouraged William of Angoulême to make a marriage alliance, the duke maintained excellent relations with his southern neighbor and *fidelis*.[17]

For this reason, whereas his father Arnold Manzer had been occupied in establishing the count's authority over the Angoumois against his cousins from the Périgord and against the bishop of Angoulême, William's reign (988–1028) was a period of territorial expansion on a large scale, both in the direction of the Poitou and the Limousin and southward toward Bordeaux. To the north, the count received from the duke a string of castles whose primary value appears to have been for keeping watch on the county of the Marche, the viscounty of Limoges, and Hugh of Lusignan.[18] To the south, the duke seems to have followed a similar policy of close cooperation with his count in controlling the region around Bordeaux and Gascony.[19]

The rule of William Taillefer, brilliant on the outside, was no less significant internally. We know from Ademar several important episodes involving insubordinate viscounts and castellans whom William dominated. In the case of the bloody rivalry among the brothers Marcillac, William intervened both to render justice and to eliminate their viscomital office entirely.[20] When Aimeri of Rancon built the castle Fractabotum "against his lord" on the borders of the Charente, about two and a half kilometers from the comital fortress of Merpins, the

[16] Olivier Guillot shows the negative conception of vassalic obligation in connection with benefices and its role in the struggles between Hugh of Lusignan and the count of Poitiers; see *Le comte d'Anjou et son entourage au XIe siècle*, 2 vols. (Paris, 1972), 1:17–18.

[17] Debord, *Société laïque*, pp. 108–10.

[18] Fortifications are known to us from this period onward: Melle (ca. 960), Chabanais (1010), Ruffec (1021), Confolens (1023), Aulnay (1032). The first mention of the castle at Rochechouart is only in 1077; see *Chartes et documents pour servir à l'histoire de l'abbaye de Charroux*, ed. Pierre de Monsabert (*Archives historiques du Poitou* 39; 1910), p. 64. But the viscounts, a cadet branch of the Limoges viscounts, are known to hold this site from the end of the tenth century and carry the surname Rochechouart as early as 1047; see *Cartulaire de l'abbaye royale de Notre-Dame-de-Saintes*, ed. T. Grasilier (Cartulaires inédits de la Saintonge, vol. 2; Niort, 1871), p. 5. William IV of Angoulême helped duke William against Boso the count of La Marche at the siege of Rochemeaux; Ademar, *Chronicon*, 3.41; p. 165. For a map of the strategic alliance between the two Williams, see Jean-Pierre Poly and Eric Bournazel, *La mutation féodale, Xe–XIIe siecles* (Paris, 1980), p. 141.

[19] This policy extended to marital strategies: William the Great to Brisque, daughter of the duke of Gascony (1011), and Alduin of Angoulême to Brisque's niece Alauzia (before 1020); for futher discussion, see Debord, *Société laïque*, p. 111.

[20] Debord, *Société laïque*, pp. 112–13.

count took the castle and gave it as a fief to his own son.[21] William's influence even reached beyond the grave. Four years after his death, his eldest son and successor, Count Alduin, died; William's dying bequest, that Alduin's progeny (the sons of William's assassin, Alduin's wife, Alauzia of Gascony) be disinherited, was honored.[22]

The authority of the count of Angoulême seems therefore to have been rather solid in 1030. His prestige is underlined by the enthusiastic welcome he received on returning from a pilgrimage to the Holy Land in 1027. This prestige and authority were built on both his great popularity and his extensive land holdings. We cannot, with any precision, determine the size of these holdings, since we only glimpse them through those portions he donated to the church. These comital donations of the later tenth and eleventh centuries were clearly localized in those sectors where the castellanies, which first appeared at the end of the tenth century, remained directly in the hands of the count: castellanies of Angoulême, Archiac, Bouteville, Châteauneuf, Marcillac, Matha, Montausier, and Montignac.[23] The convergence of these two sources of power—private landholding and banal rights— highlights the concentration of this landholding in the northwest and southwest of the county of Angoulême. In the east, however, the count had less influence.

Still another element of the count's authority came from his relations with the church. In contrast with the dukes, the counts, of Angoulême never seemed to have held direct control over the election of the bishop. But the counts did control closely the regular clergy of their county, including the prestigious abbey of Saint-Eparchius, dynastic burial site for the count,[24] which they treated as personal property and for which they appointed abbots.[25] Similar comital control can be

---

[21] Ademar, *Chronicon*, 3.60, pp. 185–86. Fractabotum is at les Landarts, commune of Chérac. Aimeri of Rancon is the same person who opposed Hugh of Lusignan in the *Conventum* studied by Garaud, "Problème," and George Beech, "A Feudal Document of Early Eleventh Century Poitou," in *Mélanges d'histoire médiévale dédiées à René Crozet*, 2 vols. (Poitiers, 1966), 1:203–13.

[22] Ademar, *Chronicon*, 3.66-67, pp. 190–94; *Historia pontificum et comitum engolismensium*, ed. Jacques Boussard (Paris, 1957), Chaps. 26–30, pp. 21–26; Debord, *Société laïque*, pp. 112–13; Monica Blöcker, "Ein Zauberprozess im Jahr 1028," *Zeitschrift für schweizerische Geschichte* 29, nos. 3–4 (1979), 533–55.

[23] Debord, *Société laïque*, p. 111–12.

[24] The counts of Angoulême, who were buried at Saint-Eparchius, often took the monastic habit at the moment of death: William II (*Cartulaire de l'abbaye de Saint-Cybard*, ed. Paul Lefrancq [Angoulême, 1930], p. 198); Arnald Manzer (*Historia pontificum*, chap. 20, p. 13); William IV (Ademar, *Chronicon*, 3.66, p. 190).

[25] For sales in the late tenth century, see Ademar, *Chronicon*, 3.36, p. 159; in the late eleventh, see *Cartulaire de Saint-Jean-d'Angély*, 2 vols. ed. Georges Musset (*Archives historique de la Saintonge et de l'Aunis*, 30, 33; Saintes, 1901, 1904), 1:395. On the free use of the abbey's wealth, see *Historia pontificum*, chap. 27, p. 22; on the prestige of control and the appointment of abbots, see Ademar, *Chronicon*, 3.65, p. 190.

found at Saint-Etienne-de-Baigne and Saint-Amantius-de-Boixe, built by the count ca. 990 and transferred together with a castle to a more strategic site only thirty years later.[26]

In general, around 1030—a convenient terminus that corresponds approximately to the deaths of William the Great, William IV, and Ademar of Chabannes—comital power was strong in the land of the Charente. But we cannot stop at this level of analysis. The political history of this period holds indices of a transformation, in both the nature of comital power and the play of social forces on which that power rested. First, it is clear that the power of the count derived in large part from the possession of castles. The major issue for the duke and his principal vassals was control of these castles. Ademar gives us a reassuring image of this conflict: public power held the upper hand. At the same time, those who held comital fortresses had a distinct tendency toward insubordination as soon as the count or duke turned their backs, and a relatively minor figure like Hugh the Chiliarc could cause the prestigious duke of Aquitaine the worst kind of difficulties.

A close reading of Ademar shows the extent to which this situation affected the institutional structures of the Carolingians. The count of Poitiers gave Aulnay as a fief to the count of Angoulême; in so doing, he made the viscount a rear vassal. The solution did not last, but it is sufficient to show that the relationships that bound the count of Poitiers and his agents in Aulnay at the beginning of the tenth century had become purely feudal by the year 1000. One can even note in the same sense the inconsistency of Ademar's vocabulary on the subject of viscounts: he referred to the *viscounty* of Melle even though that title had not been seen for more than a century,[27] as well as to that of Rochechouart, which was only the appanage of the viscounts of Limoges.

We are therefore faced with two questions. First, to what extent was the effective power of the counts transformed, and weakened, from the beginning of the eleventh century? A classic question, it is true, and many have asked it before us. We must nevertheless formulate it once again, for the indispensable comparison with previous answers and for new insights into the second question, namely, how important was the increased role castles now played in modifying the nature of comital power, and under what conditions did it develop?

---

[26] *Cartulaire de l'abbaye de Saint-Etienne de Baigne*, ed. P. F. E. Cholet (Niort, 1868), p. 63. The move underlines the count's desire to reinforce his position in a sector in which he had a rather strong landholding interest: see *Cartulaire de Saint-Amand-de-Boixe*, ed. André Debord (Poitiers, 1982), Introduction.

[27] Ademar, *Chronicon*, 3.42, p. 165. See Debord, *Société laïque*, p. 115, note 92.

A Proliferation of Castles

It has generally been suggested that the link between the castle and the ban (the power to command and constrain) originated in public (royal) power. The wielders of this public authority, with their power to constrain weakening, sought to reassert themselves by resorting to military force, that is, by relying on castles. But centrifugal forces were irreversible; the castellans, guardians of these public fortresses—and at the same time rich allodial landholders—diverted to their own profit the ban confided to them and thus became independent lords.

This analysis derives from the idea that the ban was of public origin and did not stem from private lordship. Historians therefore conclude that it must have first been confided officially by the count[28]—and the castle constructed by the count himself or on his orders—and correspondingly that the castles dating before the year 1000 were rather limited in number. This is the situation observed by Georges Duby for the Mâconnais, by Edmond Perroy for the Forez, and by Robert Fossier for Picardy. But after ca. 1000, the control of public authority weakened. Olivier Guillot notes a proliferation of castles in the Anjou throughout the eleventh century under conditions that indicate some construction not guided by the count; and this phenomenon is noted elsewhere, notably by Gabriel Fournier for the lower Auvergne, by Marcel Garaud for the Poitou, and by Tenant de la Tour for the Limousin.[29] But these scholars, for various reasons, do not seem to have investigated further the link between the ban and the castle.

And yet this is a fundamental issue. Even in those areas where the castles seem to have been of public origin, the situation was not favorable to public power. The more castles one finds in a region, the more comital power seems to have rapidly and profoundly weakened in that area, partly because the castellans became lords. But, beyond that, one should also ask whether all these castles were of public origin. And if some were of purely private origin, how did they acquire the ban? or, alternatively, how did they conflate it with customary practices (*con-*

---

[28] Georges Duby takes this position; see "Lignage, noblesse et chevalerie au XIIe siècle dans la région mâconnaise: Une revision," *Annales: E.S.C.* 27, nos. 4–5 (1972), 803–23; rpt. in *Hommes et structures du moyen âge* (Paris, 1973), pp. 395–422.

[29] Georges Duby, *La société au XIe et XIIe siècles dans la région mâconnaise* (Paris, 1953; rpt., 1972), p. 105; Edouard Perroy, "Les châteaux du Roannais du XIe au XIIIe siècle," *Cahiers de civilisation médiévale* 9 (1966), 13–28; Robert Fossier, *La terre et les hommes en Picardie jusqu'à la fin du XIIIe siècle* (Paris, 1968), p. 490; Olivier Guillot, *Comte d'Anjou*, 1:281–352; Gabriel Fournier, *Le peuplement rural en Basse Auvergne durant le haut Moyen Age* (Paris, 1962), p. 366; Marcel Garaud, *Les châtelains de Poitou et l'avènement du régime féodale: XIe et XIIe siècles* (Mémoires de la société des antiquaires de l'Ouest, 4th ser., 7; Poitiers, 1964), p. 15; Georges Tenant de la Tour, *L'homme et la terre de Charlemagne à St. Louis* (Paris, 1942), p. 297.

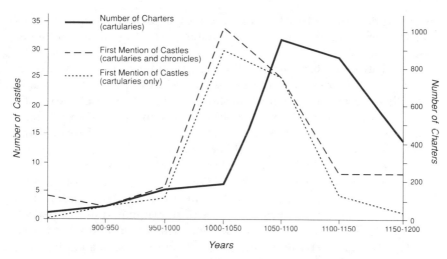

Appearance of castles and frequency of charters

suetudines)? To answer these questions, I have studied the number, location, and chronology of castles in the Charente. With the exception of Fournier's, most previous studies have used written sources only.[30] Given advances in archaeology, however, it seems both possible and valuable to inventory and analyze the evidence of undocumented fortifications to which even today the soil bears witness.

My inventory of castles in the Charente deals only with castles known before 1200, noting the oldest mention for each castle. Cases in which the first appearance of the surname (for taking a surname followed closely on the establishment of a lineage controlling a castle) predates the first formal mention of a castle are taken as indications that a castle already existed. In the same fashion, the qualification of *dominus de* or, in the work of Ademar, of *princeps de* also suggests the existence of a castle.[31] Obviously, this methodology demands caution. We are to some extent victims of the accidents of our documentation, but it may be more certain than it seems; the chronological curve in the mentions of castles in the Charente is independent of—indeed it anticipates quite remarkably—the growing abundance in our sources (see Graph 1). Moreover, we can correlate the results obtained through documentation with other elements, notably archaeological evidence. From this correlation, the chronological indications derivable from the inventory have a more certain global value in situating the principal "moments"

[30] Fossier does not really integrate the archaeological inventory of mottes in Picardy in his analysis.

[31] Debord, *Société laïque*, pp. 126–27, and Appendices I (p. 455) and II (pp. 470–71).

in the appearance of castles, even if individual items might be corrected (and therefore dated to an earlier period) by other no longer extant sources.

A most striking observation is the high number of castles known before 1200—eighty-eight. From the start, therefore, we are in an area radically different from that of the Mâconnais or the Forez, especially since of these only twelve appear before the year 1000, whereas sixty-one appear for the first time in the eleventh century and fifteen in the twelfth century. We can extend this chronological analysis. There are few castles attested during the Carolingian period or even the late Carolingian period: only six known before the middle of the tenth century. It is true that the documentation for this period is fragmentary and that certain fortresses known later may have originated in this period. It is equally clear, though, that in the ninth and tenth centuries the castle played a minor, strictly military role. It did not, for example, leave any traces in collective memory as a means of geographic localization.

This observation entails another still more important one: most of the castles first appeared well after the period of the Norman invasions. Again, within the limitations imposed by the lacunae in our documentation, one can therefore assert with some confidence that the multiplication of castles was not linked to a need for defense against an external enemy: of six castles attested before the mid-tenth century, only two (Marcillac and Matha) were formally designated as having been built "against the pagans." Similar concerns may have motivated the construction of Blaye in the south and Fronsac, as well as the ramparts of the cities of Saintes and Angoulême.

These observations formally contradict the thesis developed by R. Aubenas, and often reiterated by historians, according to which the castles of the tenth century were built by the counts to defend against the Normans.[32] In fact, construction began only in the second half of the tenth century, and the core of construction occurred after the raids ceased between 990 and 1100. A more detailed analysis shows that the principal period of construction took place right *after* the invasions, between 990 and 1050 (67 percent of those between 990 to 1100) and more precisely between 1019 and 1050 (51 percent of the first-written mentions in that period). The curves in Graph 1—which, as noted, do not depend on the growing abundance of our sources—underline that the castle became, in the first half of the eleventh century, one of the

[32] R. Aubenas, "Les châteaux forts des Xe et XIe siècles," *Revue historique de droit français et étranger*, 4th ser., 17 (1938), 548–86; Marcel Garaud, "La construction des châteaux et les destinées du la *vicaria* et du *vicarius* carolingien en Poitou," *Revue historique de droit français et étranger*, 4th ser., 32 (1953), 61.

distinctive traits retained in the collective consciousness to define the structures of daily life.

We might stop here in illustrating the new social order. But we can, it seems, make still more precise observations, particularly if we take seriously the observation that the first reference to a castle in the sources does not necessarily mark its construction. To understand the global phenomenon of the appearance of castles in texts, we must also turn to the parallel phenomenon, that of their construction on the terrain.

Ademar of Chabannes, contemporary of the events of the end of the tenth and beginning of the eleventh centuries, and highly knowledgeable about western Aquitaine, cites in this period twenty-seven different castles (not including Saintes or Angoulême) in the Limousin, the Angoumois, and the Poitou. Of these fortifications, he formally designates twelve (44 percent) as new constructions. If we restrict ourselves to the sector Ademar knew best and about which he speaks the most—the Angoumois and the Limousin—he mentions twenty-two castles, of which seven (32 percent) are cited as new.[33]

More extensive archaeological studies would give the same results. The dig we have pursued since 1971 at the castle of Andone, abandoned by the counts somewhere between 1020 and 1028, shows that this site, occupied in the third century A.D., had been abandoned throughout the early Middle Ages and reoccupied only sometime before the middle of the tenth century.[34] This castle was, however, again abandoned within a few generations, and a new one was built several kilometers away at Montignac, closer to the main road. In other words, the need for a castle in this area initially prompted the reoccupation of an ancient structure in the tenth century, but by the early eleventh the strategic location of the castle had become so important that the older one was destroyed and a newer one put up nearby.

As this example suggests, globally, the multiplication of castles mentioned in the texts corresponds closely to an intense phase of new construction. The phenomenon, localized between 1020 and 1050 by our charters, is surely a little earlier and probably coincides with the turn of the century. It clearly indicates the weakening of local public power,

[33] Ademar, *Chronicon*, 3.25–29, pp. 146–50: Limoges, Saint-Hilaire, Saint-Maixent, Montignac in Dordogne, Limoges Bourg, Rancon, Chabon; 3.34–36, pp. 156–59: Gençay, Bellac, Brosse, Brantôme; 3.42, p. 165: Rochemeaux, Blaye, Beaujeu; 3.45, p. 167: Mortemart; 3.48, p. 171: Malemort, Castro Melurensi; 3.51, p. 174: Argentan, Massai; 3.60, pp. 185–86: Fractabotum, Ruffec, Montignac, Marcillac; 3.67, pp. 193–94: Blaye (2), Archiac, Bouteville, Fronsac. On Ademar's use of various terms to designate fortifications, see the conflicting interpretations of André Debord, "*Castrum* et *castellum* chez Adémar de Chabannes," *Archéologie médiévale* 9 (1979), 97–113, and Bernard Bachrach, "Early Medieval Fortifications in the West of France: A Revised Technical Vocabulary," *Technology and Culture* 16 (1975) 531–69.

[34] André Debord, "Fouille du *castrum* d'Andone," *Aquitania* 1 (1984).

weakening that followed closely on the disorders born of the ninth-
and tenth-century invasions and the concomitant struggles of the
greats for power. The mid-eleventh century seems calmer, but after
1074 the number of new mentions once again rises (26 percent of
those in the eleventh century). Few new names appear in the twelfth
century except between 1140 and 1180, during the period of struggle
by the counts of Angoulême first with their vassals and then with
the Plantagenets.[35]

Archaeological Evidence: The Mottes

The preceding study is based entirely on written documentation. It
is impossible, however, for such sources to give us a complete list of fortifications in the first feudal age. Even a superficial investigation of the
terrain gives a rich harvest of fortifications made of either earth or
stone about which our texts do not speak. There exists in particular a
large number of feudal mottes.[36]

Some historians tend to minimize the role of the motte, a mound of
dirt on which a fortification is built. Without denying the archaeological evidence, they relegate them to the role of secondary habitat designed for knightly families, a habitat without real military value. This
treatment constitutes an excessive simplification that distorts historical
reality. One can grant that many of the mottes discovered in the countryside were built on rather modest defensive sites; even so, one should
not minimize the difficulty of assaulting a wooden tower elevated some
ten meters above the bottom of the surrounding moat. Above all, one
must not forget that many of the *castra* and *castella* about which our
texts speak are simply such castral mottes. If one also considers that 32
percent of the castles cited by Ademar of Chabannes are mottes (and
25 percent new constructions), it seems difficult to dismiss the archaeological evidence provided by these mottes.[37] The catalogue provided

---

[35] For an analysis of the geographic distribution of castles, see Debord, *Société laïque*, p.
131. Until about 1050 the castles appear in areas of old and dense settlement, but thereafter they seem to move readily into assarting areas, especially the southern Saintonge.

[36] See Guy Fourquin, *Seigneurie et féodalité au Moyen Âge* (Paris, 1970), pp. 86–89; his
conclusion: "Basically the mottes concern the history of the rural seigneury and are not
the veritable fortifications of the feudal seigneury." He paraphrases Duby here (*L'économie rurale et la vie des campagnes dans l'Occident médiéval*, 2 vols. [Paris, 1962], 2.400).
Olivier Guillot does not raise the issue, even though he made a detailed study of Angevin
castles, (*Comte d'Anjou*, 1:281–352).

[37] See note 33. Leaving aside Limoges, Saint-Hilaire, and Saint-Maixent, which are exceptional cases (*civitates* and abbeys), one should add Matha (Ademar, *Chronicon*, 3.20, p.
138), which is not a tenth- or early eleventh-century construction. Marcillac, Matha, and
Fractabotum survive in good condition to this day. The *turris* of the viscounts of Limoges
was also a motte; see Paul Ducourtieux, *Histoire de Limoges* (Limoges, 1921), pp. 407–9.

here is preliminary but sufficiently rich to be used; a more complete list would only reinforce my suggestions.

The evidence provided by this research cannot, however, be used as is. We cannot consider in the same context works that were constructed at very different times.[38] Can we nevertheless use archaeological evidence in a study of what has traditionally been called the first feudal age? Of a total of 101 mottes and earthworks I have listed, forty-two are known elsewhere thanks to a written mention (*castrum, castellum, fortalicium*); this 41 percent of datable mottes seems a representative sample. And twenty-five (60 percent) of these mottes go back to the eleventh century.

The first and without doubt most important implication of this data is the number of fortifications—101 earthworks, of which fifty-nine are known only from archaeological searches.[39] If one remembers that the texts give us the names of eighty-eight castles before 1200, we see about 150 fortified sites of various strengths in the Charente.

Where do we find these mottes? If they were simply knightly residences, we would expect to find them dispersed throughout the Charente, in close correlation with the density of major fortifications. But that is absolutely not the case. It is not that there are no relations between these mottes and the castellan fortresses, but considered globally throughout the region their construction seems to be distinctly localized in certain privileged sites: (1) the principle concentration in the upper Saintonge and the Charente Périgourdine; (2) a strong density in the lower Saintonge, between the Charente and the Gironde; (3) a series on the southern flank of the forested spine that separates the Poitou from the Charente; and (4) a concentration in the northwest of the Angoumois. Practically none exist in the heart of the Angoumois or from the plateaus of the great and little Champagne (south of Saintes).

Several reasons can be offered for this distribution. Above all, the secondary mottes are particularly abundant in sectors that are today still heavily forested, and which were sectors of assarting in the Middle Ages; this holds for the forested spine between the Poitou and the

---

Ademar's narrative indicates that Blaye 2 (built by Geoffrey in opposition to his brother Auduin II, count of Angoulême, possessor of Blaye 1), Gençay, Brantôme, and Beaujeu were mottes. The same was probably true of Mortemart and of castrum Melurensis (destroyed by fire).

[38] This is why, among the unquestionably medieval earthworks we have encountered, this list includes only—unless a text or a dig confirms its early date—mottes properly speaking, excluding, among other types, quadrangular fortifications that are more recent in other regions.

[39] Debord, *Société laïque*, pp. 470–84.

Charente and for the lower Saintonge, which was the object of a great effort of reoccupation in the eleventh century.

It seems that the sector strictly controlled by the count of Angoulême, where he most effectively controlled his fortresses, knew few or no secondary mottes; these were the zones of heaviest population density, where the count retained more effective power over his subjects. There he tolerated no construction of secondary mottes, which one should note in passing is good proof of the military value of these works for defensive purposes. Where the count of Angoulême or the count of Poitier did not effectively control the countryside, castellan lords and lords with mottes divided up control.

I have treated the subject of the castral motte elsewhere, emphasizing that certain mottes had a purely military role whereas others served in the establishment of seigneural *castellanies*.[40] Many played a crucial role in the assarting of forest land. Speaking more generally, the motte was a major factor in social differentiation; this was no common residence for the "chivalric class." The *milites* were everywhere numerous; one need only consult a cartulary to realize this—present even where no evidence indicates a motte, and too numerous for each of them to possess a motte, even were we to postulate sites for which no evidence survives. We do not really know how the *milites* lived in their villages in the eleventh century. By the end of the twelfth, we see the lesser aristocracy living in *domus*, occasionally a *maison-forte*—but the castral motte was not of their doing. Whether the foundation of an important castle or a secondary fortification, the motte played a central role in the vast phenomenon known as the "castellan revolution" carried out by the *principes*.

The Rise of the Seigneury

The great increase of fortresses from the beginning of the eleventh century indicates a rapid weakening of public power. But by whom and in whose name were these castles built? Many authors have granted, as mentioned above, that in the regions they studied the castles had public origins: either direct construction by the king and counts or with their approval. Other scholars find more independent, indeed uncontrolled, construction. These two points of view may just reflect regional

[40] André Debord, "Motte castrale et habitat chevaleresque," *Mélanges d'histoire et d'archéologie médiévale en l'honneur du doyen M. de Boüard* (Mémoires et documents publiés par la Société de l'Ecole des Chartes, 27; Paris, 1982), pp. 83–89; idem, "A propos de l'utilisation des mottes castrales," *Château-Gaillard, Etudes de Castellologie médiévale* 11 (1983), 91–100.

variations (most of those holding the latter opinion study the southern regions), but we must also recognize two different conceptions of the origins of feudalism.[41] For this reason alone, it is impossible to ignore this problem when one undertakes a regional study of the tenth and eleventh centuries. It is only after attempting to clarify this situation that one can begin to delineate the process of devolution of the ban during the course of the eleventh century.

The Origin of Castles

Historians of feudal society who argue for a uniquely public origin of most of the fortifications of the first feudal age generally build on analyses made by legal historians, most notably R. Aubenas.[42] According to this perspective, the right to build a castle was one of the attributes of sovereignty, which we know from other evidence had devolved from the king to the territorial princes and on down the hierarchy. The nadir of this trend was reached when the guardians of fortresses themselves became independent. It would be unthinkable, however, that "the first adventurer to show up" would "erect such fortifications."[43] Aubenas attempts, for that matter, in surveying the various regions of France, to show that the fortifications had all been the result of comital or episcopal authority—notably in Aquitaine where "the power of the count was so great that only in his absence would lords or even viscounts attempt to build castles without his permission, and more than one passage reveals to us the lack of success that such initiative met."[44]

Such a point of view strikes this author as without foundation, for the Charente and more generally for Aquitaine. Unquestionably, the right to construct a fortification belonged juridically to those who exercised public power; we know that where the prince remained strong, as in Normandy, he jealously guarded such a prerogative.[45] That such a power was public proves also that the ban, or *vicaria castri* (tribunal or court) attached to the castle was also essentially of public origin in a

---

[41] Michel de Boüard reviews this controversy in "Quelques données archéologiques concernant le premier âge féodale," in *Les structures sociales de l'Aquitaine, du Languedoc et de l'Espagne au premier âge féodale* (Colloques internationaux du CNRS; Toulouse, 1968; Paris, 1969), p. 43 and notes.

[42] R. Aubenas, "Châteaux forts"; Jacques Yver's study of Normandy concurs; see "Les châteaux forts en Normandie jusqu'au milieu du XIIe siècle," *Bulletin de la Société des antiquaires de Normandie* 53 (1955–56), 28–121.

[43] Aubenas, "Châteaux forts," p. 561.

[44] Aubenas, "Châteaux forts," p. 572.

[45] In 1091, the sons of William the Conqueror recalled that in the time of their father no lord had the right to dig a ditch more than a *jet de terre* (about three meters) nor construct palisades *flanqués ou à redans;* see "*Consuetudines et justitie,*" in Charles H. Haskins, *Norman Institutions* (New York, 1918), p. 282. For a recent and more nuanced discussion of this issue, see David Bates, *Normandy before 1066* (London, 1982), pp. 99–127.

juridical sense. But can one thereby deduce that all the castles were like this, born of the will of the princes? This is an unlikely extrapolation.

The great number of castles and mottes in the Charente renders the hypothesis of public origins unlikely. Why would the counts have ordered the construction of so many castles in so little time, or, for that matter, why would they have wished to multiply to excess so dangerous a means of control? Note that those who espouse the hypothesis of the public origin of castles, aware of this problem, give very low estimates of the number of new constructions right up to the end of the eleventh century.[46] Rather, if the princes insisted repeatedly on their rights where castles were concerned, it was because this right was so often transgressed and because private individuals built them without concern for their lords.[47] Beyond that, this prerogative, as Robert Boutruche pointed out, "lost its effectiveness outside of the personal domain of the princes in question."[48] In other words, the problem should be posed in terms, not of legal relations, but of the interplay of social forces.

Indeed, the arguments proposed by Aubenas to underline the strength of the duke of Aquitaine cut both ways. The events reported by Ademar of Chabannes demonstrate that the counts kept the upper hand at Ruffec, Fractabotum, and Lusignan, but they also underline the precarious positions of a power constantly threatened by the rebellion of its own purported agents. And these accounts, do not inform us of the attitudes of those involved. Where we do get a glimpse of contemporary judgment, as in the case of Fractabotum, the evidence argues for a most tenuous comital or ducal hold over castellans. Ademar nowhere reproaches Aimeri of Rancon for building a motte without permission (an "adulterine" castle), but only for having made it against his lord (*contra seniorem suum*) even though "he had sworn his lord fidelity on the sandals of Saint Eparchius."[49] These remarks suggest at most a relationship between the duties of a vassal and the permission to build a castle—and therefore a means for the count to control some clearly threatening constructions. But even this is not certain.

More generally, Aubenas's argument relies on a key notion that he merely asserts: the impossibility for just any adventurer to afford such a permanent fortification.[50] This assertion doubtless represents a sane

[46] Guy Fourquin, *Seigneurie et féodalité*, pp. 86–89 continues to espouse this approach.
[47] This holds both for the Edict of Pîtres of 864 and the *Consuetudines et justitie* of 1091 in Normandy. De Boüard thinks that even at the time of William the Conqueror ducal power was not strong enough to enforce the rule strictly; see "Quelques données," p. 58.
[48] Robert Boutruche, *Seigneurie et féodalité* (Paris, 1970), 2:37.
[49] Ademar, *Chronicon*, 3.60, p. 185; for this paragraph, see the sources cited in note 21.
[50] Boutruche takes up Aubenas's argument as well as his expression *le premier seigneur venu;* see *Seigneurie*, 2:37.

reaction against the "anarchic" vision of the birth of feudalism, but it goes too far in the opposite direction. If indeed one sees no brigand chief easily establishing enduring power in the open countryside, one must not forget that below the level of counts and bishops lay a substantial class of people—the aristocratic masters of the soil, whether allodial or feudal—with the economic means and local support to build these structures. Indeed, until the twelfth century few fortresses were built of stone; they were themselves "of the soil."[51]

We know that the Charente, like so many regions in this period, had experienced a period of political disorder, a weakening of public institutions, and therefore also an intensification of insecurity, if only from endemic brigandage. In this region in particular, the aristocrats built up their fortifications to strengthen their own position amid the struggles that opposed the bishops of Angoulême and Count Arnald Manzer (the "Bastard," † 988), or even just to protect themselves. In other words, it was from the foundations of the castles that they built their power and autonomy.

My analysis of the eighty-eight castles mentioned in the documents before 1200 yields interesting results as to their public or private origin.[52] Of the twelve castles attested before the year 1000, one alone seems to have been an independent construction, two are of unknown origin, and nine are certainly public castles at the time of their appearance in the texts, although they may later have changed their status. Of the thirty-five castles appearing in the first half of the eleventh century, fourteen (40 percent) are unquestionably public in nature, either by belonging to the count of Angoulême or of Poitiers or by being held in fiefs from the count or the bishop. The other twenty-one (60 percent) are private constructions. The masters of eight of these appear from time to time at the comital court; the others have no known association with public authority. In the following fifty years (1050–1100), the situation worsened for the count, with about two-thirds of the castles built by independent men. Only in the twelfth century did that proportion reverse itself.

One can therefore see that an important percentage of the castles in the Charente were constructed for private purposes, particularly during the eleventh century. These private castles tend to cluster in the Charente-Girondine and the upper southern Saintonge, that is, in the same sector where one finds the largest number of mottes. The twelfth century, however, represents a complete reversal of this trend and marks a strong return of the authority of the prince.

[51] Aubenas seems to think that all the castles were of stone after the tenth century; see "Châteaux forts," p. 560, note 1, and p. 580.

[52] Debord, *Société laïque*, pp. 142–53.

The Castellan Ban

The situation we have just surveyed did not remain unchanged. On the other hand, many "public" castles were usurped in the course of the eleventh century by their keepers, initially placed there by the count. On the other, castles originally public or private each served their masters as a base from which to assert their authority over the surrounding open countryside.

The problem of the ban has made historians reluctant to admit the existence of private castles. Since the ban was a parcel of public authority, they resist the notion that this authority could have been held by private individuals unless it had been legally conferred on them and only gradually been usurped. To admit the existence of private castles would be to risk repeating a long-abandoned theory, that of the origin of the ban in the private demesne. Because this old theory is surely incorrect,[53] historians have preferred to speak of all castles as arising from public authority (royal, comital, or episcopal). And those who admit the existence of purely private castles tend not to address the more general question of banal authority.[54] Olivier Guillot, however, writes that banal seigneuries can emerge "more or less independent of the count," and that therefore "what establishes banal power in customary right . . . is the castle."[55] It seems to me that this is the general direction in which one must look, thus avoiding an inappropriate legalism. It is not necessary to make an appeal to demesnal ban to understand how private castellans could have reached beyond the limits of their traditional power of patronage and landholding to establish a banal seigneury in the open country.

We have already established for the Charente, as in other regions, the chronological coincidence of three phenomena: the heyday of castle building, a transformation in the nature of comital power, and the birth of *consuetudines* (customary rights and practices). Each development was linked to the disorders and insecurity of the tenth century, to the necessities of the reconquest and the disappearance of effective royal authority in the region. From that point on, the customary power of the count relied on the fortifications he controlled in the countryside, whether they came from his landed possessions or were given in guardianship or fief. The increasing use of the expression *vicaria castri* (tribunal of the castle) makes this point clearly: custom linked the exercise of the ban to the castle. As a result, when a powerful independent landowner built a banal seigneury in the eleventh century by

[53] See a review of the positions in Jean-François Lemarignier, *La France médiévale: Institutions et société* (Paris, 1970), pp. 119–20; and Boutruche, *Seigneurie*, 2:125–26.
[54] See Fournier, *Le peuplement rural en Basse Auvergne;* and M. Garaud, *Châtelains.*
[55] Guillot, *Comte d'Anjou,* 1:307.

using his castle as a base for imposing "evil customs," the ban he established was not simply the extension of his rights of landlord or of powerful patron over the surrounding countryside. And to accomplish this seigneurial authority he relied less on the (more or less) extorted acquiescence of comital power; he called the existence of the castle itself the ban. The progressive weakening of the royal and comital ban, by fragmenting the exercise of public power, gave priority to local power politics, and naturally the owners of fortified sites (whatever their title) sought to substitute their own authority for that of failing public powers by acquiring the right of the ban. When the process involved a private castellan, he obviously needed a strong base within the landed aristocracy to have the means to build his castle—that is, land and men.

If the possession of a castle involves the ban, however, the link does not necessarily mean the existence of a castellan seigneury. This latter development results from a complex evolution that took two separate but contemporary forms: (1) the ban confided *in toto* or in part by the counts, in wardship or in fief to castellans, was taken over by these latter who would then found independent castellanies according to the classic schema delineated by Duby for the Mâconnais; (2) around their private castles, the lords gradually built a zone of influence wherein they asserted banal authority. This local crystallization of the ban occurred in both cases under circumstances of obscure, long-term struggles between castellans, since all the castles did not necessarily give birth to independent castellanies (e.g., the case for many of the anonymous mottes listed); between the counts and the holders of fortifications (most notably comital ones); and above all between the aspiring seigneurial lords and the *pauperes* (defenseless ones) and the church. The most powerful, if indirect, testimony of these struggles comes from the Peace movement.

To understand the relationship here, we must first specify the moment when the castellan transformation occurred, even if we cannot delineate all the chronological steps or all the struggles that preceded it. In the Charente, the establishment of the castellan seigneury came in a series of overlapping waves. The great period of construction occurred from 990 to 1050 and reached a peak in the final thirty years. During this feverish period of activity, the notion of *vicaria castri* took hold, appearing for the first time in 1007 and becoming a common term after 1020. It represents, in a sense, the realization of what the castle meant, of the power of constraint it conferred; from this point on, the castle tended to crystallize around it a seigneurial castellany.

The triumph of this form of political dominion seems firm from the moment it appeared as the normal element of social organization. The question is, from what moment? There was a *dominus* at Aubeterre from 1004 on, and one at Surgères only in 1199. One might hold that the seigneurial castellany existed from the moment the word *castellania* (or its synonyms) appears in the texts, even if all the castellanies had not yet been built or had not yet consolidated a seigneury; from that early time on, the dismemberment of public power had become an accepted political and geographic phenomenon. In the Charente, the first two mentions of the castellany appear in 1067 and 1068 and increase notably thereafter.[56] Therefore, the process reached a decisive stage between ca. 1020 and 1060–70. One can, however, make more precise observations by considering two specific moments: ca. 1030 and 1050–60.

The end of the long and influential reigns of William the Great (1029) and William IV of Angoulême (1028) marks the spread of the notion of *vicaria castri*. The situation still seemed good for the counts: they controlled more or less rigorously about thirteen castles (50 percent of the twenty-six we have information on), whereas seigneurial castellans seemed to control only about nine, of which six were held as direct fiefs from the counts. This picture corresponds to other indications of comital power in this period: profoundly altered in both nature and foundations, it nonetheless remained strong.

By the period 1050–60, the situation had fully evolved and the notion of castellany become habitual among scribes. When the word *castellania* entered the texts toward 1067, it reflected faithfully the situation that had developed between 1030–60—a notable decline in the counts' influence. The data suggest that the time of independent castellans derives less from the existence of obstreperous guardians of comital castles than from the initiatives of the landowning aristocracy.

Obviously one cannot push these figures too far. To an important extent they are the product of the hazards of documentation. Nevertheless, they are interesting in that they give a *minimal* point of view: given the conservative nature of diplomatic language, a more abundant and precise documentation could only give still greater support to the picture presented here, possibly even indicating an earlier and more global reach to the evolution in question. As is, the data confirm that the phenomenon of the seigneurial castellany had become preponderant between 1030 and 1050 *at the latest,* and that it grew still more powerful thereafter, with the key role played not by comital castles but by ones of private or ecclesiastical origin. It is therefore not necessary to go into much detail for the year 1200. By that time, of the seventy castles for which we can discern information about the

---

[56] Debord, *Société laïque,* p. 158, notes 66–67.

seignuery, at most thirteen were comital (18 percent), three were ecclesiastical (4 percent), and forty-eight were the center of seigneurial castellanies (68 percent).[57]

Vicaria Castri, Castles, and the Peace of God

Among the *consuetudines* mentioned in the earliest charters was the right of *vicaria*.[58] The importance of this particular right lies in its direct association with the exercise of justice, one of the basic elements of the ban. Because the word was used in the tenth century to designate a jurisdictional unit, the *vicarius*, the study of its changing meaning takes on a particular interest. At the beginning of the eleventh century the term was still used in the traditional sense to localize landed property or villages; at the same time, and in the course of the eleventh century, the term seems to have also referred to an archdeaconate.[59] But with increasing frequency from the beginning of the eleventh century, the word designated the district of a castle. In the Charente, the oldest mention came in 1007, and references multiply from the period around 1020–30.[60] Occasionally the word *castrum* does not even appear, leading some scholars to unduly prolong the life of certain Carolingian *vicariates*. In fact, there is no difference between the term *in vicaria castro Auniaco* (ca. 1038) and its contemporary *in vicaria Audenacensis* (1044).[61]

Still more frequently the term *vicaria* appears in lists of *consuetudines*. It almost always refers in such cases to the right of constraint permitting the lord to intervene in his own lands to pursue and seize delinquents—more a right of police rather than justice. But it goes without saying that the exercise of *vicaria* favors the development of the judicial

---

[57] The seventy sites in consideration are those seigneuries for which the documentation permits us to determine their nature.

[58] The issue of *vicaria* is the object of important studies: Ferdinand Lot, "La *vicaria* et le *vicarius*,"*Nouvelle revue historique de droit français et étranger* 17 (1893), 281–301; Louis Halphen, "Prévôts et voyers au XIe siècle," *Le Moyen Age* 8 (1902), 297–325; Marcel Garaud, *Essai sur les institutions judiciaires du Poitou sous le gouvernement des comtes indépendants* (Poitiers, 1910); Georges Duby, "Recherches sur les institutions judiciaires pendant le Xe et le XIe siècle dans le sud de la Bourgogne," *Le Moyen Age*, 52 (1946), 149–94, and 53 (1947), 15–38 (rpt. in *Hommes et structures*, pp. 7–60); Garaud, "Construction des châteaux"; Jacques Boussard, *Le gouvernement d'Henri II Plantagenêt* (Paris, 1956), pp. 312–27.

[59] See Debord, *Société laïque*, p. 122, notes 139–40.

[60] *Cartulaire de Saint-Jean-d'Angély*, 1:106, dated 1016 incorrectly. For further examples, see Debord, *Société laïque*, p. 122, note 142.

[61] *Cartulaire de Saint-Jean-d'Angély*, 2:107, in the same act cited in note 60. For further examples, see Debord, *Société laïque*, p. 123.

court of he who owns it.[62] The word also has a fiscal sense of collecting
fines for various infractions of the law.[63] This right of judicial constraint covered minor cases as well as crimes, and the lords always distinguished the *vicaria de quatuor rebus* (homicide, theft, rape, and
arson).[64] Just as the *vicaria* was more and more often attached to the
castle, so by similar means seigneurial justice emerged.

In a sense, there is nothing new here; the chronology corresponds
closely to that concerning castles, the ban, and customs, but one cannot over emphasize the link between the exercise of justice (*vicaria*)
and the castle; the former is one of the earliest and most important
of the *consuetudines*. Beyond any reflection on the juridical nature of
the transformation of the ban into customs, the essential fact remains
that the exercise of this ban is intimately linked to the existence of a
castle, and that, in the last analysis, for the historian as well as for
those men and women who submitted to this new authority, the ban
was the castle.[65]

Significance of the Peace Movement

Confronted with a veritable castellan revolution, the counts and
bishops made an immense effort to retain their authority, that is, to retain their power of command, justice, and police, or, as they put it, "the
Peace," whose maintenance was initially a royal attribute. Historians
have generally interpreted the Peace of God as an effort on the part of
the episcopate to substitute itself for crumbling royal authority in the
essential mission of the sovereign to maintain order.[66] The movement
was particularly precocious in Aquitaine, where the king was completely absent from the last third of the tenth century. The early case
of the council gathered at Charroux on 1 June 989 by Archbishop Gom-
bald of Bordeaux, not satisfied with reiterating the condemnations of

[62] Lot ("La *vicaria* et le *vicarius*," p. 285) and Garaud ("Construction des châteaux," pp.
69–70) assume that *vicaria* indicates rights of justice, in particular high justice. But the
texts from the Saintonge (used by Boussard, *Gouvernement*, p. 312 and notes) show that
it constitutes rights of pursuit; see Debord, *Société laïque*, p. 123, note 147.

[63] In 1067–72: *exactionem que vigerie subjaceat* (*Cartulaire de Notre-Dame-de-Saintes*, 2:43).
In 1024–30: *alaudus liber et a vicaria et ab omni redditu* (*Cartulaire de Saint-Jean-d'Angély*,
1:77).

[64] Debord, *Société laïque*, p. 123, note 149.

[65] The masters of the castles delegated the function of judicial constraint to a *vicarius*,
who has only a name in common with a Carolingian *vicarius;* see Debord, *Société laïque*,
p. 124.

[66] Emile Amann and Auguste Dumas, *L'église au pouvoir des laïques, 888–1057* (*L'histoire
de l'église depuis les origines jusqu'à nos jours*, ed. A. Fliche and V. Martin, vol. 7; Paris,
1943), pp. 489–500; Lemarignier, *France médiévale*, pp. 196–203.

those plundering church and assaulting clergy, extended its scope by anathematizing those who might ravish other defenseless people among the laity.[67]

The movement continued to expand with the active sponsorship of Duke William V: In 994, he convened a major council at Limoges, where he and his magnates reciprocally swore a pact of peace and justice in the presence of the bishops of the principality.[68] At a council assembled in his own capital of Poitiers (ca. 1000), the duke and his lay allies took control of the Peace movement. Reiterating the canons of Charroux, the council provided for the presentation of litigation concerning possible infractions "before the prince of that region [duke, counts], or before some judge of that *pagus*."[69] From that time on, the duke and his son dedicated an important part of their activity to this movement for the peace, inaugurating, according to Glaber, the great wave of councils that swept the Frankish realm at the approach of the millennium of the Passion: at Charroux and Limoges (1028, 1031) and at Poitiers (1032, 1038).[70] By taking over the direction of the Peace movement in Aquitaine, William attempted to consolidate a territorial principality in the sense proposed by Dhondt, by fully assuming, over the other Aquitanian counties he dominated, the role normally assigned to the king. The presence at all the Aquitanian Peace councils of the bishop of Limoges demonstrates this point most clearly: ecclesiastically Limoges, from the metropolitan of Bourges, did not belong in a group with the others (Poitiers, Angoulême, Saintes, Pèrigueux), which were part of Bordeaux's province; politically, however, it was part of William's duchy.

From this point of view, the Peace movement, encouraged by the duke, gives the measure of his prestige and his power: "All the princes

[67] Charroux (989), can. 2; Mansi 19:90; the text is translated in Appendix A of this volume. For a detailed analysis, see Roger Bonnaud-Delamare, "Les institutions de la paix en Aquitaine au XIe siècle" *La paix* (Recueils de la Société Jean Bodin, 14; Brussels, 1962), 1:415–87.

[68] Ludwig Huberti, *Studien zur Rechtsgeschichte der Gottesfrieden end Landfrieden* (Ansbach, 1892), p. 133. Bonnaud-Delamare tries to cast doubt on this council ("Institutions de la paix," pp. 427–28), but his argument is unconvincing in the face of the primary documentation; see Ademar *Chronicon*, 3.35, p. 158, and two independent unedited texts (see Richard Landes, Chapter 8 in this volume).

[69] See Poitiers (ca. 1000), can. 1; Mansi 19:226, translated in Appendix A of this volume.

[70] For a detailed discussion of the dates, see Bonnaud-Delamare, "Institutions de la paix," pp. 437–39, and Hoffmann, *Gottesfriede und Treuga Dei* (Schriften der Monumenta Germaniae historica, 20; Stuttgart 1964), pp. 31–38. On Poitiers ca. 1000, see Richard Landes, "The Dynamics of Heresy and Reform in Limoges: A Study of Popular Participation in the 'Peace of God' (994–1033)," *Historical Réflections / Réflexions historiques* 14 (1987), 507, note 141.

of Aquitaine were present."[71] We find yet further evidence of William's authority over the church in one of the changes between the Charroux council of 989 and the Poitiers council of 1000/14. In the first, the judgment of clerics in conflict with laypeople had been reserved for the diocesan bishop;[72] the later council brought such cases back to lay courts controlled in principle by the duke. This situation contrasts with that in the Mâconnais, as noted by Duby: there the council of Anse (994) and those that followed, by reinforcing the immunities of Cluny, were directed against the count of Mâcon, Duby saw in the Peace movement in Burgundy a cause as well as a result of the weakening of comital power.[73] It is clear that the duke of Aquitaine used the church and the Peace movement, whose initiative he took in hand, to reinforce his own power within the principality. The explicit mention of comital tribunals directly connected the princes who took the peace oaths, such as the count of Angoulême, to this substitution of the duke for the king in the role of supreme judicial authority.[74]

But the duke did not have genuine control of the enforcement of the Peace. That, at least, seems to be the indication of subsequent Peace councils, for example, at Limoges (1031). There it is no longer a matter of recourse to public tribunals but of purely ecclesiastical means of coercion—in particular, the use of the interdict if the *principes militiae Lemovicensis* became recalcitrant.[75] This turnaround seems all the more remarkable since Duke William the Fat was at this council, although he did not convene it.[76]

The reasons for this eventual setback are numerous: they relate to the growing independence of the church in this pre-Gregorian period (a point to which we return) but also to the fact that the public institutions on which the duke built his edifice were worm-eaten. The canons of the Peace councils give us valuable indications about the limits of public power and more specifically the actual state of comital justice at the beginning of the eleventh century. The traditional judicial structures still existed toward 1000, since the first canon of Poitiers places much responsibility on the tribunals of the *pagus*. But the count of Poitiers found it necessary to remind the council of the existence of these jurisdictions, normally competent to handle infractions of

[71] "Adfuerunt omnes Aquitaniae principes"; Ademar, *Chronicon*, 3.69, p. 194.

[72] Charroux (989), can. 3; Mansi 19:69.

[73] Duby, *Société mâconnaise*, p. 159–60.

[74] See note 69. The count of Angoulême is not specifically mentioned in the canon, but his well-known association with the duke makes his presence almost certain at these assemblies. Indeed, our only manuscript source for both Charroux and Poitiers come from a canonical collection from Angoulême (Vatican Reg. lat. 1127).

[75] Mansi 19:1378–80.

[76] Richard, *Histoire des comtes de Poitou*, 1:224.

peace and order. All the more remarkable then that the council explicitly anticipated situations in which one of the parties in dispute would refuse to appear before such a court (*qui sub districtione justitiae stare noluerit*) and in which the judge would be impotent to impose sentence (*si justitiam facere non potuerit*). In such cases, all the oathtakers (*principes et episcopos*) must unite in their efforts to impose justice on the recalcitrant offender.[77]

As a result, by the dawn of the eleventh century the powerful duke of Aquitaine could not guarantee the normal working of his judicial institutions. His dependence on the church to develop peace institutions bears witness not only to the growing social disorder—that is, the weakening of Carolingian military and administrative structures—but also to the profound decline of judicial structures as well, represented above all by the public power represented by the count of the *pagus*.

Institutions of Peace and the Birth of Consuetudines

Jean-François Lemarignier has shown the links between the weakening of public power in both structure and effectiveness and a new conception of the legitimacy of power, one no longer founded "on an explicit delegation of the sovereign authority but [rather] on custom and the testimony of collective memory."[78] This new conception expressed itself above all by the ever more common use of the term *consuetudines*, which referred both to the rights of ban and justice and to the profits associated with their exercise (the texts most often make reference to this latter meaning). The word appears in this sense around the year 1000 and becomes current between 1020 and 1080, according to the general observations of Lemarignier, confirmed in the Mâconnais as well as in the Poitou.

In the Charente, the documentation does not contradict these chronological parameters. The earliest certain use of the term *consuetudines* comes in 1003, applied to a tax on the transport of salt, also qualified as a *mala rapina* (evil extortion). Mentions multiply around 1030.[79] Especially noteworthy is the charter of foundation for Notre-Dame-de-Saintes in 1047, in which Geoffrey Martel, count of Anjou, in renouncing all customary rights over the property with which he endows the

[77] Poitiers (ca. 1000), can. 1; Mansi 19:226.

[78] Jean-François Lemarignier, "La dislocation du *pagus* et le problème des *consuetudines*: Xe-XIe siècles," in *Mélanges d'histoire du moyen âge dédiés à Louis Halphen* (Paris, 1951), pp. 401–10; quotation from Duby, *Société mâconnaise*, pp. 207–8; see also idem, *L'économie rurale*, 2:452–61; Garaud, *Châtelains*, p. 111–68; and Guillot, *Comte d'Anjou*, 1:370–96.

[79] *Cartulaire de Saint-Cyprien de Poitiers*, ed. Louis Redet (*Archives historiques du Poitou*, 3; 1874), p. 311. See Debord, *Société laïque*, p. 118, notes 109–10.

abbey, gives a list of those *consuetudines: arbergamentum* (billeting), *exercitum* (draft), *questam* (taxation), *procurationem* (requisitions), *cabaugada* (cavalry), *vigeria* (justice). This text deserves attention on its own: it provides a virtually complete list of the rights of public power (ban) as conceived by the Carolingians. One might add (as do other texts) some additional rights: taxes on the transport of salt (*consuetudo salis*), on riverine or maritime navigation (*ribatgium*), tolls on markets (*venda*).[80] Such a conception of power was naturally damaging to the count's authority. Rather than emanating from royal sovereignty (whose main representative was the count), power was now only a customary authority; it thus differed little in the popular mind from the private character of the landed seigneury whose demands also went under the name *consuetudines* since they too were legitimated by long usage.

The change in the juridical foundations of power weakened comital authority by lowering the count's prestige and by changing, to his disadvantage, the means of exercising power. The count gradually found himself limited to a rearguard action, trying to maintain as many of his prerogatives as possible when the situation favored him. But since customs applied to him as well, he could no longer sustain himself as the master. Olivier Guillot has described how customs imposed themselves on Fulk Nerra from the outset of his rule.[81] Furthermore, just as these customs defined authority, so they characterized the power of individual property owners. The oldest mentions of customs refer to the ruling elite (counts of Poitiers, Angoulême, Anjou) but very soon to minor officials, castellans, even private individuals (the viscount of Aulnay, Bertrand of Varaize, William of Parthenay, Isembert of Chatelaillon) and in at least one case to a ministerial (the viscount of Aulnay's senechal).[82] The customs formed an integral part of these men's patrimony, since they gave them along with men and property; indeed they were soon given as fiefs. In 1067, for example, Helias of Born retained control of the customs of Saint-Julien-de-l'Escap, land which he held as a fief (*in casamento*) from Ostendus, lord of Taillebourg, and which he ceded to Notre-Dame-de-Saintes.[83] Georges Duby has proposed a chronology of customs and banal taxation—one that the infrequent charters from the Charente neither prove nor contradict.[84]

The diplomatic texts mentioned above do not permit us to see how contemporaries reacted to the transformation and transfer of power,

---

[80] Debord, *Société laïque*, p. 118, note 111.

[81] Guillot, *Comte d'Anjou*, p. 371.

[82] See Debord, *Société laïque*, p. 119, note 113.

[83] *Cartulaire de Notre-Dame-de-Saintes*, p. 23; also, *Cartulaire de Saint-Jean-d'Angély*, 1:89 (1060–70).

[84] The new exactions first appear in the last quarter of the eleventh century according to Duby, *Economie rurale*, p. 453.

nor to determine how and to what extent "public authority" tried to counter the process. At most the charters show us pious, anxious men, in the grips of remorse, renouncing the *malae consuetudines*, that is, their (or their ancestors') earlier efforts to extend a little further and a little more intensely the power of the ban they possessed.[85] The charters also reveal the efforts of the church to protect its property by renewing emphasis on their immunities,[86] a strategy that contributed significantly to the count's growing impotence since clerics treated his ban in the same way as simple laymen's.[87] And the documents concerning the Peace movement—conciliar canons, miracle tales, sermons, historical narratives—indicate yet another response, the effort of the prince to maintain his right of arbitration, and still more the policy of the Aquitanian episcopacy to free its churches from "bad customs" and to obtain guarantees to that end.

Historians generally interpret the Peace of God as an effort to limit violence and disorder; not many deny that such concerns, which would soon give rise to the Truce of God, were fundamental.[88] But when Ademar of Chabannes, speaking of the council of Charroux in 1028, wrote that its purpose was *firmare pacem*, it would be excessive to interpret this only as an effort to suppress or minimize the ravages of war in itself.[89] Unquestionably, the Peace found a theoretical justification in the desire to restore on earth the order willed by God. But, as Bernhard Töpfer and Christian Lauranson-Rosaz have pointed out, this ideological justification should not mask the more pressing motives that drove the episcopacy to act. Granted disorder hampered the church spiritually; it also damaged it economically.[90]

The use of brute force these councils condemned could take forms other than those of pillage and warfare. The fragmentation of banal authority that took hold at the turn of the millennium in the form of *consuetudines* naturally tempted the *principes* who controlled them to extend them (*malae consuetudines*) to the detriment of those elements in the population who were not militarily strong—the church and its

[85] By 1003 the monks of Saint-Cyprien had considered a custom on the transport of their salt to be a *mala rapina* (*Cartulaire de Saint-Cyprien*, p. 311); mentions in the *Cartulaire de Saint-Jean-d'Angély:* ca. 1037 (1:130), 1039 (1:223), 1058–87 (1:31).

[86] Jean-François Lemarignier, *Etudes sur les privilèges d'exemption et de juridiction ecclésiastique normandes depuis les origines jusqu'en 1140* (Paris, 1937).

[87] Duby, *Société mâconnaise*, p. 160.

[88] For example, Georges Duby, "Les laïcs et la Paix de Dieu," in *I laici nella "societas christiana" dei secoli XI e XII* (Milan, 1966), pp. 448–61 (rpt. in *Hommes et structures*, pp. 227–40).

[89] Ademar, *Chronicon*, 3.69, p. 194; see Duby, "Laïcs et la Paix," p. 229.

[90] Bernhard Töpfer, *Volk und Kirche zur Zeit des beginnenden Gottesfriedensbewegung im Frankreich* (Berlin, 1957), pp. 7–28; Christian Lauranson-Rosaz (Chapter 5) in this volume.

rights of immunity, and still more generally the *pauperes,* the mass of free people and small free holders.[91] In fact, if the canons of the council at Charroux in 989 seem to condemn all kinds of pillage of the defenseless, those of Le Puy (994) were already more explicit: they condemned requisitions (*ad suum nihil portet, vel ad castellum bastire aut obsedire*) and the imposition of labor services (*redemptio*) on male or female peasants, in particular those working on contested land.[92] When the council of Poitiers (ca. 1000) referred to disputes over *res invasae,* it meant abuses of the ban. The echo can be heard in the charters: The monks of Saint-Cyprien called the *consuetudo de sale* (salt tax) the count collected from them a *mala rapina* (evil seizure).[93] When Geoffrey Martel ceded to Notre-Dame-de-Saintes the long and interesting list of customs cited above, he explicitly abjured the practice of raising them by force or extortion (*vi aut terrore aliquo*).[94] A text from 1039 associated the *vicarius* (right of justice) with unjust customs (*vicariam aut aliquam controversiam seu consuetudinem injustam*).[95] Often enough, when a lord renounced his "customs," he did so in order that the peasants might live in peace (*ut in pace quieti vivant [rustici]*).[96] As for the defenseless— *pauperes, villani, agricultores, rustici*—over whom the church extended the protective shelter of its conciliar decrees, they did so for the free-holding peasantry, *not* for all Christians; the canons explicitly recognized the rights of the *principes* to a free hand in dealing with their own peasants on their own land (*nisi unusquisque de sua terra aut de suo alode vel de suo beneficio*).[97]

The canons concerning the clergy and their property are, however, explicit. The canons of Le Puy condemn the imposition of any evil custom on church lands. In this sense, the most characteristic text comes from the abbey of Saint-Maixent, which preserves the trace of a council held at Poitiers around 1030.[98] The charter recorded the count of Poitiers' judgment recognizing the judicial rights of the abbey over several of its domains around Melle. The preamble reported the request of King Robert that peace councils be held throughout his kingdom and

---

[91] Duby mentions this aspect in passing; see "Laïcs et la Paix," p. 230.
[92] Le Puy (994), cans. 2, 4, in Huberti, *Studien zur Rechtsgeschichte,* p. 123.
[93] *Cartulaire de Saint-Cyprien,* p. 311, note.
[94] *Cartulaire de Notre-Dame-de-Saintes,* p. 4.
[95] *Cartulaire de Saint-Jean-d'Angély,* 1:223.
[96] *Cartulaire de Saint-Jean-d'Angély,* 1:169.
[97] Le Puy (994), can. 4, in Huberti, *Studien zur Rechtsgeschichte,* p. 123.
[98] *Chartes et docs. de Saint-Maixent,* 1:109–11; see partial translation in Appendix A of this volume. Analyzed by Bonnaud-Delamare, "Institutions de la paix," pp. 451–56, who dates it to between 1027 and 1033. But the mention of King Robert suggests that the act dates from 10 December 1030. As the text indicates, the charter in question was drawn up shortly after the council, the latter definitely dating to 1030. Hoffmann dates it to 1029–31; see *Gottesfriede,* pp. 35–36.

noted that William VI (the Fat) had just held one in his capital which stipulated respect for church property. In the aftermath, the monks complained to him at a *placitum* over which he presided at Melle shortly thereafter. They protested the *malae consuetudines* the count's prevots had imposed; and, in the spirit of the earlier peace council, the count recognized the monk's demands. This text offers exceptional evidence of a link between the institutions of the Peace and the new state of a society based on *consuetudines*.[99] There is, moreover, an interesting definition of these customs: the inquest undertaken on the count's orders went back to the earliest living memory, some seventy years into the past; thus the mid-tenth century served as the base referent.[100]

In this sense, if it is true that this council constituted an extension of the earlier Poitiers council (ca. 1000), and that William the Fat thereby indicated his will to continue his father's policies, it is nevertheless difficult to follow Bonnaud-Delamare's reasoning here that this text indicates a strengthening of the duke's justice.[101] In fact, the duke was the loser here, since his own ban (exercised in his name by his agents, the prevots, who are incriminated by the monastic scribes composing the charter) was also limited by custom. And the monks, to assure their future, extracted a new kind of immunity for the property under litigation.[102] The duke was losing the initiative, a trend indicated by the reference to the king as the source of inspiration for the Peace. As Bonnaud-Delamare himself noted, the monks thereby diminished the role of the duke.[103] At this point, the Poitou seems to approach the situation observed in the Mâconnais by Duby in which the Peace participated in the dissolution of comital power.[104] The only real difference between the two regions was the delay of a generation secured by the efforts of William the Great.

From the year 1000 on, those that the conciliar texts and the historian Ademar of Chabannes called *principes* and *milites* held the field. Behind a facade of worm-eaten institutions, a profound and irreversible crisis developed. The king was no longer—and had not been for some time in Aquitaine—capable of imposing that which, in the words

---

[99] It offers an excellent illustration to the arguments of Duby ("Laïcs et la Paix," 229–30).

[100] "[T]estatus est patrem suum judicem fuisse plusquam 70 annos, seque post mortem eius annis quamplurimis exigisse huius rei negotium"; *Chartes et docs. de Saint-Maixent,* 1:110.

[101] Bonnaud-Delamare, "Institutions de la paix," p. 456.

[102] "In totam terram supra scriptam nullus vicarius, nec ullus praepositus nullum intersignum mittat"; *Chartes et docs. de Saint-Maixent,* 1:110.

[103] Bonnand-Delamare, "Institutions de la paix," p. 455.

[104] Duby, *Société mâconnaise,* pp. 159–60.

of Odo of Blois to King Robert, was "the root and fruit of your office, that is to say, justice and peace."[105] The duke of Aquitaine tried to ride the Peace movement started by the church at Charroux in 989 to impose his own peace. But he eventually foundered on the rocks of his subordinates' castles; the castellans imposed their authority everywhere in the open countryside. By 1030, nothing qualitatively distinguished the count's ban from the ban that had fallen into the hands of his castellans.

After this time, the Peace movement fell into the hands of the Aquitanian bishops, whose councils sought to channel and domesticate not only the violence but also and above all the banal demands made by the masters of the castles. In this sense the distinctions made between good and evil customs justified the existence of a castellan ban, in the same way that the comital ban had become customary. The *vicaria castri*, the right to constraint and justice that emanated from the castle, became, little by little, the framework for a normative peace.[106] The counts and bishops could not impose their notion of peace. They had to come to terms with the *principes*, the masters of castles. One might say that around 1060–70, when the *castellania* asserted itself as the new political and judicial cadre, the castellan revolution was complete.

---

[105] Letter of Odo of Blois to King Robert II in 1023, in *The Letters and Poems of Fulbert of Chartres*, ed. Frederick Behrends (Oxford, 1976), pp. 152–54.
[106] Duby already noted the bond between the institutions of Peace and seigneurial justice; "Recherches sur les institutions judiciaires," p. 28.

7

The Peace of God and the Cult of the Saints in Aquitaine in the Tenth and Eleventh Centuries

Daniel F. Callahan

For the past decade a sweet fragrance has wafted forth from many works of medieval studies. The odor of sanctity seems to have penetrated nearly all areas of research on the Middle Ages.[1] The creative uses of saints' lives, miracles, translations, and liturgical commemorations have illuminated the past in ways never envisioned by the earliest Bollandists. This light has been especially valuable for our understanding of the early Middle Ages.[2] It is appropriate, therefore, to consider the role of the saints in that movement which was so important in the transition between the early and central medieval periods, namely, the Peace of God.[3]

The Peace of God was instituted by the church in southern France in the late tenth century to try to protect ecclesiastical property and non-combatants, such as women, merchants, pilgrims, and priests, from the restive and violent warriors of the period. It was an attempt by the

Some of the ideas in this essay were presented in a different format in a paper delivered at a meeting of the American Historical Association, San Francisco, December 1983. A portion of it was also given at a meeting of the Delaware Valley Medieval Association, Philadelphia, October 1985.

[1] A useful recent annotated bibliography appears in Stephen Wilson, ed., *Saints and Their Cults* (Cambridge, 1983), pp. 309–417. See the thoughtful review article by John Howe on this work in *Catholic Historical Review* 72 (1986), 425–36.

[2] Especially provocative in this area are Peter Brown, *The Cult of the Saints* (Chicago, 1981), and Patrick Geary, *Furta Sacra* (Princeton, N.J., 1978). The second work has been amended in its German translation. For Aquitaine, see Joseph-Claude Poulin, *L'idéal de sainteté dans l'Aquitaine carolingienne d'après les sources hagiographiques (750–950)* (Québec, 1975).

[3] Philippe Contamine, *War in the Middle Ages*, trans. Michael Jones (Oxford, 1984), pp. 270–71, expresses the significance of the *pax Dei* to the change in this fashion: "In large measure it was as a function of and around the notion of peace that a new balance of society was effected, though not without troubles and crises."

church to restore some order to a world increasingly bereft of public authority. Hartmut Hoffmann's study in the Schriften of the *Monumenta Germaniae historica* has served as the best one-volume survey, and Herbert Cowdrey's "Peace and Truce of God" the best brief introduction, to the subject.[4]

In this piece I limit myself to a consideration of the early movement between 975 and 1050, the time of its formation, the period Thomas Bisson has referred to as the "sanctified peace"—as opposed to the later "institutional peace" in which the movement was taken up by emperors, kings, and popes and made a significant part of organizational policy.[5] I focus solely on the duchy of Aquitaine, the place of origin and first home of the Peace movement, and address two specific questions: why was it in Aquitaine at this particular time in conjunction with relic gatherings that the Peace movement arose, and why did oaths play so significant a role at these assemblies? There do not seem to have been earlier ecclesiastical meetings with such large numbers of relics, often brought from great distances.

The sources on the Aquitanian Peace councils leave much to be desired. What remains to us are a few summary canons, such as those from the councils of Charroux (ca. 989), Poitiers (1000/14), and Bourges (1031);[6] brief references in saints' *vitae* or miracles, such as the material on a gathering in the Auvergne (ca. 994) and one at Bourges (ca. 1038);[7] and charter references such as those for Le Puy (ca. 994) and Poitiers (ca. 1030).[8] The vast bulk of the information about the role of the relics at such affairs comes from accounts of gatherings at

[4] Hartmut Hoffmann, *Gottesfriede und Treuga Dei*, (Schriften der Monumenta Germaniae historica, 20; Stuttgart, 1964); H. E. J. Cowdrey, "The Peace and Truce of God in the Eleventh Century," *Past and Present* 46 (1970), 42–67. Roger Bonnaud-Delamare, "Les institutions de la paix en Aquitaine au XIe siècle," *Recueils de la société Jean Bodin pour l'histoire comparative des institutions* 14 (1961), 415–87, has much useful information, although there are many inaccuracies. Hans-Werner Goetz, "Kirchenschutz, Rechtswahrung und Reform: Zu den Zielen und zum Wesen der frühen Gottesfriedensbewegung in Frankreich," *Francia* 7 (1983), 193–239, is a somewhat narrow consideration of several significant aspects of the Peace of God. It is particularly useful for its bibliographic material.

[5] Thomas Bisson, "The Organized Peace in Southern France and Catalonia, ca. 1140–ca. 1233," *American Historical Review* 82 (1977), especially pp. 292–95.

[6] For Charroux, see Mansi 19:89–90; for Poitiers, see Mansi 19:265–68; for Bourges, see Mansi 19:501–8.

[7] For the gathering in the Auvergne in the early 990s, see *Trans. et mirac. s. Viviani*, p. 283; for Bourges ca. 1038, see *Mirac. s. Benedicti*, 5.2–4, pp. 192–98, and Louis Buhot de Kersers, *Essai de reconstitution du cartulaire de Saint-Sulpice de Bourges* (Mémoires de la société des antiquaires du centre, 5; Bourges, 1912), p. 38.

[8] For Le Puy, see *Cartulaire de Sauxillanges*, pp. 52–53, and evaluation by Elizabeth Magnou-Nortier, "La place du concile du Puy (v. 994) dans l'evolution de l'idée de paix," in *Melanges offerts à Jean Dauvillier* (Toulouse, 1979), pp. 489–506; for Poitiers ca. 1030, see *Chartes et docs. de Saint-Maixent*, pp. 109–11.

Limoges (ca. 994, 1028, 1029, and especially 1031, the report of which fills over forty columns in Mansi).[9] Unfortunately, almost all this Limousin material comes from the pen of Ademar of Chabannes, a polemicist who was so intent on promoting the apostolicity of Saint Martial of Limoges that all his writings, over a thousand manuscript folios, must be treated with extreme caution, especially when one is considering the cult of the saints.[10]

Yet the sources are sufficient, I submit, to allow a tentative answer to our initial question. The Peace of God begins first in Aquitaine at this time at relic gatherings as the result of the conjunction of at least five factors. First to be considered is a feature found throughout most, if not all, of the kingdom of France ca. 1000—weak civil authority at the highest levels unable to curb aggressive warriors who were constructing a rapidly growing number of fortresses, including, especially in Aquitaine and the Loire valley, the new motte and bailey variety.[11] Hugh Capet and then Robert the Pious had little real authority south of the Loire. At the top of the duchy of Aquitaine, far and away the largest subunit of France at the time, was the ducal line of the Williams centered in Poitiers, in particular William V, the Great (ca. 993–1030).[12] It was this William who recognized the value of the Peace

---

[9] For the gathering at Limoges ca. 994, see Ademar of Chabannes, *Chronicon*, 3.35, p. 158; and Ademar, *Commemoratio abbatum S. Martialis*, in *Chroniques de Saint-Martial de Limoges*, ed. H. Duplès-Agier (Paris, 1874), p. 6. Several of Ademar's sermons in Paris, BN lat. 2469 have material on this council. I am editing with Michael Frassetto these sermons and several others in Berlin, Deutsche Staatsbibliothek, Lat. Phillipps 1664. They are to be a part of the collected writings of Ademar which will be published shortly in the Corpus Christianorum. Until the edition appears, one can consult some fragments on this gathering in Léopold Delisle, "Notice sur les manuscrits originaux d'Adémar de Chabannes," *Notices et extraits des manuscrits de la Bibliothèque nationale* 35 (1896), 290; Hoffman, *Gottesfriede und Treuga Dei*, pp. 257–59; and *PL* 141:115–20. For that of 1029, see the piece of Ademar's sermon published in Ernst Sackur, *Die Cluniacenser in ihrer kirchlichen und allgemeingeschichtlichen Wirksamkeit bis zur Mitte des elften Jahrhunderts*, 2 vols. (Halle, 1892–94), 2:484. For that of 1031, see Mansi 19:507–48.

[10] For an excellent appreciation of Ademar, see Robert Lee Wolff, "How the News Was Brought from Byzantium to Angoulême: or, The Pursuit of a Hare in an Ox Cart," *Byzantine and Modern Greek Studies* 4 (1978), 139–78. For the sermons, see Daniel Callahan, "The Sermons of Ademar of Chabannes and the Cult of St. Martial of Limoges," *Revue bénédictine* 86 (1976), 251–95. On the early career of Ademar, see Richard Landes, "The Making of a Medieval Historian: Ademar of Chabannes and Aquitaine at the Turn of the Millennium" (Ph.D. diss., Princeton University, 1984).

[11] See especially Gabriel Fournier, *Le château dans la France médiévale: Essai de sociologie monumentale* (Paris, 1978), Bernard Bachrach, "Fortification and Military Tactics: Fulk Nerra's Strongholds ca. 1000," *Technology and Culture* 20 (1979), 531–49, and idem, "Early Medieval Fortification in the 'West' of France: A Revised Technical Vocabulary," *Technology and Culture* 16 (1975), 531–69.

[12] There is great need for a full-scale study of this figure. Professor Bachrach's essay on William, "Toward a Reappraisal of William the Great, Duke of Aquitaine," *Journal of Medieval History* 5 (1979), 11–21, is correct in attacking the traditional image of William as a powerful figure, the strongest political force of this period in France. The essay, how-

movement, who was the first civil ruler to incorporate it into his own policies, and who worked creatively with the church for their mutual advantage.[13] Hence we see relatively weak civil authority at the highest levels, but power sufficiently perceptive to encourage Peace councils.

The second factor is a regional church, in particular the monasteries, which had profited greatly in a material way in the tenth century.[14] An examination of the cartularies quickly reveals the great landed wealth of the Aquitanian houses but also the extremely widespread nature of the holdings. Great houses such as those of Saint-Julian of Brioude, Saint-Géraud of Aurillac, Saint-Martial of Limoges, and the Poitevin monasteries of Saint-Maixent and Saint-Savin had holdings scattered throughout the duchy and beyond, holdings difficult to defend, holdings that were easy targets for the land-hungry warriors.[15] Cooperation was thus absolutely necessary for the churchmen, including the heavenly heads of the monastic houses, the saints. But, as Ademar of Chabannes indicates in one of his sermons, "who offends one saint offends them all."[16]

A third factor was the immense popularity of the saints in Aquitaine and the special nature of the reliquaries found in southern France.[17] The author of the first books of the miracles of Saint Faith, Bernard of Angers, states, "It is an old usage and custom in the whole region of Auvergne, in Rouergue or Toulouse, and in the whole country around, that each should set up according to his ability for his saint a statue of gold or silver or any other metal, in which the head of the saint or some other part of the body is preserved with reverence."[18] One of the first such pieces about which we have much information is a statue reliquary of the Virgin Mary seated in majesty with the Christ child.

---

ever, goes too far and leaves us with a virtual cipher who could not have functioned for over thirty-five years as duke or held the esteem of so many contemporaries, for example, Fulbert of Chartres.

[13] Daniel Callahan, "William the Great and the Monasteries of Aquitaine," *Studia monastica* 19 (1977), 321–42.

[14] See Callahan, "William the Great," pp. 321–29.

[15] Daniel Callahan, "Benedictine Monasticism in Aquitaine, 935–1030" (Ph.D. diss., University of Wisconsin, Madison, 1968), pp. 15–35.

[16] Paris, BN lat. 2469, 10r.

[17] There is a large literature on statue reliquaries. As a useful introduction to the subject, see Jean Taralon, "Arts précieux," pt. 3 of *Le siècle de l'an mil*, ed. L. Grodecki et al. (Paris, 1973), pp. 259–359. Even more valuable is Ilene H. Forsyth, *The Throne of Wisdom* (Princeton, 1972), especially chaps. 1–3. See also the recent article by Claire Wheeler Solt, "Romanesque French Reliquaries," *Studies in Medieval and Renaissance History*, n.s., 9 (1987), 165–236.

[18] "Est namque vetus mos et consuetudo, ut in tota Arvenica patria sive Rotenica vel Tolosana, necnon et reliquis nostris his circumquaque continuis, de auro sive argento seu quolibet alio metallo, sancto suo quisque pro posse statuam erigat, in qua caput sancti, vel potior pars corporis venerabilius condatur"; *Liber mirac. s. Fidis* 1.13, pp. 46–47.

Bishop Stephen II of Clermont presented the piece to his cathedral ca. 946. Placed near and eventually on the main altar where it remained until its destruction in the turmoil of the late eighteenth century, this reliquary was covered with gold and was carried in procession on feast days of the Virgin Mary.[19] This work was likely the first such statue of the Virgin in a long line that had special popularity in the Auvergne and surrounding areas in the following centuries.

Stephen II was also abbot of Sainte-Foi of Conques and there knew well another statue reliquary, that of its patron saint. This famous work, probably first fashioned in the late ninth century when the relics of Saint Faith were brought to Conques from Agen, is one of the earliest preserved, although significantly altered, reliquary statues.[20] The description of the piece by Bernard of Angers in the early eleventh century generally matches the work as it is today.[21] As a result of the growing popularity of this cult and for promotion of its pilgrimage, much ornamentation and many gems were added in the late tenth century to the original Carolingian wooden statue and metal covering.

Elsewhere in the region there are other such statue reliquaries recorded for this period. One important example is that of Saint Martial of Limoges, a golden image made after a fire at the house in 952.[22] It was seated on an altar, blessed the people with its right hand, and held the Gospels in its left. A similar piece is that of Saint Gerald at Aurillac.[23] A third example is the golden statue of Saint Privat at Mende.[24] Most, if not all, of these statue reliquaries could be brought out of the churches in processions in order to manifest more widely the presence of the saint, as we see being done with the reliquary of Saint Privat at a council at Le Puy in 1036.[25]

Bernard of Angers, who supplies so much useful information on the importance and uses of the statue reliquaries, came to these shrines of the south with a highly negative attitude toward what he initially viewed as pagan idols.[26] Yet he was won over by the genuine religious fervor aroused in Aquitaine and adjoining areas of the Languedoc by the reliquaries and accompanying miracles. He recognized the importance to the regional religious observances of the relics and their containers.[27]

[19] Forsyth, *Throne of Wisdom*, especially pp. 10, 39, 98.

[20] See Jean Taralon, "Majesté de Sainte Foy," *Les trésors des églises de France*, ed. Jean Taralon (Paris, 1965), pp. 289–94.

[21] Forsyth, *Throne of Wisdom*, p. 69.

[22] *Commemoratio abbatum s. Martialis*, pp. 5–6. See also *Chronicon B. Iterii*, in *Chroniques de Saint-Martial de Limoges*, p. 42.

[23] *Liber mirac. s. Fidis* 1.13, p. 47.

[24] *Les miracles de saint Privat*, ed. Clovis Brunel (Paris, 1912), pp. 14–16.

[25] *Les miracles de saint Privat*, pp. 14–16.

[26] *Liber mirac. s. Fidis* 1.13, pp. 47–48.

[27] *Liber mirac. s. Fidis* 1.13, pp. 47–49.

Yet, although the earliest statue reliquaries date from the Carolingian period, this widespread popularity did not become truly significant until the last half of the tenth and early eleventh centuries. Their importance grew rapidly in conjunction with the accelerating development of pilgrimages and their use in liturgical processions on the feast days of the saints and at ecclesiastical councils and synods.

In addition to portability, another item to keep in mind is the competition among the various cults of the region at this time to develop their pilgrimages. If what we know about the development of the cult of Saint Martial in this period is a fair indication of the pressures for popularity, and I think it is, it was incumbent on the impresarios of the cults, using Brown's perceptive terminology, to give as much visibility to their saints as possible.[28] Ademar's sermons have numerous references to relics being brought to Limoges to the tomb of Saint Martial for peace gatherings, thus increasing the prestige of this cult but also giving the visiting saints additional visibility.[29]

Their absence could create major problems. On one occasion the weather was dreadful for four months until the bones of Saint Leonard arrived at Limoges to join those of his fellow saints. As soon as this happened, the natural elements reflected the heavenly harmony achieved by the arrival of this previously absent member.[30]

The numerous manifestations of the heavenly order bring us to the fourth factor, the apocalypticism of the period. The religious atmosphere in southern France was supercharged with a sense of the end, if the writings of Rodulphus Glaber and Ademar of Chabannes are a representative reflection of the mentality of the time. Georges Duby in his much overlooked *L'an mil,* a little book in the tidal flood of his writings, presents a strong case for the importance of this perspective in understanding the period.[31] The argument over the degree and nature of the terrors of the years around 1000 remains very much alive.[32] How

---

[28] Brown, *Cult of the Saints,* pp. 10, 38, 67, and especially 73ff. See also chap. 6 on the power of the saints.

[29] For example, sermons 35 and 37; *PL* 141:115–20. See also Paris, BN lat. 2469, 24r and 91v, for the transporting of the relics of Saint Valeria to Limoges for the peace gatherings. One of the principal ideas Ademar was promoting was that Martial was the principal saint of Aquitaine and should be surrounded by the remains of the regional saints at peace gatherings. These affairs were seeking to achieve on earth a reflection of heavenly harmony. See also Mansi 19:531 for a reference to the relics at the council of Limoges of 1031. On Ademar's promotion of Martial as the patron of the Peace movement, see Daniel Callahan, "Adémar de Chabannes et la paix de Dieu," *Annales du Midi* 89 (1977), 21–43.

[30] Paris, BN lat. 2469, 91v.

[31] Georges Duby, *L'an mil* (Paris, 1967).

[32] A good examination of the influence of apocalypticism in the medieval period is Bernard McGinn, "Apocalypticism in the Middle Ages: An Historiographical Sketch," *Mediaeval Studies* 37 (1975), 252–86. Two older surveys of the historiography on the issue

widespread and how strong the acceptance of the apocalyptic ideas was will never be fully known, but surely they were influential, especially in the monasteries. It is not surprising that many of the charters of the period refer to the fears of the proximity of the Last Judgment more often than in the past or in the future.[33] Nor can intensified apocalypticism be dismissed as a cause in explaining the fact that the large peace gatherings with the presence of relic collections were most numerous in Aquitaine in the decade before 1000 and again in the period 1028–33, one thousand years after the death of Christ, or that at the only important one after 1033 we find Archbishop Aimon of Bourges turning somewhat away from the saints as enforcers of the peace and from the use of spiritual weapons.

The apocalyptic expectations also help to explain the numerous references in Ademar's sermons to Saint Martial as judge over Aquitaine at the time of the Last Judgment.[34] Arranged about the patron saint of Aquitaine in heaven are the other saints of the duchy, just as their reliquaries surround that of Martial at the Peace councils at Limoges. The celestial peace and harmony they enjoy is very different from the violence on earth at the time. Ademar underlines this comparison repeatedly.[35] But he also contrasts that period when the terrestrial order was most like heaven, namely, the apostolic era when Christ and his apostle Martial lived on earth, with the chaos of the early eleventh

---

of the year 1000 are Alexander Vasiliev, "Medieval Ideas on the End of the World: West and East," *Byzantion* 26 (1942–43), 462–502, and Ferdinand Lot, "Le mythe des terreurs de l'an mille," *Mercure de France* 300 (1947), 639–55. For Vasiliev and Lot there was little evidence of terrors in this period. See, on the other hand, D. Verhelst, "Adso van Montier-en-Der en de angst voor het jaar Duizend," *Tijdschrift voor Geschiedenis* 90 (1977), 1–10, and especially Landes, "The Making of a Medieval Historian," chap. 1. See also my articles "Ademar of Chabannes, Apocalypticism and the Council of Limoges of 1031," *Revue bénédictine* 101 (1991), 32–49, and "The Problem of the *Filioque* and the Letter from the Pilgrim Monks of the Mount of Olives to Pope Leo III and Charlemagne," *Revue bénédictine* 102 (1992).

[33] In particular, *Cartulaire de Saint-Jean d'Angély*, ed. G. Musset (Archives historiques de la Saintonge et de l'Aunis, 30; 1901), no. 192 (ca. 971), pp. 231–33; no. 47 (ca. 995), pp. 74–75; no. 182 (ca. 1015), pp. 217–19; no. 48 (ca. 1026), pp. 75–76. *Chartes et docs. de Saint-Maixent*, no. 31 (964), pp. 46–47; no. 47 (ca. 970), pp. 63–64; no. 51 (ca. 979), p. 67; no. 58 (ca. 988), pp. 74–75; no. 69 (tenth cent.), pp. 86–87; no. 71 (tenth cent.), pp. 88–89; no. 76 (ca. 999), pp. 94–95; no. 80 (ca. 999), pp. 98–99. *Chartes de l'abbaye de Nouaillé*, ed. Pierre de Monsabert (Archives historiques du Poitou, 49; 1936), no. 54 (942), pp. 93–95; no. 62 (ca. 978), pp. 104–6; no. 74 (ca. 991), pp. 122–25; no. 76 (991), pp. 127–29; no. 77 (991), pp. 129–31; no. 80 (ca. 994), pp. 134–35; no. 89 (996), pp. 150–51; no. 78 (ca. 1003), pp. 131–32; no. 83 (ca. 1003), pp. 139–41; no. 100 (ca. 1023), pp. 165–67. *Chartularium sancti Jovini*, ed. Charles Grandmaison (Mémoires de la Société de Statistique des Deux Sèvres, ser. 1, 17; 1854), pp. 11–12 (978), p. 17 (964).

[34] For example, Paris BN lat. 2469, 19v, 25v, 26r, 72r.

[35] This is especially true in the last sermons in Paris, BN lat. 2469.

century when the end seems so near.[36] The sermons thus provide a salvation history for Aquitaine, a set of theologized commentaries on the *vita* of Saint Martial, pieces very much imbued with a strong sense of the omega.

A fifth factor, in some ways the most important in explaining the development of relic gatherings, arises from a special aspect of the Peace of God movement, one that separates it from its Carolingian antecedent, namely, the oath taken in the presence of the relics to observe the peace. [37] In Carolingian capitularies and councils in which protection was extended to the poor and weak, it was the power of the king which gave much of the muscle to the peace rulings.[38] With the sanctified Peace of God, spiritual weapons were utilized. The saint as God's vice-regent became the principal enforcer, although the bishop exercised the power of excommunication.

An oath, however, was but one form of the nexus between heaven and earth. Before looking at the role of oaths at the Peace councils, we should examine with greater breadth the nature and significance of the bonding between the saints and their devotees in this liturgical civilization. The most appropriate means is a consideration of the supreme bonding in the medieval Christian order, the mass, and especially the tropes that play so important a part in the evolution of worship in this period. In this fashion, the special nature and importance of oaths can be set in relief.

Tropes were the insertions or additions to the common and proper of the mass in a period when the form of the eucharistic service was becoming increasingly set.[39] They were thus an opportunity for innovation, a creative outlet for the energies of churchmen, especially the monks of this period. Studies of Aquitaine are particularly fortunate on this subject because the monastery of Saint-Martial of Limoges was one of the earliest and most important centers of troping in all Christendom.[40] Dating at least from the early tenth century, the liturgical activity at Saint-Martial rapidly spread to neighboring houses.

[36] Callahan, "Sermons of Ademar," pp. 269–72, 282–85.

[37] On oaths, see Theodor Körner, *Iuramentum und frühe Friedensbewegung (10.–12. Jh.)* (Berlin, 1977).

[38] For Carolingian peace efforts, see Roger Bonnaud-Delamare, *L'idée de paix à l'époque carolingienne* (Paris, 1939).

[39] The literature on the topic of tropes is long and growing rapidly. A good initial bibliography is found in Richard W. Pfaff, *Medieval Latin Liturgy: A Select Bibliography* (Toronto Medieval Bibliographies, 9; Toronto, 1982), pp. 22–23.

[40] Two fundamental works are Jacques Chailley, *L'école musicale de Saint-Martial de Limoges* (Paris, 1960), and Paul Evans, *The Early Trope Repertory of Saint Martial de Limoges* (Princeton, N.J., 1970). A valuable work for setting the troping at Saint-Martial into its proper historical context is Richard Crocker, *A History of Musical Style* (New York, 1966), especially chap. 2, "New Frankish Forms, 700–1000."

Many of the manuscripts, with their insertions, survive. Especially important are those in the Saint-Martial collection at the Bibliothèque nationale.[41] Over a dozen Aquitanian manuscripts from the tenth and eleventh centuries offer pertinent information. Particularly important are Paris, BN lat. 1240, much of it done at Saint-Martial in the late tenth century; BN lat. 1118 from the late tenth; BN lat. 1121 from the early eleventh; and especially BN lat. 909, which contains particularly pertinent tropes of Ademar of Chabannes.[42]

Many years ago in his *Mass of the Roman Rite*, Joseph Jungmann pointed out that the tropes of the Agnus Dei from the tenth century changed the final *miserere nobis* of this part of the common to *dona nobis pacem*.[43] What he did not point out is that many of the manuscripts that first contain this change were from tenth- and eleventh-century Aquitaine. It seems likely, therefore, that this liturgical development reflects the growing Peace movement, if not in its origin then at least in its promotion.[44]

Numerous other aspects of the tropes demonstrate the powerful influence of the saints on human affairs. A series of images from these pieces throws light on the significance of the cult of the saints and the Peace movement.[45] In a trope for the feast of All Saints, they are depicted as heavenly citizens with Christ (a) or in another as his eternal companions (b). They are also presented as great throngs in heaven with him who conquered death (c).

[41] See a history and brief listing of the collection in Leopold Delisle, "Les manuscrits de Saint-Martial de Limoges," *Bulletin de la société archéologique et historique du Limousin* 43 (1895), 1–60.

[42] These pieces were published in the series *Analecta hymnica medii aevi*, ed. Clemens Blume and Guido Dreves, 55 vols. (Leipzig: (1886–1922), hereafter cited as *AH*. Most pertinent for our purposes are vol. 7, *Prosarium Lemovicense: Die Prosen der Abtei St. Martial zu Limoges*, ed. Guido Dreves (Leipzig, 1889); vol. 47, *Tropi Graduales. Tropen des Missale im Mittelalter, I: Tropen zum Ordinarium Missae*, ed. Clemens Blume and Henry Bannister (Leipzig, 1905); and vol. 49, *Tropi Graduales. Tropen des Missale im Mittelalter, II: Tropen zum Proprium Missarum*, ed. Clemens Blume (Leipzig, 1906). In addition to Paris, BN lat. 1240, 1118, 1121, and 909, also important are BN lat. 887, 903, 1084, 1119, 1120, and 1132–37. For comments on these manuscripts, in addition to the material found in Chailley, *L'école musicale*, and Evans, *Early Trope Repertory*, see Richard Crocker, "The Repertory of Proses at Saint Martial de Limoges in the Tenth Century," *Journal of the American Musicological Society* 11 (1958), 149–64, and David Hughes, "Further Notes on the Grouping of the Aquitanian Tropers," *Journal of the American Musicological Society* 19 (1966), 3–12.

[43] Joseph Jungmann, *The Mass of the Roman Rite*, 2 vols., trans. Francis Brunner (New York, 1951–55), 2:338–39, especially note 37.

[44] In several of his pieces, Ademar refers to the "kiss of peace" in the mass. For him, the mass commemorates the sacrifice of the one who was himself the true peace; see Berlin, Deutsche Staatsbibliothek, lat. 1664, 97v, 104r, 105v, 114r.

[45] Texts and sources of the tropes (a–y) in the following discussion are given at the end of this chapter; see pp. 179–83.

One of the most common images is a two-tiered depiction of reality with the saints singing praises in heaven and their adherents invoking them on earth. The authors of the tropes sought to draw as many parallels between the two orders as possible. An introit trope for the feast of All Saints depicts crowds of martyrs celebrating in heaven, worshipers on earth (d). Again, for the same feast, celebrants on earth are presented as singing to the saints on their day, while the saints in heaven give songs to Christ (e).

It is the saint who is the nexus between the two orders, with spirit in heaven and relics manifesting sacred power on earth. The saint as intermediary is surely the most common theme in the writings of the early Middle Ages. The most appropriate location for this image is in the liturgy that serves as the principal channel between the two orders. Tropes for the dedication of a church develop the liturgical texts and portray the church as a door or a bridge to the heavenly *patria* (f) or as the entrance to the heavenly Jerusalem (g).

The saints serve as the defenders of the faith and the faithful. In one trope they are portrayed as protectors throughout the world against malignant spirits attacking Christians (h). Individual saints have their militant qualities praised: Saint Stephen is honored as a *miles* for Christ (i). In another, Martin of Tours, who left behind his weapons to follow Christ, is now girded by the arms of the Word (j). In still another, Géraud of Aurillac becomes the model of strength (k).

Of all the saints of Aquitaine, the greatest intermediary and the one who obviously would receive the most attention in the tropes is Saint Martial, at whose monastery a large majority of these pieces were written. One can open the collection almost anywhere and find material on this individual. Some of the most interesting are found in the tropes to the introits of masses on the feasts of Saint Martial. In one, Martial is presented as selected by God from eternity and reigning with Him forever (l). He is the patron for Limoges (m), a patron *per saecula* for his church, over which he presides adorned with a golden crown given to him by Christ the *summus heros* (n). Another sings that the people of Aquitaine made him their monarch because he first spread the Christian message to the people of Limoges by which he made them blessed to Christ *super astra* (o). In response, the people of Limoges placed his relics in a citadel of light because he first in the west sowed the faith of the Trinity and made Aquitaine resplendent into eternity (p).

The apostolic themes that played such an important part in the new life of Martial, a *vita* from the last half of the tenth or early eleventh century and even more in the revision of this *vita* by Ademar of Chabannes, echo in several of these tropes, especially in those from the feasts of the patron of Aquitaine.[46] For example, one trope depicts Martial as a shining apostle who had God himself in the flesh (for the apostolic *vita* made Martial an immediate disciple of Christ) as his teacher in his youth. He participated in many of the principal events of Holy Week and was filled by the Holy Spirit and the dogma of Christ at Pentecost. He was a blood relative and close companion of Saint Peter the keybearer. Now he is in heaven praising God for eternity (q). Another trope says that Gaul, which he saved, venerates him as its father forever (r). And there are many more such references.

Peace is also prominent in the tropes. It is portrayed as one of the principal features of heaven (s). Christ is the path of peace (t). An introit trope for the feast of the Ascension states that the Son goes forth to the Father preserving traces of peace until the day he returns to judge the earth (u). Another makes clear that the church is the heir of Christ's peace (v). And the saints are invoked to aid in that preservation (w). As is not surprising, Martial is seen as the great *pacifer*. In a trope for a feast of Martial, Christ fortifies his saint so that his disciple may achieve peace by overcoming bands of wicked spirits (x).

It is, however, a gradual trope for a feast of Martial in BN lat. 909 which offers the most pertinent image of peace. In this trope, the congregation in the church praises Christ the king ruling forever with his *summa potentia*. The prayer goes on to rejoice in the total victory of Christ which causes the hearts of his disciples to exult. Christ is invoked as the light of the apostles and true peace and asked to grant peace and manifest his eternal *patria* (y). The last idea deserves special attention. The parallel nature of the heavenly and earthly orders will change when the earth passes away at the Last Judgment. This theme would have special meaning at a time of apocalytic expectations.[47]

The lines of this last trope were taken from a much longer piece by Ademar, a sequence that merits attention for its material on the Peace of God. The sequence was a new form developed by the Franks toward the middle of the ninth century and is found between the gospel and the preceding alleluia. Often they were many lines long and quite dramatic. As one of the principal roots of the medieval drama, the history of the sequence has drawn much attention in the past few years.[48] Like the trope, it offered an outlet for the creative energies of the monks, and as with the tropes Saint-Martial of Limoges by the end of the tenth

---

[46] See Callahan, "Sermons of Ademar," pp. 252–63.

[47] I do not make much of the point because the Last Judgment motif is not particularly prominent in the tropes examined and because this particular one comes from Ademar of Chabannes, whose life ended on a pilgrimage to Jerusalem 1033–34.

[48] Richard Crocker, *The Early Medieval Sequence* (Berkeley, 1977), and William L. Smoldon, *The Music of the Medieval Church Dramas*, ed. Cynthia Bourgeault (London, 1980), especially chaps. 1–8.

century had become an important center for the creation of sequences. Volume 7 of the *Analecta hymnica* is given over entirely to sequences from the abbey of Saint-Martial. Ten of these are from feasts of the patron saint and all of them have much important information on the evolution of the cult, especially on Martial as protector. It is the sequence Ademar wrote for the Mass of Martial the apostle in the late 1020s which is most special and pertinent.[49] In it are presented many of the peace themes he later elaborated on in his sermons.

This sequence is structured with the parallel orders, the heavenly and the earthly. It opens with the apostles in heaven praising God with alleluias. The earthly celebrants join with the angelic. All celebrate the apostolicity of Martial in heaven and on earth. The sequence then recounts some of the high points in the life of the apostle as presented in the revised *vita*. Martial is the nexus between heaven and the people of Aquitaine. He is the principal imitator of Christ for his people. Just as Christ is victor over death and bringer of peace, so is Martial.

These prayers amplify earlier tropes on the nature of true peace and underline again the heavenly and earthly orders joined for the people of Aquitaine by the saints, in particular the patron saint of the duchy. The oaths taken at the Peace councils must be understood in this context. The liturgy constantly reminds the people of the special power of the saints and thus the importance and seriousness of the oath taken on the relics.

Oaths are mentioned in the accounts of some of the earliest Aquitanian peace gatherings. At one of the first, ca. 975, Bishop Guy of Le Puy held an open-air meeting of the knights and peasants of his diocese. Returning to the Carolingian royal and episcopal directives to protect the goods of the church and the poor, Guy sought to have all in attendance swear an oath to do likewise.[50] Ademar tells us that an oath was taken by the nobles to uphold the peace at a gathering at Limoges ca. 994 after Saint Martial had performed a miracle by stopping an outbreak of a serious illness which the monk indicated had been the result of the violence in the region.[51] The most famous example of the Peace oath, however, is that taken at a gathering at Bourges, ca. 1038. Archbishop Aimon had everyone over the age of fifteen swear to a peace agreement whereby those so doing promised to act against anyone violating the peace, even to the extent of taking up weapons—the

[49] Item 169 in *AH* 7:187–88; found in Paris, BN lat. 909.

[50] *Chronicon monasterii sancti Petri aniciensis*, in *Cartulaire de Saint-Chaffre*, ed. U. Chevalier (Paris, 1884), pp. 151–52.

[51] See especially Paris, BN lat. 2469, sermon 34, fols. 86v–87r (published in part in Delisle, "Notice sur les manuscrits," p. 290, and Hoffmann, *Gottesfriede und Treuga Dei*, pp. 257–58), and sermon 35, fols. 87r–88r (*PL* 141:115–18).

famous, or infamous, war on war.[52] According to the *Miracula sancti Benedicti,* Archbishop Aimon swore an oath on the relics of the proto-martyr, Saint Stephen, to fight against the violators of the Peace of God, namely those who destroyed ecclesiastical goods, or stole them, oppressed monks or any other male or female religious or attacked the church in any way.[53] Aimon then had all the others assembled there follow his example by swearing on the remains of Saint Stephen. According to Andrew of Fleury, the powerful feared greatly this army of weak men because of their heavenly support, a statement that is much more than monastic hyperbole or wishful thinking.[54]

An oath is one of the most prominent manifestations of the bond between saint and adherent, especially at such a formal occasion as a council. Unfortunately, as I have said, the sparseness of the conciliar acts results in a paucity of information on the specific nature of the oaths. To whom, how often, in what settings, with what wording were these oaths taken? Especially to be regretted is the loss(?) of the account of what was probably the third and final day of the council of Limoges of 1031.[55] The account by Ademar of the first two days is the most detailed information we have about the content and conduct of such a gathering, albeit from a highly suspect pen. It would have been, however, the final day of the gathering when the laity, in particular the nobility, would swear an oath to uphold the peace.

The relics were important for the oaths, as was seen in Archbishop Aimon's action of having the participants of the gathering at Bourges (ca. 1038) swear on the remains of Saint Stephen. But relics had long been important in Aquitaine for this purpose. In the first half of the tenth century, Odo of Cluny had pointed out in his life of Gerald of Aurillac that "the inhabitants of that region [eastern Aquitaine] had truly ferocious habits, but gradually by his example and the reverence they have for the holy man they seem to be gentler. When they make an agreement or solemn oath in law, they have the relic brought by some monk or cleric."[56] Surely this was one of the principal reasons for transporting relics to the sites of the councils. Competition for prestige obviously also dictated attendance. But most important in the eyes of the churchmen of the period, it was imperative to make as manifest as possible that each Peace gathering be viewed as a forum for connecting the heavenly with the earthly. The holy remains were the visible sign of

[52] See the sources cited in note 7 and Thomas Head (chapter 9) in this volume.

[53] *Mirac. s. Benedicti* 5.2, pp. 193–94.

[54] *Mirac. s. Benedicti* 5.2, p. 194.

[55] Mansi 19:507–48. It is important to keep in mind that this account is found in the last part of Paris, BN lat. 2469 and is a logical conclusion to the sermons of Ademar in this manuscript; see Callahan, "Ademar of Chabannes," pp. 32–49.

[56] PL 133:700–701. The quotation is from Bisson, "Organized Peace," p. 292.

power and vitality. In one way, these relics were far more alive than the mortal participants in the church councils. In another way, they were intended to remind the warriors of their mortality. Soon the end would be at hand and the man of war must stand at the judgment seat.

At the moment of death, what is needed is a holy intercessor. What was necessary was identification with a saint. One way to achieve this relationship was to become a member of the saint's family through burial near the patron's tomb. This custom of many of the greatest nobles and aristocratic families of Aquitaine reached far back into the past.[57] By the tenth and early eleventh centuries, the counts of Angoulême were buried at Saint-Cybard.[58] Many lay powers of the Auvergne were interred near the remains of Saint Julian of Brioude.[59] In the Périgord, the tomb of Saint Front was a popular burial site.[60] In the sermons of Ademar, much is made of the fact that the legendary first Christian duke of Aquitaine, Stephen, who was converted by Saint Martial, was buried near that saint.[61] Men of the eleventh century are urged to emulate the example of the first Christian ruler of the duchy.

There is much charter evidence of lesser nobles, newly arrived in the ranks of the powerful, seeking identification with the saints. One example is that of the famous Lusignan family of castellans who in the 1020s established several priories under the control of the monastery of Nouaillé.[62] Such munificence served as a testimony to their new status.

Those warriors who failed to identify with a saint, failed to take the oath to observe the peace, or, worse, violated their oath, deserved alienation and earned for themselves excommunication, be it individual or territorial in the form of an interdict, the latter a spiritual weapon first extensively used in Aquitaine in this period.[63] What is stressed repeatedly in nearly all the Peace writings is that those who incur excommunication cannot be buried in consecrated ground and will go to hell. In Ademar's account of the council of Limoges of 1031, we read of a warrior who had violated an earlier peace, was excommunicated, and subsequently died in battle.[64] The bishop of Cahors for-

[57] J.-P. Poly and E. Bournazel, *La mutation féodale, Xe–XIIe siècles* (Nouvelle Clio, 16; Paris, 1980), pp. 315–35, especially pp. 325–26.

[58] Ademar of Chabannes, *Chronicon* 3.66, 3.19, 3.20, 3.23, 3.28, 3.35 (pp. 192–93, 137, 138, 145, 149, 157, respectively).

[59] Gabriel Fournier, *Le peuplement rural en Basse-Auvergne durant le haut moyen âge* (Paris, 1962), especially p. 416.

[60] Arlette Higounet-Nidal, *Périgueux aux XIV et XVe siècles* (Bordeaux, 1978), p. 40.

[61] For example, Paris BN lat. 2469, 13v, 6or.

[62] *Chartes de l'abbaye de Nouaillé*, nos. 104, 106, 107, pp. 172–79.

[63] Edward Krehbiel, *The Interdict* (Washington, D.C., 1909), pp. 17, 26; Emile Jombart, "Interdit," *Dictionnaire de droit canonique*, 7 vols., ed. R. Naz (Paris, 1935–36), 5:1464.

[64] Mansi 19:541.

bade his burial in order to serve as an example to others. The dead man's friends succeeded in having him buried in a church, but the consecrated ground expressed revulsion for the fetid flesh by hurling the body forth. When the corpse was discovered the following day, it was returned to its grave. That evening the earth again shook off the unwanted deposit. According to Ademar, five times the body was placed in the tomb and five times it was rejected. Eventually the companions were forced to bury the corpse far from consecrated ground and, moved by such heavenly obstinacy, decided the Peace should be observed. In several places in Ademar's sermons the unburied bodies of the excommunicated are depicted as lying about and serving as food for wild animals. The putrefying flesh reeks of dung, an interesting juxtaposition to the fragrance of the bodies of the saints.[65]

The late 1030s witnessed the end of the conjunction of the five factors in the Peace movement in Aquitaine. The year 1033 came and went without the return of Christ to Jerusalem. In 1030, the principal lay patron, Duke William V, the Great, died in retirement in a monastery. His successors were unable to sustain the Peace momentum. In 1034, the greatest propagandist for the Peace and our most voluminous source, Ademar of Chabannes, died while on pilgrimage to Jerusalem. By 1040, the Peace association of Archbishop Aimon of Bourges had been defeated in a pitched battle, thus ending his policy of war on war and discrediting further peace efforts in the area. Our sources tell us little more about relic rallies in the duchy of Aquitaine. Even the troping diminishes significantly at Saint-Martial of Limoges. The era of the sanctified peace was over in southern France. The sweet fragrance of the holy relics was no longer so overwhelming in the later eleventh-century Aquitanian aisles of power.

Tropes That Reflect or May Have Influenced
The Peace of God in Aquitaine

The tropes inserted into each passage are italicized.

a. Item 193, introit trope, *AH* 49:95; in part or whole in Paris, BN lat. 1084, 1121, 909, 1120. Gaudeamus omnes in Domino,
   1. *Annua festivis sanctis recinendo choreis,* diem festum celebrantes—gaudent angeli
   2. *Adplaudunt caeli cives super aethera Christo* et collaudant filium Dei.
b. Item 186, introit trope, *AH* 49:92; in part or whole in Paris BN lat. 1240, 1084, 1118, 1121, 909, 1120, 1119.

---

[65] Paris, BN lat. 2469, 96r, 96v.

1. *Eia, plebs devota Deo, nunc corde sereno* Gaudeamus omnes in Domino,
2. *Consonet ore simul nostrorum flos meritorum,* diem festum celebrantes
3. *Aeterni socii fulgoris geminis alti* sub honore sanctorum omnium etc.

c. Item 93, introit trope for Easter, *AH* 49:55; in part or whole in Paris BN lat. 1084, 1121, 909, 1120, 1119.

1. *Factus homo de matre, pater, tua iussa secutus Inque crucis ligno mortis acutore perempto* Resurrexi et adhuc tecum sum;
2. *Ne mihi tunc caecata cohors obsistere posset Nominis atque mei lumen fuscare serenum,* posuisti super me manum tuam.
3. *Clara dedi sanctae legis documenta patere, Agmina sanctorum traxi super aethera mecum;* mirabilis facta est scientia tua.

d. Item 35, *AH* 49:34; in part or whole in Paris, BN lat. 1240, 1084, 1121, 909, 1120.

1. *Hodie mundo festivus illuxit dies omnium sanctorum;*
2. *Hodie martyrum turba tripudiat in caelis, et nos in terris*

e. Item 195, *AH* 49:95; in part or whole in Paris, BN lat. 1084, 1119. Gaudeamus omnes in Domino,

1. *Nunc sanctis iuncti resonemus organa cunctis* diem festum celebrantes—gaudent angeli
2. *Ac caeli cives summo dant cantica Christo* et collaudant filium Dei.

f. Item 150, introit trope for the dedication of a church, *AH* 49:76–77; in part or whole in Paris BN lat. 1084, 1121, 909, 1120.

1. *Agmina perenniter, iubilant angelica, Hunc locum protestantur sacrum [sic] dicentia:* Terribilis est locus iste.
2. *Hanc domum Deo assignant prosequendo fidelium praecordia:* hic domus Dei est.
3. *Adest porta, per quam iusti properantes redeunt ad patriam,* et porta caeli.
4. *Astra, polus, terra, pontus collaetantur haec dicentes carmina:* et vocabitur aula Dei.

g. Item 145, introit trope for the dedication of a church, *AH* 49:75; in part or whole in Paris, BN lat. 1084, 1118, 1121, 909, 1120, 887, 1119.

1. *Angelicos patriarcha choros olim Dominumque Innixum scalae cernens proclamat ovanter:* Terribilis est locus iste,
2. *Spiratus Solymam deditus policam, peregrinam, Arvis quae mittit divo copiam beatorum;* hic domus Dei est.
3. *Porta haec iustitia est, caelo quae dirigit almos, Hac iusti penetrant paradisum semper ovantes,* et porta caeli;
4. *Speque fide Dominum retinent praecordia sacra, Quae templum Domini corpus quoque iure fatentur,* et vocabitur aula Dei.

h. Item 148, introit trope for the dedication of a church, *AH* 49:76; in part or whole in Paris, BN lat. 1084, 1121, 909, 1120, 1119.

1. *Plebs veneranda patrum, dictis memorare priorum, Territus in somnis quae cernens fatur Iacob:* Terribilis est locus iste;
2. *Tu prece funde pia laudes et concine vota;* hic domus Dei est
3. *Ex vivo lapide constructa et firma nitescens,* et porta caeli
4. *Pestiferos pellens, quae percipit undique lectos,* et vocabitur

5. *Fortia sanctorum praecordia fusa per orbem* aula Dei.

i. Item 347, introit trope for a feast of Saint Stephen, *AH* 49:149; in part or whole in Paris, BN lat. 1084, 1118, 1121, 909, 1119, 887.

1. *Qui primus meruit post Christum occurrere martyr, Iure suos tali testatur voce labores:* Etenim sederunt principes et adversum me loquebantur;

2. *Non ullum nocui nec legum iura resolvi,* et iniqui persecuti sunt me,

3. *Christe, tuus fueram tantum quia rite minister;* adiuva me, Domine Deus meus,

4. *Ne tuus in dubio frangar certamine miles,* quia servus tuus exercebatur in iustificationibus tuis.

j. Item 301, introit trope for a feast of Saint Martin, *AH* 49:133; in part or whole in Paris, BN lat. 1240, 1084, 1118, 909, 1120.

1. *Hic Domini famulus quia mansit iure fidelis,* Statuit ei Dominus testamentum pacis,

2. *Quo manna valeat cunctis praebere superna,* et principem fecit eum,

3. *Armis accinctum verbi vestivit honore,* ut sit illi sacerdotii dignitas

4. *Et decus eximium, mansurum firmiter usque* in aeternum.

k. Item 239, introit trope for a feast of Saint Géraud, *AH* 49:110; in part or whole in Paris, BN lat. 1084, 1118, 1120, 887.

1. *Concrepet alma cohors Christi nunc corde Geraldo, Mystice vox cuius Davidica fatur in odis:* Os justi meditabitur sapientiam,

2. *Qua gaudebit opima ferens tunc praemia miles,* et lingus eius

l. Item 293, *AH* 49:129; in Paris, BN lat. 1120.

1. *Martialem prae saecla legit cunctipotens nobisque praesulem dedit;* Statuit ei Dominus testamentum pacis,

2. *Quia dignum fore praevidit, ideoque illum digne ornavit* et principem fecit eum

3. *Lemovicam urbem tanto pastore perornans,* ut sit illi sacerdotii dignitas,

4. *Quam decenter (ad)ornans polorum adeptus est regna, ubi cum Deo regnat* in aeternum.

m. Item 290, *AH* 49:128; in Paris, BN lat. 1121, 1120, 1119.

2. *Extulit atque suis coram altaribus almis,* et principem fecit eum

3. *Lemovicis famulum statuens dicare patronum,* ut sit illi sacerdotii dignitas in aeternum.

n. Item 289, *AH* 49:128; in part or in whole in Paris, BN lat. 1084, 1118, 1121, 1120, 887, 909.

1. *Inclitus hic rutilo celebratur stemmate praesul; Plebs veneranda fratrum, modulando canamus in unum;* Statuit ei Dominus testamentum pacis,

2. *Quemque summus heros ditavit munere summo* et principem fecit eum

3. *Ecclesiae propriae firmans per saecla patronum,* ut sit illi sacerdotii dignitas

4. *Et decus, splendor, ovans vita requiesque beata* in aeternum.

o. Item 285, *AH* 49:126; in part or in whole in Paris, BN lat. 1240, 1084, 1118, 1121, 909, 1120, 887, 1119, 903.

1. *Martialis meritum quia fulsit in agmine privum,* Statuit ei Dominus testamentum pacis

2. *Plebs Aquitana suum gliscens hunc esse monarchum,* et principem fecit eum;

3. *Lemovicae genti primus nova dogmata sparsit,* ut sit illi sacerdotii dignitas,

4. *Quo Christo genitos faciat super astra beatos* in aeternum.

p. Item 286, *AH* 49:127; in part or in whole in Paris, BN lat. 1084, 1121, 909, 1120, 887, 1119.

    1. *Martialis Dominum quia gessit pectore Christum,* Statuit ei Dominus testamentum pacis,

    2. *Lucis in arce locans ipsum sua vota Lemovix,* et principem fecit eum;

    3. *Primus in occiduis fidem sparsit trinitatis,* ut sit illi sacerdotii dignitas

    4. *Hoc tellus Aquitana nitet doctore, magistro* in aeternum.

q. Item 295, introit trope for a feast of Saint Martial, *AH* 49:130; in part or in whole in Paris, BN lat. 1119, 909. Note that these are tropes to the apostolic liturgy post-1028.

    1. *Sanctus Martialis, fulgorus apostolus, ipsum Carne Deum meruit iuvenis habuisse magistrum,* Probavit eum Deus et scivit cor suum;

    2. *Fortis amore Dei nam sprevit utrumque parentem, Quem Dominus cenando suum dedit esse ministrum;* cognovit semitas suas,

    3. *Spiritus ignifluus Domini quem iure replevit Omnigenis linguis et vero dogmate Christi,* deduxit illum in via aeterna;

    4. *Clavigero caeli meritis et sanguine nexus In solio Dominum residens collaudat in aevum,* et nimis confortatus est principatus eius.

r. Item 296, introit trope for a feast of Saint Martial, *AH* 49:130; in Paris, BN lat. 1119, 909.

    4. *Gallia quem salvata patrem veneratur in aevum,* et nimis confortatus est principatus eius.

s. Item 490, gradual trope for a feast of the holy martyrs, *AH* 49:254; in Paris, BN lat. 1118.

    2. Vox exsultationis et salutis *et laetae iucunditatis, aeternae iuventutis*

    3a. In tabernaculis *iustorum, pax,*

    3b. *Lux iucundaque laetitia.*

t. Item 17, introit trope for Easter, *AH* 49:29; in Paris, BN lat. 903.

Nos Dominus, qui est lucis via et semita pacis, Dissociet a malis; dextrum quicumque, necesse est, Aut laevum gradiatur iter; sed dextra bonorum Semita; conspicuos vocat in sua gaudia iustos: Venite, benedicti patris mei, percipite regnum etc.

u. Item 123, *AH* 49:66; in part or in whole in Paris, BN lat. 1084, 1118, 1121, 909, 1120, 887, 903, 1119.

    1. *Montis oliviferi Christus de vertice scandens, Ecce, duo viri clara voce clamarunt dicentes:* Viri Galilaei, quid admiramini aspicientes in caelum?

    2. *Ad patrem pergit [filius] servans vestigia pacis;* quemadmodum vidistis eum ascendentem in caelum,

    3. *Ad diem magnum, quo iudicaturus est orbem,* ita veniet, Alleluia.

v. Item 499, gradual trope for a feast of one confessor, *AH* 49:260; in part in Paris, BN lat. 1240.

    1. *Laetetur alma fidelium ecclesia; per Christi corpus redempta felix permanet in saecula, regnat in gloria perpetua, retinens caelica in caelestibus praemia;* Alleluia.

    2a. Justus *et probitate dignus*

    2b. Germinabit *pacis et vitae dona hereditabit*

    2c. Sicut lilium *et gloria rosarum,*

w. Item 254, introit trope for the nativity of John the Baptist, *AH* 49:116; in part or in whole in Paris, BN lat. 1084, 1120.

    3. *Parcere pacificis et debellare superbos,*

x. Item 582, offeratory trope for a feast of Saint Martial, *AH* 49:300; in part or in whole in Paris, BN lat. 1084, 1121, 909, 1120, 887, 903, 1119.

    1. *Martialem Dominus roborat Davidice promens:* Veritas mea,

    2. *Pax, benignitas atque victoria* et misericordia mea cum ipso,

    3. *Asomatas fortis superabit nempe catervas* et in nomine meo exaltabitur cornu eius.

    4. *Hic quia permansit semper mihi mente fidelis,* Misericordia etc.

y. Item 526, *AH* 49:275; in Paris, BN lat. 909.

    1. Alleluia;

    2a. *Te, Christe rex, laudant agmina laeta in hac sancta aula,*

    2b. *Regnans sempiterna in gloria potentia cum summa.*

    3a. *In carne apparens in Iudaea, rex, praedicasti ipsa praesentia tua,*

    3b. *Clara victoria iam completa laetificasti discipulorum tuorum corda.*

    4a. *Lux apostolorum, pax vera, da nobis indulgentiam,*

    4b. *Concede temporum pacem, praesta aeternam patriam.*

8

Between Aristocracy and Heresy: Popular Participation in the Limousin Peace of God, 994–1033

Richard Landes

It is a fitting and trenchant irony that one of the most important councils of the Peace of God movement has left so little direct textual evidence that one historian doubted its very existence,[1] whereas the best documented case, for which detailed transcriptions of the debates and actions of the council survive, may in fact have never occurred.[2] Both councils supposedly took place in the same city, Limoges, one in 994, the other in 1031; and almost all the documentation comes from one source, Ademar of Chabannes, writing between 1025 and 1033. The irony is fitting, because it embodies the whole problem of interpreting the evanescently brilliant early Peace of God movement; in the words of one scholar, was it "Fact or Fiction?"[3] It is trenchant because through an oversight of modern historiography this documentary inversion has not yet played any role in interpretations of the Aquitanian Peace movement. Yet, understanding how the written record reversed

I thank Thomas Head and Geoffrey Koziol for their comments on my earlier attempt to present this material, "The Dynamics of Heresy and Reform in Limoges: A Study of Popular Participation in the 'Peace of God' (994–1033)," *Historical Reflections/Réflexions historiques* 14, (1987), 476–511. As a result of their comments, this new effort represents a substantially different piece in which much of the more involved discussion has been summarized in order to rework larger points. To minimize the length of both text and notes, I have often replaced either citations in Latin or bibliography with a reference to the fuller text of the earlier article or to my forthcoming book, *History and Denial in an Apocalyptic Age: The Life and Times of Ademar of Chabannes (989–1034)*, cited by chapter.

[1] Roger Bonnaud-Delamare, "Les institutions de la paix en Aquitaine au XIe siècle," *La paix* (Recueils de la Société Jean Bodin, 14; Brussels, 1962), 1:430–31.

[2] Louis Saltet, "Les faux d'Adémar de Chabannes: Prétendues discussions sur saint Martial au concile de Bourges du le novembre 1031," *Bulletin de la littérature ecclésiastique* 27 (1926), 145–60.

[3] Dolorosa Kennelly, "The Peace and Truce of God: Fact or Fiction?" (Ph.D. diss., University of California, Berkeley, 1962).

the words and deeds of contemporaries provides the modern historian with a singular means to penetrate the strange, turbulent world of the Peace of God movement at the turn of the millennium.

Ademar of Chabannes, monk of Saint-Eparchius of Angoulême, occasional resident at Saint-Martial of Limoges, historian, liturgist, grammarian, and artist, wrote some three hundred pages of sermons and historical accounts of the conciliar activity in Limoges between 994 and 1032–33.[4] This constitutes about 80 percent of the extant material directly on the Peace of God for all of Europe in the first century of the movement's history. Partly as a result of this evidential treasure trove about a clearly important but poorly documented phenomenon, Limoges holds a central place in the history of the first phase of the Peace of God.[5]

For the modern historian, however, this is literally an embarrassment of riches. Almost all this wonderful detail turns out to be the mythomanic invention of an ambitious but failed relic cult impresario who, from the recesses of his cloister, produced some five hundred folios of history the way he wished it had occurred.[6] In the end, then, this copious body of documentation for the Peace Movement contributes mostly to our confusion and confirms a healthy mistrust for the "enthusiasm" to which studies of the early Peace movement occasionally fall victim.

Yet Ademar did not create these fictions from whole cloth. Even the Burgundian monk Rodulphus Glaber, writing about the wave of Peace councils that swept through Francia in 1033, admitted that the movement started in Aquitaine.[7] And despite the evidence that no Peace councils occurred in Limoges between 994 and 1028, that city shows

---

[4] Most of this material has only been partially edited by Mansi 19:489–95, 507–48. A complete edition of Ademar's sermons is in preparation, to be published in the Corpus Christianorum. Until then, see Mansi, and Léopold Deslisle, "Notice sur les manuscrits originaux d'Adémar de Chabannes," *Notices et extraits de la Bibliothèque nationale* 35 (1896), 248–358.

[5] See, for example, H. E. J. Cowdrey, "The Peace and Truce of God in the Eleventh Century," *Past and Present* 46 (1970), 42–67, and Hartmut Hoffmann, *Gottesfriede und Treuga Dei* (Schriften der Monumenta Germaniae historica, 20; Stuttgart, 1964), pp. 25–44.

[6] See the series of articles by Louis Saltet in the *Bulletin de la littérature ecclésiastique* from 1925–31—confirmed by subsequent research despite almost thirty years of neglect from most historians; see Richard Landes, "A Libellus from St. Martial of Limoges Written at the Time of Ademar of Chabannes: *Un faux à retardement*," *Scriptorium* 37 (1983), 178–209, as well as F. G. Nuvolone, "Il *Sermo pastoralis* Pseudoambrosiano e il *Sermo Girberti philosophi papae urbis Romae qui cognominatus est Silvester de informatione Episcoporum*, Riflessioni," *Gerberto: Scienza, Storia et Mito. Atti de Gerberti Symposium* (Archivum Bobiense, 2; Bobbio, 1985), pp. 379–566; and Herbert Schneider, "Ademar von Chabannes und Pseudoisidor—der 'Mythomane' und der Erzfälscher," in *Fälschungen im Mittelalter*, 5 vols. Schriften der Monumenta Germaniae historica, 33; Hanover, 1988), 2:129–50.

[7] Rodulphus Glaber, *Historiarum*, 4.5.14. See Appendix A for text.

too many signs of cultural effervescence in this period for us to dismiss Ademar's accounts out of hand. My purpose in this essay is to trace the interaction between the earliest conciliar activity in the city (994) and the larger range of religious and social developments over the next generation—relic cults, pilgrimage, "popular heresy," church reform—which gave Limoges its prominence in the second wave of councils of the late 1020s and 1030s. This approach also helps account for Ademar's version of events. It shows how his eventual mythomania was not an eccentric aberration but, quite the contrary, a sign of the times, a sometimes disconcerting, always revealing exaggeration of tendencies and concerns that Ademar shared with many of his literate clerical colleagues. In the long run, he offers a greater chance for us to understand the dynamics of the period than would a "saner," more controlled writer.[8]

The First Peace Council of Limoges, 994

In about 1028, Ademar wrote of an unusual council held at Limoges about a generation earlier; in response to an epidemic of the "fire plague," the bishop and abbot of Limoges and the duke called a three-day fast followed by a council attended by vast throngs of people who accompanied relics from all over the region. When Martial's body was raised, a joyous miracle healed all, and the duke and his men swore a pact of peace and justice.[9] This description depicts perhaps the most famous example of a "sanctified" Peace council, that is, one in which large crowds, miracles, and great spiritual enthusiasm played a major role.[10] In this case, Ademar's comments are largely confirmed by an unusual number of independent hagiographic accounts of a council at Limoges in the late tenth century. They testify not only to the geographic scope of this event but also to its social and religious impact.[11]

---

[8] I attempt a fuller analysis in *History and Denial*.

[9] See the selections from Ademar on this council in Appendix A.

[10] Hoffman, *Gottesfriede*, p. 30. There are two accounts of the *sacer ignis* and ensuing council from Saint-Martial's scriptorium that predate Ademar (fragments in different hands from the turn of the tenth century in Paris, BN lat. 5321, fol. 1^{r-v}; 19^{r-v}).

[11] Three independent accounts survive. (1) A "foundation charter" from Charroux (ca. 1050–82) speaks of a multitude of relics and an "innumerable multitude of people," among which was Charroux's precious relic of the "Holy Virtue;" see *Chartes et documents pour servir à l'histoire de l'abbaye de Charroux*, ed. Pierre Monsabert (*Archives historiques du Poitou*, 39; 1910), no. 11 (pp. 36–39), no. 15 (pp. 51–53, dated p. x); and Jean Cabanot, "Le trésor des reliques de Saint-Sauveur de Charroux, centre et reflet de la vie spirituelle de l'abbaye," *Bulletin de la société des antiquaires de l'Ouest*, ser. 4, 16 (1981–82), 103–23 (with important bibliography). (2) A miracle, reported by Andrew of Fleury, performed by the relics of Saint Benedict brought from Sault to Limoges to counter the *sacer ignis;*

Notwithstanding traditional explanations for the Peace of God—castellan wars and social disorder—this council came in response to a natural disaster: a "plague of plagues," probably ergotism, had descended with particular virulence on the Limousin and the abbot and the bishop (brothers of the viscount), in consultation with the duke of Aquitaine, called for a three-day fast during which relics from all over would come to Limoges.[12] There seems to have been a strong line of continuity between the three councils of Charroux (989), Limoges (994), and Poitiers (ca. 1000), and the "pact of peace and justice" that concluded the assembly probably drew directly from the canons at Charroux.[13] This council, then, fused two aspects of ecclesiastical practice: the long-standing custom of dealing with natural (i.e., God-sent) calamities by holding public penitential ceremonies intended to avert the anger of the Lord;[14] and the relatively new technique—pioneered in the Auvergne and mobilized on such a grand scale at Charroux five years earlier—of drawing massive crowds of inspired people to Peace councils by gathering relics in open fields.[15] Linking together on such a vast scale this penitential tradition with the newer "peace" movement, the sponsors thus guaranteed spectacular results.[16]

Still more remarkable, the authorities who thus fanned the flames of popular religious enthusiasm did so at a time of acute apocalyptic

Mirac. s. Benedicti, 4.1, pp. 174–77. (3) The relics of Saint Vivian of Figeac (in Cahors) come to Limoges to "strengthen the peace" with great crowds in response to *sulfureo ignis; Trans. et mirac. s. Viviani,* pp. 272–74.

[12] Not only did Ademar make this point explicitly and repeatedly, but so did Andrew of Fleury. This passage comes from drafts of Ademar's *Chronicon* that predate the apostolic controversy and reflect closely the collective memory of the monks of Saint-Martial ca. 1025–27 about the incident; see Landes, *History and Denial,* chap. 9.

[13] The pact probably took as its basis that of Charroux five years earlier, since five years later (ca. 1000) a ducal council at Poitiers continued to use the Charroux canons and included a five-year retroactive clause; see Jean Becquet, "Les évêques de Limoges aux Xe, XIe, et XIIe siècles," *Bulletin de la Société archéologique et historique du Limousin* 105 (1978), 85–86.

[14] At the end of the fifth century, Bishop Avitus of Vienne instituted Rogations—a vast collective penitential procession accompanied by fasts and charity—in response to the inhabitants' fear of divinely ordained annihilation; see the account in Gregory of Tours, *Historia francorum* 2.34; *MGH SRM* 1:81–84. Also in Avitus of Vienne's seventh homily; *MGH Auctores Antiquissimi* 6:108–11.

[15] As early as the sixth century, some ecclesiastics had linked these processions to relic ostentations, a practice that became extremely frequent in the tenth and eleventh centuries according to Nicole Herrmann-Mascard, *Les reliques des saints: Formation coutumière d'un droit* (Paris, 1975), pp. 222; see also Landes, "Dynamics," p. 224. On the emergence of these relic delations, see Christian Lauranson-Rosaz (Chapter 5) in this volume.

[16] In his assertion that the popular elements of the Peace movement come only later, Karl F. Werner makes no mention of this council; see "Observations sur le rôle des évêques dans le mouvement de la paix au Xe et XIe siècles," in *Mediaevalia christiana, XIe–XIIe siècles* (Paris, 1989), pp. 159–61, and p. 180, notes 18–19.

expectation. Recent years had seen the fulfillment of an unusually complete list of apocalyptic signs, prophecies, and calculations: in 987, the last Carolingian ruling dynasty had fallen, thereby fulfilling Adso's interpretation of the fall of Rome;[17] in 989, shortly after the council of Charroux, Halley's comet made a striking appearance;[18] in 991, the bishop of Laon betrayed the last Carolingian pretender, much as Judas had done to Jesus;[19] in 992, the Annunciation and the Crucifixion coincided, a moment, according to current lore, when the End would occur;[20] and, of course, the approach of the millennium of the Incarnation loomed ever more ominously on the horizon.[21] In such circumstances ergotism must have acted like a devastating catalyst: a hallucinogenic poison that can affect entire communities at once, it provokes vivid hallucinations, from atrocious visions of hell to ecstatic ones of heaven,[22] and can produce large-scale "religious revivals."[23] So for the inhabitants of the area, for whom ergotism represented a relatively new phenomenon,[24] this terrible event would have been both

---

[17] Adso Dervensis, *De ortu et tempore Antichristi*, ed. Daniel Verhelst (Corpus Christianorum, Continuatio Mediaeualis, 45; Turnhout, 1976), p. 26.

[18] Halley's comet appeared in August 989: *Annales divionenses; MGH SS* 5:41. *Annales quedlinburgenses; MGH SS* 3:68. Thietmar of Mersebourg, *Chronicon* 4.10; *MGH SS* 6:772. Also possibly Glaber, *Historiarum*, 3.3.9, see note in John France, *Rodulfus Glaber, Opera* (Oxford, 1990), pp. 110–11, and note 4. See also P. Moore and J. Mason, *The Return of Halley's Comet* (Cambridge, 1984), p. 46.

[19] On the reaction to the betrayal of Charles, see Richard Landes, "L'accession des Capétiens: Une reconsidération selon les sources," *Religion et culture autour de l'an mil: Royaume capétien et Lotharingie*, ed. D. Iogna-Prat and J.-C. Picard (Paris, 1990), pp. 153–54, 160–62.

[20] See Abbo's remarks in his *Apologeticus* (*PL* 139: 471–72) and subsequent evidence of the power of this belief in the *Vita Altmanni* (chap. 3; *MGH SS* 12:230) (for 1065, the next occurrence), and in Lambert of Saint-Omer's *Liber Floridus*, Ghent, Bibl. Univ. 92, fols. f.2r, 27v, for a full list of cosmic events attributed to this date.

[21] See Daniel Verhelst, "Adso van Montier-en-Der en de angst voor het jaar Duizend," *Tijdschrift voor Geschiedenis* 90 (1977), 1–10, Johannes Fried, "Endzeiterwartung um die Jahrtausendwende," *Deutsches Archiv für Erforschung des Mittelalters* 45 (1989), 385–473, and Richard Landes, "*Millenarismus absconditus:* L'historiographie augustinienne et le millénarisme du Haut Moyen Age jusqu'en l'an mil," to appear in *Le Moyen Age.*

[22] The natural form of lysergic acid diethylamide (LSD), ergot has a virulent psychomimetic potency. An outbreak of ergotism in southern France in 1951 has provided the most extensive data on its collective effects; see J. Fuller, *The Day of St. Anthony's Fire* (London, 1969), pp. 38–166.

[23] See J. Massey and E. W. Massey, "Ergot, the 'Jerks', and Revivals," *Clinical Neuropharmacology* 7 (1984), 99–105, and M. K. Matossian, "Religious Revivals and Ergotism," *Clio Medica* 16 (1982), 185–92. The temptation to explain every bizarre religious phenomenon as ergotism can lead one too far; see most recently Nicholas Spanos's criticism of Matossian, "Ergotism and the Salem Witchcraft Panic," *Journal of the History of Behavioral Science* 19 (1983), 358–69.

[24] Ergot probably came with the spread of rye cultivation; the earliest recorded case appears in Flodoard, *Annales*, ad an. 945, ed. Philippe Lauer (Paris, 1906), p. 100. About five outbreaks from ca. 990–1030 receive mention in the texts, among which Limoges' case is most prominent; see Henry Chaumartin, *Le mal des ardents et le feu Saint-Antoine* (Vienne, 1946), pp. 121–24.

uncanny and unprecedented. It fulfilled the prophecy in Revelation: "Their torment was the torment of a scorpion. . . . and in those days shall men seek death, and shall not find it; and shall desire to die, and death shall flee from them" (9:5–6). Little wonder, then, that the men of the turn of the first millennium since Christ called it *sacer ignis*, the "holy fire."

This apocalyptic context underlines the significance of this council's penitential dimension. Again in opposition to the Charroux council—where the sources target a certain group within society (the warriors) as cause of the disorder—here the divine punishment (holy fire) fell on all for the sins of all, and all did penance for it.[25] For contemporaries to have attributed so dreadful an experience directly to God reveals both their predisposition to perceive His hand in their lives and their appreciation of the twin nature of this purgatorial fire: it led to hell or to heaven. This response of both fear and awe before so astonishing an experience illustrates a characteristic Christian response to disaster: "From its origins, Christian preaching about the 'last days' has been permeated by this formative tension between terror and promise of salvation; between the anguish of inescapable guilt and an aspiration towards eternal communion with God."[26] In the coming generation, such public penitential ceremonies were not rare in western Europe.[27]

Seen in this light, the course of events in Limoges this November 994 followed a distinct, highly significant pattern: (1) an unprecedented disaster that awakened a mass religious response of terror and guilt; (2) public and communal acts of penitence, including three days of fasting; (3) the arrival of vast numbers of first-class relics, and accompanying crowds, to Limoges, and the raising of Saint Martial from his crypt, as it were, to greet them; (4) a mass miracle producing euphoria among those gathered; and (5) an alliance of peace and justice mutually sworn by all the lords present. The dynamics here evoke one of the great Christian (and human) longings for collective salvation on earth. In fact, the course of events corresponded closely to the millenarian

---

[25] "And the affliction did not destroy the people of Limoges but came to correct them, whence all the people of Aquitaine did penance for their sins, and, chastised by the warning of the priests, the province became a daughter of Peace, because the peace of the bishops reigned over it; Paris, BN lat. 2469, fol. 87; *PL* 141:115B. See also the (much later) *lectiones* of the abbey, ed. J.-B. Champeval, "Chroniques de Saint Martial," *Bulletin de la Société archéologique et historique du Limousin*, 42 (1894), 307.

[26] Jean Seguy, "La sociologie de l'attente," in *Le retour du Christ* (Brussels, 1983), p. 75.

[27] For example, the procession at Rebais-Jouarre in response to celestial signs that took place at Easter in the "millennial year of the Passion"; *Miracula sancti Agili*, 1.3; *AASS*, August VI, p. 588.

scenario enunciated in so much of the canonical and extracanonical literature: from divinely sent terror and destruction, to repentance and turning to God, to collective salvation, to a new society on earth.[28]

In a palpably real sense, then, the actions of those assembled—clergy, populace, and lords—constituted a society-wide millenarian ritual, one that drew "heaven to earth and saw hope only at the end of unspeakable terrors."[29] A generation later, a hagiographer from Charroux depicted the people following the relics to Limoges in 994 as a "new Israel, leaving the slavery of Egypt, and following Moses to the promised Land"[30]; and Ademar described the same events in terms of Isaiah's messianic vision of peace.[31] Not until Glaber's description of the wave of councils at the millennium of the Passion (1033) do we have anything that approaches this level of millenarian rhetoric.[32]

Despite this (later, rhetorical) sound and fury, however, little in the documents directly confirms this millenarian reading: no further councils in Limoges for over thirty years, two distinctly tame ones in Poitiers under the firm hand of the duke (1000 and 1010),[33] no signs of masses in "hot pursuit of the millennium." A skeptical historian, inclined to admit the presence of messianic sentiments only where the documents explicitly depict them, would certainly have cause to dismiss both the material and this analysis as exaggerated.[34] Yet the events of the next generation indicate that, quite suddenly, Limoges, and more generally central Aquitaine, witnessed an exceptional level of popular and clerical religious activity that calls for some explanation. And for these phenomena ample documentation survives, particularly from the monastery of Saint-Martial.[35]

---

[28] On millenarianism as a social and religious phenomenon, see Y. Talmon, *International Encyclopedia of the Social Sciences* (New York, 1968), 10:349–62. For the Middle Ages, see Bernard McGinn, *Visions of the End* (New York, 1979), pp. 28–36.

[29] Jacques Le Goff, *La civilisation de l'Occident médiéval* (Les grandes civilisations; Paris, 1964), p. 248; see also Landes, *"Millenarismus absconditus."*

[30] *Chartes de Charroux*, pp. 36, 51.

[31] Ademar of Chabannes, Paris, BN lat. 2469, fol. 88v; *PL* 141:118. See Appendix A for text.

[32] See Appendix A.

[33] See Hoffmann, *Gottesfriede*, pp. 31–33; Bonnaud-Delamare, "Institutions de la Paix," pp. 437–47.

[34] Bonnaud-Delamare argues for over 600 pages that the Peace of God was a millenarian movement connected with the apocalyptic atmosphere that intensified at the approach of the year 1000; see "L'idée de la Paix au XIe et XIIe siècles" (unpublished thesis; Paris, 1945), summarized in "Le fondement des institutions de paix au XIe siècle," in *Mélanges d'histoire du moyen âge dédiés à Louis Halphen* (Paris, 1951), pp. 19–26. No historian of the Peace has taken up his argument; see, Hoffmann, *Gottesfriede*, p. 54.

[35] Some fifty manuscripts composed in Ademar's day survive in the Saint-Martial collection; see the discussions in D. Gaborit-Chopin, *La décoration des manuscrits à Saint-Martial de Limoges* (Paris, 1969).

The Rise of the Aurelian Legend: Martial, the Apostolic Saint, and Limoges, the *Visio Pacis*

Before the Peace Council of 994, the cult of Saint Martial, the earliest missionary to Limoges, had a modestly prominent place in Aquitaine: his relics had been guarded by monks since the time of Charles the Bald, who provided him, according to the fashion, with a new (if rather laconic) *vita* associating him directly with Saint Peter.[36] By 985, the cult had grown enough that Saint Valeria's relics were moved away from Martial's (they had been buried together) to distinguish between her miracles and his. Martial's was a modestly successful cult in a period of strong growth in relic cults, but little, liturgically or hagiographically, yet suggested the changes about to take place.[37]

Within a decade of the 994 council, the liturgical activity at Saint-Martial rose to exceptional levels—new tropes, new antiphons, possibly even a new proper,[38] and by the 1010s a new and prodigious tale of Martial's origins and deeds had emerged. According to this legend, he was Simon Peter's younger cousin and a constant companion of Jesus, towel holder at the Last Supper, witness to the Ascension, and present at the miracle of Pentecost. Martial goes on from this promising beginning to a wildly successful career as a missionary and miracle worker, converting tens of thousands at a time and resurrecting more dead than Jesus.[39]

Historians have suggested two major elements of Limousin society in these years which account for such sudden and imaginative pretension. One is the pilgrims who flocked to Martial's relics in the wake of his spectacular miracles of the 994 Peace council, making Limoges one of

[36] *Vita antiquior s. Martialis confessoris*, ed. J. Arbellot, "Etude historique sur l'ancienne vie de Saint Martial," *Bulletin de la Société archéologique et historique du Limousin* 40 (1892), 238–43. The fact that the principal text concerns this link with Peter and devotes virtually no attention to Martial's career in Aquitaine suggests that it represents the work of an outside hagiographic expert.

[37] For a detailed analysis of the evidence for the Aurelian legend before 994, see Landes, "Dynamics," pp. 473–77. Paris, BN lat. 1240, with no clear Aurelian material and few tropes to Martial, dates from the *late* tenth century; see Landes, "L'accession des Capétiens," p. 159.

[38] See Daniel Callahan, (chapter 7) in this volume, and James Grier, "*Ecce sanctum quem deus elegit Marcialem apostolum*: Ademar of Chabannes and the Tropes for the Feast of Saint Martial," in *Beyond the Moon: Festschrift Luther Dittmer*, ed. B. Gillingham and P. Merkley (Wissenschaftliche Abhandlungen, 53; Ottowa, 1990), pp. 28–74.

[39] The most accessible edition of the *Vita prolixior s. Martialis* is found in L. Surius, *De probatis sanctorum vitis* (Cologne, 1618), 6:365–74; French tr. in R. Landes and C. Paupert, *Naissance d'apotre: La vie de Saint Martial de Limoges* (Turnhout, 1991), pp. 45–103; a new edition, which includes the three recensions discussed below is in preparation for the hagiographic volume of *Ademari Cabannensis, Opera omnia*, Corpus Christianorum, Continuatio Mediaevalis. Martial resurrects four people: Austreclinius, chap. 6; Nerva's son, chap. 8; Stephan the *armiger*, chap. 13; Hildebert, chap. 15.

the central pilgrimage sites of the early eleventh century.[40] These pilgrims, to whom such a great saint must have been an apostle,[41] formed the enthusiastic audience on which the monastic imagination exercised its creativity.[42] A second factor is the prolongation of efforts to enforce the Peace oaths of 994 in subsequent years, and "Martial's especial power to mediate the peace which Christ left behind him on earth."[43] This cult was therefore no mere surge of religious enthusiasm. Martial played a significant political role in society.

A closer look at the *Vita prolixior s. Martialis* confirms these conjectures. The contents of the story read like a major statement of Peace propaganda, precisely along the lines Bernhard Töpfer has analyzed for other cults.[44] In one sense, it projected the present developments of the Peace back into an idealized past, giving Martial the scope and ability during his earthly life that he had exercised in the 994 miracle of *sacer ignis*. From opening to close it resonates with the sounds of great crowds "flowing together" to hear the good news from Jesus and Martial. Mass conversions to a gospel of peace ensue, including the ruler and his soldiers, who accept an ethic of restraint and express their collective penitence with great emotion.[45] This process of projection radically transformed Valeria's pagan fiancé Stephen from a local nobleman's son into the powerful duke of the Gauls, a mirror image of William V (993–1030), with his pilgrimage to Rome, his devotion to Martial, his love of the church and of peace.[46] Elsewhere Martial exorcises Rixoaldus, the demon leader of a diabolic band, so named because he loved strife and dissension—the very personification of that

---

[40] For a possible explanation of why, despite the evidence that Martial's constituted one of the major twelfth-century relic cults in Europe, the Pilgrim's Guide made no mention of it, see R. Landes, "The Absence of St. Martial of Limoges from the Pilgrim's Guide: A Note Based on Work in Progress," in *The Codex Calixtinus and the Shrine of St. James,* ed. John Williams (Tübingen, 1991), pp. 272-33.

[41] Gaborit-Chopin, *Décoration des manuscrits,* p. 15.

[42] See the discussion of the lay role in vernacular saint's lives by Etienne Delaruelle, "La culture religieuse des laïcs en France aux XIe et XIIe siècles," in *I laici nella "Societas Christiana" dei secoli XI et XII* (Milan, 1968), pp. 563–67. For a discussion of the possible oral, vernacular source of the Aurelian legend, see Landes, "Dynamics," pp. 481–82.

[43] Cowdrey, "Peace and Truce of God," p. 59.

[44] See Bernhard Töpfer (chapter 2) in this volume. Two historians have already made this connection between the cult of Saint Martial and the Peace movement: Cowdrey, "Peace and Truce of God," pp. 49–51, and Daniel Callahan, "The Sermons of Ademar of Chabannes and the Cult of St. Martial of Limoges," *Revue bénédictine* 86 (1976), 251–95.

[45] Compare the Carolingian *Vita,* in which little attention is given to this period of Martial's career.

[46] Note the projection of eleventh-century notions of feudal authority and military service.

bellicose temperament so rampant among the warrior class, the great enemy of the Peace of God.[47]

At the same time, by picturing the past in terms of a present ideal, the authors of the *Vita* sought to give sanction to present goals—the stable and peaceful society toward which all should strive. Aurelian's image of a peaceful, prosperous mid-first-century Aquitaine, led by a pious ruler and a charismatic saint, with a populace enthusiastically embracing the Gospels, penitential warriors, poor who received charity, and a well-endowed church—this was the ultimate social message of the *Vita prolixior*.[48] As such, it articulated a vision of the Peace movement's goal: a stable alliance between the high nobility, the church, and the populace.

In a radical reversal of the tragic tale of the martyred hero of early Christianity, the Aurelian legend presented a successful missionary and a profoundly optimistic vision of society.[49] This two-way conflation of time periods had enormous appeal: it adjusted the past to accord with Martial's present glory, and it projected Martial back into the Gospels. Such an association gave local events a heightened intensity and importance. It forged a link between Limoges and Jerusalem, between the people of Aquitaine and the children of Israel, between the Age of Peace and the Age of the Gospels.[50] For pilgrims and city dwellers, lay and clerical alike, it was a heady tale.

The genesis of the Aurelian legend and its development into the apostolic cult follows the following progression: (1) the legend first emerged in the context of pilgrim enthusiasm (after 994–ca. 1015); (2) the monks recorded a Latin version, the *Vita prolixior* I in the years after the discovery of John the Baptist's head and the beginning of construction on a new basilica (1015–21); (3) the monks pressed their claims to Martial's apostolicity in the wake of the successful consecration of their *basilica regalis* in 1028.[51] The first two stages of this process seem reasonably understandable. It made sense to spin grandiose yarns, and even to write them up at a time when the monks of Angély could successfully claim to have John the Baptist's head and those of Sens, Moses' staff.[52] Indeed, the manuscript evidence suggests that

[47] For a more extended treatment of this incident, see Landes, "Dynamics," pp. 479–80.

[48] *Vita prolixior s. Martialis*, chap. 16, p. 370.

[49] Ironically, Martial's status as confessor rather than martyr, which would soon greatly bother the monks by its low rank in the church, actually served the purpose of the story admirably.

[50] These themes all appear in Ademar's sermons and the monastic liturgy; see note 38.

[51] I treat this progression in detail in *History and Denial*, chaps. 4, 10, 14.

[52] On John the Baptist, see Ademar, *Chronicon*, 3, 56–58, pp. 179–84, and below, note 72; on Moses' staff at Sens, see Glaber, *Historiarum*, 3.6.19.

these early phases enjoyed a regional, even international, triumph.[53] But the next, apostolic step seems foolhardy; it meant rewriting ecclesiastical history, inventing new liturgical practices, and challenging Peter's solitary position at the top of the western ecclesiastical hierarchy.[54] Given that Gregory of Tours listed Martial as a third-century missionary, and that hagiographers in the region such as Letaldus of Micy and the neighboring Ademar of Chabannes cited Gregory's work—even challenged pious frauds with it—such a maneuver seems (and proved to be) perilous indeed.[55] To understand how and why the monks could attempt such an innovation, we need to look more closely at the nature of the bonds between church and people that formed the most innovative element of the Peace and the creative nexus that gave the cult of Saint Martial such power.

Popular Participation and the Peace Movement

The Aurelian legend, according to interpretation suggested above, constitutes the record of (at least one side of) a discourse between the church of the early eleventh century and the believing populace about the Peace of God and the role of the saints in society. As such, it offers insight into the vexed question of how much the Peace not only mobilized the masses but gave them an active role in public affairs. Let us then place this particular cult in a larger context of popular religious and political activity in early eleventh-century Aquitaine.

Concrete Examples: The Power of Public Opinion

Let us begin with the practical. First and foremost the large crowds at Peace councils created a powerful public arena of approval for co-operative lords and warriors and of disapproval for disturbers of the

[53] See Landes, "Dynamics," pp. 473–78.

[54] For a good discussion of the difference between *apostolus simpliciter et absolute* and *apostolus minus proprie*, and of the ecclesiastical absurdity of the innovation here attempted, see Louis Saltet, "Une discussion sur St. Martial entre un Lombard et un Limousin en 1029," *Bulletin de la littérature ecclésiastique* 26 (1925), 168–73.

[55] Gregory of Tours, *Historia francorum*, 1.30; *MGH SRM* 1:23. Letaldus had been asked by the monks of Nouaillé to write about their saint's *delatio* to what may have been the first real Peace of God council at Charroux in 989; see *PL* 137:823–24. For his historical criticism of hagiographic legends, see his preface to the *Vita s. Juliani; PL* 137:781–84. See also Thomas Head, *Hagiography and the Cult of the Saints: The Diocese of Orléans, 800–1200* (Cambridge Studies in Medieval Life and Thought, 4th sers., 14; Cambridge, 1990), pp. 217–18. On Ademar, and the likelihood that at this time he numbered among the skeptical opposition, see Landes, *History and Denial*, chaps. 6, 13.

peace.[56] This is perhaps the least quantifiable, most elusive of the effects of the Peace, partly because we have no reliable account of how many attended any given council, partly because we have no direct evidence of the effect of these crowds, partly because historically speaking, these crowds did not last long (two waves of about a decade each).[57] By the 1040s, they had been firmly pushed to the margins of the instituted peace.[58]

Around 1025, however, at least one text, the *Vita et miracula sancti Justiniani pueri*,[59] depicts the enthusiastic participation of the populace in public prayer as a millenarian norm. The text concludes with an extended depiction of the relics of Justinian at a Peace council in Limoges and offers a virtual theology of conciliar miracles.[60] At this assembly, we are told, the *popularis concursus*—every order of the population, young, old, sexes mixed—"left all wordly concerns and turned to the work of praise." They thereby gained the approval of Justinian and his celestial fellow citizens and drew down their miracles. This description itself refers back to the opening passage of the work, which compares this unanimous chorus with that of the faithful at the apocalyptic fall of Babylon and invokes it as a fitting activity for a Christian society:

> As an angelic oracle admirably commanded in the Revelation of the apostle and evangelist John, all His servants—the timid and the great—should render proclamations of praise to the Lord [Rev. 19:5]: *Magnus enim est Deus noster et laudabilis nimis*, just as the psalmist predicted [Ps. 48:1]; and therefore rightly should all the people in concert sing the greatness of His

---

[56] The "maledictions" from Limoges that L. Little has studied date from the late tenth and early eleventh centuries. See "La morphologie des malédictions," *Annales: E.S.C.* 34 (1979), 58, note 2; hence they too should be considered "Peace documents."

[57] The events of 1989 in Eastern Europe illustrate this same power of large, relatively peaceful crowds forcing otherwise authoritarian regimes to cede to the pressure of the masses.

[58] The most striking case of the exclusion of the commoners from the Peace was the defeat of the Bourges Peace league and its denunciation by a reforming monk, Andrew of Fleury; see Thomas Head (chapter 9), in this volume. More generally, the move toward an institutional Peace tended to minimize their role; see Thomas Bisson, "The Organized Peace in Southern France and Catalonia, ca. 1140–ca. 1233," *American Historical Review* 82 (1977), 290–92, whose remarks on the institutional peace are mistakenly cited by Karl F. Werner as describing the earliest stage of the movement, in "Observations sur le rôle des évêques," p. 179, note 13.

[59] The *Vita et miracula sancti Justiniani pueri* appears in the Saint-Martial manuscript, Paris BN. lat. 5240, fols, 128v–39r, ed. in the *Catalogus Codicum Hagiographicorum Latinorum in bibliotheca nationali Parisiensi*, 3 vols. (Brussels, 1889), 1:392–402. We know that the text was composed before 1029 since it originally referred to Martial as a confessor; then, like so many other codices in the scriptorium, it underwent the process of erasure and correction to *apostolus*. It is by its contents, however, one of the later developments in the Aurelian cycle. The (projected) Peace material, similar to the Aurelian, appears in four of the five miracles; see Landes, *History and Denial*, chaps. 4, 14.

[60] See the extensive theological reflections in the *Miracula s. Justiniani*, chap. 3, p. 401.

praise, those of all ages, and of each sex, of every desire and every understanding, indeed every assembly of Christianity should exult in praise of his divinity, saying with the angelic spirits, *Gloria Deo in altissimis et in terra sit pax hominibus bonae voluntatis* [Luke *2:14*].[61]

The power of this public chorus of divine praise and revivalist excitement apparently enjoyed considerable success at this time. As Töpfer and many since him have pointed out, monastic communities often used their relics to mobilize this popular enthusiasm in their war against the lay aristocracy.[62] The monks of Sainte-Foi used her relics to gather large and enthusiastic crowds in the fields where some obstreperous lord contested their claims. After each miracle, all sang Psalm 150—"Praise the Lord with harp and timbril"—as a kind of theme song joyously punctuating the manifestations of divine favor bestowed on the popular party.[63] Such an example underlines the combination of religious revivalism and show of force such tactics involved.

The most telling evidence for the power of public opinion in this period comes from indications in Limoges of the use of interdict as a major sanction during the episcopacy of Alduin (990–1014), the bishop who presided over the council of 994. "Often Alduin, in response to the sins of the populace, the rapine of the fighters and the devastation of the poor, established a new observance, [wherein] churches and monasteries ceased to perform the divine cult and the holy sacrifice and the people, like pagans, ceased from divine praises, and this observance was considered an excommunication."[64] Two unusual elements stand out in this description: (1) Ademar describes interdict approvingly as new, when in fact since Gregory I's day some form of it had been in use, most often denounced by churchmen as an unjust punishment of the innocent; and (2) he presents clergy and populace as allies in a work of social justice, when more often interdict pitted clergy against laity and involved political maneuvering.[65] In this excep-

---

[61] *Vita s. Justiniani*, preface, p. 392; see Landes, "Dynamics," p. 489, note 77. See also below, note 63.

[62] See Geoffrey Koziol's analysis of this strategy used by the monks of Lobbes to literally bring the feuding nobility to their knees before the combined force of divine and social sanction (Chapter 10, this volume).

[63] *Liber mirac. s. Fidis*, 2.4, pp. 100–104; see the discussion of this material in both Töpfer (Chapter 2) and Lauranson-Rosaz (Chapter 5) in this volume. The opening passage of the *Vita s. Justiniani* cited above also cites Psalm 150 (above, note 61).

[64] Ademar, *Chronicon*, 3.39, pp. 161–62.

[65] See Landes, "Dynamics," p. 491, note 83, and Edward Krehbiel, *The Interdict: Its History and Its Operation* (Washington, 1909), p. 26, who cites only Limousin material in this category of "causes for interdict." I thank Elisabeth Vodola for her comments on this passage.

tional context, such a policy sought to coerce the guilty through arousing the innocent to protest. Such a strategy could succeed only where there was both a strong popular commitment to ecclesiastical rituals and a significant force to such protests.[66]

This sanction constituted a potent weapon in the arsenal of the sanctified peace, and it accordingly played a central role in the debates Ademar reported for the councils of 1031 whose provisions stand out as particularly severe.[67] In the early 1030s, Ademar described the effect of a great interdict as the beginning of the celestial silence that followed the opening of the Seventh Seal in Revelation.[68] The atmosphere of collective religious enthusiasm apparently had taken on an important role in the definition of the social order: the cessation of ecclesiastical ritual, including the silence of popular prayer and rejoicing, created an intolerable situation that only the submission of the peacebreakers could bring to an end.[69]

If the Aquitanian sources seem enthusiastic about this new and unwonted popular participation, other churchmen felt quite differently.[70] Not only did the Peace councils themselves seem like dangerous innovations that threatened the traditional pillars of the social order, but the populace's active role in ecclesiastical ritual and political life was particularly subversive. "The peasants are raised to God by the prayers of those who pray [i.e., clergy]."[71] It would, in fact, be one of

[66] Berhard Töpfer, *Volk und Kirche zur Zeit des beginnenden Gottesfriedensbewegung im Frankreich* (Berlin, 1957), pp. 90–93; Hoffman, *Gottesfriede*, pp. 28–29; Landes, "Dynamics," p. 491, note 82. For a later example of how it worked, see the *Actus pontificum Cenomannis*, ed. G. Busson and A. Ledru (Le Mans, 1901), p. 392.

[67] Mansi 19:541–48 (text written by Ademar: Paris, BN lat. 2469, fol. 96, in which the expression *publica excommunicatio* appears to describe interdict). See, in addition to the works cited in the two previous notes, the discussion in Karl Josef von Hefele, *Histoire des conciles d'après les documents originaux*, 2d ed. 11 vols., trans. Henri Leclercq (Paris, 1911), 4.2: 950–59. Krehbiel offers this text and Innocent III's interdict on England in 1208 as rare examples of forbidding marriage during the interdict (*Interdict*, p. 17). On the reliability of Ademar's testimony this late in his life, see "Dynamics," p. 491, note 84, and *History and Denial*, chaps. 16–17.

[68] Paris, BN lat. 2469, fol. 97, in Delisle, 'Notice sur les manuscrits," p. 295.

[69] These were not, however, phenomena characteristic of the Peace movement alone; troping, apostolic claims, and creative forms of liturgical punishment are found in many places in western Europe in this period, even places where the Peace movement had not penetrated; see Landes, "Dynamics," p. 492, note 85.

[70] Most historians treat extraecclesiastical popular religiosity before the late eleventh century primarily as a return to pagan practices and view lay commoners as generally "indifferent to the Christian mystery strictly speaking"; see E. Delaruelle, "La pieta popolare nel secolo XI," *Congresso internazionale di Scienze Storiche* (Florence, 1955), p. 317. Writers more often lamented the absence of lay participation rather than invoked Revelation to describe it as a norm; see André Vauchez, *La spiritualité du moyen âge occidental, VIIIe–XIIe siècles* (Paris, 1975), pp. 51–65, 105–17.

[71] Gerard of Cambrai, *Gesta episcoporum Cameracensium*, chap. 52; MGH SS 4:485.

the major themes of the coming papal reform to draw the fundamental
distinction between clergy and laity.[72]

Relics and the Politics of Popular Legitimacy

At the center of popular religious and political activity stood the relic
cults, a phenomenon illustrated by the discovery of John the Baptist's
skull during Lent of 1016.[73] While the duke was on pilgrimage to
Rome, the monks of Saint-Jean-d'Angély, a monastery near the coast in
the Aunis, discovered a pyramidal box with an ancient skull, which they
claimed was the head of their patron saint. The duke, returning, received the news with elation. The skull, now housed in a worthy reliquary and correctly labeled, became an international sensation.
Pilgrims came from Gaul, Aquitaine, Italy, and Spain; indeed, even the
duke of Gascony, the king of Navarre, and the king of France came
bearing gifts.

If the duke's sponsorship of this dubious relic tells us much about the
temper of the times, the way he then deployed this new find tells us
much about his manner of redirecting the Peace movement's energies.
As in the Peace councils, the relic here played the role of bringing powerful men (*comites et principes . . . omnesque dignitates terrarum*) together
in harmony. But the duke went still farther, sponsoring a kind of relic
jamboree, a reunion of all the relics from the region at Angély. On
William's orders, the skull was displayed for an extended period, thus
enabling relics from all over to be brought.[74] The climactic moment for
this unprecedented movement of relics came in October 1016, when
some of the most important relics of the region were gathered together
for All Saints' Day.

On one level, these unusual visitors intensified the charismatic
power of the newly found skull: if the ostension were a form of proof,
the presence of huge and religiously excited crowds and all the mira-

---

[72] See the various articles in *I laici nella "Societas Christiana,"* in particular Georges
Duby's "Les laïcs et la paix de Dieu" (pp. 448–61), rpt. in *Hommes et structures du moyen
âge* (Paris, 1973), pp. 227–40.

[73] The main source for the event comes from Ademar of Chabannes, *Chronicon*,
3.56–58, pp. 179–84. His account is largely confirmed by three roughly contemporary sources: *De translatione capitis s. Johannis* (to which Ademar refers disapprov-
ingly); *AASS*, June V, pp. 650–52 (ca. 1016). *Miracula s. Leonardi confessoris*, chap. 6;
AASS, November III, p. 158 (ca. 1030–50). *Chronicon Malliacense*, 2.F; *PL* 146:126
(ca. 1060).

[74] How long is difficult to say, since Ademar's two versions of the tale place the end of
the ostension at different points in the narrative; neither account gives a specific dura-
tion or date for the event. Most accounts do speak of an extended ostension.

cles that entailed,[75] would assure a positive judgment. This technique
of gathering the relics in one site to corroborate the determinations of
the authorities places this program squarely within the framework of
the Peace of God. And as they confirmed the Baptist's presence, so did
he, theirs; his skull served as a kind of touchstone whose charismatic
presence revived the power of local relics.[76] The lining up of relics from
a large catchment area, "like troops for battle," remains one of the outstanding characteristics of the sanctified peace, thus directly associating this exceptional case at Angély with the succession of relic
gatherings begun in this region at Charroux in 989.[77]

The Rhetoric of the Peace: Exodus, Prophetic Promise, Apocalypse

The mobilization of the masses these various ecclesiastical activities
indicate, and which appears either directly or indirectly connected to
the Peace movement, had an equally remarkable corollary in the realm
of religious discourse. If the apocalyptic language of the *Vita s. Justiniani* seems extravagant, in many ways that exuberance characterizes the
rhetoric of the Peace movement. When we move from the rather laconic and often highly conservative language of the surviving Peace
oaths[78] to the hagiographic, historical, and polemical descriptions of
the Peace, we find an unusual invocation of messianic imagery that
generally comes from three biblical sources—Exodus, the prophets,
and apocalyptic literature.

A common use of metaphors identified the populace with the chil-
dren of Israel: "It was to see the sons of Israel, after leaving the servi-
tude of Egypt and crossing the Red Sea, wishing to enter the Promised
Land with Moses without any desire to follow the carnal desires of
Egypt."[79] Similarly, Andrew of Fleury described the Peace militia of
Bourges in the mid-1030s as "like unto another Israelite people."[80]

[75] On the role of large crowds in encouraging miracles, see Pierre Sigal, *L'homme et le
miracle dans la France médiévale (XIe–XIIe siècles)* (Paris, 1985), pp. 188–96. In the present
case, Ademar reports that the arrival of Saint Eparchius's relics occasioned several miraculous healings.

[76] The cult of Saint Leonard of Noblat dates from these delations to Angély. See Ademar's remarks, *Chronicon*, 3.56, p. 181.

[77] The discovery of John the Baptist's head does not appear in any discussions of the
Peace movement that I have seen: for example, Töpfer, *Volk und Kirche;* Kennelly, "Peace
of God"; Bonnaud-Delamare, "Institutions de la paix"; Hoffmann, *Gottesfriede;* Cowdrey,
"Peace and Truce of God."

[78] See Goetz's analysis in Chapter 11 of this volume.

[79] See above, note 11.

[80] *Mirac. s. Benedicti*, 5.2, p. 193; see the discussion by Thomas Head (Chapter 9) in this
volume.

This comparison became a principle theme of Ademar's sermons; he repeatedly compared the *gens Aquitana* with the children of Israel.[81] Glaber's famous description of the councils of 1033 described the populace entering a covenant (*pactum perpetuum*) with God.[82] The revolutionary tendencies the Exodus story has repeatedly elicited among oppressed populations,[83] should alert us to the daring nature of this comparison, particularly since this imagery of a new Israel became an element in subsequent lay self-perception among crusaders and communards alike.[84]

As Glaber's direct association of this covenant with the inauguration of the Lord's Jubilee at the beginning of the new millennium since the Passion shows, the notion of the Christian populace as the new chosen people moves effortlessly into feelings of millenarian expectations fulfilled. Glaber's contemporaries Ademar of Chabannes and Fulbert of Chartres shared the same prophetic framework for viewing the peace of their day—the former using Isaiah's depiction of the messianic moment to describe the 994 council and its aftermath, the latter invoking the *locus classicus* of messianic promises of peace: men of this wondrous age beat weapons into ploughshares and pruning hooks (Isa. 2:4; Mic. 4:3).[85] Such imagery comes perilously close to depicting the Peace as the fulfillment of eschatological expectations, as did citations of Revelation on interdict and public worship.

These were unusual, even dangerous, biblical passages to invoke in such situations: they came uncomfortably close to millenarianism—an expectation of an earthly kingdom of God's peace and justice which ecclesiastics since Augustine had emphatically denounced.[86] Even Ade-

---

[81] Paris, BN lat. 2469, fol. 31v, 41v–42r; see Callahan, "Sermons," p. 284.

[82] Rodulphus Glaber, *Historiarum*, 4.5, p. 193. Note that Ademar uses the two terms with which the Vulgate refers to the covenant at Sinai—*pactum* (Exod. 19:5) and *foedus* (34:27)—in his description of the 994 Peace oath at Limoges.

[83] See M. Walzer, *Exodus and Revolution* (New York, 1983), G. Lewy, *Religion and Revolution* (New York, 1974), pp. 32–38, and the literature on "liberation theology." For a striking example of what this tale of liberation inspires, see the case of the "Zionist" churches of Black South Africa, for example, in Jean Comaroff, *Body of Power, Spirit of Resistance* (Chicago, 1985).

[84] For the Crusades, see Paul Rousset, "Les laïcs dans la croisade," in *I laici nella "Societas Christiana"*, pp. 428–44. On the communes, see the role of Exodus imagery in the Bourges militia (Head, Chapter 9 in this volume) and again, for example, at Amiens in the 1090s; Charter of Guy and Ivo, counts of Amiens, *Recueil des monuments inédits de l'histoire du Tiers Etat*, 1st ser., Region du Nord, ed. A. Thierry (Amiens, 1850), 1.22; I thank Jenny Borgerhoff for this reference.

[85] *Letters and Poems of Fulbert of Chartres*, ed. Frederick Behrends (Oxford, 1976), p. 262.

[86] Millenarianism here means the expectation of a reign of peace, justice, and plenty on earth for the community of the saved, a scenario foreseeing the inversion of current power structures. The resistance of the ecclesiastical hierarchy to such revolutionary ideas constitutes one of the major themes in Christian history; see R. Landes, "Lest the

mar, despite his careful training in this Augustinian tradition,[87] used millenarian imagery (often drawn directly from Revelation) to such an extent that, taking into account his unpublished works,[88] his apocalyptic concerns rival those of his more infamous colleague, Glaber.[89] Ironically, such an association of the millennium of the Incarnation (1000–33) with millenarianism may be a kind of misconceived "chronological Augustinianism" similar to the "political" variety described by F.-X. Arquillère.[90] In fact, as some historians have pointed out, the whole concept of the Peace of God has eschatological connotations, again directly related to Augustinian ideology, which—since the location of God's peace has moved from heaven to earth—border on the millenarian.[91]

Historians should not underestimate the riskiness and significance of this messianic rhetoric. In fact, apocalyptic expectations among the populace at large posed one of the perennial threats to the stability of a Christian society.[92] And ecclesiastics did not contravene so long and powerful an ecclesiastical taboo lightly.[93] One would sooner expect from them the far more conservative, indeed seigneurial, Peace oaths that also survive. The conflict here between two different kinds of society imagined—the vertical, hierarchical one of a dominating aristocracy and the horizontal, communal one of whole people acting in

---

Millennium Be Fulfilled: Apocalyptic Expectations and the Pattern of Western Chronography, 100–800 CE," in *The Use and Abuse of Eschatology in the Middle Ages*, ed. W. Verbeke et al. (Leuven, 1988), pp. 141–211, especially the appendix on definitions.

[87] See Landes, *History and Denial*, chaps 5, 6, 17.

[88] Daniel Callahan has worked on this aspect of Ademar's work the most, and his forthcoming publications, along with his edition of the sermons for the *Opera omnia*, should go a long way toward illuminating this aspect of Ademar's preoccupations.

[89] On Glaber's apocalyptic views, see his depiction of the events of the millennium of the Passion (*Historiarum*, 4.1–6) and his explicit (and forbidden) identification of the heretics who suddenly appeared in Europe around the year 1000 with the classic millenarian prophecy, the unbinding of Satan (Revelation 20:1–7; *Historiarum*, 2.11–12).

[90] F.-X. Arquillère, *L'Augustinisme politique* (Paris, 1934). For Augustine's revolutionary exegesis of Revelation, see Paula L. Fredriksen, "Apocalypse and Redemption in Early Christianity: From John of Patmos to Augustine of Hippo," *Vigiliae Christianae* 45 (1991), 151–83. For the implications of both the exegesis and the chronology, including the issue of the "Terrors of the Year 1000," see above, note 24.

[91] See, for example, Cowdrey, "Peace and Truce of God," pp. 50–52, and Henri Dubois, "Exigences chrétiennes et contrats sociaux devant la paix de Dieu," in *La paix de Dieu. Xe–XIe siècles* (Le Puy, 1988), pp. 91–93. Both Hoffmann (*Gottesfriede*, pp. 3–4) and Goetz ("Kirshenschutz," p. 193) point out that the phrase *pax Dei* does not appear before 1033 (Vic) at the earliest, although much of Ademar's rhetoric in the years immediately preceding (1030–32) comes very close to this formula.

[92] See the examples in Norman Cohn, *The Pursuit of the Millennium* (New York, 1961; 2d ed. rev. 1972).

[93] Few periods between the fifth and tenth centuries offer so many examples of churchmen using explicit apocalyptic and messianic imagery so freely; see Landes, "Lest the Millennium Be Fulfilled," pp. 181–91, and *"Millenarismus absconditus."*

concert—points up one of the key tensions of the movement. Understanding how both voices, seigneurial and radical, could speak simultaneously may shed light on the problem.[94]

The oaths, as R. I. Moore suggests, show every sign of compromise,
an acceptance of the hard realities of the unrepentant soul wielding
power.[95] They had to pass muster both with conservative bishops like
Gerard and Adalbero and with the lords and their men who took them.
In their final, published form they probably conceded much.[96] But, at
the same time, the organizers needed popular support; and just as the
written record of oaths may reflect a clerical accommodation to aristocratic opposition to the more radical currents of the Peace, so the
oral appeals of the clergy may have conceded much to popular taste. In
the Peace of God movement, as in any mass movement, a wide spectrum probably spanned what the leaders articulated "for the record,"
what they preached "live," and what their audiences understood. And
among the beliefs invoked at these mass gatherings, apocalyptic-
millenarian imagery, so apt for describing the Peace of God and one of
the few Christian themes that consistently united clergy and laity in a
common enthusiasm, surely had an important place.[97] Indeed, as we
have seen, a wide variety of such messianic themes penetrated even the
media most resistant to them—ecclesiastical writing.

Context of Apocalyptic Rhetoric: Currents of Religious Fervor

The effect of the apocalyptic rhetoric may bear some relation to the
febrile excitation of the populace at Limoges at several points in the
early eleventh century. In 1010, for example, news of the destruction
of the Holy Sepulchre in Jerusalem reached Europe, provoking both

[94] See Georges Duby's treatment of these issues in *Les trois ordres ou l'imaginaire du féodalisme* (Paris 1978), pp. 83–104, 157–206; also see the remarks by Thomas Head (Chapter 9) in this volume. The importance of this tension in the history of the movement
makes it all the more regrettable that Susan Reynolds chose not to investigate the Peace
movement in her study of the relationship between these two forces, *Kingdoms and Communities in Western Europe* (Oxford, 1984), p. 34, note 82.

[95] See R. I. Moore, "Postscript," this volume.

[96] It is doubtful that the "letter from heaven" that mobilized the northeastern bishops
of Francia to hold Peace councils between 1024 and 1036 and aroused the abiding hostility of Bishop Gerard of Cambrai contained anything like the oaths as they survive in
the documents; see Appendix A and Goetz, "Kirchenschutz," pp. 220–29, for an analysis
of such oaths as representative of the goals of the Peace.

[97] One oft-regretted characteristic of a false prophet's or false Christ's teachings is that,
in addition to the vast crowds of ignorant rustics he or she gathers around, one finds
clerics as well; for example, Christ of Bourges (Gregory of Tours, *Historia Francorum*
10.25; *MGH SRM* 1:517–19; Thiota (*Annales fuldenses* ad an. 848; *MGH SS* 1:365). See
Landes, "*Millenarismus absconditus.*"

shock and in some cases anti-Jewish pogroms.[98] Although evidence exists for similar reactions elsewhere, Ademar's account of the situation in Limoges offers the most dramatic depiction of a city in the throes of an apocalyptic seizure: the Antichrist—the Nebuchadnezar of Babylon—had seized and trampled the Temple! Limoges was buffeted by apocalyptic signs and wonders, and one night, at the height of the terrors, Ademar claims to have seen a cross planted in the heavens with the Crucified One weeping rivers of tears over the city. In response, Bishop Alduin gave the Jews of his city the choice between conversion or death. Both symbolically and temperamentally, the reaction established the vectors that led to the First Crusade and its anti-Jewish violence.

Some eight years later, a different kind of incident revealed the volatile religious passions of the day:

> In the year 1018, a nocturnal massacre of men and women occurred at Limoges. For, in the middle of Lent, while the doors of the basilica of the Savior were opened at nocturnal vigils, the stream of the crowd, like a river flowing into the church [and rushing to the tomb of blessed Martial], by accident falling over itself, each person trampled the other. And thus more than 50 men and women were trampled by each other and died on the spot.[99]

This terrible and unfortunate incident throws a dramatic light on the size and temper of these crowds during the heyday of the Aurelian legend.[100] So many laypeople attending predawn lenten prayers constitutes an unusual level of religious activity in any period, but when fifty-two men and woman are left dead, we are dealing with high-strung emotions.[101]

---

[98] For more detail on this issue, see Robert Chazan, "1007–1012: Initial Crisis for Northern-European Jewry," *Proceedings of the American Academy for Jewish Research* 38 (1970), 101–18, and Landes, *History and Denial*, chap. 4.

[99] Ademar, *Chronicon*, 3:49, p. 173. The text here is from Ademar's first recension, Alpha, brackets from Beta and Gamma. Jules Lair printed the two other versions recorded contemporaneously by Ademar and discusses the variations in *Etudes critiques sur divers textes des Xe et XIe siècles*, 2 vols. (Paris, 1899), 2.198, note 2.

[100] Written down at least five times, thrice by Ademar: in the monastery annals, hence by the community of monks (Paris, BN lat. 5239, fol. 19r; Ademar's hand); *Commemoratio abbatum* (PL 141:83C); *Chronicon*, 3.49 (in all three drafts); and twice by Bernard Itier (1189–1215): *Chronicon*, ed. Duplès-Agier, *Chroniques de Saint-Martial*, p. 46; and in Paris, BN lat. 4281, fol. 137v, marginal note.

[101] It is difficult to estimate the size of the crowd from the number of dead, but if the casualties were caused by panic and trampling it probably numbered in the thousands. See E.-R. Labande's examples of a handful of victims in "*Ad limina:* Le pèlerin médiéval au terme de sa démarche," in *Mélanges offerts à René Crozet*, ed. P. Gallais and Y.-J. Rien (Poitiers, 1966), 1:283.

Given this volatile religiosity among the laity, the clergy tried to steer a middle course, tempering radical with conservative Christian themes. The cult of John the Baptist's head, for example, invokes an ambiguous symbolism. As a precursor to Jesus, John evokes Gospel history (i.e., the past), yet his message is messianic and prophetic: "Repent for the kingdom of Heaven is at hand."[102] The invention of his head and attendant relic jamboree could thus play on both meanings and mobilize a wide range of religious excitement. As a symbol of spiritual renewal on a collective scale, it formed a crucial bridge between the first phase of the Peace movement (990s) and the second (1020–30s).[103] As a bridge, it had the advantage of calling out the great and enthusiastic crowds without involving them in the political deliberations of the Peace councils. In yet another sense, it participated in a larger geographic unification of Europe with the Holy Land—where the apostles formerly walked those same paths westward that so many pilgrims now tread eastward, to Jerusalem.[104]

We have already seen how this new intimacy between Jerusalem and Europe led the Limousins to see a special link between their city and that City; and the evidence suggests that they were far from alone in this.[105] Clearly such passions far exceed the framework of the Peace of God; but, as the example of Limoges indicates, the Peace movement welcomed these religious strivings and amplified them. One can perhaps best see the ability of the Peace movement to focus and realize some of these religious passions in the development of the Truce of God: the last four days of the week were to be protected by a total peace that would serve to highlight the salvific process of Christ's sacrifice every week, from the Last Supper (Thursday) to the Resurrection (Sunday); and while people were engaged in such commemorative meditation, a total peace was to reign.[106] The prominent role Cluny

[102] Note the parallel in ambiguity here with the Exodus/Prophetic material on Israel.

[103] For a more detailed analysis of the incident and its role in the period's developments, see Landes, *History and Denial*, chap. 10.

[104] Ademar's chronicle informs us of many individuals (including himself, 1032–34?) and groups who made the pilgrimage to Jerusalem: from ca. 1000 to the wave of the early 1030s; *Chronicon* 3.40, p. 162; 3.45, p. 168; 3.48, p. 171; 3.65, pp. 189–90; 3.68, p. 194. Compare Ademar's description (3.68, p. 194) with Glaber's (*Historiarum*, 4.6.18–21). For secondary literature, see Landes, "Dynamics," p. 492, note 87. The tale of Charlemagne's pilgrimage also dates from this period; see Stephen Nichols, *Romanesque Signs, Early Medieval Narrative and Iconography* (New Haven, 1983), pp. 66–94.

[105] See Nichols on Orléans ca. 1000 as a kind of *translatio Hierosylimitani* (*Romanesque Signs*, pp. 17–30), and the similar symbolism in Limoges in 1010. For Germany, see Alfred Haverkamp, " 'Heilige Städte' im hohen Mittelalter," in *Mentalitäten im Mittelalter: Methodische und inhaltliche Probleme*, ed. Frantisek Graus (Vorträge und Forschungen, 35; Sigmaringen, 1987), pp. 119–56.

[106] Landes, "Dynamics," p. 493, note 91; Glaber *Historiarum*, 5.1.15; Hoffmann, *Gottesfriede*, pp. 70–89 (on the four-day peace, see pp. 83–89).

played in all this suggests that, through the Peace and Truce, that order's realized ascetic eschatology had been transferred from the cloister to the *saeculum*.[107]

Rhetoric, Fantasy, and Reality: Reading the Documents

So far we have looked at the imaginary of the Peace, the story ecclesiastics told themselves and anyone else who would listen—the story they told in stone, in painting, in tales of saints' lives and miracles, in ceremony. But did they accurately characterize the situation at this time? What the monks preached and hoped for, no matter how bound up with contemporary efforts to reform society, surely dominates our sources more than it did the crowds of laypeople—peasants and warriors—whom we can glimpse moving across a much-enlarged public stage. To what extent could these implausible visions of society have had anything to do with the hard realities of this "age of iron"?

One might answer that no fantasy is without a relation to reality. Though Saint-Martial's scriptorium may have distorted the dialogue between church and laity in this period, it nevertheless offers incontrovertible evidence that a dialogue took place. One does not compose epic accounts of first-century popular religious movements in a century with no experience or memory of collective religious enthusiasm. One does not develop notations to write liturgies for public processions in an age when the laity participates minimally in public services. One does not build larger churches when attendance is down. Ademar's sermons may never have been delivered to the public, but one does not compose a liturgical cycle of "sermons to the laity" where public preaching does not occur.[108] So, if we are dealing with monastic fabrications, they are not of whole cloth but rather fantasies of control which these literate men tried to impose on an often intractable reality. As we see below, Ademar's effort to impose his individual will on history purely through the strength of his pen represents only the most extreme example of this ecclesiastical tendency.

The question, I submit, is not whether any of this popular excitement and activity occurred but rather whether the laity behaved in the ways our documents describe. Images of unanimous choruses of

---

[107] Dominique Iogna-Prat, "Continence et virginité dans la conception clunisienne de l'ordre du monde autour de l'an mil," *Comptes rendus de l'Académie des Inscriptions et Belles-lettres*, 1985, pp. 127–46.

[108] It is remarkable that Ademar's collection of sermons rarely receives attention in surveys of preaching to the laity in the central Middle Ages; see, for example, Delaruelle, "Culture religieuse," pp. 576–81.

praise and messianic enthusiasm may describe a clerical ideal, even one that, at moments, came near realization. But enthusiastic unanimity is always short-lived, and soon enough the tensions begin to show, whether in apocalyptic anxiety and panic or in the reemergence of daily struggles for power, now conceived and articulated on a grander scale. In fact, a closer look at the material suggests a considerable divergence between clergy and laity, particularly from the 1020s on. Although we cannot expect a spokesman for the "silent majority" on the order of an Ademar to have left us his reflections, we may still find important evidence of the variety and autonomy of popular responses to both the Peace and its relic cults, especially at those points at which the *consensus omnium* broke down.

Perhaps the most revealing case of such a breakdown concerns the efforts of the monks of Saint-Martial of Limoges who, basing themselves on their recent literary success with the *Vita prolixior,* inaugurated an apostolic liturgy for their patron saint on 3 August 1029. Rather than enjoy the kind of popular support they had come to expect over the previous generation, however, the monks met unexpected opposition from both other clergy and the people of Limoges. As a result, their bold drive to make Martial an apostle failed spectacularly. The following account of this abortive effort, spearheaded by Ademar of Chabannes, is based on the highly circumstantial if partial descriptions provided by Ademar in an effort to compensate literarily for his devastating defeat in public debate. The popular opposition to the apostolicity, which Ademar ruefully concedes at two points in his letter, seems strange: up until this point the cult of Saint Martial, disciple of Jesus, had risen on the wings of popular enthusiasm. Unraveling the dynamics of popular support and opposition to the cult of Martial reveals a key to both the fate of Martial's cult and the Peace of God movement to which that cult was so closely bound.

What the material suggests is that, just at the height of the solidarity between monks and the laity implied by the *Vita prolixior* and its accompanying liturgical elaborations, something went wrong and the populace turned away from the cult of Martial. Such a development does not negate my earlier reconstruction, which placed popular enthusiasm at the core of the cult's meteoric rise; rather, it relocates the nature of the support the monks enjoyed, away from the kinds of religious issues they themselves focused on and toward ones that concerned a larger population at once flushed with a sense of moral authority and beleaguered by an intractable class of aristocratic predators. To understand what happened at Limoges on 3 August 1029, we must first review the evidence for autonomous lay religiosity in the preceding period.

The Fission of the Peace Movement:
The Populace between Heresy and Aristocracy

The period from 1015 to 1030 shows both a mounting intensity of popular activity and a growing resistance from the populace's erstwhile allies in the Peace movement, the lay and ecclesiastical aristocracy. The kind of radical Christianity the early Peace movement both needed and encouraged seems to have generated still more radical forms of religiosity. Ademar reports of their presence in 1018:

> *E vestigio* Manichees arose throughout Aquitaine seducing the *promiscuous* populace, negating holy baptism and the power of the cross, *the Church and the Redeemer of the World, marriage and the eating of meat*—whatever was sound doctrine. Abstaining from food, they seemed like monks and faked chastity. But in fact among themselves they practiced every depravity and were the messengers of the Antichrist; and they turned many simple people from the faith.[109]

This description treats a movement of great concern to both Ademar and his colleagues: popular lay heresy in western Europe.[110] Whatever their origins, heresies, both lay and clerical, constituted one of the major preoccupations of the early eleventh-century church,[111] a point underlined by the fact that this period saw the first formal executions of heretics in the west.[112] Since such heresies would become an ever more

---

[109] Ademar, *Chronicon*, 3.49, p. 173; the translation is an amalgamation of the information provided in all three recensions; text in italic material found only in Alpha, which is, exceptionally, longer than Beta or Gamma.

[110] I use "popular" here to indicate the importance rather than the exclusive presence of commoners; the salient feature of "popular heresies" seems to be the way these communities dissolve the traditional social barriers; see Brian Stock, *Implications of Literacy: Written Language and Models of Interpretation in the Eleventh and Twelfth Centuries* (Princeton, N.J., 1983), pp. 88–101.

[111] By the 1020s, suspicions and accusations of heresy within the church take on the proportions of a witch hunt; see J.-P. Poly and E. Bournazel, *La mutation féodale, Xe–XIIe siècles* (Paris, 1981) p. 387.

[112] Julien Havet, "L'hérésie et le bras séculier au moyen âge jusqu'au treizième siècle," *Bibliothèque de l'Ecole des Chartes* 41 (1880), 498–507. In addition to the famous case of Orléans in 1022, Glaber (*Historiarum*, 3.8), Ademar (*Chronicon*, 3.59, p. 185), and Anselm of Liège (*Gesta episcoporum Leodiensium*, 63; MGH SS 7:228, ca. 1050), suggest widespread executions of heretics by means both of formal tribunals and of less organized violence. See Monica Blöcker: "Zur Häresie im 11. Jahrhundert," *Zeitschrift für schweizerische Kirchengeschichte* 13 (1979), 232–34.

important element of European society throughout the rest of the
Middle Ages, historians have extensively discussed both the nature
and the causes of this rather sudden appearance of popular religious dissent.[113]

Two other Aquitanian documents confirm the existence of this heresy besides Ademar's, suggesting both that it was widespread and that
it involved laypeople and clerics together.[114] Reports from Poitiers
(1016) and the Périgord (early eleventh century) also speak with alarm
about the sudden and rapid spread of heresy.[115] The sources refer to
groups that broke down the barriers between lay and clerical, literate
and illiterate, and replaced the ecclesiastical media of salvation (e.g.,
baptism, Eucharist) with the power of radical and communitarian asceticism (celibacy, vegetarianism, poverty). Finally, these dissident
Christians often explicitly rejected many ecclesiastical forms of worship: relics, icons (especially the crucifix), lavish rituals, and chants. Despite the hints of some kind of eastern dualism and the ecclesiastical
epithets of Arian and Manichaean, it seems most useful to conceive of
these groups as "textual communities" that modeled themselves on the
early passages in Acts that describe the life of Jesus' disciples. As the
alarmed monk Heribert so bluntly put it, "they say that they lead
the apostolic life."

On the one hand, such radical ethics could not have engaged too
large a proportion of the population; entry into such a community demanded a complete transformation of lifestyle, and, after 1022 at the
latest, risking the pyre. On the other, they may have attracted a much
wider range of popular sympathy. Just like the later Cathars, whose
perfecti could arouse the sympathy and support of less committed
Christians whom one would normally consider Catholics, so these
fervent followers of the *vita apostolica* would have elicited profound

[113] See two recent general interpretations: R. I. Moore, *The Formation of a Persecuting
Society: Power and Deviance in Western Europe, 950–1250* (Oxford, 1987), pp. 13–19; Malcolm Lambert, *Medieval Heresy: Popular Movements from the Gregorian Reform to the Reformation* 2d ed. rev. (Cambridge, Mass., 1992), pp. 9–32.

[114] For greater detail on these various issues, see Landes, "La vie apostolique en
Aquitaine au tournant du millennium: Paix de Dieu, culte de reliques et communautés
'hérétiques'," *Annales: E.S.C.* 46, no. 3 (1991), pp. 573–93.

[115] "[C]um multa mala opera et ante mea tempora inaudita, Arriane heresis de radice
pullulantia, non solum in populo verum etiam in sancta prevaluisse viderem aecclesia, ut
etiam ministri ab ea recedento fugerent"; *Documents pour l'histoire de l'église de Saint-Hilaire
de Poitiers (768–1300)*, ed. L. Rédet (*Mémoires de la Société des Antiquaires de l'Ouest;* Poitiers, 1847), nos. 72a and b, pp. 80–81. On the Périgord document, which Guy Lobrichon argues may be a Cluniac forgery, I think an important body of documentation
(including the above charter) argues plausibly for its authenticity as a description, later
copied (and quite possibly altered) for all the reasons adduced by Lobrichon (Chapter 4)
in this volume.

respect and admiration from fellow Christians who did not actually join their communities.

Such an analysis may explain Ademar's curious remark linking the trampling of pilgrims at Saint-Martial during Lent of 1018 with the emergence of heresy. In his first account of the incidents, Ademar linked the trampling to the subsequent outbreak of heresy with the phrase *e vestigio*, a term he generally used to indicate causality.[116] It seems unlikely that a heresy that both predated this incident in Limoges and had a far greater scope would have actually arisen in response to the trampling. More plausibly, the trampling brought these dissenting communities to the attention of the clergy for the first time, perhaps by alienating some of the laity from the relic cults, even driving particularly committed souls to join an "apostolic community," thereby increasing the profile of these dissenting groups within Limousin society. The fact that Ademar removed any suggestion of a linkage between the trampling and the rise of heresy from his subsequent recensions suggests that readers of his initial account—the monks of Saint-Martial themselves—did not like the implication that a tragedy at their church might have contributed to a popular heresy. They preferred to remember the trampling as a result of a church too small to handle the great influx of earnest faithful.[117]

One can imagine the threat that these groups, no matter how small in number, might have posed to the church. As apostolics without the compromising institutional connections that bound monks, they surpassed the church's most ascetic population and came far closer to imitating the first apostolic community. Indeed, perhaps the most threatening, and authentic, aspects of this apostolic Christianity were the dissolution of the lay-clerical distinction and the vocation to spread the word.[118] At best, the church thereby became irrelevant; at worst, it was a dangerous hindrance and distortion. And once it executed these "heretics," the church would become—in the eyes of these apostolic

---

[116] For a fuller discussion of this issue, see Landes, "Dynamics," pp. 499–503.

[117] Ademar changed the transitional phrase to *paulo post* and interjected an account of the reconstruction of the basilica of Saint-Martial *maiori amplitudine;* see *Chronicon*, 3.49, p. 173, and Ademar's entry in the *Annales lemovicenses* ad an. 1017, inserted after the entry on the trampling ad an. 1018 (*MGH SS* 2:252).

[118] Fasting and other alimentary disciplines, for example, appear to have been some of the more objectionable practices in these heretical communities. The bishop of Cambrai, when confronted with the proposal that the Peace movement ratify a weekly fast, which itself sought to limit lay fasting, found even this unacceptable; *Gesta episcoporum Cameracensium* 3.52 (1024–36); *MGH SS* 4:485–86. See also Glaber, *Historiarum*, 4.5. The paleness of a person became a sign of fasting, and hence of heresy; see Anselm of Liège, *Gesta episcoporum Leodiensium*, 63; *MGH SS* 7:228.

Christians and their sympathizers at least—precisely what Ademar saw in them: *nuncii Antichristi.*[119]

The nature of this threat seems clear enough, but it takes on added significance in light of the Peace movement in two senses. First, it seems closely related to the penitential, revivalist aspects of the Peace: the direct lay participation, the emphasis on divine peace, the intense, even apocalyptic atmosphere.[120] In this sense these "heresies", whether they arise out of or in conjunction with the Peace, represent its radical wing.[121] Second, these apostolic ideals undermined precisely those aspects of ecclesiastical practice directly related to controlling and directing the populace. The rejection of relics, icons, and ecclesiastical chants voided the saints' cults—so strikingly represented by the *Vita prolixior*—of any power to mediate the Peace. And to reject the sacraments robbed interdict and excommunication—the Peace movement's main sanctions—of any bite.

Such developments must have struck the conservative elements of the Peace movement (as well as its still more conservative opponents) as most ominous. Convoking these large crowds had, from the start, constituted an enormous risk; and, although the initial results had been most gratifying, matters now seemed to take a turn for the worse. The genie was out of the bottle, and getting it back in posed near-insurmountable problems. The turmoil caused by the news from Jerusalem in 1010 had already marked a new and dangerous phase, in which cultural unity turned to suspicion and hostility and the Jews were only the first scapegoats in the gathering storm. Even within Christian society, the united front of the Peace, with peasants, lords, and clerics acting in concert, began to break down.[122] After all, Peace councils were organized and presided over by the highest traditional powers in society: bishops, abbots, kings, dukes, and counts. These men strove to domesticate the Peace, to divert it from the political and re-

---

[119] Note Augustine's hesitation to use the death penalty against Donatists for fear that they might paint themselves as martyrs; Epistola 100, cited in H. Deane, *The Political and Social Ideas of St. Augustine* (New York, 1963), p. 210.

[120] Historians often distinguish apocalyptic and apostolic movements in Christianity, a tendency which—for all its virtues—overlooks the fact that the apostolic community itself lived in intense apocalyptic expectation directly associated with inspiration from the Holy Spirit and the arrival of God's Peace (e.g., Luke's citation of Joel's apocalyptic prophecy in *Acts* 2:17–21). On the value of open-field Peace councils as a missionary ground for heretics who avoid churches, see Landes, "Dynamics," p. 506.

[121] Poly and Bournazel speak of the Peace as middle way between heresy and the "three orders"; see *Mutation féodale*, p. 387. Here, I suggest that it initially contained both these extremes, only to break up in the 1020s and 1030s; see Landes, "Dynamics," p. 506.

[122] My research has suggested that the events of 1010 represent a watershed in the shift from inclusive to exclusive religious dynamics, a key moment on the path to the "persecuting society" that R. I. Moore describes in *Formation of a Persecuting Society.*

ligious dangers toward which it tended, to turn the sanctified peace into the instituted peace.[123]

How did the populace respond to this *prise-en-main* of a movement in which they had played so important a role? The apostolic heresies represent only one pole of that response. One can detect more moderate, but hardly less dynamic, reactions as well. In 1019, for example, a direct confrontation developed between the inhabitants of Limoges and the vice-comital dynasty that had, for the previous generation, held the two key ecclesiastical offices of that city in their family. With the death of his uncle Geoffrey, abbot of Saint-Martial, the viscount's son, Bishop Gerard,[124] overrode the election of a new abbot and kept the position empty, thus keeping the abbey's substantial income to himself. The populace, however, reacted violently; after two years of unrest, Gerard relented.[125] The Peace movement's hallmark, the pressure of public opinion, appears this time, not in the context of an actual Peace council, but as an expression of lay religious commitment to the integrity of an ecclesiastical institution—in this case Saint-Martial.

These two expressions of popular religiosity—the emergence of lay apostolic communities and the objections to the abbatial vacancy—characterize two poles of the renewed lay spirituality of early eleventh-century Europe. In 1018, we find a radical but popular sect that utterly rejected the church; in 1019–21, a mainstream tradition that demanded the restoration of that same organization's integrity. Revolution and reform: both exhibited unusual intensity at every level of society.[126]

Popular spirituality, then, had a life and intensity all its own.[127] This autonomy illuminates the link between its arousal on a large scale

[123] For an excellent portrayal of the point of view of the "leaders" of the movement, based primarily on conciliar documentation, see H.-W. Goetz (Chapter 11) in this volume.

[124] Gerard went straight from the laity to mount the cathedra and epitomized the bellicose feudal noble against whose accession to the episcopacy the papal reform soon battled so ardently; see Becquet, "Les évêques," pp. 87–91.

[125] Ademar, *Chronicon*, 3.50, p. 174: "per biennium seditio non minime fuit civilis." This sounds the death knell for the viscount's control, which failed in both ecclesiastical offices in 1024–25.

[126] On the links between the Peace and subsequent papal reform, in which Limoges may have played a significant role, see Amy Remensnyder (Chapter 12) in this volume, especially the reference to the 1045–50 ducal grant of episcopal elections to the canons: *Sancti Stephani lemovicensis cartularium*, no. clxxxi (150), ed. Jacques de Font-Reaulx, (*Bulletin de la Société archéologique et historique du Limousin*, 68; Limoges, 1919), pp. 174–76.

[127] Curiously Töpfer, the historian who first asked to what extent the church was successful in domesticating popular spirituality with the relic cults, cites the 1018 trampling at Limoges in the context of the church's success "in bringing the masses under their control." He follows Ademar's suggestion that the trampling was caused by a too-small church; *Volk und Kirche*, p. 428.

under the auspices of the Peace movement and its crystallization in the form of antiecclesiastical apostolic cults. To imagine that the failure of the Peace movement should leave the populace bewildered and passive drastically oversimplifies what must have been a highly varied response. Accordingly, we find that Aquitaine, the region in which the Peace of God may have originated, also produced one of the most active *foyers hérétiques* of the early eleventh century. The development we can observe in Limoges passed from Peace activity (994), through pilgrimage and ceremonially elaborate relic cults that repeatedly excited the populace (1000–16, Martial, John the Baptist), to an evangelical revivalism that placed no confidence in the church (1016–22) and popular pressure for its reform (1019–21).

The next decade did not see these tensions abate. In 1028, Duke William "called a council at Charroux to wipe out the heresies which Manichaeans were spreading among the commonfolk. All the *principes* of Aquitaine were there, and he ordered them to confirm the Peace and venerate the Catholic church."[128] There is no mention here of relics or crowds of people;[129] on the contrary, Ademar's narrative clearly indicates that the populace was part of the problem.[130] So, at the site of the first relic council in the Peace movement, William, who had sought to institutionalize the Peace since the turn of the century,[131] drew a clear line between the reform of society and the creation of a new society. In Aquitaine, the duke tried to place the Peace firmly in the camp of reform; popular participation was, in principle, now neither necessary nor particularly welcome.

For the lay populace, the *inermes,* there were other activities: spectacular commemorations and liturgies. That same year of 1028, the duke also went to Limoges, where he brought great gifts in honor of the eight-day festival and relic translation in consecration of the basilica at Saint-Martial.[132] Here we find the large crowds of the earlier Peace, but, as in the case of the skull of John the Baptist, the focus of

[128] Ademar, *Chronicon* 3.69, p. 194. See also Landes, "Dynamics," p. 507, notes 137–38.
[129] Cf. Steven Sargent, "Religious Responses to Social Violence in Eleventh-Century Aquitaine," *Historical Reflections / Réflexions historiques* 12, no. 2 (1985), 223, and Landes, "Dynamics," note 139.
[130] The language of this account suggests the possibility that the task of extinguishing heresy among the populace was in some way entrusted to those *principes* attending; see corroborating evidence, note 112.
[131] See the council of Poitiers, ca. 1000; Mansi 19:256–57. Discussion in Hoffmann, *Gottesfriede,* pp. 31–32, Debord (Chapter 6) in this volume, and Landes, "Dynamics," p. 507, note 141.
[132] Landes, "Dynamics," p. 508, note 142; noted in Leiden, University Library Codex Vossiani Latini Octavo, 15 fol. 187r, in Delisle, "Notice," p. 318. Detailed account of the events in Paris, BN. lat. 2469, fols. 94–95, partial edition, Charles de Lasteyrie, *L'abbaye de Saint-Martial de Limoges* (Paris, 1901), pp. 422–26; Landes, *History and Denial,* chap. 13.

attention had shifted to more traditional ecclesiastical and less political activities. Thus, in his last year before retiring to Maillezais,[133] the seventy-year-old duke articulated a well-defined social program with a brilliant future:[134] an instituted peace, the repression of heresy, a reformed church, and elaborate relic ceremonies.[135]

Martial's Apostolic Cult and the "Climax" of the Sanctified Peace, 1029–1033

Events immediately following the assemblies of 1028 indicate that the populace had still more to say. In fact, the immediate fate of Martial's cult illustrates in spectacular detail the kinds of tension now at play within Aquitanian society. The dedication of the new, larger church in November 1028 apparently enjoyed enormous success. Indeed, evidence indicates that at least in part the crowd's fervor inspired the monk-historian Ademar of Chabannes, monk of Angoulême, to "convert" to the Aurelian legend.[136] If the duke's strategy for separating the radical, apostolic wing from the religious mainstream relied on relic cults to absorb popular enthusiasm, it is not surprising to find ecclesiastical efforts focused on swelling the appeal of relics and their liturgical cults as much as possible. And, in the increase in the aristocracy's willingness to formally approve the populist elements of the relic cults, Ademar saw his opportunity. Himself drawn by the conspicuous display of the cult's popularity and ducal approval of November 1028, Ademar was in turn able to convince the monks and abbot of Saint-Martial and the bishop of Limoges to attempt the most daring innovation yet, an apostolic liturgy to match the claims of the *Vita prolixior*.[137]

In so doing, however, Ademar and the monks pushed too far; the reversal of the cult's fortunes reveals the failed gamble, the overinflation of the Aurelian legend. The day of reckoning came immediately, at the very inaugural of Saint Martial's apostolic mass in the Limoges cathedral, 3 August 1029. The early morning meditative calm was destroyed by a pugnacious Lombard who engaged the monastery's foremost apostolic spokesman, Ademar, in a violent debate before a large

---

[133] Alfred Richard, *Histoire des comtes de Poitou*, 2 vols. (Poitiers, 1903), 1.196, note 1; 1.220, note 1.

[134] See the discussion by Amy Remensnyder (Chapter 12) in this volume.

[135] William also traveled south to Bordeaux and in September held a large *conventum* at his *castrum* at Blaye, together with the duke of Gascony. There he imposed a reform archbishop, a Frank *moribus honestum*, on the metropolitan see: *Chronicon*, 3.69, p. 194. See Landes, "Dynamics," p. 508, note 144.

[136] Landes, *History and Denial*, chap. 13.

[137] This liturgical campaign included a new version of the *Vita prolixior*. For a more detailed analysis of all these matters, see Landes, *History and Denial*, chap. 14.

public audience.[138] Despite all the evidence for popular support for the relic cult before this time, Ademar admits with a bitter sense of betrayal that on this day the crowd sided with Benedict. Indeed, the Lombard seems to have provoked a stampede away from the apostolicity similar to the panic of 1018. Ademar and the monks were stripped naked of their pretensions and made the laughing stock of Aquitaine.[139] By the time the dust had settled, Ademar was back in his old monastery at Angoulême while his enemy, Benedict of Chiusa, was attending other regional celebrations, regaling his hosts with tales of his victory.

We do not know how the monks at Saint-Martial felt, but their would-be impresario was devastated, alone in a hostile environment. There, driven by shame and isolation into an increasingly pathological attachment to his apostolic patron, Ademar dedicated a corpus of fictitious accounts and forgeries to Martial whereby the battle so ignominiously lost in reality was won on parchment. At the center of this web of deceit stood the accounts of the 1031 Peace councils of Bourges and Limoges, which debated at length on Saint Martial and, obeying a (forged) papal injunction, affirmed his apostolic status. Possibly neither of these assemblies took place.[140]

Unaware of this problem with the documents, churchmen from the twelfth century onward read the narrative as a reasonably straightforward factual account, and modern secular readers accepted their judgment.[141] So, although Benedict carried the day—there was little likelihood that the partisans of apostolicity would have dared raise the issue in any council held in the next few years,[142] and he probably drove Ademar to an early grave some five years later—Ademar won the battle with subsequent generations. For over 900 years, literate readers of early eleventh-century texts have seen Ademar's contemporaries through his inverted lenses; as a result, we have sadly misjudged them.

In particular, we have misjudged the crowds to have been typically passive, credulous, unreflecting, and eager to believe any nonsense the clergy might throw their way. But even Ademar's own text clearly indi-

[138] On the interpretation of Ademar's letter concerning this debate, see Landes, "Dynamics," p. 495, note 94, and *History and Denial*, chaps. 15–16.

[139] Paris, BN lat. 5288, fol. 57rb; *PL* 141:107.

[140] They probably did take place, although until we have a full edition of Ademar's writings in this period, and particularly the sermons, we cannot dismiss the possibility that they were entirely fabrications.

[141] Saltet's articles were passed over in silence for the next three decades, and his argument remains only imperfectly understood today; see Landes, "Libellus," p. 195, note 58.

[142] The monks of Saint-Martial probably did not try to deploy Ademar's dossier until the second half of the eleventh century, and not until the twelfth did they succeed.

cates that the populace sided with Benedict against the apostolicity.[143] In this strange story we find an early eleventh-century crowd behaving in ways historians rarely consider when thinking about the "silent majority": actively listening, rejecting claims, choosing (changing) sides.[144] Ironically, here, tacit assumptions about the nature of the populace led historians into being more gullible than the subjects of their study.[145] By September 1029, virtually no one accepted the apostolicity of Martial; but, until the late twentieth century and in many cases to this very day, most historians continue to think that all Aquitaine (and the pope to boot) accepted it.[146]

Our first task, then, is to explain this reversal of fortune, a reversal that runs so strongly counter to our understanding of eleventh-century events that even after Saltet (1925–31)—for more than a half century after him—medievalists denied its occurrence. The foregoing study, by focusing on the cult of Saint Martial in championing the Peace of God as an alliance between aristocracy and populace, suggests a way to understand Ademar's failure. In a sense, Benedict skillfully exploited the whole range of social tensions involved, from petty intramural rivalries to heretical religiosity and apocalyptic anxieties.

In pursuing the glorification of their saint to invidious levels, the monks had alienated other ecclesiastical communities, in particular the canons of the cathedral who secretly brought Benedict into town. "The abbot and his monks," Benedict claimed, "have built up this false apostolicity for still more money and because of their pride and haughtiness."[147] In pushing too far, the monks had revealed the seamy

[143] Paris, BN, lat. 5288, fol. 55vb; *PL* 141:102–3. Saltet emphasizes the critical acumen of Benedict of Chiusa rather than the crowds; see "Une discussion," p. 171. This letter predates Ademar's conscious decision to falsify an entire corpus and therefore contains major revelations that would, in time, be systematically eliminated.

[144] Ademar refers to the crowd's presence at their debate and to Benedict's disturbing preference for crude barbarisms (which they could have understood?) over the High Latin Ademar preferred; see fol.52vb; *PL* 141:93C.

[145] These assumptions of passivity and lack of discernment derive partly from the perspective the ecclesiastical sources wish to convey, partly from the fact that these illiterate groups do not participate in the medium historians most prize, documentation.

[146] In addition to those works mentioned in Landes, "Libellus," see S. Sargent, "Religious Responses"; despite being aware of Ademar's propensity to forgery (p. 230, note 46), Sargent continues to use Ademar's texts edited (anonymously) in Mansi without any critique. He claims, for example, that "the dispute [on the apostolicity] provoked heated discussions at the councils of Bourges and Limoges in 1031 and continued to be ventilated therafter" (p. 230); this is precisely what did not happen. As for the forged papal letter, which we have in Ademar's autograph, only the most recent edition of papal correspondence cites it as a forgery; see Harald Zimmermann, *Papsturkunden 896–1046* (Österreichischen Akademie der Wissenschaften, philosophisch-historische Klasse Denkschriften, 177; Vienna, 1985), pp. 1114–15.

[147] Paris, BN lat. 5288, fol. 52ra; *PL* 141:91D.

side of their liturgical choreography, staining the relic's "clean power" with their ambition.[148] To anyone who might have been influenced by the lay apostolic hostility to relic cults in general, such developments could only reinforce the argument that relics enslaved people to spiritual idols, permitting a greedy clergy to manipulate a superstitious populace.

To those in the crowd dedicated to Martial, Benedict apparently made a different appeal—to their fear of damnation. He presented the apostolic liturgy as a novelty and a sin, something that injured Martial and polluted his altar, angering the saint and his heavenly company. Since Ademar depicted Martial holding his entire flock of Aquitanians in his hand at the day of judgment, guaranteeing collective salvation for all his servants, this threat of Benedict's would have had particular potency at a time of apocalyptic expectation. The Lombard may have had precisely such anxieties in mind when he threatened dire consequences for all Aquitaine in the next five years (i.e., 1029–34), the final years of the millennium of the Passion which Glaber identified as a time of widespread apocalyptic fervor.[149]

The incident illustrates both the popular commitment to the church and its relic cults and the strength and autonomy of this lay spirituality aroused by the Peace movement. Without strong popular support for Martial's cult over the previous decades (i.e., the pilgrimage context in which *Vita prolixior* first emerged and found such success), the notion of attempting something as audacious as a public apostolic liturgy would not have occurred and certainly never could have reached the stage of enactment that it did. Without the crowd's willingness to change sides, the Lombard's attacks could not have struck home; its enthusiasm would have blunted his every attempt. One could argue that if Benedict stampeded them with apocalyptic threats then they were indeed gullible, since here we are a thousand years later reading about their lives. Possibly,[150] but in any case they were certainly not inactive, and to judge by subsequent developments like the communes and the Peasant's Crusade, the *vulgus* did not think of themselves as minor players.

It is not surprising, then, that subsequent activity in the Aquitanian Peace movement suggests unabated strains and intensities. First, an extended famine struck much of France including Aquitaine, driving

---

[148] See the difficulties Ademar has with the accusations of innovation and the rather remarkable passage on the superiority of new truths to old lies which he added to his circular letter; Paris, BN lat. 5288, fol 53va; *PL*, 141:96.

[149] On this aspect of Benedict's argument, see Landes, *History and Denial*, chaps. 15–17.

[150] On the issue of understanding those who fall prey to the "millenarian error," see Landes, "*Millenarismus absconditus.*"

some even to cannibalism. According to Glaber, contemporaries feared the end of the world;[151] for inhabitants of Limoges, this colossal disaster must have evoked memories of Benedict's ominous prophecies.[152] At the same time, a growing wave of pilgrims headed for Jerusalem, according to Glaber in order to be present at the millennium of the Passion. Described by both Ademar and Glaber, these pilgrim masses included many commoners; within five years of Benedict's triumph Ademar himself would join their ranks. In 1031–33, a series of councils convoking large crowds met in Bourges, Limoges, Poitiers, and throughout Francia.

On one hand, the clerical forces in Aquitaine found themselves in a weakened position in these years; according to Ademar, laypeople at every level of society—*sive principibus et subditis, sive urbanis et rusticis*—treated their excommunications with contempt.[153] On the other, the vast attendance the documents once again portray suggests that the populace's enthusiasm for the Peace had revived.[154] It is difficult to sort out just what happened and why, and since Ademar's testimony at this point had reached its mythomanic peak, it will be a long time before we can interpret it. The emergence of a Peace militia at Bourges in the next few years, however, enlisting everyone in the diocese over fifteen years old in a *coniuratio* of unprecedented proportions, suggests that popular participation had reached new heights and taken new forms. Its bloody defeat at the hands of the lord of Déols's mounted army, applauded by the reforming monk Andrew of Fleury, also implies that the tensions within the Peace movement had reached the breaking point.[155] Between an aristocratic *reprise en main* and programs of self help that were at once religiously radical and socially revolutionary, the commoners had few attractive options.

Whatever consensus historians eventually come to on the Peace of God in Aquitaine, at least two aspects of the problem need reconsideration. First, the bias of the documentation deserves a more systematic analysis. Ademar, for example, left us a specifically personal dossier of fabrication, one that actually inverted the deeds and

[151] Glaber, *Historiarum*, 4.4.10–13.
[152] Ademar makes much of both the apocalyptic symbolism of the famine and its role as divine punishment for lack of respect for the church.
[153] Paris, BN lat. 2469, fol. 96v, in Delisle, "Notices," p. 293. Landes, "Dynamics," p. 495, note 93.
[154] See the remarkably similar descriptions in the charter from Saint-Maixent of ca. 1032 and Glaber's description of the wave of councils that began in Aquitaine and spread to all France in 1033 (both in Appendix A).
[155] See Thomas Head's analysis (Chapter 9) in this volume.

attitudes of all his contemporaries.[156] This accounts for one part of the irony pointed out at the beginning of this essay: we have extensive documentation on a council in 1031 that may not have occurred. Second, and still more problematical, the role of the populace deserves more attention. Rather than the careful textual analysis the former investigation calls for, this issue demands conjecture and speculation. Obviously, we cannot take as accurate the rare and distorted depictions of popular thoughts, feelings, and actions provided by our documentation; but equally obviously, the commoners did think and feel and act. Somehow, if we wish to understand this period, we must try to reconstruct their mental world in its multiplicity.

In this sense, it gives too much weight to an unworthy documentation to disregard clues indicating religious enthusiasms (apostolic, apocalyptic, millenarian, totemic) because the narrative texts are insufficiently explicit, and therefore to forgo considering how these beliefs may in turn have played a role in a more aggressive, assertive, and self-organizing peasantry. However tentative, speculations about the ups and downs of people's hopes and fears, their friendships and hatreds, respect the nature of the historical process more than a narrow literalism that unconsciously assumes that, where no documentation exists, little happened. Hence we confront the second part of the opening irony: virtually no direct documentation survives about a council in 994 that, in my conjectured reconstruction of reality, set in motion the phenomenal developments of the next generation, including Ademar's mythomania.

Underlying this approach is a contention about writing history, particularly the history of a society with limited literacy.[157] The historian cannot derive narrative reconstructions from the documents alone. He or she must include the documents themselves as part of the historical events under study, must use conjectures and hypotheses to go behind their distorting lenses, to a story that also explains why they tell the tale they do. Ultimately, the verdict should favor the reconstruction that offers a convincing account both of what happened and of how those (conjectured) events led highly trained people to write, and certain privileged circles to preserve, the surviving documents. At that point, perhaps, we can produce a *narratio rediviva* that incorporates the products of a half-century of analytic social history.[158]

[156] In this sense, it differs significantly from the far more common "community" forgery of the period.

[157] I treat this theme at much greater length in *History and Denial*, chap. 2.

[158] See Lawrence Stone, *The Past and the Present Revisited* (New York, 1987), pp. 74–96.

9

The Judgment of God:
Andrew of Fleury's Account of
the Peace League of Bourges

THOMAS HEAD

The bishops who assembled in the synods that promulgated the Peace of God faced a paradox that has plagued the unarmed advocates of peace from the women of Greece portrayed by Aristophanes in the *Lysistrata* to contemporary antinuclear activists. The problem is simple: what nonviolent measures can be taken to coerce armed powers to stop fighting? Bishops of the year 1000 chose to rely on sacred power. Although they may not have enacted new laws, they did bring new religious weapons to the defense of existing laws against the growing power of the castellans and the knights.

Their efforts to enforce existing laws and to oppose the *milites* with the potent symbols and rituals of Christianity were by no means unique. Contemporary monastic communities had an entire array of sacred weapons to bear against their enemies, both secular and ecclesiastical. First and foremost, monks used the power provided by their saintly patrons against castellan opponents, as when the monks of Conques paraded the relics of Saint Faith to protect their property rights in a "place alienated from [her] by an unjust intruder," or when the monks of Fleury brought some of their relics to one of their vineyards which had been plundered by the servants of Bishop Arnulf of Orléans.[1] In both cases, according to the compilers of the collections of miracles in which these stories are found, the monks emerged victorious against their enemies. Indeed, the collections of posthumous miracle stories from the eleventh century are full of chastisement miracles in which the patron saint punished enemies of his or her *familia*

[1] Bernard of Angers, *Liber mirac. s. Fidis*, 2.4, p. 100; Aimo of Fleury, *Mirac. s. Benedicti*, 2.19, pp. 123–25.

following such ritual manipulation of the saint's relics or communal prayer directed to the saint. In still other cases, monks called on the power of their patron through elaborate curses.[2] All these actions— processions, chastisement miracles, curses—depended on what I have called elsewhere the logic of saintly patronage: the monastic *familia*— including the monks themselves, the tenants of their lands, and the donors of properties—expected that the saintly patron would protect them in this world and the next in return for their service.[3]

Saintly patronage was a potent form of sacred power in this society, but it was not the only source of power on which monks drew. Monastic scholars of this period also gathered authoritative passages from the works of the church fathers and the acts of ancient councils, seeking to create a tradition of canon law that would protect monastic institutions. As Abbo of Fleury, the ablest of these legal theorists, wrote condemning the actions of certain armed laymen, "Those who are these days called defenders of churches defend for themselves that which by law belongs to the church against the authority of laws and canons. Thus they inflict violence on clerics and monks and they rob the property of churches and monasteries for their own use and profit."[4] In a significant body of writings and speeches, Abbo called on the king of France to institute and enforce a peace of laws that would protect ecclesiastical lives, property, and power. The movement for monastic exemptions, which Abbo in large part began, was directed, at his monastery of Fleury in particular, against the power of local bishops as much as the depredations of local *milites*.[5] It is crucial to remember that in the world of the year 1000 there was no single, monolithic church

---

[2] Lester Little, "Formules monastiques de malédiction aux IXe et Xe siècles," *Revue Mabillon* 58 (1975), 377–99, and "La morphologie des malédictions monastiques," *Annales: E.S.C.* 34 (1979), 43–60; Patrick Geary, "La coercition des saints dans la pratique religieuse médiévale," in *La culture populaire au Moyen Age: Etudes présentés au quatrième colloque de l'Institut d'études médiévales de l'Université de Montréal, 2-3 avril, 1977*, ed. Pierre Boglioni (Montreal, 1979), pp. 145–61, and "L'humiliation des saints," *Annales: E.S.C.* 34 (1979), 27–42.

[3] Thomas Head, *Hagiography and the Cult of Saints: The Diocese of Orléans, 800–1200* (Cambridge Studies in Medieval Life and Thought, 4th ser., no. 14; Cambridge, 1990), pp. 187–201.

[4] Abbo of Fleury, *Collectio canonum*, chap. 2; *PL* 139:476–77.

[5] Jean-François Lemarignier, "L'exemption monastique et les origines de la réforme grégorienne," in *A Cluny: Congrès scientifique. Fêtes et cérémonies liturgique en l'honneur des saints abbés Odon et Odilon 9–11 juillet 1949* (Dijon, 1950), pp. 288–340, and "Structures monastiques et structures politiques dans la France," in *Il monachesimo nell'alto medioevo* (Settimane di studi di Centro italiano di studi sull'alto medioevo, 4; Spoleto, 1957), pp. 357–400, particularly 383–96 on Abbo; Marco Mostert, *The Political Theology of Abbo of Fleury: A Study of the Ideas about Society and Law of the Tenth-Century Monastic Reform Movement* (Middeleeuwse Studies en Bronnen, 2; Hilversum, 1987), pp. 176–96; Head, *Hagiography and the Cult of Saints*, pp. 240–55.

but rather various churches—monastic, episcopal, papal, and perhaps even lay—which competed for spiritual supremacy.

The bishops had a different set of weapons at their disposal. Chief among them was the threat of anathema or excommunication, invoked regularly in conciliar acts beginning with the council of Charroux. As representatives of Christ on earth, the bishops were empowered to separate from the body of Christ any armed man who attacked the church, its clergy, or other unarmed people under its protection. Excommunications differed significantly from monastic curses.[6] They separated offenders not simply from the *familia* of a single saint, as did a monastic *clamor,* but from all Christian society. They depended for their power on a definition of Christendom precisely as the body of Christ rather than as a collection of local *familia* and churches.[7] In the more universal definition of Christian society implicit in these excommunications, the bishops held a position of ultimate earthly supremacy. At many councils following that of Charroux, the bishops went a significant step farther: they not only threatened to excommunicate those who transgressed the Peace but also attempted to create a community of peace through the administration of oaths to the laity of their dioceses. In those oaths the potentially violent *milites* vowed, over the relics of saints, to maintain the Peace. Thus the bonds of human society were strengthened and an important new communal element was added to the episcopal definition of society We return to this communal element later.

In the late 1030s, Aimon de Bourbon, archbishop of Bourges, went yet another step farther. In the wake of a council attended by the bishops of his province, he required that all males of his diocese swear an oath to maintain the Peace. This oath does not seem to have varied significantly from earlier ones. Then, however, the archbishop formed a military force composed largely of the so-called unarmed, that is, both clerics and the *inermis vulgus,* or commoners. Some nobles and their armed retainers also chose to join.[8] The purpose of this force, which I call the Peace league of Bourges, was to ensure acceptance of the oath

[6] Roger Reynolds, "Rites of Separation and Reconciliation in the Early Middle Ages," in *Segni e riti nella chiesa altomedievale occidentale* (Settimane di studio del Centro italiano di studi sull'alto medioevo, 33; Spoleto, 1987), particularly pp. 409–25.

[7] On these two notions of church, see the suggestive, but general, remarks of Auguste Dumas, "La notion de la propriété ecclésiastique du IXe au XIe siècle," *Revue d'histoire de l'église de France* 26 (1940), 14–34, particularly 15–23.

[8] The use of the word *inermis* to describe people involved in military operations demonstrates that that term did not necessarily signify people completely lacking in weapons, but rather those who did not possess the specific trappings of the *milites.* On the problems of this term, see Bernard Bachrach, "The Northern Origins of the Peace Movement at Le Puy in 975," *Historical Reflections / Réflexions historiques* 14 (1987), 417, and the bibliography cited there.

by the *milites* and to enforce their compliance with its terms. After significant early success, the archbishop's motley force suffered a humiliating defeat at the hands of a recalcitrant noble, Odo of Déols, on the
banks of the Cher river. This was the only instance during the early
phase of the Peace movement in which armed force was used to combat
armed violence. The main source for information about these extraordinary events is a lengthy narrative contained in Andrew of Fleury's
collection *Miracula sancti Benedicti.*[9]

As an attempt to bring divine power directly to bear on certain new
and growing social problems, the Peace of God formed part of a larger
shift in mentality during the eleventh century, a shift that gradually
but inexorably altered the perceived boundaries between clergy and laity and, more generally, between heaven and earth. It is important to
remember that the Peace involved both religious and social elements;
indeed, at its very heart was a concern with reorganizing the relationship of Christianity to a changing social milieu. Andrew of Fleury was,
for his part, a keen observer of such changes. He came from a leading
monastic community in which traditions of both historiographic writing and monastic reform had long flourished. In the final analysis, he
disapproved of the actions of Archbishop Aimon as an inappropriate
attempt to employ sacred power to solve secular problems. This monk
of a traditional abbey thought that there were other ways to solve the
problems threatening Christian society. He was at odds, in this and
other instances, with partisans of the Peace of God, both monks and
bishops. To understand these differences is to understand much of
what was at stake for West Frankish clerics in the social revolution of
the early eleventh century. Thus an analysis of Andrew's interpretation
of the Peace league of Bourges, as well as of other contemporary
events, helps to illuminate the shifting perceptions of social and cosmic
boundaries which occurred during the first half of 'e eleventh century.

It is first necessary to consider Andrew and the events he chronicled
in some detail. He was born to a knightly family in the Orléanais during the reign of Robert the Pious. He was quite proud of the stature of

---

[9] Andrew of Fleury, *Mirac. s. Benedicti,* 5.2–4, pp. 192–98. The best manuscript of Andrew's work is Vatican, Reg. lat. 595. Albert Vermeesch has reedited the section of Andrew's story of the Peace league with reference to fols. 13–15 of that manuscript in *Essai
sur les origines et la signification de la commune dans le nord de la France (XIe et XIIe siècles)*
(Studies Presented to the International Commission for the History of Representative
and Parliamentary Institutions, 30; Heule, 1966), pp. 28–34, note 52. Since the Vermeesch edition makes certain important improvements on that of de Certain, I provide
dual citations for all references to Andrew's description of the Peace league of Bourges.
Otherwise, I use the de Certain edition. The episode is treated in more summary
fashion in the *Chronicon Dolensis coenobii* (in an entry under the year 1033); see *RHF*
11:387–88. A translation of extended passages from Andrew's account can be found in
Appendix A.

his family and its willingness to fulfill its moral and social obligations. In particular, he recalled how his father had once fed many poverty-striken people during a famine.[10] When Andrew entered the religious life, he did so at the leading monastery of his region. Relics of Benedict of Nursia had been enshrined at Fleury since their alleged translation from Monte Cassino in the seventh century.[11] Monks of Fleury named Adrevald and Aimo had earlier collected stories of the miracles worked at their home through Benedict's patronage.[12] Between 1041 and 1043, Andrew undertook a continuation of their work.[13] Unlike those earlier authors, however, Andrew chose to include almost exclusively stories about dependencies of Fleury rather than about the abbey itself. He arranged his stories geographically, dealing with Aquitaine, Spain, and Italy in his first book; with Fleury's priories in the Berry in the second; and finally with those in Burgundy and Neustria in the third.[14]

Andrew opened the second book of his collection by citing the solar eclipse of 8 August 1038. This event was followed the next day by the sight of blood-colored flames shooting from the sun. A description of the Peace league of Bourges immediately followed, introduced by the words *eadem nihilominus tempestate,* which indicate that in Andrew's mind it was one fulfillment of the dire omen. Archbishop Aimon of Bourges took these actions because "he wished to impose in his diocese peace through the swearing of an oath."[15] First he gathered his

[10] *Mirac. s. Benedicti,* 7.10, pp. 266–67.

[11] The authenticity of the relics of Benedict at Fleury is a vexed question, impossible to consider here. See Head, *Hagiography and the Cult of Saints,* pp. 23–24, and the bibliography cited there.

[12] In Latin, the name of Aimo of Fleury is the same as that of Archbishop Aimon de Bourbon. To ease the distinction of the two characters, I retain the spelling "Aimo" for the monk of Fleury which I used in *Hagiography and the Cult of Saints* and use "Aimon," as did Guy Devailly, *Le Berry du Xe siècle au milieu du XIIIe: Etude politique, religieuse, sociale et économique* (Civilisations et Sociétés, 19; Paris, 1973), for the archbishop of Bourges.

[13] *Mirac. s. Benedicti,* 4, prologue, pp. 173–74. Andrew's collection of miracle stories forms the fourth, fifth, and sixth books of the de Certain edition. The date of the composition is a matter of some controversy; see Head, *Hagiography and the Cult of Saints,* p. 70. The manuscripts and other editions of this work are listed by Alexandre Vidier, *L'historiographie à Saint-Benoît-sur-Loire et les Miracles de Saint Benoît,* posthumously edited and annotated by the monks of Saint-Benoît de Fleury (Paris, 1965), pp. 197–201, 203–4.

[14] A few years later Andrew went on to treat events at Fleury itself, composing first a life of Abbot Gauzlin and then a fourth book of miracles that had occurred at the mother house itself. This fourth book of miracle stories (the seventh book of the de Certain edition) was composed sometime after 1044. The last four chapters of this book were added by an anonymous continuator after 1056.

[15] "Eadem nihilominus tempestate, Aimo Bituricensium archiepiscopus, pacem sub iuris iurandi sacramento in diocesi stabiliri voluit suo"; *Mirac. s. Benedicti,* 5.2, pp. 192–93 (in Vermeesch, p. 28). The exact date of these events is a matter of some dispute. Andrew dates them to 1038, the year of the eclipse. The *Chronicon Dolensis coenobii,* however, dates them to 1033.

suffragans together for a synod and then, with their assent, required
that all the male inhabitants of his diocese over the age of fifteen take
such a binding oath to observe the peace. Aimon was himself a member
of the nobility of the Berry whom he was trying to control.[16] Andrew
inserted the purported text of the oath into his narrative. It was required of all males over fifteen and sworn in the first instance over the
relics of Saint Stephen, patron of the Bourges cathedral. Unlike oaths
sworn at earlier councils, which generally required that the oath taker
not violate the Peace themselves and not have dealings with any men
who did, the Berry oath required the men of the diocese to enforce
(*commonefacere*) the pact against transgressors.[17] In Andrew's description, the oath required that those who swore it

> would in no way withdraw secretly from the pact even if they should lose
> their property, and that, what is more, if necessity should demand it, they
> would go after those who had repudiated the oath with arms. Nor were
> ministers of the sacraments excepted, but they frequently took out ban-
> ners from the sanctuary of the Lord and attacked the violators of the
> sworn peace with the rest of the crowd of laypeople [*populus*].[18]

This unlikely army successfully cowed most of the nobility of the Berry
into taking the oath. The league focused its efforts on the castles that
dotted the countryside. Andrew likened the arrival of the Peace league
at such a fortified place to the march of the people of Israel: the doors
of castles were thrown open and violent knights submitted to the representatives of God.

So far, Andrew had described the Peace league in positive terms. The
conflict pitted the humble of society—the peasantry (*agrestes*) and the
clerics—against their noble and knightly oppressors. Faced with this
unarmed multitude (*multitudo inermis vulgi*) under divine protection,
the *milites*, "forgetting their status as knights and abandoning their fortified places, fled from the humble peasants as from the cohorts of

[16] Devailly, *Le Berry*, pp. 138–48. Aimon de Bourbon succeeded Gauzlin of Fleury as
archbishop. His departure from the policies of Gauzlin, who was a hero for Andrew,
might have been in itself sufficient to earn him bad marks from this monastic author.

[17] Vermeesch, *Origines de la commune*, pp. 37–39, discusses this innovation and the
content of earlier oaths. The verb *commonefacere* is an unusual one, similar in meaning to
the verb *commonere*. On the misguided attempts of various commentators to change it to
commune facere, see pp. 30–31. Vermeesch suggests that it expresses the idea of "putting
into effect a decision which has been made." He does not seem to realize that Andrew
later used the same word to describe the actions of a group of noblemen who sought to
prevent the bringing of a lawsuit against the monks of Fleury; see *Mirac. s. Benedicti*, 5.17,
p. 215.

[18] *Mirac. s. Benedicti*, 5.2, p. 193 (in Vermeesch, pp. 28–29).

very powerful kings."[19] For emphasis Andrew cited the book of Psalms (17:28 and 32): "For thou dost deliver a humble people, but the haughty eyes thou dost bring down, for who is God but the Lord?"[20]

Once peace had been established "in every direction," however, the laudable purposes of the league began to unravel because its members forgot their own place in the moral order. Ambition (described as *cupiditas radix omnium malorum*) began to triumph over the natural *humilitas* of the peasants and clerics. Aimon, "unmindful of his episcopal dignity," marched his forces against Beneciacum, whose lord, Stephen, was accused of breaking the peace.[21] The league laid siege to his castle and eventually set it aflame. The slaughter was described as fearful:

> The inhabitants of that region for a radius of fourteen miles had fled to this castle and, since they feared the theft of their possessions, they had brought them along. The cruel victors were hardly moved by the laments of the dying, they did not take pity on women beating their breasts, the crowd of infants clinging to their mothers' breasts did not touch any vein of mercy.

Andrew placed the death toll at a probably exaggerated figure of fourteen hundred; Stephen was spared, only to be imprisoned. The tenor of the monk's moral judgment on this military action is unmistakable: "They [the members of the league] forgot that God is the strength and rampart of his people and ascribed the power of God [*virtus Dei*] to their apostate power [*fortitudo apostata*]."[22]

After the iniquitous, indeed polluted, defeat of Stephen, there still remained one major noble who refused to assent to the oath. This man, Odo of Déols, now became the agent of a divine judgment turned against the archbishop and members of his Peace league. Supported by Geoffrey, viscount of Bourges, Aimon marched to the Cher river, where his outnumbered forces faced those of Odo. The league, once likened to the people of Israel peacefully led by God through the desert, was now compared to the warlike tribe of Benjamin. Some of the league's peasants mounted mules in order to impersonate knights and thus confuse and intimidate Odo's troops. Instead, this motley force was quickly routed. Numerous clerics perished in the melee, and the archbishop himself was severely wounded. The dead included those very people who at Beneciacum "had refused obedience to any

---

[19] *Mirac. s. Benedicti*, 5.2, p. 194 (in Vermeesch, p. 31).

[20] The numbering is as in the Vulgate. The translation is from the Revised Standard Version, where the verses are numbered 18:27 and 31.

[21] The *castrum Beneciacum* is probably Bengy-sur-Craon, thirty kilometers east of Bourges; see Vermeesch, *Origines de la commune*, p. 32, note 62.

[22] *Mirac. s. Benedicti*, 5.3, p. 195 (in Vermeesch, p. 32).

requests for mercy, and had not been moved by the smell of their brothers' being burned, and had rejoiced more than was just to have a hand in an unfortunate victory." On the day after the conflict, the river seemed to have sprouted a forest of discarded weapons and corpses. Its waters ran red with blood. This parallel to the original bloody omen in the sky concluded Andrew's account. The monk added one brief note of interest to his immediate audience: Alberic of Sully, the perpetrator of "innumerable evil injuries" against the abbey of Fleury, perished on the field of battle.[23]

What are we to make of Andrew's story? Modern historians have tended to view his collection of miracle stories as a hodgepodge of hagiographic anecdotes in which so-called historical material, such as the story of the Peace league, has been inserted virtually at random.[24] Alexandre Vidier set the tone when he remarked, "For [Andrew] the miracles are less his purpose than the pretext he used for writing history."[25] Georges Duby has more recently commented in a similar vein: "Although a hagiographer, [Andrew] did not refuse the historian's role."[26] Such an approach risks grave injustice to Andrew's method of composition and to the fact that, for an eleventh-century monk, there was virtually no difference between historiography and hagiography.[27] These historians have suggested that Andrew's opposition to the Peace movement had its roots in a conservative desire to protect the traditional social order against the forces of change: the monk who had himself come from a knightly family wished to protect the privileged position of the *milites*. I argue here that Andrew's collection was rather

[23] *Mirac. s. Benedicti*, 5.4, pp. 197–98 (in Vermeesch, pp. 33–34).

[24] See, for example, Roger Bonnaud-Delamare, "Fondement des institutions de paix au XIe siècle," in *Mélanges d'histoire du Moyen Age dédiés à la mémoire de Louis Halphen*, ed. Charles-Edmond Perrin (Paris, 1951), pp. 19–26, and "Les institutions de paix en Aquitaine au XIe siècle," in *La paix* (Recueils de la Société Jean Bodin, 14; Brussels, 1961), pp. 468–70, 474–81; Bernhard Töpfer, *Volk und Kirche zur Zeit der beginnenden Gottesfriedensbewegung in Frankreich* (Neue Beiträge zur Geschichtswissenschaft, 1; Berlin, 1957), pp. 92–94; Hartmut Hoffmann, *Gottesfriede und Treuga Dei* (Schriften der Monumenta Germaniae historica, 20; Stuttgart, 1964), pp. 34–38, and 106–9; Vermeesch, *Origines de la commune*, pp. 24–41; Georges Duby, "Les laïcs et la paix de Dieu," in *I laici nella "Societas Christiana" dei secoli XI e XII* (Miscellanea del Centro di studi medioevali, 5; Milan, 1968), pp. 448–69, and *The Three Orders: Feudal Society Imagined*, trans. Arthur Goldhammer (Chicago, 1980), pp. 185–91; Devailly, *Le Berry*, pp. 142–48.

[25] Vidier, *L'historiographie*, p. 206.

[26] Duby, *Three Orders*, p. 185.

[27] Collections of miracle stories, such as that composed by Andrew, cross the overly strict boundaries laid down by modern historians between medieval historiography and hagiography. On this problem, see Jean Leclercq, *The Love of Learning and the Desire for God: A Study in Monastic Culture*, trans. Catherine Misrahi (New York, 1961), pp. 196–206; Léopold Genicot, "Sur l'intérêt des textes hagiographiques," *Académie royale de Belgique: Bulletin de la Classes des lettres et des sciences morales et politiques*, 5th ser., 51 (1965), 65–75; Pierre-André Sigal, "Histoire et hagiographie: Les *Miracula* aux XIe et XIIe siècles," *Annales de Bretagne et des Pays de l'Ouest* 87 (1980), 237–57.

a carefully organized and argued exposition of the logic of saintly patronage, in particular as it functioned for the abbey of Fleury. It was
this traditional mentality that molded the monk's attitude toward the
Peace of God, as found both in the Berry and earlier at Limoges.

Let us first consider the two most influential analyses of Andrew's
text. Guy Devailly stresses that, contrary to Andrew of Fleury, the author of the *Chronicon Dolensis* completely ignored the role of the Peace
of God in his brief description of the events leading to the battle of the
Cher. That anonymous author instead emphasized that in the previous
year Geoffrey of Bourges had killed the eldest son of Odo of Déols.
The battle on the Cher was thus simply the solution of a blood feud.
Devailly describes Andrew's connection of the Peace movement to that
battle as nothing but a hypothesis and claims that the battle itself was
"a feudal action of the classic type." Moreover, he points out that most
historians have ignored the "precious information" provided in the
acts of episcopal synods held at Limoges and Bourges earlier in the
1030s. Although the bishops discussed the problems of violence and
peace at some length, they took no steps to develop institutional guarantees for the Peace of God. These considerations lead Devailly to dismiss the importance of the Peace league, indeed of all communal
efforts, in controlling violence in the Berry.[28]

Devailly is correct in his suggestion that the connection made by Andrew between the Peace league and the battle of the Cher was an interpretive act, but so too was the description of the battle found in the
Chronicon Dolensis. Interpretation is the essence of any historical narrative. Moreover, the notice on the battle of the Cher in the *Chronicon*
is extremely brief, and the omission of details in itself should not be
taken as significant. Also, since the implicit purpose of the Peace of
God was to control "feudal actions of the classic type," any military action—no matter how misguided—taken by the bishops within the context of the Peace was likely to have followed the form of such military
actions. More to the point, we do not have any records of other feuds
in which peasants mounted donkeys to mimic knights. Devailly's analysis is also obviated in part by the fact that the acts of the synods of
Limoges and Bourges, which he incorrectly takes to be direct reports,
are forgeries written by Ademar of Chabannes.[29] Thus, those acts lead
the historian not into the social reality of the Berry in the 1030s but
rather into the convoluted mind of the hagiographer and historian

---

[28] Devailly, *Le Berry*, pp. 142–48.
[29] Louis Saltet, "Les faux d'Adémar de Chabannes: Prétendues decisions sur saint Martial au concile de Bourges du 1er Novembre 1031," *Bulletin de la littérature ecclésiastique* 27
(1926), 145–60.

described by Richard Landes.[30] It would seem imprudent to deny the importance of the communal actions against castellan violence on the basis of the texts cited by Devailly.

Other scholars have suggested that the very involvement of peasants and clerics in such a military engagement offended Andrew's sense of the social order. Most important, Georges Duby sees Andrew's account of the Peace league as an important text in the development of the ideology of trifunctionalism. Andrew was the first writer in northern France to use the term *ordo* in reference to knights. Examining Andrew's eventual condemnation of the Peace league, Duby summarizes the monk's view of the battle of the Cher: "Enraged, God condemned the heterodox inversion of terrestrial social functions, in which serfs had brazenly attempted to dominate lords, and curates instituted as shepherds had turned into wolves."[31] In this view, Andrew was essentially a conservative who defended the trifunctional order against seemingly revolutionary attempts on the part of clerics and peasants to gain for themselves privileges that belonged by right to knights. Duby here attempts to draw a firm boundary between the uses of sacred and secular power in medieval society. In such a scheme, the use of sacred power for gain in the social order is somehow heterodox. Such distinctions are, however, overly rigid and lead to mistaken emphases in reading Andrew's text. They tend to substitute modern historical concerns— a focus on feudalism or trifunctionalism, both problematic terms—for Andrew's own interpretation.

To come to a fuller understanding both of Andrew as an author and of the events he described and interpreted, it is necessary to unpack the interpretive framework that forms and structures Andrew's attitudes toward the events he narrated. For this monk of Fleury, as for the bishops of the Peace movement, sacred power was a necessary element in any solution the church could provide to those social conflicts in which its representatives were engaged. As the mediators of divine power, clerics could quite correctly employ the power in their hands for defense against secular institutions and magnates. According to Andrew, however, the clergy involved in the Peace league had forfeited their right to divine protection through their own moral iniquity. They had refused to live up to the standards they had set for others. In their stead, a nobleman had become the instrument of divine providence. God punished the members of the league, not because of some "heterodox inversion of social functions," but because Aimon de Bourbon and his fellows had broken their own oaths through their

---

[30] See Chapter 8 in this volume.

[31] Duby, *Three Orders*, pp. 186–90 (quotation on p. 190). Contrary to Duby, I read the phrase *medio equitum ordine partiuntur equestri* (*Mirac. s. Benedicti*, 5.4, p. 196) as a reference to the line of battle formed by mounted men, not an *ordo* of society.

slaughter of the innocent at Beneciacum. They had inverted, or more accurately abandoned, their moral function. In phrases such as *virtus Dei* and *fortitudo apostata* contained within the passage quoted above, Andrew clearly distinguished between faithful and unfaithful uses of sacred power.

Since the Peace league involved a misuse of sacred power (the oath of peace) against secular authority (the power of the nobles and knights), it is important to determine what would constitute for Andrew an acceptable use of such power. A set of excellent examples can be found in the remainder of the second book of his miracle collection. These stories concern Châtillon-sur-Loire, a priory of Fleury located in the Berry. The history of that priory was marked by a series of disputes with local lords, both secular and ecclesiastical. These troubles help to explain Andrew's antipathy toward important members of the Peace league.[32] Geoffrey, viscount of Bourges and ally of Archbishop Aimon, had once laid claim to a wood that belonged to the priory. The viscount challenged a champion of the monks to a judicial duel, in which he was struck blind. When Geoffrey admitted that he had given false testimony, his sight returned, but only in his right eye. In a similar manner, the canons of the cathedral of Bourges had resorted to an ordeal to uphold their false testimony in a court action involving the lands of Châtillon. The hand of the canons' *advocatus* at first appeared to be free from harm, but then it miraculously festered, showing the truth of the claim of the monks associated with Fleury. In yet a third court case, the niece of a cleric from the Berry who had donated a church to Fleury chose to dispute the inheritance. As a result of her attempt to undo this gift to a saint, she became paralyzed. In all three cases, Andrew credited Saint Benedict with the triumph over the enemies of Fleury. The saint was not simply an effective legal advocate but a powerful warlord. When Count Landrey of Nevers led the men of the castle of Saint-Satur against Châtillon, the troops who defended the priory defeated their enemies by using the saint's name as a battle cry. The saint provided protection, in Andrew's words, "like a rampart."[33]

---

[32] *Mirac. s. Benedicti*, 5.7, pp. 203–5; 5.13, p. 211; 5.17, pp. 215–16.

[33] *Mirac. s. Benedicti*, 5.15, pp. 212–13. D. W. Rollason, "The Miracles of St. Benedict: A Window on Early Medieval France," in *Studies in Medieval History Presented to R. H. C. Davis*, ed. Henry Mayr-Harting and R. I. Moore (London, 1985), p. 86, and Carl Erdmann, *The Origin of the Idea of Crusade*, trans. Marshall Baldwin and Walter Goffart (Princeton, N.J., 1977), p. 91, both discuss this episode. Although the monks were not involved as combatants, Andrew favorably mentioned the involvement of clerics in battles against the Moslems in Spain, and he knew stories told by his predecessor of how the defenders of Fleury's properties had used the relics and banners of Saint Benedict in defeating their foes. See *Mirac. s. Benedict*, 2.15, 2.16, and 3.7. For further discussions of those episodes, see Erdmann, *Idea of the Crusade*, pp. 46–47, 90–93, and Rollason, "Miracles of St. Benedict," pp. 85–86.

The logic of saintly patronage—so well illustrated in these stories about Châtillon—formed the cornerstone of Andrew's interpretive framework. Aimo, the monk who had compiled a collection of miracles at Fleury earlier in the century, quite succinctly summarized that logic when he described one calamity at Fleury as having been possible only because Benedict had withdrawn "the right hand of his protection" from sinful monks.[34] The only striking difference between Andrew's collection and those of his predecessors was that Andrew numbered most of the secular enemies of Saint Benedict among the lesser nobility, whereas Adrevald and Aimo had described the opponents of earlier times as coming from the high nobility.[35] Numerous authors from other religious communities possessing the relics of great saints recorded similar miracle stories about saintly protection.[36]

To state simply that Andrew saw saintly patronage as a proper and acceptable form of sacred power available to religious communities for their protection against secular powers, however, does not sufficiently explain his attitude toward the Peace league in the Berry. A more detailed examination of two other episodes from Andrew's collection helps illustrate the manner in which the author from Fleury envisioned the relationship between sacred and secular in society and how that relationship allowed him to judge specific acts of social displacement to be sinful.

The first episode is the story of Stabilis, who lived near Fleury in the village of Bouteilles. Andrew described him as being in servitude (*ex servili conditione*) to Saint Benedict.[37] Under economic pressure, this serf moved to a village in Burgundy. There, while he pretended to be a freeman, his economic fortunes improved considerably. He was able to purchase all the material necessities of a knight, including a horse, weapons, and hounds. He even married a woman of free status. In Andrew's words, this man had changed his servile status (*rusticana ignobilitas*) for knightly or military privileges (*militaris commercium*). The serf's pretense of freedom included completely forsaking all his duties to Benedict, to the point that he even feigned ignorance of the saint's name. A monk of Fleury, sent to oversee various possessions in Bur-

[34] *Mirac. s. Benedicti*, 3.19, pp. 166–67.
[35] Rollason, "Miracles of St. Benedict," pp. 82–88.
[36] See, for example, Baudouin de Gaiffier, "Les revindications de biens dans quelques documents hagiographiques du XIe siècle," *Analecta Bollandiana* 50 (1932) 123–38; Pierre-André Sigal, "Un aspect du culte des saints: Le châtiment divin aux XIe et XIIe siècles d'aprés la littérature hagiographiqe du Midi du France," in *La religion populaire en Languedoc du XIIIe à la moitié du XIVe siècle* (Cahiers du Fanjeaux, 11; Toulouse, 1976), pp. 39–59; Henri Platelle, "Crime et châtiment à Marchiennes: Etude sur la conception et le fonctionnement de la justice d'aprés les Miracles de sainte Rictrude (XIIe s.)," *Sacris Erudiri* 24 (1978–79), 156–202; Head, *Hagiography and the Cult of Saints*, pp. 135–201.
[37] *Mirac. s. Benedicti*, 6.2, pp. 218–21.

gundy, discovered Stabilis and brought him before the count of Troyes, who decided to solve the case by means of a judicial duel. Stabilis designed an ingenious strategy for subverting the miraculous process of the duel. While holding a coin that symbolized his dues as a servant of the saint (*servilis testimonii obulus*) in a hidden place, he declared that he owed nothing more to Benedict. Thus his statement, made in reference to the hidden coin, was technically true, but his audience, unaware of the coin, would be unable to interpret it correctly. As he spoke, the small coin immediately grew to enormous proportions. His trick thus unmasked, the case was decided against him. Andrew concluded that the serf thereafter remained in stability (*stabilitus*) as Benedict's servant, punning on both the serf's name and the monastic vow of *stabilitas*. Stabilis had indeed revolted against the social order by pretending to be a knight. For Andrew, however, his primary offense had been his denial of his servitude to Benedict. The sin lay in the breaking of the bond between Stabilis and the divine, not in the breaking of the social bonds between the serf and living human beings.

Sin was for Andrew a form of pollution; only a supernatural patron such as Benedict could rid society of such pollution. This can be seen in his account of the famed heresy trial of 1022 in Orléans.[38] The canons of Saint-Aignan who stood trial represented a different type of revolt against the authoritative ecclesiastical and social order. The brief description Andrew provided of their trial is in general accord with several more extensive extant sources.[39] What is remarkable is the story, recounted nowhere else, of what happened at Fleury shortly thereafter. One of the monks had a vision of devils entering the cloister through the latrines. Benedict himself then appeared and attacked the demons with his abbatial staff (*baculus*), driving them through the northern door of the monastery.[40] This episode puts much of Andrew's psychopathology, particularly his fear of pollution, into sharp focus. The heretics were explicitly the servants of the devil. After their

[38] *Mirac. s. Benedicti*, 6.20, pp. 247–48.

[39] Andrew also described this heresy trial at the end of the first book of his life of Abbot Gauzlin; see *Vie de Gauzlin, abbé de Fleury: Vita Gauzlini abbatis Floriacensis monasterii*, ed. and trans. Robert-Henri Bautier and Gillette Labory (Sources d'histoire médiévale publiées par l'Institut de Recherche et d'Histoire des Textes, 2; Paris, 1969), chap. 56, pp. 96–103. An earlier letter describing the incident written by John of Ripoll, a guest at Fleury, is edited in an appendix to the *Vita Gauzlini*, pp. 180–83. All three sources from Fleury bear many similarities to one another. On their relationship to each other and to the better-known descriptions of Paul of Saint-Père-de-Chartres, Ademar of Chabannes, and Rodulphus Glaber, see Robert-Henri Bautier, "L'hérésie d'Orléans et le mouvement intellectuel au début du XIe siècle: Documents et hypothèses," in *Enseignement et vie intellectuelle* (Actes du 95e Congrès national des sociétés savantes, Reims, 1970. Section de philologie et d'histoire jusqu'à 1610, pt. 1; Paris, 1975), pp. 64–69.

[40] The description is similar to that given of Benedict in other visions by Andrew's predecessors: *Mirac. s. Benedicti*, 1.18, p. 45; 1.20, pp. 49–50; 1.40, p. 84; 2.2, p. 97.

execution, their familiar demons sought other victims and tried to invade Fleury through an appropriate break in its supernatural defenses.
The saintly patron immediately routed their forces. Andrew believed
that the monastery was surrounded by demons, as was dramatized in
the story of a sinful cellerar who was almost carried off by demons
when he wandered outside the monastic enclosure one night.[41] The
monastery was not just an island of holiness in a secular world; it was
an oasis in the midst of demonic pollution. Only Benedict's protection
kept his servants pure and safe.

In the collection of miracles performed by Saint Benedict, Andrew
presented a coherent logic of saintly patronage that shielded the servants of the saint from attack and pollution. This protection served
against supernatural, natural, and social enemies (the devil, sickness,
and the *milites*). Archbishop Aimon and the members of the Peace
league had similarly called on sacred protection through the oath they
took to maintain the Peace, but they had sinned by breaking their own
oath. The pollution of that sin, like that of the faithless Stabilis or the
heretical canons of Saint-Aignan, had to be condemned and expiated.
Andrew described—either explicitly, as in the judgment of Stabilis, or
implicitly, as in the case of the expulsion of the heretics' familiar demons—many ordeals and judicial duels as forms of supernatural
punishments.[42] So, too, Andrew employed the term for ordeal in his
description of the battle of the Cher. Odo of Déols had been "reserved
by the judgment of God [*judicium Dei*] for the punishment of evil
doers."[43] Commenting on the peasants and clerics who died in the
Cher, Andrew said: "Thus the most tempered judgment of God [*judicium Dei*] made those people, who had refused obedience to any requests for mercy, lose their lives along with their victory."[44] Andrew

---

[41] *Mirac. s. Benedicti*, 6.8, pp. 229–30.

[42] On the ordeal in this period, see, among others, Rebecca Colman, "Reason and Un-
reason in Early Medieval Law," *Journal of Interdisciplinary History* 4 (1974), 571–91; Peter
Brown, "Society and the Supernatural: A Medieval Change," *Daedalus* 104 (1975), 133–
51; Colin Morris, "*Judicium Dei:* The Social and Political Significance of the Ordeal in the
Eleventh Century," *Studies in Church History* 12 (1975), 95–112; Paul Hyams, "Trial by
Ordeal: The Key to Proof in the Early Common Law," in *On the Laws and Customs of England: Essays in Honor of Samuel E. Thorne*, ed. Morris Arnold et al. (Chapel Hill, N.C.,
1981), pp. 90–126; Charles Radding, *A World Made by Men: Cognition and Society, 400–
1200* (Chapel Hill, N.C., 1985), pp. 5–21; Robert Bartlett, *Trial by Fire and Water: The
Medieval Judicial Ordeal* (Oxford, 1986), particularly pp. 34–103.

[43] "Solusque ex omni multitudine Odo Dolensis superfuit, vindictae malorum Dei iudicio reservatus"; *Mirac. s. Benedicti*, 5.2, p. 194 (in Vermeesch, p. 31). As Morris ("*Judicium Dei,*" p. 96) points out, this was the Latin term most commonly used, outside
England, for "ordeal" at this time.

[44] "Sicque Dei equissimo vitam cum victoria amisere iudicio qui obeuntium nullis mis-
erationibus flexi, nidore fraterne nequaquam moti exustionis"; *Mirac. s. Benedicti*, 5.4, p.
197 (in Vermeesch, p. 34). Compare Andrew's language of judgment in two stories dis-

sharpened this sense of divine vengeance in his concluding reference to
the death of Alberic of Sully, an enemy of Fleury, in the battle. Earlier,
the members of the league had wrongly believed themselves vindicated
by God (*quasi Deo ex hoc praebiturus vindictam*) after the reduction of
Beneciacum. In Andrew's terms, the battle of the Cher publicly manifested God's will in the manner of an ordeal.

Andrew thus described the Peace league and its use of sacred power
in the language of saintly patronage. There are obvious similarities between the Peace of God and the traditional veneration of the saints at
monastic shrines. Many modern scholars have pointed out that the
Peace movement in general utilized many of the trappings of the cult
of relics.[45] Thomas Bisson has gone so far as to make the early, "sanctified" Peace into a virtual extension of the cult of saints: "In West
Frankland, despairing clergymen assumed not only the burden of
restoring the Carolingian institutes of peace and justice no longer enforced by the kings, but also that of pacifying the brutalized populations whose leaders were wrecking the county. And the instrument of
pacification was found in the cult of relics."[46]

The question remains, however, whether the sacred power employed
by the Peace movement was in fact the same as that which formed the
roots of Andrew's traditional logic of saintly patronage. According to
Andrew and his monastic brethren, the *familia* of Saint Benedict were
linked to God through the intercession of the saint. The living took
oaths of service directly to the saint. Benedict's relics served as the focus of the saint's continued presence in the natural world, and thus as
a conduit for that divine power his intercession had secured for his servants. In the Peace movement, however, the members of society took
promissory oaths directed to one another. The relics of the saints may

cussed above (emphases added): "Cum praefatus Geilo in illos insiliens, certaminis
primicerium Benedictum invocans patrem, illos longe numero profusiores armisque
propensiores pro libitu pessumdedit, plurimis eorum cum Landrico comite retentis. Ita
Dei aequissimo judicio, quadraginta illorum et eo amplius vitam cum victoria unius horae
amisere puncto calicem irae domini pleniter ebibentes, et fundum ad usque potantes,
quos beatorum confessorum nulla potuit terrere reverentia"; *Mirac. s. Benedicti,* 5.15, p.
213. "Deinde *aequissimo Dei judicio,* ut palpando et quodam modo poenitendo, a nemore
excedit praefato, unius arboris tam valide inliditur scopulo, ut dextro oculorum amisso,
probrum concinnatae fraudis prae se haberet perpetuo"; *Mirac. s. Benedicti,* 5.7, p. 204.

[45] See, for example, Töpfer, *Volk und Kirche,* pp. 40–54, 103–10; H. E. J. Cowdrey,
"The Peace and the Truce of God in the Eleventh Century," *Past and Present* 46 (1970),
42–67, especially pp. 44–53; Steven Sargent, "Religious Responses to Social Violence in
Eleventh-Century Aquitaine," *Historical Reflections / Réflexions historiques* 12 (1985), pp.
219–40, especially pp. 220–28. Also see Berhard Töpfer, Daniel Callahan, and Geoffrey
Koziol (Chapters 2, 7, and 10) in this volume.

[46] Thomas Bisson, "The Organized Peace in Southern France and Catalonia, ca. 1140–
ca. 1233." *American Historical Review* 82 (1977), 292.

have acted as holy witnesses and guarantors of those oaths, but it was the relationship of the living to one another, rather than directly to the saints, that provided those oaths their efficacy. The saints still held the promise of great intercessory power for the living, but they no longer served in the same central mediating position between the living and God. In the logic of the Peace movement, the social relationships of this world—policed by the episcopate—were granted the possibility of embodying God's power which had been essentially denied them according to the logic of saintly patronage. The latter, in contrast, stressed sacred relationships with the court of heaven—contracted through monastic intercession—as the primary means of dispensing God's power in this world.

The subtle but powerful difference in these contrasting logics of the relationship between the natural and supernatural worlds can be highlighted by comparing Andrew's account of the epidemic of *ignis sacer* in the Limousin in 994 to that given by Ademar of Chabannes.[47] According to Andrew, the epidemic was divine punishment for the sinful corruption of that human society. The inhabitants of the Limousin "took council in common [*commune consilium ineunt*]" and decided to petition the aid of Saint Benedict, some of whose relics were enshrined at nearby Saint-Benoît-du-Sault. The prior allowed this crowd (*caterva totius populi*) to take Benedict's reliquary on procession to Limoges to secure the help of both Benedict and the local patron Saint Martial. The epidemic ended after this pilgrimage. Ademar, who actually wrote well over a decade before Andrew, described the situation differently. For him, the epidemic was not explicitly a form of divine punishment. His description was included in a chapter in which he also enumerated the pious behavior of several nobles. Faced by the disease, the bishops of Aquitaine gathered in a council called in Limoges to consider this epidemic. There they assembled numerous saints' relics and exhumed the relics of Saint Martial. On the intervention of this saint, the epidemic ceased and an oath to maintain the Peace was promulgated. Justice was then restored through the work of the duke of Aquitaine and his deputies. In retrospect, Andrew not only added Benedict to Martial as the saint responsible for the end of the epidemic—as one might expect of a monk of Fleury—but completely ignored the association of that epidemic with the Peace oath, an aspect of the story utterly crucial for Ademar.

In Andrew's eyes, direct saintly intervention, not collective human action, brought the epidemic to an end and restored the equilibrium of

---

[47] *Mirac. s. Benedicti*, 4.1, pp. 174–177. Ademar of Chabannes, *Chronicon*, 3.35, p. 158. The two passages certainly concern the same events; see Hoffman, *Gottesfriede*, pp. 30–31.

human society. Although the people discussed the problem together, it was not their common action but rather their prayerful dedication of themselves to the saints which offered a solution. Andrew chose to ignore completely the importance of the oath of peace in describing one of the events crucial to the development of the Peace movement. For Ademar, the promulgation of peace, justice, and health came about through the work of living human beings acting with the help of a great saint, not through direct saintly or divine intervention. Certainly the Aquitanian monk was a great devotee of relic cults, particularly the cult of Saint Martial, for which he forged several texts claiming the saint's apostolicity.[48] Ademar, like the bishops who gathered the Peace councils, envisioned the relationship between human society and saintly patronage differently than did Andrew.

Andrew of Fleury and Ademar of Chabannes essentially saw the correct use of sacred power to resolve social conflicts according to two different paradigms. By the logic of saintly patronage expounded by Andrew, sacred power was mediated into human society through a court, or vertical, model. The saints were privileged above all other human beings because they sat at the right hand of God in the court of heaven. Ordinary human beings in this world of the living could best have the ear of God through the mediation of just such a saintly patron. Such saintly patrons as Benedict were the appropriate conduits of divine power. The *judicium Dei* would be rendered through their mediation on behalf of their servants. For Ademar, sacred power was mediated to human society by means of a collective, or horizontal, model. The *pax Dei* would be achieved when human beings worked together, in concert with the saints and other supernatural patrons, to solve their problems. Perhaps Ademar was so obsessed with establishing the apostolic character of his favored patron Saint Martial, by forgery if necessary, precisely because he wished to locate Martial within the collective endeavors of the original apostolic community. In any case, Ademar—and, *mutatis mutandis*, other partisans of the Peace of God—felt that collective actions such as oaths taken up by the social community had real spiritual benefit.

Communal or collective action was on the rise in the eleventh century. Historians are slowly becoming aware of its importance. One obvious sign is the ambitious attempt of Susan Reynolds to provide a general account of the "collective values and activities of lay society" in

---

[48] On Ademar's devotion to the cult of Saint Martial, see Saltet, "Les faux d'Adémar de Chabannes," and Daniel Callahan, "The Sermons of Adémar of Chabannes and the Cult of St. Martial of Limoges," *Revue bénédictine* 86 (1976), 251–95. Also see Daniel Callahan (Chapter 7) and Richard Landes (Chapter 8) in this volume.

her opposition of kingdoms and communities.[49] Despite the somewhat curious attempt by Reynolds to downplay the overall significance of the Peace movement, and despite the legitimate emphasis placed by Hans-Werner Goetz and others on the central role played by the secular and ecclesiastical nobility in it, the Peace of God was nevertheless important in this growth of collective action.[50] As organized by the bishops of Aquitaine and Burgundy, the Peace at times allowed the *populus*—that ill-defined collection of members of the lower orders who had no independent personal voice in public affairs—to become involved in political events as a collective actor.[51] Two striking examples are present in the texts we have surveyed. At the battle of the Cher, the *inermis vulgus* armed itself and stood under the banner of the church facing the power of the knights. In the Limoisin, collective oaths had the potential not only to bring about peace in the face of castellan violence but also to secure health in the face of an epidemic. In different ways, as we have seen, Andrew of Fleury sought to discount both of these collective endeavors.

Collective action on the part of the *populus* could, of course, also be turned into a revolt against power of the hierarchy, both secular and ecclesiastic. In the secular sphere, the most obvious example is the challenge mounted by urban communes to neighboring noble lords. Indeed, Albert Vermeesch argues that the Peace league organized by Archbishop Aimon was a direct precursor of the diocesan commune whose presence was first attested in Bourges in 1108.[52] In the religious sphere, the collective action of the laity could lead to the sort of heretical challenge to clerical authority for which Guy Lobrichon has found evidence in early eleventh-century Aquitaine.[53] Ademar of Chabannes, the champion of such collective action when embodied in the Peace of God or even the cult of Saint Martial, sensed this threatening potential in a way Andrew of Fleury could not fathom. According to Andrew, the heretics tried in Orléans in 1022 were only "of the clerical order." The demonic invasion of Fleury they occasioned represented a threat to the monastery which only its patron saint was ultimately able to counteract. Thus Andrew reduced this battle over heresy, in a manner similar to his description of the battle of the Cher, to a judicial duel, or *judicium Dei*, this one occurring between Benedict and the demons. Ademar, for his part, connected the heretics of the Orléanais to Manicheans active

---

[49] Susan Reynolds, *Kingdoms and Communities in Western Europe, 900–1300* (Oxford, 1984), quotation on p. 3.

[50] Reynolds, *Kingdoms and Communities*, pp. 34–35; Goetz, Chapter 11 in this volume.

[51] R. I. Moore "Family, Community and Cult on the Eve of the Gregorian Reform," *Transactions of the Royal Historical Society*, 5th ser., 30 (1980), 49–69, discusses the emergence of the *populus* in this period.

[52] Vermeesch, *Origines de la commune*, pp. 42–48.

[53] See Chapter 4 in this volume.

in Toulouse.[54] The accused heretics were themselves clerics, but they had been inspired by a *rusticus* from the Périgord and threatened to corrupt the morals of men and women in society at large. Indeed, Ademar portrayed this heresy in a manner akin to a demonic inversion of the *pax Dei*. For Ademar, the collective energies of the lay *populus* had to be carefully regulated by the clergy in such endeavors as the Peace of God or pilgrimage to the shrine of his dearly beloved "apostle," Saint Martial.

During the late eleventh century, the logic of saintly patronage expressed so forcefully by Andrew of Fleury underwent a fundamental transformation. Authors of collections of miracle stories included ever fewer chastisement miracles of the type that so delighted Andrew. Gradually the patronage of the saints came to be primarily associated with such friendly activities as the cure of disease and the release of prisoners, rather than with the chastisement of enemies. Steven Sargent has shown, for example, how the cult of Saint Leonard of Noblat, newly propagated in eleventh-century Aquitaine, could achieve practical results similar to those of the Peace movement.[55] That cult differed in certain important particulars from such traditional cults as that of Benedict at Fleury. Leonard became a specialist saint, one whose miracles almost exclusively involved the release of prisoners. This saint's patronage was not restricted to the region surrounding the saint's community; the cult soon spread through several regions, most important, Bavaria. The friends of Saint Leonard were defined in crucially different ways from the traditional *familia* of Saint Benedict.

In the High Middle Ages, Christians also turned ever more regularly for miraculous intercession to their near contemporaries, such as Thomas Becket and Francis of Assisi, rather than to those traditional heroes of the far past, such as Benedict, who had served as patrons of nearby monasteries or churches. These new saints commonly expressed their patronage on behalf of such collective bodies as guilds and confraternities—themselves largely developments of this period—rather than for the sake of their bonded servants. Monks themselves turned increasingly to the liturgical prayer they performed as a collective body as a means of both protecting themselves against outside enemies and producing revenue, which had once come from donations to patron saints.[56]

[54] Ademar of Chabannes, *Chronicon*, 3.59, pp. 184–85.

[55] Sargent, "Religious Responses."

[56] See, for example, Barbara Rosenwein, "Feudal War and Monastic Peace: Cluniac Liturgy as Ritual Aggression," *Viator* 2 (1971), 129–57; Penelope Johnson, *Prayer, Patronage, and Power: The Abbey of La Trinité, Vendôme, 1032–1187* (New York, 1981), pp. 69–102; John Van Engen, "The 'Crisis of Cenobitism' Reconsidered: Benedictine Monasticism in the Years 1050–1150," *Speculum* 61 (1986), 269–304.

The boundaries of the supernatural and the natural worlds were being redrawn during the tenth and eleventh centuries. Indeed, those boundaries have been changing constantly, if sometimes imperceptibly, throughout the history of Christianity. So, too, the ways clerics used sacred power to resolve social conflicts were also changing. The Peace movement was just such a new response to the changing social situation. It utilized forms of sacred power both to control the newly ascendant *populus* and to use that force against the power of the *milites*. Andrew of Fleury, caught up in the same changes, judged the representatives of this new movement according to the ideals of his traditional piety. That piety would survive in force for well over a century in society at large, but Andrew nevertheless expressed a logic of religious and social relations which was on the decline. The error of Archbishop Aimon and the other leaders of the Peace league of Bourges lay in their failure to trust the saints and in their attempt to usurp the power of the saints through direct collective action. A mass of pollution existed outside the comforting walls of the monastery, pollution against which only a saintly patron armed with the symbol of his divinely given authority could guard. For Andrew, comfortable with a traditional logic that was slowly losing its power in his own lifetime, only the direct intervention of the saints on behalf of their human servants would suffice to regulate and protect Christian society. For Archbishop Aimon, Ademar of Chabannes, and the other partisans of the Peace movement, the living could invoke supernatural protection through their own collective action.

10

Monks, Feuds, and the Making of Peace in Eleventh-Century Flanders

GEOFFREY KOZIOL

The Peace of God was apparently introduced into Flanders by Bishop Gerard of Cambrai in 1024 at Douai. Gerard's own biographer tells us, however, that Count Baldwin IV of Flanders was the real instigator of the declaration, since he had pressured Gerard into an action of which the bishop did not wholly approve.[1] In 1030, it was again Baldwin who had the Peace declared, this time at Audenaarde, in the diocese of Tournai, at an assembly the count apparently summoned and presided over himself.[2] Finally, Baldwin's son, Baldwin V, established a Peace for the diocese of Thérouanne in conjunction with the bishop of Thérouanne. This was probably in 1042 or 1043.[3]

[1] Georges Duby, "Gérard de Cambrai, la paix et les trois fonctions sociales, 1024," in *Compte rendu des séances de l'Académie des inscriptions et belles lettres* (Paris, 1976), pp. 136–46; also see E. Van Mingroot, "Kritisch Onderzoek omtrent de Datering van de *Gesta episcoporum cameracensium*," *Revue belge de philologie et d'histoire* 54 (1975), 281–332.
[2] *Les annales de Saint-Pierre de Gand et de Saint-Amand*, ed. Philip Grierson (Brussels, 1937), p. 891; *Sigeberti Gemblacensis Chronica, Auctarium Affligemense*, s.d. 1030, *MGH SS* 6:399.
[3] R. Bonnaud-Delamare, "Les institutions de paix dans la province ecclésiastique de Reims au XIe siècle," *Bulletin philologigue et historique du Comité des travaux historiques et scientifiques* (Paris, 1957), pp. 143–200; see pp. 184 bis and 192–95 for the text and principal commentary. For the prologue omitted by Bonnaud-Delamare, see F. Wasserschleben, "Zur Geschichte der Gottesfrieden," *Zeitschrift der Savigny-Stiftung für Rechtsgeschichte, romanische Abteilung* 12 (1891), 112–17. General works on the early Peace movement in Flanders include Bonnaud-Delamare, "Institutions de paix"; Hartmut Hoffmann, *Gottesfriede und Treuga Dei* (Schriften der Monumenta Germaniae historica, 20; Stuttgart, 1964), 59–64, 143–47, though his dating and suggestions are less perspicacious than for other regions; E. I. Strubbe, "La paix de Dieu dans le Nord de la France," *Recueil de la Société Jean Bodin* 14, no. 1 (1961), 489–501; Henri Platelle, "La violence et ses remèdes en Flandre au XIe siècle," *Sacris Erudiri* 23 (1971), 101–73; Georges Duby, *The Three Orders: Feudal Society Imagined*, trans. Arthur Goldhammer (Chicago, 1980), pp. 21–43; and J.-F. Lemarignier, "Paix et réforme monastique en Flandre et en Normandie

Much is uncertain about these assemblies;[4] but however one reads
the evidence, it is clear that there were at least three major declarations
of the Peace of God under the leadership of the counts of Flanders
within twenty years. The counts were clearly interested in the movement. Yet after the Peace of Thérouanne, the promise of the movement aborted. There were no further declarations of the Peace for
Flanders, with or without the count's participation, until 1093.[5]

A waning in formal Peace activity after the 1040s was common
throughout France. The reasons for this are again uncertain. In the
case of Flanders, one possibility, at least in the beginning, is that the
count was simply too busy fighting to concern himself with the Peace.
From 1047 to 1056, Baldwin V was at war with Henry III over control
of Lotharingia, and much of the fighting occurred in Flanders itself. In
1053, imperial forces even penetrated beyond Lille, into the very heart
of the county. The war ended only on the emperor's death in 1056, on
terms quite favorable to Baldwin.[6]

Another area hard hit in this war was Hainaut, which as an ally of
Flanders and as gateway between Flemish and Lotharingian territory
had been wasted by both armies. And among those in Hainaut who suffered most, at least by their own reckoning, were the monks of Lobbes.
The monastery had to be extensively rebuilt; but that cost money, and
money was hard to come by, not least because many of Lobbes' Flemish
estates had been lost during the preceding years, partly as a result of

---

autour de l'année 1023," *Droit privé et institutions régionales: Etudes historiques offertes à Jean
Yver* (Paris, 1976), pp. 443–68. I have not been able to consult the thesis by J. De Smet,
"De Paces Dei der Bisdommen van het graafschap Vlaanderen (1024–1119)" (Louvain,
1956), since it remains unpublished. Some of its conclusions regarding the early Peace
movement in Flanders are, however, presented by Lemarignier, Platelle, and Strubbe.

[4] Dating is especially problematic. For example, the Peace of Thérouanne can be dated
only to 1036–67; see Hoffmann, *Gottesfriede*, p. 146. A date in the early 1040s is surmised
from supplementary material of that time which shows the principals acting together. As
for the Peace of Douai, Otto Oexle has argued that the traditional date of 1036 is the
correct one, and not 1024 as proposed by Duby. Oexle's later date would, however, make
this Peace oddly eccentric to the major initiatives of 1023–24, which involved the same
actors and the same agreements. Oexle also overlooks the thematic similarity of the passages of the *Gesta episcoporum Cameracensium* that discuss the Peace of 1023 and the Peace
of Douai. In short, a date of 1024 for the Peace of Douai still makes the most sense of a
source whose chronology cannot be trusted. See Oexle, "Die 'Wirklichkeit' und das 'Wis-
sen': Ein Blick auf das sozialgeschichtliche Oeuvre von Georges Duby," *Historische
Zeitschrift* 232 (1981), 61–91, especially 74–75. See also Duby, "Gérard de Cambrai," and
Van Mingroot, "Kritisch Onderzoek."

[5] Albert Vermeesch, *Essai sur les origines et la signification de la commune dans le nord de la
France* (Heule, 1966), pp. 57–69; also see R. Bonnaud-Delamare, "La paix en Flandre
pendant la première croisade," *Revue du Nord* 154 (1957), 147–52, and "Institutions de
paix," pp. 188–98; Platelle, "Violence et ses remèdes," pp. 116–19.

[6] François-Louis Ganshof, "Les origines de la Flandre impériale," *Annales de la Société
royale d'archéologie de Bruxelles* 46 (1942–43), 124–34.

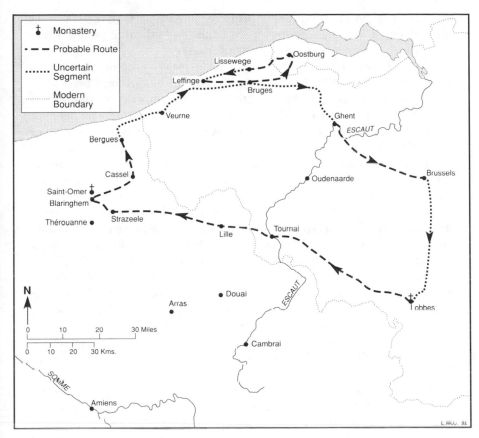

Map 3. Flanders and the *delatio* performed by the monks of Lobbes, 1060

the war itself. In 1060, the abbot therefore decided to take the relics of
his abbey's patron, Ursmer, on a tour, a *delatio*, through Flanders. He
hoped that the saint's prestige and the monks' laments would convince
the count of Flanders to restore their Flemish estates.[7] Although the

---

[7] *Miracula sancti Ursmari in itinere per Flandriam facta*, chap. 1; *MGH SS* 15.2:837–38.
The few sections not printed in the *MGH* can be found in *AASS*, April II, pp. 570–75;
unless otherwise noted, citations are to the *MGH* edition. During this period, such *de-
lationes* were becoming relatively common in the region. They are discussed, with passing
mention of the *delatio* of Lobbes, in two articles: Pierre Héliot and M.-L. Chastang,
"Quêtes et voyages de reliques au profit des églises françaises du moyen âge," *Revue d'histoire ecclésiastique* 59 (1964), 789–822, and 60 (1965), 5–32; and Pierre-André Sigal, "Les
voyages de reliques aux XIe et XIIe siècles," in *Voyage, quête, pèlerinage dans la littérature
et la civilisation médiévale* (Paris, 1976), pp. 75–104. The tour of Lobbes is also discussed
in the context of the Peace of God, but in somewhat summary and dismissive fashion, by
Hoffmann, *Gottesfriede*, pp. 146–47.

chronicler is too high-minded to admit it, one suspects that the monks also expected to garner enough gifts from the faithful to permit them to begin the reconstruction of their monastery.[8]

So it was done. For the next two or three months the monks of Lobbes covered over 300 miles, passing through three different bishoprics and at least a score of cities and towns. Shortly afterward, one of the monks wrote an account of the journey, or more accurately an account of the miracles that occurred along the way, thanks to the powers of Saint Ursmer.

The *Miracula sancti Ursmari* is a wonderful source, for its author has a fine sense of detail and drama and probably worked from notes compiled on the spot, an ordinary practice at shrines and on tours of relics a little later, as Benedicta Ward has shown.[9] The *Miracula*'s author is also surprisingly objective about the events he witnessed. Of course, these events include levitating relics and demonic apparitions, phenomena whose objective reality and reasonableness few of the age would have doubted.[10] But generally the miracles he describes are plausible enough to have occurred.[11] Certainly he does not strain the reader's trust by producing any fire-breathing dragons like that which appears in the miracles of Norte-Dame of Laon in the next century.[12] The writer is also honest enough to record one of his saint's failures and to acknowledge and address the skepticism with which some witnesses greeted an alleged cure.[13]

Detail, drama, and naturalism: these characteristics make this account a thoroughly enjoyable piece of literature. They also make it a superb source for answering the kinds of questions modern historians like to pose. In particular, we can read the *Miracula* to learn how the monks of Lobbes used their relics to resolve feuds and restore peace.

[8] Héliot and Chastang, "Quêtes et voyages de reliques"; Benedicta Ward, *Miracles and the Medieval Mind* (London, 1982), pp. 150–58.

[9] According to Ward, *Miracles*, p. 146, a notary was assigned to record the miracles of the Virgin at Rocamadour, and at Becket's tomb individuals were assigned the task of writing down whatever miracles they witnessed (pp. 90–93). Bernard of Clairvaux's preaching of the crusade in Germany was attended by many miracles, and his companions took notes on them, which they immediately collated to create a daily dossier (pp. 180–81).

[10] *Mirac. s. Ursmari*, chap. 16, p. 841; chap. 5, pp. 838–39.

[11] See, for example, *Mirac. s. Ursmari*, chap. 21, p. 842, in which a lame woman struggles to keep up with the crowd following the monks and their relics. Finally she appeals to Ursmer for aid and feels such an infusion of grace that she is able to throw away *one* crutch and catch up with the group by hobbling along on the knuckles of one hand, chimpanzee-like, while holding onto the remaining crutch with the other. A less scrupulous writer would surely have had her toss away both crutches and sprint ahead.

[12] *Miracula s. Mariae Laudunensis*, 2.11; *PL* 156:981.

[13] *Mirac. s. Ursmari*, chap. 5, pp. 838–39. *Mirac. s. Ursmari*, chap. 19; *AASS*, April II, p. 574.

For more than cures, more than displays of divine vengeance against unbelievers, this is what the writer believed had been his saint's greatest miracle in Flanders: he had simply brought peace.

The nobles of Flanders were famous for the zest with which they feuded. As Henri Platelle has written, "They fought simply for the sake of fighting."[14] The frequent campaigns and constant military preparation of recent years had doubtless only reinforced their aggressiveness, since the public competition of battle would have heightened their touchy pride and their fear of being shamed, making it that much harder for a warrior to back down from an affront to honor, estate, or family. We also know from other Flemish sources that wars could decimate the upper ranks of the nobility, the leaders from an older generation. Once they were gone, a struggle ensued to redefine the pecking order, a struggle not unlike the successional strife that still sometimes emerges between organized crime families.[15] And each assault, each murder, only embedded a feud deeper into a community, as every attack called for further vengeance. In this way, the wars between Henry and Baldwin did more than distract the count from continuing his promotion of the Peace of God; they also engendered the feuds the Peace had been designed to prevent.

Whatever the reasons, the monks of Lobbes found feuds everywhere they went. At Strazeele, wrote the author, "some knights were so hostile to each other that no mortal man could bring them to peace."[16] At Oostburg no one dared leave his house without an armed guard.[17] In

---

[14] Platelle, "Violence et ses remèdes," p. 116, and generally pp. 108–14

[15] The point is made quite clearly in Abbot Theofrid of Echternach's *Vita s. Willibrordi*, chap. 36, *MGH SS* 23:28. The men of the Walcheren united long enough to turn back an invasion by Robert the Frisian. But then they turned to fighting each other: "In perniciem exarsit mutuam et, caesis nobilioribus insulae primatibus, in tantam prorupit discordiam, ut neque libere ingredi neque egredi ulli esset copia." One might also point out that in the *Miracula s. Ursmari* two of the most important feuds involved *juvenes* at the heads of retinues and *familiae*, that is, ambitious men not yet possessing any formal authority. Their involvement in these feuds suggests that what was at stake in the feuds was just that kind of competition for supremacy after the death of former leaders described in the *Vita Willibrordi*. Similarly, the *Miracula s. Donatiani* (*MGH SS* 15.2:858) records an outbreak of feuding in 1096, during the absence of the count and the *meliores natu* on crusade. Conversely, the *Historia translationis sanctae Lewinnae* (*AASS*, July V, pp. 623–27), which records a *delatio* by the monks of Bergues in 1058—just after the war with the empire had ended—mentions not a single feud, even though the monks passed through exactly the same towns visited by the monks of Lobbes two years later. Widespread feuding therefore appears to have been not endemic in this society but periodic, erupting in concentrated bursts during moments of particular stress when the mechanisms that ordinarily kept feuds from escalating were inoperative. On the periodicity of feuds, see also William Ian Miller, "Justifying Skarphedinn: Of Pretext and Politics in the Icelandic Bloodfeud," *Scandinavian Studies* 55 (1983), 316–44.

[16] *Mirac. s. Ursmari*, chap. 5, p. 838.

[17] *Mirac. s. Ursmari*, chap. 12, p. 840.

light of what has just been said about the destabilizing effects of war, it is surely no coincidence that the monks traveled through just that area of Flanders around Lille where Henry III had concentrated his attack a few years earlier. That is where the feuds were worst, because that is where the wars had most undermined the fabric of leadership. But, wherever they found feuds the monks tried to make peace. Sometimes their efforts were in vain;[18] but for the most part they were remarkably successful.

Ending feuds was no easy task. The *Miracula* itself shows us lords who failed to make peace.[19] Other Flemish sources, like the *Vita sancti Macharii*, describe feuds that the count of Flanders himself could not end.[20] Where powerful lords failed, the monks of Lobbes succeeded— they and of course Saint Ursmer. How did they do it? Normally, eleventh-century sources are silent on such matters.[21] But, because of its attention to detail, the *Miracula* allows us to glimpse just what forces these monks could marshal to end feuds. In the process, it also gives us an insight, or at least a hypothesis, about the direction of the later Peace movement as a whole in Flanders.

Of several noteworthy incidents, two are particularly illuminating. The first occurred at Bergues, where the monks finally caught up with the count and countess of Flanders, who received them with honor.[22] It happened to be Pentecost. The next day, a great assembly was held outside the town. In addition to the monks and the count and countess, the bishops of London and Thérouanne were also present, as were a great concourse of the Flemish nobility. As the writer describes it, the monks laid down their relics and began to talk of peace and concord. We do not know what they preached, but we might infer the gist from themes the writer dwells on in the beginning of his work, in a passage that sounds remarkably like a well-honed sermon.[23] Accordingly, they said that their monastery had been destroyed in the recent wars, that their peasants had fled, that nothing remained of their church but rubble. And so they had decided to travel through the towns of Flanders that had also suffered in the wars, bearing the relics of the saint who had converted the Flemish to Christianity, that he might now convert them to the true peace of Christ.

---

[18] The only egregious failure acknowledged by the writer occurred early in the journey, at Strazeele. The incident is discussed below.

[19] As in the case of Hugh at Blaringhem, discussed below.

[20] *Vita s. Macharii*, chap. 22; *MGH SS* 15.2:617–18.

[21] Compare, for example, the laconic charters from Noyers analyzed by Stephen White, "Feuding and Peace-Making in the Touraine around the Year 1000," *Traditio* 42 (1986), 195–263.

[22] *Mirac. s. Ursmari*, chaps. 8–9, pp. 839–40.

[23] *Mirac. s. Ursmari*, chaps. 1–2, p. 838.

At some point in this sermon, the count began to second the monks' sentiments. Only the day before, he had personally shown his devotion to their saint by formally restoring the monks' property in Flanders and receiving it under his protection. Now he expected his men to follow his example. Then came the real stroke of genius: the monks not only invited the nobles to make peace among themselves but called out, one by one, the name of each man known to have a feud and challenged him to make a reconciliation with his enemy. Our writer is quite correct when he says, with his usual perspicacity, that no one present "dared to refuse" the monks' entreaties. In the presence of the count and countess, in the presence of two bishops and the relics of Ursmer, on the day after Pentecost, who in such a setting would have dared refuse to make peace when he heard his name called out for all to hear?

What the events at Bergues show is that the monks were masters at creating situations in which it was impossible not to swear peace and embrace one's enemy. They were, after all, expert liturgists—experts, that is, in using ritual and ceremony to create the right atmosphere. At least some of those sent on this journey had probably been chosen for just these skills, necessary for choreographing the masses and processions they would celebrate along the way. They used the same skills to create liturgical ceremonies that stirred up fervor for peace. Was the problem that knights were proud men, fearful of public shame, eager for public acclaim? Then the monks would force them into a setting in which they would be publicly shamed if they denied peace, publicly praised if they accepted it.

We can see this at Bergues. We can also see it in an event that transpired at Blaringhem, not far from Saint-Omer.[24] Two young knights had quarreled, and the quarrel had degenerated into a name-calling contest. The lord of the men, one Hugh, gathered his other knights and managed to reconcile them, even getting them to embrace each other and kiss—the formal, public, and ritual sign of peace. But one of the two harbored his anger—the one, says the author, "who had been more deeply wounded by the slander." And one day after the lord had left town, he approached his unsuspecting enemy and ran him through with his lance. As the author ruefully remarks, a murder "just because of a single word."

The writer sets the scene well and builds to the crisis. The murderer had been given refuge in a church when the lord returned to town and vowed to take him. As at Bergues, it just happened to be a holy day, this time the night of Ascension. This was the moment the monks chose to make their solemn entry into the city. They were probably led in by a

[24] *Mirac. s. Ursmari*, chap. 6, p. 839.

throng of people, as they usually were on their journey. And perhaps they spoke to the curious as they had spoken at Bergues, reminding their audience of the horrors of war and the blessings of peace, telling them also of the miracles their saint had already accomplished, miracles that were beginning to make the monks famous and draw crowds to them.

Early the next morning a crowd of knights gathered outside the church in which the murderer had taken sanctuary—waiting, says the *Miracula*, ranged in two groups, one ready to kill to seize the murderer, the other ready to kill to prevent him from being seized. Now our writer is hitting his stride. In the lightening dawn, he says, "the whole sanctuary glistened red as the morning sun struck the shields and rows of arms. The horses snorted and whinnied in anticipation. And Hugh's men stood surrounding the church, their swords drawn, so many men eager to shed the blood of one sinner." Suddenly, the monks seized the initiative from Hugh by passing through the middle of the crowd into the church. Up to this moment, Hugh had been quite ready to violate the sanctuary to arrest the murderer. But that was when it had just been a small local church, whose canons or priest would have been unable to resist the lord's will. The monks' solemn procession through the line of warriors into the church changed all that, because if Hugh now entered the church with armed men, he would be seen by everyone to have risked testing a strange saint of unknown powers, whose guardians had come explicitly to make peace. Hugh may still have been willing to violate the sanctuary, but the monks had upped the ante. Into a political confrontation of known dimensions they had induced a religious charge that threw everything into uncertainty.

Once inside the church, the monks found the young man lying prostrate before the altar, quite still, as if he were already dead. The monks celebrated a mass, not for the young man alone but for all the faithful of the town, and sang litanies and psalms that implored divine clemency against such dangers as its people now faced. Then, garbed in albs and vestments as for a solemn mass, they returned outside. They summoned Hugh before them, before his knights and his enemies, before the entire town, "lest for the blood of one sinner he allow the arms of the knights to clash." Hugh refused even to listen to their pleas. So all entered the church, monks and lord, knights of both sides, perhaps also some of the townspeople pressing through the narthex for a better view. Abruptly, without warning or ceremony, the monks placed the relics of Saint Ursmer on the ground in the middle of the crowd, showing by that rude gesture how much the lord's rejection of peace had hurt the saint, how the prostrate saint now himself begged Hugh for peace.[25]

> Everyone was astonished and humbly lowered their eyes. And their re-straint showed clearly enough that they recognized who lay in their midst, even though they had not known him. Tears flowed from the eyes of all. Piety and wrath vied in their hearts. At last, piety won out in Hugh, and he permitted that wretched youth to depart, safe in life and members, and even with his grace. On this occasion, among the knights present that day almost a hundred enemies made peace.

How had they done it? In understanding their success we do not need to appeal, rather helplessly, to such vague notions as the strength of popular fervor or the people's awe before the power of relics. These were surely factors. But we should also remember that these were hard-headed men, even the monks capable of laughing at a blind old woman who sought healing.[26] Fortunately, thanks to his love of detail, the author of the *Miracula* allows us to be much more specific about how fervor, awe, and even self-interest worked to resolve feuds by showing us a pattern and method to the monks' actions. For example, it is surely no coincidence that the monks often staged their grand entries on major holy days, times of bells and processions, solemn masses and sermons, times when the churches and monasteries were most visible and accessible to the public, when people's sensitivity to religious demands was sharper than usual. The monks made certain that they had religious sentiment on their side.

The monks also had an unerring instinct for identifying the key figure in a feud, the one whose yielding would bring peace. Having identified him, they isolated him and worked on him. By singling him out, they made the feud his responsibility if he denied their entreaties. So they worked on Hugh. Of course, Hugh was lord of the castle and interested in doing justice. But as Karl Leyser has noted, a lord's justice was neither impartial nor transcendent. It was a matter of politics and

---

[25] On the meaning of setting relics on the ground, see Patrick Geary, "L'humiliation des saints," *Annales: E.S.C.* 34 (1979), 27–42, trans. in *Saints and Their Cults: Studies in Religious Folklore and History*, ed. Stephen Wilson (Cambridge, 1983), pp. 123–40; and Geoffrey Koziol, *Begging Pardon and Favor: Ritual and Political Order in Early Medieval France* (Ithaca, N.Y., 1992), chap. 7.

[26] *AASS*, April II, p. 574. The monks laughed, believing that because her blindness was the natural result of age rather than of trauma or disease there could be no cure. Of course, they may have laughed less out of disdain for the woman than to distance themselves from the prospect of their saint's near certain failure. Still, it is interesting that the monks appear to have believed that some physical problems could not be cured.

friendship, and so a matter for negotiation and intrigue.[27] Hugh could have found a way out of the feud if he had wanted to—for example, by temporarily exiling the offender. The question was, did he want to? Evidently, the author of the *Miracula* did not think so, since he says that Hugh had been quite willing to kill the man and his supporters. But in pursuing the murderer so ruthlessly, was not Hugh in effect taking his own kind of vengeance on a man who had affronted his honor by violating an accord for which the lord had been personally responsible? Occurring as it did in a setting in which the rising chiefs of retinues were trying to impose or expand their power, was not this flouting of his authority, rather than the feud itself, Hugh's real concern? Moreover, people had a right to vengeance.[28] The murderer had done no more than exercise that right and redeem his honor. Perhaps he should be exiled, or forced to pay compensation both to the victim's family and to the lord for having violated the prior accord. But for Hugh to reject all compromise and utterly destroy him would have been seen by some as waging his own vendetta. It would also have been a denial of the peculiar justness of the accused's search for vengeance, and therefore a further blow to his family's honor. Viewed in this light, far from ending the feud Hugh's pursuit of justice would only have exacerbated it by identifying the lord's interests with those of the victim's faction.

At some level, Hugh must have been aware that his own vindication risked escalating the feud. If so, he must have wished for a graceful way out, but he had neither the right nor the power to impose reconciliation on the victim's family; nor did he have the option of backing down himself, since that would have shown him to be weak. The feud had become too deeply embedded to be renounced voluntarily by its participants.

The monks, however, could transcend the feud because they were strangers; strangers figuratively, because they were citizens of God's city, not of this earthly one. But that was probably less important than the fact that they were literally outsiders, not from Flanders at all but from Hainault: close enough to be familiar with the culture, concerned at its failures, and sympathetic with its problems,[29] yet distant enough

---

[27] Karl Leyser, *Rule and Conflict in an Early Medieval Society: Ottonian Saxony* (Bloomington, Ind., 1979), chap. 10, and pp. 36, 39.

[28] Hanna Vollrath, "Herrschaft und Genossenschaft im Kontext frühmittelalterlicher Rechtsbeziehungen," *Historisches Jahrbuch* 102 (1982), 61, with numerous references. This article, a sophisticated updating of Fritz Kern's idea of customary law, should be read only in conjunction with the subsequent rebuttal by Hans-Werner Goetz, "Herrschaft und Recht in der frühmittelalterlichen Grundherrschaft," *Historisches Jahrbuch* 104 (1984), 392–410.

[29] This is shown, for example, by the author's care in emphasizing that Lobbes had suffered in the wars along with Flanders, and in his tracing the origins of one feud to the insults *juvenes* often trade: "duos milites, qui aliquando disceptaverant inter se verbis asperioribus, utpote juvenes"; *Mirac. s. Ursmari*, chap. 6, p. 839.

not to be part of the structure of the feud.[30] They could therefore legitimately pose as the disinterested defenders of peace. And with that role as outsiders they brought, as we have seen, a sense of nearness to the unknown and an atmosphere of heightened expectation.

This incident also shows that, however important the monks were, the sentiments of the crowd were crucial. In fact, the monks' role was largely to create a structure that could channel and amplify those sentiments. For many in the crowd must have wanted peace and been willing to let the monks do their work: the murderer and his family, of course; but also at least some of the local nobility who did not want to be dragged into what had originally been nothing but a quarrel between two hot-headed, ill-tempered youths; and burghers and some of the local clergy, fearing that their property inside and outside the city would be attacked in a private war, new losses coming hard on the heels of the emperor's devastating campaign. Not least, there was

---

[30] The ability of holy men from outside a community to settle disputes no one within the community could settle appears frequently enough to establish a pattern. It was the case with Bernard of Clairvaux, who settled many disputes during his travels through Germany. It was also the case with Saint Macarius, a mysterious Greek who came to be regarded as a saint in Flanders and who successfully intervened to pacify feuds where even the count of Flanders failed. One also thinks of the tour of Arnulf of Saint-Médard through the towns of Flanders, a journey made purposely for the establishment of peace; *Vita s Arnulfi confessoris; AASS,* August III, pp. 230–54. Arnulf was Flemish by birth (and therefore like the Hainautian monks of Lobbes familiar with the culture); but having spent many of the past years in the Ile-de-France, he was no longer personally involved in Flemish politics—or Flemish feuds. The same pattern has occurred in other societies. According to Peter Brown, for example, holy men were frequent mediators of village conflict in sixth-century Syria. As in Flanders, the resolution of conflict was heavily imbued with a penitential character by which a small community, suffering from division, was made whole again and received, through collective penance, a "new deal." Here, too, the holy man's task was made easier because a substantial portion of the population wanted the conflict to end. Finally, the holy man was able to play this role because he was, according to Brown, "the stranger 'par excellence'." See Peter Brown, "The Rise and Function of the Holy Man in Late Antiquity," in *Society and the Holy in Late Antiquity* (Berkeley, 1982), pp. 126–37; see also G. Kingsley Garbett, "Spirit Mediums as Mediators in Valley Korekore Society," in *Spirit Mediumship and Society in Africa,* ed. John Beattie and John Middleton (New York, 1969), pp. 104–27; and Anna-Leena Siikala, *The Rite Technique of the Siberian Shaman* (FF Communications, 220; Helsinki, 1978), pp. 137–38. This is not the only possible pattern, however. In a region like the Touraine, where the power of castellans was long established and where in consequence the lay nobility shared numerous multiplex ties, including overlapping relations with local churches, abbots and monks were well positioned to act as mediators in local feuds. In contrast, Flemish nobles were only just establishing their authority over castles in the 1060s. Indeed, as argued above, the feuds were one of the by-products of the process. As a result, church and nobility had not had time to establish a stabilizing network of interlocking social bonds, so that local monks and clerics could not mediate feuds as they could in the Touraine. See White, "Feuding and Peace-Making," and E. Warlop, *The Flemish Nobility before 1300* (Courtrai, 1975), 1:105–36; note especially the sudden appearance during this period of castellans or new ruling families at Tournai, Bruges, Saint-Omer, Bergues, Veurne, Bourbourg, Cassel, Aire, Ypres, and Lille.

Hugh himself, looking for a way to back down without losing face, without losing the image of being in control.

So the monks singled out Hugh and worked on him, and in this way they transformed the very structure of the feud, because by singling out one party and making him appear responsible for perpetuating the conflict, they broke the antagonistic, factional divisions that fed the feud. Where before there had been two roughly equal factions opposed to each other, now there was just one individual who appeared to resist the desires of all the rest. Standing above the prostrate monks in a holy space, surrounded by everyone else, Hugh had been physically and socially isolated. And this was important, because whether feigned or not, the mere appearance of near unanimity within the town made Hugh's yielding that much easier, since he could now pose as the merciful and high-minded benefactor of the common good. This was the point at which the monks produced their trump, bringing out their relics and giving the avenger the religious excuse he needed to yield with honor.

Now the crowd again played an important role, this time lending confidence to the one who had backed down by taking up his example. Once Hugh had made peace and was feeling perhaps a bit anxious about what he had done, others came forward to confess their own crimes and kiss their enemies. The one individual who had stood in the way of peace had now returned to the community. The community was whole again, and what followed was a joyous celebration of wholeness, as knights came forward to confess their wrongs and beg the forgiveness of their enemies.

We know what this celebration looked like because the author described one at Oostburg, where nearly forty knights had been involved in an escalating feud.[31] The knights threw their arms to the ground, and after swearing peace on the body of the saint they embraced each other. Then everyone went into the church and sang the *Te Deum* and other holy songs "in the manner of the region." All the people sang, not just the clergy but the laity, not just the men but the women, while the bells pealed and the monks asked God to have mercy on the souls of those who had died in the feuds. At Oostburg as at Blaringhem, what had begun as a feud between individuals or individual families ended in a paroxysm of peace that united the entire community, making all its members, regardless of status or allegiance, partakers of a single religious experience.

As news of the monks' skills spread, the movement snowballed. Soon crowds came out to meet them long before they reached towns, and people threatened by vengeance took advantage of the monks' pres-

---

[31] *Mirac. s. Ursmari*, chap. 12, p. 840.

ence to prostrate themselves before their enemies and beg forgiveness. The scene at Blaringhem was repeated, the monks, their relics, the victim, and the crowd all kneeling or standing together, surrounding one person who alone appeared to resist peace, who alone threatened the unity of the community. Thanks to our author's sensitivity, we can sense the turmoil within these people's minds, torn between two nearly equal demands: the need to take vengeance, and the need to forgive and make peace. Once more, what tipped the balance toward peace was the skill of the monks in isolating them from their supporters and making them feel the weight of the pressures that worked for peace. At Lissewege, for example, the target, a *juvenis* named Robert, already the head of a large retinue of knights, lay stretched out on the ground before his enemy and the saint, themselves lying prostrate before him. Reddening and blanching in turn, gnashing his teeth, Robert clawed the ground and ate dirt in his grief. For three hours they lay there together on the ground, while the young man groaned and the monks and bearded knights stood around him, uttering no sound but sobs. It seemed that the contest had reached a stalemate, when without warning something absolutely wonderful happened, something powerful and miraculous: the saint's reliquary began to spew forth smoke and actually levitated into the air! At once everyone gasped and, beating their breasts, fell with their faces to the ground. The saint had won (*vincit*). This time, when his enemy asked Robert for pardon, Robert gave it to him.[32]

The smokescreen, the distraction of the crowd during a long ordeal that had no end in sight, the fact that a group of monks immediately and without fear ran to the reliquary and placed it on the nearby altar—one suspects a fakir's trick. But we should not follow the crowd and allow our attention to be distracted. The miracle had worked, but only because the monks had structured the confrontation in a way that let it work. They had paralyzed Robert by cutting him off from his followers and forcing him to choose between equally unquestioned but equally incompatible duties and desires. He could not have his vengeance and keep the good will of the town. He could not honor the saint and still please his comrades. He could not have justice and peace both. And, consciously or not, piously or not, that is why he recognized the levitation as a miracle instead of a fraud. It allowed the decision to make itself. In the face of the saint's power, Robert had no choice but to make peace, unless he was willing to be known as an unbeliever who had put his own private vengeance above the good of the town and the manifest judgment of God.

[32] *Mirac. s. Ursmari*, chap. 16, pp. 840–41.

The sobbing crowd that surrounded Robert and with him unquestioningly recognized Ursmer's power points once again to the considerable popular support for peace and, by extension, for the ideals of the Peace of God.[33] Indeed, by a rather natural dialectic first described by Max Gluckman, the very expansion of feuds tends to create mounting pressure for peace.[34] Without that repository of good will, the monks would have been powerless. Still, we should not ignore the existence of less altruistic motivations. It is, for example, entirely possible—even likely—that the young men in these dramatic tableaux were consciously manipulating the monks for their own ends. Thus, Hugh of Blaringhem, insulted and impotent in the face of a feud prosecuted against his will, might well have decided to play the role of a blustering lord, knowing in advance that he would never have to act on his empty threats since the script's final scene called for his wrath to turn to mercy. He would also have known that, far from weakening his authority, acting out such a transformation would only enhance his image by allowing him to appear in turn vengeful and merciful, the twin virtues of good lordship. Robert of Lissewege's marathon paralysis may also have concealed a degree of calculation. Coming as it did toward the end of the tour, his three-hour prostration and the monks' tour de force may indicate that the publicity of Ursmer's *delatio* had inflated the currency of piety, so that ever more extravagant gestures were needed to proclaim the sincerity of one's devotion (or the *virtus* of a saint).

Monks, then, were not the only ones who understood the uses of ceremonial. Laymen had mastered them as well. Nor was this true only of *juvenes* like Hugh and Robert; great lords above all knew how to use the discourse and rites of peace for their own ends. The tour of the monks of Lobbes, for example, was successful in large part because the count of Flanders had not only sanctioned it but also actively promoted it. What was true of the count was also true of the castellans who welcomed the monks into their towns.[35] Without their support, the monks would have achieved nothing. But the lords struck a good bargain, because by supporting the monks' cause they increased their own prestige and, what was no small thing, gained at least a momentary measure of peace.

Political cunning and self-interest, psychological tension, a sincere desire for peace—these are not mutually exclusive explanations of

---

[33] Bernhard Töpfer, *Volk und Kirche zur Zeit der beginnenden Gottesfriedensbewegung in Frankreich* (Berlin, 1957), although Töpfer concentrates on the ways monks created that support rather than responded to popular demands.

[34] Max Gluckman, "The Peace in the Feud," *Past and Present* 8 (1955), 1–44, rpt. in his *Custom and Conflict in Africa* (Oxford, 1973) and thoughtfully discussed by White, "Feuding and Peace-Making," pp. 258–63.

[35] In addition to the above examples, see also *Mirac. s. Ursmari*, chap. 10, p. 840, in which the castellan of Veurne receives the monks on the order of the countess.

the monks' success. All these elements were equally present, if not within the same individual then surely within the same crowd. So it was too in more formal declarations of the Peace of God, where kings, bishops, and counts enhanced their claim to God-given authority by presiding over assemblies charged with popular enthusiasm and aimed at protecting the church and the people.[36] Yet, we have also seen that not even the favor of the powerful and the support of the many were sufficient to end feuds. One also needed to know how to amplify and channel these currents of good will. Monks, skilled manipulators of liturgy and ceremonial, had just such knowledge.

In fact, the techniques used by the monks of Lobbes in ending feuds appear to have been adapted, either consciously or unconsciously, from the customs of the cloister. For example, the public naming and challenging of those who had offended the peace—the technique used in the assembly at Bergues—recalls the way violators of the monastic rule were denounced in the common chapter.[37] Monastic discipline also reinforced a sinner's sense of exclusion from the offended community by requiring long or extravagant prostrations in the presence of standing peers.[38] In the same way, the monks of Lobbes repeatedly pressured their targets into prostrating themselves in full sight of the knights and townspeople standing about them, as a means of ritually isolating them from their supporters. The monks also isolated feuders by processing around them in circles;[39] such circular processions, made with incense, and aspersions, were a common liturgical means of separating the sacred from the profane and fortifying it from attack. Thus, solemn processions around battlements protected towns from enemies.[40] Churches were consecrated and strengthened against demons with processions around their walls.[41] And altars within churches were

---

[36] See the balanced presentation by Hans-Werner Goetz, "Kirchenschutz, Rechtswahrung und Reform: Zu den Zielen und zum Wesen der frühen Gottesfriedensbewegung in Frankreich," *Francia* 11 (1983), 193–239, or, in English, Chapter 11 in this volume.

[37] *The Monastic Constitutions of Lanfranc*, ed. and trans. David Knowles (London, 1951), pp. 111–13. Ulrich of Cluny, *Consuetudines Cluniacenses*, 2.17; *PL* 149:708.

[38] Ulrich of Cluny, *Consuetudines Cluniacenses*, 2.6, 3.3; *PL* 149:705, 735. *Liber tramitis aevi Odilonis abbatis*, ed. Petrus Dinter (Corpus consuetudinum monasticarum, 10; Siegburg, 1980). pp. 216–18.

[39] *Mirac. s. Ursmari*, chap. 5, p. 838.

[40] Andrew of Fleury, *Vie de Gauzlin, Abbé de Fleury*, ed. Robert-Henri Bautier and Gillette Labory (Paris, 1969), chap 20c, p. 62; Michael McCormick, *Eternal Victory: Triumphal Rulership in Late Antiquity, Byzantium, and the Early Medieval West* (Cambridge, 1986), pp. 343–44.

[41] Rudolf Suntrup, *Die Bedeutung der liturgischen Gebärden und Bewegungen in lateinischen und deutschen Auslegungen des 9. bis 13. Jahrhunderts* (Munich, 1978), pp. 253–54. For the belief that aspersions and censings, in purifying the object blessed, protected it against demons, see pp. 342–44, 437–38.

purified by regular aspersions made in a circle around them.[42] The enclosure of bloodletters inside a circle sanctified by relics, incense, and
holy water worked in exactly the same way, with one important difference: here the impure were bound within the circle while the faithful
stood without. It was a graphic representation of everything the monks
were trying to communicate. Whereas towns, churches, and altars were
consecrated for protection against a pervasive, invisible world of demons pressing in from outside, in a feud the evil lay within the town
itself. But once contained inside the circle, the evil was forced to become visible, made to take on a familiar human face, and thus weakened. Now it was evil's turn to be besieged, and the *Te Deums* and joyous
processions—rites of military triumph— rightly marked mass reconciliations as victories of these communities over their internal enemies.

Just how important these techniques were in peace-making emerges
from the monks' one recorded failure, at Strazeele.[43] There they
gained the consent of one faction to a feud to try to make peace, but an
apparently large minority resisted. The monks then tried to force the
issue by picking up their saint and surrounding the intransigents in a
closed circle, believing that if they could ever bind them within its pe-
rimeter the power of the devil that possessed them would be destroyed.
Instead, before the monks could close the circle a black dog crossed
between the monks and their opponents, and the feuders took the opportunity to move away, refusing to be engaged. There were undoubtedly many local factors which might explain why this feud was
particularly intractable—so intractable that the author records, with a
pardonable tone of vindication, that nearly all were subsequently slain
in the contracting coils of the ensuing private war. It is also telling that
the failure occurred early in the monks' journey, that is, before their
saint's renown had been established, before the townspeople's expectations could be raised. Yet it is surely significant that in this case the
monks were not allowed to establish a foothold for their ritual, since
the circle that was such an important element in restructuring the feud
and taming evil was not only not completed but actually violated by a
profane animal, a representation of the devil. They therefore never
managed to isolate any individual within the community as they did in
their successful interventions.

If this failure underscores the importance of ritual in peacemaking,
it also reminds us just how difficult the monks' task was. So many different elements had to converge before one could hope for success.
Even then there was no guarantee that the pacts sponsored by the

---

[42] *Liber tramitis*, pp. 101, 107, 125, 133, 138. Ulrich of Cluny, *Consuetudines Cluniacenses*,
1.10; *PL* 149:653–54. Suntrup, *Bedeutung der liturgischen Gebärden*, p. 348.

[43] *Mirac. s. Ursmari*, chap. 5, p. 838.

monks would endure. In fact, neither our author nor any other source tells us whether these particular reconciliations lasted; but we know from other sources that the Flemings generally remained a tumultuous and violent people, so even if these particular feuds ended, the nobles' propensity for feuding did not. This might lead one to suspect, as Hoffmann suspected, that peacemakers like the monks of Lobbes ultimately failed in their mission; but that is too easy a conclusion.[44] In the first place, even a momentary peace was well worth struggling for and represented a considerable success. This would have been all the more true since outbreaks of feuding appear to have been not endemic but periodic, erupting during the power vacuums created by wars. Furthermore, the fact that mass reconciliations often followed the pacification of a single feud involving lords or the heads of large retinues suggests that these feuds were all linked, a conflict between the powerful generating subsidiary vendettas among their men.[45] Ending a set of feuds in this context might well have taken care of matters for a substantial period of time.[46]

Most important, we should not so emphasize the monks' short-term goal of ending feuds that we forget that over the long term they may well have succeeded in a more essential task: educating people about the ideals of the Peace of God. Historians have long tended to see this movement as a crucial turning point in early medieval culture. The creation of a new ideal of Christian knighthood, the popularization of lay piety, increasingly vocal demands for a purified clergy—all this and more has been seen as the legacy of the Peace.[47] Yet, even while acknowledging its importance, one may still be puzzled at how so much could have been accomplished by a few scattered and infrequent councils. Lessons have to be repeated to take hold.

What the *Miracula sancti Ursmari* shows is that the lessons *were* repeated, that what happened at the great Peace councils was only one aspect of the movement. The dictates of the Peace were not taught in only a few sporadic assemblies. They were also discussed in more informal assemblies, like that at Bergues. Here no articles of the Peace of God were declared, at least none that we know of. But something much

[44] Hoffmann, *Gottesfriede*, pp. 148–50.

[45] White, "Feuding and Peace-Making," pp. 214–16, 221–22, 229–31, 236–37, 241–43, 260, gives numerous examples of the way feuds between leaders might generate secondary feuds among their men.

[46] It is significant in this regard that efforts to renew the peace seem to have occurred in Flanders at regular, well-spaced intervals: the tour of Lobbes in 1060; the *elevatio* of Saint Donatian at Bruges in 1070; the mission of Arnulf in 1083–84; and another *elevatio* of Donatian in 1096.

[47] Töpfer, *Volk und Kirche*; Georges Duby, "Laity and the Peace of God," in *The Chivalrous Society*, trans. Cynthia Postan (Berkeley, 1977), pp. 123–33.

more important to the lasting success of the movement in quelling feuds and instilling the values of the Peace did happen: the monks of Lobbes, together with the count and countess, preached about the need for peace and reconciled the real feuds of real individuals.

The monks of Lobbes did not work alone. Other Flemish saints, such as Macarius and Arnulf, also preached peace and reconciled feuds. Arnulf even worked in and around the very region through which the monks of Lobbes had passed a generation earlier.[48] And there were other informal councils like that at Bergues. The *Miracula sancti Donatiani*, tells, for example, of an assembly at Bruges (a city visited by both Arnulf and the monks of Lobbes) summoned by the count of Flanders in 1070 for the dedication of the church at Hasnon. Although no mention is made of a formal declaration of the Peace, yet the setting recalled the Peace assemblies. Relics were displayed. The great of the county attended, including bishops and abbots. And miracles occurred—including the reconciliation of a feud.[49] The same source tells of a similar assembly, again at Bruges, held in 1096, while the count and the great nobles of Flanders were overseas on crusade. During their absence *bella intestina* had flared up, so severe that "brother did not fear raising a hand against brother, nor son against father." The provost of Bruges, acting in the count's place, therefore had the relics of Donatian placed outside the church, in public, where a great crowd of persons of both sexes gathered to listen to sermons. At last, inspired by the saint, "all entered a pact of peace as one."[50]

The enunciation of the ideals of the Peace of God or the reconciliation of feuds in terms of the Peace may therefore have been fairly common at local assemblies in Flanders. In other regions of France, the principles of the Peace were also recalled outside the great councils. Ivo of Chartres wrote of "the custom of our church" according to which he was about to hold a synod "in which we will deal with many issues involving ecclesiastical affairs and the peace of the entire region."[51] A Norman council held at Lisieux in 1064 decreed "that the Truce of God be frequently repeated"; Michel de Boüard, commenting on this text, believed that the Peace was in fact regularly reaffirmed in

---

[48] See above, notes 20 and 30; see also Platelle, "Violence et ses remèdes," with, however, a serious misreading of the *Vita Arnulfi* on pp. 155–56. Macarius worked in the early part of the century; but that does not invalidate the point. It only indicates how long the process of northern Europe's Christianization took.

[49] *MGH SS* 15.2:857.

[50] *MGH SS* 15.2:858, discussed briefly by Hoffmann, *Gottesfriede*, p. 150.

[51] *Correspondance*, ed. J. Leclercq (Paris, 1949), no. 62, p. 258 (1096). Although the letter was written after Urban's proclamation of the Peace at Clermont, the fact that Ivo spoke of this as a *consuetudo* indicates that the practice preceded 1095, as Hoffmann recognized (*Gottesfriede*, pp. 197–98).

Normandy.[52] It was also a custom in the diocese of Limoges to hold semiannual synods that reaffirmed the Peace. At these synods sermons about peace were delivered, those who had violated the Peace were received as penitents, and psalms of penitence were sung. Apparently only those laypeople involved in infractions of the Peace attended, but Ademar of Chabannes mentions the holding of other councils where the attending laity heard sermons about the meaning of peace.[53] Finally, the Peace canons of Lillebonne, Douai, Thérouanne, and Laon required local priests, on Sundays and feast days, to pray publicly for those who were observing the Peace of God and to publicly damn those who were violating it.[54]

Perhaps these efforts did not end feuds once and for all; but it would be incredible to suggest that they had no effect in changing the way at least some conceived of social order—and in giving those who wanted peace the courage to demand it. Certainly they help explain why Urban II's proclamation of the Truce of God in 1095 received such rapid implementation in northern France—particularly in Flanders. Urban did not preach into a vacuum. Bishops such as Ivo and Arnulf, and monks and canons such as those from Lobbes and Bruges, had thoroughly prepared the ground for him.[55]

There is in any case one tantalizing indication that the message of the peacemakers had been taken to heart. In the time of Robert II (1093–1111), the burghers of Aire-sur-la-Lys obtained from the count a confirmation of their communal organization and its customs.[56] They called this organization an *amicitia*, and its members' essential obligation was to bear each other aid as if they were brothers. This in itself recalls the language of the peacemakers. Still more striking is that, like them, the members of the *amicitia* were especially concerned with

[52] Michel de Boüard, "Sur les origines de la Trève de Dieu en Normandie," *Annales de Normandie* 9 (1959), 169–89, at p. 187 and note 55. See also Hoffmann, *Gottesfriede*, pp. 169–75.

[53] Léopold Delisle, "Notices sur les manuscrits originaux d'Adémar de Chabannes," *Notices et extraits des manuscrits de la Bibliothèque nationale* 35 (1896), 266–67, 271.

[54] The bishops of Lillebonne, for example, wrote, "Presbiteris autem precipimus ut in festivitatibus ac diebus dominicis qui hanc pacem observaverint pro illis preces agendo benedicant. Illos vero qui infregerint aut qui infractoribus concesserint maledicant." The wording of the other councils mentioned is similar: Bonnaud-Delamare, "Institutions de paix," p. 184 bis; Hoffman, *Gottesfriede*, p. 172.

[55] See Hoffmann, *Gottesfriede*, pp. 146–52, 169–75, 186–89, 195–205, 219 for references to the Peace before and immediately after Urban's decree, especially p. 195, where he argues that Urban's proclamation did not reintroduce the Truce after a long hiatus but confirmed an established custom of the French (and increasingly the Roman) church. For the Peace and Truce in Flanders at this time, see also the sources cited in note 5, above.

[56] Raoul van Caenegem, "Coutumes et législation en Flandre aux XIe et XIIe siècles," *Les libertés urbaines et rurales du XIe au XIVe siècles: Actes du colloque internationale, Spa, 5–8 septembre 1966* (Brussels, 1968), p. 125; Platelle, "Violence et ses remèdes," p. 125.

the problem of ending feuds. For example, their statutes prohibited feuds for a period of forty days following a murder, during which time judges were to attempt to achieve a reconciliation of the parties. Those who rejected such mediation were to be expelled from the brotherhood.

In its concern with feuds and its language of brotherhood, this commune, like many others, surely reflects the influence of the Peace movement as a whole. In particular, its militant appropriation of self-help betrays the influence of the Peace of Soissons in 1093 and that of Saint-Omer in 1099, both valid in Flanders and both authorizing ordinary parishioners to take up arms in defense of the peace (though only at the command of their bishops).[57] The initiative of the men of Aire also benefited by seconding a policy promoted by the count himself, since Robert had played a pivotal role in the declaration of Peace at Saint-Omer. In 1111, he even went so far as to issue a Peace on his own authority.[58] Yet Arnulf of Soissons, the canons of Bruges, and the monks of Lobbes would also have been justified in regarding the program of the *amicitia* as the fruit of their own repeated efforts. In proof one need simply point out that Aire is located within a few kilometers of Strazeele and Blaringhem, and not far from Veurne and Bruges—the very region where these three preached the virtues of brotherhood and the need to end feuds.

Thus, the great Peace assemblies were only the beginning of the Peace of God, whose ideals were literally brought home to the laity in their own towns and villages through the work of monks, bishops, and canons. Such local efforts have been ignored by historians because they did not result in articles through which one can trace the development of the Peace as an institution.[59] But it was through just such small events, simply because they were more parochial, that the ideals announced in the great councils became part of the vernacular of everyday life.

[57] Vermeesch, *Essai sur les origines,* pp. 57–69.
[58] See the references cited in note 5, above.
[59] Thus Hoffmann, *Gottesfriede,* pp. 146–49, writes that the *Miracula s. Ursmari* is primarily important because it informs us of the council at Bergues, and he dismisses Saint Arnulf's mission of peace as essentially a "personal initiative" limited to ending feuds, and therefore as largely unimportant for the history of the movement.

11

Protection of the Church, Defense of the Law, and Reform: On the Purposes and Character of the Peace of God, 989–1038

HANS-WERNER GOETZ

Whatever the causes were for the rise of the Peace of God in southern France at the end of the tenth century, it is generally agreed both that the movement was initiated by the church—particularly by its bishops—and that its dispositions were decided on in ecclesiastical councils, but also that it nevertheless had to be supported by secular powers and the populace. The movement has principally been regarded as a reaction of the church to the decline of royal and secular power, as well as to a kind of "feudal anarchy" south of the Loire in the late tenth century, a time characterized by territorial disintegration and by the rise of local powers and feudal lords. In this sense, it has been regarded as a reaction to the decline of a law unable to guarantee peace and order, as well as to the feuds of the nobles which involved either church or peasant property. According to earlier research, the church superseded the king as a guardian of law and order.

There are, however, several reasons for a revision of this traditional view. (1) The Peace of God, before the rise of the *treuga Dei* after 1033, has been regarded in retrospect as the beginning of a long movement. Nevertheless, it is worthwhile to look at the early movement as an independent period and to ascertain its immediate purposes and contents. (2) Feuding did not, in fact, play an important part in the decrees

I have prepared this free and abridged version of "Kirchenschutz, Rechtswahrung und Reform: Zu den Zielen und zum Charakter der frühen Gottesfriedensbewegung in Frankreich," *Francia* 11 (1983), 193–239. I omit many of the more general remarks from the original, concentrating on its main arguments and complementing them with some remarks on recent research. Further bibliographic details and a discussion of the research can be found in the notes in the original article. I am grateful to Thomas Head and Richard Landes for stylistic assistance and fruitful discussions.

of early Peace councils.[1] (3) Above all, more recent concepts of the institutions of late Carolingian and early Capetian society challenge the traditional view of the Peace of God. The rise of the movement can no longer be explained as a result of the king's weakness, since we know that his place was taken over by independent dukes and princes. They were the most important elements of a new constitution endeavoring to avert territorial disintegration. Even on the local level viscounts and lords were beginning to form a new means of governing.[2] Thus the decades around the year 1000 were not a period of total disorder but one in which a new order was being developed. This would, of course, imply fighting for power. There is, however, no indication that the church fought against these new constellations of power with the aid of the Peace of God. On the contrary, we recognize an eager interest in this movement on the part of dukes and powerful counts whose beginnings lay in regions of rising ducal power, namely in Aquitaine, and Auvergne, and Burgundy (the latter was governed by the king at that time).[3] It seems equally improbable that the Peace was an action on the part of the bishops against the local powers on whom they depended; at the time, the sees in southern France were regarded as part of the patrimony of the secular powers and were often occupied by members of the count's or viscount's family.[4] (4) Finally, the Peace could not have succeeded without the help of the noblemen, whose presence at the councils was frequently attested. It was therefore not a movement opposed to lay lords as an entire group. Since it was also supported by the populace,[5] it seems to have reached all levels of society.

The Peace of God ought therefore no longer to be seen as an attack on change in social structures, but as an attempt to provide a new stability for the social order parallel to that provided by new political and social organizations. It should not be seen as a substitute for a supreme power now lacking in French society; rather, it should be viewed in relation to newly ascendent powers. To prove this assertion, it becomes

---

[1] Viktor Achter, *Über den Ursprung der Gottesfrieden* (Krefeld, 1955).

[2] Karl Ferdinand Werner, "Untersuchungen zur Frühzeit des französischen Fürstentums (9.–10. Jh.)," *Welt als Geschichte* 18 (1958), 256–89; 19 (1959), 146–93; and 20 (1960), 87–119; idem, "Königtum und Fürstentum im französischen 12. Jahrhundert," in *Probleme des 12. Jahrhunderts* (Vorträge und Forschungen, 12; Konstanz-Stuttgart, 1968), pp. 117–225; Archibald Lewis, *Southern French and Catalan Society, 718–1050* (Austin, Tex. 1965).

[3] Odilo Engels, "Vorstufen der Staatswerdung im Hochmittelalter: Zum Kontext der Gottesfriedensbewegung," *Historisches Jahrbuch* 97/98 (1978), 71–86.

[4] Reinhold Kaiser, *Bischofsherrschaft zwischen Königtum und Fürstenmacht: Studien zur bischöflichen Stadtherrschaft im westfränkisch-französischen Bereich im frühen und hohen Mittelalter* (Bonn, 1981). For further discussion, see Goetz, "Kirchenschutz," notes 87, 88.

[5] Bernhard Töpfer, *Volk und Kirche zur Zeit der beginnenden Gottesfriedensbewegung in Frankreich* (Neue Beiträge zur Geschichtswissenschaft, 1; Berlin, 1957).

all the more important to ask what the organizers themselves intended when they created the Peace of God, as opposed to considering what the actual results of the movement were. Such an inquiry requires a closer look at the contents of synodal resolutions. This approach is not sufficient to uncover the whole truth about the Peace movement, but reveals an important aspect of its true nature.

Diffusion of the Early Peace Movement

The diffusion of the Peace of God may be understood slightly better with a look at its most prominent organizers, the bishops.[6] There are certain indications that the Peace that was decreed in church councils was accepted in the sees of those bishops who attended.[7] (See Table 1 for a list of Peace councils and textual sources.) It is therefore possible to reconstruct the scope of those Peace assemblies for which the lists of participants have survived.[8] However accidental this knowledge may be, we can still see, through the frequency with which certain bishops participated in Peace councils, that on the whole there were certain regions central to the Peace (that is, the church provinces of Bordeaux and Bourges), others, more marginal (to the south, east, and north), and still other regions where the Peace movement seems never to have encroached.

The division of the movement into separate phases, however, reveals that each had its own centers. The first period (989–post-1000) concentrated on Aquitaine (Charroux), the Berry, and the Auvergne (Le Puy). The first two regions were linked by the Peace of Limoges (994) in the person of Bishop Hilduin of Limoges, who had relations to both ecclesiastical provinces involved, Bordeaux and Bourges. Apart from that, however, we must distinguish a Peace movement in Aquitaine

---

[6] This aspect, which has only been touched on in my *Francia* article, has been dealt with more thoroughly in the Paris (C.N.R.S.) conference of 1987: "La paix de Dieu en France autour de l'an Mil: Fondements et objectifs, diffusion et participants," in *Le roi de France et son royaume autour de l'an mil*, ed. Michel Parisse and Xavier Barral i Altet (Paris, 1992), pp. 131–45.

[7] This is attested at Le Puy I (994), Limoges I (994), Bourges I (1031), and Toulouges (1027).

[8] Those are the councils of Charroux I (989), Limoges I (994), Anse I (994), Le Puy I (994), Poitiers I (1000/14), Verdun (1019/21), Anse II (1025), Limoges II (1028), Poitiers II (1029/31), Bourges I (1031), Limoges IV (1031), and Limoges V (1033). Because the reliability of Ademar of Chabannes is much disputed, the lists of Bourges I and Limoges IV remain uncertain; see Richard Landes, "The Dynamics of Heresy and Reform in Limoges: A Study of Popular Participation in the 'Peace of God', 994–1033," *Historical Reflections / Réflexions historiques* 14 (1987), 467–511. Yet, although Ademar must be deemed a forger regarding the apostolicity of Saint Martial, I do not believe that he invented nearly contemporary Peace councils and their participants out of whole cloth.

Table 1. Peace of God councils, 989–1038

Year	Place
989	Charroux I[a]
990	Narbonne[b]
994	Limoges I[c]
994	Anse I[d]
994	Le Puy I[e]
1000/14	Poitiers I[f]
Early eleventh century	Vienne[g]
1019/21	Verdun-sur-le-Doubs[h]
1023	Beauvais[i]
1025	Héry, Anse II, Coler[j]
1027	Toulouges[k]
1027/28	Charroux II[l]
1028	Limoges II[m]
1029	Limoges III[n]
1029/31	Poitiers II[o]
1031	Bourges I[p]
1031	Limoges IV[q]
1033	Limoges V[r]
1033	Vic[s]
1033	Auxerre[t]
1033/36	Amiens/Corbie[u]
1036	Le Puy II[v]
1036	Poitiers III[w]
1038	Bourges II[x]

[a] Mansi 19:89–90. Letaldus of Micy, *Delatio corporis s. Juniani; PL* 137:823–26.

[b] Mansi 19:103–4.

[c] Ademar of Chabannes, *Chronicon*, 3.35, p. 158. Idem, *Sermones*, nos. 1–3; *PL* 141:115–24. Idem, *Sermones*, nos. 34, 46, in Léopold Delisle, "Notices sur les manuscrits originaux d'Adémar de Chabannes," *Notices et extraits des manuscrits de la Bibliothèque nationale* 35 (1886), 290, 293. Idem, *Translatio beati Martialis de Monte Gaudio*, in Ernst Sackur, *Die Cluniacenser in ihrer kirchlichen und allgemeingeschichtlichen Wirksamkeit bis zur Mitte des 11. Jhs.*, 2 vols. (Halle, 1892–94), 1:392–96. *Trans. et mirac. s. Viviani*, chap. 32, p. 272.

[d] This council was mentioned in two charters: P. E. Giraud, *Essai historique sur l'abbaye de s. Barnard et sur la ville de Romans*, 2 vols. (1856), no. 11, 1:28–66, and *Recueil des chartes de l'abbaye de Cluny*, 6 vols., ed. A. Bernard and A. Bruel (Paris, 1870–1903), no. 2255, 3:384–88. Also see Mansi 19:99–104.

[e] Mansi 19:271–72.

[f] Mansi 19:265–68.

[g] Georges de Manteyer, *Les origines de la maison de Savoie en Bourgogne (910–1060)* (Grenoble, 1904), pp. 91–98.

[h] *Historia episcoporum Autissiodorensium*, chap. 49; *RHF* 10:172. Karl Josef von Hefele, *Histoire des conciles d'après les documents originaux*, 2d ed., 11 vols., trans. Henri Leclercq (Paris, 1907–52), 4.2:1407–10.

[i] Christian Pfister, *Etudes sur le règne de Robert le Pieux (996–1031)* (Paris, 1885), pp. lx–lxi. *Gesta episcoporum Cameracensium*, 3.27; *MGH SS* 7:474.

[j] *Historia episcoporum Autissiodorensium*, chap. 49; *RHF* 10:172. *Miracula s. Veroli*, chap. 6; *AASS*, June III, p. 385. *Chronique de Saint-Pierre-le-Vif de Sens, dite de Clarius*, ed. and

Table 1. (continued)

trans. Robert-Henri Bautier and Monique Gilles (Sources d'histoire médiévale publiées par l'Institut de Recherche et d'Histoire des Textes, 3; Paris, 1979), pp. 114–17. *Chronicon Autissiodorense; RHF* 10:275. *De diversis casibus coenobii Dervensis et miracula s. Bercharii,* chap. 27; *AASS,* Oct. VII, pp. 1019–30. *Vita s. Hugonis Enziacensis,* chaps. 27–28; *AASS,* April II, pp. 770–71. Mansi 19:423–24.

[k] Mansi 19:483–84.

[l] Ademar of Chabannes, *Chronicon,* 3.69, p. 194.

[m] Ademar of Chabannes, *Sermones,* no. 46, in Delisle, "Notices," p. 293, and Sackur, *Cluniacenser,* 2:485.

[n] Ademar of Chabannes, *Sermones,* no. 40, in Delisle "Notices," p. 291, and Sackur, *Cluniacenser,* 2:483–84.

[o] *La chronique de Saint-Maixent (751–1140),* ed. Jean Verdon (Paris, 1979), pp. 114–16 (the entry is under the year 1032). *Chartes et docs. de Saint-Maixent,* no. 91, 1:109. Mansi 19:495–98.

[p] Mansi 19:501–8.

[q] Ademar of Chabannes, *Sermones,* no. 38, in Delisle, "Notices," p. 281. Mansi 19:507–48.

[r] Ademar of Chabannes, *Sermones,* no. 46, in Delisle, "Notices," pp. 293–94, and Sackur, *Cluniacenser,* 2:487.

[s] Hartmut Hoffmann, *Gottesfriede und Treuga Dei* (Schriften der Monumenta Germaniae historica, 20; Stuttgart, 1964), pp. 260–62.

[t] *Chronicon breve Autissiodorense; RHF* 11:292. Various Peace councils are also mentioned by Glaber, *Historiarum,* 4.5.14–17.

[u] *Miracula s. Adalhardi,* chap. 4; *MGH SS* 15:861.

[v] *Miracula s. Privati,* chap. 7, ed. Clovis Brunel (Paris, 1912), p. 14.

[w] *La chronique de Saint-Maixent,* p. 116 (under the year 1036). Mansi 19:579.

[x] Andrew of Fleury, *Mirac. s. Benedicti,* 5.2–4, pp. 192–98.

(Charroux and Poitiers) from one in the Auvergne (Le Puy), at least insofar as the bishops who participated are concerned. Such a distinction is confirmed by the fact that the contents of the conciliar dispositions were more detailed at Le Puy. The Auvergnat movement nevertheless had its origins in the west and was probably brought there by the bishops of Clermont and Le Puy, who attended the council of Limoges that same year.

In the second phase (ca. 1019–38), when the Peace of God was revived after an interruption of perhaps twenty years, we recognize a considerable extension of its area: the southern part of the ecclesiastical province of Bourges, the duchy of Burgundy to the east, and parts of the provinces of Sens and Reims to the north were involved for the first time. We can, moreover, sense certain changes: the origins no longer lay in Aquitaine, but—inspired in wording by the earlier Peace of Le Puy (994)—in Burgundy at Vienne. From there the Peace decrees, with much more detailed dispositions, were transferred almost literally first to the archbishopric of Lyon and then to neighboring sees in the east (Besançon) and west (Auxerre), or, in other words, to the duchy of Burgundy and the neighboring parts of the Burgundian kingdom (Verdun-sur-le-Doubs). Subsequently with the help of Bishop

Berold of Soissons and the support of King Robert, they were transferred to the northern parts of the kingdom (Beauvais). It was not until
the second period of this phase (after 1027) that, instigated by Duke
William V, the Peace was revived in Aquitaine, where ten peace councils occurred within ten years, if we can believe Ademar of Chabannes.
In a repetition of the first phase, the Peace moved from western areas
to the province of Bourges in the early 1030s. The second council of
Bourges (1038), however, marked the end of the Aquitanian Peace
movement, which never adopted the *treuga dei*. The Peace begun in
northern Spain during the second phase (Toulouges in 1027 and Vic in
1033) developed a separate, rather regionally specific, character.

Thus, in following the scope of the Peace of God, we must acknowledge that it was not a single movement that expanded from Aquitanian
origins all over France; it was divided into several phases, each with its
own varied centers. The triumphal march of the Peace of God should
therefore not be overestimated, for periods of intensive battles for
peace alternated with "peaceless" times.

Basic Dispositions of the Peace of God

The basic tendencies of the Peace of God were already apparent in
the oldest statutes preserved, those of the council of Charroux (989).
According to that council, three offenses were to be avenged by excommunication: (1) the violent invasion of churches and robbery committed in churches (canon 1), (2) assault on unarmed clergymen (canon 3),
and (3) the theft of cattle from peasants and the poor (canon 2). These
clauses were later extended, but they were repeated in each Peace of
the period under consideration. At Poitiers (1000/14) they were renewed with explicit reference to Charroux. They may therefore be considered typical of the early Peace movement and should be examined
in more detail.

Protection of Churches

The church's desire to protect itself and its property played an exceptional role in the early Peace movement. The first intention of the
councils was to protect church buildings from burglary and theft.
Later, for example at Verdun (1019/21), this protection was extended
to the churchyard or (in the oaths of Vienne and Beauvais) to domestic
buildings and storehouses (*celleraria*). Finally, it included all houses
within a distance of thirty steps from a church. The reason for these

measures was not simply a desire to guarantee the spiritual life.[9] The council of Narbonne (ca. 990) prohibited noblemen from invading the "goods of the churches" (*ecclesiasticarum bona*). At Vienne it was forbidden to make war against the lands of the bishopric or to use them for housing the army. At Toulouges (1027) the invasion of the lands of both churches and monasteries was prohibited. It is obvious that, as a landowner, the church was especially interested in a Peace that particularly protected churches and their property.[10]

Consequently, the Peace of the church was not a purely ecclesiastical affair but an attempt to protect church property from laypeople, as at Narbonne. At Le Puy (994), for example, the usurpation of ecclesiastical, monastic, convent, and episcopal property was strictly prohibited (with the sole exception of precarial loans made by the bishop or a convent). According to the oath of Vienne, laypeople were expected not to appropriate any more ecclesiastical or monastic property *in commendam* than their ancestors had possessed in the time of Archbishop Theobald (ca. 970–1001); otherwise, such property had to be returned within thirty days. At Poitiers (1029/31) it was even decreed that appropriated church property had to be restored immediately. Damage to churches by secular lords and raids on ecclesiastical land were still the subject of Bishop Jordan's charge at Limoges (1031). At Bourges (1038) the "invaders of ecclesiastical property" were challenged.

Not only the property but also the rights and revenues of the church had to be secured. At Le Puy funerals were explicitly reserved for the clergy. This did not, however, affect the power of the bishop, who was allowed to order exceptions to those prohibitions. At Le Puy he was even allowed to invade the churches of his own see to collect taxes.

The protection of churches acquired a clear place as a central theme of the Peace movement. In this sense it was, above all, a self-protective move to secure the resources of the churches, no doubt also from social upheavals. The Peace movement was not yet, however, intended to order all public life. With their measures, the councils, in their own view, served to protect the security of the *status ecclesiae*, as in Limoges (994);[11] for "the restoration of the church," as in Poitiers (1000/14); and for "the consolidation of the holy church of God," as in the words of Bishop Jordan at Limoges (1031). The defense of churches was prominent even under secular leadership: as late as 1028, Duke

---

[9] Loren MacKinney, "The People and Public Opinion in the Eleventh-Century Peace Movement," *Speculum* 5 (1930), 181–206, particularly p. 182.

[10] Töpfer, *Volk und Kirche*, pp. 81–82, and Lewis, *Southern French and Catalan Society*, p. 317–25.

[11] *Translatio beati Martialis de Monte Gaudio*, chap. 8, in Sackur, *Cluniacenser*, 1:395.

William V of Aquitaine bade the "princes of Aquitaine" to defend the
peace and respect the church.

Protection of Certain Groups of Persons, Particularly the Clergy

The protection of the clergy can be understood as an extension of
the defense of churches to those who were in the service of the church.
It is interesting to note, however, that it was not the entire clergy who
was to be protected from assaults and arrest but only those clerics who
were unarmed.[12] Thus it seems that, in the beginning, armed clergymen did not enjoy such protection. In connection with church reform,
the council of Le Puy (994) revived the old, hardly observed prohibition against people of the church bearing weapons at all. Both clauses
should be examined together: the protection of the clergy became necessary at the very moment when priests were deprived of the possibility
of defending themselves. Or, from another perspective, it is likely that
the offer of legal protection to the clergy would have helped the prohibition against them carrying weapons to prevail.

The clergy were not the only ones so defended. The same protection
was offered to monks,[13] later to nuns,[14] sometimes, as at Vienne and
Beauvais, to widows and noblewomen who traveled without their husbands, and to the unarmed companions of clergymen and monks.[15]
The three Peace oaths of Vienne, Verdun, and Beauvais even guarded
unarmed knights (*caballarii*) during Lent. These clauses did not yet imply the existence of a season without feuds, but they were aimed at the
protection of defenseless people. Their purpose corresponded neatly
to the fact that the oath in Verdun was sworn only by knights in armor,
for it was from such men that others had to be protected. In all these
cases, the criterion for protection was defenselessness. This was extended from clergy and monks to larger circles: clergy and laity should
be able to travel about without arms and without fear.[16] By such measures, society came to be divided into two groups: those who needed

---

[12] Charroux I (989), Vienne (early eleventh century), Poitiers I (1000/14), Verdun
(1019/21), Beauvais (1023), Toulouges (1027), and Vic (1033).

[13] Le Puy I (994), Vienne (early eleventh century), Verdun (1019/21), Beauvais (1023),
Toulouges (1027), and Vic (1033).

[14] Beauvais (1023), Vic (1033), and Bourges II (1038). See also Rodulphus Glaber,
Historiarum, 4.5.15.

[15] Le Puy I (994), Vienne (early eleventh century), Verdun (1019/21), and Beauvais
(1023). Glaber, *Historiarum*, 4.5.15.

[16] Glaber, *Historiarum*, 4.5.15.

protection and those from whom they had to be protected.[17] This distinction did not coincide with the social division of *milites* and *rustici* which was to become important later. The early Peace movement, which classed the clergy with the defenseless, did not yet propose a social classification. It was simply interested in the protection of unarmed people, above all the clergy.

Protection of Cattle and of Agricultural Production

As a third element, the Council of Charroux condemned the theft of farm animals from peasants and the poor, a clause repeated in all extant Peace statutes.[18] Though these canons spoke only of farm animals, this clause has generally been interpreted as a protection of peasants. It is, however, striking that protection was restricted to animals important for food or agricultural labor: horned cattle, cows, and pigs (throughout); sheep, donkeys, goats, horses, and hens (in most places).[19] The oath of Verdun and Beauvais protected pastured animals (mules, stallions, and mares) separately. The intention of these dispositions was apparently to protect food production, an explanation confirmed by other measures. In the oaths of Vienne, Verdun, and Beauvais, protection was extended to vineyards. These oaths also prohibited the gathering of grapes on alien soil, the pillage of mills and granaries, assaults on carts bearing wine or harvest goods—including the draught animals themselves—and on ships. At Vic (1033) it was forbidden to burn down the harvest or to steal wax or bees. At Vienne the protection included peasants' tools. All these measures were meant to maintain the production of food.

That this was an essential purpose of the Peace of God is made particularly evident by the fact that the Peace synods were frequently connected with famines or plagues.[20] There even seems to be a causal nexus that involved the coming of famine, followed by the invocation of

[17] Georges Duby, "Les laïcs et la paix de Dieu," rpt. in Duby, *Hommes et structures du moyen âge: Recueil d'articles* (Paris, 1973), p. 232. For discussion of the famous social image of the "three orders," refer to Goetz, "Kirchenschutz," note 136.

[18] Anse I (994), Le Puy I (994), Poitiers I (1000/14), Vienne (early eleventh century), Verdun (1019/21), Beauvais (1023), and Vich (1033).

[19] Sheep, wethers, lambs, donkeys, and goats were protected at Charroux I, Le Puy I, Vienne, Verdun, Beauvais, and Vic. Horses were protected at Anse, Le Puy I, Vienne, Verdun, and Vic. Hens were protected at Le Puy I, Verdun, Beauvais, and Vic. Geese were protected at Verdun.

[20] Varied pestilences were attested at Anse I (994) and Limoges I (994). Famines were mentioned at Héry (1025) and Amiens/Corbie (1033).

the saints, and finally the institution of the Peace of God.[21] Thus the Peace appears to have been a result of a time of need. Alternatively, Ademar of Chabannes interpreted famine as a divine punishment for a breach of the Peace.[22] When the emergency ceased, we learn repeatedly, the enthusiasm for peace waned and the Peace was broken.[23]

Thus, in the eyes of contemporaries, famines and the Peace of God were closely related. Like the cult of relics, which was associated with the Peace movement, Peace treaties were one means of removing evils, but they were often accompanied by other means, such as fasts.[24] Since Peace regulations sometimes allowed for the feeding of three poor people instead of undertaking a fast, they also seem to be connected to the impact of famines. The Peace of God was not caused by the social and political disorders of that epoch alone; it was also inspired by the heavy blows of nature. The Peace synods of Auxerre (1033) and of Bourges (1038) were each preceded by a solar eclipse. These natural events cannot be regarded as their ultimate cause, but they no doubt provided the occasion for the synods, which dealt with central social problems and took emergency measures to alleviate need and safeguard remaining provisions.

It was only to this extent that the Peace of God protected the peasantry. *Villani* and *villanae* were indeed defended in some Peace synods,[25] but these dispositions differed distinctly from the defense of other groups such as priests and monks. Peasants were not, like churchmen, protected because they were defenseless; rather, their defense was closely associated with the protection of cattle. In the oaths of Vienne, Verdun, and Beauvais, peasants were mentioned between the dispositions concerning domestic and pastured animals; at Vic animals and peasants were joined in a single clause. Thus it seems that the peasantry were protected, not as defenseless persons, but because their work was vital in securing food supplies, a task that lay almost solely in their hands. At Verdun it was explicitly forbidden to assault and rob

[21] Roger Bonnaud-Delamare, "Les institutions de paix en Aquitaine au XIe siècle," in *La paix* (Recueils de la Société Jean Bodin, 14; Brussels, 1961), p. 432.

[22] Ademar of Chabannes, *Sermones*, no. 46, in Delisle, "Notices," p. 293.

[23] A reversed sequence was attested by Glaber, *Historiarum*, 4.5.14.

[24] Relics played an important part in the Peace movement; this is explicitly attested, though seldom in the official statutes themselves, at Charroux I (989), Narbonne (990), Limoges I (994), Verdun (1029/21), Héry (1025), Toulouges (1027), Limoges II-IV (1028–31), and Le Puy II (1036). See also Goetz, "Kirchenschutz," note 154. For the strong connection between the cult of Saint Martial and the Peace movement in the Limousin, see Daniel Callahan, "Adémar de Chabannes et la paix de Dieu," *Annales du Midi* 89 (1977), 21–43, and Landes, "Dynamics of Heresy." On fasting, see Limoges I (994), Glaber, *Historiarum*, 4.5.16, and *Gesta episcoporum Cameracensium*, 3.52; *MGH SS* 7:485–86.

[25] Le Puy I (994), Vienne (early eleventh century), Verdun (1019/20), Beauvais (1023), and Vic (1033).

those people who were harvesting. The same motivation lay behind the protection of merchants (at Le Puy, Vienne, and Beauvais).

Otherwise, protection of the *villani* was restricted to specific cases, such as the prohibition at Le Puy of ransoms (*redemptio*) demanded after kidnapping. This disposition, however, covered only those *villani* who tilled land that both belonged to other people and was the object of a dispute. Thus the council essentially decreed that peasants should not become victims of assaults against their master and that they should not become involved in his disputes; at Vienne and Beauvais it was decreed that such a peasant should not be harmed "because of a quarrel involving his master." The dispositions at Vienne, Verdun, and Beauvais were more general in prohibiting anyone from seizing, robbing, or beating *villani* or *villanae*, *servientes* or merchants, and from forcing such people to pay for their own release.

Though the Peace protected the property of peasants and merchants, it did not offer protection to an entire class. Its purpose was to provide for the security of their labor and its fruits. It would be incorrect to speak of the Peace as an antiseigneurial movement, since the rights of the landlord over his own land and his own people were explicitly confirmed at Le Puy (*nisi unusquisque de terra sua aut de suo beneficio*).[26] Consequently, the Peace did not offer protection to serfs. If, however, it is correct to regard the *villani* not simply as peasants but as specifically those peasants who worked on manses in the seigneurial *villae*, then the Peace of God did not intend to protect peasants but to protect the nobility itself and to strengthen their lordship.[27] The protection of dependent peasants—the council of Le Puy referred to those working on alien soil (*alterius terra*)—seems to have been at base a protection of the nobility and landlords.[28] Since the churches belonged to the richest landlords, these decisions complemented the measures taken for the protection of church property.

On the whole, the dispositions of the early Peace movement reveal purposes that seem much more restricted than has often been assumed. The "evils that daily accumulate among the people" (*maleficia quae in populo quotidie accrescunt*, Le Puy) consisted of those assaults on churches, defenseless ecclesiastics, and church property whose protection we can recognize as the most important purpose of the Peace treaties. From the beginning, the center of the Peace of God seems to be a defense of the church that itself organized the Peace. Its later

[26] Töpfer, *Volk und Kirche*, pp. 110–11; Hoffmann, *Gottesfriede*, p. 18.

[27] There are indications that this is the meaning of the term *villani:* for example, the differentiation made between *villani* and *servientes*, and the statement that *villani* had a *senior*.

[28] One's own property was excluded from those regulations in any case.

development is characterized by greater variety, but not by an alteration of these original ends. Peace councils tried to remove abuses but not the deeper roots of social problems. The protection of churches from the laity was not principally directed against landlords. On the contrary, by the confirmation of the seigneurial system, the social disparities were, consciously or unconsciously, strengthened. Occasionally the measures taken exceeded the strict framework of ecclesiastical protection. Thus it is now possible to resume consideration of the problems alluded to at the beginning of this essay and to ask to what extent we can recognize far-reaching tendencies—rather than short-term, problem-solving measures—to preserve public law and order in the early Peace movement.

Preservation of the Judicial Order

The Peace of God required a Christian legal order. Those central Augustinian terms, *pax et iustitia,* reappeared relatively often in Peace statutes as a unit.[29] Peace could not be achieved without simultaneous confirmation of the legal order. Law therefore was not simply an issue central to the Peace; it was its very foundation. The statutes of Peace councils consisted simply of prohibitions. To protect the church and its possessions, as well as to prevent damages to those who were defenseless, the councils had to condemn robbery and burglary. Robbers and thieves were excluded from protection under Peace regulations. Communication with such people was strongly prohibited, and fighting against them was explicitly permitted in the oaths of Vienne, Verdun, and Beauvais.

It is interesting to note the relation between the Peace of God and the established legal order. In the first place, Peace statutes did not demand punishments but only the reparation of damages. There were hardly any Peace regulations that did not repeat such words as *emendare* and *satisfacere.* In the oaths of Vienne, Verdun, and Beauvais, anyone who sheltered a breaker of the peace was obliged to persuade that offender to make reparation for the damages caused; otherwise, the person who provided shelter had to pay for such recompense. We may therefore conclude that the Peace of God endeavored to maintain the old penitential code based on atonement for damages and that it supported adequate legal title for anyone who suffered damages. Penalties were not applied unless there was no hope of satisfaction. As early as

[29] First at Limoges I (994): *pactum pacis et iustitia;* similarly at Poitiers I (1000/14): *restauratio pacis et iustitiae;* also at Limoges II-IV (1028–31) and Amiens/Corbie (1033/36).

Charroux, only those people who had failed to give due satisfaction were excommunicated; this disposition was frequently repeated.[30] It is therefore wrong to assert, as is often done, that Peace regulations punished certain crimes. Those crimes had not in any case been permitted previously. Rather, in the Peace regulations the church developed a new element—spiritual sanctions, particularly excommunication and interdict—in those cases in which reparation had not been made for an offence in accordance with current law. Consequently, violations of Peace regulations cannot be regarded as breaches of the Peace unless they were followed by a refusal to provide satisfaction. The Peace of God intended to become, not a substitute, but rather a support for current secular law. This was the intention from the first councils and not an achievement of the later German Peace movement.

The Peace of God was no more intended to undermine private legal self-defense than had been the penitential codes. The protection of specified, defenseless groups, especially church people, did not exclude someone being legally sued by a victim for a crime or debt.[31] There were few interventions against the right of judicial self-defense. The Peace of Beauvais merely obliged the victim not to demand more than the legal value of the damage suffered (*non plus quam capitale cum lege constituta*), and a guilty *villanus* was granted a reprieve of fourteen days to make satisfaction voluntarily; only then could such a person be compelled to make reparation.[32]

Thus the Peace of God lacked the tendency of the later *Landfrieden* to prohibit or restrict self-defense in favor of public jurisdiction. It did not intend to enforce judicial decrees, for there was to be no trial unless someone appealed to a court.[33] Peace conventions were based not only on current law but also on an acceptance of secular jurisdiction. According to the acts of Limoges (994), conflicts were to be settled by "those learned in the law."[34] At Poitiers the legal order, which according to common scholarly opinion had broken down, was strong enough to have conflicts settled legally (*in iustitia*) by the prince (*princeps*) of the region or by another judge of the district. Such authorities could even be compelled to administer justice by giving hostages. It was not until the ordained judges failed to maintain the law that an assembly of

[30] Anse I (994), Poitiers I (1000/14), and Toulouges (1027). It was different (excommunication *until* reparation was made) at Le Puy I (994) and Vic (1033).

[31] As for ecclesiastics at Charroux I (989), Le Puy I (994), Vienne (early eleventh century), Verdun (1019/21), and Beauvais (1023); as for peasants at Le Puy I and Vienne.

[32] For a longer discussion of the famous resistance of Bishop Gerard of Cambrai, see Goetz, "Kirchenschutz," note 201.

[33] As we learn from the statutes of Poitiers I (1000/14): *si ex contendentibus . . . unus alium interpellaverit.*

[34] Ademar of Chabannes, *Sermones*, no. 1; *PL* 141:117C.

princes (*principes*) and bishops—forming, as it were, a court of appeal—were to take charge. Ecclesiastical powers were secondary authorities subordinated to secular jurisdiction; but, when secular jurisdiction and, above all, private legal agreement failed and when atonement was lacking, those ecclesiastical powers could add the threat of spiritual sanctions.

Similarly, it was not one of the primary purposes of the Peace of God to restrict feuding, which was closely connected to legal self-defence. Feuding was not simply omitted from the dispositions of Peace councils, it was explicitly excluded from the number of infringements that were mentioned in Peace regulations. According to the oaths of Vienne, Verdun, and Beauvais, to burn or to destroy houses was not prohibited if an armed knightly enemy was to be found inside the building or if the building belonged to a castle of such an enemy. The knightly feud, then, was not forbidden, nor was the siege of castles, which were explicitly excluded from the protection offered to houses. In accordance with the defence of unarmed people, the Peace of God merely tried to reduce damages incurred by those who were not involved. At Vienne and Beauvais we learn that peasants and livestock should not be affected "because of a quarrel." At most councils, such as that of Vienne, we find a tendency to protract a feud for a fortnight in order to offer the enemy an occasion to make satisfaction. In addition, the aggrieved party was not obliged to accept the forfeit but had the right to insist on continuing the feud.

Through these observations, we discover a strong relation between the Peace of God and the established legal order (an inevitable fact if we consider the relation between peace and law in the Middle Ages). The preservation of the legal order was not the basic purpose of the Peace movement, but supporting it was an appropriate means of realizing peace. Thus it was inevitable that the Peace of God interfered with public interests. It is not by chance that the author of the *Miracula sancti Viviani* tells us that the decisions of the council of Coler (ca. 994) were made "for the arrangement of public affairs and for the assurance of an inviolable peace."[35] The church, however, did not replace a failing secular power, whose existence, in the person of *principes* and *iudices*, was taken for granted as much as was the validity of public and private law.

The Peace of God did not establish a new law; rather, it was intended to reinforce secular laws and was itself based on a secular jurisdiction that could help the movement achieve its purposes. In southern France, however, one could not expect any support from the king,

[35] "[P]ro statu rei publicae ac pacis inviolabili firmitate"; *Trans. et mirac. s. Viviani*, chap. 32, p. 263.

whose power was restricted to the royal domain, but only from dukes, counts, and other judicial powers. The application of secular laws, as at Poitiers (1000/14), was therefore not a symptom of ecclesiastical infringement on secular law but an expression of cooperation between ecclesiastical and secular powers. The council of Poitiers, as Limoges (994) before it, was convened through the efforts of Duke William V of Aquitaine.[36] Thus the resort to the jurisdiction of the *principes* and the cooperation between ecclesiastical and secular powers can be easily explained by the duke's influence, by the assistance of secular magnates, and by the dependence of the bishops on local seigneurial authorities. After all, the efficacy of the Peace ceased where public powers pertained. The oaths of Beauvais and Verdun, for example, were not valid in the case of public enemies of the king or the bishop, or in the case of a common campaign.

If the preservation of the legal order was necessary for the maintenance of the Peace, its goal, according to the Peace statutes, was, however banal this may sound, to restore peace itself, the *restauratio pacis* in the words from Poitiers.[37] It seemed thus to have an end in itself, a purpose warranted by the dispositions mentioned above. Peace was in the first place a thoroughly religious matter and thus inevitably had to be organized by the church.[38] It is therefore advisable to take a final look at the religious motives of the movement and to consider its relation to the ecclesiastical reforms that began in the same period.

The Peace of God and Ecclesiastical Reform

Monastic reform was inseparably connected to the Cluniacs. A strong relation between Cluny and the original Peace movement has often been noted in terms of the support offered to the Peace and

---

[36] Bonnaud-Delamare, "Institutions de paix," pp. 437–38. The duke also attended the councils of Charroux II (1027/28), Poitiers II (1029/31), and Limoges IV (1031).

[37] The council of Limoges (994) served, according to the author of the *Trans. et mirac. s. Viviani* (chap. 32, p. 263), *ad corroborandam pacis stabilitatem.* According to the author of the *Vita s. Hugonis prioris Enziacensis* (chaps. 27–28; *AASS*, April II, p. 770), the Burgundian councils (Héry and Anse) were assembled *ob studium reformandae pacis.* According to Ademar of Chabannes (Mansi 19:530), Limoges IV (1031) was conceived as a *conventus domini ad inquirandam pacem, ac consolandam sanctam Dei ecclesiam.* Glaber (*Historiarum,* 4.5.14) described councils that were gathered *de reformanda pace et sacra fidei institutione.*

[38] These aspects are emphasized by Roger Bonnaud-Delamare, "Fondement des institutions de paix au XIe siècle," in *Mélanges d'histoire du moyen âge dédiés à la mémoire de Louis Halphen,* ed. Charles-Edmond Perrin (Paris, 1951), pp. 19–26. On the different measures developed to secure the Peace, see Goetz, "Kirchenschutz," pp. 227–28 and the corresponding notes; for the oath, see also note 7.

Truce of God by Abbot Odilo (994–1049).[39] Earlier and less formal connections between reform monasticism and the Peace movement, however, have never been adequately investigated.[40] Therefore, the link between Cluny and the Peace of God should not be overestimated.[41] This is most particularly true since the origins of the movement should not be sought in Burgundy but rather in the Auvergne and Aquitaine. Second, Cluny was, in spite of its importance, only one of several centers of monastic reform, centers that also included Saint-Victor of Marseille, Fleury, and Dijon. Third, church reform was not restricted to monasteries; it included canons, bishops, and even laypeople. Finally, the Peace of God was not an achievement of monks but of bishops in alliance with secular authorities. The relation between Cluny and the wider church reform movement has also been much disputed.[42] An argument between Cluny and Bishop Gauzlin of Mâcon was settled by the Peace council of Anse (1025) in favor of the bishop, who maintained the right of consecrating against the monastery's papal exemption. At other times, however, when no political decisions were at stake, we recognize a close cooperation between monasteries and bishops.[43] Each had its own intentions, but they were united in their efforts to reform the church, a purpose undoubtedly shared by the Peace movement. It is not possible to explain the Peace of God as an offspring of the Cluniac reform; nevertheless, it has to be seen in the context of wider church reform.

The Peace of God was conceived as a reform—in the medieval sense of the word a restoration or renewal. Its purpose was, according to the synodal statutes, not to create something new but to restore the previous state, that is, the forgotten dispositions of earlier councils. After Charroux we can, time and again, recognize a resort to the canons of previous councils. Such a procedure, however, complied with the intentions of the ecclesiastical reform, which, of course, was also conceived

[39] Abbot Odilo was present at Anse (994 and 1025) and was one of the initiators of a letter written by the Franco-Burgundian clergy to their Italian colleagues concerning the Peace of Arles (1037/41); see *MGH Constitutiones et acta publica imperatorum et regum* 1, no. 419, pp. 596–97. See also Roger Reynolds, "Odilo and the *Treuga Dei* in Southern Italy: A Beneventan Manuscript Fragment," *Mediaeval Studies* 46 (1984), 450–62.

[40] Hoffmann, *Gottesfriede*, p. 47, notes a complete lack of elements that are characteristic of the Peace movement in Cluniac sources written before 1030.

[41] Johannes Fechter, "Cluny, Adel und Volk: Studien über das Verhältnis des Klosters zu den Ständen (910–1156)" (Ph.D. diss., Tübingen, 1966). For a discussion of this thesis, see Goetz, "Kirchenschutz," note 254.

[42] See the articles collected in *Cluny: Beiträge zu Gestalt und Wirkung der cluniazensischen Reform*, ed. Helmut Richter (Darmstadt, 1975), H. E. J. Cowdrey, *The Cluniacs and the Gregorian Reform* (Oxford, 1970), and Goetz, "Kirchenschutz," note 260.

[43] Hermann Diener, "Das Verhältnis Clunys zu den Bischöfen vor allem in der Zeit seines Abtes Hugo (1049–1109)," in *Neue Forschungen über Cluny und die Cluniacenser*, ed. Gerd Tellenbach (Freiburg, 1959), pp. 219–352.

as a restoration. The Peace council of Poitiers explicitly served "for the restoration of the church." The Peace of God and church reform originated in the same desire for order. Moreover, Peace councils—especially those of the second wave which occurred in connection with the cult of relics—were often also reform synods, or, rather, the Peace of God was preferably proclaimed at reform councils such as Bourges (1031) and Poitiers (1036). Peace and reform were supported by the same authorities.[44] It is therefore no wonder that one can discover common interests in their purposes as well.

The central purposes of the Peace of God—the protection of the church and of the clergy—were at the same time an essential aspect of the reform movements which, from a different approach, sought to protect the morals of the clergy by attacking nicolaitism and simony. The reform movement also defended the liberty of the church from the laity. Like the Peace of God, it aimed to protect ecclesiastical property and spiritual life from lay encroachment.

Peace councils, on the other hand, repeatedly promulgated acts derived from the reform movement which were especially meant to prohibit the alienation of the clergy from its spiritual duties. At Anse (994) celibacy was again made compulsory and clerics were forbidden to hunt. At Le Puy (994) they were prohibited from carrying weapons, a connection already discussed above. Priests, moreover, were not allowed to take money for baptisms (Le Puy, 994) or to accept *munera* for sacerdotal acts (Poitiers, 1000/14; Bourges 1031). Priests and deacons were prohibited from lascivious intercourse with women, celibacy and the tonsure were required, and the reception of the sons of priests into holy orders was banned. At Bourges, further dispositions concerning the reform and reputation of the clergy were combined with the decree of the Peace and completed by matrimonial prescriptions.[45] One canon was even directed against the "political" form of simony—the appointment of priests by laypeople without the consent of the local bishop.

Such reform dispositions have long been unjustly regarded as being separate from the Peace movement proper.[46] The preamble of the acts of the council of Poitiers (1000/14) ascribed the reform canons explicitly to the *pax*. The relations between church reform and the Peace of God, particularly the extensive similarity of their intentions, suggest a

---

[44] Gerd Tellenbach, "Das Reformmönchtum und die Laien im 11. und 12. Jahrhundert," in *Cluny: Beiträge zu Gestalt und Wirkung der cluniazensischen Reform*, ed. Helmut Richter (Darmstadt, 1975), pp. 371–400.

[45] At Toulouges (1027) we find decrees on incestuous marriages, the repudiation of wives, and second marriages.

[46] Only Achter, *Über den Ursprung*, pp. 6–7, regards such ecclesiastical dispositions, in addition to punishment for secular offences, as part of the Peace of God. Also see Amy G. Remensnyder (chapter 12) in this volume.

close connection between these two movements and incorporate the Peace of God into a broader movement of ecclesiastical reform. Both had their origins in the internal desire of the church for reform and protection, yet, given medieval social structures, they necessarily had to encroach on wider segments of society. In their own conceptions of themselves, however, the two movements remained ever bound to their religious background.

Although the Peace of God as well as the reform movement more generally were caused and affected, without doubt, by political, social, and economic changes, they always remained in their own understanding religious movements that regarded peace on earth as an image of, and even as a precondition for, the *visio Dei* and eternal life. At Le Puy (994) the movement was intended to establish peace "in the name of God, since without peace no one will see God." Peace thus became an urgent necessity for salvation. The Augustinian expression *pax et iustitia* also pointed to a religious context. *Pax* and *unitas,* according to the prologue of Poitiers (1000/14), belonged to the message of Christ. The consciousness that the Peace of God was a peace sanctified by God grew ever stronger. The Peace was vowed to God by an oath and pronounced in sacral forms. Pestilence and famine were interpreted as divine punishment for the lack of peace, "which the Lord especially loves and orders to be loved."[47] The Peace of Héry (1024), according to the contemporary report of the *Miracula sancti Veroli,* was established because of the fear of God and of the saints.[48] These examples show that the Peace was a devout enterprise. Furthermore, in a speech attributed to Bishop Jordan of Limoges at the synod of 1031, God himself was asked to give peace; whoever refused was said to follow the devil.[49] Peace was characterized as a divine act. Rodulphus Glaber reports that the people (*maximi mediocres ac minimi*) obeyed the decrees of the bishops "as if the voice of God himself had spoken from heaven to men on earth."[50] According to the same author's famous description of the solemn vow between God and human beings, the bishops raised their arms and croisiers toward heaven as a sign of the alliance, while the crowd cried "peace" three times.[51] The author of the *Gesta episcoporum Cameracensium* (Deeds of the Bishops of Cambrai) dropped the modal comparison ("as if") and stated that a decree from heaven had urged the people to restore peace.[52] The wordings of the dispositions

---

[47] Gerald, *Miracula s. Adalhardi,* 1.4; *MGH SS* 15:861. References to the medieval concept of peace are provided in Goetz, "Kirchenschutz," note 286; also see note 304.

[48] *Miracula s. Veroli,* chap. 6; *AASS,* June III, p. 385.

[49] Mansi 19:530. If this speech was invented by Ademar of Chabannes, it nevertheless reveals that author's ideology of peace.

[50] Glaber, *Historiarum,* 4.5.14.

[51] Glaber, *Historiarum,* 4.5.16.

[52] *Gesta episcoporum Cameracensium,* 3.52; *MGH SS* 7:485–86.

of Peace councils had become the word of God and were revealed in a "letter from heaven." The Peace militia of Bourges (1038) was considered to be God's own people, assuming the role of the Israelites.[53]

Although the characterization of the Peace movement as a "sanctified Peace" was not established until the Truce of God, the immediate relationship of the Peace of God was an essential mark from its beginnings.[54] Chiliastic ideas and the fear of the end of the world around the year 1000 were not the origins of the Peace movement, but they certainly contributed to its religious sensibility.[55] The Peace of God was not simply an ingenious means invented by the church for directing a popular movement into the right channels.[56] It was above all conceived as a religious restoration carried out by all classes and—like the passion for miracles and the unconditional belief in God—it seized the people the same way it seized the highest clergy.

This religious self-consciousness, the conviction that peace was wanted and caused by God, has to be regarded as an essential part of the Peace of God which became incorporated into the more general reform movement. The Peace of God must not be seen separately either from other religious movements of that period or from its own general concert of peace. The movement refused either to distinguish between a secular and a spiritual peace or to see a contradiction between a temporal and an eternal peace. The Peace was closely connected with relic translations and miracles that occurred during its councils. "This council," wrote Letaldus of Micy regarding Charroux, "assembled by God's will, was confirmed by the countless miracles achieved by the presence of the saints."[57] It is this religious understanding that helps to explain the later relations between the Peace of God, on the one hand, and Christian chivalry, the crusades, and the investiture contest, on the other.

Several conclusions can be drawn from the preceding observations:

1. According to the synodal acts, which reveal the purposes of its organizers, the Peace of God was conceived as taking up the goals of wider church reform, and—out of religious motivation—as applying those ideas to the actual social situation in order to realize the movement's truest goal, which was peace.

[53] *Mirac. s. Benedicti*, 5.2, p. 193. For these "letters from heaven," see Goetz, "Kirchenschutz," note 295.

[54] The first occurence of the phrase *pax Domini* was in one of Ademar's sermons concerning the council of Limoges (994); see *PL* 141:124.

[55] The argument for a strong connection of the two is made by Bonnaud-Delamare, "Fondement des institutions," p. 21.

[56] Such an interpretation has been suggested by Töpfer, *Volk und Kirche*, p. 82.

[57] Letaldus of Micy, *Delatio corporis s. Juniani*, chap. 1; *PL* 137:825.

2. The movement's point of departure was the church as an institution. Thus—in view of the political and social changes then occurring and the economic menace posed by famine—it attempted to offer protection to clergymen as well as to the churches and their estates, which provided the basis of their subsistence, from the laity. Similar protection was extended to broader circles of society through the participation of both nobles and peasants in the movement, but its objects still remained "ecclesiastical"; there was no desire to protect peasants for their own sake.

3. This protection of the church and its members—the medieval *ecclesia* included all of society—could be achieved only through the support of contemporary judicial institutions, whose validity was widely accepted. Legal feuds were approved in the same manner as were earlier penitential codes and the rights of self-defence. The Peace of God tried only to prevent future damages, or, if they had already occurred, to guarantee reparation. Thus it contributed to the restoration of an internal social order. In this sense, the religious movement adopted an institutional character.

4. Nonetheless, the Peace of God never aimed at establishing a new order or at substituting an ecclesiastical order for a failing secular one. The Peace was no doubt a reaction to the constitutional and social changes that occurred at the end of the tenth century and the beginning of the eleventh, but it was not a reaction to a kind of feudal anarchy, nor was it antiseigneurial in character. On the contrary, it fell back on new political institutions and the existing legal order, and it had high regard for the developing rights of those new local lords and territorial princes on whose support the movement depended. From the point of view of the canons of the Peace councils and complementary texts, the Peace of God was neither a fight between bishops and dukes for leadership in society (as suggested by Bonnaud-Delamare) nor an alliance between the clergy and the populace against the nobility as a whole (as suggested by Töpfer), even though it was no doubt a popular movement provoked by the misdeeds of the nobility.[58] The Peace of God was simply directed out of religious motivation against those elements that disturbed peace and order. It is not a contradiction to assert that ecclesiastical and secular organizers of the Peace were each able to consider it as a means of expanding their own power; rather, this common desire serves as further proof of the typically medieval connection between "church" and "state."

[58] See most particularly Bonnaud-Delamare, "Fondement des institutions," and Töpfer, *Volk und Kirche.* More recently, on the connections of the Peace to the populace, see Landes, "Dynamics of Heresy."

The Peace of God—as it existed from the council of Charroux (989) to the establishment of the *treuga Dei* in the 1030s—was more than the beginning of a long peace movement; rather, it was a specific phase with its own character, distinctive yet temporary. To prove this view and to defend it against older, particularly continental, views through an analysis of the intentions of its organizers has been my aim in the present article. We must, of course, not forget that, on the one hand, intentions need not coincide with results, and that, on the other, there were doubtlessly views current other than those of the movement's leaders. Such views of different groups that participated in the Peace movement are, however, much more difficult to grasp. That there were such different characteristics and aspects—that, for example, the Peace of God was also a popular movement—is not open to dispute and is proved by other articles in this volume.[59]

[59] I stress that the purpose of my original article was to emphasize certain characteristics of the Peace movement as an institution, in contradiction to older research, and to consider the purposes of its leaders, as far as they can be derived from the sources, especially the canons. It was *not* my intention to deny that there were further characteristic features of the movement, in particular that there was a strong relationship between the Peace of God and the populace. I emphasize this point in view of the misinterpretation found in the otherwise excellent historiographic sketch of Frederick Paxton, "The Peace of God in Modern Historiography: Perspectives and Trends," *Historical Reflections / Réflexions historiques* 14 (1987), 385–404. Professor Paxton, for his part, has revised his understanding of my research in the new version of his article (chapter 1) in this volume.

12

Pollution, Purity, and Peace:
An Aspect of Social Reform between
the Late Tenth Century and 1076

Amy G. Remensnyder

In a striking canon, the prelates assembled at the council of Gerona (1068) proclaimed: "Those clerics who renounce their wives and weapons shall be untroubled and in safety and have no fear. No one shall seize their possessions nor do them any harm; but they and their property shall be in the peace and truce of the Lord forever."[1] And heading the canons of this peace council was a severely worded prohibition of the "heresy of simony." These canons underscore an issue not often explored in the scholarship on the eleventh-century "peace movement"— how peace implied a disciplining of clerical as well as lay behavior.[2] As the stipulations of other peace councils reveal, Gerona was no isolated instance of this connection between clerical reform and the agitation for peace. Clerics were not to carry arms, traffic in ecclesiastical offices and services, or have wives and concubines, insisted those men and women who were trying to establish peace.

Behind these declarations lay the swelling eleventh-century preoccupation with clerical purity. Blood, money, contact (particularly sexual) with women—these were sources of pollution which defiled the

This article developed from work in two stimulating seminars at the University of California, Berkeley, one given by Thomas N. Bisson and the other by Karl Leyser. I thank particularly Professor Bisson for his encouragement and comments on this essay and Phillippe Buc for his reading of various drafts. The translations are my own.
[1] Mansi 19:1071. The manner in which the link between peace and clerical purity is so strongly stated may be due in part to the presence of the papal legate, Hugh Candidus. Nonetheless, this canon articulates a nexus described by other sources. The report of the council of Vic held in the same year described how at Gerona the peace and truce were established; Mansi 19:1076.

[2] Note that in this essay I neither capitalize "peace" nor use such terms as "the Peace of God"; it seems to me that such usages create falsely an image of one unified, coherent movement.

clergy. Certainly, like so many of the peace regulations, the canons enjoining clerics to avoid these types of pollution were hardly innovative.[3] Since the fourth and fifth centuries, councils had repeated that clerics had to conform to this ideal of purity. But in the eleventh century these canons were pronounced with a renewed frequency and a new urgency. Different too in the eleventh century was the way blood, sexual contact with women, and simony blended in the canons and narrative sources to form one complex of pollution fears.

How and why did this increasingly fervently expressed social concern with clerical purity relate to peace? But the question is too simple, for in certain ways this network of purity and pollution subsumed the laity (particularly the males) as well as the clergy. The councils proclaiming peace thus reveal a wave of anxiety about the purity of the clergy *and* of the *ecclesia,* that is, Christian society as a whole.

Here I propose to analyze peace in relation to ideas of purity and pollution expressed in sources dating (with some exceptions) between the late tenth century and 1076. This period forms one coherent moment for both peace and problems of (clerical) purity, although with certain inflections. Late in the second quarter of the eleventh century, as local and papal initiatives coincided more and more, anxiety about purity was expressed in increasingly explicit language and the sanctions became correspondingly more severe. But the real change for both peace and purity came in the late eleventh century. As they were adopted into both the papal program and developing structures of government, ideas about peace changed. After 1076, the problem of clerical purity too was transformed, in the clashes between imperial and papal parties, political concerns altered and superseded the campaign against armed, married, simoniac clerics.

First, several caveats. This is primarily a study of the language of the sources, of the metaphors chosen to represent realities. Such language reflected real concerns and influenced actions as well as being used to justify them. I do not however, mean to suggest that this interpretation completely explains the eleventh-century concern with peace, or that purity was always foremost in the minds of those who agitated for peace. In other words, there was not one Peace which automatically implied Purity. Yet the anxiety about purity illuminates certain aspects of eleventh-century conceptions of peace. Peace in this century had many facets—indeed so many that it is difficult to find in the sources and the historiography a coherent peace movement with a fixed ideology that can be labeled the "Peace of God." Consequently, tracing the peace in

---

[3] On this structural traditionalism, see, for example, Elisabeth Magnou-Nortier, *La société laïque et l'église dans la province de Narbonne de la fin du VIIIe à la fin du XIe siècle* (Toulouse, 1974), pp. 294–302.

either medieval or modern commentaries is rather like looking through a kaleidoscope. The pattern of the councils at Limoges as envisioned by Ademar of Chabannes—large crowds, penitential fervor, relics—dissolves into a different configuration with the peace oaths sworn between *milites* and bishops in the province of Reims.[4]

Here perhaps it is helpful to invoke Augustine's celebrated definition of peace:

> Peace between mortal man and God is ordered obedience, in faith, to eternal law; peace between men is ordered concord. . . . The peace of the city is the ordered concord of its citizens in ruling and obeying; the peace of the celestial city is that most ordered and most harmonious fellowship of delighting in God and being mutually in God; the peace of all things is the tranquility of order. Order is the arrangement granting to each of like things its proper place.[5]

Peace was not a particular social order but the right order.[6] In the eleventh century, various groups—bishops, nobles, monks, even peasants—attempted to proclaim their own vision of society, to impose their type of order.[7] And peace could involve not only the ordering of the hierarchy of power but also the defining and regulation of the nature of the groups composing the *corpus christianorum* in an effort to purify this social body and maintain its unity.[8]

---

[4] For Ademar, see the passages exerpted from his sermons in Léopold Delisle, "Notice sur les manuscrits originaux d'Adémar de Chabannes," *Notices et extraits des manuscrits de la Bibliothèque nationale et autres bibliothèques* 35 (1896), 241–358. For the peace oaths in the north, see Roger Bonnaud-Delamare, "Les institutions de la paix dans la province ecclésiastique de Reims au XIe siècle," *Bulletin philologique et historique (jusqu'à 1715) du Comité des travaux historiques et scientifiques*, 1955–56, pp. 143–200.

[5] *De civitate Dei*, 2 vols., ed. B. Dombart (Leipzig, 1863), 19.13, 2:329.

[6] Roger Bonnaud-Delamare, "Fondement des institutions de paix au XIe siècle," in *Mélanges d'histoire du moyen âge dédiés à la mémoire de Louis Halphen*, ed. Charles-Edmond Perrin (Paris, 1951), pp. 19–26, presents peace as an effort to establish divine order on earth. See also the suggestive remarks of H. E. J. Cowdrey, "The Peace and Truce of God in the Eleventh Century," *Past and Present* 46 (1970), 50–51, and of Jean-François Lemarignier, "Political and Monastic Structures in France at the End of the Tenth and the Beginning of the Eleventh Century," in *Lordship and Community in Medieval France: Selected Readings*, ed. Fredric Cheyette (New York, 1968), pp. 101, 111.

[7] Michel de Boüard describes the Norman peace as a ducal peace in which the episcopate played a secondary role in his "Sur les origines de la Trêve de Dieu en Normandie," *Annales de Normandie* 9 (1959), 169–89. Georges Duby presents the peace as part of an effort by the monks of Cluny to create a new society of which they would be the triumphant leaders in *The Three Orders: Feudal Society Imagined*, trans. Arthur Goldhammer (Chicago, 1980). Pierre Bonnassie argues that in Catalonia the peasants were the ones who first proclaimed peace; *La Catalogne du milieu du Xe à la fin du XIe siècle*, 2 vols. (Toulouse, 1975–76), 2:656–58.

[8] The modern anthropological treatment of problems of purity and pollution whose terminology I borrow is Mary Douglas, *Purity and Danger: An Analysis of the Concepts of*

The anxiety about purity which shimmered in the sources relating to peace belonged to the phenomenon most historians now describe as eleventh-century ecclesiastical reform rather than as Gregorian reform.[9] One aspect of this reform was a swelling wave of prohibitions of simony, of clerical marriage and unchastity, and of the clerical use of weapons, whether for hunting or warfare. This increasingly vehement protest resurrected an ideal of cultic purity which had begun to be linked with clerical office in the fourth century.[10] The laws of clerical celibacy allowed married men to be ordained, although afterward they were to abstain from sexual intercourse with their wives. But men who entered orders unmarried were to remain so.[11] And clerics were not to shed blood—either human or animal.[12] Nor were they to traffic in the Holy Spirit in any way. Such traffic, subsumed under the rubric of simony, was termed a heresy by the sixth century.[13] In other words, the clerics, the dispensers of the sacraments, were segregated from the pollution of sex and blood; the conferring of sacraments was protected from the stain of economic exchange. In the canons of councils and synods, one can trace the way this ideal of clerical purity had crystallized by the sixth century.

Pollution and Taboo (London, 1966). Throughout this essay, I use the term "purity," which corresponds anthropologically not to the medieval *puritas* but rather to *munditia* (literally "cleanness"). For this latter observation, I am grateful to Jean-Claude Schmitt.

[9] Although recently Gerd Tellenbach has protested in favor of the latter term; see " 'Gregorianische Reform': Kritische Besinnungen," in *Reich und Kirche vor dem Investiturstreit. Vorträge beim wissenschaftlichen Kolloquium aus Anlass des achtzigsten Geburtstags von Gerd Tellenbach*, ed. Karl Schmid (Sigmaringen, 1985), pp. 99–113.

[10] Dorothea Wendebourg, "Die alttestamentlichen Reinheitsgesezte in der frühen Kirche," *Zeitschrift für Kirchengeschichte* 95 (1984), 149–70. On chastity in early Christianity, see Peter Brown, *The Body and Society: Men, Women, and Sexual Renunciation in Early Christianity* (New York, 1988), pp. 120–212, 202–3, 357–60 on clerical chastity in particular.

[11] On the development of marriage regulations through the period discussed here, see, among others, A. Esmein, *Le mariage en droit canonique*, 2 vols. (Paris, 1929–35), 1:313–22; Jo Ann McNamara, "Chaste Marriage and Clerical Celibacy," in *Sexual Pratices and the Medieval Church*, ed. Vern L. Bullough and James Brundage (New York, 1982), pp. 22–33; and Jean Gaudemet, "Le célibat ecclésiastique: Le droit et la pratique du XIe au XIIIe s.," *Zeitschrift der Savigny-Stiftung für Rechtsgeschichte, Kanonistische Abteilung* 68 (1982), 1–31.

[12] Beginning in the fourth century priests were exempted from military service, and by the fifth they were forbidden to use arms; Friedrich Prinz, *Klerus und Krieg im früheren Mittelalter: Untersuchungen zur Rolle der Kirche beim Aufbau der Königsherrschaft* (Monographien zur Geschichte des Mittelalters, 2; Stuttgart, 1971), pp. 5–35.

[13] On the pre-eleventh-century history of the prohibitions of the various practices defined as simony, see Hans Meier-Welcker, "Die Simonie im frühen Mittelalter," *Zeitschrift für Kirchengeschichte* 64 (1952–53), 61–93 (particularly 63–64 for simony as heresy), as well as Jean Leclercq, "Simoniaca Heresis," *Studi Gregoriani* 1 (1947), 522–30. I have been unable to consult Joseph H. Lynch, *Simoniacal Entry into Religious Life from 1000 to 1260: A Social, Economic and Legal Study* (Columbus, Ohio, 1976).

But most historians agree that, until the late tenth and eleventh centuries, this was indeed an ideal, existing primarily at the level of canon law and hardly coinciding with social realities. Clerics bearing arms, begetting children, asking and receiving prices for baptism, and giving a *donum* for their own ordination were respected members of society. These practices were deeply embedded in and consonant with early medieval society.

The various forms of what we might call simony belonged to the network of gift giving and accorded with the Carolingian royal hegemony over the church and the power of the nobility over their *Eigenkirchen*.[14] Despite the canons, then, as Peter Damian sighed in his *vita* of Romuald (ca. 1030), "scarcely anyone knew that the heresy of simony was a sin."[15] Furthermore, clerics contracted and celebrated marriages according to the accepted norms.[16] The children they fathered were considered their legitimate heirs; indeed, hereditary priesthood—of office and benefice—was not unusual.[17] In response to Boniface's lament of 742 about the fornicating clergy of Francia, Pope Zachary merely expressed horror that clerics should be bigamous—and explained that they should have only one wife.[18] A married cleric was neither oxymoron nor monster. Furthermore, arms-bearing clergy engaged in hunting and warfare were a common enough sight. As Friedrich Prinz has argued, bishops and abbots and their followers formed the backbone of Carolingian military strength. These clerics did not just send warriors to join the kings but were required to accompany them—to the point of participating actively in battle.[19] During the late ninth and the tenth centuries, bishops and abbots increasingly assumed the role of military leaders in the face of the challenge of the Muslims, Scandinavians, and Magyars.

[14] Meier-Welcker, "Die Simonie."

[15] Peter Damian, *Vita beati Romualdi*, ed. Giovanni Tabacco (Fonti per la storia d'Italia, 94; Rome, 1957), p. 75.

[16] See the indignant letter Mantius, bishop of Châlons-sur-Marne, wrote to Fulk, archbishop of Reims, in 902 asking his advice in the case of a priest who had become engaged; PL 131:23–24. Also, Gregory VII, *Epistolae* 2.10, in *Das Register Gregors VII.*, ed. Erich Caspar (MGH Epistolae Selectae, 2; Berlin, 1920), pp. 140–41; Peter Damian, *Epistolae*, no. 40, in *Die Briefe des Petrus Damiani*, ed. Kurt Reindel (MGH Die Briefe der deutschen Kaiserzeit, 4.1; Munich, 1983), pp. 439–41; and *Opusculae*, no. 18; PL 145: 408–9.

[17] B. Schimmelpfennig discusses the history of the status of clerical offspring in "Zölibat und Lage der Priestersöhne vom 11. bis 14. Jahrhundert," *Historische Zeitschrift* 227 1978), 1–44.

[18] S. *Bonifatii et Lulli epistolae*, no. 40; *MGH Epistolae Merowingici et Karolini aevi* 1:301. How different from Leo IX's decision some 300 years later to separate all the Roman clergy from their wives and force these women to become *ancillae* of the Lateran. Peter Damian, *Opusculae*, no. 18; PL 145:411.

[19] Prinz, *Klerus und Krieg*, pp. 7, 13, 11, 81–82, 86–87.

The late tenth and early eleventh centuries witnessed an effort to align reality with the ideal of purity as enunciated in the canons. The old regulations were proclaimed with new vigor and frequency, betraying how these time-honored traditions were translated into sources of danger for Christian society. Inciting civil strife in Milan and riots in Rouen, the extirpation of these abuses became an issue that ignited the passions and polemics of opponents and adherents.[20] A new form of heresy was defined—that of the nicolaites, married (even if chaste) or unchaste clerics. By 1130, clerical marriages were considered invalid, and by the end of the century marriage had become an impediment to orders.[21] The clergy was by definition celibate. The problem of simony also loomed in a new way. In the eleventh century, the noun "simony" (*simonia*) first emerged, embodying the earlier adjective "simoniac" (*simoniacus*).[22] This reification accompanied an increasingly vigorous and vociferous battle against active and passive forms of simony. In this same period, an unmistakable discomfort with warrior bishops and even clerics who used weapons in the defense of ecclesiastical property against aggressors also began to color the sources.[23] This uneasiness translated into a concrete and concerted effort to take secular arms away from those supposed to wield only spiritual weapons.

In their campaign the reformers—clerical and lay, papal and non-papal—attacked these three "abuses" as interrelated problems, most often linking simony and clerical unchastity, but also the use of arms and unchastity and sometimes even all three.[24] These three were then

---

[20] For the unrest in Milan—the Pataria—see Andreas of Strumi, *Vita sancti Arialdi; MGH SS* 30.2:1047–75. Arnulf, *Gesta archiepiscoporum Mediolanensium; MGH SS* 8:1–31. Landulf Senior, *Historia Mediolanensis; MGH SS* 8:32–100. For the violent reaction to reform in Rouen, see *The Ecclesiastical History of Orderic Vitalis*, 6 vols., ed. Marjorie Chibnall (Oxford, 1969–80), 4, 2:200; 12.25, 6:291–95.

[21] Gaudemet believes that the concept of the invalidity of clerical marriages emerged in the period between the First and Second Lateran Councils; "Le célibat," pp. 17–23.

[22] Meier-Welcker, "Die Simonie," p. 73. On the importance of the shift from adjective to noun, see the discussion of the reification of purgatory by Jacques Le Goff, *La naissance du Purgatoire* (Paris, 1981).

[23] Prinz, *Klerus und Krieg*, pp. 171–96, and Carl Erdmann, *Die Entstehung des Kreuzzugsgedankens* (Forschungen zur Kirchen- und Geistesgeschichte, 6; Stuttgart, 1935), pp. 68, 70–71. In a typically impassioned outburst (*Epistolae* 4.9; *PL* 144:311–17), Peter Damian protested against clerics taking up arms to defend ecclesiastical property against just the type of people who infringed on what Magnou-Nortier has described as the peace of the church in Chapter 3 of this volume. Damian's letter seems to illustrate a dilemma implied by Erdmann (*Die Enstehung*, p. 68): how were the clergy to enforce the peace provisions if they renounced the use of arms? Damian's text was cited by Deusdedit in his *Liber canonum* 4.246, in *Die Kanonessamlung des Kardinals Deusdedit*, ed. Victor Wolf von Glanvell (Paderborn, 1905), pp. 532–35.

[24] Simony and arms, Reims (1049); Mansi 19:737, although Orderic reported that at this council clerical marriage and arms were banned; see *Ecclesiastical History*, 5.12, 3:120. Arms and unchastity, Coyaca (1050), can. 3; Mansi 19: 787–88. Arms, simony, and

considered, although not always explicitly, as facets of one issue: clerical purity. I need not describe the full sweep and course of the (largely unsuccessful) attempt to eradicate these practices or reiterate the various positions taken by historians on the meaning and motivation of these efforts.[25] But it is necessary to illuminate how this aspect of ecclesiastical reform was more than intertwined with the eleventh-century striving for peace. Some historians have remarked that several of the councils proclaiming peace also established canons prohibiting simony, clerical marriage, and clerical use of weapons, an observation that usually takes the form of not much more than a list of the relevant canons.[26] We need to go far beyond these canons to understand their significance, but they do provide in distilled form evidence of a structural connection between purity and ideals of peace and hence a convenient starting point.

The core of the peace canons was arguably the restrictions they placed on the use of weapons by specifying the time, location, and object of violence. The laity were not the sole subject of such canons; the councils dealt with the problem of clerics bearing arms in two ways. The councils of Charroux (989), Toulouges (1027), Vic (1033 and 1068), and Narbonne (1054) extended protection and immunity to *unarmed* clergy.[27] More pointedly, the councils of Le Puy (990/94), Gerona (1068), and Clermont (1095) stated that the clergy were not to use "secular weapons."[28] This latter, active type of prohibition may have related in part to the upper clergy's membership in exactly the arms-bearing noble class whose violence was regulated in the peace provisions. If the

---

unchastity, Compostela (1056), cans. 2, 3; Mansi 19: 856–57. Also, Tours (1060), cans. 3, 4, 7; Mansi 19:926–28.

[25] For extensive bibliography, see Uta-Renate Blumenthal, *Der Investiturstreit* (Stuttgart, 1982).

[26] Erdmann, *Die Entstehung*, pp. 64–67; Hans-Werner Goetz, "Kirchenschutz, Rechtsbewahrung und Reform: Zu den Zielen und zum Wesen der frühen Gottesfriedensbewegung in Frankreich," Francia 11 (1983), 112–13, 234–35, 237 (see also Chapter 11 in this volume). R. I. Moore, in "Family, Community and Cult on the Eve of the Gregorian Reform," *Transactions of the Royal Historical Society*, 5th ser., 30 (1980), 52–53, provides an analysis of such canons, and Bonnaud-Delamare makes some suggestive remarks in "Fondement des institutions," pp. 25–26.

[27] Charroux (989), can. 3; Mansi 19:90. Toulouges (1027); Mansi 19:483. Vic (1033), in Hartmut Hoffmann, *Gottesfriede und Treuga Dei* (Schriften der Monumenta Germaniae historica, 20; Stuttgart, 1964), p. 261. Narbonne (1054), can. 15; Mansi 19:830. Vic (1068); Mansi 19:1073. Goetz, "Kirchenschutz," p. 212, note 115, also mentions Verdun (1019/21) and Beauvais (1023).

[28] Le Puy, in *Cartulaire de Sauxillanges*, no. 15, p. 53. Christian Lauranson-Rosaz argues that this council took place at Saint-Paulien, not Le Puy, and dates it to 993 or 994; *L'Auvergne et ses marges (Velay, Gévaudan) du VIIIe au XIe siècle: La fin du monde antique?* (Le Puy, 1987), pp. 416–20. Gerona (1068), can. 5; Mansi 19:1071. Clermont (1095), can. 4; Mansi 20:817. At Anse (994), can. 4 forbade clerics to hunt; Mansi 19:101.

military activity of the aristocracy was to be controlled, that of the bishops had necessarily to be as well.

But it has been argued that these regulations of the peace councils were directed at the lower clergy, not at the bishops for whom military service had been and remained "completely traditional."[29] The infamous case of Wifred, archbishop of Narbonne, indicates the contrary. In 1059, Berengar, the viscount of Narbonne whose family was engaged in a contest with Wifred's family (the counts of Cerdagne descended from Wifred the Hairy) for the control of the Narbonnais, deposed a *querimonia* against the archbishop.[30] Prominent on his list of grievances was the accusation that the archbishop had used arms after having sworn to renounce them at a council of 1043 proclaiming peace.[31] In the presence of Raimbald, archbishop of Arles, and the assembled bishops of his province, Wifred had "renounced all military weapons and all worldly military activity. He [had] placed under the pain of excommunication and anathema himself as well as all the bishops of his diocese if they ever took up arms from that day forth. Not long thereafter, he himself used weapons like a knight [*ut miles*], his loins girded not with a girdle but with a sword."[32] Clearly, then, at this point the prohibition of bearing weapons embraced bishops as well as the lower clergy, since Wifred engaged not only himself but also his bishops in this vow. The elimination of the pollution of bloodshed thus related to all clerics.

Simony too (defined in the large sense of all traffic in the Holy Spirit) was attacked at several councils proclaiming peace. At Le Puy (990/94), Guy, bishop of Le Puy, reiterated a Carolingian prohibition: "No priest shall receive a price for baptism, for it is a gift of the Holy Spirit."[33] The council of Poitiers (1000/14) forbade clerics to solicit offerings for penance or any other sacraments they dispensed. Canon 3 of the council of Bourges (1031) proclaimed that bishops were

---

[29] Goetz, "Kirchenschutz," p. 213, note 121, citing (with some transposition) Bonnaud-Delamarc's remarks on the council of Charroux in "Les institutions de la paix en Aquitaine au XIe siècle," in *La paix* (Recueils de la Société Jean Bodin, 14; Brussels, 1961), p. 423. Prinz argues that in the Carolingian era the prohibition of the clerical use of weapons applied only to the lower clergy; *Klerus und Krieg*, pp. 72–113.

[30] Given that Berengar was openly at odds with Wifred, it is dangerous to accept his description of the archbishop's deeds as an accurate depiction of reality. What is significant here is *how* Berengar portrayed the archbishop. For a critical study of this document and an analysis of the struggle between the lineage of the viscount and that of the archbishop, see Magnou-Nortier, *Société laïque*, pp. 463–68.

[31] Jean-Pierre Poly believes that this council can be dated to 1043 and that it reiterated the peace provisions of the council of Saint-Gilles (1042/44); *La Provence et la société féodale 897–1166: Contributioin à l'étude des structures dites féodales dans le Midi* (Paris, 1976), pp. 196–97.

[32] Mansi 19:850.

[33] *Cartulaire de Sauxillanges*, p. 53.

not to receive a gift for ordinations they conferred, nor could the lesser clerics involved in the process of ordination ask any price. The first canon of the council of Gerona (1068) lashed out violently to condemn the "detestable heresy of simony." Finally, the council of Clermont (1095) reiterated the prohibition of simony.[34]

The twin of the heresy of simony—clerical marriage or unchastity—drew the fire of these councils as well. At the council of Anse (994), clerics were reminded that they should abstain from their wives (*uxoribus*); if they did not, they would no longer be permitted to celebrate mass and would lose their benefice. At Poitiers (1000/14), canon 4 recalled that no priest or deacon could have a woman hidden away in his house "because of fornication [*propter fornicationem*]." Any transgressors were to be degraded and excommunicated.[35]

At the council of Bourges (1031), the canons (as described by Ademar of Chabannes) providing for the segregation of the clergy from women were quite specific and seemed intended for immediate implementation.[36] Priests, deacons, and subdeacons who were at the moment not celibate were to renounce their spouses; any who did not do so directly after the council were to be degraded to the status of lectors and cantors. Bishops were not to ordain subdeacons until these latter promised to have neither wife nor concubine.[37] Then two rather extraordinary canons prohibited the entrance into orders of any son of a cleric (from subdeacon on up). Here children of the clergy were assimilated not only to *servi* and *coliberti* but to all children not born from a "legitimate union" who "are called cursed seed in the Scriptures and who, according to secular law, can neither inherit nor give legal testimony." In its severity, this creation of barriers between clerical children and the office of their fathers surpassed all ecclesiastical legislation until that fostered by the papal legate, Hugh of Die, at the council of Poitiers (1078).[38] At the council of Gerona (1068), canons 6 and 7 specified

---

[34] Poitiers (1000/14), can. 2; Mansi 19:268. Bourges (1031); Mansi 19:503. Gerona (1068); Mansi 19:1070–71. Clermont (1095), cans. 6, 7; Mansi 20:817.

[35] Anse (994), can. 5; Mansi 19:101. Poitiers (1000/14); Mansi 19:265–68.

[36] Bourges (1031), cans. 5, 6, 8, 11; Mansi 19:501–8. The report of this council is problematic, given that it was written by Ademar of Chabannes and hence is filled with polemic on behalf of the apostolicity of Saint Martial. Whether or not the canons were promulgated as he described them, this text demonstrates at least that the program of this fervent promoter of peace included clerical chastity. On the problems of interpreting this text, see Richard Landes, "The Dynamics of Heresy and Reform in Limoges: A Study of Popular Participation in the 'Peace of God' (944–1033)," *Historical Reflections/ Réflexions historiques* 14 (1987), 491, note 84; see also Chapter 8 in this volume.

[37] Subdeacons had often hitherto not been included in the regulations pertaining to clerical marriage.

[38] Poitiers (1078), can. 8; Mansi 20:499–500. This prohibition aroused a flood of anguished and bitter protest from the clergy of Soissons and Cambrai; see *Cameracensium et*

that priests, deacons, and subdeacons were to separate themselves from their wives and concubines. If recalcitrant, they would lose their benefice and be excommunicated. At Clermont (1095), canons 9 and 10 reiterated provisions intended to enforce clerical chastity, and canons 11 and 25 the prohibition of the ordination of clerics' sons.[39]

This summary of the canons regulating clerical purity demonstrates that the bishops, abbots, and secular lords who presided over the councils proclaiming peace were concerned with the behavior of the clergy. Their concern could become action; sometimes the councils meted out the appropriate penalties to clerics accused of simony or those who refused to give up their wives. For example, at the council of Limoges (1031), a married cleric and a simoniac were hauled forth for judgment.[40] In addition, some of the same bishops, abbots, and lords attending the councils introduced the ideal of clerical purity elsewhere; according to Ademar, in approximately 1014, William V of Aquitaine, who presided at the council of Poitiers (1000/14), restored monastic discipline at the monastery of Charroux and ejected its abbot, Peter I, "who had obtained his office through the heresy of simony."[41] Similarly, the architects of "the truce" in Provence, including Bénézet of Avignon and Raimbaldus of Arles, militated against simony.[42]

These men and councils thus participated in the ordering of the clergy. The canons they promoted defined in a newly emphatic way the ideal of a Christian clergy—an ideal that still prevails in the modern Catholic church. Clergy who did not respect the parameters of their category became monsters—anomalies contradicting the social order

---

Noviomensium clericorum epistolae; MGH Libelli de Lite 3:573–78. See also the reaction to the reiteration at Clermont (1095) of a similar prohibition; *Defensio pro filiis presbyterorum; MGH Libelli de Lite* 3:579–83.

[39] Gerona (1068); Mansi 19:1071. Clermont (1095); Mansi 20:817–18.

[40] Mansi 19:544–45.

[41] Ademar of Chabannes, *Chronicon* 3.58, p. 184. See also *The Letters and Poems of Fulbert of Chartres*, ed. Frederick Behrends (Oxford, 1976), no. 96, pp. 172, 74. For William's activities on behalf of peace, see Bonnaud-Delamare, "Institutions de la paix," and Callahan (Chapter 7) and Landes (Chapter 8) in this volume.

[42] See Poly's remarks in *La Provence*, pp. 188, 192–96, 259–62. For evidence of the concern of the nobility with simony, see Werner Goez, "Reformpapsttum, Adel und monastische Erneuerung in der Toscana," in *Investiturstreit und Reichsverfassung*, ed. Josef Fleckenstein (Vorträge und Forschungen, 17; Sigmaringen, 1973), pp. 205–40. See also Bonnaud-Delamare's argument that Jordan, bishop of Limoges, used the struggle against simony as a pretext to establish a peace between himself and the count of Poitou which specifically diminished the latter's role in episcopal elections; "Institutions de la paix," p. 472 (Delamare wrongly attributes the charter to 1032; the correct dating is 1045–50 according to "Sancti Stephani lemovicensi cartularium," ed. Jacques de Fout-Réaulx, *Bulletin de la Société archéologique et historique du Limousin* 68 [1919], 174–76). For some remarks on the significance of such restrictive clauses in charters, see N. Huyghebaert, "Saint Léon IX et la lutte contre la simonie dans le diocèse de Verdun," *Studi Gregoriani* 1 (1947), 425–32.

and contravening peace. In other words, a cleric tainted by any of the three abuses was no longer a cleric.

Indeed, this ideal of purity could serve exactly to define clerical status, as we can sense, for example, in a *notitia* (ca. 5 April 1066) pertaining to the election and installation of a reforming bishop to the see of Sisteron. This text labeled the former simoniac and married bishops of the diocese as pseudo-bishops. Their open relations with women (*uxorati publice*) were public offenses and represented an inversion and perversion of the reverence laymen had for religious women—a turning inside out of proper relations between men and women, clergy and laity: "Just as other men revere religious women, thus those bishops openly paid the utmost attention to their concubines."[43] Framing the description of their simoniacal milking of the diocese were citations of Ezekiel 34:2–3 and John 10:12–13, texts that reproach pastors who pervert what is etymologically their function—the feeding of their flocks. These bishops "were not pastors, but instead mercenaries (John 1:12–13), who were not watching over the bodies of their sheep, but were taking their wool and sucking their milk (Ezek. 34:2–3) and were seeking their own gain and not that of Jesus Christ."[44] In other words, these bishops, these "ravenous wolves," contradicted their *ordo*—and the order of the world.

Berengar's *querimonia* illustrates this same point. It also articulates how peace could relate to this defining of clerical nature. Berengar denounced Wifred for having perpetrated various offenses previous to the council of 1043—including having waged *guerra*. But in this case the viscount condemned the archbishop for devastating and despoiling the region, that is, for acting in a destructive manner. Only after having described Wifred's oath at the council did Berengar accuse him of transgressing social categories by acting "like a knight". Here the viscount highlighted the ontological opposition between cleric and *miles* which had been expressed in the oath. Arms, as Peter Damian had

---

[43] Gregory VII expressed even more explicitly the monstrous nature of married clerics, writing that anyone not included in one of the three traditional categories—*virgines, continentes,* or *conjugati*—was literally outside Christian society; *The Epistolae Vagantes of Pope Gregory VII,* ed. H. E. J. Cowdrey, (Oxford, 1972), no. 9, p. 20. For Abbo of Fleury, those who were not chaste merited punishment and not the title of cleric; *Apologeticus; PL* 139:463–64. See also Abbo's *Epistolae,* no. 14; *PL* 139:449–59. Also, Abbo, *Collectio canonum,* chaps. 39, 40; *PL* 139:495–96. For a discussion of Abbo's ideas about clerical chastity, see Marco Mostert, *The Political Theology of Abbo of Fleury: A Study of the Ideas about Society and Law of the Tenth-Century Monastic Reform Movement* (Hilversum, The Netherlands, 1987), pp. 96–99.

[44] "Pièces justificatives, no. 1," in Noel Didier, *Les églises de Sisteron et de Forcalquier du XIe siècle à la Révolution* (Paris, 1954), p. 182. See pp. 1–60, and Poly's remarks in *La Provence,* pp. 251–52, on the situation and the resulting installation of a reforming bishop.

written, were reserved for the laity.[45] Thus, by disarming Wifred, the peace council of 1043 rendered him a cleric in a new way.

In a very general sense, this is Augustine's peace—the establishment of the right order, with everything in its place. The regulations against simony, the use of arms, and sexual contact with women contributed to and reflected the process of social ordering which Georges Duby and others, focusing on the laity, have proposed as an interpretive framework for the peace councils and the eleventh century in general.[46] This ordering of the clergy paralleled the defining of the *milites*. The process of categorization elevated as it distinguished, clothing each group with its particular type of authority. The attack against the three clerical evils at these councils thus participated in the forging of an ideal of spiritual power which contrasted and competed with the armed power of the warrior class.[47]

This relatively simple interpretation of the relation between clerical purity and peace is, however, somewhat deceptive, for it does not articulate the very specific and intimate nature of the connection. Indeed, one might object that these were two separate issues, though both were promulgated through the forum of the councils. After all, little of the evidence thus far cited explicitly links the two. But these matters were inextricably related, as the preamble of the council of Poitiers (1000/14) hinted. Quoting a letter dated 364 of Hilary of Poitiers, it declared: "Indeed the name of peace is beautiful and the name of concord which Christ ascending to heaven left behind to his disciples is fair." This preamble continued to explain that William, "duke of Poitiers," and various ecclesiastical prelates were gathered "for the restoration of Christian society . . . this restoration of peace and justice."[48] As noted above, the canons of this council included not only the peace provisions but also prohibitions of clerical relations with women and the buying and selling of clerical services. Hence, the process of reestablishing this peace originally brought by Christ embraced the regulation of clerical as well as lay behavior.

---

[45] "Si sacerdos arma corripit, quod utique laicorum est, quid meretur?" Damian made it clear that armed clerics reversed the proper order by usurping the physical sword reserved for the secular power; *Epistolae* 4 9; *PL* 144:314–15.

[46] Georges Duby, "The Laity and the Peace of God," in his *The Chivalrous Society*, trans. Cynthia Postan (Berkeley, 1977), pp. 123–33; Otto Gerhard Oexle, "*Tria genera hominum*: Zur Geschichte eines Deutungsschemas der sozialen Wirklichkeit in Antike und Mittelalter," in *Institutionen, Kultur und Gesellschaft im Mittelalter: Festschrift für Joseph Fleckenstein zu seinem 65. Geburtstag*, ed. Lutz Fenske, Werner Rösener, and Thomas Zotz (Sigmaringen, 1984), pp. 483–500.

[47] R. I. Moore stresses how the peace councils created an ideal of power for the unarmed—the clerics and the "people"; see "Family, Community and Cult," p. 63.

[48] Mansi 19:265. For Hilary's letter, *PL* 10:609.

A most stunning piece of evidence makes absolutely explicit what was implied at Poitiers: canon 8 of the council of Gerona (1068), cited above. Here the link between peace and a pure clergy was unmistakably underlined. Only those clerics unsoiled by blood or sex had a place in the order of peace; those who were not clean disturbed and contradicted peace. The penalty prescribed for the latter was the same as that for lay *corruptores* of peace—excommunication. To understand the significance of the connection between peace and clerical purity so blatantly declared at Gerona, we need both to consider other aspects of peace and to turn to other evidence to supplement that of the somewhat disembodied and often laconic accounts of conciliar proceedings. How did clerics who carried arms, had wives, or trafficked in the Holy Spirit pose a barrier to the bringing of peace—of both a social and a celestial nature—to earth?

At a most practical level, an ideal of clerical behavior was necessary for the creation of peace. *Disruptores, violatores,* and *raptores*—from the sixth century onward these were the terms employed in narrative sources and conciliar canons to brand those who perturbed the "peace of the church."[49] Fixed in form, this vocabulary could, however, metamorphose in meaning—or at least in its "signified."[50] In the eleventh century it was used to stigmatize not only laypeople who threatened the physical fabric of the church but also simoniacs, unchaste clerics, and clerics who bore weapons. Impure clerics were considered to be *violatores* of the peace of the church in a concrete way just as were laypeople who infringed any of the peace regulations.

For example, clergy waging warfare disrupted churches as much as the *milites* did. Berengar accused the arms-bearing Wifred of Narbonne of having left in the wake of his *guerra* destroyed churches, burned relics, and wounded and dead people.[51] Simoniacs too were seen to damage the churches in their care. The sources depicted these latter clerics as concrete embodiments of the biblical text traditionally applied to them: "thief and robber [*fur et latro*]" (John 10:1–2, 8–10). Humbert of Silva Candida, for example, whose monumental *Adversus simoniacos* (ca. 1059) is sparsed with this Johannine reference, called simoniacs "invaders and devastators of ecclesiastical property."[52] In a discussion of the origins and the consequent flourishing of simony, Humbert chronicled a progressive despoiling of the church. He wrote

---

[49] See Chapter 3, this volume.
[50] Here I diverge somewhat from the interpretation proposed by Magnou-Nortier.
[51] Mansi 19:851–52.
[52] Humbert of Silva Candida, *Libri tres adversus simoniacos*, 3.5; *MGH Libelli de Lite* 1:203.

that the earliest simoniacs had reached into their own pockets to purchase office, but that later ones extracted the sums exchanged from ecclesiastical revenues, thus impoverishing churches. Humbert painted a vivid picture of the miserable lot of such churches, formerly rich in lands and servants, now so poor that they possessed not even a small hovel. He concluded this passage by describing how simoniacs transferred to laypeople tithes and the offerings of the living and the dead—a common enough complaint in charters of the period.[53]

Married clergy were considered to plunder the church as well. As Atto of Vercelli explained and Peter Damian reiterated, clerics with wives and children had a tendency to enrich themselves permanently from ecclesiastical patrimonies, leaving the church destitute;[54] hence, the prohibitions of clerics' sons inheriting their fathers' office, and benefice, that is, to prevent the transformation of ecclesiastical property into familial inheritance.

The *notitia* of Sisteron made particularly clear how its married *and* simoniac bishops had ruined the diocese, leaving it, head and body, "devastated and broken."[55] After briefly describing how the marquesses had initiated the despoiling, it expanded on the deeds of the greater offenders, the "so-called bishops." Among the metaphors analyzed above was the very concrete complaint: "And that which had not already been destroyed, they ruined for the benefit of their sons and daughters. Whether tithes or vineyards, cultivated or uncultivated land, or any kind of rent, they gave it away or sold it in its entirety."[56] The leitmotiv was how these "rapacious wolves" treated the church's possessions as theirs to pass on to their children and felt free to sell whatever was left for their own profit—just as they had already trafficked in ecclesiastical offices. The language was that used to describe the violence and devastation caused by the "enemies of the peace." Peace, then, at this nuts-and-bolts level, involved a disciplining of the clergy so that they would change from *raptores* into *pastores* of their churches.

[53] Humbert, *Adversus simoniacos*, 2.35; *MGH Libelli de Lite* 1:183–84. For similar complaints in charters described in language very reminiscent of that used to describe lay offenders of peace, see, for example, Poly, *La Provence*, pp. 251–52.

[54] Atto of Vercelli, *Epistolae*, no. 9; *PL* 134:116–17. For a suggestion of the same concern, see Peter Damian, *Opusculae*, no. 18; *PL* 145:419–20. Alienation of ecclesiastical property through the children of clergy also emerges as a concern at the council of Pavia (1012/24); Mansi 19:44–54. See Jack Goody's interpretation of eleventh-century reform as an effort to recuperate ecclesiastical property, *The Development of the Family and Marriage in Europe* (Cambridge, 1983), especially pp. 95, 133–34.

[55] Didier, *Eglises de Sisteron*, p. 181.

[56] Didier, *Eglises de Sisteron*, p. 182. See also the texts Poly cites in *La Provence*, p. 251, note 8, and p. 252, note 11.

But clerical impurity threatened more than the physical peace of the church; it could also undermine social peace. In his *Apologeticus* (ca. 994) addressed to Hugh Capet and his son Robert, Abbo of Fleury presented simony (the "avarice" of the clergy) as fomenting discord within the kingdom as well as harming churches. Indeed, throughout this passage he used the social images of concord and discord, reconciliation and excommunication. Through bishops who gained their office by simony, "harm and the seeds of discord grow in the kingdom. . . . these prelates, intent only on avarice, are allowed to ruin churches completely and they corrupt the *mores* of those subject to them whom they ought to instead correct by setting an example." Because simony attacked the political order, Abbo assigned to his royal audience the task of its repression. First, in the passive sense, Robert and Hugh were to avoid contact with simoniacs (of course no Christian was to have contact with any heretic or excommunicate). Second, in the active sense, it was part of the royal office to combat simony by supporting councils condemning this evil so that "through reconciliation the state is made better and grows." And if Hugh and Robert did not do so, Abbo menaced, invoking the topos of the king as pastor and judge of his subjects and responsible for their sins before God, "this evil will rebound on you who occupy the highest position in the kingdom for just this reason: to render just judgment to all."[57] Simony thus eroded the civil peace and harmony which it was the king's function to maintain.

A yet greater peace was at stake—that peace which bound Christians together to form one mystical-social body, one church. This peace was engendered by the bonds of charity between human beings.[58] Beginning in the first century, Christian writers had richly developed this theme. Paul wrote: "And above all these, have [the virtue of] charity, which is the bond of perfection. And let the peace of Christ, into which you were called in one body, rejoice in your hearts" (Col. 3:14–15). Augustine further elaborated this image, making the nexus of peace, charity, and the social body of Christ explicit: "Just as the body of Christ is held together, so are the social members bound together and united in charity and the bond of peace [*in charitate et in vinculo pacis*]."[59] He defined exactly this social glue of charity as peace: "Peace is the bond of holy society, the spiritual joining, the edifice composed of living stones [1 Peter 2:4–5]. Where is this to be found? Not in one

---

[57] *Apologeticus; PL* 139:467–68. On Abbo's conception of the king's role within the church, see Mostert, *Political Theology,* pp. 92–93, 195.

[58] On the long history of the complex of social order, charity, and peace, see Roger Bonnaud-Delamare's discussion in his *L'idée de la paix à l'époque carolingienne* (Paris, 1939).

[59] Augustine, *Enarrationes in Psalmos, CI–CL,* ed. E. Dekkers and J. Fraipont (Aurelii Augustini Opera, 10.3; Turnhout, 1956), 125.5.13, p. 1854.

place but throughout the whole earth."[60] In the ninth century, Pseudo-Isidore recuperated this imagery.[61] Similar language characterized the writings of Gregory VII and Damian, both of whom had a predilection for such phrases as "the glue of charity" and "the bond of peace."[62] This was the peace referred to by the council of Poitiers—the peace Christ brought to earth to make all Christians one in one body—in his body.

In the eleventh-century sources, simony was represented as exactly the enemy of this peace. It tore the fabric that was Christian society and dissolved the bond of charity. Even a cursory reading of Humbert's *Adversus simoniacos* makes this clear. In a passage that flows from tropology to allegory and back again, Humbert transformed the general catch-all topos of the heretic as the enemy of Christianity to show specifically how simoniacs' actions ripped apart Christ's mystical body.[63] He first accused simoniacs of utterly lacking in charity and hating their fellow human beings (here simony seems to be the buying and selling of sacraments such as baptism rather than office):

> In what way could they possibly have [charity], those who so despise God that they indeed strive to sell [Him] for any price whatsoever, and so hate their neighbor that they completely close their heart toward him in order that he might not receive free that which divine generosity wished and ordered them to give him free? . . . these [simoniacs] . . . despoil their happy neighbor of all his goods of both body and soul. They are so hardened against charity that, without the intervention of money given or promised, they will not open their mouth to God for either love of Him or of their neighbor.

Their dearth of charity made simoniacs, in Humbert's eyes, heretics; their avarice denied the social significance of Christ's incarnation and destroyed the correspondence between the mystical and physical bodies of Christ:

> For why did Jesus come in the flesh, if not so that out of the diverse types of human beings and all the peoples and nations for whom He gave His soul with His exceedingly great love, with this same charity He should

---

[60] Augustine, *Enarrationes in Psalmos, CI–CL*, 149.1.2, p. 2178.

[61] *Epistola Eusebii secunda*, in *Decretales pseudo-isidorianae et capitula angilramni*, ed. Paul Hinschius (Leipzig, 1863), p. 238.

[62] Damian, *Epistolae*, no. 28, in *Die Briefe*, pp. 255–56. *Disceptatio synodalis; MGH Libelli de Lite* 1:93. *Vita Romualdi*, chap. 43, p. 104. Gregory VII, *Epistolae* 1.3, 2.69, 9.25, in *Das Register*, pp. 6, 227, 608; Henry IV used a similar expression in a letter to Gregory, 1.29a, p. 48.

[63] *Adversus simoniacos*, 2.31; *MGH Libelli de Lite* 1:179–80. For other examples of Humbert's use of corporal imagery, see 1.14, p. 123; 2.30, p. 178; 2.47, p. 195.

form for Himself the glorious church without stain or wrinkle or any other sort of blemish? . . . Thus with all His own gathered into one in Himself, the one God should be "all things in all" (1 Cor. 15:28). It is of this miraculous and desirable union that those who do not fear to sell the Holy Spirit . . . are violently jealous and against which they plot.

Through the incarnation, Christ had incorporated all human beings into the one untarnished church that was his body. And it was the Holy Spirit—or charity, that of Christ and of human beings—which held together the *corpus christi:*

Through the Holy Spirit, a very great diversity of limbs is brought together, bound and united beneath one head, Christ, in an irreproachable and mysterious arrangement. . . . This [the Holy Spirit], like a most powerful and fervent *bitumen* or *gluten,* glues together and joins the body of Christ with charity which is diffused in the hearts of the saints . . . and makes it grow in the augmentation of God when it forms from men of different professions and ways of life one body and one spirit in one hope according to the vocations by which they are called.

Precisely because they bought and sold the Holy Spirit, which was charity, simoniacs destroyed the ineffable integrity and order of this sociomystical body:

When these heretics dare to steal this most efficacious cement (so to speak) of God's construction, how great and miserable are the ruins they create! In them, just as in tumble-down old walls, nothing is to be found that is ordered [*ordinatum*], nothing that is not confused. There is no pleasing beauty, nothing but the squalor of nettles and thorns, of desire and avarice, and the horror of a serpent's lair.

The image is striking; it recalls what was seen to be the concrete result of the clerical abuses. All that would be left of the church and the churches after such clerics had finished with them would be a heap of crumbling stone, the dismembered body of Christ.

This idea of corporal damage is reminiscent of the sweeping first canon of the council of Narbonne (1054): "For the first of all our provisions . . . we exhort and prescribe according to God's commandment and our own that no Christian shall kill any other Christian, for without a doubt, whoever kills a Christian sheds Christ's blood."[64] Implicit

---

[64] Mansi 19:827.

in this canon is the continuum of the Christian, the *corpus christianorum* and the *corpus christi*—and peace. Simony and violence offended, indeed destroyed, the peace that was Christ.[65]

It was not only by rending the *corpus christi* that simoniacs and unchaste clerics were dangerous. Mixed with the corporal imagery used by Humbert in these passages were hints of what emerged unmistakably elsewhere in his writings: simony and clerical unchastity represented sources of contagious pollution which infected the body of Christ, stained the church, and hence threatened the *corpus christianorum*. This terminology of purity and pollution colored a vast number of eleventh-century sources, becoming more exaggerated in the somewhat overwrought polemical texts of the later eleventh and early twelfth centuries.

Peter Damian, for example, described the highly contagious pollution of simony in phrases such as "the leprosy and lethal contagion [*lethiferae contagionis lepra*],"[66] "venality contaminates," and "the obscenity of unclean commerce soils,"[67] even using various forms of the word "pollution" itself. In a letter to the bishop of Fonte Avellana, Damian described the fate of a simoniac priest: he contracted leprosy.[68] The metaphor used for simony thus incarnated itself. The emphasis of purity and pollution is equally a leitmotiv in Humbert's *Adversus simoniacos*.[69] This was more than an elaboration of the old topos of the pollution of heresy; instead, there was a focus on how venality and money introduced impurity.[70]

---

[65] In his early twelfth-century *vitae* of Gregory VII and of Herluca, a disciple of William of Hirsau, Paul of Bernried linked the nature of clerics, the sacramental body of Christ, and his physical body. He related several visions in which Christ with torn clothing or wounds dripping with blood appeared to simoniacs or unchaste clerics and accused them of thus abusing his body when they celebrated mass. These visions are hagiographic illustrations of Gregory VII's denial of the validity of the sacraments of such clerics: Paul of Bernried, *Vita Gregorii*, in *Pontificorum Romanorum . . . vitae*, 2 vols., ed. J. M. Watterich (Leipzig, 1862), 1:542. *Vita b. Herlucae; AASS* April 2:554.

[66] *Opusculae*, no. 12, *PL* 145.469. Here Damian insisted (contrary to Humbert) that the sacraments of simoniacs were valid; see also *Epistolae*, no. 40, in *Die Briefe*, pp. 421–22.

[67] *Epistolae*, no. 13; *PL* 144:220.

[68] *Epistolae*, no. 14; *PL* 144:146–47.

[69] For vivid examples, see *Adversus simoniacos*, 1.19, 2.26, 2.28, 2.30, 3.4; *MGH Libelli de Lite* 1.132–33, 165–72, 174, 179, 201.

[70] For two examples of a more traditional use of the formula "simony is heresy and hence pollution," see *Letters of Fulbert*, no. 2, p. 10, and Abbo of Fleury, *Apologeticus; PL* 139:462. R. I. Moore discusses the images of disease used for heresy in "Heresy as Disease," in *The Concept of Heresy in the Middle Ages (11th–13th c.)*, ed. W. Lourdaux and D. Verhelst (Louvain, 1976), pp. 1–11. The topos of simoniacs and pollution was certainly not invented in the eleventh century, but such imagery became a leitmotiv and was tailored in a new way just as the money economy was developing. For two interpretations of the emergence and sociocultural consequences of the money economy, see Lester Little, *Religious Poverty and the Profit Economy in Medieval Europe* (London, 1978), and Alexander Murray, *Reason and Society in the Middle Ages* (Oxford, 1978).

This language of impurity blossomed in descriptions of unchaste clerics and the female companions with whom they "fornicated."[71] In a long apostrophe addressed to the female consorts of clerics, Damian provided a fabulous catalogue of the names of various unclean creatures with which he branded the women to whom earlier centuries had accorded the titles of not only "wife" but sometimes even *episcopissa* or *presbytera*.[72] Damian's more restrained contemporaries contented themselves with terms such as *concubina, meretrix*, and *pellex*. As Damian's letters, replete with luxuriant imagery, show, this pollution was not confined to women but came from the unchaste clerics themselves.[73]

The contagion of clerical unchastity is highlighted by the language Adam of Bremen (1072–76) chose to describe the deeds of two reforming archbishops of Bremen-Hamburg. Between 1029 and 1032, Archbishop Libentius ordered the women with whom his canons "were openly and criminally married" to leave the city. After this purge, the city was restored to health: "This illness ceased [*cessavit hic morbus*]." But the pollution returned soon thereafter. Archbishop Alebrandus (1035–45), "seeing moreover that the pestiferous illness [*pestiferum morbum*] of the marriages of the clergy was growing day by day, decided to follow in the footsteps of his predecessor, Libentius, in order finally to guide the church and cloister back to their previous condition."[74] Reform thus involved a containment and eradication of this source of pollution.

The imagery of sexual pollution could be applied also to simony. At least once, Humbert of Silva Candida portrayed simoniacs with images hinting at sexual pollution.[75] Venality, heresy, and the implication of sexual impurity were woven together by Gregory VII in his vilification of the simoniac Gottfried of Milan: "He dared to buy, as if she were a vile servant woman, the bride of Christ and to prostitute her to the devil [*diabolo prostituere*]. Trying to separate her from the catholic faith, he strove to stain her with the crime of the heresy of simony [*symonicae*

[71] This latter verb was that preferred by Leo IX, Alexander II, and Gregory VII; see Gaudemet, "Le célibat," p. 12.

[72] Damian, *Opusculae*, no. 18; *PL* 145:410. On earlier terminology for priests' wives, see McNamara, "Chaste Marriage," pp. 23–25.

[73] See, for example, *Opusculae*, no. 18; *PL* 145:387–424. Also, *Epistolae* 5.4; *PL* 144:344. For Damian, this pollution was more powerful than that of simony; he urged avoidance of the sacraments of unchaste clerics; *PL* 145:400.

[74] Adam of Bremen, *Gesta Hammenburgensis ecclesiae pontificum*, 2, schols. 43, 54; *MGH SS* 7:328, 331. See also 2.29, schol. 77; 7:346–47.

[75] *Adversus simoniacos*, 2.32; *MGH Libelli de Lite* 1:180. Although Humbert went to develop this image according to a well-established topos—heretics as fornicators and adulterers—he first articulated how the pollution resulted precisely from the venality of simony.

heresis scelere maculare]."[76] As this overlapping vocabulary reveals, these two "abuses"—simony and clerical unchastity—could arouse one and the same fear for the church.

This language of purity and pollution embraced liturgical objects and the sacraments—the eucharistic *corpus christi*—as well as clerical persons and behavior. Rather of Verona described elaborate provisions for the celebration of mass.[77] Closer in time and space to the councils and people who are the focus here, canon 3 of the council of Coyaca (diocese of Oviedo, 1050) prescribed the materials to be used in the fabrication of liturgical objects and the proper dress of the priest, ending with a distinct emphasis on the necessity of the physical purity of the sacraments themselves:

> The host should be made from grain that is whole and healthy [*sana et integra*]. The wine and water should be clean [*mundus*]. This is in order that the Trinity may be symbolized by the wine, host, and water. The altar should be properly clothed and on it should be a clean [*mundum*] linen covering. Above and beneath the chalice there should be a clean and unblemished [*mundum & integrum*] corporal.[78]

The council of Narbonne in 1054 placed the olive under its protection in canon 9.[79] This canon invoked the olive's value as a typological and physical sign of the return of peace to the earth, its sacramental function within the church as the source of oil for chrism, and its practical one of providing oil for lamps illuminating altars. Any Christian who stole the fruit or cut a branch of this physical pledge of the longed-for peace had to make recompense according to the preceding provisions of the council. Despite Hartmut Hoffmann's materialist interpretation of this canon, might we not consider this concern with the olive to form a continuum with that obsession with sacramental purity which emerged in a more extreme form in the violent and spectacular rejection of chrism consecrated by clerics suspected of simony and unchastity?[80] It is significant that chrism was used for the rites of the

---

[76] *Epistolae*, 1.15, in *Das Register*, p. 24. See also the transposition of imagery usually reserved for simony to nicolaism in Bernried, *Vita Gregorii*, p. 484.

[77] Rather's text is replete with words such as *mundissimus, nitidus*, and *abluere* and includes an indirect prescription for clerical chastity; *PL* 136:538–39.

[78] Mansi 19:787. This clause is immediately followed by prohibitions for the clergy of contact with women and the bearing of arms.

[79] Narbonne, can. 9; Mansi 19:829.

[80] "Die eigentliche Absicht . . . wird in dem Schutz zu suchen sein, welcher der wirtschaftlichen Aktivität zukommen sollte"; Hoffmann, *Gottesfriede*, p. 96. The Milanese under the sway of Arialdus and his followers refused to use the chrism of simoniacs; Peter Damian, *Opusculae*, no. 30; *PL* 145:525. In the late eleventh century the legate

incorporation of the Christian into the church and into particular orders: baptism, confirmation, priestly and royal unction.

Indeed, R. I. Moore interprets Rather of Verona's detailed prescriptions for the celebration of mass as the counterpart of "the anxiety that began to dog the people and their leaders in the period of the reform, whether the masses celebrated by priests so unclean as those they denounced could possibly be valid."[81] Moore proposes that such fears and the struggle against clerical impurity in the forms of simony and clerical marriage related to the presumably increased (though explicitly unrecognized) social power of priests and women in a time of great social strain and change. Accordingly, the ideal of clerical purity represented in part a reaction against their power, an attempt to resolve the contradiction within the system by loading clerics and women with pollution taboos. And, although he discusses in a general way social tensions that engendered a thirst for reconciliation and community, priests and women remain for him the locus and focus.

But are women and priests really the sum total of the problem? The evidence Moore himself cites shows that taboos could be directed at the laity as one group without necessarily singling out women.[82] Pollution fears were not engendered only by women and clerics, separately or together. The concern about the nature of the ministers and of the sacraments they dispensed betrays an anxiety about the status in terms of pollution and hence about salvation of Christian society as a whole.

From clerics polluted by contact with women or blood or traffic in the Holy Spirit (or by contact with the laity[83]), the stain could spread to the rest of the *corpus christianorum*, the same *corpus* created by the bonds of charity. The conduit of the contamination was precisely the sacraments which served to unite Christians in this one body—and which were the focus of renewed theological attention in this period.[84] Humbert made explicit how impure clerics defiled the body of Christ and

---

Amatus of Oloron supposedly poured onto the ground chrism consecrated by a bishop accused of simony; "Notitia de Ecclesia de Viancio," in *Miscellanea novo ordine digesta et non paucis ineditis monumentis*, 4 vols., ed. S. Baluze, rev. ed. J. Mansi (Lucca, 1761–64), 1:125.

[81] Moore, "Family, Community, and Cult," p. 64.

[82] In addition to Moore's evidence, note that the council of Gerona (1068) prescribed that "nullus teneat ecclesiastica ornamenta, qui sit laicus; neque sit inde sacrista, aut bajulus"; Mansi 19:1071.

[83] Humbert described lay investiture as pollution in *Adversus simoniacos*, 3.11; *MGH Libelli de Lite* 1:211–12.

[84] In this renewal of sacramental theology, the priest's role was magnified, making his purity even more critical; Christopher Brooke, "Gregorian Reform in Action: Clerical Marriage in England, 1050–1200," in his *Medieval Church and Society: Collected Essays* (New York, 1971), p. 733. Moore, "Family, Community, and Cult," p. 65, argues that the

infected the people through the sacraments. Deriding the Byzantine church for being still in "the embraces of the heresiarch Nicolas," he sarcastically described how candidates for entrance into orders who as yet had no wives were forced to marry. Then, playing on the contrast between the two bodies handled by these newly married and newly ordained men, he wrote,

> Completely enervated and exhausted by the recent pleasures of the flesh and thinking in the midst of the holy sacrifice about how to pleasure their wives, they handle the immaculate body of Christ [*immaculatum christi corpus*] and distribute it to the people. Immediately afterward they turn their sanctified hands [*sanctificatas manus*] to touch the limbs of women. Thus it shall be that: "just as the people, so the priest" [Isa. 24:2] and in the end the people will be evil just like their priests.[85]

The pollution of the priest was not confined to himself and to his social role; it spilled out to infect the people to whom he gave the sacraments.

But the *ecclesia*, the *corpus christianorum*, had a body as well as a head. Even a purified clergy could not lead an impure people toward salvation. As the text of Isaiah which Humbert cited implied, the state of the priests mirrored that of the people. Pollution fears tend to form a complex by engendering one another and overlapping, and in the eleventh century this nexus included the laity.[86] They were increasingly subject to strictures relating to two of the same areas of impurity as the clergy—marriage and the use of arms. Hence, one cannot say that what was polluting for one group was pure for the other.

Lay use of weapons and the shedding of blood became controlled and defined—subject to taboos, if you will—in part precisely through the provisions for peace.[87] These councils declared increasingly limiting regulations of the time, place, and object of the lay use of weapons. Without minimizing the very practical motivations of such provisions, cannot we also perhaps interpret them at a more metaphorical level as an effort to contain the pollution of the shedding of blood?

---

fears about clerical impurity reveal the importance accorded the priest as the mediator in what John Bossy has described for a much later period as the social miracle of the mass; John Bossy, *Christianity in the West, 1400–1700* (Oxford, 1985).

[85] Humbert, *Contra Nicetam; PL* 143:1000. In the Eastern Church, the laws of clerical celibacy were much more liberal and there was no major move in the eleventh century to tighten them; Esmein, *Le mariage*, 1:316–18.

[86] On conflation and complexes of pollution imagery in general, see R. I. Moore, *The Formation of a Persecuting Society: Power and Deviance in Western Europe, 950–1250* (Oxford, 1987), pp. 62–65.

[87] Duby, "Laity and the Peace."

Lay sexual relations were increasingly framed by what Duby has called the "ecclesiastical model" of marriage, which involved a degradation of the status of the concubine and especially an escalation of the degrees of consanguinity within which marriage was prohibited.[88] By the eleventh century, the slow coalescence of the Germanic and Roman definitions of incest had culminated in an extension of the concept of consanguinity to include a full six if not seven generations calculated in the Germanic fashion. Regardless of exactly when this change occurred, in the eleventh century this incest prohibition became a much debated issue.[89]

At some peace councils, incest regulations appeared: Toulouges (1027), Bourges (1031), and Gerona (1068).[90] Augustine's discussion, cited by Gratian, of the incestuous but necessary marriages among Adam and Eve's children hints at how incest might have been conceived of as inimical to peace. Marriage involved a bond of charity. Since such a tie already existed between natural relatives, incest created an improper concentration of charity among a reduced number of people. Incestuous marriages had therefore to be avoided so that "thus the social bond [*vinculum sociale*] would not be confined among a few small groups but would be diffused more widely and among more people, establishing more abundant ties of kinship."[91] For Augustine, it was exactly this bond of charity—perverted and inverted by incest—which created peace.

This antithetical relationship between peace and incest was made explicit in a letter written in 1023 to Sancho III the Great of Navarre by Oliba, bishop of Vic, who some years later actively proclaimed peace

[88] On the increasing gulf between the dignity of marriage and the ignominy of concubinage, see Brooke, "Gregorian Reform," p. 98, and Georges Duby, *Le chevalier, la femme, et le prêtre: Le mariage dans la France féodale* (Paris, 1981), p. 56. But Raymund Kottje argues that, until at least 1050, concubinage retained its status in canon law as a valid and respectable union; see "Konkubinat und Kommunionwürdigkeit in vorgratianischen Kirchenrecht: Zu c. 12 der römischen Ostersynode von 1059," *Annuarium Historiae Conciliorum* 7 (1975), 159–65. See Gregory VII's view that a layman with a mistress should be excommunicated in *Epistolae vagantes*, no. 9, p. 20.

[89] The history of this coalescence is murky and has not been clarified by the conflicting theories proposed by historians: Duby, *Le chevalier*, pp. 40–41; Esmein, *Le mariage*, 1:372–94; Goody, *Development of Family*, pp. 56, 134–46; David Herlihy, *Medieval Households* (Cambridge, Mass., 1985), pp. 61–62. On the intricate methods of counting degrees of consanguinity, see E. Champeaux, "*Jus sanguinis:* Trois façons de calculer la parenté au Moyen Age," *Revue historique de droit français et étranger*, 4th ser. 12 (1933), 241–90.

[90] Toulouges; Mansi 19:483–84. Bourges, cans. 17, 18; Mansi 19:505. Gerona, can. 3; Mansi 19:1071.

[91] Augustine, *De civitate dei*, 15.16, 2:79. Gratian cited this chapter in *Decretum*, II, causa 35, quaestio 1, in *Corpus iuris canonici*, 2 vols., ed. Emil Friedberg (Leipzig, 1879–1881), 1:1262.

at several councils.[92] The king had asked the bishop for his advice in the matter of a marriage he desired to arrange between his sister Urraca and Alfonso V of Leon, who were related within the prohibited degrees. The bishop responded sternly in the negative.[93] The centerpiece of the letter was his rejection of the idea that peace could possibly result from an incestuous union. Here he moved from political peace and the physical ecclesiastical peace to the peace Christ brought to earth:

> But perhaps someone will say, "If the king grants to the emperor marriage with his sister, this will mean the long continuance of peace, the destruction of the pagans and, in their realms, the amelioration of the churches in the laws of God. If he does not, this will cause the sundering of peace. . . ." This way of thinking is completely specious . . . for never [have] peace . . . or . . . the secure establishment of religion resulted from such an incestuous marriage. . . . Are they not the coequals of heretics, those who suggest insidiously that from the pledge of such a union, peace and justice [*pacis and justitiae*] will be obtained? . . . Since indeed peace originates in chastity and modesty, "Christ who is our peace" [Eph. 2:14] came among men as the son of the chaste and most modest Virgin so that he would make peaceful those things which are in heaven and those on earth.[94]

Oliba denied the king any political or ecclesiastical justification for an alliance created by such a marriage. Indeed, he likened Sancho to heretics—to offenders against the proper order, to those who pollute.[95] The king's project was a perversion of his royal function to maintain just this order, or *pax et justitia*. An incestuous marriage that contradicted Christ's message could never be the foundation for peace of any sort. Thus the peace councils called for the eradication of incest.

Incest not only negated peace but, as the closing flourish of Oliba's letter with its emphasis on chastity shows, belonged to the category of the defiling. Oliba's words recall Isidore of Seville's definition of incest: "The judgment of incest is designated for [matters involving] holy

[92] For Oliba's involvement in councils proclaiming peace, see Anselm M. Albareda, *L'abat Oliva fundador de Montserrat (971?–1046)* (Montserrat, 1931), pp. 146–59, and, more recently, Ramon d'Abadal i de Vinyals, *L'abat Oliba, bisbe de Vic, i la seva època* (Barcelona, 1962), pp. 215–42. See also the text edited by Hoffmann, *Gottesfriede*, pp. 259–60.

[93] Oliba did not succeed in deterring Sancho. On the 1024 marriage and the relations between Sancho and Oliba, see d'Abadal, *L'abat Oliba*, pp. 246–47.

[94] *Cartulario de San Juan de la Pena*, ed. Antonio Ubieto Arteta (Textos medievales, 6; Valencia, 1962), no. 38, pp. 113–14.

[95] Incest was not, however, considered a heresy in the eleventh century. Commenting on two councils in 1065 of Alexander II, Goody writes that the pope attacked "the heresy of incest." Goody has mistaken the words of the editors for original text; see *Development of Family*, p. 161, citing Mansi 19:1037.

virgins or blood relations. Whoever has intercourse with such persons is considered to be incestuous [*incesti*] and thus unchaste [*uncasti*]."[96] The incestuous, guilty of unchastity, were stained and impure. Fulminating against the masters of law at Ravenna who were agitating for a return to the Roman way of computing generations, Peter Damian described incest as pollution. He accused these proponents of Roman law who "in the guise of marriage introduce the filth of incest [*incestus sordes*] and strive to defile the purity of the church's chastity [*aecclesiasticae castitatis munditiam foedare*]."[97] In his *De contemptu saeculi*, when Damian lamented the lack of impact that preaching had "nowadays" on the laity, his most developed example involved the "thousands" of people who refused to dissolve their incestuous unions, which he called "an abomination."[98] Perhaps, then, the flurry of excommunications for incest and the frequency with which incest prohibitions were pronounced in the eleventh century reveal an anxiety about the purity of lay sexual relations.[99]

As Oliba implied, incestuous marriages, which he described as "bond[s] of fornication," posed a threat to more than the partners themselves. He cited Osea 4.2–3, a text in which the pollution of various crimes—homicide, lying, theft, adultery, and "blood touching blood"—caused the earth to sicken. "Blood touching blood" was, he explained, incest. Given the text he chose, did he not see this latter as a source of contagious pollution?[100] This problem thus related to the health of the social body; canon 9 of the council of Tours (1060) proclaimed that those who committed incest were to be excommunicated and "in all ways cut away with the sword of the spirit like a putrid limb from a healthy body [*putridum membrum a sano corpore*]."[101]

As a few tantalizing fragments of evidence hint, this concern about the purity of lay marriage could intertwine with the attack against cler-

---

[96] *Etymologiarum sive originum libri XX*, 2 vols., ed. M. Lindsay (Oxford, 1911), 5.26, no pagination.

[97] Peter Damian, *Epistolae*, no. 19, in *Die Briefe*, p. 198.

[98] Peter Damian, *Opusculae*, no. 12; *PL* 144:284.

[99] Duby, (*Le chevalier*), Goody (*Development of Family*), and Herlihy (*Medieval Households*), propose various interpretations of the causes and implications of the inflation of the concept of incest—including an imposition of clerical concepts of marriage (Duby), a reaction against "resource polygyny" (Herlihy), and ecclesiastical machinations to gain control of the maximum amount of lay property possible (Goody). But none of these historians have remarked on how the preoccupation with incest in the eleventh century might have related to an anxiety about purity. Duby notes only the polluting quality that incest had for Burchard of Worms; *Le chevalier*, p. 77. I am not suggesting that this anxiety about incest originated among the laity; as Duby has shown, there was a divergence in lay and clerical conceptions of an acceptable marriage.

[100] Jerome's exegesis of this passage makes no mention of incest; *In Osee commentariorum libri tres*, 1.4; *PL* 25:847.

[101] Mansi 19:928.

ical unchastity. Peter Damian drew an explicit parallel between clerical *copulatio* and lay incest. He compared clerics having intercourse with women who by virtue of baptism were their spiritual daughters to fathers corrupting their natural daughters through incest.[102] Abbo of Fleury lumped together unchaste clerics and incestuous laypeople as those entangled in "detestable sexual unions."[103] Canon 7 of the council of Gerona (1068) subjected clerics who refused to divorce themselves from their weapons or women to the same penalties as the incestuous.[104] The adulterous cleric was thus guilty of incest, and the incestuous lay person of unchastity—one complex of pollution fears.

But surely taboos reveal a concern with purifying, with rendering sacred. The regulating of lay marriage and the lay use of arms resulted in a purification of both—and hence of the lay nobility. Incest prohibitions ensured that marriage would be a nonpolluting bond of charity, restriction of the use of arms that the shedding of blood would not pollute Christianity. And, beginning in the eleventh century, marriage was increasingly elevated from the level of the profane to the sacred, eventually being defined in canon law as a spiritual and not a carnal union. Marriage, one of the defining characteristics of the laity, was transformed from the possibly polluting into a sacrament.

The ideal of the Christian knight was constructed along with that of the Christian marriage. By the eleventh century, penance was no longer automatically required for the shedding of blood in battle. The activity of the *milites* was more than justified; it was elevated to the plane of the salvific. The Christian knight wielding his reliquary sword and dying in the service of God was sure, in the words of the *Chanson de Roland*, of going straight to heaven. The peace councils played no small role in this Christianization and consecration of the knights and their shedding of the blood of those defined as pagans and heretics.

In the eleventh century, there was a new and intertwined emphasis on lay and clerical purity which related to a distinct ordering of the

---

[102] *Opusculae*, no. 17; *PL* 145:384–85. Goody remarks, "For a long period it was . . . maintained that the sacrament of confession established a . . . relationship of spiritual kinship between confessor and confessant, with the consequence that intercourse between them was incestuous, at the time when priests were not necessarily celibate," but he gives neither references nor dates; *Development of Family*, p. 199. But cf. Joseph H. Lynch's remarks in *Godparents and Kinship in Early Medieval Europe* (Princeton, 1986), pp. 166–69.

[103] Abbo of Fleury, *Apologeticus; PL* 139:463. In the ninth century, Haymo of Auxerre discussed in succession unchaste clerics and incestuous laypeople; see Guy Lobrichon, "L'ordre de ce temps et les désordres de la fin: Apocalypse et société, du IXe à la fin du XIe siècle," in *The Use and Abuse of Eschatology in the Middle Ages*, ed. Werner Verbeke, Daniel Verhelst, and Andries Welkenhuysen (Louvain, 1988), p. 321, note 23.

[104] Mansi 19:1071.

social world—to peace. For the clergy, marriage, the use of arms, and simony—all formerly accepted (though formally rejected) practices—became sources of pollution. Thus cleansed, the clerics were ideally to command a spiritual power consonant with the institutional weight of an increasingly centralized church. The (male) lay aristocracy was purged as well through the regulation of its defining attributes, marriage and warfare. At first glance it seems that the resulting two groups were antithetical, with the clergy delineated as distinct from all the *milites* were—married, bearing arms, and exchanging money for services. But the aristocracy and the clergy were also fit into one overarching paradigm. Each group was defined and made Christian in a new way. A process of purification with respect to two of the same sources of pollution—women and arms—embraced them both.[105] And, in a time of increasing social differentiation and tension, all Christians were integrated into one harmonious order, the pure body of Christ.

Those who did not conform to the paradigms of purity were considered enemies of peace. At a concrete level, clerics bearing arms, having wives or women, or involved in simony—as well as laypeople arbitrarily using arms—broke the ecclesiastical peace by threatening the physical fabric of the church. At the metaphorical level, such clerics and laypeople transgressed the order that was peace, the order that fixed the boundaries of lay and clerical roles. Finally, still in the realm of representation, impure clerics and laypeople polluted the *corpus christianorum* that was Christ, who was peace. The physical realities and the metaphors were not divorced from one another; these fears for the peace of the mystical body of Christ and that of its terrestial counterparts, the church and the churches, were captured in similar language—that of damage and integrity, of purity and pollution. This is evident in Rodulphus Glaber's celebrated description of how the "sanctified peace,"[106] engendered by collective penitential practices at councils, was ruptured. Here in one indissoluble complex appear the offenses of the laity and the clergy:

Inclining toward evil like a dog to its vomit or a washed pig to its mud wallow, the human race rendered void in many ways the pact it had made of its own will. . . . Indeed, the prelates of both orders turned to avarice and began to commit many acts of rapine and cupidity. . . . Then, provoked by the example of the great, the middling and lesser people sank to monstrous, disgraceful deeds. Indeed, when ever had such cases of incest and

[105] And in the late eleventh and twelfth centuries the third source—money—became an issue for the laity as well.

[106] Thomas N. Bisson, "The Organized Peace in Southern France and Catalonia, ca. 1140–1233," *American Historical Review* 82 (1977), 293.

adultery, such illicit minglings between blood relations, so much wanton-
ness of concubines, so much malevolence of evil people been heard of? . . .
since there was no one among the people, or only a very few, who
would . . . confute the others, the prediction of the prophet was fulfilled:
"And it shall be, just as the people, so the priest" [Isa. 24:2]. . . . And indeed the universal pope himself [Benedict IX] as a boy of almost ten years
was elected by the Romans with the intervention of a considerable amount
of money. . . . It was gold or silver and not merit that had raised up the
remaining prelates of that time [to their positions].[107]

This pollution created by people, pastors, and princes together was the
very abrogation of peace. The whole *corpus christianorum* had to be
cleansed if this peace—the peace that was Christ—was to return to
earth.

[107] Rodulphus Glaber, *Historiarum*, 4.5. A similar pollution complex appears in the
Lombard redaction (ca. 1047) of Sibylline texts; *Sibyllinische Texte und Forschungen:
Pseudomethodius, Adso und die Tiburtinische Sibylle*, ed. Ernst Sackur (Halle, 1898), pp. 183–
84.

Postscript: The Peace of God
and the Social Revolution

R. I. MOORE

Anyone who was looking for a simple account of the eleventh-century Peace movement will not have found it in this volume. A century's research, here lucidly appraised by Frederick Paxton, has added levels of complexity, if not of confusion, to what once appeared as a straightforward popular reaction to the anarchy and disorder traditionally associated with the approach of the millennium. Almost everyone who has looked seriously at any aspect of the Peace movement, including many of the present contributors, has added a new layer of interpretation, discerned a new facet of activity, found someone else doing something else—and often done so without invalidating, even without calling into question, the findings of their predecessors. The implications of the essays collected here for students of other aspects of the history of northwestern Europe in the eleventh and twelfth centuries, and for the interpretation of the period as a whole, are correspondingly diverse. I do not pretend to address all the issues to which they direct attention. I attempt no more than to explore, by way of example, some of the implications of the findings reported in these pages for a single question of long-standing and enduring interest, the nature of the connection between the religious excitements of the years around the millennium and the broad and deep changes in social structure and relations which, though still only spasmodically in progress and only fragmentarily visible, heralded a transformation

In expressing my gratitude to the editors for the privileged access to these essays which the invitation to add this Postscript has conferred on me, I must also emphasize that I have appropriated their materials and some of their conclusions to a use for which they were not designed, and for which their authors (who have not had the opportunity of commenting on my work as I have on theirs) are in no way responsible.

that the classic syntheses of successive generations have agreed in hailing as the beginning of a new age—"the European takeoff," "the making of the Middle Ages," "the birth (followed, naturally, by the infancy) of Europe."[1]

The late tenth and early eleventh centuries in western Europe were a time of sudden, rapid, and all-transforming change, a moment—and there have not been many of them in European history—when an old world began to burst apart and a new one to thrust its way forth from within. The Peace of God expressed and embraced a series of responses to changes as profound as their causes were mysterious. Peace itself was a word with many meanings, all of which implied that its breach was catastrophic, because they were all derived from Augustine's famous identification of peace with the divinely ordained order—*pax omnium rerum tranquillitas ordinis.*[2] Every wrong, whether in the social or the moral domain, constituted a breach of the peace, and every response to a perceived evil might properly aspire to restore it. More particularly, peace was the most precious gift of the king, and keeping the peace his most elementary duty and the primary source of his authority. It was a duty that the Carolingian and Capetian kings of the tenth century were increasingly unable to discharge. One of the most important ways the Peace movement is to be understood is as the reactions of different groups of their subjects, in different circumstances, to that fact.

The cause of the upheavals that took place around the millennium was neither the invasions of Vikings, Magyars, and Saracens, who had plagued Carolingian Europe between the middle of the ninth and the middle of the tenth centuries, nor any recovery from them. The long decline of the Carolingian order was rooted in the impossibility for a military aristocracy of continuously securing new supplies of loot and land when continuous military expansion was no longer assured. For territorial empire there is no stability; it must expand or decline. The difficulties of Charlemagne's empire began at the height of his success, in the early years of the ninth century, and became steadily more acute as the century proceeded. In the absence of conquest, internal competition produced factionalism and particularism, which undermined royal power and created the fissures that admitted the new barbarians. In the second half of the tenth century, for reasons which are still poorly understood, the need, or greed, of the nobles became still more

[1] Louis Halphen, *L'essor de l'Europe* (Paris, 1932); R. W. Southern, *The Making of the Middle Ages* (London, 1951); Robert S. Lopez, *La naissance de l'Europe* (Paris, 1962) (in English, *The Birth of Europe* [London, 1967]); Robert Fossier, *Enfance de l'Europe, Xe–XIIe siècles* (Paris, 1982).

[2] *De civitate dei,* 19:13.

acute. No doubt the customary division of properties between children
in each generation was bound to produce a crisis of noble subsistence
sooner or later, as estates became too small to support their propri-
etors, though such crises have occurred often enough at other times
and places without provoking the radical and complex response that
occurred here. It does seem probable that the position was exacerbated
by a sudden flood of donations to monasteries in the decades before
the millennium, though if so it remains effectively unexplained.[3]

Whatever the reasons for the crisis, a series of responses to it which
together reshaped the social order it is clearly visible from very early in
the eleventh century, or even before. First, in many parts of Francia
(and in Italy too, though there in a somewhat different form) the laity
set about repossessing, as violently as need be, lands that had been
given to churches, especially monasteries, by members of their families; no doubt they were not always scrupulous to take only what had
been given.[4] Second, they sought to increase their revenues by taking
more from their dependent peasants and by using brute force, disguised as an extension of the rights of public power and private lordship, to reduce independent cultivators to dependence, bringing all
under a similar, uniform regime. This was the extension of the seigneurie through the power of the ban, which everywhere reduced free
and independent landowners to serfdom, as is graphically described
for Aquitaine in this volume by André Debord.[5] And third, the nobles

[3] Georges Duby, *La société aux XIe et XIIe siècles dans la région mâconnaise* (Paris, 1953),
pp. 57–65; Barbara Rosenwein, *Rhinoceros Bound: Cluny in the Tenth Century* (Philadelphia, 1982), pp. 36–37; Daniel Callahan, Chapter 7, this volume. Note, however, Rosenwein's recent suggestion that, since in the tenth century the exchange of land was at least
as important as a means of social bonding as it was as an economic transaction, the multiplication of transactions toward the end of the century can be seen not only as a cause
of instability but also as a response to it; Barbara Rosenwein, *To Be the Neighbor of St. Peter:
The Social Meaning of Cluny's Property, 909–1049* (Ithaca, N.Y., 1989), p. 205. The weak-
nesses of previous attempts to explain the pace and scale of donation to Cluny in the
second half of the tenth century are crisply exposed by Constance B. Bouchard, *Sword,
Miter, and Cloister: Nobility and the Church in Burgundy, 980–1198* (Ithaca, N.Y., 1987), pp.
225–46, but Bouchard's own willingness to settle for the pious sentiments of the formulas
must be taken as an admission of defeat, at least in the absence of any clear chronological
or other correlation between the trajectory of donation and other indications of mounting religious enthusiasm.
[4] Steven Weinberger, "Les conflits entre clercs et laïques dans la Provence du XIe
siècle," *Annales du Midi* 92 (1980), 269–79.
[5] For the process in general, J.-F. Lemarignier, "La dislocation du *pagus* et la problème
des *consuetudines*," in *Mélanges dediées à la mémoire de Louis Halphen*, ed. Charles-Edmond
Perrin (Paris, 1951), pp. 401–10, remains the indispensable starting point. Compare
Bachrach's conclusion that at the council of Saint-Germain-Laprade Guy of Le Puy "attempted nothing less than to put the *pagus* together again"; Bernard Bachrach, "The
Northern Origins of the Peace Movement at Le Puy in 975," *Historical Reflections/Réfle-
xions historiques* 14 (1987), 405–21, quotation on p. 419.

sought to protect the integrity of their patrimonies by diminishing or nullifying the claims of daughters and younger sons on them, so that the land might descend undivided from eldest son to eldest son in each generation.[6]

These stratagems were not, of course, attempted simultaneously or uniformly in every part of Europe. Most notably, to the east of the Rhine, where the politics of expansion still prevailed,[7] they did not develop until much later and then in very different forms. But in different degrees and combinations these three strategies were applied so widely and generally through most of what had been the Carolingian empire that the perception of classical feudalism as a social formation characteristic of the lands "between the Rhine and the Loire"[8] has been superseded by a general recognition that, from around the third decade of the eleventh century until the seventh or eighth decade of the twelfth, the similarities arising from domination by private retinues operating from castles were a good deal more important throughout the Carolingian lands (including those to the south not only of the Loire but of the Alps and Pyrenees)[9] than the differences between particular forms of domination that arose from local variations of circumstance and tradition.[10]

One of this volume's merits is that it links the Peace movement clearly and specifically to all three developments. What is now generally accepted as its first manifestation, the council summoned by Bishop Guy of Le Puy at Laprade-Saint-Germain in 975 or soon after to secure the restoration of lands and revenues that had been, as he saw it, usurped from his church and others in the region, was a direct assertion, or reassertion, of royal authority. The skillful analysis by Bernard Bachrach of Guy's background and conduct makes it quite clear how conservative were his objectives.[11] Guy, the brother of Count Geoffrey Greygown of Anjou, was appointed to the see with the direct

---

[6] As classically expounded by Georges Duby, from *La société dans la région mâconnaise* to the essays collected in *The Chivalrous Society*, trans. Cynthia Postan (London, 1977; for the most part also in *Hommes et structures du moyen âge* [Paris, 1973]) to *The Knight, the Lady, and the Priest: The Making of Modern Marriage in Medieval France*, trans. Barbara Bray (New York, 1983). See R. I. Moore, "Duby's Eleventh Century," *History* 69 (1984), 36–49.

[7] K. J. Leyser, *Medieval Germany and Its Neighbours* (London, 1982), for example, pp. 23–25, 88–91.

[8] F. L. Ganshof, *Feudalism* (Paris, 1944; trans. Philip Grierson, London, 3d ed., 1964), p. xvii.

[9] For a useful discussion on this point, see Chris Wickham, reviewing *Structures féodales et féodalisme dans l'occident méditerranéen* (Rome, 1980), in *English Historical Review* 98 (1982), 835–37.

[10] Georges Duby, *The Three Orders: Feudal Society Imagined*, trans. A. Goldhammer (Chicago, 1981), pp. 147–66; Jean-Pierre Poly and Éric Bournazel, *La mutation féodale, Xe–XIIe siècles* (Paris, 1980), pp. 129–36; Fossier, *Enfance de l'Europe*, pp. 951–64.

[11] Bachrach, "Northern Origins."

approval of the Carolingian King Lothar. It seems plain that his appointment carried with it, in the Carolingian fashion, the powers and duties of the count as well as those of the bishop. He was quite ready to use the prerogatives of either office as the occasion required. Thus, in 975, although his chief objective was the restoration of ecclesiastical lands and revenues, there was nothing ecclesiastical about his methods: he called the *milites ac rustici* of the region to what was in effect a summons of the host, and he got what he wanted from them by means of a direct and carefully orchestrated threat of military force, assembled in ambush under royal authority. At a second council, at Saint-Paulien in 993–94, Guy joined other bishops and counts of the region in issuing a set of canons that dealt mainly with spiritual matters and were to be enforced by spiritual sanctions. But the two first and most important of them forbade the exercise of certain powers of taxation and coercion except by those—counts and bishops—to whom they properly pertained.

Guy was here resisting two powerful though not novel forces that had destroyed by usurpation the authority of the crown and used the usurped authority to attack the wealth of the church. As Elisabeth Magnou-Nortier here demonstrates so forcefully, Guy's tactics and language belonged to a much older and broader tradition. Those who disturbed the peace of the church—the peace, that is, which had protected the church's people, possessions, and revenues in the earliest Germanic law codes—had been denounced as *invasores, usurpatores, violatores ecclesiarum,* and so forth since the sixth century. The *invasiones* the Frankish councils had denounced so regularly were often not simple acts of brigandage but attempts to reclaim or repossess gifts made earlier to the church. In the late tenth century, any such action must have been directed with particular force against Cluny and its dependencies, which had recently been accumulating property with great rapidity in just the areas where the Peace movement appeared—Burgundy, the Auvergne, and Aquitaine. In a new study of profound significance, published after these essays were written, Barbara Rosenwein has shown how the tension between monastery and aristocracy arising from these donations was exacerbated by a developing difference of understanding between them, in consequence of which the church expected increasingly to defend as permanent acquisition—property in the modern sense—land that may often have been handed over with the intention, based on the perceptions of an earlier age, that it should be treated rather as part of a fluid, imprecise, and custom-governed pool of reciprocal gifts and favors.[12]

[12] Barbara Rosenwein, *Neighbor of St. Peter,* particularly pp. 109–25.

As Elisabeth Magnou-Nortier demonstrates in this volume, the instruments of depredation, or at any rate its pretext, were *rapinae, praedae, redemptiones*—not mere looting, as we translate so casually, but specific powers of requisition and coercion granted by the Carolingian kings to those whose responsibility it was to levy and provision their armies and to afford military protection to churches and their lands. These were among the powers of the ban, which everywhere were annexed during the late tenth and early eleventh centuries by local magnates and *milites* intent on extending their possessions and revenues, and which Guy of Le Puy reclaimed and reserved for episcopal and comital control in the acts of his two councils. By 975, however, the view on which Guy had acted that royal power should be vigorously asserted can hardly have been widely shared. By 993, the Carolingian house had been replaced by the Capetian, which secured little recognition or influence south of the Loire. Though the proclamations of peace continued to reflect the language and traditions of the royal prerogative, a more effective guarantor was required. In 989,

> when evil doers had sprung up like weeds, and wicked men ravaged the vineyard of the lord like thorn bushes and briars choking the harvest, the abbots and bishops and other holy men decided to call a council at which *praeda* would be forbidden, what had been taken unjustly restored to the church, and other blemishes on the face of the holy church of God scraped away with the sharp blade of anathema. The council was summoned to the monastery of Charroux, and great crowds of people went from Poitou, the Limousin, and neighboring regions. The bodies of many saints were brought along, to reinforce the pious by their presence and dull the threats of the wicked. The divine will, moved as we believe by the presence of the saints, illuminated that council by frequent miracles.[13]

In particular, the archbishop of Bordeaux and five of his suffragans pronounced anathema on those who robbed churches and the poor or offered violence to unarmed clerics. A few years later, probably in 994, Archbishop Burchard of Lyon presided over a large assembly at Anse, in Burgundy, which placed Cluny and certain of its lands under the protection of its anathema, banned clerks from the hunt and from marrying, prohibited magical divination, and forbade (agricultural) work, commercial transactions, and holding pleas on Sundays.[14]

These were the first councils to display clearly the form traditionally associated with the Peace of God, though they had been foreshadowed

---

[13] *Delatio corporis s. Juniani in synodum Karrofensem; PL* 97:824–25. For the acts of the council of Charroux, see Mansi 19:89–90.

[14] Mansi 19:99–102.

in various ways. During the next fifty years or so they were followed by many more, especially and most vigorously in southwestern France. In view of both the traditional commitment of the Cluniac monks to peace and their place among the foremost targets of the aggressors, it is not surprising that Cluny and its abbots took a leading role, orchestrating the great assemblies at which crowds of people swore on relics the monks brought out into the fields to support each other and the oppressed church against the *milites* who had destroyed the peace. On these occasions the prelates who presided over the assemblies exercised the royal office of keeping the peace. In doing so, even when like Aimon of Bourges in 1038 they led into battle armies gathered for the purpose, they did not act inconsistently with the office and duties of the Carolingian episcopate, which was regularly entrusted with public powers. Nevertheless, the long-term effect of their intervention, as such conservative observers as Gerard of Cambrai and Adalbero of Laon saw very clearly, was not to reinforce royal authority but to undermine it, by taking into the hands of the lay magnates and the prelates who supported them the powers of peacekeeping that the king should have exercised.[15]

From only a slightly less elevated perspective, however, the view was different. For William V of Aquitaine (duke ca. 993–1030), striving to assert his lordship over a broad territory, the Peace movement he promoted so energetically provided the opportunity of consolidating his authority by assuming, as Debord observes, the role normally filled by the king in his capacity as arbiter of the peace. Thus the council of Poitiers (1000/14) over which he presided enhanced his authority by ordering those accused of *invasiones* to do justice or appear before the duke himself or the count of the *pagus* in question, though by threatening recalcitrants with spiritual sanctions it also implicitly conceded that the disintegration of comital authority was proceeding apace, here as elsewhere.[16] Whether it follows, more generally, that there was any essential contradiction between the goals of the Peace and the interests of the lords is very much to be doubted. The second canon of this council's predecessor, that of Charroux in 989, had famously anathematized "anyone who should take [*praedaverit*] a sheep or an ox or a cow or an ass or a goat or a billygoat or pigs from any of the farmers or other poor"—unless, it adds less famously, by reason of an offence they have committed (*nisi per propriam culpam*).[17] The profits of justice, the most fundamental and lucrative constituent of the seigneury, were not to be affected. Similarly, several essays in this collection emphasize the ex-

---

[15] Duby, *Three Orders*, pp. 36–40, 53–55, 125–39.
[16] Mansi 19:267.
[17] Mansi: 19:90.

clusion clauses in some of the Peace agreements, which have too often been overlooked. Guy of Le Puy's council at Saint-Paulien in 993, for example, forbade unauthorized levies on flocks and crops, the building and besieging of castles, the exaction of arbitrary payments and services from peasants and of evil customs (*malae consuetudines*)—except by lords acting on their own lands or on lands over which they exercised authority: *nisi unusquisque de suis terra, aut de suo alode vel de suo beneficiu vel de sua commanda.*[18] The council, in other words, did not resist the consolidation of the seigneuries in the hands of the lords; it endorsed it, on condition that each should respect the boundaries of the others. One reason for this delicacy is indicated by the next clause, according to which nobody shall dare to take such levies from "ecclesiastical, episcopal, canonical, or monastic land"—unless, the council adds thoughtfully, it has been acquired from the bishop or the brethren as a voluntary gift. The protection is not extended to those who work the land, from whose surplus the exaction in question must come, but to the church that claimed its lordship. In part, this was consistent with Guy's position as the representative of public power, but the construction of private castles had long been clearly seen as a fundamental threat to the authority of the king and his representatives. Its acceptance here, even if it was no more than a recognition of the inevitable, is a plain testimony of the abandonment of public authority by those who might have been thought most willing to uphold it.

In the context of the exercise of lordship, this self-imposed limitation on the scope of the canons was of the greatest importance. It meant that, although (at least in theory) the protection of the Peace would be extended to independent (allodial) landholders who were resisting absorption by the great, no obstacle was offered to the oppression or exploitation of those who were tenants already, whether free or unfree. Far from condemning the subjugation of the countryside by the castellans and the reduction of free tenants to serfdom which created the seigneurial regime, the council legitimized them. If this was not a direct return to the lay aristocracy for leaving the church in undisturbed possession of its acquisitions, it was, at the very least, an acknowledgment of a community of interest between secular and ecclesiastical lordship which precluded any possibility that the church might take the side of the oppressed against the oppressors. The concern of Bishop Guy's peace, in short, was strictly limited to regulating conflict between lords, and especially to protecting one of those lords, the church, against the rest. That context underlines the significance of Barbara Rosenwein's demonstration that the lands listed in the acts

---

[18] On the *commenda*, see Poly and Bournazel, *Mutation féodale*, pp. 98–99.

of the council of Anse, convened the next year in response to Cluny's complaints of harassment by "malignant and importunate men," had been carefully selected and accumulated by gift and exchange over some generations and "had come, by 994, to make up the core of St. Peter's holdings," the strategic center of Cluny's developing seigneurie.[19]

The new preoccupation with the immovable character of landed property which Rosenwein has shown to have lain behind the proliferation of disputes between monasteries and their erstwhile patrons also gave additional clarity and urgency to the distinction between the secular and the ecclesiastical. Land was coming to be seen more as the prime constituent of a permanent and deliberately assembled estate—and less as a parcel of gifts to be broken up and passed back and forth between the members of a social network these transactions defined and renewed.[20] The structure of the families of its secular lords also began to change. Control was vested in particular individuals—usually the eldest sons—rather than in the kinship group as a whole, and the integrity of the patrimony was protected by a variety of devices against the progressive fragmentation which under partible inheritance normally resulted from the marriages of siblings. Consequently, eldest sons and the churches had a common and growing interest in proclaiming the sanctity of property rights and rallying opposition to those who challenged them. It was in this context that the Peace councils endorsed, and doubtless did something to realise, the third strategy for the protection of the noble patrimony mentioned above. Their strictures against incestuous marriage—marriage, that is, within the seventh degree of kinship, newly defined according to the Germanic reckoning, which multiplied the number of potential marriage partners forbidden to a given individual by a factor of about twenty—were an essential part of the campaign to enforce primogeniture and bring about the reconstruction of the noble family.[21]

[19] Mansi 19:177–80; Rosenwein, *Neighbor of St. Peter*, especially pp. 85–98, 162–72, noting particularly the map on p. 169. The comment quoted is on p. 88.

[20] Rosenwein, *Neighbor of St. Peter*, especially pp. 199–200, 205–6; cf. Jean Dunbabin, *France in the Making, 843–1180* (Oxford, 1985), pp. 199–21, 222–23.

[21] Moore, "Duby's Eleventh Century," pp. 40–42; Duby, *The Knight, the Lady and the Priest*, pp. 35–37, 51–53, 69–70; Jack Goody, *The Development of the Family and Marriage in Europe* (Cambridge, 1983), pp. 134–46. This point is not necessarily inconsistent with the sense of Amy Remensnyder's discussion in Chapter 12, but it should be borne in mind that in one respect at least the incest prohibition might work against the interests of peace, by making it harder to contract, and easier to prevent, diplomatically useful marriages. An obvious example, though at too elevated a political level to bear on the present discussion, is Henry I's securing of an annulment of the marriage between William Clito and Sybil, second daughter of Fulk IV of Anjou, on the grounds of

The church also had its part of the bargain to keep. After his triumph over the *milites ac rustici* in 975, Guy of Le Puy reorganized the
lands of his cathedral, which he had just replenished so firmly, so that
one third would support the canons, living in common, and one third
defray his own expenses.[22] In requiring his canons to lead the common
life (and so to surrender themselves to chastity, poverty, and obedience), Guy fulfilled what had been the first goal of reform since the
time of Odo of Cluny. From the bishop's point of view, the rule of
chastity coupled with the prohibition of personal property would protect church lands against being broken up and alienated to the descendants of the canons. From the point of view of his brother, who
remained in the world, it ensured that the lands he had granted or restored to the church would not become the patrimony of a rival dynasty to his own but, on the contrary, would support his dynastic
strategy by remaining available to provide benefices for the younger
sons of his own descendants.

The losers were the younger sons—or, at any rate, those younger
sons who did not become clerks or monks but *milites*. Finding a place
for them in the new order was a long and critical business, in which the
Peace movement played a leading part. In the first place, its role was
defensive. Those who threatened to disrupt the new deal had to be
branded and characterized clearly as enemies of society, and sanctions
had to be organized to bring them under control. In the longer term,
a more positive solution was required and was found in the order of
chivalry and the idea of Christian knighthood—in the establishment of
a knightly order that embraced the entire secular aristocracy from
kings to landless adventurers and proclaimed special spiritual and material goals and rewards (including the prospect of fame, wives, and
land won in far-off places) for those who accepted the long apprentice-
ship and still longer exclusion from the breeding cycle which the new
social order required.[23] While this was slowly achieved during the rest
of the eleventh century and beyond, lay rulers all over Carolingian Europe began to appropriate the claims of the Peace and Truce of God in

---

consanguinity, in order to reopen the question of the Norman succession and clear the
way for the marriage he desired between his daughter Matilda and Geoffrey of Anjou.
Plainly, the matter needs further consideration in specific regional and local contexts.

[22] *Chronicle of St. Pierre du Puy,* in C. Devic and J. Vaissette, *Histoire du Languedoc* (Toulouse, 1875), 5:15.

[23] Georges Duby, "Laity and the Peace of God" (especially pp. 123–33), "Youth in Aristocratic Society" (pp. 112–22), and "The Origins of Knighthood" (pp. 158–70), all in
Chivalrous Society; I. S. Robinson, "Gregory VII and the Soldiers of Christ," *History* 58
(1973), 169–92; Maurice Keen, *Chivalry* (New Haven, Conn., 1984), pp. 44–50.

support of the reassertion of their own authority, extending in the
name of peace their claims to do justice, maintain order, and even levy
taxes.[24]

As it emerged in the early decades of the eleventh century, therefore,
the Peace of God foreshadowed a new social order founded on a firm
and sharp distinction between the lay and the ecclesiastical. It was not
designed to express or correct the grievances of poor laypeople except
to the limited extent (though perfectly genuine as far as it went) that,
since the alleviation of distress through charity was a principal object
and justification of ecclesiastical (and notably Cluniac) wealth, there
were grounds to fear that the impoverishment of the churches would
lead to its decline. The *pauperes* so regularly referred to as the objects
of the movement's protection were most often the monks themselves,
appealing with perhaps more thought of principle than practice to the
ideal humility and helplessness of their order. In asserting the legitimacy of lordship over men and the exploitation that went with it, the
vocabulary of these councils contrasted sharply with that of the contemporary monastic movement in Tuscany, in which dissociation even
from legitimate domination and its fruits was rapidly becoming the
sine qua non of holiness[25]—an attitude whose conquest of the reforming spirit in the north would not be registered until the end of the eleventh century, when the Cistercians and other new orders refused to
accept tithes and cultivated lands on the ground that they were stained
with the blood of the poor.[26]

In the long run, and largely in retrospect, the results of the social
revolution set in train by these events came to be understood and the
rearrangement of the mental landscape it involved—"l'imaginaire du
féodalisme"[27]—to be described as the establishment of the society of
three orders. It was not so at the time: the concept of the three orders
which Adalbero of Laon and Gerard of Cambrai advocated described
the old world whose passing they sought to resist; the harbingers of the
new, which they deplored, were the Peace movement, the Cluniacs, and
heresy.[28] To those on the other side of the argument, the first two and

[24] H. E. J. Cowdrey, "The Peace and Truce of God in the Eleventh Century," *Past and
Present* 46 (1971), 58–67; David Bates, *Normandy before 1066* (London, 1982), pp. 163–64;
Thomas F. Bisson, "The Organized Peace in Southern France and Catalonia, c. 1140–
1223," *American Historical Review* 82 (1977), 290–311.
[25] R. I. Moore, "Family, Community and Cult on the Eve of the Gregorian Reform,"
Transactions of the Royal Historical Society, 5th ser., 30 (1980), 53–55, where, however, I had
not seen the contrast between the French and Italian movements emphasized here.
[26] Giles Constable, *Monastic Tithes, from Their Origins to the Twelfth Century* (Cambridge,
1964), pp. 136–42.
[27] As in the French title of Duby, *Three Orders: Les trois ordres ou l'imaginaire du féodalisme*
(Paris, 1978).
[28] Duby, *Three Orders*, pp. 129–46.

a good part of the third of these sinister forces marched behind the banner of "reform." We have already seen why the restoration of ecclesiastical property was inseparable from a far-reaching reconstruction of the moral landscape of both clergy and laity. In this volume, Amy G. Remensnyder illustrates in detail how the Peace councils, in successive lists of canons, adumbrated with increasing comprehensiveness and precision the essentials of the program of ecclesiastical reform which would dominate the rest of the eleventh century and shape the medieval church—the abolition of simony, the enforcement of clerical celibacy, the separation of the laity from the clergy and the clergy from the world, regularity and purity in the celebration of the sacraments, and so on. She also shows how in the process all the enemies of reform were drawn together into a single comprehensive menace by being designated as the agents of pollution. Conversely, by welding the elements of reform into a single, coherent program the councils compelled their champions to accept what were now defined as the consequences of their positions: for both clergy and laity, property and power became conditional on the scrupulous performance of their designated roles in their designated sphere, each defined and unmistakably declared by adherence to an appropriate code of sexual morals and conduct.

The subsuming of all the targets of reform into a single threat of pollution that Remensnyder describes was also an essential preliminary to the marshalling of popular enthusiasm against them which was the indispensable cutting edge of the Peace of God. Bernhard Töpfer showed long ago, in a classic essay whose appearance here in English translation is very much to be welcomed, how in the absence of effective royal protection the monks of the tenth century used their ceremonial, their liturgy, and above all the relics of their saints to rally support against their oppressors.[29] How these weapons were turned to the service of reform we are graphically reminded by Rodulphus Glaber: "The bishops and abbots and other devout men of Aquitaine summoned great councils of the whole people, to which were borne the bodies of many saints and innumerable caskets of holy relics . . . [and they] came rejoicing and ready, one and all, to obey the commands of the clergy no less than if they had been given by a voice from heaven speaking to men on earth."[30]

---

[29] See also Benedicta Ward, *Miracles and the Medieval Mind* (London, 1982), pp. 36–49; D. W. Rollason, "The Miracles of St. Benedict: A Window on Early Medieval France," in *Studies in Medieval History Presented to R. H. C. Davis*, ed. Henry Mayr-Harting and R. I. Moore (London, 1985), pp. 73–90; Thomas Head, *Hagiography and the Cult of Saints: The Diocese of Orléans, 800–1200* (Cambridge Studies in Medieval Life and Thought, 4th ser., 14; Cambridge, 1991), especially pp. 172–81.

[30] Rodulphus Glaber, *Historiarum*, 4.5.14. For the passage in full, see Appendix A of this volume.

This volume contains striking confirmation that the alliance between church and people which the literary sources describe so movingly was quite deliberately constructed. In a highly original application of liturgical to social history, Daniel Callahan shows us how the regional tradition of mobilizing relics as a focal point of popular action was replicated and reinforced in the liturgy by the tropes and sequences added to the mass whose composition was a distinctive and prolific Aquitanian innovation of this same period—and which contain numerous invocations of peace, including the first examples of the change from *miserere nobis* to *dona nobis pacem* in the common. One of the major centers of this work was the great monastery of Saint-Martial at Limoges, where in the years after the council of Limoges in 994, as Richard Landes shows, the monks composed a new biography of their founder, persuasively disguised as a very old one and carefully constructed to display the same idealized union of church and people under a wise and generous ruler.

The active and explicit involvement of the people in the liturgy (in direct contrast to the firm distinction that Gerard of Cambrai made a few years later between those who prayed, the *oratores*, and those who worked), the oath taken by all present at the rallies, which as Callahan points out distinguished these proclamations of the peace sharply from their Carolingian counterparts, and the reliance on excommunication, which provided the movement's most general and evidently most effective sanction, all bring out clearly the essential role of popular enthusiasm in the early Aquitanian Peace movement, dignified though it was by the patronage, and no doubt the initiative, of the duke and the prelates. Yet, if the *populus* appears in the vocabulary of this period as "that part of the population whose members were deemed by the rest to have no *independent* political role,"[31] it was largely because it was still the case, as Peter Brown observed of late antiquity, that what popularity implied was "the ability of the few to mobilize the support of the many."[32] Who the people were, and why they should have been so responsive to the appeal of the monks, are questions we are still some way from resolving. It is not too difficult, in general terms, to identify groups that were losers by the changes taking place, at greater or lesser speed, all over eleventh-century France. Among them perhaps the most conspicuous, or at any rate those likeliest to win the historian's attention, were the free landholders (*alodii*) of insufficient substance to protect their lands and eventually their freedom against the pressures exerted by their more powerful neighbors. In principle, as we noted in

[31] Moore, "Family, Community and Cult," p. 51; emphasis added.
[32] Peter Brown, *The Cult of the Saints: Its Rise and Function in Latin Christianity* (Chicago, 1981), p. 48.

the context of the council of Saint-Paulien, the Peace protected their interests, and there are indications that they were to be found among its forces. The militia of Aimo of Bourges was drawn from the *populus*, included *rustici*, was a *multitudo inermis vulgi*—meaning, comments Bachrach,[33] not that its members were unarmed but that they lacked the heavy defensive armor of the knight. The militia Andrew of Fleury described in these terms plainly included serfs. Bachrach sees both Guy of Le Puy and Aimon of Bourges remobilizing the Carolingian levy, of which free smallholders would have formed the backbone[34]—though a backbone now made militarily obsolescent by the enormously superior equipment and training of the knights as well as being dispossessed by the superior power of their lords. Nor was usurpation only a matter of property, at least in the Auvergne; Christian Lauranson-Rosaz's contribution to this collection brings out the importance of the reassertion of ancient rights of popular assembly and jurisdiction which had been eroded by the Carolingian colonization of the region among the impulses that rallied around the Peace. Yet, even of a group so manifestly and universally on the losing side, our fragmentary information warns us against too easy generalization, for those from whom Guy of Le Puy extracted promises in 975 "to keep the peace, not to oppress the goods of the poor and the churches [that is, not to raise taxes on their own account], and to give back what they had taken," were the *milites ac rustici* of his diocese.[35] In this there is a reminder of the magnitude of the changes that were under way. Two centuries later the ranks of the *milites* would include kings and great nobles as well as small-time desperadoes, and *rustici* would mean *serfs* and would have acquired a range of pejorative connotations, including those of heresy and illiteracy, which reflected the dominance of the new culture by the aspirations and values of an essentially urban intelligentsia.[36] It would be inconceivable to find the two lumped together as common actors, as they are so casually by the chronicler of Le Puy.

[33] Bachrach, "Northern Origins," p. 417.
[34] Bachrach, "Northern Origins," p. 416.
[35] *Chronicle of St. Pierre du Puy*, 5:15.
[36] Alexander Murray, *Reason and Society in the Middle Ages* (Oxford, 1978), pp. 237–44; for other examples, see Brian Stock, *The Implications of Literacy: Written Language and Models of Interpretation in the Eleventh and Twelfth Centuries* (Princeton, N.J., 1983), pp. 27–29, 249–50, 319, 356, 521. Ian Wood, who kindly read a draft of this essay, points out that the pejorative use of the word *rustici* was not new in the twelfth century; see Peter Brown, "Relics and Social Status in the Age of Gregory of Tours," in his *Society and the Holy in Late Antiquity* (London, 1982), pp. 230–33; cf. J. Le Goff, *Time, Work and Culture in the Middle Ages* (Chicago, 1980), pp. 92–97. This, however, is a very different and subtler denigration, cultural rather than social in the first instance, and makes it all the more striking that the word could be used without any pejorative imputation at the end of the tenth century.

The Peace movement was one of the first and most eloquent expressions both of the distress and resentment caused by the massive transformation in the distribution of power and wealth which brought about a far more complex and sharply articulated social hierarchy and of the means by which such a transformation was carried out in a society that lacked all but the most elementary, and elemental, mechanisms for enforcing and adapting to change. It is not at all surprising that its actual role in articulating and implanting the goals and values of the social revolution contrasts so sharply with the accounts presented by its chroniclers, who were themselves in the front line of the battle. The fact that as members of the monastic order they had an obvious interest in depicting the monasteries as champions of the weak against the brutalities of unbounded power does not mean that they were altogether wrong. An indispensable premise of the astonishing stories they have to tell is that, whatever the church and its saints might undertake, and however bizarrely, they always needed to establish legitimation by popular acclaim against the brute force of those with whom they competed for order, property, and influence. The chroniclers describe the Peace of God as they envisaged it, as an alliance of church and poor against the greed and despotism of the lords, the restoration of a lost social order in which church and king protect the poor against abuse by the powerful—precisely what could no longer be guaranteed in the real world. The appeal to the yearning for the restoration of a golden past so evident in passages like those quoted above, in the *Vita prolixior* of Saint Martial of Limoges, and in Lauranson-Rosaz's account of the subversion of Auvergnat popular assemblies was the surest way of rallying those who felt themselves the victims of change and of focusing resentment on the exploiters of new forms of power so brilliantly symbolized by the *milites* and the castles from which they rode.

Putting the chroniclers' dramatic and elevating descriptions of bishops and abbots heading a crusade for justice to the poor in their proper context confirms that they had no intention of fomenting a social revolution—or rather, that for the most part they were prepared to support and legitimate the social revolution that in fact occurred at this time, of which not the people but the eldest sons of lords, and through them the entire aristocracy, were the chief beneficiaries. Indeed, Thomas Head provides us with a sensitive and illuminating account of how one chronicler, Andrew of Fleury, distrusting the entire strategem of manipulating the saints, in however worthy a cause, found himself gradually separated from the goals of the movement with which he had initially sympathized. And we are afforded by Richard Landes's examination of the successive drafts of the chronicle of Ademar of Chabannes a glimpse of a more violent disillusion, a uniquely revealing

insight into the crisis provoked in Aquitaine when the contradiction between the interests of the leaders and the hopes they had excited in the
people became apparent. The circumstances in which this occurred are
essentially conjectural, but among them we must count two striking incidents. In 1018, fifty people were trampled to death in the basilica at
Limoges, in circumstances that Ademar went to some length to obscure. In the following year, Abbot Geoffrey of Saint-Martial, son of the
vicomte of Limoges, died. His nephew, and the son of the *vicomte*,
Bishop Gerard, refused to consecrate his duly elected successor, thus
keeping the revenues in his own hands, until after two years he was
forced by popular unrest to climb down. That the 1010s and 1020s saw
the final breakdown of ducal and comital control over the castellans
which the council of Poitiers had tried to avert in 1010 is confirmed by
the charter of Saint-Maixent, which records that another council at
Poitiers, in 1030, appealed to custom instead of ducal authority to protect the lands of the abbey against *invasores*: the ban was no longer at
the duke's disposal, the seigneury had established itself, and though
the churches might sometimes be the losers in particular instances they
were also lords like other lords.

Whatever its immediate cause, the impact on popular sentiment of
the manifest divergence between popular and seigneurial interest, lay
or ecclesiastical, was plainly, even harshly, displayed in 1029 when an
itinerant monk named Benedict of Chiusa engaged Ademar of Chabannes, liturgist, historian, and ardent devotee of Saint Martial, in
public debate and scored an easy and humiliating victory.[37] Popular
endorsement of Benedict's claim that the apostolicity of Saint Martial,
the cause to which Ademar had dedicated his work and passion, was no
more than a fraudulent attempt to raise money and power on false pre-
tences was a shattering humiliation. Ademar devoted the rest of his life
to obliterating it from the historical record, with great success. Nothing
could better display precisely the attitude to the growing power and
wealth of the church which inspired the heresies of Leutard of Vertus
in Champagne shortly after the millennium, or of the men of Arras
who told Gerard of Cambrai in 1025 that salvation lay in earning their
food by their own hands and doing injury to no one.[38] In Aquitaine
those in authority had already reacted to popular skepticism of the
propriety of their claims and the beneficence of the earthly dispensa-
tion. At Charroux in 1028, Duke William "summoned a council of

[37] For a full description of the confrontation, see Robert Lee Wolff, "How the News
Was Brought from Byzantium to Angoulême; or, The Pursuit of a Hare in an Oxcart,"
Byzantine and Modern Greek Studies 4 (1979), 169–209.
[38] Rodulphus Glaber, *Historiarum*, 2.11. *Acta synodi Atrebatensis; PL* 142:1272. See also
R. I. Moore, *The Origins of European Dissent* (Oxford, 1985), pp. 35–38.

bishops and abbots to wipe out the heresies which the Manichees had been spreading among the people. All the princes of Aquitaine were present, and he ordered them to keep the peace and respect the Catholic church."[39] The extent to which Ademar had come to see the influence of heretics among the people as the source of pollution and disruption is further emphasized by his account of the trial at Orléans in 1022, a purely political affair which (as Thomas Head remarks) Ademar attributed not only to the baleful influence of Manichaeans but to the corruption of the guilty clerks by "some peasant" (*quidam rusticus*)—a telling betrayal of the collapse of the alliance so recently celebrated between church and people.[40]

Whether or not real Manichaeans were to be found in Aquitaine— and it is most unlikely[41]—the proclamation of their presence and influence represents a realignment of the political relations between the prince and the church, on the one hand, and the people, on the other, an assertion of hierarchical authority, and a repudiation of the power of popular spiritual judgment which had been implicit in the rallies around the relics and the acclamation of miracles. This was not the only occasion when it seems that criticism of the consquences of the Peace movement, as opposed to its stated goals, led to the allegation of heresy against the critics. In another unexpected and singularly revealing reappraisal of a familiar source, Guy Lobrichon not only redates from the mid-twelfth to the early eleventh century a famous but anomalous description of heretics alleged to be active in the Périgord but also shows us that it is not a description of real heretics at all, only a clever caricature of opponents within the Cluniac order of the burgeoning elaboration of Cluny's famous liturgy and the extension of its control ever more tightly over an ever-growing number of monasteries—developments particularly associated with the abbacy of Odilo in the first half of the eleventh century and with the region to the southwest, through the Auvergne and Aquitaine. The "Letter" of Heribert

[39] Ademar of Chabannes, *Chronicon*, 3.69, p. 194.

[40] Rodulphus Glaber, *Historiarum*, 3.8.26, also inserts a member of the lower orders into his account—*mulier quaedam ex Italia;* see Stock, *Implications of Literacy*, pp. 115–18, 145–50. On the affair at Orléans, see R.-H. Bautier, "L'hérésie d'Orléans et le mouvement intellectuel au début du XIe siècle," *Actes du 95 Congrès national des sociétés savantes (Reims, 1970), Section philologique et historique* (Paris, 1975), 1:63–88.

[41] Despite Poly and Bournazel, *Mutation féodale*, pp. 382–427, there is no evidence of either theological dualism or the influence of Bogomilism among the heretics of the eleventh-century west. Neither does their discussion, or to the best of my knowledge any other, demonstrate any necessity to postulate it; in that respect I stand by the conclusions in R. I. Moore, "The Origins of Medieval Heresy," *History* 55 (1970), 21–36, and *Origins of European Dissent*, pp. 38–45, 164–67, and (1985 ed.) 285–89. It seems to me that the light Richard Landes has thrown on these events makes the *manichaeus ex machina* even more superfluous than he was before.

may now take its modest place alongside the much more serious and substantial dossier of documents prepared to support the canonization of Abbot Maiolus of Cluny (994), also under the direction of Abbot Odilo, also associated with the scriptorium of Saint-Germain at Auxerre, and also designed to support the claims of Cluny to privilege and property as the reward of the sacrifice their vows of poverty, chastity, and obedience represented to its monks.[42]

The movement for the Peace and Truce of God still had a long future before it when Ademar was jeered from his debate with Benedict of Chiusa. As it spread to the north and east through the rest of the eleventh century, it met the fate of many a radical movement, as Thomas Bisson showed some years ago, in being gradually taken over as part of the repertory of claims and techniques with which a new generation of kings and princes gradually began to reassert their power.[43] It also had another future, which Geoffrey Koziol reveals in his fascinating account of the settlement of Flemish feuds by the relics of Saint Ursmer, as its goals and techniques were continued and diffused at local levels through agencies which were not Peace councils and which issued no canons but which answered a continuing and often desperate need for services of conciliation and the resolution of conflict. But, if the construction offered here is correct—and it must be emphasized that it does not bear the endorsement of those whose work has been pressed into its service—the first fine careless rapture never was recaptured. The Aquitanian Peace of God was, in its first phase, a truly millennial movement, in the sense that it represented and expressed the aspiration of an ideal society in which division and dissension were submerged in the common dream of princes, prelates, and people that they might banish force and corruption from the world to usher in a reign of peace, justice, and perfect order. The crisis of the Aquitanian Peace movement represents in miniature, as it were, the entire course of the eleventh-century revolution. It displays in full the dilemma more familiar at center stage during the papal reform a generation later. Again and again as the eleventh century proceeded, the dream would be invoked to bring the force of popular enthusiasm to the aid of reform, most dramatically and devastatingly by the pope himself

---

[42] Dominique Iogna-Prat, *Agni immaculati: Recherches sur les sources hagiographiques relatives à saint Maieul de Cluny (954–994)* (Paris, 1988), pp. 305–57. His conclusions allow us the rare pleasure of supplying a deficiency of Gibbon: "I remember reading somewhere the confessions of a Benedictine abbot: my vow of poverty has brought me an income of an hundred thousand crowns a year; my vow of obedience has brought me the power of a sovereign prince. I forget the consequence of his vow of chastity"; Edward Gibbon, *The Decline and Fall of the Roman Empire*, chap. 37, Everyman ed. (London, 1910), 4:14, note 5.

[43] Bisson, "Organized Peace."

when Gregory VII called on the people of Europe to sit in judgment of their priests and bishops and boycott the services of those whom they found simoniac or uncelibate. In that case too the reform ushered in a new order before it lost its radical vision and accommodated itself to the realities of power. In that case too some of those who felt that their revolution had been betrayed lost faith in the integrity and authority of the church and were repressed as heretics by the victors.

Perhaps we have been sufficiently reminded at the approach of the second millennium of the Christian era how sudden, how mysterious, and how irresistible may be the conviction of a seemingly helpless and quiescent populace that the brutality and corruption of an old order can be tolerated no longer. Like much else, that force was new in the eleventh century and contributed indispensably to the building of a new Europe. Yet if, as has been alleged, the eleventh century was the first in European history in which the crowd played its part on the stage of public affairs, we had best remember also that when the play was over the people of Europe were a good deal less free than they had been before, even if they did have a new civilization to show for it. In all these respects the movement for the Peace of God was, for better or for worse, the harbinger of a new age.

Selected Documents on the
Peace of God in Translation

DOCUMENT 1. The acts of the council of Charroux (989). Mansi 19:89–90. Translation by Thomas Head.

Supported by the authority of the councils of our predecessors and in the name of God and of our savior Jesus Christ, I, Gunbaldus, archbishop of the second province of Aquitaine have gathered together along with my fellow bishops in this court which is called Charroux on this first day of June. These bishops, as well as clerics and monks, not to mention laypeople of both sexes, have beseeched the aid of divine justice. Our purpose is that the criminal activity, which we know has for some time been sprouting up through evil habit in our districts because of our long delay in calling a council, will be rooted out and more lawful activity implanted. Therefore we who are specially gathered together in the name of God decree, as will be made manifestly clear in the following canons, that: (1) If anyone attacks the holy church, or takes anything from it by force, and compensation is not provided, let him be anathema. (2) If anyone takes as booty sheep, oxen, asses, cows, female goats, male goats, or pigs from peasants [agricolae] or from other poor people [pauperes]—unless it is due to the fault of the victim—and if that person neglects to make reparation for everything, let him be anathema. (3) If anyone robs, or seizes, or strikes a priest, or a deacon, or any man of the clergy [ex clero] who is not bearing arms (that is, a shield, a sword, a breastplate, or a helmet), but who is simply going about his business or remaining at home, and if, after examination by his own bishop, that person is thus found to be guilty of any crime, then he is guilty of sacrilege, and if he furthermore does not come forward to make satisfaction, let him then be held to be excluded from the holy church of God.

[signed by] Gunbaldus, archbishop of Bordeaux; Gilbert, bishop of Poitiers; Hildegar, bishop of Limoges; Frotarius, bishop of Périgueux; Abbo, bishop of Saintes; Hugh, bishop of Angoulême

DOCUMENT 2. Letaldus of Micy: *Delatio corporis s. Juniani ad synodem Karoffensem* (989). *PL* 137:823–26. Composed mid-990s(?). Translation by Thomas Head.

Brother Letaldus gives salutations to Lord father Constantine and to the other brothers of the monastery of Nouaillé. The angel Gabriel was once sent by the Lord to alleviate the labors of Tobias. The angel not only delivered him from toil but also gave him the support of the kindness of divine piety. Then he returned to him by whom he had been sent, going forth from whom does not make one absent. Gabriel first taught those who had benefited from heavenly kindness and addressed them, saying, "It is good to hide the secret of a king, but gloriously to reveal the works of God" [Tobias *12*:7, RSV]. Therefore it is fitting that we reveal and confess the works of Christ which are allowed to happen in our times through his most glorious confessor Junianus, both for the praise and glory of the saint's name and for the edification of those who will hear the story. All people should learn these things, for such works as were done in the days of our fathers and are still done for us now do not happen on account of our own merits but through the kindness of piety and the intervention of those fathers who are provided as intercessors for us. They provide something for us to copy in the important correction of our own lives.

We therefore approach the task of writing this work which we have promised, not trusting in the help of men, but supported by the aid of divine largess, which comes from him who said, "Open your mouth wide and I will fill it" [Psalm 81:10, RSV]. Reverend fathers and brothers, you have begged us with your prayers and you have enjoined me by your charitable command. Do not allow our rustic speech to be displeasing to you, if only so that truth alone may bring forth the whole narrative, as it was told by you. At that time sinners were rising up like stalks of wheat. Evil people wasted the vineyard of the Lord just as briars and thorns choke the harvest of the land. Therefore it pleased bishops, abbots, and other religious men that a council be held at which the taking of booty [*praeda*] would be prohibited and the property of the saints, which had been unjustly stolen, would be restored. Other evils that fouled the fair countenance of the holy church of God were also struck down by the sharp points of anathemas. I think that this council was held at the monastery of Charroux and that a great crowd of many people [*populus*] gathered there from the Poitou, the Limousin, and neighboring regions. Many bodies of saints were also brought there. The cause of religion was strengthened by their presence, and the impudence of evil people was beaten back. That council—convoked, as it was thought, by divine will—was adorned by frequent miracles through the presence of these saints. Along with these various relics of the saints honored by God, the remains of the glorious father Junianus were brought with proper honor.

Several things occurred when the relics of the holy father Junianus were brought forth from their monastic enclosure. Not far from the monastery [of Nouaillé], those who carried the bundle containing the saint stopped and put down their holy burden. After the most holy relics departed, the faithful in their devotion erected a cross in order to memorialize and record the fact that the relics of the holy father had rested there. From that time to this, whosoever suffers from a fever and goes there is returned to their former health through the invocation of the name of Christ and the intercession of this same father Junianus. When the party came to the little village called Ruffiacus, they sought out the manse house and passed the night there in a vigil singing hymns and praise to God. The next day they resumed their journey. At the place where the relics had rested, faithful Christians erected a sort of fence from twigs, so that the place where the holy body had lain might remain safe from the approach of men and animals. Many days later a wild bull came by and wantonly struck that same fence with his horns and side, when suddenly he retreated from the fence, fell down, and died. In that same place a little pool was created by placing a gutter tile to allow run-off water to be stored up. Because of the reverence for the holy relics, this pool served as an invitation for many people to wash. Among these there was a woman who suffered from elephantiasis. When she washed herself with that water, she was returned to her former health.

DOCUMENT 3. Ademar of Chabannes on the first council of Limoges (994). *Chronicon*, 3.35, p. 158. Composed ca. 1026(?). Translation by Richard Landes.

In those times, the pestilence of fire burned over the Limousin, for the bodies of men and women without number were devoured by an invisible fire and everywhere their wailing filled the earth. Therefore

Gosfridus, abbot of Saint-Martial . . . and Alduin the bishop [of Limoges] held council with William the duke [of Aquitaine] and declared a three-day fast. Then all the bishops in Aquitaine came together in Limoges, and bodies and relics of the saints were solemnly brought there, and the body of Martial, patron of Gaul, was raised up. Whence an enormous joy filled everyone, and all sickness everywhere ceased; and a pact of peace and justice was then concluded by the duke and his lords.

DOCUMENT 4. The acts of the council of Poitiers (1000/14). Mansi 19:265–68. Translation by Phillippe Buc.

Handsome indeed is the name of peace, and beautiful the belief in unity, which Christ ascending to heaven left to his disciples. Therefore on the first of January, William duke of Poitiers summoned a council, and five bishops convened in Poitiers, Siguinus archbishop of Bordeaux, Gilbert bishop of Poitiers, Hilduin bishop of Limoges, Grimoard of the city of Angoulême, Islo bishop of Saintes, and twelve abbots, to restore peace. The duke and the other princes swore this restoration of peace and of justice [*iustitia*] by providing hostages and by accepting the threat of excommunication.

Canons:
1. All shall stand trial about disputed possessions in the presence of the prince or of a judge.

[The princes and bishops] decreed that, for disputes that would arise in the counties whose princes were present there concerning whatever possessions had been usurped during the preceeding five years or would be usurped from the time of the council onward, if one of the parties [to the dispute] called the other party to justice for these possessions, they should come into the presence of the prince of that region or of one judge of that county and stand trial [*iustitia*] for these possessions. And should one refuse to submit to the strictures of judgment [*iustitia*], let the prince or judge of this guilty party either enforce judgment [*iustitia*] or forfeit his hostages. And should he be unable to do justice [*iustitia*], let him convoke the princes and bishops who ordained this council and let all unanimously set out to destroy and trouble him, and let him endure this persecution and troubling until he returns to the rectitude of justice [*iustitia*]. Therefore, to confirm these things, hostages were given and a threat of excommunication laid down at the council, so that from that day on no one might break into a church, and so on, as had been decreed at the council of Charroux.

2. A bishop shall not demand gifts for penitence or confirmation.

Let no priest receive a gift for penance or for any gift of the Holy Spirit,[1] unless it is freely given.

3. Priests or deacons who have women in their house shall lose their clerical order.

Let no priest or deacon hold a woman in his house, or in the cellar, or introduce her in a secret place to fornicate. For should he attempt to do this, let him know that he shall lose all clerical orders and not celebrate the sacred mysteries [of the mass] with other men. Indeed, whoever eats and drinks unworthily eats his own damnation [see 1 Cor. 11:29]. And blessed Gregory [says]: "There is no good work without chastity, nor indeed is chastity much without good works" [see Homily 13; *PL* 76:1124].

DOCUMENT 5. Bernard of Angers: a miracle worked by the relics of Saint Faith at a council in the Rouergue (ca. 1012). *Liber mirac. s. Fidis*, 1.28–29, pp. 71–73. Translation by Thomas Head.

I do not think that the following should be omitted. Among the many bodies of saints that are carried to councils according to the custom of this province, that of Saint Faith, who holds as it were the princely role, particularly shines with the glory of miracles.[2] Of the many that have occurred [at these councils], we think it sufficient to note [the following], lest we seem to be dragging this book out tediously. The most reverend Arnaldus, bishop of Rodez, called together a synod from his parishes, to which the bodies of saints were brought in golden reliquaries, which took the form of both chests and statues, from various communities of monks and canons. In the field of Saint-Felix, which is about one mile from the town, the battleline of the saints was drawn up in tents and pavilions. The following images decorated that place: the golden statue reliquary [*maiestas*] of Saint Marius, confessor and bishop; the golden statue reliquary [*maiestas*] of Saint Amantius, also a confessor and bishop; the golden chest reliquary [*capsa*] of Saint Saturninus, martyr; the golden image [*imago*] of Mary, the holy mother of God; and the golden statue reliquary of Saint Faith.[3] Besides

---

[1] That is, for any sacrament or church ritual or clerical ordination.

[2] Saint Faith was a girl from the city of Agen who, according to legend, had been martyred at the age of twelve in 303. In the ninth century the monks of Conques had stolen her body from the monastery of Figeac. Bernard of Angers, a student of Bishop Fulbert of Chartres, made three pilgrimages to Conques and composed a large collection of miracle stories in the saint's honor.

[3] Saint Marius was a bishop of Clermont and patron of the abbey of Vabres. Saint Amantius was an early bishop (ca. 400) and patron of the diocese of Rodez; his relics were venerated in a monastery named in his honor located near the cathedral. Saint

these there were many relics of other saints, whose number cannot be listed in the present pages. Among the other events that occurred there was one of fame and marvel which was chosen in its goodness by the almighty as a means of glorifying his faithful servant. A boy who had been born blind and lame, deaf and dumb, was supported by his kinsmen and placed before the image that held the honor of the chief rank. Remaining there for about an hour, he was granted [a cure from] divine medicine. Endowed with complete deliverance through grace, he arose speaking, hearing, seeing, and even walking happily about on untroubled feet. When the cries of the commonfolk [*vulgus*] went up over such a prodigy, the lords of the council, who were deliberating at some remove, began to inquire among themselves, saying, "What are the people making this racket about?" Countess Berthilda answered, "What could it possibly be, except Saint Faith making jokes [*ioca*] as usual?" When the matter had been investigated, everyone there was filled with wonder as much as with joy. They urged the entire assembly to divine praise and recalled with great happiness how the venerable lady had said that Saint Faith was only joking.[4]

DOCUMENT 6. Peace oath proposed by Bishop Warin of Beauvais to King Robert the Pious (1023). Vatican, Reg. lat. 566, fol. 38v.[5] Translation by Richard Landes.

I will not invade a church for any reason. Nor will I invade the storehouses on the premises of a church because of its protected status, unless to catch [someone who has committed] a homicide, or a wrongdoer who broke this peace, or a horse. But if I invade a storehouse for such a reason, I will, to my knowledge, take out nothing more than that wrongdoer or his equipment. I will not assault an unarmed cleric or monk, nor anyone walking with him who is not carrying a spear or a shield, nor will I seize their horse unless they are committing a crime or unless it is in recompense for a crime for which they would not make

---

Saturninus was the first bishop and patron of Toulouse. Saint Faith's body was kept in a reliquary at Conques; her head, encased in a jewel-encrusted golden statue, remains today one of the most famous works of metalwork dating to the Romanesque period in France.

[4] According to the testimony of Bernard of Angers, there seems to have been an entire category of miracle ascribed to Saint Faith at Conques which were considered such playful jokes.

[5] Published in Christian Pfister, *Etudes sur le règne de Robert le Pieux (996–1031)* (Bibliothèque de l'Ecole des Hautes Etudes, 64; Paris, 1885), pp. lx–lxi; and Roger Bonnaud-Delamare, "Les institutions de paix dans la provence ecclésiastique de Reims au onzième siècle," *Bulletin philologique et historique du comité des travaux historiques et scientifiques (jusqu'à 1715)*, 1957, pp. 148–53.

amends, fifteen days after my warning. I will not seize bulls, cows, pigs, sheep, lambs, goats, asses or the burden they bear, mares, or their untamed colts.

I will not seize villeins of either sex, or sergeants or merchants, or their coins, or hold them for ransom, or ruin them with exactions on account of their lord's war, or whip them for their possessions. I will not exact by extortion mules and horses, male and female, and colts pasturing in the fields from the first of March to All Souls' Day, unless I should find them doing damage to me. I will not burn or destroy houses unless I find an enemy horseman or thief within, and unless they are joined to a real castle. I will not cut down or uproot the vineyards of another, or harvest them for reasons of war, unless it is on my land, or what, to my knowledge, ought to be my land. I will not destroy a mill, or seize the grain that is in it, unless I am on a cavalcade, or with the host, or it is on my land.

I will not, to my knowledge, harbor or assist an admitted and notorious public robber. And that man who will break this peace knowingly, I will not protect him after I learn of it, and if he did it unknowingly and came to me for protection, either I will make amends for him, or I will make him make amends within fifteen days after I have been informed, or I will deny him my protection.

I will not attack merchants or pilgrims or take their possessions unless they commit crimes. I will not kill the animals of villeins except for my consumption or that of my men. I will not plunder a villein or take his property at the perfidious instigation of his lord. I will not assault noble women in the absence of their husbands, or those who travel with them, unless I should find them committing misdeeds against me; and the same holds for widows and nuns. I will not take wine from those who carry it in carts or take their oxen. I will not capture hunters or take their horses or dogs, unless, as it is said, I find them doing me damage. And from those who will have sworn this [oath] and keep it in my regard—with the exception of lands that are mine by freehold or benefice or by delegation, and except when building or besieging a castle, or when I am in the host of the king or our bishops, or on cavalcade—I will accept only what I need for subsistence, and I will take nothing home with me except horseshoes, and I will not break into the protected areas of churches while on the aforementioned military expeditions, unless they refuse to sell me what I need to live.

From the beginning of Lent until the end of Easter, I will not assault unarmed horsemen or take their possessions, and if a villein should do damage to another villein or horseman, before I seize him, first I will make complaints about him and await fifteen days for satisfaction before punishing him, but no more than the law allows.

The above-written was sworn in these words. You heard this, King Robert, just as recorded in this brief text, and as I, Bishop Warin, in this last hour set forth and just as those present now heard and understood. Thus I expect from my part against those who swear this oath now and will swear it between now and the feast of Saint John next June, and from the festival for six years, with the exception of royal war . . .

DOCUMENT 7. The acts of the council of Elne-Toulouges (1027). Mansi 19:483–84. Translation by Phillippe Buc.

The twenty-seventh year after the millennium of the Lord's incarnation, on the sixteenth day of May, Oliba pontiff of Vic, in the stead of Berengar bishop of Elne (at that time a pilgrim to the Holy Land) met along with Udalcher archpriest of the holy church of Elne and archdeacon Gaucelin and Ellemachus, churchwarden and precentor, and Gauzbert, and the aforementioned see's other canons and an assembly of the sacred dukes and a crowd of the faithful (not only men, but also women). They met in the county of Roussillon, in the meadow of Toulouges. And when they met there, they first asked for the Lord's mercy, that he might convert his faithful's heart and direct their minds and deeds to himself. They inquired whether the statutes hitherto laid down by the aforesaid bishops were observed. But when they found that all of them were not only trampled underfoot but also forgotten, they strove to renew them in those terms in which they had been first established.

Therefore, the aforesaid bishops (along with all the clergy and faithful people) established that no one dwelling in the aforesaid county and diocese would assail any enemy of his from the ninth hour on Saturday to the first hour on Monday, so that everyone would render the honor owed to the Lord's day. And no one would assail in any way a monk or cleric traveling without arms, or any man going to or returning from church with his kin,[6] or any man accompanying women. Nor should anyone dare to violate or assault a church or houses located within a radius of thirty yards [from a church]. And they established this pact or truce [*truce*] because the divine law and almost all of the Christian way of life had been reduced to naught (as it is read), and because iniquity was rife and love was becoming cold. And therefore we the aforesaid bishop, along with the clergy and every order serving the Lord's cult, ordered and forbade before God that no man or woman

[6] The manuscript reads *consilia* (councils), for which we have interpolated *familia*.

should presume to defile or infringe anything of what is written above, or invade willfully the rightful possessions of the holy church of Elne, of other churches, or of the monasteries. Nor should anyone knowingly remain in an incestuous marriage up to the sixth degree [of consanguinity]. And should one have done this (and continue to do so from now on), unless he comes to his right mind and amends as far as he can and gives full satisfaction within a space of three months to holy mother church in the presence of the aforesaid canons, let him remain excommunicate and outside the limits of the holy church and of the community of all Christians.

And let you all know how great a sin it is to associate with excommunicates. No Christian should eat or drink with them, or give them a kiss, or speak with them (unless about making amends). Nor should they be buried in churches if they die excommunicate, nor should any cleric or faithful pray for them. And should they spurn excommunication after three months have lapsed, let them be bound with the bond of anathema, that is, to be condemned to perdition like the traitor Judas. And should they (may God prevent this!) die in this faithlessness, their bodies shall not be led to burial with psalms and hymns or spiritual chants, and their names shall not be recited at the altar among those of the faithful dead. And since they sinned up until their death, unless they do penance, they shall be condemned to endless and eternal damnation.

In the presence of God and of his saints, we forbid all the canons of the aforesaid see lest any of them should dare absolve any of these faults without the consent of the aforesaid archpriest and archdeacons, and of the churchwarden and master of the school, and of the other brother canons. Let the divine ministries be performed without interruption for the excommunicate for the space of three months, so that God grants them penance and they recover from the devil's snares (in which they are caught to do his will). And should one refuse to accomplish this, let him know that, unless he comes to his senses, he shall be punished with the excommunication laid down above. But let the Lord Jesus Christ grant eternal peace and mercy to all those who shall observe the aforesaid. Amen.

DOCUMENT 8. Excerpts from the *Gesta episcoporum Cameracensium* (1024–36). *MGH SS* 7:475, 585. Translation by Richard Landes.

3.27. At the same time, seeing that the condition of the realm tottered on its foundations, and that the incompetence of the king and the sins [of men] confounded the laws and profaned the customs of the fathers as well as all manner of justice, the bishops Berold of Soissons and Warin of Beauvais tried to save much of the public interest by following the opinions of the Burgundian bishops. These [bishops], surely devoid of all authority, had made a common decree, that all men should be constrained by an oath, themselves as well as others, that they should become servants of peace and justice. Aroused therefore by such a device, the aforementioned bishops, conspiring with their fellow bishops of upper Gaul, all urged even Lord Bishop Gerard to join them. He, considering issues more deeply, thought to reject it completely, and considering this council pernicious and impossible gave no assent to them. This plan, he answered, seemed not so much impossible as inappropriate, since they claimed for themselves what was royal right. In this way they actually confounded the condition of the holy church, which ought to be administered by twin persons, that is, the royal and priestly. The latter are assigned to pray, the former to fight. Therefore it is the job of kings to put down sedition with strength, and to check wars, to spread the commerce of peace; and it is [the task] of bishops to urge the kings to fight vigorously for the safety of the fatherland, so that they might conquer in prayer. Therefore this decree was most dangerous to all; all either had to swear or be anathematized. All indeed would be caught up in this common sin, were they to use this idea. And thus the other bishops rejected the dissenting bishop with private censures, saying that he who disagreed with those desiring peace was not a friend of peace. But afterward, yielding unwillingly to urgent exhortation, especially from the abbots of Saint-Vaast and Saint-Bertin, he agreed. But what he had warned of beforehand, events later proved correct. Very few escaped the crime of perjury . . .

3.52. In the same fashion, the French bishops promulgated a decree for their subjects. One of them claimed he had a letter sent from heaven which demanded that peace on earth be renewed. He communicated this matter to the others and gave these issues to be conveyed to the people: no one should bear arms, or attack for plunder; an avenger of his own blood or of his neighbor's should be compelled to forgive the murderers; let [all] observe fasting on bread and water every Friday, and on the Sabbath [abstention] from meat and fat; and content with this fast alone for the satisfaction of all sins, they should know that no further penitence may be added.

And they should confirm by oath that they will observe these things; and those who refuse should be deprived of Christianity. And they passed many other rules that would be burdensome here to recount. Our bishop, alarmed by this novelty, and condescending to the weakness of sinners, prepared a speech according to the decrees of the holy fathers. He showed that the human race had been divided from the beginning into three parts: prayers, farmers, and fighters; and he gave a clear document showing that each of these fosters the others with right and left hand.

DOCUMENT 9. Charter from the abbey of Saint-Maixent (1032). *Chartes et docs. de Saint-Maixent*, no. 41, p. 108. Translation by Richard Landes.[7]

When the status of the holy church, wandering among the choppy waves of the world, seemed to fail, and innumerable diabolically inspired crimes were destroying holy religion, the compassionate Lord, not allowing Zabulus to prevail and long dominate the world, at length permitted a solution with the [following] keys, and thereby to call back [men] to the pristine practices of holy religion.

Therefore, with the mercy of the most benevolent creator, it was established under the princes of the Aquitanians, by the king, that is, by Robert, justly ordering the kingdom of the Franks, and by the dukes living under his rule, and also many bishops, and various priests together with every order of clerics, that councils should be celebrated in every city. And with an innumerable multitude of people [*plebs*] gathered there, as much of nobles as of the powerless, they should treat matters concerning the Catholic faith and the holy church of God, so that a faith improved in all things be affirmed by God.

Among others in various parts it happened that a council was held at the town of Poitiers by the duke, that is, most noble William [VI], under Isembert the bishop of that same town, and Jordan the bishop of Limoges, and Arnold the bishop of Périgueux, and various orders of Christians, that is to say, abbots, monks, and clerics as well as the faithful people. When, therefore, they had discussed many things, they decreed that if any man should dishonestly or violently take possession of the property of the holy church, or unjustly seize it, he should restore it with the greatest zeal, so that the church might obtain the lands of the monasteries whole and free. And thus all decreed that it be done, and they confirmed it with oaths and excommunication.

[The text goes on to deal with a specific case in which the monastery of Saint-Maixent objected to "evil customs" (*malae consuetudines*) that the duke's agents and justices committed through "lies and cupidity, passing unjust judgment and condemning the powerless." The duke then acknowledged the monastery's independence from his agents.]

[7] Dated on the basis of an entry in *La chronique de Saint-Maixent, 751–1140*, ed. and trans. Jean Verdon (Les classiques de l'histoire de France au moyen âge, 33; Paris, 1979), p. 114.

DOCUMENT 10. Rodulphus Glaber on events in the year 1033. *Histori-arum* 4.5.13–17. Composed late 1030s(?). Translation by Richard Landes.

4.5.13. As a result of the sins of men, the destruction of this plague raged over the world for three years. . . . It seemed as if the order of times and elements, which had from the beginning controlled past ages, had plunged into perpetual chaos and the destruction of the human race was at hand.

4.5.14. [But] at the millennial anniversary of the passion of the Lord [1033], the clouds cleared in obedience to divine mercy and goodness, and the smiling sky began to shine and blow gentle breezes, declaring with its serenity the magnanimity of the Creator. . . . At that point, in the region of Aquitaine, bishops, abbots, and other men devoted to holy religion first began to gather councils of the whole people [*populus*]. At these gatherings the bodies of many saints and shrines containing holy relics were assembled. From there through the provinces of Arles and of Lyon, then through all of Burgundy, and finally in the farthest corners of France [*ad ultimas partes Franciae*], it was proclaimed in every diocese that councils would be summoned in fixed places by bishops and by the magnates of the whole land for the purpose of reforming both the peace and the institutions of the holy faith. When the news of these assemblies was heard, the entire populace [*tota multitudo universae plebis*] joyfully came, unanimously prepared to follow whatever should be commanded them by the pastors of the church. A voice descending from heaven could not have done more. For everyone was still under the effects of the previous calamities and feared the future loss of sweet abundance.

4.5.15. A notice divided by chapters contained the list of forbidden actions and sacred commitments made to God. The most important was to observe an inviolable peace so that men of either condition, whatever previous threats had hung over them, could go anywhere completely tranquil and without arms. Whoever stole or broke into the property of another was to be constrained by the full rigor of the law [*legum distinctione artatus*] and was to be most energetically punished with the most energetic fine or physical punishment.

4.5.16. There were many other decisions made at those councils, one of which was to dignify the sixth day by not drinking wine and the seventh day by abstaining from meat unless one was gravely ill or it was a most important holy day. If one had to relax this prohibition for some reason, he should feed three poor people in compensation.

Innumerable sick people were healed at these gatherings of the saints. But lest someone find these miracles frivolous, it happened many times that at the moment the twisted arm or leg returned to its pristine rectitude, skin cracked, flesh tore, and blood flowed copiously. This then proved the validity of those other miraculous cures where doubt might have remained. These miracles aroused such enthusiasm that the bishops raised their staffs toward heaven and all present stretched their palms to God, shouting with one voice "Peace! Peace! Peace!" It was as the sign of their perpetual covenant [*signum perpetui pacti*] which they had vowed between themselves and God. It was also understood that every five years throughout the globe everyone would confirm this grace of peace in a marvelous manner. And that year there was such an abundance of grain and wine and other fruits of the earth that one could scarce hope for so many in the next five years. Indeed, any human victuals could be had for nothing that year, aside from meat and delicacies: it was the beginning of that antique great jubilee of Moses. In the next, the third, and the fourth year, similar abundance prevailed.

4.5.17. But alas! how painful! the human race, ever forgetful of the beneficence of God, prone to evil like a dog returning to its vomit, or a sow wallowing in the stye, repeatedly violated its own covenant [*pactum sponsionis*] and, as it is written: "You grew thick, you grew sleek and you kicked" [Deut. 32:15].

DOCUMENT 11. Andrew of Fleury: activities of the Peace league of Bourges in 1038. *Mirac. s. Benedicti*, 5.1–4, pp. 192–98. Composed 1040–43. Translation by Thomas Head.

5.1. In the 1038th year after the incarnation of the Lord, on the eighth day of August, in the middle of the day, the sun was darkened and hid the rays of its splendors for a space of almost two hours. Again the following morning it remained under the same appearance for the entire day and unremittingly gave off bloody flames.

5.2. At this very same time, Archbishop Aimon of Bourges wished to impose peace in his diocese through the swearing of an oath. After he had summoned the fellow bishops of his province and had sought advice from these suffragens, he bound all men of fifteen years of age and over by the following law: that they would come forth with one heart as opponents of any violation of the oath they had sworn, that they would in no way withdraw secretly from the pact even if they should lose their property, and that, what is more, if necessity should demand it, they would go after those who had repudiated the oath with arms. Nor were ministers of the sacraments excepted, but they often took banners from the sanctuary of the Lord and attacked the

violators of the sworn peace with the rest of the crowd of laypeople
[*populus*]. In this way they many times routed the faithless and brought
their castles down to the ground. With the help of God they so terrified the rebels that, as the coming of the faithful was proclaimed far
and wide by rumor among the populace, the rebels scattered. Leaving
the gates of their towns open, they sought safety in flight, harried
by divinely inspired terror. You would have seen [the faithful] raging
against the multitude of those who ignore God, as if they were some
other people of Israel. Presently they trampled [the rebels] underfoot
so that they forced them to return to the laws of the pact which they
had ignored.

We thought it fitting to insert in writing that which was agreed to in
the pact which the archbishop himself, along with various fellow bishops, promised under oath in the following way: "I Aimon, by the gift of
God archbishop of Bourges, promise with my whole heart and mouth
to God and to his saints that I shall discharge with my whole spirit and
without any guile or dissimulation everything that follows. That is, I
will wholeheartedly attack those who steal ecclesiastical property, those
who provoke pillage, those who oppress monks, nuns, and clerics, and
those who fight against holy mother church, until they repent. I will
not be beguiled by the enticement of gifts, or moved by any reason of
bonds of kinship or neighborliness, or in any way deviate from the path
of righteousness. I promise to move with all my troops against those
who dare in any manner to transgress the decrees and not to cease in
any way until the purpose of the traitor has been overcome."

He swore this over the relics of Stephen, the first martyr for Christ,
and urged the other [bishops] to do likewise. Obeying with one heart,
his fellow bishops made among everyone age fifteen or older (as we already said) in their separate dioceses subscribe [the pact] with the same
promise. Fear and trembling then struck the hearts of the unfaithful so
that they feared the multitude of the unarmed peasantry as if it were
a battleline of armored men. Their hearts fell so that, forgetting their
status as knights and abandoning their fortified places, they fled from
the humble peasants as from the cohorts of very powerful kings. The
prayer of David fitted the situation most aptly: "For thou dost deliver
a humble people, but the haughty eyes thou dost bring down, for who
is God but the Lord?" [Psalm 18:27, 31, RSV]. . . . Odo of Déols remained alone among the whole multitude [of rebels], reserved by the
judgment of God for the punishment of evil doers.

5.3. When by the will of God they had, trusting in the help of divine
strength, established peace in every direction, ambition (the root and
aid of all evil) began to seep along the stalks of such good works. They
forgot that God is the strength and rampart of his people and ascribed
the power of God to their apostate power. . . . Thus the aforemen-

tioned bishop was touched by the sting of mammon and raged around and around in blind ambition. Unmindful of his episcopal dignity, he attacked Beneciacum, the castle of one Stephen, along with a multitude of the people [*populus*] of Bourges. He reproached Stephen for the fault of having ignored the peace, he tried to burn the castle with flames and ordered it to be leveled to the ground, as if he were exacting the vengeance of God upon it. They burned the castle, which was hemmed in on all sides by the siege, with more than one thousand four hundred people of both sexes inside. Stephen alone of that great number escaped, although his brothers, wife, and sons were all consumed by the fire, and he placed the laurel wreath of his great victory on their wretched heads. The inhabitants of that region for a radius of fourteen miles had fled to this castle and, since they feared the theft of their possessions, they had brought them along. The cruel victors were hardly moved by the laments of the dying, they did not take pity on women beating their breasts, the crowd of infants clinging to their mothers' breasts did not touch any vein of mercy. . . . And so the just bore responsibility for the crime of the iniquitous and the just perished in place of the impious. Having been granted this great triumph, the people returned to their homes dancing with a pitiable joy. Stephen was placed under guard in a prison in Bourges.

54 Almighty God wished to avenge the blood of his servants and, not long after this, set the aforesaid bishop against Odo, the sole rebel. The bishop sought to force Odo to join in the pact common to all, but he would not delay in making an armed attack. Discovering that Odo's spirit remained inflexible, as was God's will, Aimon began—while the blood of the innocents was not yet dry—to collect allies together from all sides, including a large contingent of God's ministers. Confiding in lesser things, he directed his battleline against the enemy. When both armies stood almost at grips, a sound was made heavenward [indicating that Aimon's forces should] retreat, since they no longer had the Lord with them as a leader. When they made no sign of following this advice, an enormous globe of flashing light fell in their midst. Thus it came to pass, as it is said, "Flash forth the lightning and scatter them, send out the arrows and rout them!" [Psalm 144:6, RSV]. Then the people [*populus*] perceived that they were much inferior to their adversaries, since those exceeded in number the sands of the sea. They decided that some foot soldiers should be mounted on various animals and mixed into the cohorts of mounted warriors [*milites*] so that they would be judged mounted warriors by their opponents, more because of the appearance of their being mounted than because of the setting of their weapons. Without delay up to two thousand of the plebeian rabble were mounted on asses and arrayed as knight [*equestri*] among the order of knights. But these men were terrified and they took flight

along the banks of the Cher. They were killed in such numbers that they blocked the river in such a way that they made a bridge out of the bodies of the dying over which their enemies proceeded. More fell by their own swords than by those of their pursuers. . . . The number of the dying could not be comprehended: in one valley seven hundred clerics fell. Thus the most tempered judgment of God made those people—who had refused obedience to any requests for mercy, and had not been moved by the smell of their brothers' being burned, and had rejoiced more than was just to have their hands in an unfortunate victory—lost their lives along with that victory.

DOCUMENT 12. Rodulphus Glaber on the Truce of God (1041). *Historiarum* 5.1.15–16. Composed ca. 1044(?). Translation by Richard Landes.

5.1.15. It happened about that time [*1041*] that, by the inspiration of divine grace, a pact was confirmed starting in Aquitaine and then gradually spreading throughout Gaul; according to this men agreed, through both love and fear of the Lord, that from Wednesday evening to dawn the following Monday no man might presume to steal by force from another, or take vengeance on an enemy or even take a pledge from an oathtaker. Whoever broke this public decree should either die or be driven from his own country and the company of Christians. It further unanimously pleased all that this should be called, in the vulgar tongue, the Truce of God [*treuga Dei*], since it was upheld not only by human sanctions but also by oft-displayed divine terrors.

Various raging fools in their audacity did not fear to break the pact, and immediately divine retribution or the avenging human sword appeared. This happened so often in so many places that I cannot record individual instances. This was only just. For just as Sunday is considered holy in recollection of the resurrection of our Lord (and called the octave), so the fifth, sixth, and seventh days, out of reverence for the supper and passion of our Lord, should be free of iniquitous deeds.

5.1.16. And it happened that while this statute was, as we have said, strictly observed throughout almost all of Gaul, the people of Neustria refused to adopt it. [Glaber details the devastation of the war between Henry I and the sons of Odo of Blois.] Then, by a hidden judgment of God, divine vengeance rained furiously upon that people. A deadly fever consumed many people, as many from the magnates as from the middling and the least of people. It spared some, indeed, with an arm or a leg amputated, to serve as examples for future generations. And then the people of almost the entire world endured a famine for lack of wine and wheat.

"To Control Military Requisitions": A Letter from Hincmar of Reims to Charles the Bald (859)

SUMMARY: Hincmar knows that King Charles must deplore the evils that pagans and even Christians themselves have caused in the kingdom. Even more must the king lament those evils that occur in the palace, which is called "sacred," or in the places he either stays or traverses in his journeys. When the impending arrival of the royal entourage is announced in any given place, there is a reaction as if the army of the Antichrist were coming, an army that is always accompanied by evils. The archbishop knows that the king fears that the whole church in such a situation will pray to God: "Arise O Lord God and your hand be exalted!" [Psalm 10:12, RSV] Equally, he is sure that the king is aware of the misfortunes the people suffer.

TEXT: This is why, oh Lord, I do the only thing I can do, that is, to pray for God's mercy. Consequently I inform you that I have directed written instructions to the priests of the *villae* where your purveyors, who are actually great thieves, go to requisition supplies, so that the priests may read them out loud to these men. I send to your lordship a copy of these directions. Keep it secret and then, on the day that you fix, order your followers [*fideles*] to come to you. Then announce that you wish them to know whatever it is that it pleases you to tell them and then, before they return to their own estates, admonish them according to the wisdom God has given you.

PL 125:953–56. Translation by Elisabeth Magnou-Nortier (from Latin to French) and Amy G. Remensnyder (from French to English, with reference to the Latin). The purpose of this procedure was to reflect as exactly as possible in the English version Professor Magnou-Nortier's own rendering of the passage.

SUMMARY: Hincmar suggests to the king that he rely on his uncle Rudolph, a godfearing man who labors for the good of the realm. The archbishop also exhorts the king to exercise firmness but also discretion vis-à-vis his followers in order to sift out those who serve him well from among those who do not. The king, Hincmar remarks, is the one who best knows the qualities of each of his followers and thus is in the best position to do this.

TEXT: To those men whom you do not need to keep near you and who move from one of their estates to the next with nearly their whole household, and thus live off the labor of others, specify exactly the length of the sitting and the contributions they should bring there.[1] Then let them either return to their lands or stay with you with just a few followers so that they live according to justice. You should establish yourself in one of the more secure places of your realm until that time when you call for a full assembly of your followers in order to confront some new matter effecting the kingdom.

But I greatly fear that these men who thus offend against God and scarcely correct themselves will be able to help neither you nor themselves when it is necessary. Thus, as your predecessors customarily did, send ahead men who will prepare the stopping points for long journeys and who will have the mission of ensuring peace. But choose men unlike those of whom the apostle [Paul] said: "You, who preach that men should not steal, yourself steal" [Rom. 2:21]. As I have said, I send along to you a copy of the instructions that I gave to the *villae* so that you can, if you so desire, order them to be read out loud in your presence to your followers [*fideles*] after your own admonition. Announce to them that these are the words of God and that those who execute them are sent by God and that hence they must in no way ignore them or allow their men to do so.

Keep the copy I have sent you and the suggestions I have made secret so that no one except you knows anything beforehand. If anyone should, you might not benefit fully from these provisions. I urge that you decide to do the following: someone should daily in your name read these instructions out loud to those who have not yet heard them as soon as they arrive at your residence.

SUMMARY: Hincmar also recommends that the king reread carefully the provisions of the synod of Quierzy which had been sent to both him and his brother Louis but which had been drafted for his benefit rather

---

[1] The translation of the phrase *commendate quae vobis sunt placita et necessaria* is a provisional suggestion.

than that of Louis. In addition, three things had come to Hincmar's attention about which he had first judged it best to remain silent. But then he decided the contrary, believing that if he submitted these matters to the king for remedy it would be to the advantage of both of them.

TEXT: Of the three, I could not believe two; the third I had to, though unwillingly. This is the first. Many people say that you assert that you have no duty to get involved in cases dealing with requisitions and forced contributions [*rapinis atque depraedationibus*] and that everyone must defend himself as he can.[2] Although I know this to be a lie, as you indeed prove through your actions it to be, I wanted to inform you that evil-minded people and those who have certain complaints defame you with such rumors. Indeed, it is the office of the king to direct himself and his followers who do good toward what is better and to deflect bad people from evil. Hence it is not consonant with this office to demand from the realm and its subjects *dona et servitia* while not providing for them so that they might have the wherewithal to meet the exactions they do owe. Equally, it is contrary to the royal office to order and impose things that please the king while not forbidding or eliminating those things that displease God.

I presume to suggest these things to your lordship because the lands where fiscal revenues are the most concentrated have decreased in productivity since the realm of your father and grandfather was divided up.[3] It is necessary and in accord with the royal honor befitting you that there should be no further diminution of the revenues which your predecessors received from these lands and which pagans and false Christians have usurped along with the greater part of your kingdom. If you thus ruin the modest part where you and your followers must live, neither you nor they will have any hope of holding out there.

The second matter that has been brought to my attention is that those with complaints who come to your palace receive not only no solace but not even a good word. I did not want to believe this rumor any more than I had wanted to the first because I know that you keep in your heart what the Lord says: "He who stops his ears to the lamentations of the poor shall also complain and not be heard" [Prov. 21:13].

---

[2] *Depraedatio* is here distinguished from *rapina*. This distinction suggests that *rapina* would correspond to a requistition for which an indemnity was paid and *depraedatio* would correspond to a requisition for which there was none. This is, however, only a hypothesis. Devisse saw the exceptional significance of Hincmar's letter but did not exactly understand it, because he did not give the words their exact meaning; see J. Devisse, *Hincmar, archevêque de Reims (845–882)*, 3 vols. (Paris, 1975), 1:327–30.

[3] The expression *capitalia loca* has not yet drawn the attention of historians. It merits in particular that of economic historians.

SUMMARY: God, from whom nothing is hidden, cannot be made to listen to one who disobeys divine orders. It is in vain that such a person presents himself before the gates of the celestial kingdom.

TEXT: The third case, which I have to believe is true, is that, once all the necessary food and drink has been collected, the *raptores* demand a payment in cash [*redemptio*] from the churches and threaten to break in forcibly if they do not receive it. It is with deep sorrow that I admit that Christians can do such things. Paul reveals what he considers to be more grave than the gravest of sins, saying, "You, who abominate idols, commit sacrilege" [Rom. 2:22]. They add sacrilege to all their other sins and they do not abominate idols, since the same Saint Paul writes: "Avarice is the service of idols" [Eph. 5:5]. May the omnipotent God according to this same apostle grant that you may desire to and manage to accomplish in good will that task which has been commended to you and to us and to the realm entrusted to you.

The Latin Texts of the "Letter" of Heribert

Document 1. Paris, BN lat. 1745, f. 31r (early eleventh century). Originating from the scriptorium of Saint-Germain of Auxerre.

De quadam secta hereticorum [early thirteenth-century title]

Omnibus christianis qui sunt in oriente et occidente, meridie et aquilone, cre-
dentibus in Christo, pax et gra[-]
tia in Deo patre, filioque eius unigenito domino nostro, et spiritu sancto. Nova
heresis horta est in mundo,
incipiens hoc tempore a pseudo apostolis; ab ipso sui exordio sunt ministri totius iniquitatis.
qua de causa studemus ne in illorum heresim incidatis haec uobis scribere, et
cautos ac sollicitos
per omnia uos reddere. Surrexerunt igitur sicut veritas rei se habet nostri tempore in petra[-]
gorensem regionem quamplurimi heretici, qui pro eo ut christianitatem radic-
itus pervertant.
dicunt se apostolicam vitam ducere. Carnem non comedunt, uinum non bibunt
nisi per mo[-]
dicum tertio die. Centies genua flectunt, pecuniam non solum non recipiunt,
sed et habitam prout
uidetur decenter dispertiunt. Sed est illorum secta valde perversa, occultaque
ac decipiens. Nam ecclesiam
non intrant, nisi causa seductionis. *Gloria patri et filio et spiritui sancto* nusquam
dicunt, sed pro illa

These editions were prepared by Guy Lobrichon. They are exact renderings of the manuscript texts; no corrections whatsoever have been made. Document 1 is set to reproduce the line breaks of the manuscript.

dicunt *quoniam tuum est regnum, et tu dominaris omni creaturae in secula seculorum, amen.* Elemosinam dicunt

nihil esse, quia nec unde fieri possit debere possideri. Missam pro nichilo ducunt, nec communionem

debere percipi nisi solummodo fracmenta panis benedicti. Canticum ecclesiasticum vanum esse asserunt,

ac pro fauore hominum inuentum. Missam si quis horum decantaverit causa seductionis, nec canon

dicit, nec communionem recipit, sed aut retro aut iuxta altare uergit. Hostiam vero,

in missalem aut post altare proicit. Crucem seu vultum domini non adorant, sed et adorantes

prout possunt prohibent, ita ut ante uultum stantes fando dicant "O quam miseri sunt qui te

adorant, dicente psalmista. *Simulacra gentium*, et cetera" [Psalm 113:4; 134:15, Vulg.]. In hac itaque seductione

quamplurimos iam non solum laicos propria omnia relinquentes, sed etiam clericos, presbyteros, mona[-]

chos et monachas pertraxerunt. Itaque sunt mersi ut uelint inuenire qui eos crucient

et morti tradant. Faciunt enim multa signa. Nemo namque tam rusticus se cum eis iungit,

qui non infra octo dies sit sapiens, litteris, uerbis et exemplis, ut nec superari a quoquam

ulterius ullomodo possit. Ledi non possunt, quia etsi capiuntur. seruari nulla uinctione possunt.

Nam fui ego Erbertus monachorum omnium minimus auctor scripti huius ubi ferreis compedibus uincti

fuerunt missi in tonnam uinariam, fundum patentem habens, sursum clausum, deorsum custodibus

adhibitis. In crastinum non solum non sunt inuenti, sed nec semita eorum est inuenta usquequo se repre[-]

sentauerunt. Uas uini uacuum, ex suo uino parum intus misso, in crastinum plenum inuenitur.

Sed et alia quam mira faciunt, quae non possunt scribi. Has namque ceterasue regiones occulte

modo aggrediuntur.

DOCUMENT 2. Vesoul, BM 1, f. 165r. Manuscript copied in the third quarter of the twelfth century. Originating from the scriptorium of Luxeuil. Heribert's "Letter" is a contemporary addition on a folio the bottom part of which has been severely mutilated.

Omnibus christianis notum esse cupio ego Heribertus monacus ut se caute agant a pseudo apostolis qui christianitatem peruertere nituntur.[1] Surrexerunt

---

[1] Written over an erasure of *cupiunt*.

enim in Petragoricensi regione quamplurimi heretici, qui se dicunt apostolicam uitam ducere. Carnes non comedunt, uinum non bibunt nisi per modicum tercia dies, cencies in die genua flectunt. Pecuniam non solum non recipiunt, sed etiam habitam prout uidetur decenter despiciunt. Sed illorum secta ualde est peruersa occultaque atque despicabilis. *Gloria Patri* nunquam dicunt, sed pro *Gloria Patri* dicunt, *Quoniam tuum est regnum et tu dominaris universe creature in secula seculorum amen.* Elemosinam nil dicunt esse quia non unde posset fieri deberet possideri. Missam pro nichilo ducunt, nec communionem debere percipere, nisi fragmen panis. Missam si quis eorum decantauerit, presbyter causa seductionis non canonem dicit, non communionem recipit, sed aut retro aut iuxta uergit hostiamque autem in missale aut retro altare proicit. Crucem seu uultum Domini non adorant sed adorantes prout possunt prohiben[nt],[2] ita ut ante uultum Domini dicant "O quam miseri sunt qui te adorant dicente psalmista *Simulacra gencium arg[entum] et aurum* usque *similis illis fiant.*" In hac seductione quamplurimos non solum laicos nobiles propria relinquentes, sed [/ / / / /] prebyteros monacosque pertraxerunt. Nullus enim est si se cum eis iungit, quin infra octo dies sit sapiens, lit [/ / / / / /] nec exemplis superari poterit, nec ullo modo detineri poterit. Si capiuntur ulla uinctione seruar[/ / / / / / /] eos liberante. Et ita sunt miseri ut uelint inuenire qui eos crucient et morti tradent. Fa[/ / / / / / / /] Nam si alicubi ferreis cathenis uel compedibus uincti fuerint, et missi in tonnam uina[/ / / / / / / / /] clausum custodibus adhibitis, in crastinum non semita eorum inuenitur, usquequo se repres[/ / / / / / / / / /] ex suo uino parum inmisso plenum inuenitur. Aliaque permira faciunt que non p[/ / / / / / / / / / / / /] deficiente. Nam has cetereasque regiones occulto modo ingrediuntur, et n[/ / / / / / / / / / / / / / / / / /]quia cum eis sum satis altercatus, sed uerbis superari non possunt. Quicumque hec le[/ /] ac Germaniam cautos faciat, quia modo disperguntur Prince [pȝ]. [/ /].

DOCUMENT 3. Paris, BN Lat. 16208, f. 135v. From the last quarter of the twelfth century, or ca. 1200. Originating from the Sorbonne (Parisian hand).

Omnibus christianis Heribertus salus. Exierunt de petragorensi regione pseudo apostoli nostram pervertere cupientes christianitatem. Carnem non comedunt uinum non bibunt. nisi tertio die. et hoc parum. Cenies flectunt genua in die. *Gloria patri* non dicunt, sed pro *gloria patri* dicunt. *Quoniam tuum est regnum domine et tu dominaris universe creature in secula seculorum amen.* Missam pro nichilo reputant. et sanctam communionem. Cruces et uultus domini adorare prohibent. miseros eos uocantes qui ea adorant. prosternentes illud psalmiste. *Aures habent et non audient.* et cetera. usque *similis illis fient.* Elemosinam dicunt non debere dare. Multa miracula faciunt. Nemo est tam rudis. si cum eis.VII. diebus demoratus fuerit quin omni scripturarum scientia ita

---

[2] From here on, the end of each line has been cut off to a greater and greater degree.

edoctus sit. ut nec uerbis nec exemplis superari possit. Si in uase uacuo de vino quod portant guttam unam miserunt. cras plenum erit. nec uinculis nec catenis. nec quolibet modo teneri possunt. Magister eorum uocatur Pontius nomen cuius maledictionibus repleatur. Amen.

Hoc fuit anno domini Mo Co LXa IIIo.

Contributors

DANIEL F. CALLAHAN is Associate Professor of History at the University of Delaware. He has written several articles on the works of Ademar of Chabannes and is currently coediting, with Michael Frassetto, two volumes of the sermons of Ademar of Chabannes which will appear among his collected works in the Corpus Christianorum. He is completing a book entitled *When Heaven Came Down to Earth: The Peace of God in Aquitaine in the Tenth and Eleventh Centuries* and working on studies of Saint Michael the Archangel and the changing idea of Jerusalem in the west during the Benedictine centuries.

ANDRÉ DEBORD is Professor of Medieval History and Archeology at the University of Caen. He is the author of *La société laïque dans les pays de la Charente: Xe–XIIe siècles* (Paris, 1984) and of *Châteaux et société dans la France médiévale* (Paris, forthcoming). He has directed the excavations at the comital castle of Andone in the Charente throughout the 1980s and has published numerous articles on medieval archeology and social history.

HANS-WERNER GOETZ is Professor of History at Hamburg University. He is the author of *Leben im Mittelalter vom 7. bis zum 13. Jahrhundert* (Munich, 1986), which will appear shortly in English translation from Indiana University Press, and has published numerous articles on medieval historiography and historical consciousness. He has just completed an introduction to medieval studies and is working on a study of women's ways of life in the early Middle Ages.

THOMAS HEAD is Associate Professor of History at Yale University. He is the author of *Hagiography and the Cult of Saints: The Diocese of Orléans,*

800–1200 (Cambridge, 1990) as well as articles on both eleventh-century France and the role of women in medieval and early modern Christianity. He is currently completing a study of the trial of heretics at Orléans in 1022 and working on a comparative study of the the ordeal in legal, liturgical, and hagiographic sources.

GEOFFREY KOZIOL is Associate Professor of History at the University of California, Berkeley. He is the author of *Begging Pardon and Favor: Ritual and Political Order in Early Medieval France* (Ithaca, 1992). He is currently working on cross-cultural comparisons of state development.

RICHARD LANDES is Assistant Professor of History at Boston University. He is coordinating a group of American and European scholars in editing the collected works of Ademar of Chabannes for the Corpus Christianorum. He has completed a full length study of Ademar, *History and Denial in an Apocalyptic Age: The Life and Times of Ademar of Chabannes (989–1034)*, and is currently working on a companion volume concerning apocalyptic expectation and social transformation in early Capetian France.

CHRISTIAN LAURANSON-ROSAZ is Maître de Conférence at the Université Jean Monnet (Saint-Etienne). He is the author of *L'Auvergne et ses marges (Velay, Gévaudan) du VIIIe au XIe siècle: La fin du monde antique?* (Le Puy-en-Velay, 1987) as well as various articles on the French Midi in the early Middle Ages. He is currently engaged in research on the continuance of late antique structures of society and of the mentality in southern France around the year 1000.

GUY LOBRICHON is Maître de Conférence at the College de France (Paris) and the University of Paris I. He is now participating in a large collective project on symbolic and ideological creations in early medieval Burgundy; the group's most recent publication is *L'Ecole carolingienne d'Auxerre* (Paris, 1991). He has edited several books on these subjects and on other topics in medieval Christianity. He has published numerous articles on a variety of cultural and historical issues as well as *Assise: Les fresques de la basilique inférieure* (Paris, 1985) and is currently preparing another book on the history of Venice as seen through its painting.

ELISABETH MAGNOU-NORTIER is Professor of History and Geography and Director of the Centre de Recherche sur le Haut Moyen Age Occidentale at the University of Lille III. She is the author of *La société laïque et l'Eglise dans la province ecclésiastique de Narbonne de la fin du VIIIe à la fin du XIe siècle* (Toulouse, 1974) and *Foi et fidélité: Recherches sur l'évolution des liens personnels chez les Francs du Ve au IXe siècles* (Toulouse, 1976). She is currently completing a study of the relationship between church and state in the Frankish kingdom from the fifth to the twelfth century as well as organizing a series of biennial colloquia titled "Public Administration in the West during the Early Middle Ages."

R. I. MOORE is Reader in History at the University of Sheffield; he has also taught at the University of Chicago. He is the author of *The Birth of Popular Heresy* (London, 1975), *The Origins of European Dissent* (London, 1977), and *The Formation of a Persecuting Society: Power and Deviance in Western Europe* (London, 1987). He is currently working on a general account of popular religion and social change in the eleventh and twelfth centuries.

FREDERICK S. PAXTON is Associate Professor of History at Connecticut College. He is the author of *Christianizing Death: The Creation of a Ritual Process in Early Medieval Europe* (Ithaca, 1990) in addition to articles on canon law, codicology, and Carolingian church history. He is currently studying illness and healing in late antiquity and the early Middle Ages.

AMY G. REMENSNYDER is Assistant Professor of History at the University of Pittsburgh. She is the author of an article on the cult of Saint Faith of Conques and the problem of popular culture. She is currently working on a book concerning the social and political implications of monastic foundation legends in the south of France during the period 1000–1250.

BERNHARD TÖPFER is Professor of History at Humboldt University (Berlin). He is the author of *Volk und Kirche zur Zeit der beginnenden Gottesfriedensbewegung im Frankreich* (Berlin, 1957) and *Das kommende Reich des Friedens* (Berlin, 1964).

Index

Abbo, bishop of Saintes, 328
Abbo of Fleury, 14, 91, 94, 124, 220, 294, 305
Adalbero, bishop of Laon, 92, 133, 202, 314, 318
Adam of Bremen, 298
Adelarius of Fleury, 43
Ademar of Chabannes, 33, 59, 95, 99–101, 136–41, 145–46, 150, 161, 163, 167, 170–75, 178–79, 184–86, 194, 197, 200–201, 206–10, 213–17, 234–38, 264, 268, 282, 288–89, 322–25, 329
Ademar of Montcil, 120
Adrevald of Fleury, 223
Adro of Montier en Der, 188
Agde, council of (506), 61
Agobard of Lyon, 63, 90, 97
agricultural production, 10, 70–74, 267–70, 327, 333, 339
Aimeri of Bourbon, 109
Aimeri of Rancon, lord of Fractabotum, 139, 150
Aimon of Bourbon, archbishop of Bourges, 7, 36, 68, 94, 171, 176–79, 221–38, 314, 321, 339–41
Aimo of Fleury, 223, 230
Aimo of Valence, 117
Aire-sur-la-Lys, 257–58
Alauzia of Gascony (wife of Alduin, count of Angoulême), 140
Alberic, lord of Sully, 226
Alduin, bishop of Limoges, 196, 203
Alduin, count of Angoulême, 140
Alebrandus, archbishop of Bremen, 298

allodial landholders, 112–16, 132–34, 142, 320–21
Amalarius of Metz, 90, 97
Amantius, Saint, relics and cult of, 51, 127, 331
Ambrose of Milan, 90
Amiens and Corbie: council of (1033/36), 262, 267n, 270n
Anastase, archbishop of Sens, 97
anathema, 221, 313–14, 327–29, 334–36. See also curses; excommunication
Andone, 145
Andrew of Fleury, 7, 177, 199, 217, 222–30, 253n, 321–22, 339–42
Angoulême, 140, 144–45; bishop of (see Grimoard; Hugh); counts of, 151 (see also Alduin; Arnald Manzer; William IV)
Anse: council of (994), 68, 110, 121, 158, 261n, 262, 267nn, 271n, 288, 313; council of (1025), 261n, 262, 274–75, 316
Antichrist, 97–99, 207, 210, 343
Anzy-le-Duc, priory of Saint-Martin of Autun, 45–46
apocalypticism, 97–99, 170–71, 175, 187–90, 199–205, 216–17
apostolic era, 171, 174–76, 193, 204
apostolic life (vita apostolica), 11, 84–86, 96–98, 208–12
Aquitaine: cult of saints and pilgrimage in, 41–57, 165–79, 191–218; dukes of (see William I; William III; William IV; William V; William VI); noble power in, 135–55; Peace of God in,

Aquitaine (*cont.*)
   3–7, 33–34, 135–64, 166–72, 184–90, 194–218, 313–15 (*see also* Bourges; Charroux; Limoges; Narbonne; Poitiers; Rouergue)
archeology, 142–48
Archiac, 140, 145n
Arians, 208
Arles: archbishop of (*see* Ithier; Raimbald); council of (ca. 1024), 7; ecclesiastical province of, 7, 117–18, 338
Arnald Manzer, the Bastard, count of Angoulême, 139, 151
Arnold, bishop of Périgueux, 337
Arnold, bishop of Rodez, 127
Arnulf, bishop of Orléans, 91, 219
Arnulf, Saint, bishop of Soissons, 256–58
Arquillère, F.-X., 201
Arras, 323; condemnation of heretics at, 101
Artaud, archbishop of Reims, 67
assarts, 147–48
asylum, 60, 76
Atto of Vercelli, 293
Aubenas, R., 144, 149–51
Aubeterre, 154
Audebert I, count of the Marche, 137
Audenaarde, Peace declaration at (1030), 239
Augustine of Hippo, 90, 100, 200–201, 302. *See also* peace
Aulnay, viscounts of, 141, 160
Aurillac, abbey, 111–14; assembly held at (972), 110–11
Auvergne: cult of saints and pilgrimage in, 125–32; Peace of God in, 104–34, 261–63, 311–15 (*see also* Clermont; Le Puy; Saint-Germain-Laprade; Saint-Paulien)
Auxerre, council of (1033), 262, 268
Azalais, 119, 128

Bachrach, Bernard, 19n, 311, 321
Baldwin IV, count of Flanders, 239
Baldwin V, count of Flanders, 239–40, 243
ban (*bannum*), 12–14, 113–14, 133–34, 140–42, 149–56, 159–63, 313, 323. *See also* lordship
Barnard, Saint, relics and cult of, 127, 130
Beauvais: bishops of (*see* Warin); council of (845), 64; council of (1023), 262, 266–69, 271; Peace oath of, 264, 266, 268, 270–73

Bego of Calmont, bishop of Clermont, 47, 121, 124, 129
Beneciacum, 225, 228, 233, 341
Benedict, abbot of Chiusa, 213–17, 323, 325
Benedict, Saint, relics and cult of, 43–44, 54, 223, 234, 237
Benedict IX, pope, 307
Bénzét, bishop of Avignon, 289
Bercharius, Saint, relics and cult of, 5
Berengar, bishop of Elne, 334
Berengar, viscount of Narbonne, 287, 290, 292
Berengar of Tours, 83
Bergues, 244–45, 253–55
Bernard of Angers, 48–52, 55–56, 126, 130, 169, 331–32
Bernard of Clairvaux, 81
Berold, bishop of Soissons, 264
Bertrand of Varaize, 160
bishops: organization of Peace councils and assemblies by, 2–8, 29–30, 37–40, 105, 110–11, 116–22, 127–29, 196, 236–39, 256, 259–64, 289; relation to monks, 91–93, 219–21, 273–77; relation to *populus*, 26–28, 119–20, 196–97, 210–11, 221–22, 321–26; relation to secular nobility, 14–15, 31–32, 38–40, 60–65, 93–94, 107–11, 117–19, 219–21, 270–73, 276–79. *See also* Bourges: Peace league of; *entries for individual bishops*
Bisson, Thomas, 34, 166, 233, 325
Blaringhem, 245–51, 258
Blaye, 144–45
Bloch, Marc, 12–13, 116, 118
Bogomils, 81
boni homines, 112–15. *See also* judicial institutions
Bonnassie, Pierre, 35–36, 105, 122
Bonnaud-Delamare, Roger, 27–29, 33, 38, 163, 278
Bordeaux, archbishops of. *See* Gunbaldas; Siguinus
Boüard, Michel de, 256
Boudet, Marcellin, 116
Bourges: archbishops of (*see* Aimon of Bourbon; Dagbert); council of (1031), 166, 214, 217, 261nn, 262, 287–88, 302; council of (1038), 166, 227, 262, 264–66, 268; Peace league of, 7, 29, 36, 94, 176–77, 199, 217, 221–38, 277, 339–42; viscounts of (*see* Geoffrey)
Bournazel, Eric, 9
Bouteilles, 230
Bouteville, 140, 145n

Boutruche, Robert, 150
Brown, Peter, 320
Bruges, 256–58
Burchard, archbishop of Lyon, 313
Burgundy: cult of saints and pilgrimage in, 41–57; dukes of (*see* Gilbert); Peace of God in, 3–7, 261–64, 336, 338, 342. *See also* Anse; Auxerre; Beauvais; Coler; Héry; Verdun-sur-le-Doubs; Vienne
burial, 178–79, 335

Calixte, 109
Callahan, Daniel, 6, 17, 19, 320
Calmin, Saint, relics and cult of, 130
canon law, 61–69, 280–307
Carolingian empire, collapse of, 1, 15, 31, 38, 107–8, 309
castellan revolution, 1–2, 12–17, 106–8, 135–64; and origins of Peace of God, 21, 24, 31, 38, 58–59, 108–9, 132–34, 155–64, 259–60, 278, 308–11
castellans, 1–2, 11–16, 135–64, 178, 225–29, 252. *See also* lords
castles, 12, 114, 135–64, 167, 224–25, 229, 311. *See also entries for individual castles*
Cathars, 81–82, 208
celibacy, 275, 283–85, 319
Chambon, priory of Saint-Martial, 46, 53
Charente, castles in the, 143–55
Charlemagne, 63, 73
Charles the Bald, king of the Franks, 64–67, 73–75, 343–46
Charroux, abbey, 124, 289; abbot of (*see* Peter); council of (989), 68, 110, 121, 156–58, 162, 166, 187–89, 199, 221, 261n, 262, 264–68, 271n, 277, 286, 313–14, 327–30; council of (1027/28), 157, 161, 262, 273n, 329
chastity, 99, 207, 294–98, 302, 305, 331
Châteauneuf, 140
Châtillon-sur-Loire, priory of Fleury, 229–30
Cher river, battle of the, 222, 225–28, 232–33, 236
Cheyette, Fredric, 15
chrism, 299–300
Chronicon Dolensis, 227
Cistercians, 11, 318
clergy, secular: armed, 223–26, 266, 280–84, 290–92, 306; assaults on, 4, 157, 327–28, 332–34, 339–42; prohibited from bearing arms, 65, 266, 275, 280, 283, 285–87; protection of, 157–

58, 266–67; relation to monks, 91, 123, 215. *See also* celibacy; marriage; nicolaitism; simony
Clermont: assembly at (958), 116; bishops of (*See* Bego of Calmont; Stephen II); council of (1095), 26–27, 34, 120, 286–89; viscount of (*see* Robert)
Cluny: abbey of, 312–13, 315–16, 324; abbots of (*see* Odilo; Odo); Cluniac monasticism, 71, 89–98, 102, 109, 324–25; and cult of saints, 12, 47, 56–57; immunities of, 158, 313; and Peace of God, 11–12, 105, 125, 204–5, 273–74; and reform, 42, 91–93, 132, 273; and Truce of God, 7–8, 204–5, 273–74. *See also* liturgy; reform
Coblenz, council of (922), 67
Coler: council of (ca. 980), 121–25; council of (1025), 262
common people. *See* merchants; *populus*
communes, 18, 23–32, 38, 236, 257–58
Compostela, pilgrimage to, 50–51
concubinage, 280, 283, 288, 302
Conques, abbey, 47–52, 131, 196, 219, 331–32
consuetudines. See customs
Corbie, council of. *See* Amiens and Corbie
Cornards, confraternity of the, 120–21
corpus christi (*corpus christianorum*), 282, 295–97, 300–301, 306
courts. *See* judicial institutions
Cowdrey, H. E. J., 33–34, 39, 166
Coyaca, council of (1050), 299
crucifix, 83–85, 99, 203, 206
crusades, 18, 26–27, 30–31, 37–38, 132. *See also* Clermont; First Crusade; Urban II
cult of saints, 11, 41–57, 121–32, 165–83, 186–217, 219–20, 229–38, 241–56. *See also* relics; *entries under individual saints*
curses, 195n, 221. *See also* anathema; excommunication
customs (*consuetudines*), 14, 59, 70–71, 92, 106, 115, 152–56, 159–64, 315, 337

Dagbert, archbishop of Bourges, 128
Dalmas, viscount, 108
Debord, André, 13, 310, 314
Deusdet of Rodez, 129
Devailly, Guy, 36, 227–28
Donatian, Saint, relics and cult of, 256
Douai, Peace declaration at, 257
Duby, Georges, 12, 31–32, 37, 104, 142, 153, 163, 170, 226–28, 291, 302

Durand, Ursinus, 82–83
Duval, Frédéric, 25, 37n

Ellemachus, precentor of Elne, 334
Elne-Toulouges: council of (1027), 7, 262, 264–66, 268n, 286, 302, 334–35
Ennezat, tribunal at, 107–8
Erdmann, Carl, 26–27, 30, 37
ergotism (*ignis sacer*), 6, 48, 176, 186–92, 234–35, 329–30, 342
eucharist, 83–85, 208
excommunication, 118, 172, 176–79, 196–97, 210, 221, 288–89, 292, 294, 319, 328, 330–31, 335–36. *See also* anathema; curses; interdict

Faith, Saint, relics and cult of, 47–52, 55–56, 219; "jokes" (*ioca*) of, 53, 331–32; *maiestas* of, 51–52, 126–27, 131, 169
famine, 48, 69–70, 216–17, 223, 267–68, 338, 342
fasting, 186–87, 330, 336, 338, 342
feast days, 43–48, 170, 173–76, 198
feud and private warfare, 1, 15–16, 72, 227, 243–57, 259–60, 278, 325; and origins of Peace of God, 22–38, 259–60
Figeac, abbey, 45, 52, 122–23, 331n
First Crusade, 8, 26, 203
Flanders: counts of, 239–40, 244–45, 252, 256, 258 (*see also* Baldwin IV; Baldwin V; Robert II); Peace of God in, 239–58
Fleury (Saint-Benoît-sur-Loire), abbey, 43–44, 52, 222–23, 230–32
Flodoard of Reims, 67
fornication, 284, 288, 298, 304, 331
Fossier, Robert, 9, 142
Fournier, Gabriel, 142
Fractabotum, 139, 145n, 150
Frankfurt, synod of (794), 43
Fronsac, 144–45
Front, Saint, relics and cult of, 130–31, 178
Frotarius, bishop of Périgueux, 111, 328
Fulbert, bishop of Chartres, 138, 200, 331n
Fulcran, bishop of Lodève, 70, 129
Fulk Nerra, count of Anjou, 136, 160

Garaud, Marcel, 142
Gaucelin, churchwarden of Elne, 334
Gauzbert, bishop of Cahors, 111
Gauzbert of Elne, 334
Gauzlin, bishop of Mâcon, 274
Geary, Patrick, 15

Gelasian doctrine, 59–60, 61, 64
Genulph, Saint, relics and cult of, 46
Geoffrey, abbot of Saint-Martial, 211, 323
Geoffrey, viscount of Bourges, 225–29
Geoffrey Greygown, count of Anjou, 311
Geoffrey Martel, count of Anjou, 159, 162
George, Saint, legend and cult of, 130–31
Gerald, Saint, count of Aurillac, 111–15, 174; relics and cult of, 51, 126, 169, 177
Gerard, bishop of Cambrai, 202, 239, 314, 318, 320, 323, 336–37
Gerard, bishop of Limoges, 211, 323
Gerbert, archbishop of Reims, 94
Gerona, council of (1068), 280, 286–89, 292, 302, 305
Gilbert, bishop of Poitiers, 328, 330
Gilbert, count of Autun and duke of Burgundy, 44
Gluckman, Max, 16, 252
Goetz, Hans-Werner, 4, 17, 38–40, 69–72
Görris, Gerhard, 25
Gorze, abbey, 11
Gosfridus, abbot of Saint-Martial, 330
Gratian, 302
Gratus, Saint, relics and cult of, 46–47
Gregorian reform. *See* reform: Gregorian
Gregory, bishop of Tours, 194
Gregory I, the Great, pope, 196
Gregory VII, pope, 4, 295, 298, 326
Grimoard, bishop of Angoulême, 330
Gui, viscount of Limoges, 137
Guigo, bishop of Glandèves, 128
Guigo, bishop of Valence, 128
Guillot, Olivier, 142, 152, 160
Gunbaldus, archbishop of Bordeaux, 124, 156, 313, 327–28
Guy of Anjou, bishop of Le Puy, 3, 106, 116–21, 127–29, 134, 176, 331–17, 321

hagiography, 2–3, 52–54, 97, 122–23, 130–31, 166–67, 191–94, 205–6, 213, 222–23, 226–27, 242–56
Halley's comet, 188
Head, Thomas, 7, 17, 19, 322, 324
heaven, 171–77, 179–83
Helias of Born, 160
Henry of Lausanne, followers of, 81–84
Henry I, king of France, 342
Henry II, emperor of Germany, 6, 89

Henry II, king of England, 82
Henry III, emperor of Germany, 240, 243–44
heresy, 7, 17, 36, 57, 80–103, 207–13, 323–25, 347–50. *See also* apostolic life; Arras; Orléans
Heribert. *See* "Letter of Heribert"
Hervaeus, archbishop of Reims, 67
Hervaeus of Buzançais, 97
Héry, council of (1025), 4, 92, 262, 267–68nn, 276
Hilary of Poitiers, 291
Hildegar, bishop of Limoges, 328
Hilduin, bishop of Limoges, 261, 330
Hincmar, archbishop of Reims, 74–78, 343–46
Hoffman, Hartmut, 18, 30–31, 58, 116, 122, 128, 166, 255, 299
Huberti, Ludwig, 23–25
Hugh, bishop of Angoulême, 328
Hugh, Saint, relics and cult of, 45–46
Hugh Capet, king of France, 90–91, 167, 294; election of (987), 1, 13, 188
Hugh of Blaringhem, 245–50
Hugh of Chalon, bishop of Auxerre, 92–93
Hugh of Die, papal legate, 288
Hugh of Lusignan, 138–41
Humbert aux Blanches Mains, 72
Humbert of Silva Candida, cardinal, 292–302

ignis sacer. See ergotism
incest, 60, 302–5, 316, 325
interdict, 178, 196–97
invasions: ninth-century, 65; tenth-century, 10, 54, 124, 144, 284, 309
Isarn, bishop of Grenoble, 129
Isembert, bishop of Poitiers, 337
Isembert of Chatelaillon, 160
Isidore of Seville, 303
Islo, bishop of Saintes, 330
Ithier, archbishop of Arles, 118
iuvenes, 243, 248–52, 317–18
Ivo, bishop of Chartres, 256

Jerome, 90
Jerusalem, 17; destruction of Holy Sepulchre in, 202–3, 210; pilgrimage to, 50–51, 55, 179, 204
Jews, 203
Joachim of Fiore, 89
John the Baptist, discovery of relics of, 49, 193, 198–99, 204
John the Scot, 99
Jonas, bishop of Orléans, 63

Jordan, bishop of Limoges, 265, 276, 337
Judas, 62
judicial institutions, 15–16, 91–92, 102–3, 106–20, 149–64, 270–73, 278–79, 312; decline of, 95; history of, 21–25
Julian of Brioude, Saint, relics and cult of, 178
Jungmann, Joseph, 173
Junianus, Saint, relics and cult of, 328–29
Justinian, Saint, relics and cult of, 195–96

Kennedy, Dolorosa, 29–30, 32
Kienast, Walther, 136
kings: Capetian, 1, 11–13, 167, 294, 309; Carolingian, 1, 24, 31, 63–67, 73–75, 107–8, 141, 188, 309; failure of, 4, 13, 20, 94–95, 107–8, 156, 163–64, 167, 294, 309, 335; as guarantors of peace, 107, 259, 294, 303, 309; Merovingian, 24, 62–63; Ottonian, 241–43; Plantagenet, 146; weakening power of, 1–2, 12, 31–33, 38, 138, 167, 172, 259–60. *See also entries under individual kings*
Kluckhohn, August, 21–25, 37
knights (*milites*), 1–4, 8, 13, 18, 31, 111, 147–48, 192–93, 220–28, 232, 236, 238, 243–51, 255, 266–67, 291–92, 306, 312–14, 317–18, 321–22, attack participants at Peace assembly, 131; presence of, at Peace councils and assemblies, 116–20, 125, unarmed, 266
Körner, Theodor, 34–35
Koziol, Geoffrey, 8, 15, 17, 19, 325

Lambert, count of Chalon-sur-Sâone, 46–47
Landes, Richard, 6, 17, 19, 320, 322
Landfrieden, 8, 21–24, 35, 271
Landrey, count of Nevers, 229
Landric, count, 6
Laon, Peace declaration at, 257
Last Judgment, 171, 175, 178–79, 182, 216
Lauranson-Rosaz, Christian, 4, 13, 17, 161, 321–22
Lemarignier, Jean-François, 159
Lemasson, Anne-Marie, 122
Leonard of Noblat, Saint, relics and cult of, 95, 130, 237
Le Puy: bishops of (*see* Guy of Anjou); council of (990/994), 4, 68, 71, 162, 166, 176, 261–69, 271nn, 275, 286–87;

council of (1036), 262, 268n. *See also*
Saint-Paulien: council of (993/994)
Letaldus of Micy, 53, 194, 227, 328–29
"Letter of Heribert," 17, 80–103, 208,
    347–50
Leutard of Vertus, 100, 323
Leyser, Karl, 247
Libentius, archbishop of Bremen, 298
Liber quare, 97
Lillebonne, Peace declaration at, 257
Limoges, 185–86; bishops of (*see* Ger-
    ard; Hildegar; Hilduin; Jordan);
    council of (994), 6, 110, 157, 167, 176,
    186–92, 196–97, 234–35, 261n, 262,
    265, 268nn, 270n, 271n, 273, 320,
    329–30; council of (1028), 157, 167,
    261n, 262, 268n, 270n; council of
    (1029), 167, 262, 268n, 270n; council
    of (1031), 42, 157–58, 167, 177–78,
    197, 214, 217, 261n, 262, 265, 268n,
    270n, 289; council of (1033), 261n,
    262; viscounts of (*see* Gui)
Limousin, Peace of God in the, 184–218
Lisieux, Peace declaration at (1064),
    256–57
Lissewege, 251–52
liturgy, 172–74, 210, 212, 243–47, 250–
    54, 319, 324. *See also* mass; sequence;
    tropes
Lobbes, abbey, 240–41; monks of, 240–56
Lobrichon, Guy, 7, 17, 19, 324
lords: changing status of, 1–2, 13–16,
    28, 31–32, 106–16; donations by, to
    ecclesiastical institutions, 55, 60–63,
    65, 79, 310–16; as founders of monas-
    teries, 46–47, 111, 159–60, 178; lin-
    eages of, changing structure of, 13–16,
    309–11, 315–16; power of, 135–41,
    149–61; presence of, at Peace coun-
    cils, 3–6, 17–18, 111, 116–20, 128–29,
    186, 212, 221–24, 309; relation to
    bishops, 14–15, 31–32, 38–39, 93–94,
    107–11, 117–19, 219–21, 270–73,
    276–79; relation to monks, 53–55,
    91–93, 130, 161–63, 229–30, 240–55;
    relation to *populus*, 12–14, 153–54,
    161–62, 224–25, 236, 271, 310–11;
    support of Peace councils and assem-
    blies by, 105, 118–19, 157–59, 167–
    68, 186, 260, 265–66, 289, 314–15.
    See also castellans; *iuvenes;* knights;
    Landfrieden; Truce of God
lordship, 12–14, 31, 113–16, 130–34,
    142–55, 314–18
Lothar, king of the west Franks, 312
Louis I, the Pious, king of the Franks,
    63–64, 73

Louis IV, d'Outremer, king of the west
    Franks, 107–8
Louis the German, king of the east
    Franks, 344–45
Luchaire, Achille, 23, 25
Lusignan, 150
Luxeuil, abbey, 82, 92

Mabillon, Jean, 81–83
Macarius, Saint, 256; *Vita s. Macharii,*
    244
MacKinney, Loren, 18, 26–28, 37
Magnou-Nortier, Elizabeth, 17, 35, 312–
    13
maiestas, 51–52, 126–27, 168–70, 331
Maiolus, Saint, abbot of Cluny, 124, 325;
    relics and cult of, 47
malae consuetudines. See customs
mallus, 112–13
Manichees, 99, 207–208, 212, 323–24
manuscripts: Berlin, Staatsbibliothek,
    lat. 1664, 173n; Ghent, Bibl. Univ. 92,
    188n; Paris BN lat. 887, 173n, 181–
    83; Paris BN lat. 903, 173n, 181–83;
    Paris BN lat. 909, 173, 175, 179–83;
    Paris BN lat, 1084, 179–83; Paris BN
    lat. 1118, 173, 179–82; Paris BN lat.
    1119, 173n, 180–83; Paris BN lat.
    1120, 173n, 180–83; Paris BN lat.
    1121, 173, 179–83; Paris BN lat.
    1240, 173, 179–82, 191n; Paris BN
    lat. 1745, 84–86, 90–91, 102; Paris
    BN lat. 2469, 167–71nn, 176n, 189–
    90nn, 197nn, 200n, 217n; Paris BN
    lat. 2627, 122n; Paris BN lat. 4281,
    203n; Paris BN lat. 5239, 203n; Paris
    BN lat. 5288, 214–16nn; Paris BN lat.
    5321, 186n; Paris BN lat. 11685, 89n;
    Paris BN lat. 16208, 82n; Vatican,
    Reg. lat. 566, 332; Vatican, Reg. lat.
    1127, 158n; Vesoul, Bibliothèque mu-
    nicipale, 1, 82–83
Marcillac, 140, 144–45
Margam, abbey, 92; *Annales de Margan,*
    82
Marius, Saint, relics and cult of, 51, 127,
    130, 331
marriage, 302–5, 316, 335; clerical, 36,
    275, 280, 283–93, 298, 300–301, 305–
    6, 313
Martène, Edmund, 82–83
Martial, Saint, 6, 176, 178; Aurelian leg-
    end of, 191–97, 203, 213; claims for
    the apostolicity of, 6, 33, 50, 167,
    174–76, 193–94, 206, 213–16, 235;
    relics and cult of, 126, 169–70, 174–

76, 186–94, 203, 206–7, 209–16, 234–35, 330; *Vita prolixior s. Martialis*, 191–93, 206, 210, 213, 216, 320, 322
Martin of Tours, Saint, 174
Mary Magdalene, saint, relics of, 49–50
mass, 85, 96, 172–76, 246–47, 299–300
Matha, 140, 144–45
merchants, 333
Merpins, 139
Micy, abbey, 48–49, 53
milites. See castellans; knights
millenarianism, 200–201
millennium: as anniversary of life of Christ, 17, 27–28, 31, 157, 171, 179, 188, 190, 201, 216, 338, 342; and religious fervor, 12–13, 51, 323; "terrors of the year 1000," 170, 188, 201, 277; turn of the, Europe at the, 1–2, 9–12, 17, 52, 308–9
miracles: chastisements, 53–56, 219–20, 229–32; cures, 47–49, 111, 122–24, 176, 189, 191, 234–35, 329–32, 338–39; liberation of prisoners, 95; meteorological, 170; parodic, 85, 88; reconciliations, 242–56. *See also* portents and signs
Molompise, village, 55
monastic immunity, 31, 79, 90–91, 130, 158, 161–62
Monforte, condemnation of heretics at, 101
monks: and the cult of saints, 41–57, 122–32, 191–94, 219–21, 229–98, 341–50; presence of, at Peace councils, 4–7, 34; promotion of Peace councils and assemblies by, 99–101, 122–25; protection of, 266–67; relation to bishops, 91–93, 219–22, 273–77; relation to *populus*, 41–50, 56–57, 131–32, 230–31, 318–23; relation to secular clergy, 91, 123, 215; relation to secular nobility, 53–55, 91–93, 130, 161–63, 229–30, 240–55. *See also* monastic immunity; property; reform
Montausier, 140
Monte Cassino, abbey, 223
Montfaucon, abbey, 67
Montier-en-Der, abbey, 5
Montignac, 140, 145
Moore, R. I., 11, 18, 20, 36–37, 202, 300
Mozac, abbey, 130

Narbonne, archbishop of (*see* Wifrid); council of (ca. 990), 110, 121, 262, 268n; council of (1043), 68, 287, 290–

91; council of (1054), 8, 68, 70, 72, 286, 296, 299; viscount of (*see* Berengar)
nicolaitism, 285, 301
nobles. *See* lords
noblewomen, 266, 333
Notre-Dame-de-Saintes, abbey, 159–62
Nouaillé, abbey, 136, 178, 328–29
nuns, 266, 333, 340

oaths: communal, 30; of keeping the Peace, 32–35, 68–70, 78, 117–19, 125, 133, 166, 172, 176–78, 186–89, 200–202, 217, 221, 224, 233–34, 264–73, 282, 330, 332–34, 336, 339–42; of vassalage, 107
Odilo, abbot of Cluny, 12, 92, 94, 324–25
Odo, abbot of Cluny, 124, 177, 317
Odo, king of the west Franks, 67
Odo, lord of Déols, 222, 225–27, 340–41
Odo II, count of Blois, 164, 342
Odorannus of Sens, 90, 94
Oliba, bishop of Vic, 302–4, 334
Oootburg, 249, 250–51
ordeal, judicial, 229–36
Orléans: bishop of (*see* Arnulf; Jonas); council of (538), 62; council of (541), 62; trial of heretics at (1022), 101, 207n, 231, 236–37, 324

pagus, 12, 113, 157–59, 314
palace, royal, 343–46
Paray-le-Monial, abbey, 46–47
Paschasius Radbertus, 63, 83
Paxton, Frederick, 2–3, 19
peace: Augustinian notion of, 12, 25, 28, 200–201, 270, 282, 291, 302, 309; "of the church," 59–60, 292; concepts of, 27–28, 59–60, 97–98, 107–8, 171, 175, 182–83, 270–71, 276–77, 281–82, 291, 294, 303, 306; kisses of, 173, 245, 250; *pax Dei*, 201n; *pax Domini*, 277n; restoration of, 273. *See also* kings
Peace of God: documentation for, 2–3, 111, 122–23, 128, 166–67; historiography of, 2–3, 21–40, 58–61, 104–6, 226–28; origins of, 3–4, 21–25, 29–31, 38–40, 56, 58–60, 69–70, 104–34, 259–64
peasants: armed, 3, 223–26, 236, 321; changing status of, 12–14, 15, 109, 114–15, 321; serfs, 12–14, 71–72, 162, 230–31, 288, 310, 315. *See also* allodial landholders

Perigord, heresy in the, 80–103, 208
Périgueux, 85; bishops of (*see* Arnold; Frotarius)
Perroy, Edmond, 142
Peter, abbot of Charroux, 289
Peter, bishop of Viviers, 128
Peter, Saint, 130, 191, 194
Peter Damian, 284, 290–98, 305–6
pilgrimage, 11, 17, 41–57, 169–70, 175, 179
pilgrims, protection of, 333
pillage, 1, 14–16, 53–55, 106–10, 113–16, 157–63, 225, 264–70, 312–15, 327–28, 330–42, 345–46; vocabulary of, 58–79
Pirenne, Henri, 23, 25
Pîtres, council of, 65–66
placitum, 107–9, 116
Platelle, Henri, 243
Poitiers: bishops of (*see* Gilbert; Isembart); council of (1000/14), 68, 157–58, 162, 166, 187, 261n, 262–65, 266–67nn, 270–71nn, 273–76, 287–89, 291–92, 314, 323, 330–31; council of (1010), 323; council of (1029/31), 68, 162, 166, 217, 261n, 262, 265, 323, 337; council of (1036), 262, 275; council of (1078), 288; counts of, 141, 151. *See also* William III, William V, William VI
Poly, Jean-Pierre, 9
Poncius, 81–83
populus: definition of, 2; *inermis vulgus*, 212, 221, 224, 236, 321; presence of, at Peace councils and assemblies, 2–7, 17–18, 26–29, 34–37, 109–11, 116–25, 187–89, 312, 329, 332, 334, 337–40; protection of, 162, 267–70; public action of, 17–18, 238, 320; relation to bishops, 26–28, 119–20, 221–22, 321–23; relation to monks, 41–50, 56–57, 131–32, 230–31, 318–23; relation to secular nobility, 12–14, 162, 224–25, 236, 271, 310–11; religious practices of, 11, 43–50, 55–57, 120–21, 125–27, 236–37
Porcian, Saint, relics and cult of, 45
portents and signs, 188, 223, 242, 251, 339
Praemonstratensians, 11
primogeniture, 13–14, 316
Prinz, Friedrich, 284
Privat, Saint, relics and cult of, 130, 169
private warfare. *See* feud and private warfare
property: disputes over, 16, 312–16; ecclesiastical, 4, 14–15, 38–40, 53–56,

60–69, 76, 90–94, 109, 117–20, 130–32, 161–63, 168, 229–34, 240–42, 264–66, 312–16, 321, 327–37, 340; merchant, 333; noble, 71–72; peasant, 4, 14, 63, 113–15, 119–20, 132–34, 162–63, 267–70, 314–15, 321, 327, 333; protection of, by judicial institutions, 34, 220–21; protection of, by Peace councils, 3–6, 108–9, 119–20, 161–63, 264–73, 313–15, 327, 333; protection of, by saintly patronage, 53–56, 95, 219–20, 229–34. *See also* allodial landholders, pillage
prostration, 246–47, 250–51, 253
pseudo-Dionysius, 99
pseudo-Isidorian decretals, 64–67, 79, 295
publicani, 82–84

Quierzy, council of, 64, 344–45

Raimbald, archbishop of Arles, 287, 289
Rather, bishop of Verona, 299–300
Ratramnus of Corbie, 83
Raymond, count of Toulouse, 119, 129
Raymond III, count of the Rouergue, 55
reform: ecclesiastical, 4, 36–38, 212–13, 319, 273–77, 280–307, 319, 324–26; Gregorian, 11, 18, 31, 91, 132, 283, 326; monastic, 4, 11–12, 42, 56–57, 90–94, 99–104, 124–25, 273–74
relics: discovery of, 49–50, 193, 198–99; journeys of, 128, 187, 198–99, 241–52, 328–29; at Peace councils, 2–9, 26, 29, 95, 105, 122–28, 166–72, 186–89, 256, 282, 319–20, 328–32, 338–40; translations of, 43–47; used in taking oaths, 125, 150, 172, 176–78, 224, 314, 340; used to defend ecclesiastical property, 55–56, 95, 196, 219–20. *See also* cult of saints; *maiestas*; *entries under individual saints*
Remensnyder, Amy G., 4, 19, 319
requisitions, military, 73–78, 159–60, 332–34, 343–46
Reynolds, Susan, 236
Robert, count of the Rouergue, 55
Robert, viscount of Clermont, 109
Robert of Lissewege, 251–52
Robert II, count of Flanders, 257–58
Robert II, the Pious, king of France, 6, 78, 90–91, 97, 162, 164, 167, 264, 294, 332, 334, 337
Rodez, diocese of, 127, 331
Rodulphus Glaber, 6, 11–12, 18, 33, 50–51, 89, 99–101, 170, 185, 200–201, 216, 276, 306, 319, 338–39, 342

Roman law, 61–62
Rosenwein, Barbara, 15, 312, 315–16
Rouergue: council in the (ca. 1012), 127, 331; counts of the (*see* Raymond III; Robert)
Rousillon, 334
Ruffec, 150
Ruffiacus, 329
Rufinus, 90

sacraments, 287, 299–301
Saint-Aignan, college of canons in Orléans, 231–32
Saint-Amand, abbey, 92
Saint-Amantius-de-Boixe, abbey, 141
Saint-Barnard, abbey, 128–29
Saint-Basle-de-Verzy, council of (991), 91
Saint-Benoît-du-Sault, priory of Fleury, 234
Saint-Benoît-sur-Loire, abbey. *See* Fleury
Saint-Bertin, abbey, 336
Saint Chaffre, abbey, 130
Saint-Cybard, abbey, 178
Saint-Cyprien, abbey, 162
Saint-Eparchius, abbey, 140
Saintes, 144–45; bishops of (*see* Abbo; Islo)
Saint-Etienne-de-Baigne, abbey, 141
Saint-Genou-de-Lestree, abbey, 46
Saint-Germain-Laprade, council at (975), 116–21, 311, 317
Saint-Germain of Auxerre, abbey, 84, 90–93, 102, 325
Saint-Hilaire, abbey, 136
Saint-Jean-d'Angély, abbey, 49, 136, 193, 198–99
Saint-Léonard of Nobalt, abbey, 95
Saint-Macre, council of (935), 67
Saint-Maixent, abbey, 136, 162, 168
Saint-Martial, abbey, 48–50, 93, 168–70, 191–94, 205, 320; abbots of (*see* Geoffrey; Gostridus); dedication of the *basilica regalis* at, 193; liturgical manuscripts of, 172–76; trampling of pilgrims in the church of, 48, 203, 209, 323
Saint-Omer, Peace declaration at, 258
Saint-Paulien: council of (993/994), 127–29, 166, 312, 315; identification as *Ruessium*, 129
Saint-Philibert, abbey, 44–45; abbot of (*see* Stephen)
saints, cult of. *See* cult of saints
Saint-Satur, 229
Saint-Savin, abbey, 168
Saint-Vaast, abbey, 336
Saltet, Louis, 215

Sancho III, king of Pamplona, 302
Sarlat, abbey, 93
Saturninus, Saint, relics and cult of, 331
Sauxillanges, abbey, 109, 128
Seguinus, archbishop of Sens, 97
Semichon, Ernest, 21–25, 37
Senlis, council of (989/90), 67
sequence, 175–76
Siguinus, archbishop of Bordeaux, 330
simony, 36, 280, 283–99, 306, 319, 331
Sisteron, *notitia* of, 290, 293
Soissons: bishops of (*see* Arnulf; Berold); Peace declaration at (1093), 258
Souvigny, priory of Cluny, 47
Stephen, abbot of Saint-Philibert, 44–45, 52
Stephen, legendary duke of Aquitaine, 178, 192
Stephen, lord of Beneciacum, 225, 341
Stephen, Saint, 174; relics and cult of, 177, 224, 340
Stephen of Thiers-Huillaux, 109
Stephen II, bishop of Clermont, 107–11, 119, 126, 168–69
Strazeele, 243, 254, 258
Surgères, 154

Te Deum laudamus (hymn), 250, 254
Tenant de la Tour, Georges, 142
Thérouanne, diocese of, Peace declaration for (1042/43), 239–40
Thibaud, archbishop of Vienne, 128
three orders. *See* trifunctionalism
tithes, 66, 73
Töpfer, Bernhard, 17, 19, 28, 30, 37, 38, 161, 192, 278, 319
Toulouges, council of. *See* Elne-Toulouges: council of
Tournai, diocese of, Peace declaration for, 239
Tours: council of (567), 62; council of (1060), 304; council of (1163), 82
towns and townspeople, 10, 242, 245–46, 249–51, 254, 257. *See also* communes
trifunctionalism, 32, 105, 114, 210n, 226–28, 318–20, 336–67
tropes, 172–76, 179, 180–83, 191, 319
Trosly, council of (909), 67
Truce of God (*treuga Dei*), 7–9, 22, 56, 132, 256–57, 289, 342
Tulle, abbey, 115, 130

Udalcher, archpriest of Elne, 334
Urban II, pope, 26, 257
Ursmer, Saint, relics and cult of, 8, 241–56, 325

Valeria, Saint, relics and cult of, 46, 49, 130, 191–92
Valerian, Saint: relics and cult of, 44–45; image of, 52
vassalage, 136–41, 150, 160–61
vengeance, 243, 248, 250–52
Verdun-sur-le-Doubs: council of (1019/ 21), 92, 261n, 262–64, 267–68nn, 271n; Peace oaths of, 266, 268, 270, 272–73
Vermeesch, Albert, 32, 37, 222n
Vézeley, abbey, 49–50
Vic: bishops of (*see* Oliba); council of (1033), 262, 264–68, 271n, 286; council of (1068), 286
vicarius (vicaria), 14, 109, 112–13, 131, 149, 152–56, 162–64
Vidier, Alexandre, 226
Vienne: council of, 262, 265–69, 271n; Peace oaths of, 264, 266–68, 270, 272
Virgin Mary, *maiestas* of, at Clermont, 126–27, 168–69, 331
Vivian, Saint, relics and cult of, 45, 51–52, 122–23, 127, 130

Wala, 63
Ward, Benedicta, 242

Warin, bishop of Beauvais, 71, 78, 332–34, 336
White, Stephen, 15
widows, 61, 266
Wifrid, archbishop of Narbonne, 287, 290–92
Wifrid, the Hairy, count of Cerdagne, 287
William I, the Pious, duke of Aquitaine, 108
William III, Caput-Stuppae (Towhead), duke of Aquitaine, 107–8
William IV, Ironarm, duke of Aquitaine, 135n
William IV, Taillefer, count of Angoulême, 136–41, 154
William V, the Great, duke of Aquitaine, 135–38, 154, 157, 163, 167–68, 179, 192, 212, 264, 266, 273, 289, 291, 314, 323, 330
William VI, the Fat, duke of Aquitaine, 157–58, 163, 337
William of Newburgh, 82
William of Parthenay, 160
women: consecrated, 61. *See also* noble-women; nuns; widows

Zachary, pope, 284

Library of Congress Cataloging-in-Publication Data

The Peace of God : social violence and religious response in France around the
 year 1000 / edited by Thomas Head and Richard Landes.
 p. cm.
 Includes bibliographical references and index.
 ISBN 0-8014-2741-X (alk. paper). — ISBN 0-8014-8021-3 (pbk. : alk. paper)
 1. Peace—Religious aspects—Christianity—History of doctrines—Middle Ages, 600–
1500. 2. Peace movements—France—History 3 France—Social conditions—
987–1515. 4. France—Religious life and customs. I. Head, Thomas (Thomas F.)
II. Landes, Richard Allen.
DT746.4.P4405 1992
274.4'03—dc20   92-52758